Practicum and Internship Experiences in Counseling

This ready-to-use resource provides the practical information and hands-on skills interns and practicum students need to successfully complete their clinical experiences and join the counseling profession with confidence.

Designed to accompany students as they advance through practicum and internship, *Practicum and Internship Experiences in Counseling* helps bridge the gap from theory to practice. It covers the day-to-day elements of practice in agencies and schools that are often missing from the theory-based courses. Chapters are packed with case examples, activities, voices from the field, and self-assessments, including tools for assessing and addressing ethnocentrism, intersectionality, and bias in counseling practice.

This resource orients clinical students to the field, while providing them with the day-to-day skills they need to thrive.

Special focus on:

- **Expectations** and how to get the most out of the supervision process.
- **Assessment and intervention** with clients in danger and crisis.
- **Wellness and developing healthy work and personal habits** to carry through one's entire career.

Readers see clearly how to:

- **Apply the laws and ethics** in everyday clinical practice.
- **Work with special issues** (neuropsych and psychopharmacology) and populations.
- **Market and position oneself in the job market**, with an eye toward growing/marketing a counseling practice after graduation.

Included in each chapter:

- **Several self-assessment activities** encouraging self-reflection and self-assessment on the concepts of the chapter.
- **Voices from the field features** providing firsthand, in-the-trenches perspectives from counselors who have "been there and done that."
- **Realistic case examples** challenging readers to apply knowledge and skills to realistic cases they are likely to encounter in the field.

Included are separate chapters on:

- Relationship building.
- Goal setting.
- Record keeping.
- The integration of theory into practice.

Bradley T. Erford, PhD, is a professor in the Peabody College at Vanderbilt University. He was the 61st president of the American Counseling Association and is an ACA fellow and the author of more than 30 books and 100 journal articles.

Practicum and Internship Experiences in Counseling

Edited by Bradley T. Erford

Routledge
Taylor & Francis Group
NEW YORK AND LONDON

First published 2023
by Routledge
605 Third Avenue, New York, NY 10158

and by Routledge
4 Park Square, Milton Park, Abingdon, Oxon, OX14 4RN

Routledge is an imprint of the Taylor & Francis Group, an informa business

Some material in this book was previously published by Pearson Education, Inc.

ISBN: 978-1-032-30487-8 (hbk)
ISBN: 978-1-032-30486-1 (pbk)
ISBN: 978-1-003-30552-1 (ebk)

DOI: 10.4324/9781003305521

Typeset in Sabon
by Apex CoVantage, LLC

This effort is dedicated to The One: the Giver of energy, passion, and understanding, who makes life worth living and endeavors worth pursuing and accomplishing, the Teacher of love and forgiveness.

Contents

Preface and Acknowledgments xiv
About the Editor xvii
List of Contributors xviii

1 **Matching Goals, Developing Skills, and the First Impression** 1
ROBIN WILBOURN LEE, RACHEL M. O'NEILL, JENNIFER JORDAN, MICHELLE STEVENS, AND BRADLEY T. ERFORD

Preview 1
Beginning Your Field Experience 1
Differentiating Between the Goals and Objectives of Practicum and Internship 2
Practicum 2
Internship 2
Working With a Multidisciplinary Team 4
Intake Session/Interview 6
Reviewing Informed Consent 6
Confidentiality 6
What to Do With Parents and Guardians in the Initial Session 7
Gathering Information and Client History 7
Psychosocial History 8
Mental Status Exam 8
Diagnosis 22
Treatment Planning 23
Developing a Treatment Plan 25
Identifying the Problem 26
Defining the Problem 26
Developing Goals 26
Developing Objectives 26
Selecting Interventions 27
Diagnosis 27
An Example Treatment Plan 27
Summary 28

2 **The Supervision Process** 30
CATHERINE Y. CHANG, CAROLINE O'HARA, AND LINDY K. PARKER

Preview 30
Your Roles as a Counselor and a Supervisee: Where the Student and Professional Align 30
Your Role as a Counseling Practicum Student and Intern 31
On-Site Supervision and Your Site Supervisor's Role 31
University Supervision and What You Can Expect 32

Developing Positive Relationships With Your Supervisors 33
Developing Learning Goals with Your Supervisors 35
Supervision Versus Counseling 36
Barriers to Effective Supervision 37
Learning From Different Philosophies and Theoretical Orientations: Growing and Changing 38
Making Case Presentations 40
Summary 41

3 **Integrating Theory Into Practice** 43
DANA HELLER LEVITT AND BRADLEY T. ERFORD

Preview 43
The Significance of Theory 43
Ethics of Applying Counseling Theory 43
What Makes a Good Theory? 44
Theoretical Paradigms 45
Psychodynamic Paradigm 48
Humanistic-Existential Paradigm 51
Behavioral/Cognitive-Behavioral Paradigm 54
Systems Paradigm 61
Postmodern Theories 63
Integrating Theory Into Practice 70
View of Human Nature 70
Goals of Counseling 70
Role of the Professional Counselor 71
Techniques and Approaches 71
Flexibility 71
Theoretical Integration 72
Integrative Versus Eclectic Counseling 73
Why an Integrative Approach? 73
Summary 77

4 **Record Keeping: What to Include and What to Leave Out** 78
JAMES JACKSON, LATOFIA P. PARKER, AND CHARLOTTE DAUGHHETEE

Preview 78
The Importance of Record Keeping 78
How to Keep Case Notes 79
Process Notes 80
Standard Format 80
SOAP Notes 80
Time-Sequenced Notes 82
The Line Between Too Much and Not Enough Information 84
Instances Where Detail Is Necessary 85
We Are What We Write: The Importance of Professional Written Communication as Keys to Effective Writing 85
Progress Notes and Supervision 86
Tips to Avoid Record Keeping Problems 87
When Clients Request Their Records 91
Summary 93

5 Putting Ethics and Law Into Practice 94
BY LYNN E. LINDE AND BRADLEY T. ERFORD

Preview 94
Ethical Standards and Laws 94
Ethics in Clinical Practice 95
American Counseling Association Code of Ethics 95
AMHCA Code of Ethics 101
Codes of Ethics From Marriage, Couple, and Family Counseling Organizations 102
The American School Counselor Association (ASCA) Ethical Standards for School Counselors 103
Making Ethical Decisions 106
Common Ethical Dilemmas for Beginning Counselors 107
Professional Competence 107
Misrepresentation 107
Pressure to "Upcode" 108
"Can I Be Sued?" and "What Is Malpractice?" 108
Subpoenas 109
Confidentiality 110
Limits to Confidentiality 111
Confidentiality and Privileged Communication 112
Minor Consent Laws 113
Records and Personal Notes 114
Educational Records 114
Personal Notes 116
The Health Insurance Portability and Accountability Act (HIPAA) of 1996 117
Child Abuse and Neglect 117
Custody Issues' 118
Harm to Self and Others 118
Summary 122

6 Special Populations and Issues 123
VICTORIA E. KRESS, MATTHEW J. PAYLO, NICOLE A. STARGELL, AND CHRISTINE A. MCALLISTER

Preview 123
Special Populations and Issues 123
Child Maltreatment 124
Children With Learning Disabilities or Giftedness 127
Intellectual Disability 127
Giftedness 128
Nonsuicidal Self-Injury 130
Intimate Partner Violence 131
Substance Abuse 132
Older Adults and the Terminally Ill 134
Military Populations 136
Counseling Military Service Members and Veterans 136
Treatment Considerations and Issues 137
Evidence-Based Treatments 138
Counseling Mandated and Unmotivated Clients 138
Low Motivation and Non-Compliance 138
Legal Offenders 140

Court-Ordered Counseling 140
Transference and Countertransference 141
Transference 141
Countertransference 142
Summary 143

7 **Applying Multicultural Counseling** 147
JOSÉ VILLALBA AND BRADLEY T. ERFORD

Preview 147
Developing Cultural Sensitivity: Historical and Current Contexts 147
Historical Context 148
Current Social, Political, and Economic Contexts 148
Application: How Contexts Help and Hinder Development of Cultural Sensitivity 149
The Multicultural and Social Justice Counseling Competencies: Attitudes and Beliefs, Knowledge, and Skills 152
Applying the Multicultural and Social Justice Counseling Competencies 152
Confronting Oneself: Self-Awareness, Overcoming Bias, and Working With Differences 154
Expanding Our Notion of Self-Awareness 154
Overcoming Biases 155
Working With Differences 156
Application: Self-Awareness, Overcoming Bias, and Working With Differences 156
Counseling Diverse Clients From a Strengths-Based Perspective 158
Social Capital as a Framework for Strengths-Based Perspectives 159
Eliciting Client Strengths Through Strengths-Based Counseling 159
Application: Counseling From a Strengths-Based Perspective 160
Summary 161

8 **Assessing and Intervening With Clients in Danger and Crisis** 163
LINDA FOSTER, PAUL HARD, AND ERIC DARCH

Preview 163
The Importance of Training in Risk Assessment and Suicide and Crisis Prevention 163
Assessing Client Suicide Risk 166
Risk Factors, Warning Signs, and Protective Factors 166
Evidence-Based Suicide Risk Assessment 166
Assessment Instruments 167
Determining Risk Level 168
Some Best and Not So Best Practices 169
Interventions With Suicide 170
Documentation of Assessment and Intervention Efforts 171
Duty to Warn 174
Homicidal Clients 175
Assessment of Homicide Risk 175
Media Influence 176
School Violence 176
Workplace Violence 177
Intimate Partner Violence 177
Assessing Your Views 177
Counselor Safety Plan 178
Threat Level Assessment 178

Homicide Survivors 179
Legal and Ethical Concerns 180
Disaster: Large-Scale Shock 180
Disaster Response Phases 180
Survivor Responses 181
Safety Issues 181
Intervention Approaches 182
Training Programs 183
Disaster Legal and Ethical Issues 184
Death Notification 185
Termination 185
Wellness 185
Large-Scale Shock, Disasters, and Cultural Considerations 186
Summary 186

9 Practicing Professional Responsibility 188
STEPHANIE G. PULEO, CHARLOTTE DAUGHHETEE, AND JASON M. NEWELL

Preview 188
What Does It Mean to Practice Responsibly? 188
The Counselor Is Responsible To . . . 189
Counselors Are Responsible for Being . . . 191
How Do Counselors Know If They Are Practicing Responsibly? 197
Responsibility Is Revealed in Professional Dispositions 197
Assessment of Professional Dispositions 202
Summary 205

10 Wrapping It Up 207
NICOLE A. STARGELL AND BRADLEY T. ERFORD

Preview 207
Termination 207
Termination of Supervisory Relationships 208
Termination of Counseling Relationships 214
Meta-Learning: Learning From What You've Learned 217
Summary 220

11 Other Pertinent Issues in Counseling Practice 221
ELISABETH BENNETT AND MARK A. YOUNG

Preview 221
A Day in the Life of a Counselor 221
The Role of the Counselor 222
Consultation 223
Career Guidance 226
Academic Advising 232
Advocacy in Counseling 233
Psychopharmacology 235
Frontal Lobe 235
Parietal Lobe 235
Occipital Lobe 236
Temporal Lobe 236

Limbic System 236
Endocrine System 236
Neurons and Synapses 237
Psychological, Educational, and Vocation Assessment 242
The "Business" of Counseling: Third-Party Payers 246
Summary 248

12 Counselor Self-Care 250
KERRY THON

Preview 250
Stress and the Helping Professions 250
Our Obligation to Help Ourselves 251
Helpful Models for Understanding Stress 252
Identifying Personal Stressors 252
Coping With Personal Stressors—Dimensions of Health and Intervention 253
Counselor Self-Care 253
Recognizing and Avoiding Burnout 259
Vicarious Trauma, Compassion Fatigue, and Secondary Trauma 260
Common Sources of Stress for the Beginning Counselor 262
Lack of Delegating 262
Difficulty With Boundaries 262
Inability to Compartmentalize 264
Role Confusion 264
Being All Things to All People 265
Feelings of Incompetence 265
Personal Counseling 266
Summary 267

13 From Envisioning to Actualization: Marketing Yourself in the 21st Century 268
NICOLE A. STARGELL AND JESSICA A. HEADLEY

Preview 268
From Envisioning to Actualization: Marketing Yourself in the 21st Century 268
Temet Nosce 268
Select Strengths 268
Examine Values, Biases, and Beliefs 269
Live With Limitations 270
Formulate Your Counseling Approach 270
Understanding the Field Around You 271
Using Networking Opportunities and Embracing Mentorship 272
Securing a Job the Old-Fashioned Way 273
Preparing a Curriculum Vita or Resume 273
Using Your Resume or CV 278
Cover Letters 279
The Job Search 279
Landing the Interview and Following Up 281
Carving Out Your New-Age Niche 281
Reaching Out with Social Networking 282
Selling Yourself on the Virtual Job Market 282

Building a Professional Website 283
Virtual Liabilities 284
The Advantages of Continued Learning 284
Keep Up to Date 285
Become an Expert 285
Summary 286

References 287
Index 302

Preface and Acknowledgments

Practicum and Internship Experiences in Counseling provides much more than a basic review of practicum and internship. In this text, students will experience a series of "ah-ha" moments where issues, only partially understood before, are brought to life in practical situations; where the information from one's course of study comes together to form a complete picture; and where an intern understands the counseling profession and process holistically. A special feature of the text is the frequent integration of self-assessments of personal beliefs, professional knowledge, and personal characteristics used to identify areas of strength, as well as areas in need of further improvement. Thus, *Practicum and Internship Experiences in Counseling* serves as a road map to optimize the practicum and internship experience, allowing the student to draw confidence from a knowledge base, continually self-assess in every area pertinent to competent practice, and integrate theory into intentional practice under supervision.

Practicum and Internship Experiences in Counseling emphasizes numerous issues often overlooked in clinical seminars and experiences, yet repeatedly experienced by the beginning counselor, including:

1. Clarification of the confusion surrounding the counseling profession.
2. The importance of goodness of fit between student skills and placement.
3. The importance of understanding and operating from theoretical perspective.
4. The essentials of the initial meeting with a client.
5. Common ethical dilemmas experienced in counseling practice.
6. Multicultural issues related to not only ethnicity, but also gender, religion, sexual orientation, and disability.
7. How to respond to large-scale crises.
8. How to respond to a client who intends to harm self or others.
9. How to deliver evidence-based practice.
10. Management of counselor self-care.

Chapter 1, "Matching Goals, Developing Skills, and the First Impression" by Robin Wilbourn Lee, Rachel M. O'Neill, Jennifer Jordan, Michelle Stevens, and Bradley T. Erford, introduces the student to the wonderful world of the counseling field experience. We differentiate between practicum and internship experiences, focusing on the goals of each, and then discuss helpful orientation information, such as working in multidisciplinary teams and matching your assets with preferred client populations and sites. A specific focus is placed on self-reflection, self-assessment, and identification of personal strengths and areas of challenge. Clinical experiences may also be a time of trepidation, as many trainees ask themselves questions like, "Do I really have the skills for this?" or, "What if my supervisor doesn't like me?" or, "What if I have a client with issues I can't handle?" All these questions are a normal part of entering a new experience. An important goal for students at this point is to prepare for the anxiety one may experience as the student moves from practice to real-life situations. Chapter 1 provides an in-depth review of intake and treatment planning procedures.

In Chapter 2, "The Supervision Process," Catherine Y. Chang, Caroline O'Hara, and Lindy K. Parker unveil the supervision process as a complicated process that involves various individuals (i.e., supervisor, supervisee, and client) and organizations (i.e., the university and the practicum/internship agency or school) and transpires through various stages. In this chapter, we explore supervision processes, the various roles you will hold as you begin your practicum–internship sequence, and what you can expect from your on-site and university supervisors. We will also cover the development of positive supervision relationships and learning goals as well as the differences between supervision and counseling. In addition, we will discuss barriers to effective supervision, different theoretical approaches, and ways of making case presentations. Throughout this chapter, several self-assessment activities are provided to help students identify strengths, growing edges, needs, and goals.

Chapter 3, "Integrating Theory Into Practice," by Dana Heller Levitt and Bradley T. Erford, answers the question: Why do professional counselors study theories? Whether working with individuals, families, or groups, regardless of the setting, professional counselors have a professional responsibility to develop a foundation and clear rationale for their theoretical orientation to serve clients best. Professional counselors operate out of theories that best fit their personal philosophies of human change and the counseling process, but also choose approaches that effectively address the client's issues. Selecting a theoretical orientation is a career-long process that begins during professional training. In Chapter 4, the significance of integrating theory into counseling practice is explored, and a brief overview of the major theoretical paradigms is presented. Students also begin to explore their own initial preferences for theoretical orientation with the intent of continuing one's personal and professional exploration to discover a personal, integrated counseling style.

Chapter 4, "Record Keeping: What to Include and What to Leave Out," by James Jackson, Latofia P. Parker, and Charlotte Daughhetee, asserts that appropriate clinical record keeping is essential to ethical practice. When documenting counseling services, it is imperative that counselors be mindful of the legal, ethical, and agency requirements regarding documentation. Good comprehensive record keeping promotes quality treatment and documents that treatment falls within accepted standards of care, thereby providing protection from liability risk. By following standard therapy note-writing formats and allowing time for note-writing immediately following a session, counselors can produce precise yet thorough documentation of their practice. In addition to client records, counselors engage in other types of professional writing, including communication with other professionals and the production of practice marketing materials. The ability to write professionally is vital to professional responsible practice.

Chapter 5, "Putting Ethics and Law Into Practice," by Lynn E. Linde and Bradley T. Erford, addresses some ethical and legal issues in counseling commonly encountered by counselors-in-training. Professional counselors must always remember that how one conducts oneself personally and professionally reflects not only on oneself, but also on colleagues and the counseling profession. Knowledge and understanding of the issues reviewed in this chapter on ethics and laws are only a starting point. Counselors must keep up to date with the laws, ethics, policies, and procedures that govern professional practice in your state and workplace. The implementation of professional responsibilities will require undivided attention every day of one's professional life.

Chapter 6, "Special Populations and Issues," by Victoria E. Kress, Matthew J. Paylo, Nicole A. Stargell, and Christine A. McAllister, provides ample evidence that professional counselors are regularly faced with myriad complex client or student presenting issues that require the synthesis of information spanning multiple areas. The topics presented in this chapter cover a variety of issues and populations that counselors will confront in practice and are those that were likely not addressed in detail in other areas of the counseling curriculum. In approaching these topics, an emphasis was placed on presenting basic, practical information that may help counselors navigate their work with these populations. The presentations provided are intended to serve as a starting point for considering one's work with the indicated populations.

Chapter 7, "Applying Multicultural Counseling," by José Villalba and Bradley T. Erford, will enhance the reader's clinical experiences by exploring the historical and contextual nature of cultural sensitivity, examining the development of the Multicultural and Social Justice Counseling Competencies, delving into the reader's self-awareness and the role self-awareness plays when working with individuals identifying with different societal groups, and finally, emphasizing the benefits of working with clients from a strengths-based approach. To facilitate the reader's heightened multicultural counseling competence while in their clinical placement, each of the four sections of Chapter 8 concludes with a series of self-assessment activities and case study scenarios related specifically to the content of a particular chapter section.

Chapter 8, "Assessing and Intervening With Clients in Danger and Crisis," by Linda Foster, Paul Hard, and Eric Darch, focuses on assessment and intervention of clients in crisis. Counselors must be prepared to assess and intervene with clients who may be a danger to themselves (i.e., suicidal), others (i.e., homicidal), or have experienced traumatic events due to either natural disasters or man-made events. Topics of suicide, homicide, and large-scale shock can be uncomfortable for counselors-in-training, so self-assessment examples and activities are included to help students gain insight and create a personal philosophy for working with these issues.

Chapter 9, "Practicing Professional Responsibility," by Stephanie G. Puleo, Charlotte Daughhetee, and Jason M. Newell, explores the theoretical foundations of ethical, proficient counseling practice and the developmental process of ongoing advancement of therapeutic expertise. In particular, the chapter discusses the sacred nature of the counseling relationship and the professional behaviors that are expected of the counselor in service of that relationship. Clients entrust aspects of their lives to counselors, placing a daunting amount of responsibility on them. The counseling relationship and the welfare of the client are contingent on professional, responsible practice by the counselor; therefore, the continuing improvement of one's counseling practice is fundamental to best practice. A major key to proficient counseling practice is the self-awareness of the counselor and the counselor's ability to assess areas of personal and professional growth. Commitment to continuing competency as a lifelong professional value is stressed, and the importance of advocacy for the profession and for clients is posited as essential to responsible professional practice.

Chapter 10, "Wrapping It Up," by Nicole A. Stargell and Bradley T. Erford, focuses on how best to terminate therapeutic relationships or transition clients from intern care to the care of another mental health professional. Clinical experiences also offer opportunities to reflect on what has been learned and to provide formative and summative performance evaluations of the student, supervisor, and training program.

Chapter 11, "Other Pertinent Issues in Counseling Practice," by Elisabeth Bennett, provides an overview of other pertinent issues/roles in counseling practice, including consultation, academic advising and career guidance, and advocacy. Supportive and collaborative services such as psychological, educational, and vocational assessment; compliance support for the psychopharmacological regimen set by a medical professional; and practice consistent with the requirements of third-party payers or managed care companies are also discussed. Understanding the role and function of the counselor is imperative in maintaining an ethical position and providing best practice throughout one's counseling career. A self-assessment at the end of each section will assist the reader in the application of knowledge in each area to the practice of counseling.

Up until this point, the focus has been primarily on your relationship and interactions with clients, how to provide outstanding services, and how to get the most out of your practicum and internship. In the final two chapters, the focus shifts and is now squarely on you as the counselor-in-training. Chapter 12, "Counselor Self-Care," by Kerry Thon, reviews the importance for all counselors to have an effective self-care plan to help prevent burnout and to deal with the stressors inherent in the counseling field. Clinical supervision allows you to seek advice and consultation from experienced counselors as you might seek knowledge from others who have gone before you. This can assist you in sidestepping common pitfalls and mistakes made by beginning counselors and provide much-needed support as you come to the limits of your competence. Your self-care plan is much like your protective gear, which can help you weather the storms as you navigate through your first counseling experiences. Many professionals have tools of their trade that they need to keep in tip-top shape. As counselors, we are our own best therapeutic tool, so we have an obligation to keep ourselves in shape mentally, physically, and spiritually. What you learn about stress and wellness applies to not only your clients but yourself as well.

Finally, Chapter 13, "From Envisioning to Actualization: Marketing Yourself in the 21st Century," by Nicole A. Stargell and Jessica A. Headley, addresses the importance of finding your place in the counseling market as a 21st-century counselor. The first part ("*Temet Nosce*") will address the significance of self-evaluation and reflection, using the SELF acronym. The second part ("Understanding the Field Around You") will highlight current trends and opportunities in the field. The third part ("Securing a Job the Old-Fashioned Way") will cover the logistics of the job search and traditional self-promotion strategies. The fourth part ("Carving Out Your New-Age Niche") will outline how social media can be used to establish counselor identity and credibility. Finally, the final part ("The Advantages of Continued Learning") will discuss how advanced training and postgraduate education can increase your marketing opportunities. Ultimately, the integration of information from all these sections will enhance your ability to promote yourself to potential employers and clients, giving you the edge you need to compete in this current market.

In summary, *Practicum and Internship Experiences in Counseling* emphasizes understanding one's roles as a counseling practicum student or intern, practicing competently, continuing to assess what is not yet understood, and understanding the duty to continually grow and learn as a professional counselor.

Acknowledgments

Anna Moore, my editor at Routledge, deserves special mention for her stewardship during the writing and production of this book. Additional thanks go to Makenzie Crouch, an outstanding copy editor at Apex CoVantage; and to Spandana Bakthavachalam, my project manager at Apex CoVantage for outstanding service.

About the Editor

Bradley T. Erford, PhD, LCPC, NCC, LPC, LP, LSP, is a professor and director of the human development counseling program of the Department of Human and Organizational Development in the Peabody College at Vanderbilt University. He was the 61st president of the American Counseling Association (ACA) for 2012–2013 and an ACA past treasurer. He is a Fulbright Specialist and is the recipient of the ACA Research Award, ACA Extended Research Award, ACA Arthur A. Hitchcock Distinguished Professional Service Award, ACA Professional Development Award, Thomas J. Sweeney Award for Visionary Leadership and Advocacy, and ACA Carl D. Perkins Government Relations Award. He was also inducted as an ACA Fellow. In addition, he has received the Association for Assessment in Counseling and Education (AACE) AACE/MECD Research Award, AACE Exemplary Practices Award, AACE President's Merit Award, the Association for Counselor Education and Supervision's (ACES) Robert O. Stripling Award for Excellence in Standards, Maryland Association for Counseling and Development (MACD) Maryland Counselor of the Year, MACD Counselor Advocacy Award, MACD Professional Development Award, and MACD Counselor Visibility Award. He is the editor of numerous texts, including: *Orientation to the Counseling Profession*, *Crisis Intervention and Prevention*, *Group Work in the Schools*, *Practicum and Internship Experiences in Counseling*, *Group Work: Process and Applications*, *Transforming the School Counseling Profession*, *Professional School Counseling: A Handbook of Principles, Programs and Practices*, *Assessment for Counselors*, *Research and Evaluation in Counseling*, and *The Counselor's Guide to Clinical, Personality and Behavioral Assessment*; and co-author of several more books: *Mastering the NCE and CPCE*, *45 Techniques Every Counselor Should Know*, *Free Access Assessment Instruments for Common Mental Health and Addiction Issues*, *Educational Applications of the WISC-IV*. and *Group Activities: Firing Up for Performance*. He is also the General Editor of *The American Counseling Association Encyclopedia of Counseling*. His research specialization falls primarily in outcome research and development and technical analysis of psychoeducational tests and has resulted in the publication of more than 90 refereed journal articles, 150 book chapters, and 20 published tests. He is Editor Emeritus of *Measurement and Evaluation in Counseling and Development* (MECD) and Senior Associate Editor of *Journal of Counseling & Development* (JCD). He was a representative to the ACA Governing Council and the ACA 20/20 Visioning Committee. He is a past president and past treasurer of AARC, past chair and parliamentarian of the American Counseling Association—Southern (US) Region; past chair of ACA's Task Force on High Stakes Testing; past chair of ACA's Standards for Test Users Task Force; past chair of ACA's Interprofessional Committee; past chair of the ACA Public Awareness and Support Committee (co-chair of the National Awards Sub-committee); chair of the Convention and past chair of the Screening Assessment Instruments Committees for AACE; past president of the Maryland Association for Counseling and Development (MACD); past president of Maryland Association for Measurement and Evaluation (MAME); past president of Maryland Association for Counselor Education and Supervision (MACES); and past president of the Maryland Association for Mental Health Counselors (MAMHC). He was an associate editor of the *Journal of Counseling & Development*. Dr. Erford is a licensed clinical professional counselor, licensed professional counselor, national certified counselor, licensed psychologist, and licensed school psychologist. A graduate of the University of Virginia (PhD), Bucknell University (MA), and Grove City College (BS), he teaches courses in assessment, research, and evaluation in counseling and stress management (not that he needs it!).

Contributors

Elisabeth Bennett, PhD, is a counselor educator at Gonzaga University, where she is a professor and senior faculty. She has been providing counseling services to the community for over 35 years in various settings, including hospital, agency, school, clinic, and private practice. Her education, training, and experience range across several specialties, including neuropsychology and assessment, gerontology, trauma and abuse, child and adolescent development, marriage, couple, and family issues, peri and postpartum concerns, and organizational leadership, functioning, and productivity. Her greatest education pleasure remains with her students and their clinical training.

Catherine Y. Chang, PhD, is a professor in the Department of Counseling and Psychological Services at Georgia State University. She is Director of International Programs for the College of Education and Human Development. Her areas of research interest include multicultural counseling and supervision, professional and social advocacy in counseling, and Asian and Korean concerns.

Eric Darch, PhD, received his doctorate in counselor education and supervision, an MEd in school counseling, and a BA in foreign language (Spanish), all from Auburn University. He has over 20 years of Title 1 public school experience serving as a teacher and school counselor within all grades PK–12. He is a nationally certified counselor (NCC) and a nationally certified school counselor (NCSC). His professional interests include: the role of the school counselor, children and adolescents, ethics in school counseling, translating research to practice in the school setting, behavior management, and multicultural and linguistically diverse students. He has several publications and has presented on these topics.

Charlotte Daughhetee is Professor Emeritus at the University of Montevallo. She is an NCC, LPC, and LMFT, and has counseling experience in K–12, university, and private practice settings. She earned her MEd in school counseling and PhD in counselor education from the University of South Carolina. She has experience in crisis intervention in school and university settings and has presented and published on crisis intervention.

Linda Foster, PhD, NCC, NCSC, LPC-S, is a core faculty member in the clinical mental health counseling program at Walden University. She received her undergraduate degree from Samford University, master's and education specialist degrees in community counseling from the University of Alabama in Birmingham, and a PhD in counselor education at Mississippi State University. Dr. Foster worked as a licensed professional counselor for over ten years at the elementary, middle, and high school level, maintained a small private practice, supervised graduates for licensure, and has been a full-time counselor educator since 2007. She has served on local, state, national, and international counseling boards and editorial boards. Dr. Foster's research interests include professional identity of counselors, counselor education faculty dynamics, and the use of single subject research methods by counselors. Dr. Foster has presented various topics at the state, national, and international level and has published numerous articles in peer-reviewed journals, as well as several book chapters.

Paul Hard, PhD, LPC-S, NCC, is Department Chair of Counselor, Leadership, and Special Education with Auburn University at Montgomery, where his concentrations are in clinical mental health and marriage and family counseling. He has over 26 years of agency counseling and private practice. His clinical foci have been in the areas of addictions, relationship counseling, sexual minorities, and trauma. His research interests have been in the areas of ethics, counselor/professional impairment and wellness, complicated grieving in pre- and postnatal loss, professional credentialing and advocacy, sexual minority issues in counseling, and ministerial termination.

Jessica A. Headley, PhD, LPCC-S is an assistant professor at Ursuline College in the Counseling and Art Therapy Department and a licensed professional clinical counselor–supervisor. She has served as a professional counselor for over ten years in various settings, including hospitals, community mental health, colleges, and private practice. Currently she serves as the CEO of a private practice, Wellness Grove, in Ohio, where she specializes in women and gender issues, career development, gerontology, and creativity in counseling. She has numerous presentations and publications in these areas, as well as counseling leadership and advocacy.

James Jackson, PhD, LPC, NCC is a professor and coordinator of the Clinical Mental Health Counseling track at the University of Montevallo in Montevallo, Alabama. His clinical specialties include play therapy, trauma-focused cognitive-behavioral therapy, and advocacy services with abused children and adolescents in schools, foster homes, and group homes, as well as serving adults and families through private practice, in-home, and community mental health agencies.

Jennifer Jordan, PhD, LPCS, NCC, is a professor in the counseling and development program at Winthrop University. She is the president of the South Carolina Board of Examiners for licensed professional counselors, marriage and family therapists, addictions counselors, and psychoeducational specialists and the executive director of the South Carolina Counseling Association.

Victoria E. Kress, PhD, LPCC-S, NCC, CCMHC, is a counseling clinic director, distinguished professor, and the coordinator of the clinical mental health and addictions counseling programs at Youngstown State University. She has 30+ years of clinical experience in various settings, including community mental health centers, hospitals, residential treatment facilities, private practice, and college counseling centers. She has published five textbooks and over 140 journal articles and book chapters on counseling youth and adults.

Robin Wilbourn Lee, PhD, LPC/MHSP, NCC, ACS, is a professor in the professional counseling program at Middle Tennessee State University. She received her doctoral degree in counselor education and supervision from Mississippi State University. Her interests include counselor professional issues, advocacy, and ethical and legal issues.

Dana Heller Levitt, PhD, is a professor of counselor education and department chair at Montclair State University. She received her master's and doctoral degrees from the University of Virginia. Dr. Levitt's research focuses on ethics and counselor development, eating disorders, and body image.

Lynn E. Linde, EdD, is the Executive Director of the Center for Counseling Practice, Policy, and Research at the American Counseling Association. She formerly was Coordinator of Clinical Experiences in the school counseling program at Loyola University Maryland. She received her doctorate in counseling from George Washington University. She is a former Branch Chief for Pupil Services at the Maryland State Department of Education. She was the 2009–2010 President of the American Counseling Association and 2012–2103 Treasurer. She was the Southern Region representative to the ACA Governing Council, past chair of the ACA–Southern Region, and past president of the Maryland Association for Counseling and Development, and has served on numerous committees and task forces, including the 2014 ACA Ethics Revision Task Force. She is an ACA Fellow, a recipient of the Carl Perkins Award, and a number of awards from ACA, its entities, and the State of Maryland.

Christine A. McAllister, MSEd, is a licensed professional counselor. Her clinical and research interests include trauma, suicide, chronic illness, and LGBTQ+ affirmative care. She has published several articles and book chapters, presented at several counseling conferences, and engages in servant leadership for counseling organizations, including Association for Humanistic Counseling, Ohio Counseling Association, and Chi Sigma Iota.

Jason M. Newell, PhD, LICSW-PIP, is a professor and social work program director in the Department of Behavioral and Social Sciences at the University of Montevallo. His research and specialty areas include clinical social work practice; treatment of anxiety, trauma-related, and mood disorders; and professional resilience. He teaches introductory courses in social welfare and social work practice, human behavior and the social environment, research methods, practice with individuals and families, and practice in mental health care.

Caroline O'Hara, PhD, LPC (GA), NCC, is a scholar and advocate working as an assistant professor at Syracuse University. She primarily publishes and presents in the areas of microaggressions, social justice, and advocacy (both client and professional). Most of her counseling experience has been in college counseling centers providing campus outreach as well as individual, group, career, and disability counseling. She has also worked in partial hospitalization, hospital, and hospice settings. Dr. O'Hara has also held multiple leadership positions at local and national levels.

Rachel M. O'Neill, PhD, is a clinical director at a behavioral health organization and adjunct faculty member in the counseling programs at Youngstown State University and Walden University. She has authored over 15 scholarly journal articles and book chapters and has presented over 70 times at national, state, and local conferences and workshops. She has experience working in a variety of settings, including addictions treatment, community-based mental health, inpatient psychiatric services, and college counseling.

Latofia P. Parker, PhD, LPC, NCC, BC-TMH, completed her doctoral study at the University of Alabama and is an associate professor in the counselor education program at the University of Montevallo with primary teaching responsibilities in grief and loss, ethical and legal issues in counseling, and clinical supervision. Her research interest includes crisis intervention, counselor education pedagogy, and ethical and legal issues in counselor education.

Lindy K. Parker, PhD, is a licensed professional counselor and currently serves as a clinical assistant professor at the University of Georgia. She has clinical experience in multiple settings, including college counseling centers, psychiatric hospitals, substance abuse programs, adolescent outpatient facilities, alternative schools, and private practice. Dr. Parker has designed new undergraduate, graduate, and dual degree programs, and she has enhanced existing academic programs to better prepare graduates for mental health, public health, law, and maternal and child health positions. She has received external funding from the Department of Education, the Health Resources and Services Administration, and the Department of Defense for her program development efforts. Dr. Parker has conducted research in the areas of gatekeeping, career counseling, professional advocacy, animal-assisted therapy, and school counseling.

Matthew J. Paylo, PhD, is a professor of counseling at Concordia University Irvine. He has over 12 years of experience in counselor education and 20 years of clinical experience in various settings, including community mental health centers, prisons, hospitals, adolescent residential treatment facilities, and college counseling centers. Dr. Paylo is passionate about implementing evidence-based interventions within therapeutic relationships that highlight empathy, unconditional positive regard, and genuineness. Matthew co-authored two books on assessing, diagnosing, and treating mental and emotional disorders. In addition, he has published numerous journal articles and book chapters on trauma, evidence-based treatments, offender treatments, adolescent counseling, social justice counseling, and the implementation of the DSM.

Stephanie G. Puleo, PhD, LMFT, LPC, NCC is a retired counselor educator who held faculty appointments at the University of Florida and the University of Montevallo. She earned her PhD in counselor education at the University of Alabama. She also earned master's degrees in school psychology and community counseling and is certified by the American Red Cross in disaster mental health. In addition to providing counseling and supervision services in the Birmingham, AL, and Atlanta, GA, areas, Dr. Puleo continues to enjoy writing and creative endeavors.

Nicole A. Stargell, PhD, is an associate professor at the University of North Carolina at Pembroke (UNCP). She is a licensed school counselor and licensed clinical mental health counselor, as well as a national certified counselor. Dr. Stargell serves as the chair of the Department of Counseling at UNCP, the testing coordinator, and faculty advisor for the Phi Sigma Chapter of Chi Sigma Iota. She is a member of the UNCP Institutional Review Board and serves on the editorial board for the national journal *Counseling Outcome Research & Evaluation* and the regional journal *Teaching and Supervision in Counseling*.

Michelle Stevens, PhD, is an adjunct faculty member in the professional counseling program and the inaugural director of the Center for Fairness, Justice, and Equity in the College of Education at Middle Tennessee State University. Prior to joining the clinical mental health faculty, Stevens instructed at Youngstown State

University, Cleveland State University, and Kent State University. Past positions held by Stevens include president of the MTSU Black Faculty and Staff Association from 2018 to 2020 and assistant director of the Center for Counseling and Psychological Services. Other areas of interest include the study of cultural issues and historical trauma in the Black community and mentoring throughout the pipeline.

Kerry Thon, MA, LCPC, is a licensed clinical professional counselor (LCPC) in Illinois. She earned a MA in professional counseling from the Illinois School of Professional Psychology. She has over 16 years of direct clinical experience working with children, adolescents, and families. She has worked in residential treatment facilities, therapeutic day schools, private practice, and within community agencies. Her clinical experience, as both a clinical therapist and clinical director, focused on addressing trauma symptoms, mood disorders, anxiety disorders, and aggression and self-injurious behaviors. She has been an affiliate faculty member at The Family Institute at Northwestern University since 2017. She has over 15 years of experience as an adjunct faculty member with several university counseling programs throughout Illinois. She is a past president of the Illinois Mental Health Counselors Association and maintained a board position for ten years. Her clinical interests include trauma work, mood and anxiety disorders, and self-care and wellness-based practices for counselors and other mental health professionals.

José Villalba, PhD, received his doctorate in counselor education from the University of Florida. He is Vice President for Diversity and Inclusion and Chief Diversity Officer. Prior to his current position, José served as Senior Associate Dean for Faculty, Evaluation, and Inclusivity in the Office of the Dean of the College. He also is a professor of counseling. He has been affiliated with the Department of Counseling since arriving at Wake Forest in 2011. Prior to arriving at Wake Forest, he was an associate professor of counseling at the University of North Carolina at Greensboro, as well as an assistant professor of counseling at Indiana State University. He teaches courses in multicultural counseling, school counseling, and health and human services. His research interests include health disparities in Latina/o youth, as well as Latina/o access to and completion of higher education option.

Mark A. Young, PhD, LMHC, NCC, completed his doctorate at Idaho State University and is currently an assistant professor and director of the Marriage and Family Counseling Program at Gonzaga University. His teaching and research interests are in couples and family counseling, live supervision, and attachment based interventions.

1

Matching Goals, Developing Skills, and the First Impression

Robin Wilbourn Lee, Rachel M. O'Neill, Jennifer Jordan, Michelle Stevens, and Bradley T. Erford

Preview

This initial chapter introduces you to the wonderful world that awaits in your counseling field experience. We differentiate between practicum and internship experiences, focusing on the goals of each, and then discuss helpful orientation information such as working in multidisciplinary teams and matching your assets with preferred client populations and sites. A specific focus is placed on self-reflection, self-assessment, and identification of personal strengths and areas of challenge. Finally, we review where you are heading, including information related to certification, licensure, and employment. Entering the field experiences of practicum and internship is often a time of excitement because it is an opportunity to work with real clients rather than practicing counseling skills by role-playing skills with peers. It may also be a time of trepidation, as many trainees ask themselves questions like, "Do I really have the skills for this?" or, "What if my supervisor doesn't like me?" or, "What if I have a client with issues I can't handle?" All these questions are a normal part of entering a new experience. An important goal for you at this point is to prepare for the anxiety you may experience as you move from practice to real-life situations. But remember, this is what you have trained for in your many classes and experiences. In addition, this is your career choice, and hopefully, you are excited about finally being able to begin your career as a professional counselor.

Beginning Your Field Experience

Congratulations! You are embarking on one of the most exciting periods of your graduate training: the field experience! Your practicum and internship experiences afford you the opportunity to interact with clients and put all the knowledge and skills that you've learned in the classroom into practice. Practicum and internship experiences give you an opportunity to practice counseling skills and techniques under supervision. It's important that you are prepared to take full advantage of the field experience. This chapter and the entire text will help provide you with resources to make the most of your practicum and internship placements. This text is designed to be read in its entirety; yet, it will also be helpful as a reference for special issues in the future. Each chapter will help inform a different aspect of your practicum and internship experiences.

A few years ago, an intern stated, "I wish I knew exactly what my client was going to say *before* I went into session. That way, I could be prepared with exactly how to respond." The idea of feeling unprepared to work with client concerns is one of the most common themes we hear as counselor supervisors. Trainees often feel overwhelmed at the thought of finally putting all their education into practice. Feeling overwhelmed is natural and can actually be helpful in motivating you to be more effective as a counselor trainee. After all, it would probably be concerning if you weren't at least somewhat anxious about your first experiences working with a client.

Although anxiety is normal, there are steps that you can take to prepare for your field experience (see Think About It 1.1). Being proactive in developing good relationships with supervisors, coworkers, and peers can be especially helpful in ensuring a successful field experience. The intent of this text is to impart strategies for a successful field experience. This chapter will provide a brief overview of the field experiences (i.e., practicum and internship) and will serve as the foundation for the rest of the text. Now, let's dive right into the wonderful world of the field experience!

DOI: 10.4324/9781003305521-1

Think About It 1.1

As previously mentioned, many students experience anxiety when considering their first practicum or internship experience. Reflect on the following questions:

1. What am I most anxious about with regard to practicum or internship?
2. What am I most looking forward to with regard to practicum or internship?

Now consider and reflect on your goals for practicum or internship.

3. How do you define a successful practicum or internship experience?
4. What skills will you hope to develop during practicum or internship?
5. What steps can you take to ensure that you'll develop these skills?

Differentiating Between the Goals and Objectives of Practicum and Internship

Practicum and internship are often referred to as the field experiences. Combining the two field experiences can often lead students to believe that these experiences are quite similar. However, it's important to note that practicum and internship serve very different functions in counselor training. In this section, we will review the differences between practicum and internship experiences.

Practicum

In most counselor education programs practicum represents the first introduction to the field experiences. In some cases, students may complete practicum experiences *on-site* (e.g., at a university counseling center under faculty supervision) or *off-site* (e.g., at a community-based agency or school). Regardless of the location, the practicum experience is designed to serve as an introduction to the practice of working with clients. During practicum, you will learn how to complete client-related documentation (e.g., progress notes, individualized service plans) and become oriented to your practicum location and the field of counseling.

Orientation is ordinarily an overarching goal of the practicum experience. Practicum is a time for you to learn about your site's policies and procedures, become familiar with standards of practice, and basically become acclimated to the site and your supervisor's expectations for your performance. You will get to know the other employees at the site and learn your way around the facility. Your practicum experience also provides you with the opportunity to observe client sessions and the resulting process of documentation. Many practicum students find this helpful, as it allows an opportunity to see other professionals interact with clients. Finally—at long last—practicum experiences allow students to counsel real live clients with real presenting concerns.

For students who are enrolled in a Council for Accreditation of Counseling and Related Educational Programs (CACREP) accredited program, all field experiences will follow the requirements set forth by CACREP (2016) standards. These requirements include the provision of at least 100 practicum clock hours, 40 of which must include direct service (i.e., face-to-face contact) with clients. The other 60 hours can be accrued in a variety of ways, including researching treatments, reviewing site policies and procedures, and completing client documentation.

CACREP requirements also provide specific direction related to the provision of counselor trainee supervision. Later in this chapter we will discuss the purpose of supervision and how you can maximize the effectiveness of your interactions with your supervisor. For now, it is important to mention that CACREP standards require one hour per week of individual (dyadic or triadic) on-site supervision with an approved clinical supervisor. In addition to on-site supervision, you are also required to complete an average of 90 minutes of group supervision with an approved faculty member from your university. This weekly group supervision usually takes place in the classroom, with a faculty member providing group supervision to students who are enrolled in the practicum course for that particular term.

Internship

Internship generally represents a full foray into the counseling profession—living the life of the counselor. Most internship sites will require interns to complete all the responsibilities generally associated with the counseling position, such as documentation, billing, and productive counseling practice. In schools, interns will run groups and conduct developmental classroom activities. Students who are enrolled in a CACREP-accredited program will be required to complete at least 600 clock hours of internship work, which will typically occur over the course of two to three semesters or three to four quarters. Of these hours, at least 40% must occur in direct service activities, whereas the remaining hours can result in non-direct care. Supervision requirements remain the same as in the practicum, with students receiving at least one hour of individual (dyadic or triadic) supervision on-site and an average of 90 minutes of group supervision weekly, usually provided in a group seminar on a university campus.

In internship, you will generally be assigned a caseload of clients. Caseloads will vary according to your setting; outpatient interns might be responsible for five to ten clients at a time, whereas inpatient interns might be responsible for only two to three patients at a time. In schools, an intern will generally share responsibility for student cases from the supervising school counselor's caseload. It is important to have open discussions with your supervisor related to the number of active clients with whom you feel comfortable working. Whether enrolled in practicum or internship, field experiences will help you to hone your counseling skills with real clients and students who present with real-life challenges.

Voices From the Field 1.1 My Internship Experience, *by Rick Fawcett*

I remember sitting in my first internship counseling session. I was dressed nicely, seated in the proper SOLER position (sit squarely, open posture, lean slightly, eye contact, relax), and I was absolutely terrified as I waited for the client to arrive. The room felt like a sauna, and I was sweating bullets as I waited for the session to begin. Would the client cry? Would I cry? Would my faculty and site supervisors cry when they saw my sessions? I felt like the session began and ended within the span of five minutes, and the client and I both survived tearlessly.

I became more comfortable as my internship progressed. My internship site, a residential addiction treatment facility, was intimidating at first. I had never worked with clients in the community, much less with clients who have such a critical issue to deal with, one that could actually kill them. The counselors and staff at the facility were very helpful. I asked a great number of questions, but they were always there to help. When in doubt, I asked the question, and they were always available with an answer, probably recalling their own days as an intern.

Humility and ambition have been very important in my internship. I had to have a lot of humility to realize exactly how much I did not know. My professors had done a great job preparing me, but there is no substitute for real experience. If I was unsure, I asked. Sometimes my hunch was right, but sometimes it was wrong, so it was best to ask. Ambition helped me to make my own opportunities, which was crucial. I could have sat in an office all day, but I sought out opportunities in co-counseling, group counseling, assessments, and getting involved in other areas. I asked for more responsibilities, and that made my experience more valuable and enriching.

In the following sections, we will review some important components of a successful field experience. However, attending to seemingly minor details can also lead to a smooth field experience (see Personal Reflection 1.1).

Personal Reflection 1.1

I completed my doctoral internship at a private, for-profit psychiatric hospital that provided acute care to children and adolescents. Although the facility was new to me, I was a licensed counselor, and I had worked in the field for a couple of years. On my first day, a Friday, I went to the agency dressed in my typical business attire. I was surprised, however, to notice that all the staff were dressed rather casually with most—even the psychiatrists—wearing jeans and casual shirts. Although I was surprised, I noted that several area hospitals had adopted an informal dress code policy, and I assumed that perhaps this hospital had decided to follow suit. In retrospect, I should have checked with my supervisor; however, it felt trivial to ask him about dress code when I had so many other pressing issues to address during our brief meeting that first day. So, instead, I returned to my internship on Monday dressed in jeans and a sweater. You can imagine my surprise (and horror!) when I noticed that everyone was dressed in business attire. I quickly approached my supervisor to apologize for my casual attire and explain my mistaken assumption that the hospital endorsed a casual dress code policy. My supervisor chuckled and reminded me that my first day had been a Friday, which meant that the staff members were dressed for *casual Friday*. Naturally, I spent the rest of the day completely uncomfortable with my attire and wishing that I would have just asked my supervisor about appropriate dress during my first day. The moral of the story? *Nothing* is too insignificant to talk about with your supervisor. If you're confused, if you have a question, or if you need clarification, then you need to speak with your supervisor. Remember, your supervisor signed on to work with you knowing that you are new to the profession; thus, the supervisor expects that you will have a lot of questions about the internship process. ~RO

There are many components to a successful internship. In the following sections, we will provide a brief overview of some of the major areas of practicum and internship work. However, it is important to note that all field placement sites are unique; thus, it's important to talk with your site supervisor about important policies, procedures, and expectations specific to your site.

Working With a Multidisciplinary Team

A multidisciplinary team, sometimes referred to by other names, such as a treatment team, consists of a group of professionals from various professional backgrounds working together in the interest of effective client care. Depending on your field placement, you may be expected to work closely with a multidisciplinary team for the purposes of integrated coordination of client care. Multidisciplinary teams may consist of counselors, physicians (e.g., general practitioners, psychiatrists, pain management specialists), nurses, psychologists, social workers, occupational therapists, rehabilitation specialists, vocational specialists, supportive case managers, and paraprofessional support staff. Again, the type of setting that you work in and the client population that you serve will generally dictate the variety of team members assigned to work with the client. For example, counseling interns at an addiction treatment facility work as part of a team with an addictionologist (i.e., MD with a specialty in addiction medicine), nurses, social workers, case managers, and family counseling specialists. Another example of coordination of client care might include working with a client who has an eating disorder. In this example, it would be important for the counselor to work with the client's primary care physician to ensure proper management of the physical effects of the eating disorder. It would also be necessary to coordinate meal planning services and weight restoration with a nutritional counselor. Last, psychiatric services might be needed to help alleviate comorbid symptoms of depression or anxiety.

Working as part of a multidisciplinary treatment team has both advantages and challenges. In terms of advantages, working as part of a treatment team allows for different perspectives, which can contribute to a better overall understanding of the client and the presenting concern. Conversely, treatment teams can often make it difficult for some professionals, especially new professionals, to feel comfortable contributing to the team and advocating for the client. As part of a multidisciplinary treatment team, you must be prepared for all team meetings and be able to effectively articulate your clients' needs (see Case Study 1.1). Remember, you may be sharing your case with individuals who are approaching the client's care from a different perspective. As such, it is important that you are prepared to communicate your perspectives on the client's care in a clear and concise way that makes it easy for those with different professional backgrounds to understand. As noted earlier, your internship is an opportunity to begin to transition from the role of the student to the role of the professional counselor. It is important that you work to develop skills to effectively work and interact with other professionals.

Case Study 1.1 Shannon

Imagine you are a counseling intern in an outpatient counseling center who has been assigned to work with Shannon, a client who has, in the past, demonstrated resistance to the counseling process and has been a frequent no-show for her counseling appointments. During a recent team meeting, Shannon's psychiatrist noted that she missed an appointment with her last week, and the case manager also reported that Shannon has been late to several of her scheduled sessions. As Shannon's primary counselor, you know that her car recently broke down, and she's been having difficulty getting to her appointments on time; however, when she does attend her appointments with you, she seems motivated and willing to work on counseling goals. During the meeting, the case manager and psychiatrist wonder if perhaps Shannon should be discharged from treatment for non-compliance.

- Would you feel comfortable advocating for her continued involvement in treatment?
- Explain.

Many interns assume that they can simply refer clients with whom they do not wish to work. However, referring clients is not always a clear-cut process, and there are times when the referral might not be in the best interest of the client. Consider the case of Carlos (Case Study 1.2). It can be helpful to remember you are not expected to always *agree* with your clients' thoughts and behaviors. In fact, it is not necessary to be in agreement with your clients; it is, however, necessary to understand and validate the worldviews of clients.

Case Study 1.2 Carlos

Carlos is a 46-year-old Hispanic male who presented for counseling services with depression. Carlos is initially quite guarded and hesitant to open up to a counselor. After meeting for several sessions with Carlos, you've developed a good rapport with him, and he begins to open up about his past. Carlos reports to you that he used to be addicted to heroin, and while in his active addiction, he sexually assaulted a female. Carlos expresses remorse and regret over the event and identifies the experience as contributing to his current feelings of depression. Imagine if, as the assigned counselor, you informed Carlos that you would be facilitating a referral to another provider because you refused to work with sexual offenders.

- What effect might this notification have on Carlos?
- Is it possible that such behavior would damage the trust Carlos had placed in his counselor and potentially impact his future relationships with treatment providers?
- What would be a proper course for the intern to take?

Carlos's case illustrates that it is important for counselors to be prepared to deal with complex client cases and demonstrate compassion and good judgment, even under trying circumstances.

Hopefully, by this point in your professional development, you've considered areas that you consider personal strengths, as well as potential areas for growth or how to improve on demonstrated weaknesses. At this time, read Think About It 1.2, and consider what additional growing edges you need to develop.

Think About It 1.2

- What personal and professional learning experiences have you had that will contribute to your field experience? What do you do well? What strengths have you developed that will be helpful in working with your clients, supervisor, and coworkers?
- What personal and professional learning experiences will you need to continue your development as a counseling professional? In what areas do you need to grow? What will be the most difficult part of working with your clients, supervisor, and coworkers?

Voices From the Field 1.2 Maintaining Balance and Engaging in Self-Care, by *Julie Lenyk*

The process of being a counselor intern requires a lot of extra work both during scheduled hours and on your own personal time. During internship I learned that in the counseling profession, it is easy to become overinvolved with work and lose sight of taking care of your own well-being. However, over time I have learned that to be an effective counselor, it is important to be invested in your work, but it is also important to find a balance between your professional and personal life.

When I first started my internship, I realized that it was not going to be easy. I had to put in a lot of work to develop my skills as a counselor and a professional in this field. I spent a lot of time during regular work hours and outside work researching, practicing interventions, and prepping for my sessions. I also spent a lot of time completing the necessary paperwork, including progress notes and treatment plans. I found that on most days I had to come to work early and leave work late just to maintain all my professional responsibilities.

What I didn't realize at the time was that along with developing my professional skills and my passion for counseling, I was also developing poor self-care habits. Most days I would not take a lunch break or take time off to take care of my basic needs. I also spent many weekends studying and thinking about my clients. This did not offer me much time to engage in fun activities or interact with family and friends. I often put these things to the side because I did not think they were necessary for me to become a better counselor.

What I have learned is that self-care affects not only your personal well-being, but also your professional well-being and your ability to be an effective counselor. Self-care is just as important as researching interventions and preparing for sessions. It may take some time to develop a balance between work and personal priorities, but it is important to start maintaining a balance even before internship begins.

I now practice better self-care and engage in activities that enhance my overall well-being. I take time in between sessions to laugh with a colleague, meditate for a few minutes, or just get something to eat. I also spend time outside work practicing yoga, spending time with family and friends, and walking my dogs. It is important to make time for yourself and find what works for you. Maintaining a balance between work and leisure and engaging in self-care are important factors to ensure your success as a counselor.

Intake Session/Interview

Reviewing Informed Consent

The initial session has many purposes, one of which is an opportunity to ensure that your clients clearly understand their rights and responsibilities, which are typically included in some type of disclosure statement. Disclosure statements can take many forms. An agency will more than likely have a prepared set of documents that clients review and sign, whereas a school counselor may use a personally designed brochure. Informed consent is about your client's right to be educated about the process. It is important to recognize that although informed consent is typically presented in the initial session, it is also an ongoing process and should be reviewed and discussed multiple times as you are working with your clients. Regardless of your work setting, your skill regarding informed consent means being able to effectively explain the informed consent elements that relate to your site and your clients. Informed consent will be addressed comprehensively in Chapter 5.

Confidentiality

Of all the elements to be discussed during the informed consent process, confidentiality could be considered the most important. Confidentiality is a cornerstone of the counseling process. It affords the client the opportunity to discuss intimate details without the risk of having that information shared outside the sessions. Without confidentiality, it is doubtful that clients would choose counseling as a means to helping them resolve issues. However, although we need to make sure that clients understand confidentiality, they must also understand the limits to confidentiality. Confidentiality and the limits to confidentiality need to be reviewed multiple times while working with clients. Counselors must also consider how best to explain confidentiality to their clients, based on the population being served. If you are working with children, you know choosing language they can understand is crucial. If you are working with adolescents, understanding how important confidentiality is to them is crucial. Thus, explaining the limits may be challenging. The limits to confidentiality include (a) client waives privilege; (b) death of the client; (c) sharing information with subordinates for billing or record-keeping purposes; (d) consultation with fellow professionals; I protecting someone in danger; (f) counseling multiple clients in the same session; (g) counseling minor clients; (h) court-ordered disclosures; and (i) legal protections for counselors in disputes.

Although you may not choose to discuss all these limits with your clients, you should make sure that you are covering the limits most appropriate for your population. One key consideration is to make sure to provide enough information for your client to understand the information without overwhelming them with too much complicated jargon.

What to Do With Parents and Guardians in the Initial Session

If you are working in an agency setting, you should consider how to handle the parents of your minor clients. There are several factors to consider. First, you will need to help parents understand the counseling process. According to the ACA *Code of Ethics* (2014), parents are to be considered a resource for counselors. This differs from previous codes that stated counselors should only act in the best interest of the minor client. Second, you will need to discuss confidentiality as it relates to their children. Considering confidentiality and children, the law and ethical standards may diverge. According to most helping professions' ethical guidelines, children are afforded the same ethical rights to confidentiality as adults. However, the law states that a minor child has no privacy, and that privileged communication belongs to the parents/guardians. This can cause a dilemma for professional counselors. How do you keep your minor client's information confidential while respecting the parent's/guardian's rights to know? The following steps are recommended:

- Determine whether the minor is willing to disclose the information to the parents/guardians.
- Try to persuade the parent/guardian that it is in the best interest of the child not to disclose the confidential information.
- Schedule a joint meeting for the minor child and parent/guardian to resolve the issue; assume the role of the mediator.
- If you are disclosing to the parent/guardian, be sure to inform the minor prior to the disclosure.

Depending on the case, there may be a time when you feel that disclosing is not in the best interest of the minor client. In this case, you may decide not to disclose. When choosing this option, you should involve your supervisor to ensure that you are not held liable. Although cases in which you would not disclose to the parents/guardians have been described, it is important to remember that child abuse is always an exception to confidentiality and should be disclosed to authorities immediately.

Gathering Information and Client History

The first session with a client is often more structured and counselor driven than subsequent sessions. The first meeting is the time to conduct an intake. Different agencies have specific policies of how they handle the intake process, and it is important that you understand agency policy prior to your first client visit. Some agencies appoint an intake counselor to conduct the intake interview with all new clientele prior to assigning them a counselor. When gathering information in the intake interview, it is important to remember that this is also a time of relationship building with your client. Explaining the counseling process to them as well as how counseling will be conducted in the future helps to alleviate unnecessary anxiety. Most agencies have a specific intake protocol that includes demographic questions and a psychosocial history of the client. Standardized tests such as symptom and behavior inventories are often used to supplement the intake process to deepen the understanding of the client's treatment needs. Other options for gathering information in the intake include interviewing family members, friends, or teachers, after gaining the permission of the client, or parent/guardian of a minor client.

When gathering information, a professional counselor relies on the basic counseling skills mentioned earlier in the chapter. A heavy emphasis is placed on questioning, and in general, the more open-ended questions the counselor can ask, the more effective the interview will be. It is important to note when a client does not answer a question or hesitates, as what a client doesn't say can be just as important as what they do say. Do not force a client to answer questions with which they are uncomfortable. You can always go back to those more difficult questions at a later date and clarify or explore those issues as needed. Pushing the client turns the intake into more of an interrogation than an interview.

During the intake interview it is crucial to distinguish between the presenting problems and the etiology of the problem. Presenting problems are the symptoms a client is currently experiencing that bring them to counseling. These include changes in mood, sleep, eating, thoughts, behaviors, and attitudes, to name a few. In the sample intake that follows, you will see a presenting problems checklist that allows the counselor to explore a wide range and depth of presenting concerns. The etiology, on the other hand, refers to relevant psychosocial factors that have exacerbated presenting symptoms. In the following section is a list of relevant psychosocial factors that need to be unearthed to determine etiological factors.

Psychosocial History

A psychosocial history is a history of the client's social and psychological functioning; it explores the presenting problem, the current context of the problem, and resources and barriers to treatment. It also helps the professional counselor to create a case conceptualization and determine the best method of treatment. A comprehensive approach to intake interviews is available in Erford (2021). The psychosocial history usually includes:

- *Personal history*, which includes educational background, employment history, military history, family of origin, marital status, current living situation and relationship status with friends and family, and abuse, legal, and religious histories.
- *Drug/alcohol use/abuse history* in self and family. This includes what types of substances are being used, how much, how often, date of first use, and progression of use. Prior treatment for drug or alcohol abuse and family history of abuse are also explored.
- *Counseling history* comprises any past treatment for mental health issues and medications prescribed for such issues. An inquiry into past and current suicidal or homicidal ideations or actions is assessed. Family mental illness is also investigated.
- *Medical history* is important to research from personal and family history perspectives. Oftentimes medical issues can mimic psychological symptoms and need to be ruled out prior to diagnosis.
- *Current symptoms* include what has brought the client into counseling. Assessing the client's beliefs about these symptoms and gaining an understanding of how disruptive they are to the client's current functioning is important. How long have the symptoms been occurring? How often do the symptoms occur? Can you pinpoint when the symptoms began? Is there a time when the symptoms are less intense or seem to disappear altogether?
- *Client resources* consist of social or community supports, client strengths, and motivations. Assessing how the client approaches counseling and how receptive the client is to you as a counselor can be a resource toward change.

Mental Status Exam

As mentioned earlier, counselors are listening to both verbal and nonverbal messages in the intake interview. At the conclusion of the intake interview, counselors complete a mental status exam based on their perceptions of a client during the interview process. Kress et al. (2021) listed 12 categories within the mental status exam that a counselor should be aware of:

1. **Appearance:** well groomed, adequately groomed, poorly groomed.
2. **Behavior:** calm, psychomotor agitation, psychomotor retardation, poor eye contact, poor impulse control, guarded, poor balance or coordination.
3. **Speech and language:** rate, volume, coherence, abnormalities, deficits.
4. **Emotions:** mood such as euthymic, depressed, irritable, anxious, euphoric, and affect such as appropriate, broad, flat, blunted, and the congruencies of mood and affect.
5. **Orientation to reality:** hallucinations, delusions.
6. **Concentration and attention:** attentive, scattered, focused.
7. **Thought processes:** word usage, thought blocking, racing thoughts, flight of ideas, loose associations, magical thinking.
8. **Thought content:** suicidal ideation, fears and phobias, obsessions and compulsions, delusions.
9. **Perception:** hallucinations, illusions, depersonalization, derealization, dissociative.
10. **Memory:** normal, long-, or short-term deficits.
11. **Intelligence and knowledge:** above average, average, below average.
12. **Judgment and insight:** good, fair, poor.

Case Study 1.3 and Table 1.1 provide a sample intake for client "Sophie Sheppard" that includes all the preceding information related to intake interviewing.

Case Study 1.3 Sophie

Sophie appears to be a young woman in her mid-twenties employed as a marketing manager for a popular clothing company in a large city. She reports that she is single with no children. Sophie states that the reason she is seeking counseling at this time is to discuss possible options for her future. She states that she is very good at her job and is financially self-sufficient. Now that her career is well underway, Sophie's thoughts have turned toward settling down and starting a family, but she has yet to find "the one." She is concerned because her relationships tend to be short term, and she spends a lot of time thinking that she may never find a mate.

Table 1.1 Client intake form

Date: 9/13/23 Client Number: 2841

I. CLIENT INFORMATION

Last Name Sheppard First Name Sophie MI O

Sex: ___ Male √ Female ___ Nonbinary Date of Birth 09/04/95 **Age** 27

Ethnicity: __ Asian __ Black √ Hispanic √ Native American √ White ___ Other (___)

Current Address 570 W. Steet 4th St., Apt. H City Rock Hill State SC Zip Code 27922

Primary Telephone Number (803) 555-1234 **Other Telephone Number** ( ) NA

How may we contact you regarding your appointment? *(Check all that apply.)* √ Primary Telephone

___ Other Telephone

May we leave a message on an answering machine or with anyone who answers your phone? √ Yes or No

In an emergency, who we should contact: Erica Sheppard (704) 555-9876

Relationship to you Mother

Work Telephone ( ) NA Home Telephone ( ) NA

How did you learn about the Community Counseling Clinic? Referred by friend, Molly Smith

II. PSYCHOSOCIAL HISTORY

Educational History

Education: (check all that apply) ___ GED √ HS Grad √ College-# of years 4

Degree/Major BA, Marketing and Management Vocational training NA

Do you have a history of learning difficulties? Yes___ No √

COMMENTS

___

(*Continued*)

Table 1.1 (Continued)

Do you have any barriers to learning such as the inability to read or write? Yes____ No __√____

COMMENTS

____

Employment History

Employed: (please check one) __√__Full time _____Part time ______Unemployed-date last worked __/__

Not in labor force: (please check one) _______disabled ________retired _______homemaker ________

student _____living in institution ______other ____

If you checked disabled, please explain further ______________________________________

If employed, employer name: ____Urban Utopia______________________________________

Occupation ____Marketing manager____

Are you currently under financial distress? Yes ____ No __√___

Military History

Are you now or have you ever been a member of the military? Yes ___ No __√___

If yes, what branch ____

Please list any pertinent duties or trauma experienced during your service

____

Social History

Marital Status: ___√__Single _____Married _____Separated _____Divorced _____Widowed ______Remarried

______Cohabitating

What is your current living situation? ____L ves alone_

Household Members	Relationship	Age	Quality of Relationship

Table 1.1 (Continued)

Is there a history of mental illness in your family? Yes_______ No __√__ **If yes, please explain**

____

____

Are you currently or have you ever been physically, mentally, sexually, or emotionally abused?

Yes __√__ No _____ **if yes, please explain** While in college, CL suspects drink was drugged at a party, and she was raped by one or more males.

Is there a history of drug or alcohol abuse in your family? Yes _√_ No_____ **If yes, please explain**

Mother is a recovering alcoholic with 5 years sobriety

What do you believe are your strengths? "I am outgoing and friendly. I do really well at my job; time management and the structure I create in my life."

Describe what type of support system you have "I'm really close with my family and have a lot of friends. I believe in God and go to church sometimes."

Drug/Alcohol History

Have you ever had a problem with drug/alcohol abuse? __No__ If yes, please explain ____________

Illegal drug use past 12 months _____**yes**__√__**no**

Prescription drug abuse past 12 months _____**yes**__√__**no**

Nonprescription drug abuse past 12 months __√__**yes** _____ **no**

Alcohol use past 12 months __√__ **yes** _____ **no**

Drug/Substance /Alcohol	Age of 1st use	Date of last use	Frequency	Amount	Method
Benadryl	16	Monday	nightly	2 tablets	orally
Alcohol	16	Monday	nightly	6 ozs.	orally

III. COUNSELING HISTORY

Have you previously received counseling services? __√__ No ___Yes

If yes, respond to all items below.

(*Continued*)

Table 1.1 (Continued)

Name(s) of Facility________________________________

Location(s) of Facility (City and State) ________________________

Type of Facility ____Outpatient ____Inpatient (hospital)

Type of Counseling (check all that apply): ____Psychological ____Substance Abuse

Dates of Counseling: Start____________________________

End ________________________________

Previous

Problem(s) ________________________________

Success in resolving previous problems (check one): ____Unsuccessful ___Partially Successful ______Highly Successful

What did you find to be particularly helpful or not helpful about your previous counseling experience? __
____

Were you prescribed any medication for dealing with the above issue? Yes_____ No ______

If yes, what medication were you prescribed? ________________________

IV. MEDICAL HISTORY

Name of *current* physician "I don't have one. I go to a clinic."

Name of psychiatrist, if one is seen NA

Please check all *current* and previous medical conditions from the list below.

___Problems with Vision/Hearing ___Headaches

___Thyroid Problems ___Dizziness

___Lung Disease ___Chest Pains

___Stomach Problems ___Joint Pain

___High Blood Pressure ___Diabetes

___Heart Disease ___Seizures

___Weight Loss ___Weight Gain

Physical Exercise: times per week 3 for how long "about 30 minutes" ___Pain (explain) ________________________ ___Environmental Allergies: (explain) ________________________ ___Food Allergies: (explain) ________________________ ___Other (explain) ________________________

Table 1.1 (Continued)

Do you *currently* take prescription or "over-the-counter" medications? ___No _√__Yes

If yes, please provide all requested information below.

Name of Medication	Dosage	Times/Day	Start Date	Side Effects
Valtrex	5 mg	2	as needed	lethargy, headaches

Do you *currently* take vitamins or herbal supplements? ______No __√__Yes **If yes, please provide**

Name of Supplement	Dosage	Times/Day	Start Date	Side Effects
Multivitamin		1	age 12	NA
Calcium	200 mg	1	age 12	NA
Vitamin C	10 mg	2	age 25	NA

V. PRESENTING PROBLEM

PRESENTING PROBLEMS CHECKLIST Please rate each of the following items according to the following scale: 1 Not at all, 2 A little, 3 Moderately, 4 Quite a bit, 5 Extremely

	1	2	3	4	5
1. School and/or job performance too low.	√				
2. Too critical of others.				√	
3. Unhappy or anxious without knowing why.			√		
4. Have difficulty studying and/or concentrating.		√			
5. Worry about things I have done.			√		
6. Parents or others too critical of my behavior.		√			
7. Have fears that seem unrealistic.			√		
8. Not interested in my courses or job.	√				
9. Problems with sleeping.				√	
10. Worry about my drinking/smoking/drug use.		√			
11. Dislike being dependent on parents/spouse/others.	√				
12. Problems in romantic relationships.					√
13. Parents or others oppose my ideas/values/beliefs.		√			
14. Lack of interest in school or work.	√				
15. Experience frequent mood fluctuations.			√		
16. Don't know what I want out of life.	√				
17. Feel others do not like me/no one seems to care about me.		√			
18. Feel lonely.			√		
19. Have trouble making decisions.			√		
20. Worry about my physical health.				√	

(*Continued*)

Table 1.1 (Continued)

21. Worry about my mental health.			√		
22. Other people disappoint me.				√	
23. Nothing I do seems meaningful or important.		√			
24. Feel very anxious in new situations.		√			
25. Can't seem to control my own thoughts/behaviors.		√			
26. Doubt my ability to meet goals/standards.	√				
27. Concerned about family members.		√			
28. Confused about questions of morals/religion/spirituality.	√				
29. Feel depressed.	√				
30. Concerned about my sexual identity.	√				
31. Feel tired, dizzy, and/or weak.		√			
32. Have difficulty trusting other people.			√		
33. Afraid to speak up in class or at work.	√				
34. Cannot seem to budget my time and/or money.	√				
35. Worry about what others think of me.		√			
36. Concerned with sexual functioning/thoughts/behaviors.					√
37. Low self-esteem.			√		
38. Thoughts/feelings of ending my life.	√				
39. Easily annoyed or irritated.	√				
40. Feeling hopeless about the future.	√				
41. Having urges to break or smash things.	√				
42. Having urges to beat, injure, or harm someone.	√				
43. Concerned with weight/eating habits/physical appearance.	√				
44. Thoughts of death or dying.	√				

Comments regarding the presenting problem checklist: Relationship problems. CL is never as interested in men as they are of CL. Since rape incident, has not been sexually active; "I'm afraid to tell my boyfriend about my past because I don't want to lose him."

What problem(s) brings you to counseling? CL wants to discuss options for her future, decide whether or not to go forward in her relationship with boyfriend, and figure out why she continues to be awakened by recurring nightmare.

How *long* have you experienced this problem? (Specify): ___Days ___Weeks_√_ Months ___Years

How *often* do you experience this problem? (Check one): __Hourly _√_ Daily __Weekly __Other

How *intense* is this problem? (Check one): ____Mild ____Moderate _√_Severe

Table 1.1 (Continued)

The following is to be filled out by counselor after the session.

VI. CLIENT STRENGTHS

_√_ Person states and/or displays a **high degree of motivation** for insight, change, etc.

_√_ Person has **identifiable skills and/or talents** that may be utilized in the service of coping.

_√_ Person **relates openly and is receptive in interaction** with interviewer.

_√_ Person is **verbally articulate and/or is well able to identify his/her concerns.**

_√_ Person appears to display **at least average degree of psychological mindedness** (versus resistant

to considering psychological causes and contributions to presenting problems).

_√_ Person has relatively **few** and **well-defined goals.**

_√_ Person has identifiable and consistent sources of **psychosocial support** (e.g., family, friends,

belief system).

_√_ Person is **not experiencing significant impairment** in academic/occupational functioning.

g. ***VII. MENTAL STATUS and BEHAVIORAL OBSERVATIONA.*** **APPEARANCE** *(note height, weight, distinguishing physical characteristics, grooming, hygiene, etc.):*

_√_ Well dressed/groomed ___ Adequately dressed/groomed ___ Poorly dressed/groomed

B. BEHAVIOR *(note particularly rapport and interaction with interviewer):*

___ Calm, no excesses or deficits

_√_ Displays psychomotor agitation

___ Displays psychomotor retardation

___ Poor posture, balance, or coordination

___ Poor eye contact

___ Shows difficulties of impulse control

___ Reluctant or guarded in interview

___ Shows abnormalities of gait, limb usage

C. SPEECH (*note rate, volume, coherence, abnormalities or deficits, etc.*):

_√_ Fluent, no abnormalities or deficits

(*Continued*)

Table 1.1 (Continued)

D. EMOTION:

1. MOOD:

___ Normal/Euthymic	___ Irritable	___ Elevated (mild)
___ Depressed/Sad	___ Angry	___ Euphoric (moderate)
_√_ Anxious or Fearful	___ Pain (emotional)	___ Expansive (severe)

2. AFFECT:

_√_ Appropriate/Euthymic	___ Broad	___ Labile	___ Constricted
___ Animated (as in mania)	___ Flat	___ Blunted	

3. MOOD and AFFECT are

_√_ Congruent	___ Incongruent

E. THOUGHT PROCESSES AND CONTENT (*note irregularities of word usage, thought blocking, racing thoughts, flight of ideas, loose associations, delusional or near-delusional ideations, magical thinking, etc.*):

_√_ No irregularities reported or noted

F. PERCEPTION (*note hallucinations, illusions, depersonalization, derealization, dissociative processes*):

_√_ No irregularities reported or noted

G. OTHER (*e.g., notable difficulties of orientation, attention, memory, judgment, intelligence, insight*)

Attention/Concentration	Judgment	Intelligence	Insight	Memory
_√_ Intact	_√_ Good	_√_ Above Avg.	_√_ Good	_√_ Intact
___ Distractible	___ Average	___ Average	___ Fair	___ Short-term deficit
___ Impaired	___ Poor	___ Below Avg.	___ Poor	___ Long-term deficit

VIII. CLINCAL SUMMARY:

Client is single, 27-yr.-old self-identifying as a biracial (Caucasian/Native American) female of Latin Origin & oldest of 4 siblings (1 bro/2 sis). Good relationship w/immediate family but entire extended family is estranged. Mom is recovering alcoholic w/5 yrs

Table 1.1 (Continued)

sobriety. CL is employed full time (extremely satisfied). Seeking services for relationship issues stemming from her reluctance to commit to intimate relationship w/BF she "really likes a lot" & thinks he may be "the one" due to overwhelming fear of disclosing her past, which includes a rape, abortion, and STD (Herp II) while in college. CL has remained abstinent since incident. Describes problem as extremely severe. CL also concerned about physical health & spot on leg she fears may be skin cancer but afraid to see medical doctor. CL reports difficulty sleeping & self-medicates w/alcohol & OTC sleep aids to avoid recurrent dream of having forcible sex as a child w/unknown male. Dream has increased in frequency past 6 months. CL relates this to rape incident. CL states readiness to commit to intimate relationship w/current BF but cannot bring herself to disclose her past to him because "he'll leave me" but if she does not tell him or waits too long "he'll get tired of waiting & leave anyway." CL withdraws from BF's pressure to commit by isolating. CL moderately concerned about critical attitude ("being too picky"), realistic versus unrealistic fears, disclosing her past (today is the first time ever), moodiness & tendency to isolate, and difficulty trusting others & making decisions. CL pleasantly dressed & well groomed, articulate, appears above average in intelligence, good insight & thought processes, judgment & (conscious) memory appear intact w/no perceptual irregularities. Displays congruent mood/affect & mostly appropriate/euthymic affect—constricted at times. CL's emotional anxiety & fear displays by psychomotor agitation (heavy breathing, hand wringing, restless legs, squirming). CL stated goals are to explore options for her future & decide how/when/whether to disclose past to BF or just end relationship. CL also wants to be able to sleep w/out having to medicate & wants dream "to go away." CL highly motivated to change, open & receptive w/strong identifiable skills (self-reports "I'm outgoing & friendly"), & few well-defined goals. Strong family support system, no significant impairment noted in job performance but presenting problem does impair significant personal relationship. Limits of confidentiality & emergency services/procedures reviewed w/CL, who stated understanding.

Rhonda Bradley, LPC

Counselor Signature ______________________ Date ______________

LuAnn Sizemore, LPC-S

Supervisor Signature (if necessary) ______________________ Date ______________

Understanding the Client's Issues

Counselors-in-training are often overwhelmed by the issues and information a client brings into session. It feels as if the client has come in and given you a handful of random puzzle pieces. If you don't know how to organize the pieces, structure the foundation, and fit the pieces together, you are left with chaos and confusion. In this case, the counselor begins to focus on arbitrary pieces of the puzzle without a clue of how to connect. Case conceptualization is the process counselors use to learn how to organize, structure, and assemble the puzzle.

Case conceptualization is undoubtedly one of the most important aspects in the counseling process. In essence, it is the process of synthesizing and analyzing the data gathered from the client intake, psychosocial history, mental status, and other assessment instruments to create a "framework" for treatment. When looking at the information gathered as a whole, what does it tell us?

- Who our clients are.
- What difficulties they are facing.
- How they are functioning.
- What patterns in behaving they are exhibiting.

- What patterns in thinking they are experiencing.
- What patterns in emoting they are experiencing and exhibiting.
- What patterns of relating they utilize.
- What they have tried in the past.
- How long the problem has been occurring.
- How motivated they are.
- How strong a support system they have.
- What their trauma history is.

So, how do we use case conceptualization to make sense of all this seemingly unrelated information? What do we do with it? We choose a model of case conceptualization to generate a plan. H. Stanley Judd said, "A good plan is like a road map: it shows the final destination and usually the best way to get there." That, in effect, is what case conceptualization is to the counseling process. Each conceptualization will detail diagnostic, clinical, and treatment information. Sperry and Sperry (2012) described three types of case conceptualization: provisional, full-scale, and brief case conceptualizations. Berman (2018) took this a step further by describing four styles of writing case conceptualizations within a theoretical framework: assumption-based, symptom-based, interpersonally based, and historically based. These will be discussed further in the following section.

Symptom Focused

The symptom-focused model, derived from the medical model of therapy, focuses on the symptomology presented by a client followed by a treatment plan centered on the reduction of these symptoms. The symptom-focused conceptualization is grounded in behavioral modification techniques and employs language consistent with the behavioral approach. Symptoms and treatment objectives are reported in concrete, measurable terms. The emphasis is placed on diagnosis and treatment of specific quantifiable symptoms. This type of case conceptualization is straightforward and is rather easy to implement, create, and monitor. Due to the simplicity and ease of monitoring progress, this type of conceptualization is preferred by most third-party payers.

For entry-level counselors, this may be the least challenging of the three types of conceptualization. There are also resources available to guide counselors through this process in the way of treatment planning manuals. These manuals provide an outline to: (a) aid in the definition of the problem in behavioral terms, (b) create long-term goals, (c) create short-term objectives, (d) specify treatment in behavioral terms that are easily measured, and (e) offer diagnostic suggestions (Berghuiset al., 2014).

Although a new counselor may be drawn to this type of conceptualization to reduce anxiety and to secure their developmental need for concrete explanations and solutions in counseling, there are drawbacks to this type of conceptualization. First and foremost, this type of conceptualization ignores the origins of the symptomology being presented. This leads to treatment that may act as a temporary Band-Aid for the presenting problem, yet may not address the issues needed for long-term symptom reduction. This style is also limited with client issues that are more abstract and ambiguous in nature.

Client Focused

The client-focused case conceptualization is motivated by the client's wants and desires. The information gathered is processed with the client to generate an understanding of the client and treatment for the client that is specific to their needs and wants. Sperry and Sperry (2012) conceded that clients come into counseling with their own schema of how they view their problems, how severely the problem is affecting them, what they anticipate from treatment, and how motivated they are to carry out the strategies identified to reach their therapeutic goals. The client may not be consciously aware of the schema they have developed; therefore, it is the counselor's task to work with the client to uncover and explore these schemas. Sperry and Sperry contended not only that counselors must identify and unearth these schemas but that they also have a duty to collaborate with the client to create a shared schema or conceptualization, which in turn leads to enhanced treatment outcomes.

Teyber and Teyber (2017) created a client-focused case conceptualization model based on an interpersonal process approach to counseling (see Table 1.2). This model specifically addresses the client's interpersonal style and personality dynamics with others as well as the counselor.

Table 1.2 Sample case conceptualization using Teyber's client-focused model

Case Conceptualization

During the intake interview, Sophie revealed the following information about herself: While in college, Sophie believes she was drugged and raped by multiple men. The rape resulted in Sophie being pregnant, which lead to her having an abortion. Also, Sophie contracted type II herpes from the traumatic event, and she feels too ashamed to tell anyone, including a physician.

I. Identifying Data

Sophie is 27 years old, is biracial (Caucasian/Native American), and lives alone in a high-rise apartment near the center of the city within walking distance to work. She oversees seasonal sales marketing campaigns for a higher-end clothing chain especially popular with young professionals. Sophie is the oldest of four siblings, and her mother is a recovering alcoholic. While in college, Sophie was raped by multiple men and has had substantial anxiety ever since.

II. Presenting Problems

Sophie wonders why she is unable to commit to a relationship. She indicates that men usually like her more than she likes them. She has turned down two marriage proposals since college. She reports that her family and friends tell her she is "too picky." This adds additional stress and worry to her life because most of her friends have married and started a family, and she feels pressure to do the same. She knows this would please her parents. Though she describes herself as outgoing and friendly, she struggles with feelings of inadequacy.

III. Relevant History

Sophie is the oldest of four children. She was raised Presbyterian in a rural community where her parents still live. Her brother and oldest sister live near their parents in the same town and are married with children.

Her younger sister attends college at the local university but continues to live at home. She has German, French, and Native American ancestors. She describes her relationship with her family as close. Her mother is a recovering alcoholic with five years continuous sobriety. They gather together almost every Sunday, on holidays, and on birthdays. She remembers a tumultuous family life while she was in high school and, as the oldest, tried to keep peace in the family, often covering for her mother when she was under the influence to reduce household turmoil. Sophie made good grades and was very popular with her peers in high school and college. As a student, she participated in a sorority as well as several clubs and organizations. Mostly, she was determined to set a good example for her siblings by getting a good job after graduation and having a successful career. To her knowledge, no one in her family has a history of mental illness, and only her mother has a history of addiction. Extended family members are rarely mentioned. Sophie is reluctant to commit to her boyfriend due to her overwhelming fear of disclosing her past trauma. Sophie remains sexually abstinent and stated that if her boyfriend finds out the truth about her trauma, he will leave her. In addition, Sophie stated if she doesn't tell him about her trauma, "He will get tired of waiting and leave anyway."

A. Medical: Sophie is a little concerned about her health. She spent a lot of time in tanning beds and for some time has ignored a spot on her leg hoping it would go away, but it seems to be getting bigger. She believes this is the least of her concerns but may see a doctor soon. Sophie has long been troubled by a reoccurring nightmare. In the dream she is a little girl having sex in the dark with an unknown man. She tries but is unable to resist or scream for help. She reports using sleeping pills and alcohol before bedtime in an effort to avoid dreaming.

B. Educational: Sophie has a bachelor's degree in marketing and management. She considered pursuing an MBA but because she has such a good job right now, she decided to postpone furthering her education. She appears to be of above-average intelligence and describes herself as responsible and independent.

C. Military: Sophie has never served in the military.

D. Vocational: Sophie was hired for her present position immediately after graduation. After working part time in one of the company's retail stores during high school and completing an outstanding internship in the corporate office during her senior year in college, she required minimal training for her position. She receives excellent performance reviews and has a good rapport with company employees at every level. She rates her job satisfaction as very high.

Table 1.2 (Continued)

E. Sexual: Sophie contracted a sexually transmitted disease years ago. She is not sexually active. She aborted one pregnancy. While in college, she remembers passing out at a party after drinking one bottle of beer. She recalls being in and out of consciousness and some males she did not know taking her to her apartment. The next morning, she realized she had had sex but could not remember with whom. Several bruises appeared on her body, and she hid them under long clothing until they healed. She did not seek medical attention and kept the incident to herself. After a missed period, a pregnancy test revealed a positive result. She went alone to have an abortion at a clinic using a false name. Several days later, she developed very painful blisters in her genital area and tested positive for type II herpes at a health department. Since then, she manages outbreaks with medication prescribed by a doctor and filled at a pharmacy in another town. She has never revealed this to anyone nor has she had sex since. She has been dating a man for quite some time and is pretty sure he thinks she is "the one" and is ready to commit. His name is Sam, and she really likes him. They are both tiring of the rat race of city dwelling and dream of moving to the country. Recently she has been turning down his invitations to spend time together because he persists in wanting to take their relationship to the next level, which she feels ready to do but is horrified by the thought of telling him about her past. Until now, she has not discussed this with anyone.

F. Counseling: Sophie reports that she has never participated in counseling. She has attended Al-Anon and open AA meetings in the past.

IV. Interpersonal Style

Sophie's typical interpersonal style is to move toward others. She likes to please and is an overachiever in the workforce. She avoids confrontation with family and friends. When she is confronted with a situation she cannot handle in that way, she will retreat and become isolated. In counseling Sophie's style is similar to her patterns with others. She is eager to please me as the counselor as displayed by being early and alwlys doing her homework. She becomes quiet when confronted and often tries to explain the contradictions mentioned to settle the issue in her mind.

V. Environmental Factors

Her environmental stressors are limited and her support system fairly strong such that on a typical day, Sophie gets up, usually walks to work, has lunch out with coworkers, walks home, changes clothes, has dinner, and does more work at home. Some evenings she goes out to dinner and/or to the movies with her boyfriend or a group of friends. On weekends, she goes to the library or the park, shops for groceries, cleans house, does laundry, attends church, and often drives to the country to visit her parents, brother and sisters, and their families. Sometimes the man she is dating accompanies her. She reports keeping to a strict schedule and maintaining order as priorities in her life.

VI. Personality Dynamics

a. Cognitive fac-tors: Sophie has above-average intelligence, is mentally alert, focuses on positive cognitions, has an innate ability to understand her own and others' behaviors, and has a high ability to make decisions and carry out the practical affairs of daily living. Sophie has not processed her history of trauma.
b. Emotional factors: Sophie's typical emotional state is anxious, which was displayed during the intake interview. Her affect was appropriate and congruent with her verbalizations and mood; her range of emotions is normal, not blunted.
c. Behavioral factors: Sophie exhibits psychomotor agitation through hand wringing, heavy breathing, restless legs, and squirming. She experiences frequent nightmares, which she tries to avoid through self-medication. She avoids sexual functioning due to her trauma, which has led to embarrassment and fear of rejection. Her eating patterns are normal. Sophie drinks alcohol and ingests sleeping pills to avoid an uncomfortable and reoccurring sexual dream.

VII. Counselor's Conceptualization of the Problem

What are the common themes identified by the client? Sophie shows a common theme of fear of being rejected. She worked hard in every aspect of her life to keep the peace and to avoid confrontation and unease. This is consistent with her growing up in an alcoholic household and being the parentified child and the one to keep the peace.
What ties all the information together? Her personality style of moving toward others and her fear of rejection tie the information together leading to effective treatment possibilities.

Theory Focused

Theory-focused case conceptualization uses a theoretical base to formulate the ways you will (a) form a relationship with a client, (b) understand a client given all the information gathered, and (c) determine what interventions to use with a client (Zubernis et al., 2017). The heart of theory-focused conceptualization is determining why a person is experiencing the difficulties they are and how they are perpetuating the symptoms based on your theoretical modality. The answer to this is the driving force toward determining an appropriate intervention. Theory-focused case conceptualization has been criticized for being counselor driven and forcing a one size fits all mentality. However, integrated theory has become popular to meet the diversity of needs each client brings to the counseling process.

For beginning counselors, the first step in theory-focused case conceptualization is identifying a theory. This is an arduous task for some. When learning theories in your counseling program, you are often exposed to a significant variety at a rapid pace, leaving some confused and retaining only surface-level information for any given theory. It is important to spend quality time exploring theory and finding one that is the best fit for you and your personality style. Betan and Binder (2010) referred to the concept of metabolizing theory; they found that with time and experience, seasoned counselors are able to use theory almost unconsciously. It becomes part of the counselor's cognitive process, thereby considerably limiting the time spent on the immense task of case conceptualization. For beginning counselors, this process is slow and cumbersome, requiring much conscious thought, practice, and persistence.

Berman (2018) suggested a two-step process for organizing a case conceptualization by theory. She stated that creating a premise is an important first step to help the reader understand what will be covered in the conceptualization. The second part of the Berman model includes the supporting material that provides evidence for the material written in the premise. Berman suggested this material can be written in a multitude of styles, depending on the counselor's preference and theoretical orientation. Several of the styles she mentioned are (a) assumption-based, (b) symptom-based, (c) interpersonally based, and (d) historically based.

Assumption-based conceptualizations use the major assumptions from a counseling theory to organize the written format (see Table 1.3). Symptom-focused counseling organizes the information in the case conceptualization in terms of the symptoms the client presents and uses these to guide the long- and short-term treatment goals. Interpersonally based written conceptualizations focus on a systems perspective and how the client relates to others in their life. The information is organized around the relationships with others, the counselor, and with self. Historically based written conceptualizations organize information in terms of time periods that are relevant to the client's presenting problems, noting time periods when feelings, behaviors, and patterns emerged and were learned.

Table 1.3 Person-centered theoretical case conceptualization written from an assumption-based style

Premise

1. Client demographics.
2. Reason for referral:
   - Strengths and weaknesses based on theoretical assumptions.
3. Theoretical supporting material:
   - Basic tenant: people will move forward in a constructive manner if they have the appropriate conditions fostering growth. Therefore, people who do not have a positive environment around them may grow in unconstructive ways.
   - List what aspects of the following conditions are missing in the client's current relationships:
     1. Congruency.
     2. Unconditional positive regard.
     3. Accurate empathic understanding.
   - When these conditions are met, a person becomes less defensive and more open to themselves and their world.
   - When people are free, they are able to find their own way. What is stopping this person from being free?

Table 1.3 (Continued)

- Counseling focuses on the constructive side of human nature, what is right, what assets they have.
  1. What is blocking their growth? (Look within and outside self.)
  2. What is the client doing that is enabling them to live an authentic and full life?
  3. How well does this client know himself or herself? Those that know themselves best discover more appropriate behavior.
  4. How much responsibility is the client taking to fully encounter reality?
  5. Focus is on the here-and-now experience. How are they not keeping this focus?
  6. What masks are your client wearing? These are developed through socialization and enable people to lose themselves.
- During intervention, to assess the case, Rogers (1957) describes four traits of people who are becoming actualized:
  1. Openness to experience.
  2. A trust in themselves.
  3. An internal source of evaluation.
  4. A willingness to continue growing.
- Give examples of what you may see or hear from your client that lets you know they are becoming actualized.
- The best source of assessment in person-centered counseling is not assessment devices but the individual client.

Diagnosis

The Diagnosis Debate

There has been some debate about whether counselors should diagnose mental disorders. Traditionally, counselors have used a wellness/developmental model of conceptualization and treatment as opposed to the medical model. However, to communicate with other professionals and to receive third-party reimbursement, diagnosis is necessary. In addition, the Council for the Accreditation of Counseling and Related Educational Programs (CACREP) stated in the 2016 standards that counselors-in-training must demonstrate knowledge and competency related to the DSM-5 in order to effectively diagnose and treat (Remley & Herlihy, 2020). Similarly, state counselor licensure boards often require training in diagnosis and treatment planning. Dougherty (2005) noted several ethical issues associated with diagnosis that beginning-level counselors should be aware of, including time restraints, bias, stereotyping, and lack of consistency from one clinician to another, to name just a few. There is often pressure generated by managed care companies to provide an accurate, speedy diagnosis. Yet, without the proper time to assess the client and consult other professionals, the likelihood of making faulty diagnoses increases. Formulating a diagnosis is not a one-time process; it must be reevaluated often.

Kress et al. (2021) suggested viewing diagnosis as one part of the person in a holistic context of the developmental model of counseling, providing a guide for the counselor to determine the most effective treatment plan, to understand the course of the disorder, and to help the client identify the symptoms in the context of a disorder. On one hand, a client may feel relief knowing that there is a diagnosis that can explain what they have been going through; on the other hand, diagnosis can stigmatize a person and prevent them from obtaining certain jobs or insurance policies, as well as allowing the client to perpetuate the problem by blaming the disorder and not taking any responsibility for treatment.

Several assessment guides are available that may help the beginning counselor feel more at ease in the diagnostic process, but one should always proceed with caution because there is no substitute for knowledge and experience. Clients do not want to feel like they are only being assessed based on symptoms and diagnosis, and standardized assessment procedures should be mixed with other interview questions and empathic understanding.

The Role of Diagnosis in Treatment

Understanding the diagnostic process is crucial to the formation of the treatment plan. This is a complex topic, and professional counselors ordinarily take entire courses in diagnosis and treatment of mental disorders. In the DSM-5 (APA, 2013), all physical, mental, and personalities disorders are listed in the same place, unlike the prior axis system in the DSM-IV TR. You will use the diagnoses to inform your treatment goals and interventions.

A sample diagnosis for Sophie might be as follows:

F43.10 Posttraumatic stress disorder
F10.20 Alcohol use disorder
Herpes zoster

Treatment Planning

Treatment planning is an integral but too often neglected piece of the counseling puzzle. As mentioned earlier in the chapter, case conceptualization is referred to as a road map for working with your client. Using that analogy, let's consider that the treatment plan is your GPS (Global Positioning System); it actually provides more detail than a map, and if you follow the specific directions, you are much more likely to reach your desired destination. The treatment plan (GPS) should be influenced by your theoretical orientation (road map), but there are many more intricate pieces involved in developing a treatment plan. Ingram (2012) stated that a treatment plan should address the specifics of what will happen in the session, skills that the counselor will use, the type of relationship to be formed, and any specific processes that may be used. Table 1.4 shows an example of a completed treatment plan.

Table 1.4 Individualized treatment plan

Client Name (First MI Last): Sophie O. Sheppard				Client # 12345
Goals	Goal #	Linked to Treatment Recommendation # from Intake:		Start Date: 10–5–12
State Goal below in collaboration with client:	Client has read? ☒ Yes ❑ No	Client agrees? ❑ Yes ❑ No	Client's Initial: SOS	Target Completion Date: 3–5–12
To ↓ Sx of Anxiety				Adjusted Target Date:
				Reason for Adjustment:
Desired Results in client's words:				
"I want to find out if I have a future with Sam or not and stop feeling trapped and stuck in my life."				
"I want a future with him but he needs to know what he's getting into."				
Strengths and how they will be used to meet this goal:				
CL displays a desire to seek help as evident by confiding in counselor.				
CL values honesty.				
CL is resilient.				
Skills/Knowledge needed:				
CL needs further sexual education in regard to STDs.				
CL needs regular medical care to address health concerns.				
Address sexual trauma; recognize cognitive distortions.				
Natural/Community Supports needed:				
Family support				
Primary care physician				
Continue w/work				

(*Continued*)

Table 1.4 (Continued)

OBJECTIVE #__*1*__:		Start Date: 10–5–12	Target Date/ Duration: 3–5–12
Client will ↓ Sx of anxiety as evidenced by ↑ exercise level and stress reducing activities			
Client will:			
CL will participate in rigorous exercise for at least 30 minutes once per day.			
CL will research yoga classes and meditation groups.			
CL will engage in 1 pleasurable activity per week.			
Parent/Guardian/Community/Other will: □ Not Clinically Indicated			
Therapeutic Intervention	Service Description	Frequency	Responsible: Provider/Credential
Identify anxiety relieving activity	Counseling	1x/wk	
Encourage new/diverse activities	"	"	
Assign/Process pleasurable activity	"	"	

OBJECTIVE #__2__:		Start Date:	Target Date/ Duration:
CL will address and process history of sexual trauma as evidenced by ↑ reporting of emotions tied to trauma; identify fears; demonstrate improved coping (↓ in anxiety self-rating).			
Client will:			
Learn progressive muscle relaxation techniques & practice daily.			
Address/Process but not relive trauma.			
Role-play conversation with b/f.			
Parent/Guardian/Community/Other will: ❑ Not Clinically Indicated			
Therapeutic Intervention	Service Description	Frequency	Responsible: Provider/Credential
Teach/coach prog. Relaxation	Counseling	1x/wk	
Guide in trauma process	"	"	
Role-play inter-/intrapersonal situations	"	"	

Table 1.4 (Continued)

Actual Date of Goal Completion:	Goal Discontinued Date:	Reason for Discontinuation or refer to Progress Note of ____________ (date):

Other Agencies Involved	
Name of Agency: Community Health Clinic	
Name and Title: Doctor available	
Services Provided: Continued medication monitoring	
Transition/Level of Care Change/Discharge Plan	
Level of Care/Transition/Discharge Criteria: For D/C CL needs to report: process history of sexual trauma as evidenced by ↑ reporting of emotions tied to trauma; identify fears; demonstrate improved coping (↓ in anxiety self-rating).	Anticipated Date:
Team Signatures	
Client: Sophie Sheppard	Date: 3–5–12
Client received copy of Individualized Treatment Plan? ☒ Yes ☐ No	Initial to confirm copy:
Parent/Guardian(s) (If Applicable):	Date: 9–15–12
Primary Provider/Credential: *Rhonda Bradley, LPC*	Date: 9–15–12
Supervisor's Signature/Credential: *LuAnn Sizemore LPC-S*	Date: 9–15–23

Conceptualizing a treatment plan for each specific client involves several data-gathering steps, discussed earlier in this chapter. Whether in the form of an initial intake, a psychosocial history, general questioning to understand the client's story, or some combination of methods, assessment is imperative and must be an early piece of the counseling relationship. All these pieces of information help to clarify case conceptualization, may lead to a diagnosis, and definitely inform the treatment plan.

At this stage it becomes more apparent why it is so important to gain as much accurate information as possible during the assessment phase. Without accurate information, your GPS may take you to Alexandria, Louisiana, when you actually intended to go to Alexandria, Virginia; 1200 miles off course could be very frustrating in a counseling session.

Developing a Treatment Plan

The process of conceptualizing and writing a treatment plan may vary from one client to another and among counselors. In addition to considering your theoretical orientation, the goals of the client, and the setting in which you practice, the plan may also be influenced by the intended purpose (Maruish, 2019). The most obvious use is planning a course of treatment, but the treatment plan may also be used in dealing with third-party payers to support requests for continued services or to meet accreditation requirements with organizations such as TJC (The Joint Commission, formerly The Joint Commission on the Accreditation of Healthcare Organizations). Formalized treatment plans for purposes other than the use of the counselor may require additional information. However, here we will outline the basic steps of treatment planning that are useful for treating a client.

Berghuis et al. (2014) suggested six steps for developing a treatment plan that are helpful in providing some guidance. The steps are (a) problem selection (identifying the problem), (b) problem definition (defining the problem), (c) goal development (developing goals), (d) objective construction (developing objectIs), (e) intervention creation (selecting interventions), and (f) diagnosis determination (diagnosis). Each of these steps will be discussed in more detail next.

Identifying the Problem

The first step in developing a treatment plan is identifying what the problem is. A familiar concern from counseling interns is, "I don't feel like I'm getting anywhere with this client." To which a supervisor typically responds, "What goals have been identified for counseling?" Facilitating the client's exploration of possible goals for counseling is an important part of your job as the counselor. Berghuis et al. (2014) pointed out that the client may identify many issues throughout the assessment phase, and it is the counselor's job to help the client prioritize the most important concerns on which to focus in counseling. Some of the issues may need to be "tabled" and dealt with at a later time because the treatment plan should not contain more than a few problems to focus on at any one time. However, it is important to note that the treatment plan should be reviewed and revised over time as goals are achieved and change (Maruish, 2019).

Defining the Problem

The next step in the process is defining the problem as it specifically relates to the client Berghuis et al., 2014 Maruish, 2019). For example, let's assume that the counselor and client identify the problem to be that the client is depressed. As you know, depression can manifest itself in many ways (e.g., not eating, eating too much, not sleeping, sleeping too much, social isolation, abusing drugs or alcohol, loss of interest, poor performance at work or school). Therefore, it is important to provide a behavioral definition of how the identified problem is manifesting.

Developing Goals

Once the counselor and client have identified, prioritized, and defined problems to be addressed in counseling, the next step is developing long-term treatment goals. Berghuis et al. (2014) recommended setting "broad goals for the resolution of the target problem" (p. 5). In other words, what will it look like if the client achieved the desired effect? Each problem identified for the treatment plan will have a minimum of one goal statement, and each goal will have several related objectives. Maruish, 2019). asserted that goals and objectives should be achievable, sustainable, realistic, measurable, and stated in the positive rather than in negative.

Developing Objectives

There are typically two or more objectives associated with each long-term goal. Objectives can be thought of as short-term goals that are measurable. Therefore, objectives must be written in behaviorally measurable language. Objectives can be thought of as a series of steps that, when completed, will result in the achievement of the long-term goal (Berghuis et al., 2014).

Sample Goals and Objectives

To help with your conceptualization of goals and objectives, we offer the following examples:

Goal #1—Elevate mood and show evidence of increasing social interaction.
Objectives

1. Identify cause of depressed mood.
2. Specify past or present contributing factors to sadness.
3. Engage in social interaction with family and friends.

Goal #2—Reduce the significance (frequency and intensity) of anxiety so that social and occupational functioning are not impaired.

Objectives

1. Increase participation in exercise activities that decrease level of anxiety.
2. Engage in pleasurable activity with family and friends at least once each week.
3. Participate in relaxation activities such as yoga or meditation.

Selecting Interventions

Interventions are what you, the professional counselor, actually plan to do to achieve the objectives. These are action items, and there should be at least one intervention for every objective identified in the treatment plan. Berghuis et al. (2014) suggested that interventions be selected after taking into account both the client's needs and the counselor's abilities. For example, you should not choose systematic desensitization as an intervention if you have little to no experience with that technique. As counseling interns, you might also take into consideration the experiences of your supervisors when selecting interventions. It's possible to select an intervention that you do not have experience or expertise with if your supervisor is experienced in that technique and willing to supervise you as you are learning new tools for your toolbox.

Diagnosis

Diagnosis may or may not be included in your role as a counselor practicum student or intern. If diagnosis is part of your training placement, the steps you have taken toward assessment and case conceptualization up to this point should inform the diagnosis. Diagnostic categories from the DSM-5 are typically expected to be included in a treatment plan, especially by third-party payers. You are encouraged to practice this piece of the treatment plan process under supervision, even if it is not required at your internship site.

An Example Treatment Plan

The steps outlined here and included in Case Study 1.4 make up the core of any treatment plan. However, it's important to note that, depending on who the treatment plan is being written for, additional information might be included. Maruish (2019, p. 136) identified the following components that may be included in formal treatment plans: (a) referral source and reason for referral, (b) presenting problem, (c) problem list, (d) diagnosis, (e) goals and objectives, (f) treatment, (g) patient strengths, (h) potential barriers to treatment, (i) referral for evaluation, (j) criteria for treatment termination or transfer, (k) responsible staff, and (l) treatment plan review date.

Case Study 1.4 Treatment Plan: Problem #1: Depression

Definition: Client reports experiencing decreased appetite (loss of 10 lbs. in 2 weeks without trying), increased sleep (up from 8 hours a night to 14 hours in a 24-hour period), lack of energy or desire to engage in social activities previously enjoyed, feeling worthless.

- **Goal:** Alleviate depressed mood, return to previous level of functioning.
- **Objective**: Describe symptoms of depression client is experiencing.
- **Intervention(s):** Ask client to make a list of symptoms, describing as specifically as possible each symptom; process list in session.
- **Objective:** Identify source of the depression.
- **Intervention(s):** Ask client to identify possible causes of depression, make a list, and process in session.
- **Diagnosis:** Major Depressive Disorder, Single Episode.

Summary

The field experience is a time to begin practicing your skills, while under supervision, with the intent of learning and growing from your experiences. If you expect to be perfect as a counselor trainee, then you will likely be disappointed to learn that we all have areas in which to grow. The field experience is the perfect time to seek supervision, guidance, and support from your site-based supervisor and your faculty supervisor. This initial chapter differentiated between practicum, an initial experience in which one observes and works to develop basic counseling skills, and the internship experience, in which the intern dives deep into the counseling role and lives the life of the professional counselor. We discussed helpful orientation information such as working in multidisciplinary teams and matching your assets with preferred client populations and sites. Multiple opportunities were provided for self-reflection and self-assessment to identify personal strengths and areas of challenge.

Finally, we reviewed the services provided by, and importance of, professional counseling organizations like the American Counseling Association, its divisions and branches, and Chi Sigma Iota, the international counseling honorary society. We encourage all professional counselors to obtain the national certified counselor (NCC) credential offered by the National Board for Certified Counselors (NBCC), as well as the relevant state certification or licensure to attain and maintain employment opportunities as a professional counselor—to take your rightful place as a member of the counseling profession.

When working with clients, there are many details of the first impression. One of your first decisions will be to focus on either building the relationship or gathering information, although both will be a focus in the helping process at some point. In developing the relationship, we focus on building rapport, characteristics of helpers, and counseling skills. When the priority is on information gathering, we focus on the intake process, informed consent, and treatment planning and diagnosing.

Initial sessions encompass the legal and ethical aspects of the counseling relationship, defining client rights, confidentiality, and duty to warn through the informed consent process. This chapter also detailed the importance of confidentiality with minors and how to work with parents regarding their child's rights within the counseling relationship.

Although many skills are used with the client in session, there are also more advanced skills related to the counselor's process, which focus on internal processing or working outside the client session. These skills include case conceptualization, treatment planning, and diagnosis. These are imperative for understanding what issues will be addressed, in planning sessions, determining the best treatment, and theoretical modalities to be used.

Many agencies have specialized intake forms to help gather information about the client in a structured format, which is highly recommended for beginning counselors to use while gaining experience in the field. During this initial intake process, counselors are beginning to assess the client's needs, goals, and wants through both formal and informal assessment tools. Gathering a psychosocial history and conducting a mental status exam are the most commonly used tools.

When working with clients, counselors use specific skills to develop the relationship and gather information. These skills should be maintained throughout the relationship even as more advanced skills are used. Another key aspect mentioned in the chapter is the amount of research that shows the person, or the “self,” of the counselor is one of the key ingredients in successful counseling, therefore making counselor self-assessment and self-awareness a necessity to becoming an effective counselor.

2

The Supervision Process

Catherine Y. Chang, Caroline O'Hara, and Lindy K. Parker

Preview

The supervision process is complicated and involves various individuals (i.e., supervisors, supervisees, coordinators, and clients) and organizations (i.e., the university and the practicum/internship agency or school) and transpires through various stages. In this chapter, we explore supervision processes, the various roles you will hold as you begin your practicum–internship sequence, and also what you can expect from your on-site and university supervisors. We will also cover the development of positive supervision relationships and learning goals, as well as the differences between supervision and counseling. In addition, we will discuss barriers to effective supervision, different theoretical approaches, and ways of making case presentations. Throughout this chapter, we will provide several self-assessment activities to help you identify your strengths, growing edges, needs, and goals.

Your Roles as a Counselor and a Supervisee: Where the Student and Professional Align

Entering practicum and internship is an exciting time for any professional counseling student. This experience marks the beginning of your transition from didactic learning in the classroom to supervised experience with real clients. One shift includes the addition and integration of field learning into your classroom learning. You will be shifting from learning *what* and *why* to learning *how*. You will also experience role shifts from being exclusively a student to becoming a counselor/clinician (a student intern) and supervisee. As you start your field experience, consider the questions in Think About It 2.1.

Think About It 2.1

As you begin your field training, reflect on the following questions:

1. What are you most excited about as you think about becoming a professional counselor?
2. What are your greatest fears about working with a student or client?
3. What population do you think you will have the most difficult time counseling? Explain.
4. What characteristics do you embody that will enhance your experience and that may be potential challenge for you?

As a counseling practicum student or intern, you may counsel individuals, couples, families, or groups in diverse settings. Regardless of where you are working as an intern (e.g., school, hospital, community health center, correctional facility, private practice, college counseling center), you will employ your counseling skills and use the knowledge gained from your program of study. It is common for students entering the field to feel excited about finally applying all that they have learned!

During practicum and internship, you will learn and gain experience as you counsel clients in a real-world setting under the supervision of established professionals. To understand what this means, we will begin by examining some important terms.

Supervision has been defined by Bernard and Goodyear (2019) as

> an intervention provided by a more senior member of a profession to a more junior colleague or colleagues who typically (but not always) are members of that same profession. This relationship is evaluative and

DOI: 10.4324/9781003305521-2

> hierarchical, extends over time, and has the simultaneous purposes of enhancing the professional functioning of the more junior person(s); monitoring the quality of professional services offered to the clients that she, he, or they see; and serving as a gatekeeper for the particular profession the supervisee seeks to enter. (p. 9)

Supervision formats include individual, triadic, or group sessions (Association for Counselor Education and Supervision [ACES], 2011). It is common for interns to participate in both individual/triadic and group supervision at their university and at least individual/triadic supervision on-site.

Supervisors are generally more experienced professionals who guide and evaluate other, often newer, professionals in their counseling work. Supervisors may be located on-site and/or at the student's university. Commonly, supervisors are professionals in the same field as their supervisees; however, many supervisors you will encounter are in other mental health fields (e.g., psychology, social work). Supervisors will work with you to ensure client welfare and facilitate your development as a professional counselor. Often, counseling doctoral students serve as university supervisors for master's-level supervisees. These doctoral students are also supervised in sessions called supervision-of-supervision.

Supervisees are those individuals who participate in supervision and are evaluated by one or more supervisors. Supervisees may include both students who are in graduate training programs and individuals who have finished graduate studies and are pursuing licensure or certification (Bernard & Goodyear, 2019).

Your Role as a Counseling Practicum Student and Intern

As a counseling practicum student and intern, your role as a clinician involves the practice of professional counseling with clientele while under supervision at your university and on-site. Interns may engage in many facets of counseling, including, but not limited to, (a) conducting intake or follow-up assessments; (b) providing group, individual, couples, and family counseling; (c) documenting case notes; (d) reporting potential abuse/neglect; (e) attending in-services and treatment team meetings; (f) providing psychoeducational and outreach workshops; (g) being available for student drop-ins; and (h) conducting classroom guidance sessions. In this role, counseling interns gain experience and increase competence as they engage in behaviors of professional counselors in the field.

Your Role as a Supervisee

In addition to your counseling activities, you will participate in regular, weekly supervision. As a supervisee, you will use supervision to explore client concerns and issues relating to your own development. In supervision, supervisees discuss their caseload of clients, provide evidence of performance in sessions (commonly by audiotape or videotape clips or by self-report), discuss supervisee self-awareness, and process supervisor feedback (Bernard & Goodyear, 2019). Commonly, individual and triadic supervision sessions are at least one hour per week, and group supervision sessions are an average of 1.5 hours long.

A common expectation, especially during group supervision, is for supervisees to conduct case presentations about their clientele. A case presentation is more than just playing a section of a counseling session recording and processing feedback. Case presentations frequently involve a discussion of student/client demographics and characteristics, goals, interventions, assessment tools, the impact of client and counselor culture, conceptualization, ethical concerns, and theoretical orientation. We will discuss case presentations more fully later in this chapter.

On-Site Supervision and Your Site Supervisor's Role

The main role of the on-site supervisor is to ensure client welfare and attend to the needs and policies of the site. In this capacity, the site and the on-site supervisor are primarily concerned with service delivery (Bernard & Goodyear, 2019). In other words, the main goal of the site is the quantity and quality of services offered to the population they serve. The on-site supervisor typically has administrative and managerial responsibilities in addition to client care and is often classified as an **administrative supervisor**. For example, on-site supervisors may also deal with fiscal concerns of the site, personnel issues, and site regulations. Commonly, on-site supervisors are professional counselors, case managers, program coordinators, or other professionals in leadership positions.

It is important to remember that practicum students and interns are guests of their sites and should adhere to all site protocols. Sites expect that interns will comply with the rules and regulations of the site and follow standards for client care, crisis management, termination of services, proper releases of information, and other situations. It is the responsibility of the site and site supervisor to provide the practicum student or intern with an orientation and any training materials regarding expectations, site policies and procedures, and emergency/crisis protocols (Bernard & Goodyear, 2019). In addition, sites and on-site supervisors typically expect that practicum students and interns will perform their duties during the site's normal hours of operation. Many universities have periods of time where classes are not held. However, do not expect that your site will mirror your university semester schedule. In fact, taking weeks away from your counseling work (e.g., during university breaks) could raise ethical concerns. If you do not see your clients for an extended period of time, this may be considered abandonment. Furthermore, your site may not be aware of or sympathetic to additional pressures on you from your university (e.g., exam weeks).

University Supervision and What You Can Expect

As previously discussed, university supervision and on-site supervision have areas of overlap and differences. Whereas on-site supervisors are primarily concerned with site needs (service delivery) and client care, university supervisors are primarily concerned with the education and skill development of the counseling student (Bernard & Goodyear, 2019). University supervisors usually hold the role of a **clinical supervisor**. Thus, they are primarily focused on your growth and development as a professional counselor as well as the client care you provide. University supervisors are responsible for developing evaluation standards and disclosing to the intern the ways in which grades are assessed.

As with any professional endeavor, it is wise to keep accurate, up-to-date, and succinct records summarizing your supervision sessions. Your university supervisor may prompt you to provide this information, but you should keep careful records regardless of which type of supervisor directs you to do so. Licensure boards and certification agencies may require you and your supervisor(s) to provide documentation of the dates, hours, and brief synopses of your professional work and supervision for you to obtain licensure or certification. It is also possible that professional agencies may audit your records and request such documentation throughout your career. Please refer to Chapter 3 for more information on record keeping.

It is important that you know that university supervisors will not **cross-supervise**. This means that, generally, they will not tell you to do something that goes against the direction of your site supervisor or the policies of your site. The idea here is that the university supervisor does not want to "step on anyone's toes" at the site, and vice versa. They do not want to tell on-site supervisors how to do their jobs. However, it is possible that a situation may arise in which there is an ethical or legal disagreement between supervisors or an emergency situation that requires action (see Think About It 2.2). If these concerns are unresolvable or urgent, your university supervisor may intervene.

For example, supervisors may disagree about mandated reporting and breaking confidentiality regarding a certain client. Perhaps the on-site supervisor has explored the issue with the supervisee and does not think reporting is necessary, but after exploring the issue with the supervisee, the university supervisor does think reporting is necessary. If we take this example further, then the university supervisor will weigh the concerns of the client, the supervisee, the site, and ethical and legal codes. If the university supervisor deems it necessary to report, they will aid the supervisee in how to do this, even though the on-site supervisor did not deem it necessary. This is an instance in which a university supervisor would be going against the on-site supervisor. Hopefully, these occasions are rare.

Think About It 2.2

As previously mentioned, during the course of your internship, you will likely have multiple individual and group supervision sessions each week. As a result, it is also likely that you will discuss some of your students/clients in multiple supervision settings.

- What happens if one supervisor makes one suggestion and a different supervisor makes another suggestion?
- What if you receive feedback from your university group supervision that you could develop more of a discussion about the impact of cultural differences between you and a particular client, and yet, you receive feedback from your on-site group supervision that you are on just the right trajectory with this same client?
- How do you proceed?

Part of the answer may depend on your theoretical orientation, of course. However, one method of approaching this conundrum is to discuss the differences in feedback with all parties involved before proceeding with your client. On the other hand, this may take some time, and it may be that you have another appointment scheduled with this client before you are able to discuss all feedback with all parties. In general, it is a good idea to (at the minimum) discuss any changes you intend to make in your approach with clients with your on-site supervisor before doing so.

University supervisors may facilitate discussions about many topics, such as your reactions to students/clients, your use of basic counseling skills, case conceptualizations, professional identity, and your theoretical orientation. University supervisors will want to observe you with a wide variety of clients and across a wide range of activities. For example, if you have been counseling female clients and have had limited opportunities to counsel male clients, your university supervisor may encourage you to obtain more diversity in your clientele. Or if you have had the opportunity to counsel clients/students with a high socioeconomic status (SES), can you also have the opportunity to counsel clients/students with limited financial means? Also, your supervisor will need to observe you demonstrating proficiency at different stages in the counseling process. In other words, how do you typically open an initial session, how do you work with people after several sessions, and how do you terminate sessions? These are examples of the types of objectives that will contribute to your evaluations and grades.

Developing Positive Relationships With Your Supervisors

As a professional counselor, part of your training includes the development of interpersonal skills. These skills, such as active listening, reflecting, and clarifying, can help you build relationships in many spheres of your life, including supervision. In general, the characteristics expected of a competent professional counselor can also be applied to develop a positive **supervisory alliance** (working alliance with your supervisor), such as the ability to manage conflict, genuineness, and respect (Bernard & Goodyear, 2019). A strong supervisory alliance is important to establish and maintain because the supervisory alliance is correlated with supervisees' satisfaction with supervision, supervisee self-efficacy, supervisee self-disclosure, and supervisee working alliance in counseling (Park et al., 2019). Several factors contribute to the supervisory alliance: supervisee and supervisor attachment styles, resistance, power, shame, anxiety level, need to feel and appear competent, and transference and countertransference between the supervisor and the supervisee (Bernard & Goodyear, 2019).

To develop positive relationships with your supervisors, it is helpful to know what they need and expect (e.g., attending weekly treatment team meetings, providing one tape per week for review). Conversely, it is also important for your supervisors to know what you need and expect (e.g., ability to maintain the required number of hours, explanation of site crisis protocols, process for increasing your caseload). Thus, one of the paramount goals of a positive supervisory relationship is explaining, clarifying, and understanding expectations from the beginning and throughout your journey through practicum and internship. In many ways this parallels the principles of informed consent. However, your supervisor should ideally be providing information and asking questions to help initiate and facilitate this process, especially because you are new to counseling and supervision.

Haynes et al. (2003) reported on a study that gathered information from supervisors regarding supervisee characteristics that facilitated successful supervision experiences. Several factors emerged, with the supervisee's desire to learn, grow, and improve being rated as the most helpful and important. Other ideal factors included non-defensiveness, openness, appropriate knowledge and counseling skills, preparedness, initiative, and the willingness to take risks. Conversely, participants reported that poorer supervisory alliances and outcomes resulted with supervisees who exhibited the opposite of these traits.

Openness About Concerns, Missteps, and Feedback

One of the foundations of a positive supervision relationship is to share your concerns and missteps as early and often as possible. Even in a trusting environment, this is easier said than done. In other words, if you have a question on how to proceed or how to make a decision about a certain client, ask your supervisor early. If you wait several days or weeks, the situation may become more difficult to resolve and may place additional stress on you, your clients, your supervisor, and your site. Supervisors know that you are learning, and they are there to support you in your work. Use their expertise and perspectives.

Giving and receiving feedback are also key elements in building and maintaining a positive supervisory relationship (see Personal Reflection 2.1). In essence, feedback is communication that can affirm something done well or critique something that could have been done differently. Remember that although you will be receiving regular feedback from your supervisors, you also can and should provide feedback to them as well. According to Ivey et al. (2017), feedback provides information about how someone perceives another person. Ideally, effective feedback includes the following guidelines: (a) the receiver should be in charge; (b) feedback should focus on strengths and positive assets; (c) the topic should be something the receiver can change; (d) feedback should include concrete and specific ideas; (e) feedback should be nonjudgmental; (f) present tense feedback is ideal; and (g) feedback should be concise. After feedback is offered, the sender and receiver should confirm that they accurately understand each other. See also the later section entitled "Barriers to Supervision," which also explores feedback processes in supervision.

Personal Reflection 2.1

When I was a young child, I can recall some of my mother's guidance around household stains and spills. She would tell me that she would vastly prefer if I would tell her early rather than hide something until later. I remember her reassuring me that she would not be angry with me, but that it would be easier to clean a mess when it was freshly made than after it had set. She even demonstrated her claim by cleaning something just after a spill and showing me how easy it was. She contrasted this with stains that would not clean because they were not addressed quickly. Thus, through her explanation, demonstration, and reassurance, I felt confident that I could inform her if I made a mess without feeling guilty or fearful. As I hope you can tell, this story represents a parallel with supervision. Although your supervisors are not your parents or caregivers, they are in a position to guide and support you if you make a misstep or if something does not feel right. As with my childhood lessons, I urge you to inform your supervisors early if anything might need a quick spot or deep clean. ~CLO

Supervisee Responsibilities

Another major aspect to building positive supervision relationships is to fulfill your responsibilities as a supervisee. Some of these responsibilities include being prepared for supervision sessions, actively engaging in self-reflection and increasing your self-awareness, identifying/developing your goals and asking for what you need, and completing tasks and commitments in a timely fashion. As with any professional meeting, supervisors expect that you will come prepared with specific questions or concerns to address and not waste time trying to think of something to talk about after you begin your session (Haynes et al., 2003). One way to avoid this is to keep a notebook, binder, or electronic file that can store notes, questions, and reflections that you have for supervision. This could include anything related to your direct individual or group work or even the field of professional counseling. For instance, if someone asks you a question you do not know how to answer, you could document this in your list of questions or reflections to be ready to address during your next supervision session. You could also discuss reactions you are having to your clients, theory and technique questions, self-care strategies (for some ideas, see Think About It 2.3), roadblocks you are experiencing, and ways to advocate for clients and the counseling profession. Truly, supervision is what you make of it, and the possibilities are endless.

Think About It 2.3

As professional counselors, we discuss the importance of self-care as a central part of professional practice. But what does this abstract term really mean when self-care can vary so much from person to person? When professional counselors are able to engage in self-care, we have observed what an asset it can be in promoting wellness among counselors and those whom we serve. We have also witnessed, unfortunately, when self-care is pushed aside for various internal or external reasons to the detriment of the counselor and client. So, what does all this mean? In the spirit of our prevention-oriented wellness model, we suggest that you (ahead of time) consider:

1. What does self-care represent to you?
2. What does self-care *specifically* look like for you?
3. What are the benefits and obstacles to self-care?
4. What happens when you are not able to engage in self-care?

Some examples might include setting boundaries around work; making time for regular eating, sleeping, and exercising; and noticing the physical aches and pains you carry in your body when you are stressed. Try to generate concrete examples about thoughts, feelings, behaviors, and circumstances/contextual factors. After considering your specifics, discuss your reflections with other interns, instructors, supervisors, and loved ones to develop ideas about how to strengthen your self-care practices. Once you have a solid awareness and foundation, you will be able to rely on this existing knowledge when you are being tested during your practicum and internship experiences.

Another way to build positive relationships with your supervisor is by actively engaging in self-reflection and discussions to increase your self-awareness. It may be helpful to ask yourself what you hope and expect from supervision. Do you expect your supervisor to have "all the answers," and is this what you prefer? What do you know about yourself as a multicultural being (e.g., sexual identity, ability status, religious affiliation, race) and how might this affect your work with your supervisor(s) and your clients? Consider how you would like to assess and monitor your supervision relationship. It also may be helpful to reflect on how you approach, manage, and resolve interpersonal conflict (Bernard & Goodyear, 2019).

An additional aspect of fulfilling your responsibilities as a supervisee includes identifying and developing your goals and asking for what you need. This may be easier or more difficult, depending on a number of factors such as interpersonal style, personality, topic, nature of your supervision relationship, and contextual factors such as race and gender (Bernard & Goodyear, 2019). One way to take a preventative approach is to communicate clearly your program's requirements and your particular goals in your first interview at your site or your first meeting with your on-site supervisor. At that time, it is important and appropriate to explain the requirements of your program (e.g., how many direct service hours you need each semester) and your specific objectives and interests (e.g., equal experience with individuals and classroom developmental guidance groups). This way, if you are into your third week at your site and still have not held any individual sessions, you could refer back to the initial conversation to prompt your supervisor so that they can work toward making changes to your caseload. Taking this example further, you may also discover that you want to work with students in a group setting, and so you will need to bring this to your supervisor's attention to see what changes might be made and what additional opportunities you may have at your site. Remember, it may or may not be possible for you and your supervisor to work out different arrangements, but it will help your supervisory relationship if you can be aware of your needs and communicate them clearly (and often).

By completing tasks and commitments quickly, regularly, and efficiently, you also build a positive relationship with your supervisor. When your site assigns you clients, when you meet with clients, and when you document your sessions, your on-site supervisor must "sign off" on your activities. For instance, during staff meetings, your supervisor might need to know the status of each of your clients before assigning you additional clients. If you fall behind on your documentation, it is difficult for your supervisor to have the information needed to make decisions about altering your case load. Not only can this be a nuisance for your supervisor to have to follow up with you, but it may be a legal, ethical, or site protocol violation to be slow or late in providing documentation. For these reasons, supervisees should complete documentation and case notes on a regular basis. One suggestion is to designate a specific time slot daily or weekly to attend to the administrative parts of professional counseling. If you build this time into your schedule, you are more likely to complete documentation in a consistent and timely fashion.

Developing Learning Goals with Your Supervisors

Initially, your goals for supervision may be broad and include things like becoming a competent counselor, developing autonomy, and being properly prepared for your future career as a counselor (Morgan & Sprenkle, 2007). As supervision progresses and you become more self-aware of your own development as a counselor, you will likely add more specific goals and objectives to your list. Your university and on-site supervisors may also be able to suggest some learning goals for you.

Learning goals help to focus the efforts of your own work and development. They can also focus the content of the supervision session. For example, a supervisor who knows the supervisee has a goal of becoming more multiculturally competent will likely provide extra psychoeducational material relating to diverse cultures and multicultural counseling. The supervisor may even become acutely attuned to any biases the supervisee might display, and the supervisor can point those out to the supervisee as areas for potential growth.

Borders and Brown (2005) suggested creating a separate contract with your supervisors that is composed entirely of your stated learning goals (see Self-Assessment Activity 2.1). Sharing your stated goals and collaborating with your supervisors on any possible additions to the goal contract can help your supervisors get to know you more and likewise help you to better know your supervisor. This two-way interaction enriches the supervision relationship, which in turn leads to an enhanced supervision experience.

Self-Assessment Activity 2.1 Learning Goals

Learning goals are the agreement between the supervisor and supervisee and help focus the supervision sessions. Learning goals can include specific counseling interventions or techniques, relationship issues, cognitive skills related to conducting counseling, self-awareness, and so on. List three to five learning goals that you have for your supervision experience.

Supervision Versus Counseling

During supervision, you may notice your supervisor using techniques that look similar to the counseling skills you have recently acquired. You may also find the supervision experience feels therapeutic at times. Still, it should be clear that supervision is not intended to be personal counseling for supervisees. For example, consider the situation in Think About It 2.4. Although supervisees may find that personal issues arise during their practicum and internship sequence, a supervisor is only to address those issues that influence the supervisee's work with clients (Bernard & Goodyear, 2019). Anything beyond that, where a supervisor begins to act as the supervisee's personal counselor, is an ethical violation. That being said, supervisees in need of their own professional counseling are encouraged to seek that counseling from their university counseling center or another qualified professional in the field.

Think About It 2.4

Imagine you are a supervisee dealing with the loss of your mother. Your mother has been ill for some time, so her death was not unexpected, yet you are finding yourself having a difficult time dealing with her death. As a part of your field experience, you find yourself working with many women who remind you of your mother. You openly discuss your grieving process and your reactions to your clients with your supervisor.

- How appropriate is it for your supervisor to assist you in your grieving process?
- How much time should the supervisor spend in discussing your reactions to your female clients?
- How receptive would you be to your supervisor referring you to a counselor to assist in your grieving?

Bernard and Goodyear (2019) stated that evaluating supervisees is the most important difference between supervision and professional counseling. Unlike professional counseling, where most counselors refrain from evaluating their clients, evaluation of a supervisee is required. And although this evaluation can include some of the supervisee's stated goals, it is largely based on criteria outlined by professional standards. Moreover, practicum and internship supervision is generally conducted within a prescribed time frame, during which supervisees must achieve the required objectives and meet the professional standards; counseling, on the other hand, usually progresses at the client's pace. Finally, the option to enter supervision is usually not optional, per se, whereas the decision to enter counseling usually is. To achieve counseling career goals, a supervisee should be required to receive supervision during training, and supervisors are often assigned to supervisees at the outset of their supervision process. In other cases, supervisees may have some freedom in choosing a supervisor (see Personal Reflection 2.2).

Personal Reflection 2.2

Less than a year into my counselor training program, my cohort, including myself, was required to choose which supervisor we would have for our practicum–internship experience. We made this choice by registering for that supervisor's course section of practicum–internship. Although some of my cohort members registered for the section offered at the most convenient time, a mentor of mine advised me against this common mistake. Instead, before registration began, I reviewed the curriculum vitae of the available supervisors. I also attended my university's Chi Sigma Iota chapter meetings with the objective of speaking to more advanced students in the program and soliciting their feedback on the potential supervisors. I narrowed down the list of possible fits with my chosen client population and interests, and I even made appointments with some of those potential supervisors. Being proactive and investing this time was invaluable to my training, as it informed my choice and helped create a supervision experience that was extremely positive for me.

Barriers to Effective Supervision

When done well, supervision can facilitate one of the most rewarding and enjoyable parts of your counselor training program. There are, however, numerous potential barriers to effective supervision that can originate from multiple sources (e.g., the supervisee, the supervisor, the site), despite each entity having only the best intentions. Being mindful of some of the common barriers is the first step toward preventing them and puts you on a path toward your best potential supervision experience.

One of the most straightforward barriers is lacking competence, from either the supervisee or the supervisor or both. Although it is nearly impossible for a supervisor to be knowledgeable about every situation and population, a supervisor should be competent and experienced in the area in which their direct supervisee is working (ACES, 2011). All efforts should be made to remedy mismatched supervisees and supervisors. To facilitate this, supervisees should gather as much information about their field placement as possible so that a fully informed match can be made with available supervisors.

Also, supervisors should be trained and should have achieved competence in the skill of supervision itself in advance of taking on a supervisee of their own. Before entering into a supervision relationship, prudent supervisees will seek assurance that their potential supervisor is trained in supervision, as well as competent in their chosen population. Still, even with adequate planning and preparation, supervisees may find themselves in negative supervision relationships, with either their university supervisor or site supervisor. Although these situations do appear to be rare, they can be stressful and confusing for the supervisee. Some supervisees have had some success in resolving these conflicts in supervision by discussing them directly with their supervisor. Many supervisees use their own coping strategies to navigate and endure these supervision conflicts and also seek the support of peers and partners partners (Baird & Mollen, 2019). Other supervisees have had to involve a neutral third party—perhaps a site director or university clinical internship coordinator or faculty member—to facilitate a change in supervisor or internship placement. Of course, each situation is different and should be handled with thoughtful care. In all cases of a suspected ethical violation by a supervisor, though, a supervisee should consult with a trusted faculty member and/or senior staff member at their site on the appropriate reporting policies and procedures. Although being in a negative supervision relationship can be discouraging, supervisees should be reminded that the field facilitates multiple supervision relationships and opportunities—so hopefully one problematic supervisor will be only one among many positive supervisors a supervisee (and ultimately novice professional counselor) will encounter and learn from within their counseling career.

It is unreasonable to expect a supervisor to be competent in every type of population and counseling setting (see Personal Reflection 2.3). It is equally unreasonable to expect a supervisee to be able to deliver best counseling practice to their chosen population at the start of their practicum and internship experience. There would be no need for supervision if this were the case. Throughout the practicum and internship experiences, you will undoubtedly be confronted with gaps in your counseling knowledge, as well as counseling skill areas that need further development. Yet, in an effort to appear competent, some supervisees may not readily express these identified shortcomings. It is in the best interest of both yourself and the clients you serve that you identify and express these areas to your supervisors and perhaps even make them working goals for the supervision relationship. Any supervisory relationship that lacks openness and space for the supervisee to express these doubts and vulnerabilities is facing a barrier to truly effective supervision.

Personal Reflection 2.3

I immediately developed a strong supervisory relationship with my post-master's supervisor. I felt safe to share my incompetence, and she knew just the right ways to push me toward growth and best counseling practice. I was also extremely proud to call her my supervisor, as her reputation was well respected in the field.

When an entry-level opportunity to work at a child and adolescent treatment center was presented to me, I jumped at the chance to get experience in this area of counseling. Yet my supervisor expressed concerns about me having her as my only supervisor as I took on this new client population. Her concern was grounded in her knowledge that, although she had some past training and experience working with children, it had been many years, and her current practice was now focused exclusively on adults. Just weeks into my new practice, we mutually agreed that I needed to seek other supervision, specifically with a supervisor who had more competence in the area of children. Although I was saddened to leave that supervision relationship, I was soon matched with a supervisor who actively worked with children in her own ongoing practice, and we also developed a wonderful working alliance. It was an invaluable training experience.

In hindsight, it was my fear of the unknown and my resistance to change that almost got in the way of some crucial growth and learning. Although most in the field hope for students to have one valuable and impactful supervisory relationship, I now expect students to have at least two.

Discussions about the supervisee's underdeveloped skills or even incompetence are likely inevitable, so a supervisee who is unable or unwilling to hear feedback from a supervisor will not experience an effective supervisory relationship. It is not uncommon for a supervisee to experience some level of anxiety, especially around these critical discussions (Borders & Brown, 2005). Yet, being unable to receive and make use of feedback can impair development. Equally, a supervisor who has not invited feedback from supervisees is also doing a disservice to the supervisory process. Being able to express to your supervisor what works and does not work for you is essential to creating a better, more productive working alliance (see Self-Assessment Activity 2.2).

Self-Assessment Activity 2.2 Feedback

Is feedback an area that makes you anxious? One way to alleviate that anxiety is to express to your supervisor the way you most like to receive feedback. Perhaps you like to hear things directly, along with concrete examples of ways to improve. Or maybe you prefer to receive feedback on opportunities for improvement when that feedback is presented along with identified areas in which you are excelling.

- How do you like to receive feedback?
- How can you communicate this preference to your supervisor(s)?
- Do you know the way in which your supervisor(s) prefers to give and receive feedback?

Perhaps the part of supervision that has the greatest potential to create anxiety and unease for both supervisor and supervisee is evaluation. Although you may be accustomed to evaluation coming only at the end of a course, evaluation should be ongoing throughout your supervision experience (Bernard & Goodyear, 2019; Campbell, 2006). Because the ability to remain on your chosen counseling career path can depend on the evaluation of your supervisor, as a supervisee, you should know exactly how your supervisor currently evaluates your performance and that you are doing what is necessary to receive a final endorsement toward licensure or certification. Although supervisors are ultimately responsible for providing this ongoing evaluation, supervisees should have a full understanding of when and how their supervisor will conduct and provide these evaluations, as well as the criteria used in those evaluations. If you are unsure about the criteria on which you will be evaluated, when evaluations will occur, if a specific evaluation instrument will or will not be used, or how evaluations will be communicated to you, then you are at risk of encountering a barrier to supervision.

A growing area in supervision includes addressing cultural issues and advocacy within the supervision process. Specifically, both supervisors and supervisees must be able to articulate their own cultural values and beliefs, as well as recognize those of others. Counselors-in-training are often lacking in multicultural and advocacy competencies and may hold biases based on cultural group membership (Goodyear et al., 2016). Other research has shown that when appropriate and sufficient attention is given to cultural issues in supervision, the supervisee has a more positive supervision experience (McLeod, 2008). Although it is preferable for these discussions to originate with the supervisor at the beginning of the supervisory relationship, supervisees should feel increasingly comfortable discussing multicultural issues during supervision, and eventually supervisees can initiate those conversations. Ignoring cultural issues—whether your own, your client's, or your supervisor's—will likely be a barrier to effective supervision.

Learning From Different Philosophies and Theoretical Orientations: Growing and Changing

As a part of both the counseling and supervision processes, you will be exposed to a great deal of information (e.g., client demographic information; client behavior and attitude; your reaction toward the client and supervisor; the interaction among you, your clients, your supervisor). This information can become overwhelming if you do not have a mechanism to assist you in organizing and interpreting that information. Counseling theories help us to make sense of this potentially overwhelming information. Schermer (2002, p. XI) stated, "The facts never just speak for themselves. They must be interpreted through the colored lenses of ideas: percepts need concepts." Theory can serve as these lenses to help us focus our attention and to assist us in organizing the multitude of information that we gather during a counseling session (Bernard & Goodyear, 2019). As a part of your development, you will be encouraged to develop your own theoretical orientation and to apply that theory when appropriate to your work. As you begin your journey to developing your own theoretical approach to your work with your clients, consider the following questions: How do you think people change? How do you make changes in your own life? In the next chapter, you will be introduced more thoroughly to the importance of integrating theory into practice with a focus on developing your own theory.

As you are encouraged to develop your theoretical orientation, it is important to remember that your supervisors also have their own theoretical orientations that guide their practice with their clients as well as their practice with their supervisees. In fact, many supervisors operate from a theoretical orientation that guides how they conceptualize client and supervisee change as well as a supervision model that guides how they structure their supervisory process. Your supervisor's theoretical orientation and supervision model will also guide how they structure and process case presentations.

Bernard and Goodyear (2019) described three broad categories of supervision models: (a) models grounded in psychotherapy theory, (b) developmental models, and (c) process models. To these three categories, we suggest adding multicultural supervision models. Models grounded in psychotherapy theory include psychodynamic supervision, person-centered supervision, cognitive-behavioral supervision, systemic supervision, and constructivist supervision. Developmental models include the integrated developmental model (IDM; Stoltenberg & McNeill, 2009) and the Loganbill et al. model (1982). Examples of process models include the discrimination model (Bernard & Goodyear, 2019) and the systems approach to supervision model (Holloway, 1995). Examples of multicultural supervision models include the racial identity developmental model (Chang et al., 2004) and the heuristic model of non-oppressive interpersonal development development (HMNID; Ancis & Ladany, 2010). It is outside the scope of this chapter to discuss each of these supervision models; however, it is important for you as a beginning counselor to understand that many supervisors operate from a particular supervision model and that their model for supervision will influence the supervisory process and your relationship. Therefore, it is important for you to inquire about your supervisor's approach to supervision and how that may affect your supervisory process and alliance. Although we believe it is the responsibility of supervisors to discuss their supervision models with supervisees at the beginning of the supervisory relationship, if your supervisor does not initiate this discussion, you can do so with the following questions: (a) What supervision model do you follow?; (b) What is your approach to organizing the supervision session?; and (c) What is your approach to providing feedback?

Voices From the Field 2.1 Becoming Myself, *by Julia Whisenhunt*

Prior to my doctoral studies, I had not considered the importance of having a theory of supervision. As part of my graduate education, I had trained in clinical supervision and even engaged in the supervision of supervisors. I was familiar with the process—the multiple roles the supervisor plays, the legal and ethical responsibilities, and ways to facilitate growth in my supervisee. I had the critically important knowledge and skills necessary to supervise another counselor. I was competent in supervision, but my style was inconsistent, and I didn't rely on a conceptualization of my supervisee to inform our process.

The doctoral program I attended at Georgia State University requires an intense supervision of supervision training experience. At the beginning of the experience, I felt relatively confident in my supervision skills; I knew basically what do to and how to do it. Throughout my first two years in the program, my major professor had stressed the importance of approaching every professional role (i.e., counseling, supervision, teaching, and research) from a theoretical perspective. She believes that one's theory should be consistent across the professional domains—an idea that I had only partially endorsed. So, I knew I would be expected to demonstrate how what I did during my supervision sessions was reflected in my theory.

I began my supervision sessions with the explicit thought that I needed to balance the roles I played—consultant, teacher, and counselor—and integrate my counseling theory throughout. It was choppy and unnatural.

I was generally doing and saying the "right" things, but I was so focused on my performance that I was missing some underlying themes and opportunities to facilitate awareness in my supervisees. I knew something had to change. My next approach was to enter each session relaxed, abandoning my mission to "perform" well and demonstrate my theory. As each session progressed, though, I found myself reverting to the familiar stereotypic roles. It became clear to me that I wasn't allowing *myself* to be in the session. My professor even commented once, "this doesn't sound like the Julia I know." I was acting out the role of what I expected of myself and what I thought was expected of me. How was I supposed to be natural in my supervision sessions and still uphold my responsibilities as a supervisor? For me, the answer came through letting go.

At that point in my professional development, I had already integrated my counseling theory and felt confident in my ability to let my theory guide me during counseling sessions without being cognitively preoccupied with evaluating myself and justifying each intervention. I came to the realization that I had to trust myself in supervision as well. I had the fundamental knowledge and skills in supervision. And, through my counseling theory, I knew how I conceptualized the process of growth and change. My task, then, was to modify my counseling theory to fit the supervision relationship. I began analytically evaluating how the components of my counseling theory fit or did not fit into the supervision relationship. It wasn't long until I realized that the components fit equally well into both relationships. My major professor was right! My theory *is* consistent across the professional domains. Once I accepted that my counseling theory also guides my supervision, I was free to be natural in sessions because I knew that what I was doing was informed by my theory and guided by my beliefs about growth and change.

This isn't to say that I am a counselor to my supervisees. Rather, my point is that, in my opinion, the process of supervising another counselor is essentially a process of facilitating development, which is not altogether very different from the underlying goal of counseling. And, just like in counseling, if I were not guided by a theory of how development occurs, my work with supervisees would be haphazard. As my major professor says, it's great if an intervention works well once, but how can you be expected to replicate those results if you don't know why you're doing what you're doing?

Making Case Presentations

Making case presentations is an essential skill in the development of a supervisee. Case presentations are an important learning tool because they provide not only a structure for helping us articulate our work with our students/clients but also us a structure for seeking supervision and consultation. Your supervisor's theoretical orientation and model of supervision will also influence the structure of case presentations. Table 2.1 provides sample guidelines for developing a case presentation.

Borders (1991) provided a systemic approach to peer group supervision, which can be used to structure the case presentations. This model was adapted by Lassiter et al. (2008) to include a greater focus on multicultural

Table 2.1 Guidelines for an oral or written case presentation

In preparing for your group presentation, select a client with whom you are having some difficulty or challenge. Prior to the meeting, organize information about your client and your experiences. Please include a brief audio/video presentation of the session. Your introduction and review of the tape should last no more than 15 to 20 minutes. This leaves the majority of the time for feedback and comments from your peers and supervisor. Your case presentation should include the following information:

1. Description of student/client.
2. Statement of the problem/concern.
3. Cultural information.
    a. What cultural biases might you have toward your client?
    b. What cultural biases might your client have toward you?
    c. What cultural values might enhance or impede your relationship with this client?
4. Your theoretical approach to working with this client.
5. Assessment/diagnosis.
6. Your treatment goals for this client.
7. Your goal for this session.
8. Are there any ethical considerations for working with this client?
9. Solicit feedback. What questions do you have for the supervision group?

counseling competence. The structured peer group format is designed to encourage skill development, conceptualization skills, supervisor feedback, and self-monitoring. According to Lassiter et al. (2008), the structured peer group procedure includes the following steps:

1. The supervisee solicits specific feedback about their counseling performance.
2. Peers in the group are assigned or choose a specific role, perspective, or task to focus on while reviewing the counseling tape segment. These tasks may include observing counselor or client nonverbals, assuming the role of the counselor or the client, viewing the segment from a specific theoretical orientation, or generating a metaphor for the counseling process.
3. The supervisee presents the taped segment.
4. The group members provide feedback based on their roles or tasks.
5. The supervisor facilitates the discussion serving as both moderator and process observer.
6. The supervisor summarizes the feedback and the discussion.

A modification to this process that we have made in supervision groups is that we end the discussion with "If this were my client I would . . ." This stem offers the counselor trainee with specific things to consider in their future work with their clients, while keeping in mind that this is from the perspective of their peer group members.

Summary

The process of supervision is complex and multifaceted, involving multiple individuals and agencies. In this chapter, we have discussed your transition from being a classroom-bound student to a counseling practicum student or intern. As you move into your practicum and internship, you will experience both excitement and anxiety at the opportunity to put into practice your classroom learning. As a counselor trainee, you will be expected to be involved in all aspects of the counseling profession under supervision including, but not limited to, conducting classroom developmental guidance sessions; engaging in crisis protocols; conducting intake interviews; providing individual, couples, and group counseling sessions; keeping accurate documentation; and participating in in-service and team meetings.

A part of the supervisory process includes working with both your university supervisor and your on-site supervisor. Although both supervisors are concerned with student/client welfare and your development as a professional counselor, each will have different foci as their primary emphasis based on their role as either your university supervisor or your on-site supervisor. On-site supervisors are also often referred to as your administrative supervisor because they are concerned with the quantity and quality of services offered to the clientele that the agency serves. Your university supervisor may also be referred to as your clinical supervisor. Your clinical supervisor is concerned with your growth and development as a professional counselor. It is important that both the site and university supervisors work collaboratively to provide an optimal supervisory environment that will enhance your training.

An important aspect of the supervisory process is the relationship (i.e., supervisory alliance) that you will develop with each of your supervisors. To develop a positive supervisory alliance, it is helpful for both you and your supervisors to be clear about your expectations and needs from the supervisory process. In addition, in conjunction with your supervisor, you will want to create an atmosphere of openness where concerns and missteps can be shared.

Developing learning goals with your supervisors assists in fostering the supervisory alliance. Learning goals help to establish the agreement between your supervisors and yourself, and they help to provide structure for your supervisory sessions. The learning goals can include specific interventions or techniques, relationship issues, cognitive skills related to conducting counseling, and goals related to self-awareness. It is important to note that these learning goals are specifically related to your development as a counselor and are separate from your treatment goals that you will establish with your clients.

Effective supervision results in a positive growth experience for both supervisees and supervisors. However, there are barriers to effective supervision that you must be aware of and work toward preventing. These barriers include supervisor and supervisee competence, lack of effective and timely feedback, and cultural competence. Being mindful of these potential barriers to effective supervision is the first step toward preventing them.

This chapter has focused on the various aspects of the supervision process. It is important to note that how supervisors choose to structure the supervisory process is largely influenced by their theoretical orientation and supervision model. Theory provides a lens to filter and organize the vast amount of information that you will gather in the counseling and supervision processes. Just as you are encouraged to develop your theoretical orientation for your work with your clients, your supervisors are encouraged to apply a supervision model to their approach to supervision. Your supervisors' theoretical orientation and their supervision model will influence how they use case presentations in your supervision. In this chapter, we presented the structured peer group model as one method for processing the case presentation. The supervisory process is a dynamic process that involves multiple individuals and agencies. To achieve a successful outcome in supervision, it is incumbent on both the supervisor and the supervisee to actively engage in the supervisory process, being mindful that both the supervisor and the supervisee are responsible for a successful supervision experience.

3

Integrating Theory Into Practice

Dana Heller Levitt and Bradley T. Erford

Preview

The nature and quality of the counseling relationship is more significant than any other factor in counseling. Given this perspective, why do professional counselors study theories? Whether working with individuals, families, or groups, regardless of the setting, professional counselors have a professional responsibility to develop a foundation and clear rationale for their theoretical orientation to serve clients. Professional counselors operate out of theories that best fit their personal philosophies of human change and the counseling process, but also choose approaches that effectively address the client's issues. Selecting a theoretical orientation is a career-long process that begins during professional training. In this chapter, the significance of integrating theory into counseling practice is explored, and a brief overview of the major theoretical paradigms is presented. You will also begin to explore your own initial preferences for theoretical orientation with the intent of continuing your personal and professional exploration to discover your personal style.

The Significance of Theory

Theories ground us as professional counselors. Theories provide a means to understand what we are doing, how we are serving clients, and how to explain counseling to clients. People entering counseling are generally not interested in hearing a detailed description of their counselor's philosophical beliefs about the nature of the counseling relationship and human change. Rather, they are seeking guidance about the change process and how the professional counselor can help them to accomplish that goal. Theories represent clients' realities and what we know to be important and effective elements of the counseling relationship (Hansen, 2006a). Professional counselors must have a firm sense of the counseling process alongside their own philosophies about what works in counseling and how individuals change and grow.

A firm understanding of your beliefs about counseling can help you explain the process to clients, helping them understand the nature of counseling and what can be expected (Gladding, 2018). This road map for counseling can help you generate new ideas with the client to determine the best course of action and the means to reach goals.

Theories provide a framework for conceptualizing client problems and determining a course of action in counseling (Halbur & Halbur, 2018). For example, a professional counselor who operates from a cognitive-behavioral standpoint would identify a client's struggle with bulimia as faulty logic and plan a course of treatment to reshape thoughts and behaviors. A psychodynamic-oriented professional counselor would view the issue through the lens of the client's past and spend counseling time uncovering early triggers and sustaining factors for the disorder.

Ethics of Applying Counseling Theory

One theory does not fit for all clients. A successful approach with one client may be problematic with another. Professional counselors have an ethical responsibility to be culturally competent and to address each client's needs as such. There is no cookie-cutter, "one size fits all" approach to counseling. Despite what some clients may be seeking, professional counselors do not have a handbook of problems and solutions. Professional counselors instead must use their understanding of theory to provide the best possible services to clients. Operating

DOI: 10.4324/9781003305521-3

from a clear theoretical framework also means being flexible with that approach to know when it will not work. Self-Assessment Activity 3.1 provides an opportunity to explore some of the theoretical underpinnings of your counseling approach.

Self-Assessment Activity 3.1 Theoretical Underpinnings

A 7-year-old girl is referred for counseling. Recently, she has been having difficulty staying on task during class and making friends. Her parents were never married and no longer live together. Her teacher reports that the girl came to her the previous day and mentioned something about other students making fun of her on the playground because she does not have a "real" family.

- As a professional counselor, how would you establish rapport?
- What types of questions would you ask her during the first session?
- What strategies would you employ to begin solving some of the problems she is having in school?
- Now, if the student were a 21-year-old male Asian college student with a history of distractibility and poor peer relations, what types of alterations would you make to your approach and strategies?
- Finally, if the client were a 42-year-old woman returning to college or graduate school, and with a history of distractibility and poor peer relations, how might you change your approach and strategies?

From an ethical standpoint, professional counselors must be clear about their professional orientation to serve clients best. As will be discussed in Chapter 6, the American Counseling Association (ACA) *Code of Ethics* (2014) provides guidelines for professional and ethical counseling practice. All professional counselors and counselors-in-training are expected to abide by the principles stated in the *Code of Ethics*. Sections of the *Code of Ethics* pertain specifically to learning and practice associated with theories. Professional counselors must be aware of new trends and best practices in the profession. Professional counselors must also be competent to use the theories they choose to employ in counseling and must have a firm foundation for the work they perform with clients.

Closely related, and perhaps one of the most fundamental aspects of professional and ethical practice, is continual counselor self-reflection. **Self-awareness** is crucial to counselor development. Professional counselors must regularly assess their beliefs about the counseling process and their effectiveness with clients. By this manner of self-awareness, professional counselors can determine and strengthen their theoretical beliefs and practices. Self-Assessment Activity 3.2 encourages exploration and refinement of your theoretical approach by exploring the approaches used by practitioners in the field.

Self-Assessment Activity 3.2 Theory in the Field

Interview three practicing counselors about their theoretical orientations. Discuss with them the importance of theory in their current work, how they arrived at their personal theories, how they transitioned from intellectual to practical application of theoretical principles in practice, and the relationship of their theories to personal philosophies. Are there differences when working with individuals, groups, or families? How do the counselors' theoretical orientations compare and contrast with yours?

What Makes a Good Theory?

In their classic text, Hansen et al. (1993) suggested that a good counseling theory is (a) clear and easily understood; (b) comprehensive; (c) explicit and heuristic, generating further research; (d) specifically geared to help clients reach their deIed outcomes; and (e) useful to practitioners. Theories must be sound to be plausible to professional counselors. Literally hundreds of theories exist, and more continue to emerge (Ivey et al., 2017). All these theories can be overwhelming to beginning counselors who are trying to do what is in the best interests of their clients. Professional counselors need a means of organizing the information about theories, applying what works, and building on natural helping capabilities.

Intentionality, or making conscious and intentional decisions, is a necessity in applying the basic helping skills (Halbur & Halbur, 2018). As mentioned in Chapter 5, skill application is both an art and a science. Technical expertise, although important, will not always make the professional counselor most effective. A firm, philosophical understanding of the counseling profession and practice, and knowledge of the research behind what you do, will help you in your selection of and adherence to a theory that best fits your natural style of helping. Considering theories with respect to their common elements can help professional counselors determine what works best for whom and most notably for you as the counselor.

Theoretical Paradigms

Through self-awareness, professional counselors strengthen their approaches and learn new ways to work with clients. Theoretical orientation usually remains relatively constant through counselors' development given the connection to personal philosophy. Changes that occur tend to be within the general categories of theories, referred to as **paradigms**. These paradigms are a means of grouping theories based on common characteristics. Multiple theories exist within each paradigm. Table 3.1 provides summary characteristics of the five most prominent paradigms, and Table 3.2 summarizes the techniques and multicultural considerations of the important theories ordinarily associated with each paradigm. We will explain each of these paradigms in detail throughout the remainder of the chapter.

Table 3.1 Theoretical paradigms: theories and theorists

Paradigm	*Major Theories*	*Prominent Theorists*
Psychodynamic	Psychoanalysis Adlerian	Sigmund Freud Alfred Adler
	Ego psychology	Carl Jung
Humanistic-existential	Person-centered Existential	Carl Rogers Victor Frankl, Irvin Yalom, Rollo May
	Gestalt	Fritz Perls
Behavioral/cognitive-behavioral	Behavioral	John Watson, B. F. Skinner, Albert Bandura, John Krumboltz
	Cognitive	Aaron Beck
	Cognitive-behavioral therapy	Donald Meichenbaum
	Rational emotive behavior therapy	Albert Ellis
Systems Postmodern	Family systems Narrative Constructivist	Murray Bowen, Virginia Satir Michael White, David Epston George Kelly
	Feminist	
	Interpersonal therapy (IPT)	

Table 3.2 Theoretical paradigms: techniques and multicultural considerations

Paradigm	*Principles*	*Techniques*	*Considerations*
Psychodynamic	Predetermined	Free association	Ego and past cultural identity development
	Relationship of events and current functioning	Interpretation	Id, ego, superego development
	Bring unconscious into conscious	Dream analysis	Limited views of women
		Analysis of transference	
Humanistic-existential	Innate goodness of people	Counseling relationship	Attention to individual's unique perspective
	Self-actualization	Empty chair	Lack of structure

(*Continued*)

Table 3.2 (Continued)

Paradigm	*Principles*	*Techniques*	*Considerations*
	Freedom and responsibility	Genuineness, empathy, unconditional positive regard	Limited attention to external factors
	Finding meaning	Role play	Common values of love, death, anxiety
	Anxiety	Role reversal	
		"I" statements	
Behavioral/cognitive-behavioral	Changing behavior, negative thought patterns, beliefs	Specify automatic thoughts	Understanding beliefs as identity
	ABCDEs of REBT	Homework	Structure
	Disputing irrational beliefs	Thought stopping	Caution when challenging belief systems
		Cognitive restructuring	
		Token economy	
Systems	Family provides framework for understanding individual	Genograms	Identity patterns
	Differentiation of self	Questioning	Caution when attempting to change multigenerational patterns
		Coaching	Resistance to external input on family
		"I" position	
		Detriangulation	
Narrative	Retell story to create favorable outcomes	Deconstruct problems	Many cultures emphasize storytelling
	Person is not the problem	Externalize problems	High-level processing required
		Miracle question	
		Sparkling moments	
Constructivism	Personal reality	Card sort	Insight required
	Personal construct	Identify constructs	Challenges test beliefs and principles
		Repertory	
Feminist	Application of feminist principles: equality, empowerment	Gender role analysis	Addresses shared experiences of oppression
	Mutuality	Empowerment	Political action may be against belief
	Androgyny	Egalitarian relationship	Limited application with men
		Sociocultural exploration of gender	
Interpersonal psychotherapy	Improve interpersonal functioning, social network	Therapeutic alliance	Flexible and adaptable to unique individuals
	Attachment, social, and communication theories	Communication analysis	
	Present focus	Interpersonal incidents	
		Content and process affect	
		Role playing	

Theories can be described as having specific and common factors. **Specific factors** are the unique characteristics of a given theory. They are elements that distinguish one theory from another and are often the basis of association with a theory. For example, the empty chair technique is a specific factor for gestalt, a humanistic-existential theory. Disputing irrational beliefs is unique to Albert Ellis's rational emotive behavior therapy (REBT) and the behavioral and cognitive-behavioral paradigm. **Common factors** are characteristics that appear in most if not all theoretical perspectives. For example, a therapeutic alliance and a healing setting that promotes client trust through professional counselor competence are common factors. A coherent rationale and set of procedures are also common to all theories. These are important principles to keep in mind as you review the major paradigms and begin to formulate and solidify your approach to counseling. To illustrate further the application of theoretical principles, consider the case of Terry in Case Study 3.1, and then answer the questions posed in Self-Assessment Activity 3.3. We will return to this case throughout our discussion of the paradigms and theories in the chapter.

The following discussion of theories and paradigms is broad in nature. We encourage you to read further about theories in the references provided throughout this chapter and to research in greater depth the specific theories of interest.

Case Study 3.1 Terry

Terry is a 23-year-old graduate student in microbiology. Terry recently relocated to the area to pursue graduate study after completing her undergraduate degree at a small college near her hometown. Now living two states and hundreds of miles away from her family, Terry feels that she is experiencing her independence for the first time.

Terry first became interested in science when she received a science kit for her seventh birthday. Her parents encouraged her to study science throughout high school and pushed her toward a major in biology when she entered college. Terry has heard on more than one occasion that she is the family's "only hope for a doctor." As first-generation immigrants to the United States, Terry's parents feel that their only daughter must be successful to prove their culture's ability to thrive in a competitive American environment.

Terry was referred to counseling following the midterm period of her first term in graduate school. Her roommate discovered numerous cuts on her arms and reported that Terry seemed down over the past few weeks. When she finally agreed to see a professional counselor, Terry reported that she did not perform well on her midterm exams and was questioning whether she could make it in graduate school. She was concerned about disappointing her parents and bringing shame to their family.

Self-Assessment Activity 3.3 Presenting Issues

Considering the case of Terry, write your initial reactions to her presenting issues for counseling. Specifically:

1. What is the problem?
2. Who is involved in Terry's dilemma?
3. How is the dilemma affecting Terry?
4. What would you hope to see as the goal of counseling for Terry?
5. What might counseling entail?
6. How will you know that counseling is complete?
7. How does your conceptualization attend to Terry's culture?

Keep your responses in a convenient location as you review the remainder of the chapter. These responses may relate to your emerging theoretical orientation.

Psychodynamic Paradigm

At the time of his work, Sigmund Freud was considered revolutionary in his thinking and conceptualizing of the problems experienced by people, primarily women. Today, many theories are based on Freud's work, additive to what he developed or created as an alternative explanation to a theory heavily focused on the past and the subconscious mind. For this reason, the psychodynamic paradigm serves as an introduction and foundation to the other paradigms of counseling theories.

Theories that fall under the psychodynamic paradigm are based largely on insight, unconscious motivation, and personality reconstruction. The psychodynamic paradigm holds that most problems clients face are the result of unresolved issues from their early development. The focus in counseling from a psychodynamic framework is on the relationship of past events with current functioning. In the case of Terry, the professional counselor may question how childhood messages of expected success are affecting her current performance in graduate school and the subsequent feelings she experiences. The psychodynamic approach is very analytic in nature and may require a good deal of time to uncover past issues and make headway into current and future functioning.

Psychoanalysis

Freud's psychoanalytic theory is probably the most widely recognized theory in the psychodynamic paradigm. Many people may have the image of a wise therapist sitting behind a couch, on which a client lays and contemplates the meaning of past events. Many popular media depictions do little to ameliorate this stereotype and may perpetuate the public's mistaken beliefs about the nature of counseling in general. Although this image may have been the form of psychoanalysis in early renditions of the theory, much has changed since Freud's groundbreaking approach to counseling to challenge the means by which professional counselors with a psychoanalytic orientation help their clients.

Freud believed that personality is completely formed in childhood, and that challenges later in life are the result of unresolved conflicts. Consistent with the idea that theories emerge from our personal philosophies and experiences, Freud's background demonstrates his emphasis on childhood and the family. The eldest of eight siblings of an authoritarian father, Freud was particularly close to his mother. His upbringing and religious affiliation (a Jew in Vienna, Austria, in the mid- to late 1800s) limited his career aspirations to medicine or law. One might see the basis of Freud's intense self-analysis and his subsequent theories of personality dynamics as based on his own life experiences.

In psychoanalysis, the personality is perceived as being composed of three parts: the **id**, or pleasure principle; the **ego**, or reality principle; and the **superego**, or morality principle (conscience). Conflict among these structures creates anxiety in the individual. The subsequent anxiety is often managed by the ego by employing **defense mechanisms**. These mechanisms help the individual to cope with the anxiety and not be overwhelmed. Defense mechanisms can be either adaptive or damaging. For example, Terry may be turning her frustrations with her parents' expectations inward and harming herself, rather than expressing these feelings to her parents. This process of projecting unwanted emotions to oneself in this case is maladaptive in the sense that Terry is being harmed both physically and emotionally.

The goal of psychoanalytic counseling is to bring unconscious drives into consciousness and develop insight into intrapsychic conflicts. Techniques such as free association, interpretation, dream analysis, and analysis of resistance and transference may be employed to assist in the development of insight. As might be expected (and is often a criticism of this approach), this process can be quite lengthy and time consuming.

The psychoanalytic counselor is like a blank screen. Listening, analyzing, and attending to **transference** (i.e., a client projects feelings for another person onto the counselor, such as when the client perceives the counselor to be a "father figure") and **countertransference** (i.e., a counselor reciprocates by engaging in interactions with the client similar to what the client experienced in a primary relationship, such as when the counselor behaves as the parent figure would toward the client who perceives the counselor to be a "father figure") issues are essential to successful counseling in the psychoanalytic approach. The therapeutic relationship takes the form of the professional counselor as expert, teaching the client about the intrapsychic processes occurring.

The culturally sensitive counselor may encourage individuals from ethnic and racial minority groups to develop an overall ego identity as well as a cultural identity. It is also important for psychoanalytic counselors to address their own potential biases and recognize how countertransference could unintentionally play a part in the counseling process. A limitation for multicultural counseling in psychoanalysis is in the area of gender issues. Women are seen as inferior to men because they do not resolve the Electra complex (attraction to the male parent) as completely as it is thought that men resolve the Oedipal complex (attraction to the female parent). This concept and other similar concepts, such as penis envy, have been largely discredited and discontinued. For independent study on psychoanalysis, consult the following foundational resources:

Freud, A. (1936). *The ego and the mechanisms of defense* (J. Strachey, Trans.). International Universities Press.
Freud, S. (1933). *New introductory lectures on psychoanalysis* (W. J. H. Sprott, Trans.). Norton. (Original work published 1923.)
Freud, S. (1947). *The ego and the id* (J. Strachey, Trans.). Hogarth. (Original work published 1923.)
Freud, S. (1955). *The interpretations of dreams* (J. Strachey, Trans.). Hogarth. (Original work published 1900.)

Adlerian Counseling

Alfred Adler, a student of Freud, developed his theory as a result of disagreement with many of the principles his mentor proposed. Adler commended Freud's work on dream interpretation, yet the generalizations Freud drew from dreams and his emphasis on sexual trauma and development did not resonate with Adler. Herein lies another example of the need to formulate a personally relevant theory of counseling. Adler left Freud's tutelage to develop his approach of focusing on the whole person. This holistic viewpoint approached the client as a whole, indivisible being, capable of growth, seeking social interest and connections with others. Similar to Freud, Adler emphasized the role of childhood in personality development and problem (and solution) formation.

Adler's work has been widely used, yet not widely researched or developed. Adler's work is best known for its emphasis on and analysis of birth order and sibling relationships. Sweeney (2009) and Watts (2017) are among the few modern Adlerian scholars. Traces of Adler's work are evident in the wellness movement in the counseling profession. Commonly used Adlerian-based techniques include the use of "I" messages, "acting as if," (or "reflecting as if") and "spitting in the client's soup."

The Adlerian concept of **social interest** lends to the theory's cultural sensitivity. **Social interest** means individuals are encouraged to move beyond themselves to learn about and understand different cultural groups and how they may contribute to society. Cultures that emphasize the family find that many Adlerian concepts fit with their value systems. However, limitations exist where emphasis is placed on changing the autonomous self and in the exploration of early childhood experiences. Some clients may find it inappropriate to reveal family information or may not want to delve into the past because they may not see the connection to current pressing concerns. For more information regarding Adlerian counseling, the following resources may be useful.

Adler, A. (1927). *Understanding human nature*. Fawcett.
Adler, A. (1964). *Social interest. A challenge to mankind*. Capricorn.
Adler, A. (1969). *The practice and theory of individual psychology*. Littlefield, Adams.
Dreikurs, R. (1953). *Fundamentals of Adlerian psychology*. Alfred Adler Institute.
Maniacci, M. P., Watts, R. E., & Carlson, J. (2005). *Adlerian therapy: Theory and practice*. American Psychological Association.
Peluso, P. R. (2008). Adlerian therapy: Theory and practice. *Journal of Counseling & Development*, *86*(4), 505–507.
Sweeney, T. J. (2009). *Adlerian counseling and psychotherapy: A practitioner's approach* (5th ed.). Routledge.

Other Psychodynamic Theories

Jungian theory (also referred to as ego psychology) and object-relations theory are other approaches that fit within this paradigm. Although many principles of these theories are used today, more modern adaptations of psychoanalysis and Adlerian counseling are seen more readily in practice. Table 3.3 provides a listing of strategies and techniques aligned with the psychodynamic paradigm. To study a foundational work by Carl Jung, refer to:

Jung, C. G. (1961). *Memories, dreams, reflections.* Vintage.

Table 3.3 Psychodynamic strategies and interventions

- Analysis of transference and countertransference.
- Analysis of private logic.
- Parent or teacher consultations.
- Encouragement.
- Analyze Adlerian goals of misbehavior (attention, power, inadequacy) and build social interest through group activities.
- Teach "I" statements and other skills.
- Encourage insight into unconscious aspects of problem through creative processes.
- Adlerian play therapy to discover the child's lifestyle and private logic.
- Teach parents techniques for encouraging the child.
- Family constellation and family atmosphere.
- Lifestyle analysis.
- Striving for significance and belonging.
- Natural and logical consequences.
- Early recollections to understand the child's behavior patterns.
- Adlerian family counseling for family to learn to operate cooperatively.
- Variation of activities between play and talking can be used, such as during sand play or drawing.
- The use of metaphor and exploration of developmental themes highlighted in movies, TV, and books.
- Focus on helping to become more self-aware through the use of pictures, stories, and metaphors.
- Help accept responsibility for the life choices that come with becoming an adult and to avoid regression toward childhood, where decisions were made on their behalf.
- Assist with adult identity formation in a culturally sensitive fashion.
- Explore recurrent themes in the child's fantasies and play.
- Play therapy techniques may be used to understand the current emotional state of the student.
- Acting (or reflecting) "as if."
- Free association.
- Determine events of childhood that may have a larger impact later in life.
- Empty chair.
- Role-play.
- Sand tray play and puppets may help younger children project angry feelings outside themselves.
- Try a projection game such as "Parallels with Animals," in which the counselor asks the child what different animals look, act, and sound like when they are angry (Vernon, 2004).
- Artwork.
- Incomplete sentences.
- Psychoeducational lessons/handouts on self-understanding.
- Recognizing feelings and basic motivation.
- Mutual storytelling.
- Draw a tree, and make a branch for each person the student feels he can trust.
- Analysis of avoidance (e.g., refusing to come to school).
- Talk about the fears and worries that may be embedded in the unconscious.
- Relationship of events and current functioning.
- Dream analysis.
- Analysis of ego development (fragile ego, under/overdeveloped superego).
- Analysis of anxiety and defense mechanisms (especially avoidance).
- Use of sand tray and symbolic play to better understand conscious and unconscious struggles.
- Patterns of similar behavior for family members.
- Interpret the reason for behavior based on dialogue, drawings, or dreams.
- Explore relationships between current behavior and past or current life events.
- Attachment assessment and introduction of stable adult figure.
- Explore relationship with teachers perceived as "safe" or "unsafe."
- Explore unconscious themes through use of a timeline to chart significant life events.
- Verbally explore the past and how this affects current behavior.
- Use various art mediums such as drawing or sculpture to allow clients to explore and work through early childhood stressors.
- List some positive things about self to draw on strengths, encourage, and build self-esteem.
- Analysis of relationship with father and mother throughout childhood.
- Assist in achieving industry vs. inferiority, identity vs. role confusion.
- Expressive techniques in uncovering unconscious struggles.

Table 3.3 (Continued)

- Uncover and process attachment issues, childhood conflicts, and motivation for behavior.
- Explore conflicts regarding maintaining power/status quo in classroom.
- Process childhood interests and experiences and how one views family and self-roles.
- Explore use of emotion (e.g., anger) to mask hurt.
- Analyze immature/neurotic defenses (projection, regression, acting out, splitting, devaluation, displacement, rationalization, intellectualization).

Humanistic-Existential Paradigm

In contrast to the subconscious focus in the psychodynamic paradigm, the humanistic-existential paradigm is relationship oriented. Rather than focusing on an individual's unresolved conflicts in the past, the focus here is on current and future functioning. Humanism and existentialism are similar in the belief that human nature is fundamentally good, and people have the freedom and responsibility to grow and develop.

Humanists believe that goodness and worth are qualities that people possess. In the journey toward self-actualization, it is believed that people are purposeful, active, and capable of determining their own behavior. Similarly, existentialists place an emphasis on the importance of anxiety, freedom, values, and responsibilities and on finding meaning in one's actions (Gladding, 2018). Another parallel between humanists and existentialists is that both emphasize the importance of the client–counselor relationship. The professional counselor must enter the client's subjective world to focus on client perceptions of the presenting issue.

Person Centered

Person-centered therapy, developed by Carl Rogers (1951, 1957), is a major theoretical approach in the humanistic framework. Over time, this approach has also been identified as nondirective, client centered, and Rogerian. According to Rogers, the primary motivating force of humans is **self-actualization**, the tendency to move in the direction of growth, adjustment, socialization, independence, and self-realization (McWhirter & Miesch, 2009).

Because people have the basic need for a high self-regard, they attempt to organize their internal and external experiences into an integrated self. During this process of self-actualizing, unhealthy psychological or social influences may hinder an individual from realizing potential as an integrated, productive self. In other words, conflicts develop when individuals' basic needs and their needs to obtain approval from others are inconsistent. Terry, for example, is experiencing conflict between her basic needs for self-actualization and her need for approval from her parents. The professional counselor working with Terry will need to be present and congruent to assist her in moving toward the discovery of Terry's true self.

Rogers (1957) identified three essential characteristics a professional counselor must employ for a therapeutic relationship to be established: genuineness (or congruence), unconditional positive regard, and empathy. **Genuineness** is displaying honesty, sincerity, and directness, while avoiding any personal or professional façade. **Unconditional positive regard** is defined as the professional counselor's ability to accept every aspect of the client's personality, while remaining nonjudgmental and nonevaluative toward the client's feelings, thoughts, and behaviors. **Empathy** is the ability to understand the client's world in the way the client understands it. With Terry, the professional counselor must be open to hearing Terry's experiences and acknowledging her challenges with the situation, regardless of personal opinion. Creating a nonthreatening, anxiety-free relationship would allow Terry to resolve conflicts and reach self-understanding.

Person-centered counseling has had a significant impact in the area of human relations with diverse cultural groups. Many countries have adopted person-centered concepts in counseling as well as cross-cultural communication and education. Multicultural limitations include lack of structure, difficulty translating core conditions to practice, and focus on internal evaluation, rather than external evaluation (Corey, 2016). The following resources provide more information about person-centered counseling:

Rogers, C. (1942). *Counseling and psychotherapy*. Houghton Mifflin.
Rogers, C. (1951). *Client-centered therapy*. Houghton Mifflin.
Rogers, C. (1961). *On becoming a person*. Houghton Mifflin.
Rogers, C. (1980). *A way of being*. Houghton Mifflin.

Existential

Existentialism stems from Søren Kierkegaard, a 19th-century philosopher who focused on the pursuit of becoming an individual. There are many contributors to existentialism as a therapeutic approach, including Ludwig Binswanger, Fyodor Dostoyevski, Friedrich Nietzsche, and Abraham Maslow. In more recent years, notable figures in existential psychotherapy include Rollo May, Victor Frankl, and Irvin Yalom.

The essence of existentialism is that humans are believed to have the capacity for self-awareness and the freedom and responsibility to make choices that would bring about meaning in their lives. However, along with this freedom comes the reality of living with the consequences of those choices, which could lead to **existential anxiety**. May (1977) asserted that normal anxiety can be healthy and motivational.

Frankl (1963) maintained that despite negative conditions, individuals can preserve their own independent thinking, spiritual freedom, and opportunities for choice. In contrast, an individual who sees life as meaningless and without value would be thought to be in what Frankl termed an **existential vacuum**. A well-functioning person is an individual who authentically experiences reality and expresses needs in a way that is not determined by others. Terry may not be in the existential vacuum but may be questioning the meaning of her current experiences. While having her first taste of freedom, it will be important for Terry to explore her choices and needs as self-determined and not those of her parents.

Other than concentrating on the client–counselor relationship, there is no systematic way that existential counselors help others. Still, Yalom (2017) was able to emphasize three significant qualities within the existential counseling process: (a) helping clients attend to the **here and now** (i.e., being present in the current moment); (b) being open and authentic with clients; and (c) cautiously using self-disclosure.

Specific goals in existential counseling include making clients sensitive to their existence, identifying characteristics unique to each client, assisting clients in enhancing interactions with others, helping clients pursue meaning in life, and promoting present and future decision making that will affect the client's direction in life. Few specific techniques are offered in an existential approach. All interventions are undertaken with the intention of assisting clients to find meaning in their actions.

The existential focus on love, suffering, anxiety, and death, all of which are the universal elements of human life, makes this theory applicable cross-culturally. In contrast, a limitation of multicultural existential counseling involves the emphasis on self-determination and the lack of focus on the environment and the social context. Some clients may feel powerless in the face of external realities such as discrimination, racism, and oppression. Refer to the following classic resources for more information on existential counseling.

Frankl, V. (1963). *Man's search for meaning*. Beacon.
May, R. (1953). *Man's search for himself*. Dell.
May, R. (Ed.). (1961). *Existential psychology*. Random House.
Yalom, I. D. (1980). *Existential psychotherapy*. Basic Books.

Gestalt Therapy

Gestalt therapy began in response to the reductionist emphasis in theories of counseling such as psychoanalysis and behaviorism, which attempted to break an individual's personality or behavior into understandable parts. In contrast, **gestalt therapy** promoted the idea of wholeness. Frederick (Fritz) Perls and his wife Laura Perls were the major theorists associated with this school of thought.

Similar to person-centered counseling, gestaltists believe that people have the tendency to move toward wholeness or self-actualization. Emphasis is placed on the present as indicated by Perls's (1970) statement: "To me, nothing exists except the now. Now = experience = awareness = reality. The past is no more and the future is not yet. Only the *now* exists" (p. 14).

In contrast to psychoanalysis, which focuses on predetermined and unconscious forces, the gestalt view of human nature is anti-deterministic; people can become responsible, grow, and change from past events. For example, Terry is experiencing difficulties in her life that are a result of her earlier thoughts, feelings, or experiences. This phenomenon is otherwise referred to as **unfinished business**—in Terry's case, asserting her own interests. The role of the gestalt counselor is to provide an atmosphere that allows Terry to identify and pursue what she needs to grow. Being honest as well as deeply and personally involved with Terry would allow the counselor to help her redirect energy in more positive and adaptive ways of functioning.

Gestalt counselors also directly confront clients with their inconsistencies. They focus on the polarities within people and push clients to correct misconceptions, to genuinely express emotions, and to take responsibility for change. Gestalt techniques may include exercises and experiments such as empty chair, role playing, role reversal, dream analysis, and the use of "I" statements (Erford, 2020). Other characteristics of gestalt counseling that help clients develop and become mature in the now include awareness of nonverbal and verbal expressions and shedding neurotic tendencies. Perls (1970) identified five layers of neurosis that were thought to impede a client's ability to be in touch with oneself. Only when individuals reach the final, or explosive, layer can they be truly authentic and in touch with themselves and others.

Gestalt counseling can be viewed as a culturally sensitive theory because the experiments employed by professional counselors may encourage clients to integrate the polarities that exist between the cultures to which they belong. Gestalt techniques can also be tailored to fit with a client's distinct perception and interpretation of a personal cultural framework. In contrast, gestalt counseling has an individualistic focus, which may be a conflict for people from cultures that emphasize group values. Table 3.4 provides strategies and techniques aligned with the humanistic-existential paradigm. Consult the following resources for further study of gestalt therapy.

Perls, F. (1969). *Gestalt therapy verbatim.* Real People Press.
Perls, F. (1972). *In and out of the garbage pail.* Bantam.
Polster, E., & Polster, M. (1973). *Gestalt therapy integrated: Contours of theory and practice.* Brunner/Mazel.
Zinker, J. (1978). *Creative process in Gestalt therapy.* Random House.

Table 3.4 Humanistic-existential strategies and interventions

- Therapeutic conditions (genuineness, unconditional positive regard, empathy).
- Model active listening, congruence, unconditional positive regard and empathy with family.
- Use role play and reverse role play to assist in finding meaning of current behavior while encouraging responsibility.
- "I" statements.
- Focus on the present, immediacy.
- Active listening and reflection of feelings.
- Building relationship.
- Provide opportunity for empathy and safe exploration of thoughts, feelings, and behaviors.
- Encourage self-awareness and choice leading to acceptance of self and others.
- Gently confront inconsistencies.
- Teach family members to (a) focus on the here and now; (b) take responsibility for their own thoughts, actions, feelings, and sensations; and (c) accept personal responsibility for change.
- Teach family members to substitute the use of *won't* for *can't* and to substitute the use of *what* and *how* for *why*.
- Teach parents to use self-esteem building activities with child.
- Encourage self-exploration and self-discovery through a warm, supportive, affirming therapeutic relationship.
- Through the relationship, the student can learn to accept themselves and begin the journey toward self-actualization.
- Provide support around goal setting.
- Counseling is seen as a way of *being with*, rather than *doing to* the client.
- Culturally sensitive play therapy techniques could be used, giving children and individuals with different learning abilities the opportunity to *play out* rather than *talk out* feelings.
- Appreciation for student uniqueness.
- Focus on choice, taking responsibility for actions and the present and future.
- Redirect energy or actions.
- Focus on the person they desire to be through art therapy techniques (mask activity).
- Avoid using desks to be more personal than authoritative.
- Respect the client regardless of acting out behaviors.
- Create a job or role for the student to feel a sense of meaning.
- Create a memory box to feel a sense of accomplishment and connection when adding to the box.
- Examine anxiety and behavioral issues related to safety, belonging, and personal and global responsibility and freedom (to classmates, classroom, school, community).
- Mentoring relationship.
- Minimal encouragers and few questions.
- Acceptance and trust.
- Puppets and expressive art therapies for social issues and familial issues.

(*Continued*)

Table 3.4 (Continued)

- Reflective play therapy to process anxiety and substance abuse.
- Cautious self-disclosure.
- Music and art as adjunctive techniques.
- Help parents and staff understand the student's perspective.
- Role-play potential scenarios relevant to responsible and irresponsible behavior.
- Identify emotions and appropriate expression.
- Examine anxiety and behavioral issues and a sense of belonging to classmates, classroom, school, and community.
- Informal "lunch bunches" with student and potential friends to foster relationships among peers and sense of accomplishment and connection.
- Redirect energy or actions.
- Encourage student to write a letter to their ideal self.
- Use humor to lighten the mood.
- Explore significant changes in student's life, both good and bad.
- Help to find meaning by having student work with even younger students.
- Develop self-awareness.
- Demonstrate respect for the client's unique self.
- Consult with familial environments/guardians.
- Frame understanding of self in the context of community.
- Help to find a place through a major life transition.
- Develop activities that correct behavior but with respect and regard for the client as an individual.
- Explore parent feelings toward clients and any incongruence.
- Help to provide a sense of belonging by creating a special role for the student (i.e., mentor younger students, special job to complete daily).
- Help the client to work through the feelings of "stuckness" that can accompany transitions.
- Explore life scripts.
- Analyze ads for messages.
- Consider clients' roles in society and the meaning of their choices.
- Explore conflict regarding future plans.
- Provide decision-making models for present and future use.
- Explore scenarios using the empty chair technique.
- Explore the meaning of place in the world at this time.
- Identify and resolve incongruencies.

Behavioral/Cognitive-Behavioral Paradigm

Clients seek action. Terry wants to act to change her current dilemma. The behavioral or cognitive-behavioral paradigm is the most action-oriented of the theoretical groupings. Clients are guided to pursue specific tangible changes in behavior and thought. From a practical standpoint, many beginning professional counselors are drawn to this paradigm because of the many tools and techniques it employs. In addition, professional counselors and clients alike can more readily observe progress in counseling from this perspective.

Behavioral Counseling

John B. Watson was one of the first advocates for **behaviorism**, as he was able to establish that human emotions were acquiescent to conditioning. Over time, behaviorism has incorporated various ideas, practices, and theories. Other theorists associated with this approach include Burroughs Frederick (B. F.) Skinner, Joseph Wolpe, Hans Eysenck, Albert Bandura, and John Krumboltz.

Behavioral theory focuses on how to reinforce, extinguish, or modify a wide range of behaviors. Specifically, it emphasizes the association between feelings and environmental stimuli and the learning or unlearning of behaviors accordingly. Professional counselors are mainly concerned with the science of observing behavior with the resulting consequence of whether to reward positive behavior or extinguish negative behavior. This is accomplished by eliminating the cause or condition that triggered the behavior. Terry might be presented with alternatives to handle the emotional and academic stresses she faces, with the goal of developing a new set of more adaptive behaviors that can be used in everyday situations. A specific behavioral technique is the **token economy**, where clients gain or lose tokens depending on whether or not they have reached a mutually agreed-on target behavior. Other behavioral techniques include the use of the Premack principle, behavioral contract, time out, response cost, and overcorrection (Erford, 2020). Techniques based on social learning theory include modeling, behavior rehearsal, and role play.

Another behavioral approach involves the stimulus-response model. This model applies **classical conditioning**, or learning through the association of two stimuli. The most well-known example of this model is from Pavlov and his laboratory experiments with dogs. He found that when he paired two stimuli, food and the sound of a bell, the dogs would eventually associate the sound of the bell with food and begin salivating in response to the bell before the food was served. Similarly, certain human emotions such as phobias develop because of paired associations. Once these associations are learned, they can be unlearned and replaced in a procedure referred to as **counterconditioning** or **systematic desensitization.**

The nature of the client–counselor relationship in behavioral counseling differs dramatically from the humanistic-existential approaches. Behavioral counselors function as active teachers, reinforcers, and facilitators who help clients learn, unlearn, or relearn specific ways of behaving. It is also common for professional counselors to enter into the client's environment to instruct people who are a part of helping the client's change process. Beyond the use of reinforcers, behavioral counselors may use other techniques, including systematic desensitization, assertiveness training, implosion and flooding, contingency contracts, and aversive techniques. The ideal outcome of most behavior modification programs is to have the client's new behavior continue after the program has terminated (**response maintenance**) and to have the desired behaviors generalized to environments outside the counseling setting.

Behavioral counseling has advantages for individuals who are from cultures that do not focus on the experience of catharsis. For example, emphasis is placed on specific behaviors that the client wants to change and the development of problem-solving skills. Behavioral counseling takes into account an individual's environmental conditions that could be contributing to psychological problems, such as sociocultural, political, and social influences. A limitation exists when professional counselors fail to recognize conditions beyond the individual, such as Terry's cultural emphasis on family. Other resources on behavioral counseling include the following.

Bandura, A. (1969). *Principles of behavior modification.* Holt, Rinehart & Winston.
Skinner, B. F. (1953). *Science and human behavior.* Macmillan.
Watson, J. B. (1925). *Behaviorism.* W. W. Norton.

Cognitive-Behavioral

In the 1970s, many professional counselors recognized that behavioral approaches were too limited and saw value in combining them with cognitive approaches. Aaron Beck developed cognitive therapy, an approach that focuses on recognizing and changing negative thoughts and maladaptive beliefs into more realistic and constructive thoughts and beliefs. The essence of cognitive therapy is to focus on the cognitive content or automatic thoughts associated with an individual's reaction to an event. Beck asserted that psychological problems were derived from common processes, such as making incorrect inferences based on incorrect information, being unable to distinguish between reality and fantasy, and faulty thinking. In short, he maintained that how people think determines how they feel and behave.

Donald Meichenbaum (1995) is one of the founding theorists of the cognitive-behavioral therapy (CBT) approach. Similar to Beck, Meichenbaum thought that helping people change the way they talk to themselves into more constructive cognitions was central to the counseling process. The maladaptive self-statements that affect individuals' behaviors are termed "cognitive distortions." Following are nine ways of mentally assessing a situation: all-or-nothing thinking, catastrophizing, labeling and mislabeling, magnification and minimization, mind reading, negative predictions, overgeneralization, personalization, and selective abstraction (Gladding, 2018).

The CBT counselor collaborates with the client by sharing the responsibility of selecting goals and bringing about change. Specific techniques, such as specifying automatic thoughts, assigning homework, thought stopping, and cognitive restructuring, are useful in identifying and challenging distorted thoughts. With Terry, the professional counselor may address her all-or-nothing perception of success with being a doctor and being accepted by her parents. Homework might include exploration of others' career decision making to challenge cognitive distortions. There are dozens of creative CBT techniques; they are usually active, time limited, and structured (Erford, 2020). Consult the following resources for further study on cognitive and cognitive-behavioral counseling.

Beck, A. T. (1976). *Cognitive therapy and emotional disorders.* New American Library.
Beck, A. T. (1987). *Love is never enough.* Harper & Row.
Meichenbaum, D. (1977). *Cognitive behavior modification: An integrative approach.* Plenum.

Rational Emotive Behavior Therapy

Rational emotive behavior therapy (REBT) is similar to counseling theories that emphasize behaviors and cognitions by placing emphasis on thinking, judging, deciding, analyzing, and doing. Albert Ellis, the founder of REBT, assumed that people contribute to their psychological problems by how they interpret life circumstances and events. This assumption is based on the idea that there is a cause-and-effect relationship between behaviors, cognitions, and emotions. It is thought that people have the potential for both rational and irrational thinking.

In other words, although people have a tendency to move toward growth, self-preservation, happiness, and self-actualization, they also have a propensity for self-destruction, intolerance, self-blame, and avoidance of actualizing growth potentials. Ellis stresses the point that people generally feel the way they think. Minimizing irrational beliefs and replacing them with practical and effective beliefs is a central tenet of REBT.

The REBT counselor encourages clients to identify irrational ideas that contribute to their disturbed behavior, challenges clients to validate their beliefs, uses logical analysis to dispute the irrational beliefs, and teaches clients how to replace their ideas with more rational beliefs. One way to accomplish these goals is to use the ABCDEs of REBT (Figure 3.1). The letter *A* (Activating Event) represents the activating experience, the letter *B* (Belief) represents what the person believes about the experience, and the letter *C* (Consequence) refers to the subsequent emotional reaction or behavioral response to *B*. The letter *D* (Dispute) represents disputing irrational beliefs, and the letter *E* (Evaluation) refers to the development of a new response. Other specific techniques that may be used in REBT include humor, changing one's language, rational emotive imagery, role playing, and other behavioral techniques.

The cognitive-behavioral counseling approaches have advantages from a cultural perspective. For example, in the process of identifying and understanding clients' values and beliefs, professional counselors are able to understand fully the clients' conflicting feelings. Also, the emphasis on cognition and behavior and relationship issues and the structure provided can be beneficial for people from various populations. A limitation of these approaches exists when the professional counselor does not fully understand the cultural background of the client. It is important for professional counselors to proceed with sensitivity and caution when challenging

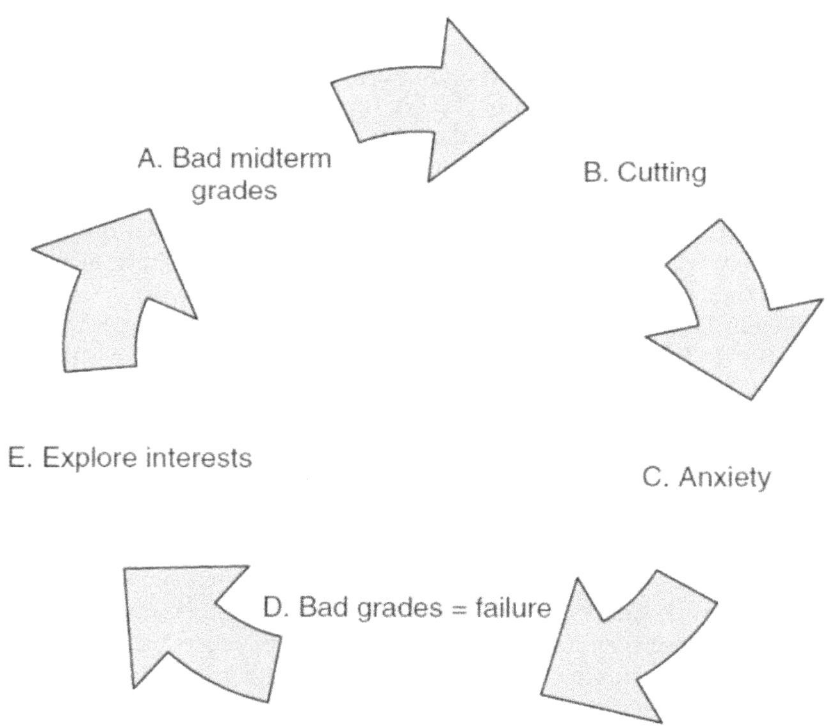

Figure 3.1 The ABCDEs of REBT in Terry's case

beliefs, values, and ideas because they may infringe on clients' cultural foundations. For more information on REBT, refer to the following resources.

Ellis, A. (1973). *Humanistic psychotherapy: The rational-emotive approach*. Julian Press.
Ellis, A. (1994). *Reason and emotion in psychotherapy revised*. Birch Lane.
Ellis, A. (1996). *Better, deeper, and more enduring brief therapy: The rational emotive behavior therapy approach*. Brunner/Mazel.

Reality Therapy and Choice Theory

William Glasser developed choice theory, which is based on the assumption that all behavior is purposeful and a choice. Glasser contended that most people do not have a clear understanding of why they behave as they do; they choose behaviors they think will help them cope with frustrations caused by unsatisfactory relationships, which constitute many of the problems people have.

Also central to choice theory is that humans make choices based on the physiological need of survival and four psychological needs: love and belonging, power, freedom, and fun. Survival relates to how to maintain good health and a satisfying life. Love and belonging signify the importance of involvement with people and the need to love and be loved. Power refers to the need to be in charge of one's life and to have a sense of accomplishment and achievement. Freedom is the need to make choices, whereas fun is the need to laugh, experience humor, and enjoy life. Individuals attempt to control their world to satisfy these five basic needs, which differ in degree. Importantly, choice theory provides the theoretical underpinnings of Glasser's approach, whereas reality therapy is the counseling application of choice theory.

Reality therapy stresses the present, thereby helping people solve current problems. Instead of emphasizing feelings, the focus is on thinking and acting to initiate change (Glasser, 2001). Reality therapy, whether employed in an individual or a group setting, is active, didactic, and directive; it teaches clients to look at whether their actions are getting them what they want, examine their needs and perceptions, and make a plan for change.

One of the basic premises of reality therapy is that connection and interpersonal relationships are very important, which leads to wide applicability of reality therapy to groups. With this in mind, a primary role of a counselor is to establish a good relationship with the client by engaging in warm and caring interactions, but also direct and confrontational interactions as appropriate.

According to Glasser (2001), counselors must be responsible individuals who can fulfill their own needs to help others do the same. Furthermore, they must be mentally and emotionally mature, supportive, involved, accepting, and respectful of all. Professional counselors can serve as role models of responsible behavior and help clients to assume responsibility for their own actions. Professional counselors help clients to find effective ways to meet their needs and to develop specific action plans that will help clients make the changes needed to attain their goals. Counselors are active, teaching and encouraging clients to take control of their lives by thinking and acting differently. Of course, professional counselors need to develop their own style so they can employ it with sincerity. It is critical that professional counselors demonstrate openness to their own growth and a willingness to explore their own values with the client.

Wubbolding (2016) identified four techniques commonly employed in reality therapy: humor, paradox, skillful questioning, and self-help procedures. According to Wubbolding, humor helps clients to develop an awareness of a situation and should be used only after considering the timing, focus, and degree of trust. Paradox, where clients are asked to perform the problematic behavior under certain circumstances while restraining the behavior's expression under all other circumstances, can be effective for some clients, but should be used cautiously in school settings. Skillful questioning involves using open-ended questions to help clients explore issues. It is also important to focus on positive behaviors that clients would like to target.

Advantages of reality therapy are that it stresses accountability and includes a structure that helps individuals develop action plans for change. In addition, choice theory is straightforward, flexible, and a relatively brief approach to counseling. Clients learn to accept responsibility for their behavior, realize that they can control themselves but not others, and develop their problem-solving abilities. Clients also learn how to engage in self-evaluation and deal with present concerns in a supportive environment. Limitations of this approach include the de-emphasis on feelings and lack of exploration of the past; counselors are cautioned against being too simplistic or acting as moral experts. For more information on reality therapy, refer to the following resources.

Glasser, W. (1965). *Reality therapy*. Harper & Row.
Glasser, W. (2001). *Counseling with choice theory*. HarperCollins.
Wubbolding, R. E. (1990). *Expanding reality therapy: Group counseling and multicultural dimensions*. Real World.
Wubbolding, R. E. (1991). *Understanding reality therapy*. HarperCollins.

Solution-Focused Brief Counseling (SFBC)

Brief counseling approaches have become increasingly popular since the 1980s due to managed care and other accountability initiatives, as well as societal emphasis on quick resolution to personal challenges. Brief counseling approaches go by many names, but currently the most prominent orientation is called solution-focused brief counseling (SFBC). SFBC is difficult to categorize under a specific paradigm and could easily be placed elsewhere. However, given the action-oriented, brief strategies employed in SFBC, we have included it under the behavioral/cognitive-behavioral paradigm.

SFBC is a social constructivist model underlain by the observation that clients derive personal meaning from the events of their lives as explained through personal narratives. SFB counselors value a therapeutic alliance that stresses empathy, collaboration, curiosity, and respectful understanding, but not expertness. de Shazer (1988, 1991) and O'Hanlon and Weiner-Davis (1989) are often credited as scholarly and theoretical forces behind the prominence of SFBC, which de-emphasizes the traditional therapeutic focus on a client's problems and instead focuses on what works for the client (i.e., successes and solutions) and exceptions in the client's life during which the problems are not occurring. Berg and Miller (1992, p. 17) summed up the SFBC approach very nicely by proposing three basic rules on which SFB counselors operate: (a) "If it ain't broke, don't fix it," (b) "Once you know what works, do more of it," and (c) "If it doesn't work, don't do it again." It is easy to see the basic appeal of this commonsense approach to counseling.

Walter and Peller (1992) proposed five assumptions that expand on these three basic rules: (a) Concentrating on successes leads to constructive change; (b) clients can realize that for every problem that exists, exceptions can be found during which the problem does not exist, effectively giving the client the solutions to their problems; (c) small, positive changes lead to bigger, positive changes; (d) all clients can solve their own problems by exposing, detailing, and replicating successes during exceptions; and (e) goals need to be stated in positive, measurable, active terms. Sklare (2014) successfully applied SFBC to children and adolescents using the preceding rules and assumptions to focus on changing student actions, rather than insights. Sklare concluded that insights do not lead to solutions; successful actions lead to solutions.

Five techniques are commonly associated with SFBC (Erford, 2020): scaling, exceptions, problem-free and preferred future dialogue, miracle question, and flagging the minefield. Scaling is a very commonly used technique with counseling individuals of nearly any age and from any theoretical perspective. Basically, scaling presents clients with a 10-point (or 100-point) continuum and asks clients to rate where they currently are with regard to, for example, sadness (1) or happiness (10); calm (1) or irate (10); hate (1) or love (10); totally unmotivated (1) or motivated (10). Scaling is helpful in gauging a client's current status on a wide range of issues. It is even more helpful when it is reused periodically to gauge the progress of a client. Scaling is a very quick and helpful assessment technique with wide applicability in counseling.

Exceptions (Erford, 2020) are essential to the SFBC approach because exceptions provide the solutions to the client's "problems." Counselors probe and question the client's background for times when the problem wasn't a problem, determining exceptions, and providing the client with alternative solutions to act on. Problem-free and preferred future dialogue is a technique that allows the counselor to turn the counseling intervention from a problem-focused environment to a solution-focused environment. SFB counselors hold the core belief that when clients focus on problems, they become discouraged and disempowered, and any insight they might gain into the origin and sustenance of the problem is not therapeutically valuable. A complementary belief is that finding exceptions/solutions to problematic circumstances encourages and empowers students, leading to actions and successes. The miracle question helps to reconstruct the way a client perceives a problematic circumstance into a vision for success, which motivates the client to pursue the actions that will lead to future successes.

The final technique is a treatment adherence technique called flagging the minefield (Erford, 2020). Treatment adherence is critical in any field in which individuals seek and receive help. Many, even most, receive the help they seek but then do not follow the treatment regimen, for whatever reason, basically guaranteeing the treatment will not be effective. For example, a patient may go to a doctor to address a medical condition, but then not follow the doctor's advice. If medication is prescribed, the patient may not have the prescription filled or may not take the medication according to the doctor's directions. Flagging the minefield is a technique ordinarily implemented during termination that facilitates clients' thinking about situations during which the positive outcomes and strategies learned during counseling may not work and to think ahead of time about what should be done in those circumstances to persevere and succeed. Treatment adherence is a critical issue in counseling; what good is all that hard work and effort to alter problematic thoughts, feelings, and behaviors if the student will return to problematic functioning shortly after termination?

SFBC is a culturally respectful approach to working with clients of diverse backgrounds because it discourages diagnoses, focuses on the client's personal frame of reference, and encourages clients to integrate and increase actions that have already been shown to be a successful fit for that personal frame of reference. The SFBC approach proposes that the client is the leading expert on what works for the client, and the counselor's role is to help the client recognize what the client knows to already work. The professional counselor then encourages the client to alter actions and "cheerleads" for the client's successes. SFBC approaches are particularly appreciated by clients who prefer action-oriented, directive interventions and concrete goals. SFBC is one of the more effective cross-cultural approaches because it empowers clients' personal values, beliefs, and behaviors and does not try to dispute or alter these. As a brief review of the theoretical approaches described so far, complete Self-Assessment Activity 3.4. Table 3.5 provides strategies and techniques aligned with the behavioral/CBT paradigm. For more information on SFBC, refer to the following resources.

De Jong, P., & Berg, I. K. (2002). *Interviewing for solutions* (2nd ed.). Brooks/Cole.
de Shazer, S. (1988). *Clues: Investigating solutions in brief therapy*. W. W. Norton.
de Shazer, S. (1991). *Putting difference to work*. W. W. Norton.
Metcalf, L. (1998). *Solution focused group therapy: Ideas for groups in private practice, schools, agencies, and treatment programs*. Free Press.

Self-Assessment Activity 3.4 Review of Paradigms

There are numerous action concepts and approaches in the first three paradigms discussed. Test your knowledge by matching the following theorists with the important concepts.

___ 1. Adler	a. Wholeness
___ 2. Freud	b. Social interest
___ 3. Meichenbaum	c. Self-actualization
___ 4. Ellis	d. Spiritual freedom and choice
___ 5. Frankl	e. Interpretations of life events
___ 6. Perls	f. Defense mechanisms
___ 7. Rogers	g. Cognitive distortions

Table 3.5 Behavioral/CBT strategies and interventions

- Positive reinforcement.
- Token economy.
- Premack principle.
- Behavior charts.
- Behavior contracts.
- Disputing irrational beliefs.
- Cognitive restructuring.
- Specify automatic thoughts.
- Analyze negative self-talk and practice positive self-talk.
- Visual imagery.
- Modeling.
- Behavioral rehearsal.
- Role playing.
- Time-out.
- "Picture in your mind"; what it would look like if . . .
- Exceptions.

(Continued)

Table 3.5 (Continued)

- Miracle question.
- Overcorrection.
- Response cost.
- Flagging the minefield.
- Behavioral play therapy.
- Parent/guardian or teacher consultations.
- Brainstorming.
- Bibliotherapy/biblioguidance.
- Recognize and dispute negative thoughts and beliefs replacing with rational self-talk.
- Thought stopping.
- Behavioral homework.
- Develop action plans for change.
- Identify positive behaviors and exceptions to the problem and strive to do more of the positive behaviors.
- Scaling.
- Teach family about basic needs (survival, autonomy, control, belonging).
- Responsibility.
- Teach parents about the common irrational beliefs of children and parents.
- ABCDE model.
- Analyze the client's shoulds, oughts, musts, catastrophizing, and awfulizing.
- With children younger than 8 years, focus on concrete skills such as problem solving and behavior rehearsal.
- With older children, the therapeutic alliance is essential to help the child to "buy in" to the therapeutic process and establish goals for behavioral change.
- Develop coping strategies.
- Consider contextual/environmental factors.
- Guided imagery/relaxation.
- Behavior intervention plans.
- Scaling questions to address degree of catastrophizing.
- Positive reframing to challenge negative predictions.
- Assess triggers through drawing, role play, puppets, or sentence completion.
- Postulate different points of view.
- Practice healthier self-talk.
- "Picture on paper."
- Examine a recent situation in which the client may have made a bad choice and ask to tell you what a better choice may have been.
- Set up a reward system for completed class work and homework.
- Develop coping strategies.
- Psychoeducation groups (e.g., friendship building, conflict resolution, emotional regulation).
- Positive feedback focusing on resources.
- Reframe weaknesses into strengths.
- Journal or draw about feelings and thoughts.
- Understand one's perceptions of the issue and how those perceptions lead to feelings and actions.
- Address negative predictions.
- Functional behavior assessment.
- Instruct parents to assist in helping the student change the behavior.
- Assigning a job to foster a sense of belonging and responsibility.
- Teach the stages of change with emphasis placed on timing and choice to modify behavior.
- Build on perceived strengths and use culturally relevant examples.
- Help understand that people think (and therefore feel) differently.
- Teach about choice theory and help the client make a list of some of the good and poor choices made that have contributed to the current situation.
- Monitor to determine compliance with writing homework down and coming to school prepared.
- Adopt a strengths-based approach that emphasizes successes, not failures.
- Make situationally intelligent decisions based on the context and salient cultural factors.
- Consideration of the consequences of behavior can help to manage and direct thinking and actions to meet personal goals.
- Collaborate to set up clear and tangible goals.
- Explore realities of impact of behaviors/circumstances on future life plans (e.g., relationships, family planning).
- Facilitate an increasing awareness of reality testing to discover how the world works.

Systems Paradigm

In contrast to the counseling approaches discussed so far, the systems approach focuses on the interactive perspective or the communication patterns within the client's family system or some other societally constructed system. In other words, the family provides the framework for understanding how the client behaves and functions in interpersonal relationships. There are many pioneers in family therapy; Murray Bowen developed one of the most comprehensive views of human behavior of any approach to family therapy. The essence of Bowen's model is **differentiation of self**, which is the ability to maintain one's individuality in the face of group influences—the pressures of a person's family (Nichols & Davis, 2020).

Bowen (1966, 1976) asserted that clients have less emotional autonomy than they imagine, and that clients are more dependent and reactive than we realize. Bowenian theory explains how the family, as a multigenerational structure of relationships, shapes the interaction of individuality and togetherness using six concepts: differentiation of self, triangles, emotional cutoff, nuclear family emotional process, multigenerational transmission process, and societal emotional process.

Normal family development is thought to occur when anxiety is low, family members are well differentiated, and partners are emotionally sound with their families of origin. This becomes difficult as most people leave home during the adolescence-to-adulthood transformation. The result often is that adults react with adolescent sensitivity in their relationships with their parents and with others who interact in a way that is reminiscent of their parents (Nichols & Davis, 2020). This is evident in Terry's struggle to communicate her anxiety and pressure to her parents. Bowen stated that individuals are likely to repeat problematic behaviors in their own families that have been passed down from past generations unless they explore and resolve these patterns (Kerr & Bowen, 2009).

To help family members identify intergenerational patterns and to help members differentiate from one another, a professional counselor must remain calm, neutral, and objective and be differentiated from his or her own family. A Bowenian counselor may work with all members of a family, although it is not necessary because it is believed that changing just one family member may have a direct impact on the entire family system. Specific techniques that may be used include genograms, asking questions, going home again, detriangulation, person-to-person relationships, differentiation of self, coaching, and the "I-position" (Gladding, 2019; Nichols & Davis, 2020).

The **genogram** can be an appropriate tool for professional counselors to identify cultural aspects that influence family members' behaviors. A genogram is a visual depiction of family structure. Lineage, nature of relationships, and interactional patterns are displayed and analyzed with the counselor to understand better one's current system. The genogram helps individuals and families to see the relationships between familial patterns and present behaviors. Evidence suggests that differentiation can be applied with several cultural identities. In contrast, some concepts may be limited in their application to people from diverse backgrounds. Table 3.6 summarizes some family systems strategies and interventions aligned with the family systems paradigm. More information regarding genograms can be found in the following resource.

McGoldrick, M., & Gerson, R. (1985). *Genograms in family assessment.* W. W. Norton.

For more information regarding family systems counseling, refer to the following resources.

Bowen, M. (1972). On the differentiation of self. In J. Framo (Ed.), *Family interaction: A dialogue between family researchers and family therapists* (pp. 111–173). Springer.
Bowen, M. (1976). Theory in the practice of psychotherapy. In P. J. Guerin, Jr. (Ed.), *Family therapy: Theory and practice* (pp. 42–90). Gardner Press.
Bowen, M. (1978). *Family therapy in clinical practice.* Aronson.

Table 3.6 Family systems strategies and interventions

- Caregiver or teacher training for dealing with relevant behavioral, academic, and social issues and family dynamics.
- Play therapy.
- Parent/guardian or teacher consultations.
- Teacher training on helping children cope with relevant issues.
- Reach out to caregivers to engage them in school.
- Explore the family system through development of a genogram to identify behaviors and patterns passed down.
- Coaching.
- "I" position.
- Teach family members to recognize harmful communication patterns.
- Assist in building each family member's self-esteem.
- Teach family members differentiation by modeling "I" statements.
- Focus on familial relationships and times when the family successfully overcame difficulties.
- Emphasize strengths, community, and resources.
- Educate parents on signs, process, and interventions related to issues (e.g., bullying, divorce).
- Focus on interpersonal relationships.
- Family as framework for understanding individual.
- Use parent skills training for promoting family connectedness and involvement.
- Analysis of family rules and expectations.
- Evaluation of family communication style.
- Exploration of family conflict management techniques.
- If family members are unavailable, ask students what they would be doing or saying if family members were there.
- Highlight strengths in the existing system.
- Use metaphors and narrative to indirectly guide clients to healthier ways of behaving and coping.
- Miracle question.
- Sparkling moments.
- Exploring interpersonal incidents.
- Role playing.
- Exceptions.
- Flagging the minefield.
- Provide resources in the community to support the family.
- Teach individuality despite family pressure.
- Collaboration with parents about expectations.
- Counseling for siblings and/or parents.
- Parent education about school support systems available.
- Education and collaboration with school personnel to assist student.
- Assess family needs.
- Teach caregiver skills to support developmental needs, consistency, and availability and explore alternative solutions.
- Autobiography/timeline of family events through sand, art, or play.
- Family sculpting.
- Analyze family dynamics.
- Referral to local agency for family intervention.
- Identify triggers.
- Coaching.
- Assess basic needs of family.
- Build a pattern of communication conducive to emotional expression.
- Identify key school and community persons who can assist the family in getting an evaluation for student.
- Consult with faith-based and community leaders for assistance.
- Community member participation in career day.
- Get students involved in job shadowing programs.
- Teacher training on exposing all students to the college option.
- Educate families on the change in family dynamics common in transitional situations.
- Link with community resources to support family stability and locate extracurricular activities.
- Discuss triangulation and work toward detriangulation.
- Help the client to differentiate between self and family and to develop mature peer relationships.
- When working with parents, try to reframe misbehavior using a developmental and emotional context.

Table 3.6 (Continued)

- Use family dynamics as a framework for understanding the situation.
- Communication analysis.
- Try to learn what values are important to the family.
- Assist client in discussing feelings with parents.
- Consult with parole officers, community counselors, and other community service agents working with the client.
- Determine student's perceived and actual role in the family, school, and community.
- Facilitate healthy peer relationships and connections with mentors.
- Revisit discipline policies that continue to affect academic progress.
- Although the student must follow the school protocol, explore ways that school staff, students, and parents can reinforce success.
- Encourage adolescent to explore "going home again" and work on differentiation from emotional reactivity in family of origin.
- Support the client through identity development.
- Help the family to understand changing parent–child relationships and the need for independence that defines adolescence.
- Connect the family to resources to support the student in pursuing postsecondary options.
- Work with parents to identify possible community resources to assist in understanding client behavior.
- Identify cultural beliefs and values that will help contextualize client behavior.

Postmodern Theories

Theories take time to develop and become empirically validated for use in the counseling profession. Postmodern theories constitute a fifth paradigm of counseling theory. Many can fall into this paradigm, including postmodernism (Hansen, 2006a), decisional counseling (Ivey et al., 2017), motivational interviewing, narrative or constructivist approaches, and feminist counseling.

Some newer theories were developed for specific purposes. For example, motivational interviewing is an approach designed to work with individuals struggling with substance dependency. Many postmodern theories have been criticized for lacking empirical evidence that the approach works. Some (e.g., feminist) have even been viewed as lacking specific techniques and being more of a philosophy. Hansen (2006b) has posited that it is some philosophical perspective that makes us most effective as professional counselors. In addition, theories take time to develop. Professional counselors want to avoid the "conference syndrome" approach of applying any new theory they hear or read about in professional development opportunities.

Instead, we propose a more systematic approach to learning about postmodern theories, seeing what fits with one's personal style of counseling, and applying principles as opportunities arise and the theories become more solidified. For the purposes of this chapter, and to avoid overwhelming the reader, we will discuss four postmodern theories: narrative, constructivist, feminist, and interpersonal counseling.

Narrative Theory

Terry has a story to tell. She has created a story about her life and present situation, one that she might say needs to be retold. The professional counselor can help Terry to see and create success by helping her to retell her story of wanting to fulfill parental expectations and continual concerns about measuring up to her potential into a story that more accurately fits her desires. Such is the nature of narrative counseling: help clients to retell the stories of their lives to create outcomes that better reflect what they would like to be (Monk et al., 1997).

One way to conceptualize narrative counseling is to consider a book with many chapters. We can read a book and think we know how it will end in the final chapter. As a metaphor for our lives, we may be comfortable with the opening chapter and a few in between, but we may be dissatisfied with the contents of the book as a whole. Rather than looking to change the problems, a narrative approach suggests rewriting the chapters themselves to create a better perspective on the problems that lie therein. In essence, narrative counseling contends that we are the authors of our own lives (White & Epston, 1990).

Michael White and David Epston (1990) are the primary individuals associated with narrative counseling. The concepts of the theory are originally derived from family counseling. White and Epston drew from family therapy expert Gregory Bateson, who suggested that the means for change is to compare one set of events in time with another. In counseling practice, the goal of narrative counseling is to develop alternative stories for one's life. The counselor would help Terry identify what she would truly like her life to be like, evaluate the possibilities, and determine what must occur in the interim to make this story a reality. The counselor would want Terry to understand that she or her parents are not the problem; rather, the problem itself is the problem. Narrative counseling can assist Terry to shift her perspective of the problem and create a new outlook (story) for her life and circumstances.

The narrative counselor asks many investigative questions to understand what underlies the story and one's self-perception. Techniques used in narrative counseling are encompassed within this idea of questioning and investigating as it relates to retelling one's story. The narrative counselor helps to deconstruct problems, externalizing and separating them from the person and avoiding blame and self-recrimination (Monk et al., 1997). The professional counselor seeks exceptions to the story, times when the outcome of one's actions is inconsistent with what one says or does in the story. These exceptions are referred to as **sparkling moments**, the positive shifts that begin to occur when one can exert control over the problem and begin to create a new story (White & Epston, 1990).

The client and professional counselor work together "against" the problem to identify more favorable stories (Monk et al., 1997). From a cultural standpoint, narrative therapy is consistent with the storytelling nature of some ethnic populations. For example, the Chinese culture is built on a series of stories handed down from generation to generation and appearing in the form of mythical beliefs. For individuals who come from cultures where storytelling is a part of their practice, narrative therapy can feel familiar and productive. The shift to identifying one's role in changing stories can be challenging, and the narrative counselor must exercise patience and caution to deconstruct problems and not beliefs.

Narrative theory tends to provide an overarching and organizing vision of the problem as separate from the person. This approach can be empowering and eye-opening. Narrative therapy requires a level of insight from the client to be able to tell and then retell the story. For more information on narrative theory, refer to the following resources.

White, M., & Epston, D. (1989). *Literate means to therapeutic ends*. Dulwich Centre Publications.
White, M., & Epston, D. (1990). *Narrative means to therapeutic ends*. W. W. Norton.

Voices From the Field 3.1 Narrative Therapy With Children Who Have Been Abused, *by Victoria E. Kress*

When counseling children and adolescents who have been abused or traumatized, I like to integrate strength-based approaches, such as narrative therapy (NT), with evidence-based treatments for addressing trauma, such as trauma-focused cognitive-behavioral therapy. Narrative therapy presupposes our clients possess the inner strengths and resources they need to resolve their own problems. As professional counselors, it is our job to develop, identify, and apply clients' strengths. Children who have been abused often feel a deep sense of shame, guilt, and/or embarrassment and can benefit from approaches that are inherently empowering.

One technique that I often use with this population in individual and group counseling is *Letters From the Future*. In this activity, clients are asked to imagine that they are writing a letter to themselves (in the present) from a future time period when they are much older and wiser. Clients are invited to provide suggestions, advice, and words of hope and wisdom to themselves from this future state.

As a variation of this activity, when I do this activity in a group setting, I often have the group members write a *Letters From the Future to a Friend* (i.e., a friend inside the group, outside the group, or a fictitious person) who has recently experienced sexual abuse. Group members are invited to provide wisdom, encouragement, and direction to their friend. What follows is a letter written by a 12-year-old African American girl who was sexually abused by her mother's boyfriend for two years. She wrote this letter from the future, to a friend, during her third session of a group I facilitated for children and adolescents who had been sexually abused:

Dear Friend,

Hi. How are you doing? Well . . . fine? I would like to share something about the sexual abuse which was when I was raped. It was painful, so I talked to my mom about the abuse. It helped but it still hurts but I see I am going strong anyways. And the man is in jail for what he did to me and I thank God for that. I have had the wisdom to talk to people, but before I didn't do that. And even though you have lost a little part in you, I hope that you will keep your self-confidence and always love yourself because whatever happened to you is not your fault. So keep up the good work and keep up having the words of good courage. So keep your mind POSITIVE and look ahead. You have to not do drugs and drink because that is not going to help you neither. When you want to do those things you need to talk to your good friends and to your mom and your counselor. You have to keep going to church and believe God will help you get through this to. Because he will. I promise.

Well, bye-bye. See you soon. And just remember, stay POSITIVE and STRONG.

In providing advice from a future orientation, she was able to identify positive coping skills (e.g., the value of talking about her experiences, using her spirituality and faith to ground herself, avoiding substances as a coping mechanism, engaging in positive self-talk, avoiding self-blame) and ways she could evolve and grow secondary to her abuse experiences. A counselor can give a client guidance and suggest adaptive ways of coping, but ultimately our goal is to help our clients connect with and internalize these resources on their own. This narrative therapy technique provides an opportunity for clients to readily connect with solutions and answers to their struggles that fit with their values and beliefs. It is ironic that sometimes getting out of the present can help people better connect with solutions and more adaptive realities.

Constructivist Theory

Is one person's perception of a problem another person's reality? How do we derive meaning from our lives, and how do we make sense of this reality? Constructivist theory, based on the work of George Kelly's (1963) **personal constructs,** suggests that people create their own meaning and realities based on personal experiences. Constructivism holds that we create our own meaning, and it is the job of the counselor to respect and work with that reality, not to contradict or deny it (Hansen, 2006a).

Terry believes that she must be a successful scientist to please her parents. She is operating under the belief system that success is equal to parental approval. She also believes that people should have personal responsibility for upholding the expectations of a culture. The constructivist counselor would see that Terry is operating under a set of personal constructs, or belief systems, that guide her actions and goals. Personal constructs, as defined by Kelly (1963), are self-beliefs. They guide us in determining the courses of action we take, the people with whom we associate, and the decisions we make about our own lives. The process of identifying and integrating these personal constructs is at the heart of constructivist counseling.

The constructivist counselor is inquisitive. Constructivism is often paired with narrative techniques such as storytelling and searching for alternative explanations to problems. The goal of constructivism is to create and construe personal reality actively through examination of personal constructs. The professional counselor and client work collaboratively to identify constructs and their origins. Often clients do not emerge with specific strategies to handle situations, but instead focus on personal learning and examination of how they are living authentic lives based on these identified constructs.

One specific technique that stands out from this theory is the use of a card sort. The **card sort** is a means of organizing beliefs into categories to help illustrate the organization of one's system of understanding and operating (Kelly, 1963). The constructivist counselor might help the client to develop a repertory test or grid to illustrate and organize belief systems. For example, Terry might be assisted to determine the major beliefs she has created about family, career, success, and failure. The professional counselor and Terry may identify the basic belief systems to explore further how they are operating in her interactions and decisions regarding her future. In doing so, Terry develops insight and explores the meaning she places on her constructs and the actions she is taking to find meaning in her life.

Similar to narrative theory, constructivism requires significant insight and a higher level of processing than many traditional approaches. The theory may have limitations in its cross-cultural application in that some cultures expect adherence to their principles. Clients engaged in constructivist counseling are questioning and at times even challenging fundamental belief systems. In Terry's case, the exploration of personal constructs may reveal that culture is not as strong a belief to her as it is to her parents. This may contradict her culture's expectation of respect for parents and elders and challenge Terry in creating a new perspective of her situation. Conversely, proponents of constructivist counseling hold that the exploration of beliefs can be the ultimate goal of the theory and can work effectively with most cultures. The following resources are for further reading about constructivist counseling.

Kelly, G. A. (1955). *The psychology of personal constructs: A theory of personality*. W. W. Norton.
Neimeyer, G. (1992). *Constructivist assessment: A casebook*. SAGE.

Feminist Counseling

A feminist approach to counseling has been criticized as challenging fundamental cultural beliefs. Feminist counselors operate from the basic philosophy of feminism and support, respect, and high valuation of the role of culture in one's life.

The feminist philosophy espouses the equality and rights of women. The feminist movement began during the 1800s and abolition, wherein women were fighting for their voices to be heard (Wood & Fixmer-Oraiz, 2019). This movement continued through voting rights and what is more commonly perceived as the start of feminism, the women's rights movements of the 1960s. The principles of feminism held that women should be perceived as equals with men, have equal rights for employment and opportunities, be given certain inalienable rights to make their own choices, and essentially be treated with a fundamental human respect.

Because of this history, one often perceives feminist counseling as benefiting (or being provided by, for that matter) only women. Much of the literature regarding feminist counseling suggests a woman-centered focus. Chester and Bretherton (2001) identified six themes in feminist counseling from their research with practicing professional counselors: woman-centered, egalitarian, feminism as belief, feminism as action, critique of patriarchy, and a positive vision of the future. Gilbert and Scher (2009) further assert elements of feminist counseling to include empowerment, androgyny, and mutuality within the counseling relationship. The latter citation emphasizes the importance of equality in counseling and in one's life and carries a more universal position that can benefit women and men. Gender sensitivity in counseling may be a more accurate (and perhaps more palatable) position in applying feminist principles in counseling (Bartholomew, 2003).

How feminist counseling appears to the observer seems to be more questionable. The fact that this approach is an application of feminist principles makes it difficult to identify key feminist counseling theorists. We may look to the work of Carol Gilligan, a preeminent theorist on women's development, Judith Jordan and her colleagues at the Stone Center, and others who all have had an important role in the creation and proliferation of feminist approaches to counseling. The feminist counselor values the female as well the male perspective—ideally the role of gender in our lives (Bartholomew, 2003).

A **gender role analysis** is one of the primary techniques used from this perspective. Gender role analysis is a means of examining with clients messages they have received about what it means to be male or female, where these messages are derived, and how they have been employed and are affecting one's functioning (Bartholomew, 2003). Gender role analysis may address another important principle of feminist counseling: **androgyny**.

Based on the pioneering work of Sandra Bem (1981), androgyny challenges the traditional gender roles for men and women. **Androgyny** suggests that we should value individual characteristics for what they are, regardless of a predefined category. Professional counselors addressing androgyny see that stereotypically masculine and feminine roles are valuable within each individual. A woman who is more assertive in the workplace and athletic with her peers may also be very sensitive and caring with her partner. Feminist counselors employ gender role analysis to examine these roles and to help the individual put them in an historical and societal context (Hoffman, 2001). The client is helped to see that all these attributes create her uniqueness. It is often society's views that perpetuate her beliefs that she is somehow aberrant or unacceptable (Chester & Bretherton, 2001). Feminist counseling addresses the societal perceptions and the means by which the individual can take action to implement change. This sociocultural perspective and action as well as a degree of assertiveness are the goals of feminist counseling.

The sociocultural history and viewpoint of feminism contribute to the multicultural sensitivity of this approach in counseling. Feminism has a rich history of working toward equality. Pioneers such as bell hooks and Alice Walker in the 1970s addressed the concern that feminism addressed the concerns of only White, upper-class women (Wood & Fixmer-Oraiz, 2019). Current feminist movements have evolved and now emphasize and work toward the equal rights of all, including intersectionality and issues of gender, race, ethnicity, sexual orientation, and other cultural variables.

Challenges with the feminist theory may be the push for political action. Critics argue that suggesting individuals must see personal issues as political and engage in social change imposes the professional counselor's values, which may be inconsistent with one's cultural beliefs. We instead argue that feminist counselors simply suggest the societal context of issues and explore what, if any, role they would like to have to shape the understanding of one's issues from a broader perspective.

Terry's case is an example of the cultural context and challenges from a feminist perspective. Terry is attempting to fulfill her parents' wishes for her success, a message that may suggest cultural values of parental respect and collectivism. We might also wonder about messages she received about what it means to be female in her culture and in her family. Are there expectations that she will unquestioningly accept her role as a daughter and follow her parents' career aspirations for her? Terry's pursuit of a career in science is nontraditional for women in the United States (even in the 21st century). From a feminist counseling perspective, our gender role analysis might include an exploration of Terry's role in a traditionally male field and a more fluid understanding of gender identity. This is completed without bias or suggestion that she must stay in or leave the profession. Instead, there is an exploration of what this means to Terry in terms of being female and her identity as a whole. In other words, how does Terry perceive herself and her presenting concern through a gendered lens? Additional resources regarding feminist counseling include the following.

Bem, S. L. (1993). *The lenses of gender*. Yale University Press.
Brown, L. S. (1994). *Subversive dialogues: Theory in feminist therapy*. Basic Books.
Enns, C. Z. (1997). *Feminist theories and feminist psychotherapies: Origins, themes, and variations*. Haworth.

Interpersonal Psychotherapy

Interpersonal psychotherapy (IPT), originally developed for adults with depression, is time limited and specifically focuses on interpersonal relationships. Goals of IPT include helping clients improve their relationships or their expectations about them and helping clients improve their social support systems to alleviate their presenting distress. For IPT, the view of human nature is based on the assertion that psychological symptoms are connected to interpersonal distress (Stuart & Robertson, 2012). This approach is derived from three theories: (a) attachment theory, (b) communication theory, and (c) social theory.

Attachment theory is based on the premise that individuals have the intrinsic drive to form interpersonal relationships, a result of the need for reassurance and the desire to be loved. Attachment theory describes the way individuals form, maintain, and end relationships and hypothesizes that distress occurs as a result of disruptions in an individual's attachment with others. Problem areas specifically addressed by IPT include interpersonal disputes, role transitions, and grief and loss.

Whereas attachment theory is useful in understanding the broader, or "macro," social context, **communication theory** works on a "micro" level, describing the specific ways in which individuals communicate their attachment needs to significant others. In other words, maladaptive attachment styles lead to specific ineffective communications. The result is that the individual's attachment needs are not met.

Social theory contributes to IPT by placing emphasis on interpersonal factors and how those factors contribute to depression or anxiety. One's social support system may be disturbed as a result of an individual's maladaptive response to a particular life event. The level of social support one has directly influences how one handles interpersonal stress. Social theory hypothesizes that poor social support is a fundamental factor in the development of psychological distress (Stuart & Robertson, 2012).

There are three main goals of counseling for IPT: (a) relieving the client's disturbing psychological symptoms; (b) examination of conflict, loss, and transition in the client's relationships; and (c) establishing the client's needs to aid in more effective use of one's social support system. In contrast to CBT, where the focus is on the client's internal cognitions, IPT focuses on interpersonal communication. Where IPT may focus on cognitions, they are not the primary targets. Likewise, CBT and the other theories of counseling may touch on interpersonal issues, but they are not the focus.

In contrast to analytically oriented theories, which tend to focus on early life experiences in relation to current psychological distress, IPT has a present, here-and-now focus that helps the client improve the current communication and social support systems. In light of its time-limited approach and here-and-now focus, IPT aims to resolve psychological distress and improve interpersonal communication, rather than to change the underlying cognitions.

The IPT counselor uses the client–counselor relationship to develop insight into the client's interpersonal functioning and to assess the client's attachment style. In the case of Terry, the professional counselor first would need to establish a therapeutic alliance with her to understand her experiences with school and the pressure from her parents. Together, the counselor and Terry would examine Terry's communication patterns and her social support system. What does Terry need to improve her here-and-now interpersonal relationships to build a more effective social support system? What about Terry's attachment style or communication patterns with her parents need to be addressed?

Common techniques of IPT include establishing a therapeutic alliance, communication analysis, describing interpersonal incidents, using content and process affect, and role playing. Because IPT has a solid theoretical foundation and a solid structure, it can be useful for clients from diverse backgrounds. The process and content of IPT counseling is flexible and adaptable, and highlights the unique needs of individuals. IPT takes into account the components of several theoretical paradigms and creates a unique approach to address the individual needs of the client. Consult the following resources for further reading on IPT.

Bowlby, J. (1969). *Attachment*. Basic Books.
Kiesler, D. J. (1996). *Contemporary interpersonal theory and research: Personality, psychopathology, and psychotherapy*. Wiley.
Sullivan, H. S. (1953). *The interpersonal theory of psychiatry*. W. W. Norton.
Weissman, M. M., Markowitz, J. C., & Kleman, G. L. (2000). *Comprehensive guide to interpersonal psychotherapy*. Basic Books.

Table 3.7 provides strategies and techniques aligned with the postmodern theories paradigm. These discussions of the various counseling paradigms offer a sampling of the many theories that exist. The information provided can be very challenging to digest and even more challenging to determine what fits you as a professional counselor. Now, complete Self-Assessment Activities 3.5 through 3.7 to begin considering what you would do as a professional counselor and how that fits within the theoretical perspectives. The next section of this chapter addresses the means by which you can apply theory in your counseling practice.

Table 3.7 Postmodern strategies and interventions

- Miracle question.
- Sparkling moments.
- Empowerment.
- Communication analysis.
- Interpersonal incidents.
- Role play.
- Reading stories (bibliotherapy).
- Creating drawings.
- Storytelling.
- Provide with age-appropriate information about various aspects of issues.
- Deconstruct the problem-laden story, identify unique outcomes, and help co-author a new story that is strength based.
- Externalize the problem, and work against the problem.
- Celebrate success.
- Address attachment issues.
- Here-and-now focus.
- Work on communication skills and accessing social support.
- The process of change results from dialogue between counselor and family members.
- Empower each family member to reauthor a more successful story.
- Focus on communication skills, building friendships, and development of personal goals.
- If the student and family desire it, attend to development of identity and fluency in both the mainstream and native cultures.
- Examination of interpersonal relationships.
- Social support system analysis and improvement.
- Motivational interviewing.
- Narrative therapy to deconstruct and externalize problems.
- Examine personal constructs.
- Identify and improve personal support systems.
- Fill-in-the-blank exercises.
- Sentence stems.

Table 3.7 (Continued)

- Word sort activities.
- Coat of arms.
- Listen to story without blame.
- Explore gender roles.
- Empower in healthy ways to decrease feelings of helplessness.
- Use content of current situations to process affect.
- Parent/student collaboration building and negotiating.
- Caregiver/teacher training for dealing with relevant behavioral, academic, and social issues.
- Explore family, school, and community dynamics.
- Write a short story about how the student successfully accomplished a goal.
- Bibliotherapy about other peoples' experiences that are similar.
- Explore alternative explanations to problems.
- Question and challenge the status quo.
- Focus on resiliency factors.
- Mentoring.
- Encourage to self-advocate and be competent and confident.
- Scaling to determine needs and levels of anxiety.
- Use expressive therapies (art, music, play) to tell life stories.
- Stress reduction and mindfulness.
- Psychoeducational and support groups to construct new realities.
- Assist in developing positive social networks.
- Assist in creating a story about the situation and identify a more favorable outcome.
- Break problems down into pieces.
- Assess ability to code switch in the school environment, if applicable.
- Explore beliefs and attitudes toward working with diverse clients. What are these beliefs and assumptions, and how do they affect interactions?
- Help staff ponder multicultural considerations and biases regardless of racial self-identification.
- Analyze your expectations of teachers and what historical life events have shaped your expectations or concerns about school staff.
- Read stories about different careers and issues.
- Create drawings to understand career interests.
- Focus on positive relationships with peers and adults.
- Improve interpersonal relationships by rehearsing behaviors to achieve desired goals.
- Identify someone in the client's life who would be the least surprised to see them planning for the future.
- Shape application of discipline policy.
- Identify cultural strengths the client and family bring.
- Identify cultural strengths and capital within the family and community and harness these strengths to gain support and encouragement for parenting client.
- Share stories about people the student might be aware of, their learning process, and how they pursued their careers.

Self-Assessment Activity 3.5 Review of Postmodern Theories

Match the component with each of the postmodern theories identified. Expand on your understanding by applying concepts from Terry's case.

___ 1. Family systems	a. Personal constructs
___ 2. Narrative	b. Clients are more dependent and reactive than we realize
___ 3. Feminism	c. Develop alternative stories for one's life
___ 4. Constructivism	d. Highly value the role of culture in one's life
___ 5. Interpersonal theory	e. Relationships are key to development and wellness

When considering Terry's case, what specific issues do each of these theories indicate?

Self-Assessment Activity 3.6. Relating Skills and Theories

How do the basic helping skills of counseling (e.g., empathy, active listening, reflection of feeling, paraphrasing, challenging, and confronting) fit within the theoretical paradigms discussed? Do all helping skills have a place in all theories, with differing emphasis in each? Attend to your personal preference in using each skill. How do these helping skills fit with your early leanings toward the theories?

Self-Assessment Activity 3.7 Revisiting Terry's Case

Review your previous perceptions of Terry's case. How do your beliefs about her situation and how *you* might approach counseling align with the counseling theory paradigms discussed in this section?

Integrating Theory Into Practice

These discussions of the various counseling paradigms offer a sampling of the many theories that exist. The information provided can be very challenging to digest and even more challenging to determine what fits you as a professional counselor. After reviewing the paradigms and considering culture, counselors must begin to integrate theory into their counseling practice. As an intern or practicum student, what are the critical components of your approach at this point in your counselor preparation?

A means of organizing thoughts about theory selection is to consider whether the underpinnings of a theory are aligned with your basic beliefs about counseling. The elements of a theory highlight the specific and common factors, personal philosophy, and multicultural considerations discussed in this chapter. However, to be philosophically aligned with the paradigm or theory, professional counselors should consider each of the following elements: view of human nature, goals of counseling, role of the professional counselor, and the techniques or approaches used.

View of Human Nature

How do people change? What motivates people to behave, think, and feel the ways that they do? What do you believe will best help someone grow and develop? These are important questions to ask yourself when considering your own **view of human nature**. The manner in which you believe individuals change will be directly related to the counseling theories to which you subscribe. For example, if you believe that personality is more or less fully constructed in childhood, and change can occur only through regression back to those times, you may be more suited to one of the psychodynamic theories. Conversely, if you believe people are self-determined and control their own destinies, a humanistic-existential approach may be a better match.

Regardless of varying beliefs about how people change, practitioners across settings can agree that change happens only when one is ready to engage in the process. The pioneering work of Prochaska and DiClemente (1982) proposed stages of the change process to explain the manner in which individuals move through changes in thought, behavior, or emotion. Their work originally studied smoking cessation in an adult population and has since been adapted to many issues and populations. Table 3.8 outlines Prochaska and DiClemente's five **stages of change** and how they might appear in counseling practice.

Goals of Counseling

A second important aspect in applying theory to practice is the perceived goals of counseling. Clients may enter counseling wanting immediate answers to difficult problems. We understand that as a profession we are not

Table 3.8 Stages of change

Stage	*Description*	*Application in Practice*
Precontemplation	No intent to change; Unaware that problem exists	Identify problem as others have presented it to the individual; create ownership
Contemplation	Awareness of problems, but not yet committed to act to change	Weigh pros and cons of problem and solutions
Preparation	Intent and commitment to act	Address fears, impact of possible change in life
Action	Modify behavior, experiences, or environment to overcome problems	Discuss experience of the change and subsequent feelings; Consider means to sustain change
Maintenance	Prevent relapse and sustain gains achieved through change	Monitor and discuss new approach to problem

Source: Adapted from "Transtheoretical Therapy: Toward a More Integrative Model of Change," by J. O. Prochaska and C. C. DiClemente, 1982, *Psychotherapy: Theory, Research and Practice, 20*, pp. 161–173.

prone to give direct advice or be problem solvers. Instead, we give individuals the tools to manage their own problems and to apply them in future situations. An overarching goal of counseling is to help individuals more effectively manage problems in everyday living.

At first glance, the identification of an overarching goal of counseling may seem to answer all our questions about this subtopic. However, further examination shows that theories have different beliefs about what counseling should accomplish. Person-centered counselors believe counseling should result in greater self-awareness, behaviorists want to see physical evidence of change in actions, and REBT-oriented counselors assert that changes in thinking and behavior are the ultimate goals of the counseling experience. Your personal beliefs about what individuals should gain from their time in counseling will dictate your determination of approach.

A word of caution: Many new counselors jump to the conclusion that it is their role to determine specific goals for their clients. Specific goals, such as to stop smoking, build a healthy romantic relationship, stay out of prison, or get into college, must be established by the individual seeking counseling. Goal setting is a collaborative venture between professional counselors and clients. The emphasis on elements of goals and the manner in which counseling can assist in reaching the goals is determined by counselor orientation.

Role of the Professional Counselor

Relative activity or passivity as a professional counselor will help apply theory into practice. As you have read, theories differ in their perceptions of the roles professional counselors play in the therapeutic process. Whether one is collaborator, expert, equal, or indifferent, the role of the professional counselor differs across theories. We have also learned that many theorists were most successful in being genuine and true to their own preferences for interactions with one another. The professional counselor's role must be consistent with the other elements of theory and can in great part be determined by your personality and style of interaction. Some professional counselors teeter on the edge of offering advice, whereas others may utter only a few words throughout their time with clients.

Techniques and Approaches

Professional counselors entering the profession may be drawn to approaches that outline specific techniques to be used with clients. For this reason, we have seen many professional counselors begin with a cognitive-behavioral orientation and gradually shift to approaches that offer more flexibility in the process. This phenomenon may be due in part to the level of ambiguity we are willing to endure as we enter into new situations. So much of what we do as professional counselors does not contain a "how-to" manual. We do not have guidelines suggesting, for example, that if a client states his disdain for his mother, we should offer him the opportunity to role-play a preferred interaction with her. We must instead rely on what seems to be consistent with our beliefs about counseling as outlined in the other elements of theory selection.

Some theories are more heavily laden with techniques, whereas others are more amorphous in providing general guidelines about approaches. As you review the theories, what seems to stand out to you as most meaningful and effective? As you enter into the professional counselor role, what do you notice consistently about your approach? Are there certain techniques to which you are more drawn? Do you work more effectively when you can rely on a general approach and employ techniques as needed? A helpful guide to understanding and applying techniques to counseling practice is Erford's (2020) *45 Techniques Every Counselor Should Know*.

Flexibility

Beginning to integrate theory into practice requires contemplation of the aforementioned elements. Applying theory also requires flexibility. No two counseling interactions are alike. What works well with one individual may fall flat with another. As we will discuss shortly, few professional counselors operate from truly purist perspectives and instead combine principles that fit best with their goals, beliefs, and desired roles in counseling. Selecting theory relies on a careful examination of your own personal style. The focus questions presented in Self-Assessment Activity 3.8 are intended to assist you in beginning to consider your counseling style and application of theory. Then complete Self-Assessment Activity 3.9.

Self-Assessment Activity 3.8 Relating Personal Beliefs and Theory

Answer the following questions as honestly as possible as they relate to each element of theoretical orientation. Consider your own beliefs and preferences as you answer the questions.

View of Human Nature

1. How do people change?
2. Are people able to change (self-determined), or is our destiny determined for us?
3. What motivates people to change?

Goals of Counseling

1. What are the common goals for all people in counseling?
2. What is the possibility of change as the result of counseling?
3. What can be reasonably accomplished in the context of counseling?

Role of the Professional Counselor

1. How do you perceive the relationship between professional counselor and client? Equals? Experts?
2. To what extent are you willing to let the client dictate the direction of the session, and to what extent do you believe the professional counselor should determine the focus?
3. To what degree should professional counselors provide guidance through personal disclosure and perspective?

Techniques and Approaches

1. What tools do you believe will be most helpful in communicating with clients?
2. Which basic counseling skills (i.e., reflecting feeling, challenging) are most appealing to you in counseling?
3. What do you believe would be most beneficial to you if a professional counselor was to help you with a present concern?

Review your answers to these questions and compare them with the information in Tables 3.1 and 3.2 to delineate which theories may be most appealing as you enter into your counseling practice.

Self-Assessment Activity 3.9 A Theory in Detail

Research a specific theory to discover the basic elements of the theory (e.g., the way of looking at human nature, techniques, goals). You may wish to begin your research with the references listed after each theory discussion in the chapter.

- What types of clients and presenting problems would most likely benefit from the use of this theory?
- For what types of clients and presenting problems would it be inappropriate?
- Would you use this theory? Explain.

Theoretical Integration

With so many sound theories from which to choose, it is challenging to select just one. Many professional counselors, as previously stated, rely on more than one theoretical perspective. **Theoretical integration** is the synthesis of the best aspects of several theories with the belief that doing so will produce richer and more meaningful outcomes (Bradley et al., 2011). Professional counselors operating from an integrative perspective combine the best of what works for them with intentionality. Although employing diverse perspectives and techniques, the integrative counselor holds fast to one underlying, foundational theoretical orientation. For example, we might at our core believe and operate from the existential standpoint of finding meaning in life and searching for ultimate existence. Yet, working with adolescents in an alcohol treatment facility might require that we employ person-centered techniques to build rapport and behavioral techniques to demonstrate change required for discharge. At our core, however, remains the fundamental belief system of existentialism, which guides the use of supplemental approaches.

Integrative Versus Eclectic Counseling

We are intentional in differentiating integrative and eclectic modes of counseling. **Eclecticism**, in contrast to theoretical integration, is more haphazard in nature. The eclectic counselor is a technical expert, relying on knowledge of approaches and techniques and applying what seems to fit at a given time. Eclectic counselors select approaches based on client presenting issues and symptoms. Eclectic counselors use techniques from several areas without regard for theory (Cutts, 2011). There is a lack of a unified or guiding theory for the professional counselor employing this approach. In many ways, eclecticism feels safe for beginning counselors who feel that they are "flying by the seat of their pants" every time they are faced with a new client and presenting issue. A challenge with an eclectic approach is a lack of organized understanding of what principles of a foundational theory are most appropriate to a given client (Lazarus & Beutler, 1993). Without the complete knowledge of a guiding theory, it is difficult to know which pieces of the theory to extract and which to apply. Although tempting, always consider more fully what you believe about counseling and use that as your guide.

Why an Integrative Approach?

With myriad research to demonstrate best practices in counseling, there is ironically a lack of consensus on a single most effective theory. Professional counselors rely instead on the "it depends" mentality of counseling. Not to be confused with eclecticism, theoretical integration offers the professional counselor flexibility in working with various issues and presenting concerns. There exists a level of multicultural responsibility to meet clients where they are when they enter counseling. You must be sure that what you do matches what clients need. Professional counselors can remain authentic in so doing, as the application of elements of theories will differ based on one's underlying belief systems. Theoretical integration offers at the core a guiding theory; this guiding theory assists the counselor in making informed decisions about how to proceed in counseling while maintaining flexibility in the techniques used to assist the client in reaching goals (Cutts, 2011).

One must also acknowledge the limitations of a purist approach. As discussed earlier, professional counselors work in settings with specific requirements for their clients. For example, community mental health often requires that individuals reach counseling goals and implement change within a shorter time. How can a psychodynamically oriented counselor work under such managed care dictates? One answer may be simply to maintain the fundamental principles of psychodynamic approaches in selecting cognitive-behavioral strategies to employ in practice. In a school setting, which often offers even more limited time for individual counseling, existentially oriented counselors can help youth explore what is most meaningful in their lives by challenging them to face issues and work in the present-focused framework of reality therapy or gestalt theory.

Integrative counseling was developed initially to help clarify the conceptual understanding of theories and their applications (Norcross & Goldfried, 2005). Being an integrative counselor requires you to be a knowledgeable counselor. Knowledge of the many theories, or at minimum the paradigms, is required to determine consistency in applying varying techniques to support one's foundation. A guiding theory at the core of an integrative approach is necessary in conceptualizing client presenting issues and determining a general direction for counseling (Cutts, 2011). In addition, exploring one's own beliefs about counseling, as in the previous section, builds a better foundation on which to add supporting approaches. Counseling is a profession valued for flexibility and ability to see multiple dimensions of a problem. Professional counselors must put this in practice by employing what works best to meet a client's needs. Complete Self-Assessment Activity 3.10 to explore your personal integrated approach to counseling.

Self-Assessment Activity 3.10 Your Integrated Orientation

Using Figures 3.2 and 3.3, indicate the various theories you believe will be part of your integrated style of counseling. Consider not only which theories appeal to you for their consistency in beliefs, but also how they will be used. For example, what do you assume to be your core, guiding theory? On what part of the figure do you identify the core? As a humanistically oriented counselor, I (D.H.L.) would identify my core of existentialism at the midsection, or belly, of the figure because I operate from my "gut" in counseling (Figure 3.2). I tend to "use my hands" as a counselor and supplement my work with approaches in person centered and CBT. Of course, your integration must be consistent. It would not work well to have a core existential approach and supplement

Figure 3.2 Author's integrated theory (D.H.L.). Core: belly; theory: existential; tools: hands; supplemental theories: person-centered, CBT

Figure 3.3 My integrated theory. Core: __________; theory: _______ tools: __________; supplemental theories: ____________

with psychodynamic eyes because of the very different philosophies of these two theories. Place your own core theory at your own identified core on Figure 3.3. We have started our own visual depiction of our integrated orientation to help you begin.

As you complete and review your integrated theory, provide a rationale for how these different theories work well together. How do their philosophies complement one another? How is the overall approach depicted here consistent with your own personal beliefs? How is the overall approach depicted here consistent with your beginning beliefs about the counseling process and change?

Voices From the Field 3.2 How My Counseling Theory Has Informed My Practice, *by Randall M. Moate*

I recall quite clearly the first day of my counseling theories class in my master's degree program. After taking a look at the syllabus and glancing in the textbook, I asked myself, "*How in the world will this stuff ever help me?*" The material seemed interesting in an academic sense, but far removed from what I envisioned counseling actually being. My thinking was along the lines of "*Real counselors probably don't spend time thinking about this stuff!*"

Through my development as a practicing counselor, I have developed a deep appreciation for the importance and utility of connecting with a counseling theory. Reflecting back on my development as a counselor, cultivating a solid theoretical foundation has been invaluable to me. In fact, I cannot envision what it would be like to practice *without* having a counseling theory to work from. The following paragraphs briefly detail how I have come to appreciate and use a counseling theory in my work.

As I began reading about the various theories, I approached this experience similarly to how I would approach a first date. I tried to keep an open mind about things and not have any serious expectations, and then see where things went from there. Needless to say, there were several "bad" first dates, but also some pretty good ones. Eventually I came across a theory that was the perfect fit for me—love at first sight, you might say. I recall reading about the theory and found myself nodding my head frequently, and saying to myself "*This totally makes sense to me*," and "*I have always looked at the world this way*." At this point I wasn't exactly sure how I would use my theory, but I did feel a sort of kinship with it. I felt reassured that there were other likeminded counselors out there.

As soon as I met with my first "real" client in practicum, the utility of espousing a counseling theory or approach became readily apparent to me. I noticed that during a 50-minute counseling session, my client wanted to share a lot of information with me. I also noticed that our conversation wasn't linear, and that my client moved around onto several different tangents. At times I felt like my head was spinning and that the session was moving very fast. What allowed me to persevere through this experience was having my theory to help filter and organize what was being said. My theory functioned like having a personal assistant with me in session. It helped me to organize and prioritize all that was being said.

Typically, when I am working with clients, the first couple of sessions seem to go by rather quickly. In general, clients I have worked with tend to want to focus on their presenting problems, share their story, and have me deeply listen to what they have to say. This generally seems to be a good starting point for our therapeutic relationship, as we build trust, rapport, and understanding. However, as we continue our work together, I have several questions that start to tug at the back of my mind: "How is our work together going?" "Do we have a direction and focus in session?" "Am I helping the client achieve their goal(s)?" and "Am I doing a good job?" I am able to fall back on my counseling theory to help me answer these questions. My theory helps to provide a context that I can use as a measuring stick to evaluate how I am doing as a counselor and whether I am helping the client make progress.

"Who am I as a counselor?" "How do I help people?" and "What are my strengths and weaknesses?" are questions I frequently find myself reflecting on. During times of doubt and stress, I find answering these questions to be sustaining and comforting. It helps me to reaffirm who I am as a counselor, how the process of change occurs, and what I hope to achieve as a counselor. My counseling theory—in part—influences how I answer these questions. Rather than being left on my own to sort through these things, I have the bulwark of my theory to fall back on.

I have come to regard a counseling theory as a lens through which I see the world. After several years of practicing from a counseling theory, it has become integrated with who I am as both a professional and a person. Looking back over my education experiences, my theoretical development was critical to my development as a counselor. Starting as a skeptical student who was cynical about the "real-world" utility of counseling theories, I have become very appreciative of all the ways in which theories support the work I do as a counselor.

Summary

In this chapter we discussed the significance of integrating theory into the practice of counseling. It is the professional counselor's ethical responsibility to understand theory and to employ techniques with flexibility sensitive to the client's needs. The case of Terry, as well as the self-assessment activities provided throughout this chapter, help to encourage the reader to apply theory to personal practice by focusing on human nature, goals of counseling, the role of the counselor, and techniques employed with flexibility.

Given the vast array of theories to choose from, this chapter attempted to compartmentalize many theories and their specific factors into larger, more cohesive paradigms. The five major paradigms discussed include psychodynamic, humanistic-existential, behavioral/cognitive-behavioral, systems, and postmodern. By providing examples of the major theoretical paradigms in psychotherapy, we emphasized the fundamental principles of each theory and attempted to familiarize beginning counselors with the common factors in these various theories. Without evidence of a single most effective theory, most professional counselors today employ an integrative approach. Integrative approaches rely on the application of theories that work best with a client and attempt to synthesize different treatment strategies to serve the unique needs of the client, as well as foster growth and development in the personal philosophy of the counselor.

Determining a counseling theory is an involved and lengthy process. The five paradigms discussed here are a starting point to learn more about the counseling theories as you enter into practice. Before foreclosing on a specific theory, we strongly encourage beginning counselors to reflect on their beliefs about themselves, human nature, and counseling. Aside from the ethical and professional responsibilities for using theory in practice, understanding how counseling works will better prepare you to help clients. A unique perspective on your client's issues that is embedded in your beliefs about how people change and develop will enable you to select appropriate interventions to assist clients to reach their goals. An intentional counselor is a successful counselor, employing a unique integration of personal characteristics and counseling theories.

Answer Key

Activity 3.4 1. b, 2. f, 3. g, 4. e, 5. d, 6. a, 7. c.
Activity 3.5 1. b, 2. c, 3. d, 4. a, 5. e.

Record Keeping

What to Include and What to Leave Out

James Jackson, Latofia P. Parker, and Charlotte Daughhetee

Preview

Appropriate clinical record keeping is essential to ethical best practice. When documenting counseling services, it is imperative that counselors be mindful of the legal, ethical, and agency requirements regarding documentation. Good comprehensive record keeping promotes quality treatment and also documents that treatment falls within accepted standards of care, thereby providing protection from liability risk. By following standard therapy note-writing formats and by allowing time for note-writing immediately following a session, counselors can produce precise yet thorough documentation of their practice. In addition to client records, counselors engage in other types of professional writing, including communication with other professionals and the production of practice marketing materials. The ability to write professionally is vital to professional responsible practice.

The Importance of Record Keeping

The creation and maintenance of clinical records has been significantly influenced by the climate of managed care and evidence-based practice. One outcome of this influence is that the process of keeping clinical records has taken on increased importance and complexity. Record keeping is an important aspect of providing effective services to clients, documenting that appropriate services were rendered, and maintaining continuity of services when a change in mental health providers occurs (Welfel, 2015). Two primary areas of responsibility that must be considered with regard to keeping clinical records are legal and clinical responsibilities (Gutheil & Hilliard, 2001).

From a legal perspective, the information documented in the clinical record is often the most compelling evidence of the facts when a complaint or legal suit is brought against a professional counselor. Courts and regulatory boards typically give considerable weight to clinical records made during the course of treatment (Gutheil & Hilliard, 2001). Most states require counselors to maintain client records and may have regulations and statutes concerning the content of records. The American Counseling Association's (ACA's) *Code of Ethics* (ACA, 2014) mandates that counselors maintain records in accordance with institutional, agency, and legal requirements. Although inpatient records require specific categories of data with stiff penalties for facilities and clinicians not in compliance, the requirements for outpatient records are generally not as structured or strict (Gutheil & Hilliard, 2001). It is incumbent on counselors in both inpatient and outpatient settings to learn the requirements for and maintain good clinical records.

Good record keeping may help reduce the professional counselor's legal risk of liability by demonstrating that the services provided are within the bounds of a reasonable standard of care; thus, clinical records should document the counselor's decision-making and treatment processes and the response of clients to treatment. Koocher et al. (2013) identified 15 content domains that should be present in a comprehensive clinical record.

- **Identifying information:** Client name, contact information, gender, date of birth, marital status, parent/guardian (or next of kin), employment status, and billing information.
- **First contact:** Referral source and date of the initial contact.
- **Legal notifications:** Information for clients as required by HIPAA, consent forms, confidentiality, and limits.

DOI: 10.4324/9781003305521-4

- **Pertinent history and risk factors:** Detailed medical, social, vocational, and educational history, including sufficient information to form a diagnosis and treatment plan. Important to ask in the first session are the questions: "Tell me about the most violent or impulsive act you have ever done" and "Have you had thoughts of harming yourself or others recently?" Obtain permission to contact prior mental health practitioners and secure records of prior treatment.
- **Medical or health status:** Obtain information regarding medical status, name of the client's primary care physician, and pending medical tests or conditions.
- **Medication profile:** Identify past and current medications and illicit drugs taken by the client and note any referrals for medication.
- **What brought the client to the office?** Provide a detailed description of the client's current condition, including presenting problems or symptoms and the reason for the referral. Inquire what brought the client for help at this time and document the reasons.
- **Diagnostic impressions:** Describe diagnostic formulations and clinical impressions based on the most current edition of the *DSM*. Do not "upcode" or "downcode."
- **Treatment plan:** Design a treatment plan that includes short-term and long-term goals and a description of planned therapeutic interventions. The treatment plan should be updated as needed.
- **Progress notes:** Indicate progress toward counseling goals using clear, precise language and observable facts. Write as if the client and client's lawyer were reading the note with a lawsuit in mind, and you are demonstrating you are a dedicated, serious, and concerned professional.
- **Service documentation:** Document each session and the client's response to treatment.
- **Document follow-up:** Document any referrals for treatment and missed appointments. Maintain copies of any notices, reminders, and correspondence with clients, and note in the record any significant telephone conversations.
- **Obtain consent:** Maintain copies of all releases of information and consent forms, including consent for any form of recording (video, etc.).
- **Termination:** Write a termination summary or discharge note for the client. As termination approaches, make sure that case notes reflect the planning and progress toward the end of treatment.

Koocher et al. (2013) noted that developing a comprehensive record as just described would likely require several sessions. Obviously, certain documentation such as consent forms, HIPAA agreements, and so on should be secured before treatment is initiated, whereas other documentation artifacts will be captured over the course of therapy.

Keeping appropriate case notes is both an important component and indicator of ethical practice. The *ACA Code of Ethics* (ACA, 2014) sections A.1.b., A.6.c, and B.6.g. offer additional guidelines related to maintaining case notes, which include: (a) counselors are responsible for maintaining such records as necessary for providing professional services to clients; (b) accurate, timely, and sufficient documentation should be kept to facilitate the continuity of services; (c) interactions of a nonprofessional nature between counselors and clients, including former clients, should be documented in case records and should also include the rationale, possible benefit, and likely consequences of the interaction; (d) after counseling services are terminated, records are maintained to permit future access as required by state and federal statutes; and (e) when records are disposed of, this must be done using a method that protects client confidentiality. Although necessarily broad in scope, these guidelines underscore that ethical counseling practitioners are intentional in maintaining appropriate professional records documenting their work with clients.

How to Keep Case Notes

Progress notes serve the dual purposes of documenting both client progress toward counseling goals and the work done during sessions. Piazza and Baruth (1990) identified four components required in a progress note. First, the counselor's goals for the session must be identified. Goals should be linked to the treatment plan and should demonstrate continuity of the work conducted in previous sessions. Second, an evaluation of client progress toward the identified goal for the session should be included, as well as the counselor interventions implemented. Third, clinical impressions based on behaviors observed by the counselor should be noted. The fourth and final component is an action plan, which will serve as the goal of the therapeutic work to be conducted in the following session. Formulating goals for the next session based on the work done in the previous session promotes continuity over the course of treatment.

Process Notes

Under HIPAA, process notes are referred to as **psychotherapy notes**, which may present some confusion due to the terminology. This terminology came about when the federal government included provisions under HIPAA that the client's signature on the Notice of Privacy Practice would allow providers to communicate information required for treatment and payment without the need to secure separate client consent for each contact. Although these provisions greatly streamlined the consent process, this also permitted third-party payers access to the complete clinical record of clients, which presented concerns for mental health practitioners with regard to maintaining confidentiality of client information. In response, professional mental health associations negotiated an exception to such access for documents specified as psychotherapy notes (Welfel, 2015). Thus, process notes differ from progress notes and are not considered part of the clinical record. Due to the special status of psychotherapy notes under HIPAA, these notes are not included under a signed waiver of medical records unless specifically mentioned in the waiver (Koocher & Keith-Spiegel, 2016).

Essentially, process notes consist of information written down by the counselor for the purpose of reflecting on personal reactions to the counseling process such as countertransference, as well as any working drafts of the counselor's impressions concerning treatment (Koocher & Keith-Spiegel, 2016). Process notes may be kept for the purpose of increasing counselor competence; for example, reviewing supervisee cognitive processes through the use of process notes can be a valuable supervision technique. However, due to the impressionistic nature of process notes, after the relevant information has been extracted from these working notes and incorporated into the formal clinical record, it is recommended that these notes be destroyed. Any process notes that are not destroyed may be subpoenaed in legal proceedings. See Think About It 4.1.

Think About It 4.1

Imagine that a colleague tells you that he keeps personal notes of his sessions on a flash drive that he carries around with him in addition to the clinical records kept at the agency where he works. What ethical or legal concerns might be associated with such a practice? What, if any, suggestions might you make to your colleague?

Standard Format

Maintaining up-to-date case notes is a challenge for most practicum and internship students, in part because agencies differ widely on the format used for therapy notes. Agencies often are subject to either in-house or external audits and, to ensure compliance, may have guidelines or even training specific to writing case notes. Agencies also commonly have certain expectations for clinical records to facilitate reimbursement for services and demonstrate therapeutic effectiveness. These expectations represent a "learning curve" as interns learn to write the narrative of their work in the session within the structured format of the template used at the site. A good practice for practicum students, interns, and new counselors to follow when first joining an agency is to carefully examine the note format in use at the site and clear up any questions concerning documentation procedures. Even in agencies where guidelines aren't specified, such as schools, supervisors typically have clear ideas about what constitutes a good—and bad—case note.

Agencies with formalized note-writing templates generally include places on progress note forms for information such as Time In, Time Out, Participants, Content, Intervention/Client Response, and Progress. Also, agencies often have specific abbreviations commonly used in writing notes. For example, an agency might have a standardized sentence at the beginning of client notes for each session to indicate client presentation, orientation, and the presence or absence of symptoms of particular concern. This could be noted with an initial sentence such as "Client presented appropriate attire, O x 4, no s/i, h/i, or a/v/h," which would indicate that in this session the client is Oriented to Person, Place, Time, and Situation, demonstrates no Suicidal Ideation, Homicidal Ideation, or Audio or Visual Hallucinations. Examples of exemplary notes (minus identifying client information) and commonly used abbreviations at the site may be available for review and might save the counselor much time by preventing the need to rewrite notes.

SOAP Notes

The acronym **SOAP** stands for Subjective, Objective, Assessment, and Plan and is a standardized format for writing case notes that is part of an organizational system of medical records called the problem-oriented medical record (POMR; Kettenbach, 1995). The SOAP documentation format has been adapted for use across the allied health fields and is a common format used in the mental health field. Cameron and Imani Turtle-Song (2002) provided an excellent description of the use of the SOAP format for writing therapy notes for mental health practitioners. The information appropriate to include under each heading follows.

Subjective

This section and the objective section of the SOAP format are for the purpose of data gathering. Information should be both clear and brief. A common difficulty is deciding whether content is subjective or objective. Content is classified as subjective if it is reported to, versus observed by, the counselor. This includes client perceptions of the problem such as reports of affect, behaviors, cognitions, goals, symptoms (including descriptions of symptom frequency, intensity, and duration), and the impact of symptoms on client relationships. Reports from other outside sources such as client friends and family, as well as information from other agency representatives such as probation officers, and so on should also be included in this section.

Direct quotations of client statements should generally be avoided. Some exceptions to this are situations in which the client makes specific statements of intent to do harm to self and/or others. In this circumstance, it may be important to record the client statements precisely to support the clinical decision to take protective actions, which involve breaking confidentiality. Another circumstance potentially requiring a direct quote includes statements by the client suggesting a change in mental status. Negative statements made by the client about other treatment providers should not be included in the client record (Cameron & Imani Turtle-Song, 2002).

Objective

Information included in the objective section of the note should be factual and quantitative in nature. Two sources of objective data are written records and counselor observations. Counselor observations should be directly witnessed by the counselor and include data that is interpersonal, physical, and psychological in nature. Counselors should strive for precision and clarity and avoid using words with negative connotations and that are open to interpretation such as *manipulative*, *spoiled*, and *drunk* to describe client presentation. Counselors should generally avoid using terms such as *seemed* or *appeared* to qualify observations and should instead support observations by phrases like *as evidenced by* (Cameron & Imani Turtle-Song, 2002).

Assessment

The counselor's clinical formulations concerning client problems, including DSM-5 diagnosis (American Psychiatric Association, 2013), should be summarized in this section. Clinical impressions related to diagnostic criteria should also be included to provide a record of information used in diagnosis and treatment planning; such information should be clearly identified as the counselor's clinical impressions. Some authors Piazza & Baruth, 1990) contend the inclusion of clinical impressions in the clinical record is inappropriate due to the risk of such information being wrong and recommend such information be kept in the counselor's personal notes. However, keeping clinical impressions in a separate location in the form of personal notes presents serious ethical and legal considerations. Documentation of the clinician's reasoning for diagnostic decisions and the evolution of the treatment are kept most appropriately in the clinical record (Cameron & Imani Turtle-Song, 2002).

Plan

The plan section is divided into two sections consisting of the action plan and the prognosis. The action plan includes information such as interventions, client education, progress of treatment, and the therapeutic work intended for the next session. Any consultation or referrals are also documented in this section. The prognosis is a prediction of the possible outcomes of treatment based on the client's diagnosis, motivation, and resources. Common terms used in prognosis assessments include *excellent*, *good*, *fair*, *guarded*, and *poor*. Supporting information substantiating the prognosis should be provided (Cameron & Imani Turtle-Song, 2002).

Time-Sequenced Notes

Baird and Mollen (2019) indicated that the most common format for recording information from counseling sessions is time-sequenced notes. In this format, the significant material that the professional counselor wishes to include in the record is recorded in the same sequence in which it occurred. The counselor may record material as it occurs during the session or may wait until the session has concluded. The sequence of the material as presented by the client may provide valuable information about the relationship between significant themes. Obviously, the theoretical orientation of the counselor will affect the selection of the material focused on during the session, as well as what is considered important to include in the therapy note. Although this style of note-writing is common, additional information (e.g., a treatment plan) is often required to satisfy agency requirements and secure reimbursement from third-party payers. Case Study 4.1 provides a context to illustrate how a clinician might capture the essentials of a session using the SOAP and time-sequenced formats.

Case Study 4.1 Ebony

Ebony is a 34-year-old Black female who was referred for counseling by a friend to address her symptoms of grief. She arrived for her 2:00 p.m. intake appointment on time wearing casual attire. Ebony is a physician assistant at a local hospital. Ebony and her husband have been married for two years and do not have children. Six months ago her father passed away from pancreatic cancer. Ebony reported that her father refused to undertake chemotherapy and she respected his wishes to forgo medical treatment. She reports that she took a leave of absence from work to move home to help her mother take care of her father during his last days. She reported that she returned back to work a week after his death and has been extremely sad since her father's death.

Ebony doesn't have a desire to spend time with family, go to work, or engage in hobbies. She cries herself to sleep at night and has starting experiencing unexpected moments of emotional outbursts at work. She states that she feels like she is on an "emotional rollercoaster." Ebony says there are times that she thinks about her dad and gets angry. She doesn't understand why he refused chemotherapy; her anger then makes her feel guilty. Ebony feels guilty for being angry at her deceased father but also feels guilty that she couldn't help him. She states that she helps sick people for a living, so how is it possible that she couldn't help her own dad. Ebony describes other symptoms such as being easily irritated and feeling lonely and lost.

Initially, the emotional outbursts occurred only at home and usually once per week, but now they are occurring at work and have increased to the current level of two to three days a week. Ebony went to her pastor for spiritual help but believes that she needs more than just spiritual guidance. Ebony demonstrated both positive and negative affect during the interview. When discussing her father, Ebony often cried but otherwise she was able to competently answer the intake questions. Ebony reports that she is not currently taking any prescription or nonprescription drugs; she does not smoke or use illicit substances. Ebony reports drinking wine and cocktails on special occasions or when hanging out with friends. Her physician had prescribed her a sleeping pill, but Ebony indicates that she doesn't want to become dependent on pills to help her sleep. She described herself as a typical easy-going person with an average middle-class background. When discussing her work as a physician assistant, she indicated that she was very satisfied with her career prior to her father's death. But now she is not sure if she wants to continue working in a health care setting because it is becoming too draining. Ebony is concerned about the outbursts at work. They have not occurred in front of patients, but she is concerned that she might start crying in front of a patient who is receiving treatment for a terminal illness.

Ebony is an only child. She indicated she has several cousins with whom she grew up so she never really felt like an only child. She indicated that she has a satisfying, loving relationship with her husband and good support system in her friends and work colleagues. Ebony reports that her friends, family, and coworkers have been extremely supportive of her during her time of grief.

Ebony noted that she and her husband are trying to get pregnant, and it makes her sad that her kids will never get to know their grandfather. Ebony began to cry while describing how she envisioned her father as a grandfather. She said her father would jokingly say that he wanted to be called "Gramps." Ebony noted that her grief has become unbearable. She agreed to record in the coming week the thoughts, feelings, and behaviors she experienced in relation to her grief and bring the journal to the next session for discussion. Following is a SOAP note example for Ebony.

SOAP Note Format

Subjective (S)

Client is a 34 y/o Black female referred by a friend for symptoms associated with grief. Client stated no use of medications or illicit substances; however, she reported she occasionally drinks wine and cocktails at social events and with friends. Client described unexpected emotional outbursts in the form of crying and becoming easily agitated with self and others occurring over the past 3 months, increasing from once/week and only at home to current frequency of two or three/week both at home and work. Reports onset of grief symptoms occurred after the death of her father. Symptoms include increased irritability and agitation, extreme sadness, feelings of isolation and loneliness, anger, and guilt. Client reports active family and social support systems.

Objective (O)

Client presented appropriate attire and demonstrated appropriate affect; evidenced significant emotional distress and sadness when discussing loss of her father. Client stated she is questioning if she wants to remain in the health care profession because she is worried about how she would respond to terminally ill patients after the loss of her father. Client appears motivated for counseling, as evidenced by being on time for appointment, answering all questions, and statements expressing her needs for more than spiritual guidance to ameliorate her grief symptoms.

Assessment (A)

V 62.82 Uncomplicated Bereavement

Plan (P)

Implement bereavement interventions with client to address grief symptoms. Homework: Client will identify affect, behaviors, and cognitions surrounding the occurrence of grief symptoms and record these in a journal to discuss in the next session.

Prognosis: High level of functioning prior to onset of bereavement and good insight suggest positive prognosis for treatment.

Following is an example of a time-sequenced note format.

Time-Sequenced Note Format

Client is a 34-year-old married Black female referred by friend to address grief symptoms. Client presented appropriate attire and affect. Client is a physician assistant at a local hospital. Client lives with husband; father died of pancreatic cancer six months ago. Client began experiencing unexpected emotional outbursts 3 months ago coinciding with father's death.

Client describes main symptoms as sadness, anger, guilt, irritability, sleeplessness, and isolation/loneliness. Client noted she sought the help of her pastor but feels she needs more than spiritual guidance. Initial frequency of outburst once/week and only at home, currently two or three/week and now at home and work. PCP prescribed sleeping pill to help with sleeplessness; however, client doesn't want to take a sleeping pill. Client reports no use of prescription or nonprescription drugs, does not smoke, or use illicit substances. Client reported she occasionally drinks alcohol at social events.

Client is concerned about having emotional outbreaks at work, especially in the presence of clients. Client is concerned that she no longer wants to work in hospital setting around terminally ill patients. Client demonstrated appropriate negative affect when discussing loss of father. Client noted good social support system. Client identified main stressors as grief symptoms being unbearable. High level of functioning prior to onset of bereavement and good insight suggest positive prognosis for treatment. Client will record in the coming week the thoughts, feelings, and behaviors she experiences in relation to her grief symptoms and bring the journal to the next session to discuss.

Current diagnosis: Uncomplicated Bereavement.

The Line Between Too Much and Not Enough Information

A common challenge faced by beginning counselors is deciding what should be included in the therapy note. When writing case notes, style is generally not as critical as brevity, precision, and clarity. The objective of recording essential information is to do so with an efficient use of space and time. By striving for economy of expression, the counselor will save time as well as the time of other professionals who will read the case notes (Baird & Mollen, 2019).

Although records must contain enough detail to accurately represent the counseling process, counselors should always be mindful that others may view or inspect records in the future. For instance, clients can request copies of records or they may ask that you transfer copies to other professionals. If your records are subpoenaed, they will be viewed by those involved in the case. State mental health authorities might view records at a state agency as part of an auditing visit. Always write with the knowledge that although your records must be thorough, they should not contain unnecessary detail.

Cameron and Imani Turtle-Song (2002) noted that "few counselors are able to write clear or concise clinical case notes, and most complain of feeling frustrated when trying to distinguish what is and is not important enough to be incorporated in these notes" (p. 287). The difficulty in deciding what should be included and what to omit from the record may be related to the concern of leaving out information that is clinically significant. In the beginning experiences of clinical work, every detail of client verbalizations and behaviors during sessions may appear equally important to include. Deciding what is clinically relevant may be further complicated by unfamiliarity with a theoretical framework that emphasizes certain aspects of treatment; for example, a site may approach treatment from a theoretical framework with which the intern is not as well acquainted. Reviewing examples of case notes provided by the site may help the new counselor identify the elements of sessions typically included in case notes as well as common phrases associated with these elements. This may in turn facilitate the process of learning to write notes that conform to the protocols of the site. As you consider issues around case notes, see Think About It 4.2.

Think About It 4.2

Suppose a colleague confides in you that he is "way behind" on completing his case notes—in fact, he has no written documentation of his work with clients over the last three weeks. As your colleague sits down and begins writing his notes from memory, what legal, ethical, and standard of care concerns do you have in relation to his lack of timely documentation?

Instances Where Detail Is Necessary

Certain events in the course of treatment may warrant additional detail to be included in the case note. Baird and Mollen (2019) noted that one situation requiring special consideration for record keeping is when an abused spouse is receiving counseling, and the abuser does not know. In this case, the record should include some special indicator noting exactly how and where to contact the client and also specific protocols for billing so that it is not possible to inadvertently reveal that the client is coming for treatment. Unauthorized release of client information is one basis for malpractice suits evidenced in case law.

As a source of evidence of appropriate diagnosis and treatment, the information contained in the clinical record is critically important in circumstances when clients threaten harm to themselves or others. If a client expresses a desire to harm self or others, it is important to document the implementation of the appropriate intervention to promote safety. Documentation may include noting compliance with agency protocols, including a record of consultation with outside agencies and resources. Significant client statements that have a direct bearing on the clinician's decision regarding the level of intervention necessary to protect the client or others (e.g., client responses to a risk assessment) should be included as well (Zuckerman & Kolmes, 2008). If a no-harm agreement is used, a copy of the agreement with accompanying behavioral strategies addressing the risk behaviors should be provided to the client, and the counselor should document that the client received a copy of the agreement. When documenting incidents involving risk of harm, a good guideline to keep in mind is that the only evidence of action taken is that which is written in the record (Harris, 1995), commonly expressed as "If you don't write it down, it didn't happen."

We Are What We Write: The Importance of Professional Written Communication as Keys to Effective Writing

Rawson et al. (2005) noted the importance of professional writing for clear, precise, and succinct communication among colleagues regarding cases and treatment. Professional writing encompasses not only case documentation but also communications among professionals, as well as informational and promotional materials read by the public. Often, the written word is the first contact a counselor has with clients and other professionals. Written expression errors, typos, and an unprofessional tone can create a negative impression that can have an adverse effect on a counselor's reputation and standing. The tone and the requirements of professional writing differ from academic assignments and informal writing. Thus, practice and assessment of professional writing ability is beneficial for all counselors, and writing should be considered a fundamental practice skill. Professional writing not only involves understanding the mechanics of written communication and the use of appropriate terminology to accurately communicate in professional contexts, but also entails planning and carving out sufficient time to clearly construct text that expresses authentic meaning.

Make Time for Documentation

A commonly overlooked challenge faced by new counselors related to writing notes is making sure that adequate time is reserved at the end of each session to complete the case note. The therapy record should be written immediately after the session. Although the most obvious advantage of writing notes after each session may be to facilitate recall of significant material from the session (Cameron & Imani Turtle-Song, 2002), this documentation practice has several other potential benefits, which may include

- Facilitating the processing of reactions to the session, such as countertransference.
- Reducing "clutter" in working memory and promoting focus on the client in the following session.
- Contributing to a sense of competence as a counselor through demonstrating the ability to appropriately structure sessions within the available resource of time.
- Reducing "paperwork fatigue" by completing notes through several short periods of writing one note after each session instead of one long period of writing several notes at the end of the day.
- Requiring the counselor to identify significant themes that may assist with case conceptualization.
- Reminding the therapist of homework assigned to the client so the therapist will check on this in the next session.

Other Professional Writing

In addition to client documentation, writing is required in other facets of a counselor's career. The practice of counseling is often collaborative; therefore, counselors must frequently communicate via letters or email with other professionals, including mental health practitioners, medical personnel, and lawyers. It is prudent to construct such communications with care. First of all, remember that email and faxed documents are not secure communications, and it is essential to protect client confidentiality (Wheeler & Bertram, 2019). Professional communications should never be rushed. Dashing off an email or typing a letter quickly without thought can lead to confusion, embarrassment, or misinformation. Always take time to read over what you have written to make sure you are communicating clearly and competently. Careless mistakes can miscommunicate information about a client and could create a negative impression of a counselor's competency.

Another aspect of professional writing is the development of materials to promote one's practice. Ads, brochures, and other materials are often the initial interface with a new client, and the impression such documents create can make or break a practice. Of course, promotional materials should be eye-catching, but more important, they must be accurate and concise. This is another case where less is more because too much text often ceases to be communicative and simply becomes confusing.

Counselors may be asked to write columns for local newspapers or school newsletters, or they may choose to write informational blogs on practice websites. Such venues are excellent platforms to communicate general mental health and wellness ideas and can also serve as effective public relations tools. The following tips may be helpful to keep in mind when writing professional letters, columns, and blogs or when developing promotional materials.

- Write and then rewrite. The first draft gives you the basic framework of information that needs to be communicated. Subsequent drafts serve to enhance the readability and style of the document.
- Always proofread carefully. If the information being written is not confidential, it is best to ask a colleague to proofread for you and give you feedback. Another set of eyes can be extremely helpful because people tend to read what they meant to write and may miss actual errors.
- Ask yourself (and your proofreader) if the meaning is clear. Have you clearly communicated your message as you intended? If there is a chance that your meaning could be misconstrued, rewrite.
- When writing promotional materials, you must represent yourself, your credentials, and your expertise accurately. Follow the ethical and legal guidelines of your state regarding promotional material and advertising.
- Promotional materials should be succinct; verbose brochures get tossed aside.
- Avoid using jargon or professional buzzwords that could be confusing to clients.
- When writing columns or blogs, take care that you do not use real-life examples that breach client confidentiality. Examples should be broad, general, and not identifiable as a particular person.
- Relax and enjoy writing. Although you must take care to proofread and have clarity in your writing, you must also let your voice express itself. Allow your genuineness to shine through in your written communication.

Progress Notes and Supervision

Supervisors are responsible for the welfare of their supervisee's clients (Welfel, 2015), and reviewing case notes plays a fundamental role in the supervisory process. By reviewing notes, a supervisor can evaluate the extent to which a supervisee is adhering to standards of care and can monitor client progress. Without examining case notes, supervisors cannot be fully informed on the progress of the client and the skill development of the supervisee (Heller et al., 2010). Perhaps more importantly, Prieto and Scheel (2002) highlighted the role case documentation can play in the development of the supervisee's case conceptualization skills. The use of notes in supervision provides an opportunity to help supervisees recognize relevant facts, identify presenting problems, and know when to seek out additional information. Examining notes in supervision strengthens treatment planning and highlights the importance of examining what is happening within each session, using this information to continually assess and modify treatment. Harris et al. (2009) suggested that graduate programs invite legal experts and practicing counselors as guest speakers in classes to provide students with opportunities to hear about documentation practices and concerns. In addition, programs should have students observe a court proceeding involving counseling records; this would be instructive and would also emphasize the critical importance of following best practice in case documentation and record keeping.

Tips to Avoid Record Keeping Problems

The *ACA Code of Ethics* (2014) is quite clear on the ethical responsibilities of record keeping. As stated earlier in this chapter, client records not only serve to document actions taken within the therapeutic relationship, but also guide treatment planning and the therapeutic process. Furthermore, in the event a counselor is sued for malpractice or faces a complaint before a licensure board, the case record is the key method by which a counselor can prepare a defense; it is often stated that records are your first line of defense. This is not to say that the only reason one keeps records is in self-defense, but the realization of the possibility of a malpractice lawsuit or a licensure board complaint should keep counselors mindful of the importance of clear and accurate record keeping. Magen and Magen (2010) pointed out that some practitioners who are overly cautious about possible litigation may write vague summaries of sessions, noting aspects of the case that could be generalized to most clients. Such nebulous descriptions are not conducive to quality care because this practice fails to adequately describe the counseling process. Magen and Magen provided the following basic guidelines for appropriate professional writing (p. 803):

- Simple, avoid jargon.
- Objective.
- Parsimony—keep it brief and to the point.
- Avoid adjectives.
- Write in simple declarative sentences.
- Relevant—writing should serve the professional purpose.
- Ethical—write in accordance with ethical and legal standards.

Not only do records clarify the degree to which a counselor has fulfilled standards of care, but also, according to Wheeler and Bertram (2019), appropriate record keeping is the standard of care: "Counselors have an explicitly stated legal and ethical duty to create and maintain client records on every client" (p. 115). Therefore, if a counselor fails to maintain suitable records, the counselor has violated standard of care.

How long should client records be kept? Ultimately, counselors should be guided by state law regarding how long to keep client records. Basic HIPAA standards recommend a minimum of six years after termination of treatment, and for minor clients, a counselor should store records for seven years past the date the minor client reaches adulthood. State licensure laws may require practitioners to keep records for a longer period of time; thus, counselors should follow the requirements of their licensure. In the event a practitioner has dual licensure, the counselor should keep records for the longest period required by one of their licenses. Now complete Self-Assessment Activity 4.1 to hone your documentation skills.

Self-Assessment Activity 4.1 Professional Writing

The following activities can be done in small groups or in pairs. Practicing common writing situations and obtaining feedback from your peers will strengthen and polish your writing skills. For each of these activities, take your peer feedback and rewrite the activity. Remember, your writing is a reflection of your professionalism.

1. Choose a television show or movie that has psychotherapy scenes. Some suggestions are: *Sopranos*, *In Treatment*, *Analyze This*, or any television or movie scene that contains a lengthy monologue by a character. View the scene with your activity partner/small group. After viewing, each person should write SOAP notes as if the counselor for the character. Exchange SOAP notes and provide feedback to one another. Did you and your peer(s) emphasize different aspects of the scene? If so, why? Did you write too much? Not enough?
2. Write a social media post describing a new program or group that you will be offering in your practice. This post will be shared on your business pages and shared with other local businesses. Exchange this with your activity partner/small group and provide feedback to one another. Is your post professional yet welcoming to potential clients? Did you portray yourself and your services appropriately?

3. You are an LPC and have opened a private practice, and you want to send a letter to local lawyers and doctors announcing your practice, your credentials, and the services you provide. Write a letter and exchange with your activity partner/small group and give feedback to one another. Is the tone of your letter professional? Does the letter communicate competency to the reader?
4. Have each person choose a wellness or life skill topic (e.g., stress management, self-care, goal setting). Write a brief blog on this topic. Exchange with your activity partner/small group and give feedback to one another. Is the blog informational, and is the information factual? Does it appeal to the reader?

Double-Lock Guideline

Counselors are responsible for the safeguarding of client records. Records should be stored in a secure locked manner where they will be safe from theft or from dispersal or damage due to a natural disaster such as a tornado or hurricane. Because client records should never be accessible to unauthorized individuals, keeping records under double-lock is best practice. Essentially, the double-lock guideline means that someone must get through two locks to access files. Client files should always be under lock when not in use. Although it may be easier for a counselor to simply leave a file on a desk while they pop out of the office for a few minutes, those few minutes could result in a breach of confidentiality that might be harmful to a client and could expose the counselor to litigation.

With the advent of electronic record keeping, counselors must possess technological expertise regarding file security (Reamer, 2017). Confidential files should be password protected or encrypted (Mills, 2012). Counselors should use extreme caution when storing files on laptops or devices such as flash drives, as these can be easily stolen. Wheeler and Bertram (2019) pointed out the importance of making sure files are secure and having a backup system to guard against loss of information if a computer crashes. There are software systems developed specifically for mental health practice that can assist counselors in setting up a thorough framework for the development and maintenance of client records. Although these systems are extremely useful, it is important that counselors research the security properties of a program before investing in it for their practice. Case Study 4.2 illustrates some security considerations.

Case Study 4.2 Keith and Ibrahim

Keith and his colleague Ibrahim have a part-time private practice located in a large office building. Their office space has a waiting area and two offices for counseling. The office building houses several types of businesses and is conveniently located. Keith and Ibrahim see clients in the evening, and although many of the businesses in the building are closed, there are always a few lawyers working late, and the custodial crew comes in around 9:00 pm to clean, so they are never alone in the building. It has been a good arrangement. Ibrahim has a locked filing cabinet in his office. Keith keeps his client files in the unlocked file drawer in his desk. When confronted by Ibrahim about this practice, Keith noted that because the main door is locked and his personal office door is locked, he is complying with double-lock guidelines. What do you think? Is Keith complying? In what ways could his client files be compromised? Is Ibrahim complying with the double-lock guideline?

Confidentiality With Client Communication

Remley and Herlihy (2020) pointed out that informed consent is linked to the foundational ethical concepts of self-determination and autonomy and is crucial to the development of the counseling relationship. Essentially, a clear explanation of the limits of confidentiality is vital to true informed consent. As a fundamental aspect of the counseling process, informed consent should be accurately documented in the client record with a signed copy of the informed consent document and case file notation that the counselor and client have discussed the document. Informed consent provides clients with all pertinent information about the process of counseling so that clients can know what they are entering into and can make an informed judgment about the counseling process.

One of the most important aspects of informed consent is the explanation of the limits to confidentiality. In most jurisdictions, counselors must breach confidentiality when a client is a danger to self or others or when they suspect abuse or neglect of a child or vulnerable adult. In addition, in states with counselor privilege, a counselor may attempt to quash a subpoena; however, a judge can require the counselor to testify. In some states, counselors do not have privilege and therefore must respond to subpoenas without first attempting to quash them. It is important for counselors to be aware of all their state's laws regarding privilege and confidentiality.

Electronic communications such as phone messages, emails, or texts are not considered secure, and care must be taken to inform clients of this fact. Bradley et al. (2011) suggested that counselors include in the informed consent a discussion with clients about the risks of third parties accessing emails that exist even with data encryption and firewalls in place. As part of the informed consent, the counselor should discuss with the client the security limitations of such communications and also clarify if and how counselors should contact clients using emails, texts, and phone messages (Zur, 2010). Not only could information be hacked, but more likely, another person may have access to the client's phone or email account and could see confidential information. The counselor has no guarantee that the client is the person on the receiving end of texts and emails. However, these types of communications are part of everyday life, and clients may prefer to receive communication via text. Counselors should take precautions to minimize the information imparted in emails, texts, and phone messages and communicate simple direct statements such as, "We need to reschedule your appointment."

An important consideration regarding client-generated email, text, and phone message communication is how to appropriately include such artifacts in case documentation. (Zur, 2010) noted that if a phone message, text, or email has clinical significance, it should be included in the client's record. However, emails, messages, and texts that have no clinical significance (e.g., appointment scheduling messages) are not included in the client record. For some messages, the content can simply be noted in the record with the date and time that the message was left. However, counselors might receive voice mail messages where it would be prudent to record the message as part of the clinical record. There are various methods by which client voice mail messages can be saved (VOI or MP3), but counselors must be cognizant of specific security risks with such technologies and include these risks in their informed consent documents. See Self-Assessment Activity 4.2 to reflect on how you would handle such messages.

Self-Assessment Activity 4.2 Documenting Voice Mail

Which of the following client voice mails have clinical significance and should be included in the client record? Could some of these messages simply be documented, or should you record and save the actual message? What ethical and legal concerns might be raised by introducing into the clinical record a verbatim copy of client statements? Do clients know in advance that the message might become part of their clinical record, and should this be a factor in deciding whether or how client statements might be maintained in their files?

1. " "Just wanted to let you know that it worked! Timmy did his homework each night this past week."
2. "I was right, the meeting will be over at 3:00 so the 3:30 appointment works fine."
3. "Jim is acting the same way; he isn't doing any of the things you suggested. I'm really getting fed up."
4. "The school counselor signed the release; I'll bring you a copy next week."
5. "I really feel something special happened in our session yesterday. I'm getting so much out of our counseling."
6. "The self-talk statements we worked on just don't ring true. If I say them, I know I'm just lying to myself."
7. "Hey Doc, just wanted to let you know I got the job!"
8. "Susan is on a business trip next week, but Jenny and I can make the family counseling appointment."
9. "Sorry I forgot the checkbook. I just put the check in the mail so you should get it in a couple of days."
10. "The insurance people called me, and they got the paperwork. Thanks."

Considering that significant voice mail messages may become part of the clinical record underscores the importance of discussing with clients the appropriate content of voice mail as part of informed consent procedures. This discussion might appropriately be part of the process of providing clients with the contact information of agency and community resources to access in times of crisis. Imagine the potential consequences if a counselor neglected to discuss with clients the appropriate use and implications of leaving voice mail messages after agency hours. A client in crisis might call and leave an emotionally charged phone message on the counselor's answering machine with the intent that the counselor listen to the message and assist in processing the crisis with the client in the next session. Such an exchange would resemble the dynamic of asynchronous counseling, which would not be appropriate for a client in crisis . Also, if the counselor did not inform the client about the frequency with which the counselor typically checks and responds to voice mail, the client might have the expectation that leaving the voice mail would initiate an immediate response from the counselor to assist with managing the crisis. Consider these questions in regard to this circumstance:

- How might leaving clinically significant messages affect the dynamics of the person-to-person interactions during sessions? How might this impact the counseling relationship? Could this represent a change of service modality?
- If a client calls with the intent of venting on your voice mail and, in the process of venting, becomes even more overwhelmed, what are some other possible adverse consequences?
- If a client leaves information on voice mail that indicates a danger of harming self or others, what might be your responsibility?
- What if a client leaves a message on your voice mail with the expectation you will immediately respond to the crisis and fails to contact emergency services? What if the client follows through and does harm?
- What challenges might the counselor face in appropriately documenting the content of the voice mail in the client record?

As the preceding scenario demonstrates, clients should be provided information during the informed consent process concerning protocols for communicating with counselors via voice mail as well as resources to contact when the counselor is not available.

In addition to providing clients with structure concerning what is appropriate to record on the counselor's voice mail, counselors must also take steps to reduce the likelihood that client phone messages might be accessed by others. For example, a client might leave a message after agency hours on an answering machine. If the machine is located in an accessible place, other staff (e.g., security, cleaning staff) might be able to hear messages as these are recorded or might even be able to play back and listen to recorded messages, thus breaching client confidentiality. To address this risk, voice mail messaging machines should be placed in secured locations.

As noted previously, communicating outside face-to-face interactions via email and text messaging technology also poses significant concerns that should be discussed with clients. If substantial interactions take place between counselor and client through technological means that are not discussed as part of the informed consent process, these interactions could arguably fall outside the parameters of the established therapeutic modality. Clients who interact with their counselors using email through an office network should be made aware that others can directly access their messages. Clients who send email from a shared home computer should also consider that others may also have access to their messages (Recupero & Rainey, 2005). The counselor's limited ability to confirm the identity of clients when using text-based messaging takes on particular significance when considering treating minors and managing crisis situations. Even when clients are provided with an identification code to verify identity, the possibility exists that this code could be compromised, and the counselor might unknowingly breach confidentiality while interacting with a person who falsely presents as the client.

A unique challenge presented by text-based interaction is the lack of nonverbal cues facilitating communication. The use of emoticons or other nonverbal expressions such as <<laughing>> have limited utility in the therapeutic context and do not fully compensate for this challenge. In addition, the therapeutic intervention of calling attention to discrepancies between verbal and nonverbal messages when communicating via text-only interaction might literally be "virtually impossible."

Recupero and Rainey (2005) divided the risks associated with communicating with clients via the Internet into two categories: general security risks and content-specific risks. General security risks are represented by hackers who might intentionally intercept private information through unauthorized means. Also in this category are emails sent to the wrong address through inadvertent typos in the "to" field. Content-specific risks refer to "the 'unsanitized' nature of e-therapy communications" (p. 323) represented by exact transcripts of client emails. As has been noted previously, these artifacts might include inappropriate, irrelevant, or misleading information that should not be included in the client's clinical record, and the clinician should consider client welfare and best practice in deciding how such information might be appropriately documented.

Electronic records are increasingly being used by agencies and counselor education programs (Magruder et al., 2018). Electronic record programs designed specifically for mental health professionals, such as Therascribe, assist with not only documentation of counseling sessions, but also processes such as billing, diagnosis, and treatment planning. Although the benefits of such programs are substantial, so are the potential risks associated with their use. For example, access to client information typically requires the counselor to enter login information such as a username and password. If the counselor's login information is compromised, the client's records would then be accessible.

The process of keeping electronic records has potential risks as well. The ease of editing electronic word processing documents might suggest that making changes to previously documented entries in an electronic clinical record can be accomplished quickly and without detecting the change; however, under HIPAA, such changes could represent a serious violation of standards. HIPAA requires that covered entities protect the confidentiality information stored in electronic records against "reasonably anticipated threats." To address this requirement, electronic record-keeping systems commonly include safeguards to record system activity, identify security violations, and discover when documentation is destroyed or altered. It is critical that electronic health records are kept in compliance with HIPAA rules to avoid substantial penalties.

Another risk associated with electronic records is that when stored on a computer hard drive, any documents may be retrievable by others even if intentionally deleted by the counselor. Conversely, in the event of data corruption or the physical loss or destruction of hard disks, client records that are not also maintained as hard copies could be irretrievably lost. Electronic storage and backup devices should be subjected to the same double-lock guidelines as prescribed for paper-based records.

When Clients Request Their Records

According to the *ACA Code of Ethics* (2014), clients may request access to their records as decreed in B.6.d.

> B.6.d. Client Access Counselors provide reasonable access to records and copies of records when requested by competent clients. Counselors limit the access of clients to their records, or portions of their records, only when there is compelling evidence that such access would cause harm to the client. Counselors document the request of clients and the rationale for withholding some or all of the record in the files of clients. In situations involving multiple clients, counselors provide individual clients with only those parts of records that related directly to them and do not include confidential information related to any other client.
>
> (ACA, 2014)

Welfel (2015) noted that providing clients access to records is based on the foundational ethics principles of autonomy and beneficence; however, access to records does not necessarily mean files are immediately copied. There are several matters to consider. First of all, Welfel pointed out that when writing notes, it is a good idea to remember that a client could one day read the notes. A counselor who has kept this advice in mind will likely not have major concerns regarding the contents of the record. Remley and Herlihy (2020) stressed that records are kept for the benefit of the client, and the client should have access to such records. However, in the event that the counselor believes it would be detrimental for the client to see the records, the counselor can prevent access. In these cases, Remley and Herlihy suggest the following steps: (a) Explain why you believe it would be best if the client did not see the record and the client might retract his or her request; and (b) offer to make a summary of the record for the client rather than a copy. The client could still demand to see or have a copy of the records, and if the client takes legal action, the law will most likely be on the client's side regarding the client's right to record access. Counselors should document their reasons for not wanting to release information and should document that they explained these reasons to the client.

If the records contain confidential information related to other people, a situation that might occur in family or group counseling, the counselor should explain that releasing the records would infringe on the privacy of others. If the client refuses a summary of the part of the records related to them and still insists on having a copy of the records, the counselor should expunge from the copy all references to other people. Grossman and Koocher (2012) pointed out that to release unredacted copies of case records of couple or family counseling, the mental health practitioner would need to have written permission of each person discussed in the record. Before releasing any information, counselors must have the consent of the client for release (Grossman & Koocher, 2012; Remley & Herlihy, 2020). In legal situations, a camera review, whereby a judge or other impartial party goes over the records and identifies for release only those parts of the record that are pertinent, might be called for (Gladding, 2017). However, Stansbury (2010) pointed out that a camera review does have "the disadvantage of providing information to a judge out of context and without any foundation or explanation" (p. 537). Again, it cannot be stressed enough that counselors must be ever mindful of the fact that their client records could one day be read by the client or others. Strict observance of ethical best practice regarding documentation is crucial.

Under HIPAA, when releasing information about a client, counselors should release the minimum amount of essential information and not a copy of the entire file (DeLettre & Sobell, 2010, Grossman & Koocher, 2012). In addition to the protection provided by minimum disclosure, HIPAA also provides protection by allowing state laws that surpass the privacy protection of HIPAA to supersede HIPAA regulations, and by allowing the exemption of "psychotherapy notes" from being released, thus only requiring the release of the clinical record (Grossman & Koocher, 2012). Grossman and Koocher noted that the clinical record should consist of the following:

> 1. Medication prescription and monitoring; 2. Counseling session start and stop times (i.e. duration); 3. Modalities and frequencies of treatment; 4. Results of clinical tests (including raw test data); 5. Summaries of: a. Diagnosis, b. Functional status, c. Treatment plan, d. Symptoms, e. Prognosis, f. Progress to date.
>
> (p. 44)

The Family Educational Rights and Privacy Act (FERPA), which applies to public educational institutions as well as private educational institutions that receive federal funding, pertains to records at educational institutions. Regarding educational records, school officials should remain mindful that under FERPA, parents of minor students and students 18 years or older can request to view records and can challenge information contained in such records (Remley & Herlihy, 2020). Counselors may maintain clinical case notes separate from the educational records covered by FERPA, and these clinical case notes are not subject to FERPA. FERPA does contain a clause to allow the release of private information in emergency situations in the event that a student is a danger to self or others and the release of such information could protect the health and safety of others.

If a client brings a malpractice lawsuit or a complaint before a licensure board against a counselor, the client must sign a release and relinquish the right to confidentiality, and the client records will be released (Welfel, 2015). Counselors have a right to use client records to defend themselves in a lawsuit or an ethics complaint. However, Welfel stressed that counselors should be certain that the client has signed a release before using case information in a defense. Once again, it is wise to remember that your records could be seen and read by others, and you must have documented your treatment clearly, professionally, and ethically. Your defense will hinge on the extent to which you observed ethical best practice and standards of care. Failure to clearly document what transpired in the counseling relationship will mean that you have no defense. Remember—if it's not documented, it didn't happen.

Other Administrative Responsibilities

If a counselor works in a school or an agency, the school or agency is the custodian of the records. However, private practitioners must store and eventually properly destroy client records. The length of time a client record should be kept has been discussed previously in this chapter. What happens to the records of a counselor who dies? Again, if the counselor works in an agency or school, continuity of client care and the security of client records are assumed by the agency or school (Mills, 2012). However, private practitioners must address what will happen to their practice in the event of their death. Wheeler and Bertram (2019) pointed out the necessity of private practitioners appointing a records custodian who will assume the secure storage and disposal of client records on a counselor's death or incapacity. This is in keeping with section C.2.h. of the ACA (2014) *Code of Ethics*, which identifies the need for counselors to prepare in advance a plan by which the records custodian will appropriately carry out the transfer of files and clients. Thus, the designated custodian should also be able to contact clients and provide referrals, thereby ensuring ongoing care. The identity and role of the custodian should be outlined in the informed consent document. If a counselor dies without a custodian, the counselor's clients would be abandoned, and the confidentiality of their records could be comprised if the records are simply tossed into a dumpster or if the counselor's computer is sold with client information remaining on it. These types of actions could result in the counselor's estate being sued for breach of confidentiality.

When it is time to destroy a file, how should this take place? For paper records, the counselor, or an administrative clerk who has been trained in handling confidential information, should shred the documents to ensure that confidential material cannot be obtained. Electronic data should be deleted and then deleted again from the computer recycle bin. In addition, the data should be wiped or overwritten on the hard drive.

Summary

Although record keeping has always been important in counseling, the emergence of managed care and evidence-based practice has emphasized the necessity of appropriate documentation in counseling services. In addition, legal and regulatory requirements actually codify appropriate documentation into law, and the *ACA*'s *Code of Ethics* (ACA, 2014) contains specific directives regarding ethical and best practice in documentation and records. Developing and keeping proper client records is a counselor's ethical, legal, and clinical responsibility.

Progress notes document how a client is progressing in treatment and also provide documentation about what is happening in treatment sessions. Progress notes include goals for the session, which are linked to the treatment plan and can establish continuity of treatment. Progress notes should also include counselor interventions, client progress, and the counselor's clinical impressions. Finally, notes should contain an action goal connecting to the next session.

Process notes, also referred to as psychotherapy notes, are notes written by the counselor for the purpose of personal reflection. They can be useful for analyzing treatment impressions and can also be valuable in supervision. After relevant information has been obtained from process notes, it is recommended that they be destroyed.

A standard record format is the SOAP notes system. SOAP stands for Subjective, Objective, Assessment, and Plan. The Subjective section includes client perceptions of the problem and client report; the Objective section is factual and quantitative and includes written records and counselor observations. The Assessment section is the counselor's clinical and diagnostic impressions. Finally, the Plan section consists of an action plan and the prognosis. Beginning counselors often struggle with writing too much or not enough information. Reviewing examples of notes can help novice counselors to refine their ability to synthesize important elements into notes and also become familiar with agency protocols. It is important to keep in mind that certain situations in counseling call for more detail. For example, cases involving domestic violence or instances where a client indicates harm to self or others.

Clear inclusive documentation is imperative to appropriate practice; counselors should be knowledgeable in documentation procedures and schedule sufficient time for writing thorough notes that accurately reflect client treatment. The therapy record should be written immediately after the session to generate a precise record of therapy. In addition, by making time to write notes after the session, counselors are more likely to identify significant themes, and they also avoid the danger of end-of-the-day paperwork pileup.

5

Putting Ethics and Law Into Practice

by Lynn E. Linde and Bradley T. Erford

Preview

This chapter addresses some ethical and legal issues in counseling commonly encountered by counselors-in-training. As a professional counselor, you must always remember that how you conduct yourself personally and professionally reflects on not only yourself but also your colleagues and profession. Knowledge and understanding of the issues reviewed in this chapter are only a starting point. Keep up to date with the laws, ethics, policies, and procedures that govern professional practice in your state and workplace. The implementation of your professional responsibilities will require your undivided attention every day of your professional life.

Ethical Standards and Laws

The cornerstone of the counseling relationship rests on the public's trust in the services provided. Each professional counselor has an enormous responsibility to uphold the public trust and must seek high levels of training, education, and supervision in the ethical application of counseling practices. This is particularly essential in a profession such as counseling because counselors usually work with clients and students as lone professionals, often with little oversight and behind closed doors in confidential circumstances.

One of the greatest challenges facing most professional counselors daily is how to handle appropriately the many different ethical and legal situations they encounter. Because of the nature of counseling, professional counselors must be prepared to help clients who present a variety of challenges. At the beginning of your career, it is often difficult to know all you need to understand and be able to do. Numerous resources and sources of information can help guide professional counselors as they strive to assist clients in an ethical and legal manner. The professional associations for counselors have created ethical standards for professional behavior and provide a wealth of current information, resources, and training. Federal and state governments continually enact laws and regulations that affect counselors, including the judicial branch, in which courts hand down decisions that directly affect counselors' behavior. In addition, agencies, insurance companies, state boards of education, and local school systems create policies, guidelines, and procedures that counselors must follow.

Practicum students and interns are sometimes confused by the difference between ethical standards and laws and what one should do when these seem to be in conflict with each other. It may be helpful to take a look at the origin of both. **Ethical standards** are usually developed by professional associations to guide the behavior of a specific group of professionals. According to Herlihy and Corey (2014), ethical standards serve three purposes: to educate members about sound ethical conduct, to provide a mechanism for accountability, and to serve as a means for improving professional practice. Ethical standards change and are updated periodically to ensure their relevance and appropriateness.

Ethical standards are based on generally accepted norms, beliefs, customs, and values. Codes of ethics ordinarily are based on Kitchener's five moral principles of autonomy, justice, beneficence, nonmaleficence, and fidelity (Forester-Miller & Davis, 2016). Autonomy refers to the concept of independence and the ability to make one's own decisions. Professional counselors need to respect the right of clients to make their own decisions based on their personal values and beliefs, and not impose their values on clients. Justice means treating each person fairly, but it does not mean treating each person the same way. Rather, counselors should treat clients according to the client needs. Beneficence refers to doing good or what is in the best interests of the client. In counseling, it also incorporates the concept of removing conditions that might cause harm. Nonmaleficence means doing no harm to others. Finally, fidelity involves the concepts

DOI: 10.4324/9781003305521-5

of loyalty, faithfulness, and honoring commitments. This means that professional counselors must honor all obligations to the client. ACA (2014) added a sixth principle to the *Code of Ethics*, veracity, which basically means that counselors behave and respond truthfully in all professional interactions.

Laws are also based on these same, generally accepted norms, beliefs, customs, and values. However, laws are more prescriptive, have been incorporated into code, and carry greater sanctions or penalties for failure to comply. Laws and ethical standards exist to ensure the appropriate behavior of professionals within a particular context to ensure that the best interests of the client are met. When ethics and laws seem to be in conflict, the professional counselor must attempt to resolve the conflict in a responsible manner (Cottone & Tarvydas, 2021). Professional counselors must make their clients aware of this conflict. Because there are greater penalties associated with laws, the counselor will often follow the legal course of action if there is no harm to the client. Many ethical standards recognize that other mandates must be followed and suggest that professional counselors work to change mandates that are not in the best interests of their clients. Self-Assessment Activity 5.1 provides an opportunity to explore the nuances of an ethical/legal conflict.

Ethics in Clinical Practice

Professional codes of ethics form the foundation of effective, moral practice. This section highlights the essential practice elements of the American Counseling Association's (ACA's) *Code of Ethics* (2014), American School Counselor Association's (ASCA's) *Ethical Standards for School Counselors* (2016), American Mental Health Counselors Association's (AMHCA's) *Principles for AMHCA's Code of Ethics* (2020), and the American Association of Marriage and Family Therapists (AAMFT; 2022) and International Association of Marriage and Family Counselors (IAMFC; Hendricks et al., 2011) codes of ethics. Whereas the ACA *Code of Ethics* serves to promote ethical practice across all disciplines and settings of the counseling profession, other associations' codes of ethics and guidelines speak more directly to their specialty area and setting. For example, the ASCA's *Ethical Standards for School Counselors* discusses what ethical behavior consists of in a school setting, whereas the *Principles for AMHCA's Code of Ethics* applies specifically to agency and private practice settings.

Many professional counselors belong to multiple organizations, each of which may have its own code of ethics. They may also hold credentials from organizations or state credentialing boards that have a code of ethics as well. Many counselors are National Certified Counselors, a credential offered by the National Board for Counselor Certification, Inc. (NBCC), which also has a code of ethics. Although most of the specific ethic provisions align across codes, differences do exist. It is often hard to know which code takes precedence. Although each professional will have to make that determination individually, there are two general guidelines. First, what is the setting in which one is practicing (e.g., school, clinic), and is there a particular code that applies specifically to that setting? Second, in what capacity (e.g., licensed professional counselor, marriage and family therapist, certified school counselor) is the professional operating? So, if you are a marriage and family counselor working in an agency, the IAMFC or AAMFT codes may be most applicable, whereas the ACA or AMHCA codes may be most applicable if working in a university counseling center. In addition, all codes are similar, and all concern behaving in an appropriate professional manner, operating in the best interests of the client, and practicing within the scope of one's education, training, and experience. If a professional counselor is doing all these things, the existence of multiple codes of ethics should not be a significant issue. Because the ACA *Code of Ethics* is a more comprehensive and encompassing code, summaries of the main emphases of the ACA code will be provided. However, the practicum student or intern should review the ACA code and the specific applicable practice setting code in depth to become familiar with all expectations for professional conduct.

American Counseling Association Code of Ethics

The ACA revises its *Code of Ethics* about every ten years. The seventh and most recent revision took effect in 2014 and reflects some significant changes from the 2005 *Code of Ethics*. Each section begins with an introduction, which sets the tone for that section and is a beginning point for discussion (ACA, 2014). Parts of the ACA *Code of Ethics* have been updated to reflect the current thinking and practice in the field, and several new issues were added, such as an increased focus on the use of technology and social media in counseling and electronic records. The six main purposes of the 2014 *Code of Ethics* include:

> The *Code*
> 1. The *Code* sets forth the ethical obligations of ACA members and provides guidance intended to inform the ethical practice of professional counselors. 2. The *Code* identifies ethical considerations relevant to professional counselors and counselors-in-training. 3. The *Code* enables the association to clarify for current and prospective members, and for those served by members, the nature of the ethical responsibilities held in common by its members. 4. The *Code* serves as an ethical guide designed to assist members in constructing a course of action that best serves those utilizing counseling services and establishes expectations of conduct with a primary emphasis on the role of the professional counselor. 5. The *Code* helps to support the mission of ACA. [and] 6. The standards contained in this Code serve as the basis for processing inquiries and ethics complaints concerning ACA members.
>
> (p. 3)

The 2014 ACA *Code of Ethics* can be viewed at www.counseling.org/docs/default-source/ethics/2014-code-of-ethics.pdf?sfvrsn=2d58522c_4. It addresses the responsibilities of professional counselors toward their clients, colleagues, workplace, and themselves by delineating the ideal standards for conducting one's behavior. All members of ACA are required to abide by the *Code of Ethics* as a condition of membership, and action is taken against any member who fails to do so. In effect, as these are the ethical standards of the profession, all professional counselors are held to the *Code of Ethics* by the mental health community, regardless of whether they are members of the ACA.

The *Code of Ethics* is divided into nine areas: (A) The Counseling Relationship; (B) Confidentiality and Privacy; (C) Professional Responsibility; (D) Relationships with Other Professionals; (E) Evaluation, Assessment, and Interpretation; (F) Supervision, Training, and Teaching; (G) Research and Publication; (H) Distance Counseling, Technology, and Social Media; and (I) Resolving Ethical Issues. Each of these areas details specific counselor responsibilities and standards. In general, the *Code of Ethics* discusses respecting one's client and the background each client brings to the counseling setting; maintaining professional behavior with clients and other professionals; practicing with the best interests of the client in mind; and practicing within the limits of one's training, experience, and education. Section H provides direction for members resolving ethical dilemmas. Highlights from each of these areas are summarized next, but at this point, readers should locate the actual ACA *Code of Ethics* on the ACA website and peruse it in detail.

Section A: The Counseling Relationship

A key issue addressed in this section is boundaries with clients and dual relationships. The period of time that a professional counselor and former client must wait to engage in romantic or sexual relationships was changed from two to five years, and the language was expanded to include not just clients, but also romantic partners or family members of former clients. This change highlighted the vulnerable nature of clients in a helping relationship. Although nonprofessional relationships with clients outside the formal counseling relationship ordinarily should be avoided, the current *Code* recognizes that this is not always possible and also recognizes that nonprofessional relationships with clients may even benefit clients (e.g., attending formal ceremonies, hospital visits, membership in community organizations, commerce), albeit when conducted with caution.

Continued emphasis was placed on critical issues, including general client welfare and avoiding harm, appropriate termination of services (see Chapter 11), fees and bartering, and informed consent. The informed consent provision is particularly important because many state counseling boards now require written consent so that clients can choose a counseling relationship with a qualified provider from an informed consumer position. Section A.2.b specifies that informed consent includes, but is not limited to, purposes, goals, techniques, procedures, limitations, potential risks, and benefits of services; the counselor's qualifications, credentials, and relevant experience; the intended use of tests and reports, fees, and billing arrangements; the right to confidentiality and limitations; the continuation of services should the counselor become incapacitated; obtaining clear information about their records; participating in ongoing treatment planning; and the right to refuse treatment at any time and the potential consequences for doing so. In addition, the *Code* addresses the need to balance assent from minors and others incapable of giving consent without the assent of parents and family members who hold the legal rights of consent, protection, and decision making on their behalf. Examples of informed consent forms that address these are provided in Table 5.1.

Table 5.1 Professional disclosure statement*

Bradley T. Erford, PhD
Address
Telephone Numbers & Email

I welcome you as a new client, and I look forward to working with you. The purpose of this form is to let you know about my approach to counseling, what you can expect from counseling, and my background. This form will also give you an opportunity to give consent for counseling or assessment services.

In my view, the relationship of feelings and thoughts to behavior is crucial to understanding the issues that affect being successful in life. I use a variety of strategies that can help people make sense of their world, strategies that are mostly humanistic and cognitive-behavioral in nature; that is, they are strategies based on the notion people often experience personal difficulties because of relationship issues, and that the way people think about and see themselves and the world influences how they feel and behave. You will be encouraged to engage in strategies to address these issues both during and between our sessions.

Individual counseling offers you a chance to express ideas and concerns to understand your situation better and learn new ways to solve problems. However, there are risks and limitations to counseling. At times, you might experience feelings that are uncomfortable and hard to face. I often compare this process to taking medicine: it may not taste great, but it also is usually better for you in the long run. I will do my best to provide an accurate and fair assessment and diagnosis that will help guide our treatment planning and goal setting. We will also discuss this assessment/diagnosis and your resulting treatment plan/goals throughout the counseling process. Counseling is a collaborative process done with your best interests in mind and the ultimate goal is for you to reach a level of healthy and independent personal functioning.

Of course, you have the right to refuse or terminate treatment at any time, and should you believe either of these options appropriate, I hope you will discuss the potential benefits and risks associated with your decision with me. If at any time I become unavailable to continue providing services to you as a result of incapacitation or other cause, I will help transition you to another mental health care provider who can either continue treatment or ensure appropriate referral so that your best interests are served.

I specialize in working with children, adolescents, and their families, and provide psychoeducational assessment, as well as individual, group, and family counseling. I am particularly experienced in working with individuals presenting with disruptive, anxious, and depressed behaviors, as well as individuals experiencing learning, divorce, or grief adjustment difficulties, or in need of stress management.

Everything you discuss with me will be kept confidential by me except matters pertaining to (1) suicide or harm to another person; (2) physical/sexual abuse or neglect of minors, persons with disabilities, and the elderly; (3) legal activity resulting in a court order; and (4) anything else as required by law. For those matters, legally and ethically, I would have to break confidentiality and involve others. Except for these conditions, any written information or report that I possess cannot be shared, orally or in writing, with another individual or agency without your express written permission. Tests are administered and reports are produced to facilitate personal diagnosis and treatment. Of course, I would be willing to share information with any other professional or agency that you wish, provided that you sign a written release-of-information form, which I can provide for you. Alternatively, you may share results from written reports or sessions at your discretion because confidentiality applies to my communications, not yours. Ethically guiding my behavior is the ACA *Code of Ethics* published by the American Counseling Association in Alexandria, VA, the National Board for Certified Counselors (NBCC, Inc.), and the Code of Ethics adopted by the Maryland Board of Professional Counselors and Therapists. Legally, I adhere to U.S. and Maryland statutes.

As for my background, I have been a licensed professional counselor since 1988. I earned my bachelor's degree (BS) in biology from Grove City College (PA), master's degree (MA) in school psychology from Bucknell University (PA), and PhD in counselor education from the University of Virginia. I am a member of the American Counseling Association, and I am a licensed clinical professional counselor (LCPC), which allows me to practice mental health counseling in Maryland. My LCPC state license was issued by the Board of Professional Counselors and Therapists in Baltimore, MD. I also am a national certified counselor (NCC), which is a designation given by the National Board for Certified Counselors (NBCC).

As far as counseling/assessment session fees are concerned, I charge $____ per hour. This same rate applies to time spent on providing special services, such as court appearances. Cost for a standard psychoeducational assessment is $_____, which includes a written report and up to 1 hour for a feedback/interpretation consultation session. I do not participate with third-party payers, such as managed care organizations and insurance companies. By signing this form, you are agreeing to pay this fee on the day the service is provided. Missed appointments without a 24-hour notice will have to be paid for, except for genuine emergencies.

(*Continued*)

Table 5.1 (Continued)

I have attached a business card to this letter. Please feel free to contact me at any time during business hours. If I am unavailable, you can leave a message, and I will get back to you as soon as possible. In the event of an emergency, please call 911 or go to the nearest emergency room.

I hope that you will find this counseling experience to be successful and, in some ways, enjoyable. I thank you very much for taking time to read this. Please sign below to indicate your consent to pursue counseling or assessment services.

Bradley T. Erford, PhD, LCPC, NCC

LC#

Contact Information:

Board of Professional Counselors and Therapists 4201 Patterson Avenue Baltimore, MD 21215–2299 410–764–4732	American Counseling Association 5999 Stevenson Avenue Alexandria, VA 22304 800–347–6647

Note: You do not have to sign this; you have the right to refuse counseling or psychoeducational assessment.

I, ________________________, fully understand what I have just read and offer my consent for counseling or psychoeducational assessment, free of any pressure to do so. Here is my signature and the date of the signature (that expires one year from now).

____ Signature	__________________ Date
____ Signature of a custodial parent is required in cases where the child/adolescent is a minor	__________________ Date

Source: *This information is required by the Board of Professional Counselors and Therapists, which regulates all licensed clinical professional counselors in Maryland. You can contact the Board at Board of Professional Counselors and Therapists, 4201 Patterson Avenue, Baltimore, MD 21215–2299, or 410–764–4732.

Section A also includes standards for serving the terminally ill and facilitating end-of-life decisions, making the ACA one of the first national associations to address these issues. In doing so, the ACA directs counselors to receive adequate supervision and seek multiple professional collaborations and help clients to exercise self-determination and participate maximally in decision making.

Section B: Confidentiality and Privacy

Several major changes were made to the confidentiality and privacy section of the *Code of Ethics*. Standard B.1.a reminds professional counselors to maintain sensitivity and awareness of cultural meanings of privacy and confidentiality. Counselors should also be respectful of differing views and inform clients with whom, when, and how information will be shared. Another addition was Standard B.3.e, which took into consideration the transmission of confidential information and reflected the growing use of technology throughout the counseling process. This Standard advised counselors to take precautions to ensure confidentiality when using technologies such as computers, electronic mail, or voice mail. Confidentiality and privileged communication are covered more comprehensively later in the chapter.

A new and important addition was Standard B.3.f, which asserted that professional counselors should maintain the confidentiality of deceased clients as is consistent with legal requirements and policies. Another significant change involved Standard B.4.b, Couples and Family Counseling. The *Code* stated that professional counselors must clearly recognize who is considered to be "the client," must discuss limitations and expectations of confidentiality during couples and family counseling, and should seek and document an agreement with all involved parties as to their individual rights to confidentiality or obligations to protect the confidentiality of the known information.

Finally, Section B.5 was expounded on to address confidentiality and privacy when counseling clients who are minors or adults lacking the capacity to give informed consent. Professional counselors are directed to inform parents and legal guardians of the confidential nature of the counseling relationship as well as to establish a working relationship with them to serve clients better. Counselors must also seek permission from the appropriate parties to disclose information. When working with this specific population, counselors are reminded to uphold written policies, federal and state laws, and ethical standards as applicable.

Voices From the Field 5.1 Managing Boundary Issues in Counseling, *by Victoria E. Kress*

As I pulled into my driveway, I noticed someone lying in the grass on my front lawn. My initial reaction was, "That's strange." I went into the house and peered out the window only to realize it was one of my clients. My next reaction was, "Wow, this is creepy. Do I call the police? Do I go and talk to her? How did she know where I live? Why is she on my lawn?" Sadly, in graduate school, no one had taught me what to do when situations like this arise.

When in doubt, peer supervision is always the way to go. So I called my friend who is a counselor, but she didn't answer the phone. I thought about calling the state counseling board to consult, but it was a Saturday and no one there was working. I considered reviewing my ethics textbook from graduate school, but I knew the answer couldn't be found there.

Knowing this client was unpredictable and volatile, worst-case scenarios went through my head: "Is she going to attempt suicide on my lawn? Is she going to harm me and my dog?" As I pondered my options, she left. She ostensibly wanted me to know that she had been there, and once that end was met, she was able to leave.

What to do next? Naturally, I decided to address the issue with my client. "Tell me about what was going on when you were laying on my lawn Saturday." She was coy in her explanation of why she was at my home, but I was direct in my response. I set boundaries with her and explained the importance to her—and to me—of her honoring those boundaries. We discussed that if she couldn't navigate those boundaries and regulate her affect around our relationship, we would need to explore finding a counselor with whom she could have a more successful therapeutic relationship. As her core issues were related to self and other boundaries, the experience did provide good fodder in helping her work toward reaching her goals. Thankfully, she did not return to my lawn.

Section C: Professional Responsibility

This section continues to place emphasis on issues such as professional competence, advertising and soliciting clients, professional qualifications, and public responsibility. One area that was significantly expanded on involves counselor impairment (Standard C.2.g). Professional counselors must be alert to signs of personal impairment and refrain from providing or offering services if the impairment could potentially harm a client. If the problem reaches the level of professional impairment, the counselor should seek assistance. Professional counselors are now also required to assist supervisors or colleagues in recognizing impairment and, if necessary, to provide assistance, intervention, or consultation.

Standard C.2.h was added to address further the issue of counselor impairment or subsequent termination of practice. This standard states that counselors should follow a prepared plan for the transfer of files and clients when they leave a practice. Counselors need to designate a specific colleague or "records custodian" and create a proper plan for file and client transfer in the case of their incapacitation, termination of practice, or death.

Standard C.7 acknowledges that professional counselors must use techniques, modalities, or procedures that have a scientific or empirical foundation and are grounded in theory. If not, counselors should note their procedures or techniques to be "unproven" or "developing." The potential risks and ethical considerations of the procedures or techniques should be explained to the client, and counselors should take all necessary steps to protect the client from any potential harm. Counselors are still required to monitor their effectiveness and take any necessary actions to improve as professionals.

Section D: Relationships With Other Professionals

This section stresses the importance of interaction and relationships between counselors and other professionals. Professional counselors should become knowledgeable about their colleagues and develop positive working relationships and communication systems. It is also recognized that counselors may often be a part of an interdisciplinary team. Several standards reflect this development.

Professional counselors are reminded to be respectful of differing approaches to counseling services and the traditions and practices of other professional groups (Standard D.1.a). Standards D.1.b and D.1.c specifically address interdisciplinary relationships and teamwork, respectively. Professional counselors must work to develop and strengthen relationships with interdisciplinary colleagues. Professional counselors must also keep focused on how best to serve their clients when working in a team environment. To do so, counselors can contribute to and partake in any decisions that could potentially affect the well-being of clients using the values, experiences, and perspectives of the counseling profession and other disciplines. When working with an interdisciplinary team, it is the counselor's responsibility to clarify the ethical and professional obligations of individual members and the whole team. Professional counselors are encouraged to attempt to resolve ethical concerns initially within the team. If a resolution cannot be made within the team, counselors should pursue other means to address the concerns consistent with the well-being of the client.

Section E: Evaluation, Assessment, and Interpretation

A noticeable change to this section involved the replacement of the word *tests* with *assessment*, which has a more integrative and broader connotation. In addition, "career assessment" was added to several standards, and further details were included. For example, Standard E.1.a now includes specific examples of measurements, including but not limited to "educational, mental health, psychological, and career assessments" (ACA, 2014, p. 11) It is still recognized that assessment is only one part of the overall counseling process, and that professional counselors must consider cultural, social, and personal factors.

Historical and Social Prejudices in the Diagnosis of Pathology (Standard E.5.c) states that professional counselors should be aware of social and historical prejudices in the pathologizing and misdiagnosis of historically oppressed individuals and groups. In addition, counselors should be cognizant of the role of mental health professionals in the continuation of these problems. Not only does the revised ACA *Code of Ethics* take into consideration historical factors, but it was also changed to reflect the current trends in counseling.

The inclusion of Section E.13, Forensic Evaluation: Evaluation for Legal Proceedings, denotes the increased presence of professional counselors in legal proceedings and subsequent legal matters. This new section outlines the primary obligations for counselors, the consent for evaluation, and the necessity to avoid potentially harmful relationships regarding forensic evaluations. The primary obligation of professional counselors conducting forensic evaluations is to generate objective findings that are supported by appropriate techniques and information. Counselors are entitled to form their own professional opinions but must define any limitations in their testimonies or reports.

Section F: Supervision, Training, and Teaching

Section F now encompasses more than three pages within the ACA (2014) *Code of Ethics*, but the focus remains on fostering professional relationships and creating appropriate boundaries between supervisors and practicum students or interns. The ethical obligations of both parties are clearly set forth, and counselors should be accurate, honest, and fair during the training and assessment of students. Areas of focus include counselor supervision and client welfare, counselor supervision competence, supervisory relationships, supervisor responsibilities, counseling evaluation and remediation, responsibilities of counselor educators, student welfare and responsibilities, evaluation and remediation of students, roles and relationships between educators and students, and multicultural/diversity competence in counselor education and training programs. As with Section A, Section F includes standards to address the change from dual relationships to potentially beneficial relationships between counselor educators or supervisors and students.

Section G: Research and Publication

An important change from previous versions is replacement of the term *human subjects* with *research participants*. The revised *Code* also recognizes that independent researchers who may lack access to an Institutional Review Board might also design and conduct research programs. These independent researchers are advised to seek out and consult with researchers who are acquainted with Institutional Review Board procedures to make appropriate safeguards available to research participants.

Further additions or clarifications include the disposal of research documents and records of relationships with research participants when there are intensive or extended interactions. Professional counselors are obligated to take the appropriate steps to destroy any documents or records that contain confidential data or may identify research participants within a reasonable period after the completion of a research study or project. Section G.3 outlines the restrictions on relationships with research participants that include nonprofessional relationships, sexual or romantic interactions, and sexual harassment, as well as potentially beneficial interactions.

Finally, in the publication section Standard G.5.b specifically states that professional counselors do not plagiarize or present another person's work as their own. In addition, the standard concerning professional review of documents presented for publication was expanded to include making valid publication decisions, reviewing materials in a timely manner, avoiding biases, and evaluating only those documents that fall within one's field of competency.

Section H: Distance Counseling, Technology, and Social Media

Section H is new to the ACA (2014) *Code of Ethics* because of the rise in importance of technological issues in counseling and addresses issues of technology in providing counseling services, record keeping, research applications, and use of social media. It recognizes that counseling is no longer always in person and was a timely addition that was tested throughout the COVID-19 pandemic when nearly all counseling and counselor training went online for months to in some cases more than a year. These timely guidelines helped counselors navigate counseling through a variety of modalities. Counselors must become knowledgeable about various resources to help continue navigation of various technology-based counseling modalities, and the benefits and challenges of using technology in counseling, especially the challenges to confidentiality and the ethical and legal requirements of use of technology.

Section H.1 addresses the legal and knowledge considerations. Clients have the right to decide upon the use of technology in counseling and such provisions should be included in the informed consent process. Limitations of confidentiality when using technology must be shared with the client (H.2.c) and counselors must use appropriate encryption (H.2.d). Counselors take precautions to accurately verify the identity of the client when employing distance counseling, social media, or other forms of technology (H.3, H.4).

Boundary maintenance is especially important when employing distance counseling, social media, and other forms of technology. Counselors must maintain professional boundaries (H.4.b) and separate their personal and professional presence on social media (H.6.c). Counselors must receive the consent of a client before viewing client information on social media or on Internet Web sites. Counselors must also avoid public disclosures on social media of client information. Section H recognizes that technology and communication continue to evolve but solidifies the stance that counselors must maintain client confidentiality. Thus, counselors must stay abreast of ethical and legal applications to the use of emerging technologies to practice.

Section I: Resolving Ethical Issues

This final section provides information and suggestions pertaining to the resolution of ethical issues. Standard I.1.c states that if there is a conflict between ethical responsibilities and laws, professional counselors should make known their commitment to the *Code of Ethics* and work to alleviate the conflict. Counselors may follow legal requirements or regulations if the ethical conflict cannot be resolved in this manner.

Procedural details were increased for professional counselors reporting a suspected ethical violation (Standard I.2.b). When informal resolution is inappropriate for an ethical violation, or the issue is not correctly resolved, professional counselors are directed to seek further action, such as referring to voluntary national certification bodies, state or national ethics committees, state licensing boards, or any suitable institutional authorities. It is further stated that this standard is not applicable if a professional counselor has been retained to review the work of the counselor who is in question, or if it would violate any confidentiality rights.

The addition of Standard I.2.f states that professional counselors absolutely should not deny a person's advancement, admission to academic programs, employment, promotion, or tenure based only on their having made an ethics complaint or being the subject of an ethics complaint. This standard provides some protection against unfair discrimination for counselors who have made an ethics complaint or been the subject of one. In addition to the ACA, other counseling organizations have established codes of ethics.

AMHCA Code of Ethics

The *Principles for AMHCA Code of Ethics* (2020) can be viewed online at www.amhca.org/publications/ethics. The AMHCA code aligns consistently with the ACA *Code of Ethics* (2014) and is structured into six sections:

Section I—Commitment to Clients, which includes counselor–client relationship (primary responsibility, confidentiality, dual/multiple relationships, exploitive relationships), counseling process (counseling plans, informed consent, multiple clients, clients served by others, termination and referral, technology-assisted counseling, clients' rights, end-of-life care for terminally ill clients), counselor responsibility and integrity (competence, nondiscrimination, conflict of interest), assessment and diagnosis (selection and administration, interpretation and reporting, competence, forensic activity), record keeping, fee arrangements, and bartering, and other roles (consultant, advocate); Section II—Commitment to Other Professionals, which includes relationship with colleagues and clinical consultation; Section III—Commitment to Students, Supervisees, and Employee Relationships; Section IV—Commitment to the Profession, which includes teaching, research and publications and service on public or private boards and other organizations; Section V—Commitment to the Public, which includes public statements and advertising; and Section VI—Resolution of Ethical Problems.

The ethical provisions in the AMHCA code are directed at mental health counselors who work in diverse institutional, agency, and private settings. As a result, the statements often clarify practice behaviors in those settings. For example, AMHCA (2020) states, "Information received about a client by another agency or person should not be forwarded to another person or agency without the client's written permission" (p. 2), a provision that fosters compliance with the Health Insurance Portability and Accountability Act (HIPAA) of 1996. The code also specifies that "When CMHCs choose to exceed state minimum requirements for maintaining records, they must notify clients in their informed consent" (p. 11).

Mental health counselors do not enter a counseling relationship with a client being served by another mental health professional unless all parties are aware of and consent to the service arrangement. Likewise, counselors protect client confidentiality as they create, maintain, store, transfer, and dispose of client records and should plan for client termination procedures due to counselor death or incapacity by assigning a custodian to help transfer clients and files. In each of these instances, clients should be offered appropriate referrals. In addition, AMHCA offers a helpful listing of what supervisors of practicum students, interns, and graduate licensees in training should include in a signed supervision informed consent document (Section III.A, p. 14).

A particularly helpful section of the AMHCA code is I.B.7—Clients' Rights. The client informed consent provision indicates that clients must be informed of their rights (I.B.2.b), and the following section provides succinct provisions for a client informed consent document:

> *7. **Clients' Rights.*** Clients have the right to be treated with dignity, consideration, and respect at all times. Clients have the right to:
>
> a. Quality services provided by concerned, trained professionals and competent staff.
> b. Confidentiality within the limits of both federal and state law, to be informed about the exceptions to confidentiality, and to expect that no information will be released without the client's knowledge and written consent.
> c. Information such as time of sessions, payment plans/fees, absences, access, emergency procedures, third-party reimbursement procedures, termination and referral procedures, and advanced notice of the use of collection agencies.
> d. Clear information about the purposes and goals of counseling.
> e. Appropriate information regarding the CMHC's education, training, and practice limitations.
> f. Full, knowledgeable, and responsible participation in the ongoing treatment plan to the maximum extent feasible.
> g. Obtain information about their case record and to have this information explained clearly and directly.
> h. Request information and/or consultation regarding the progress of their therapy.
> i. Refuse any recommended services, techniques, or approaches and to be advised of the consequences of this action.
> j. A safe environment for counseling free of emotional, physical, or sexual abuse.
> k. A clearly defined termination process, and to discontinue therapy at any time.
>
> (p. 7)

Codes of Ethics From Marriage, Couple, and Family Counseling Organizations

Two marriage, couple, and family counseling organizations have published codes of ethics. The International Association of Marriage and Family Counselors (IAMFC) is a division of the ACA, and the IAMFC code

(International Association of Marriage and Family Counselors [IAMFC], 2017) is consistent with the ACA code. It can be viewed online at www.iamfconline.org/ethics. The IAMFC code outlines nine sections: A. The Counseling Relationship and Client Well-Being; B. Confidentiality and Privacy; C. Competence and Professional Responsibility; D. Collaboration and Professional Relationships; E. Assessment and Evaluation; F. Counselor Education and Supervision; G. Research and Publication; H. Ethical Decision Making and Resolution; and I. Diversity.

The American Association for Marriage and Family Therapists (AAMFT) also publishes a code of ethics (2022), which can be viewed online at www.aamft.org/Legal_Ethics/Code_of_Ethics.aspx. The AAMFT code outlines nine principles: I. Responsibility to Clients; II. Confidentiality; III. Professional Competence and Integrity; IV. Responsibility to Students and Supervisees; V. Research and Publication; VI. Technology-Assisted Professional Services; VII. Professional Evaluations; VII. Financial Arrangements; and IX. Advertising. The IAMFC and AAMFT codes each address the diverse work settings of marriage, couple, and family counselors, but modify the previously discussed codes to the family context.

The American School Counselor Association (ASCA) Ethical Standards for School Counselors

The ASCA (2016) developed a parallel set of ethical standards that specifically addresses counseling practice in the schools. These standards discuss putting the counselee's best interests first, treating each student as an individual and with respect, involving parents as appropriate, maintaining one's expertise through ongoing professional development and learning, and behaving professionally and ethically. There are six sections of the ASCA *Ethical Standards for School Counselors*, which are meant to guide the ethical practice of school counselors, provide self-appraisal and evaluation information by peers, and inform stakeholders of responsible counselor behaviors. Although many of the provisions overlap with the ACA *Code of Ethics* explained earlier, what follows is a discussion of additions, extensions, and clarifications provided in the ASCA code.

A. Responsibilities to Students

School counselors are concerned with and make available to students comprehensive, developmental, data-driven programs that address the academic, career, and personal–social needs of all students. They respect and accept the diverse cultural and individual values and beliefs of students and do not impose their own values on the students or students' families.

School counselors disclose the limits of confidentiality and gain informed consent as appropriate. Confidentiality and informed consent are challenging issues when dealing with minor children, and school counselors involve important persons and support networks and consider laws, regulations, and policies, as appropriate to ensure that parents/guardians are active partners in their minor child's school experiences. School counselors acknowledge and support the parent's legal and inherent rights. When students participate in small-group counseling experiences, school counselors notify parents/guardians. As with adult clients, a student's right to confidentiality is surrendered when the student presents serious and foreseeable harm to self or others.

School counselors use brief, solution-focused approaches when possible and strive to maintain an appropriate professional distance from students so as not to engage in a dual relationship that would jeopardize the effectiveness of the primary counseling relationship. School counselors especially avoid online social networking relationships with students through various communication mediums. School counselors also take steps to ensure that students understand the nature of and how to report the occurrence of cyberbullying.

School counselors separately store sole-possession notes used as memory aids and destroy these notes when the student transfers to another school or school level, or graduates. If the notes may possibly be needed in a future court proceeding, the school counselor uses best judgment in the maintenance of these sole-possession records. This issue of sole-possession notes is covered in more detail later in this chapter.

B. Responsibilities to Parents/Guardians, School, and Self

School counselors establish appropriate collaborative relationships with parents and respect parental rights and responsibilities. Unless prevented by court order, school counselors honor parental requests for student records and periodic reports. This especially applies to noncustodial parents who may ask for periodic performance reports that the custodial parent may chose not to provide. Legally, a noncustodial parent is allowed access to the student's information, unless a judge has ordered otherwise.

As an advocate for all students within the school community, school counselors notify appropriate officials of conditions that systematically limit the effectiveness of the school counseling program or other curricular components. School counselors also engage in community partnerships to obtain resources that support their comprehensive program and promote student success. School counselors advocate for the hiring of only qualified and appropriately trained school counselors and only accept employment for a position for which they are qualified.

As do all counselors, school counselors function within the boundaries of their training and experience. They are responsible for maintaining physical and mental self-care and wellness and engage in continuous personal and professional growth throughout their careers. This presumes that school counselors will remain current with research and practice innovations in broad areas that influence school counseling practice (e.g., advocacy, cultural competence, technology, leadership, assessment data). Recall that as counselors become more experienced, the standard of care expectations increase. Thus, as school counselors become more experienced, the expectations for their ethical and legal performance also increase. School counselors use culturally inclusive language, create equity-based programs that promote the performance and achievement of all students, and maintain current membership in professional associations.

C. School Counselor Administrators/Supervisors

District-level school counselor supervisors and administrators make sure that resources are distributed fairly to school counselors and school counseling programs, which include opportunities for professional development. Supervisors/administrators make sure that school counselors under their supervision adhere to ASCA ethical standards and address/eliminate systemic barriers to ethical practice. Supervisors/administrators ensure their school counselors implement data-driven, competencies-based comprehensive school counseling programs, and understand release-of-information procedures.

D. School Counseling Intern Site Supervisors

Site supervisors must be appropriately educated, trained, experienced, and licensed or certified prior to committing to supervise a school counseling intern. Site supervisors also acknowledge the numerous responsibilities needed to support interns, including an understanding of school counseling ethics, comprehensive developmental school counseling programs, performance assessment, cultural competence, technological competence, virtual counseling and supervision practices, and procedures for communicating with university faculty and supervisors to evaluate, remediate, and express concerns about intern performance. Site supervisors do not supervise close acquaintances, friends, or family members.

E. Maintenance of Standards

This section provides school counselors with specific guidance on how to handle ethical dilemmas in the field and by colleagues. It is important that school counselors work through the appropriate channels and steps to remedy ethical challenges. Although a colleague who behaves in an unethical manner is problematic and needs to be addressed when evident, ethical codes and hearing committees often serve an educative function to promote high standards and good practice. These procedures are relatively common across ethical codes of conduct and will be addressed more comprehensively in the next section.

F. Ethical Decision Making

The ethical decision-making steps suggested by ASCA include:

> Define the problem. . . . Apply ASCA Ethical Standards and law . . . consider . . . developmental levels . . . setting, parental rights and minors' rights . . . apply beneficence, autonomy, nonmaleficence, loyalty and justice. . . . Determine potential courses of action and their consequences. . . . Evaluate the selected action. . . . Consult [and]. . . . Implement the course of action (p. 8).

Self-Assessment Activities 5.1 and 5.2 will help you integrate the information on ethical and legal issues in counseling and apply ethical decision-making principles to numerous scenarios.

Self-Assessment Activity 5.1 Discerning Ethical Actions

Place a checkmark in the appropriate column. How ethical is it for a professional counselor to?

	Never	Rarely	Sometimes	Usually	Always
1. Barter with a client for services.					
2. Invite a client to a personal party or social event.					
3. Provide counseling to a friend who is in a crisis.					
4. Accept a gift from a client if the gift is worth less than $10.					
5. Accept a gift from a client if the gift is worth more than $50.					
6. Accept a client's invitation to a special event.					
7. Go out for coffee with a client after a counseling session.					
8. Become friends with a client after termination of the counseling relationship.					
9. Give the home phone number to a client.					
10. Share personal experiences as a member of a self-help group when a client is in attendance.					
11. Occasionally hire a client to baby-sit.					

Self-Assessment Activity 5.2 Understanding the ACA Code of Ethics

Answer the following questions regarding the ACA *Code of Ethics* (2014).

1. Are the ethical standards sufficiently comprehensive and specific to guide you in working with diverse client populations? Are you aware of any subtle biases you may have against individuals who are different from you? How can you guard against racial and sexual stereotyping in your counseling relationship with clients?
2. How can you recognize when you are meeting your personal needs at the expense of a client? Do you think it is possible to continue your work as a professional counselor if you do not meet your own needs? Can you think of any values you hold that you might impose on certain clients? If you became aware of personal problems that were negatively affecting your work, what would you do?
3. What might you want to tell clients about the exceptions to confidentiality? Do you think that informing clients about the limits to confidentiality increases or decreases trust? What are your thoughts about confidentiality as it pertains to contagious, fatal diseases? What are your thoughts about confidentiality as it pertains to minor clients?
4. Under what circumstances might you consult with another professional regarding your ethical obligations to a client? How can you determine when a client's condition represents a clear and imminent danger to the client or others? How can you assess the degree of danger?
5. When might you make use of tests as a part of the counseling process? What factors do you need to take into account in selecting, administering, scoring, and interpreting tests? What are the ethical considerations in testing diverse client populations?
6. How can appropriate relationship boundaries between counselor educators and students be determined? What ethical, professional, and social relationship boundaries between counselor educators and students do you see as important? What ethical, professional, and social relationship boundaries between supervisors and supervisees do you see as important?

Making Ethical Decisions

Counseling professional organizations have developed guides to ethical decision making that can be used when a professional counselor is concerned about a particular situation and needs to determine if an ethical dilemma exists. The ACA's model involves seven steps: (a) identify the problem, (b) apply the ACA *Code of Ethics*, (c) determine the nature and dimensions of the dilemma, (d) generate potential courses of action, (e) consider the potential consequences of all options and choose a course of action, (f) evaluate the selected course of action, and (g) implement the course of action (Forester-Miller & Davis, 2016).

C. B. Stone (2017) has taken the ACA model and applied it to the school setting. As Stone and others caution, professional counselors using either of these models or any other ethical decision-making model would not necessarily come to the same conclusion. There is seldom one correct way of handling any given situation, and each counselor brings different background, values, and belief systems to each dilemma. However, if one reflects on the moral principles and continues to practice with these in mind, it is likely that the dilemma can be resolved in the client's best interests.

Remley and Herlihy (2020) suggested four self-tests to consider when a decision has been made. First, in thinking about justice, would you treat others this same way if they were in a similar situation? Second, would you suggest to other counselors this same course of action? Third, would you be willing to have others know how you acted? Fourth, do you have any lingering feelings of doubt or uncertainty about what you did? If you cannot answer in the affirmative to the first three tests and in the negative to the fourth test, perhaps the decision was not ethically sound. It is always appropriate and ethically sound to consult with a colleague when working through a dilemma to ensure that all aspects of the issue have been examined and that all possible problems have been discussed.

Failure to understand the law, and by extension policies, procedures, and guidelines, is an unacceptable legal defense. It is incumbent on the professional counselor to become familiar with all the various sources of information and guidance that are available to perform one's responsibilities in an ethical and legal manner. There are many ways of maintaining current information.

In most work settings, with the exception perhaps of private practice, professional counselors have a supervisor or other individual in authority who can help them become familiar with the regulations, policies, and guidelines relevant to that setting. Most schools and many community agencies have administrative manuals that incorporate all these sources of information into continually updated binders. The ACA newsletter, *Counseling Today*, highlights issues and important, timely topics in counseling, as do other professional journals and newsletters. Many commercially available newsletters cover recent court rulings and their impact in different work settings.

The Internet has become a valuable tool for current information and resources, although one must be careful to authenticate this information. Guillot-Miller and Partin (2003) identified more than 40 sites that include information relevant to ethical and legal practices for professional counselors. The professional associations for counselors and other mental health professionals, institutions of higher education, state and federal government agencies, government-funded organizations, and professional and legal publishers all continuously update their websites and are good sources of current information.

Sometimes mandates seem to be in conflict with each other. In such cases, common sense should prevail. There may be a therapeutically logical reason to follow one particular mandate rather than another one. Professional counselors should follow the logical course of action and document what they did and why. For example, if a counselor is working with a suicidal teenage client but believes that telling the parents would perpetuate an abusive situation, the counselor should handle the situation as an abuse case and also inform Child Protective Services about the suicidal behavior. In addition, if a particular policy, guideline, or regulation is not in the best interests of the clients in the counselor's work setting, as per the ethical standards, the counselor should work to change the mandate.

Two other issues are sometimes confusing for professional counselors. The first concerns the different ways in which counselors in different settings operate. Some mandates cover all counselors, particularly mandates that are the result of federal or state legislation or court cases. For example, child abuse and neglect laws apply to all counselors regardless of the setting in which they work. However, the implementation of some mandates, particularly as they become policy and guidelines, may look different in different settings.

Schools have perhaps the greatest number of mandates under which staff must operate, yet professional school counselors seldom need permission to see students (Remley & Herlihy, 2020), particularly if there is an approved comprehensive developmental program. A mental health counselor, employed by an outside center or agency but working either in a school or in a school-based health center, needs signed, informed consent to see the same students. In some cases, local school systems have mandated an opt-in program, which is a program that requires signed, informed consent for students to participate in different aspects of the comprehensive guidance program. In such cases, professional school counselors working in nearby systems or schools may operate differently, perhaps using an opt-out program in which all students participate unless a parent or guardian has expressly (in writing) forbidden the student from participating.

A second issue concerns professional counselors who hold multiple credentials. A counselor may work as a professional school counselor but hold state certification or licensure and work as a mental health counselor outside school. The counselor may need permission to do something as a professional school counselor, but not need permission as a mental health counselor, or vice versa. Under which set of mandates should the counselor operate?

The answer to both of these questions is the same: Employees must follow the mandates that apply to their work setting. Professional counselors are required to operate under the mandates of the system that employs them or, in the case of volunteers, the mandates of the entity under whose auspices they are working. If a counselor is employed by an agency or a private practice, he or she must follow the mandates of that entity. If a counselor is employed by a school system as a counselor, he or she must follow the mandates of the local school system. Teachers who have degrees in counseling or another related mental health degree but continue to be employed as teachers do not have the same protections as counselors because they are not employed in a mental health capacity. They need to check the policies of their school system carefully to see if they are covered by any protections such as confidentiality.

Common Ethical Dilemmas for Beginning Counselors

Professional Competence

In addition to being knowledgeable about mandates, as was previously discussed, there are further steps that professional counselors should take to ensure ethical and legal behavior. Several of these are mentioned in the ACA *Code of Ethics* (2014), but it is important to reemphasize them. As reported by Cottone and Tarvydas (2021), professional counselors should

- Maintain professional growth through continuing education. Although counselors must attend continuing education opportunities to renew national credentials, state credentials, or both, it is important to stay current with the theories, trends, and information about clients and different populations.
- Maintain accurate knowledge and expertise in areas of responsibility. Information changes so quickly that professional counselors must ensure they are providing quality and effective services to their clients. One way of achieving this goal is through professional development, but counselors may also gain information through reading, consultation with colleagues, supervision, and other means.
- Provide services only for which they are qualified and trained. The easiest way for professional counselors to get into trouble professionally is to provide services for which they are not qualified, either by training or by education. This is particularly true when using counseling techniques. Counselors should have training in using a particular technique before using it. Reading about a technique is not equivalent to implementing it under supervision. Also, professional counselors should not try to work with clients whose problems go beyond their expertise. If professional counselors are put in a situation where there are no other counselors to whom to refer the client, the counselor should consult with colleagues and ask for supervision to ensure the effectiveness of the counseling.

Misrepresentation

Accurately represent your credentials. As stated in the ethical standards, professional counselors should claim only the credentials they have earned and only the highest degree in counseling or a closely related mental health field. Counselors who hold doctorates in non–mental health fields should not use the title "doctor" in their work as a counselor. This is a particular problem in school settings, where counselors might earn doctorates in administration, supervision, or related fields but continue to work as counselors and use the title "doctor" in their job. Counselors should not imply in any way that their credentials allow them to work in areas in which they are not trained.

Pressure to "Upcode"

Everyone wants for clients to get the help that they need. In the current culture of managed care and accountability, however, it is not unusual for third-party payers to limit the number of sessions, or even to deny services because a mild mental health concern is not considered serious enough to warrant treatment. To help clients obtain services, some counselors might consider upcoding clients' diagnosis or reported severity. Upcoding means changing a client's diagnosis to a more serious condition, for example from adjustment disorder with depressed features to dysthymic disorder, or a V-code like bereavement to major depressive disorder. Upcoding also occurs when the client's severity level is changed to make it seem that the client is in more urgent need or in need of longer-term treatment. More sessions mean the client has more time to respond to and benefit from the treatment regimen, but it is also skirting the issue of fraud. Fraud is a legal term that in this instance basically means that the counselor is petitioning for services the client is not entitled to and at the same time financially benefiting from the effort. Fraud is a legal issue, and counselors found guilty of insurance fraud face stiff fines, penalties, and even jail.

There are also several ACA ethical clauses that are operational here. Section E.5.a. Proper Diagnosis states, "Counselors take special care to provide proper diagnosis of mental disorders" (p. 12). One of the issues that counselors sometime do not think about is that an upcoded, improper diagnosis becomes a part of the client's insurance history and may have unintended consequences in the client's future. Looking at the issue from the other side of the coin (i.e., downcoding), Section E.5.d. Refraining from Diagnosis states, "Counselors may refrain from making and/or reporting a diagnosis if they believe it would cause harm to the client or others" (p. 12). Thus, downcoding is ethically allowable if the counselor believes applying the diagnosis may not be in the client's best interest. For example, it may occur that a client with some psychotic phasing and a concomitant mood disorder may be diagnosed with just major depressive disorder or a bipolar disorder, rather than a more serious schizo-affective disorder. Upcoding and downcoding should be avoided when possible, and pressure on a practicum student or intern by an agency to do so should be immediately addressed with a supervisor.

"Can I Be Sued?" and "What Is Malpractice?"

The answer to "Can I be sued?" is, of course, yes. Anyone can be sued for almost anything, particularly in our litigious society. The more important question is, "Will I be found guilty?" The answer to this question is much more complex.

If professional counselors fail to exercise "due care" in fulfilling their professional responsibilities, they can be found guilty of **civil liability**—that is, the counselor committed a wrong against an individual. **Negligence** may be found if the wrong committed results in an injury or damage—in other words, if the duty owed to the client was breached in some way. In counseling, it is more common for counselors to be sued for malpractice. **Malpractice** occurs during performance of a professional duty when either misconduct or an unreasonable lack of skill occurs. Generally, for a counselor to be held liable in tort for malpractice, four conditions have to be met (Stone, 2017): (a) a duty was owed to the plaintiff (client) by the defendant (counselor), (b) the counselor breached the duty, (c) there is a causal link between the breach and the client's injury, and (d) the client suffered some damage or injury.

An example of negligence would be a professional counselor who failed to report an abuse case. The counselor had a duty to the client and failed to fulfill that duty. With malpractice, the client suffered because of lack of skill or inappropriate behavior on the part of the counselor. An example of malpractice would be if a counselor treated a client with an eating disorder through hypnosis when the counselor was not trained to use the technique of hypnosis. The situation may be further complicated if this technique is not recognized as effective for treating eating disorders.

The standard of practice will be used in any liability proceeding to determine if the professional counselor's performance was within accepted practice. The standard of practice question is, "In the performance of professional services, did the counselor provide the level of care and treatment that is consistent with the degree of learning, skill, and ethics ordinarily possessed and expected by reputable counselors practicing under similar circumstances?" and and it will be established through the testimony of peers. These peers, who are called expert witnesses, are considered to be experts in the field under question. For professional school counselors, the expert witnesses would be other school counselors (Stone, 2017). For rehabilitation counselors, the expert witnesses would be other rehabilitation counselors. For mental health counselors, the expert witnesses would be other mental health counselors. The standard is an ever-evolving level of expectation and is influenced by two major factors: education and experience. The standard is not an absolute one, but a variable one. It will be much higher for a professional counselor who has practiced for many years and pursued advanced graduate training or professional development than it will be for a counselor in the first year of practice immediately after graduate school. The more training and experience a counselor possesses, the higher the standard to which the counselor will be held accountable. The assumption is that a professional counselor should know more each year he or she practices through experience and training and should be held to a higher standard with each additional year. Using this standard of practice, a counselor will usually be found guilty of malpractice if one or more of the following situations occurs:

- The practice was not within the realm of acceptable professional practice.
- The counselor was not trained in the technique used.
- The counselor failed to follow a procedure that would have been more helpful.
- The counselor failed to warn or protect others from a violent client.
- The counselor failed to obtain informed consent.
- The counselor failed to explain the possible consequences of the treatment.

Sexual misconduct is the primary reason that liability actions are initiated against professional counselors. School staff, counselors, and other mental health professionals have been accused of committing sexual abuse or misconduct. It may be that other problems, such as failure to use a more appropriate technique, are actually more common, but that most clients lack the ability to recognize therapeutic problems and may just have a general sense that "it isn't working or helping" and choose to terminate.

Although the number of professional counselors who are sued is increasing, the number still remains small. In schools, parents are more likely to request their child not be included in certain school counseling program activities or to complain to the principal or central administration about a program or behavior. In rare cases, parents may sue. Most cases against school counselors have been rejected by the courts. In school or agency settings, violating or failing to follow mandates would get a professional counselor in trouble faster than almost any other behavior. Depending on the counselor's action, the professional counselor may be reprimanded. In extreme cases, the counselor's employment may be terminated. In clinics and agencies, few counselors are sued over professional practice issues; counselors are more often sued because of sexual conduct or illegal activities. Professional counselors must be knowledgeable about their communities. They may have a legal right to implement certain programs or conduct certain activities, but if the community is not supportive of those activities, they are going to face opposition.

When a professional counselor is faced with any legal action, the first thing the counselor should do is call a lawyer, and then let the counselor–supervisor, if there is one, know. Most agencies, clinics, practices, and schools are accustomed to dealing with such legal issues and may even have a procedure for what needs to be done. Professional counselors should never attempt to reason with the client or contact the client's lawyer without advice of counsel. It is important to not provide any information to, or discuss the case with, anyone except the counselor's lawyer or the person designated to help the counselor. Just as professional counselors advise clients to get professional mental health help when they have personal problems, counselors must get legal help when they have legal problems.

Subpoenas

Many professional counselors will receive a **subpoena** at some point in their professional career. Probably the most common reason counselors, and particularly professional school counselors, receive subpoenas is in cases involving custody disputes, child abuse or neglect allegations, and special education disputes. In most cases, the client an attorney is representing believes that counselors may have some information that will be helpful to the case. Professional counselors need to pay attention to subpoenas because they are legal documents. At the same time, consider whether the information being requested is confidential because professional counselors may be limited in what they can share. Under no circumstances should the counselor automatically comply with the subpoena without discussing it first with the client, the client's attorney, or both, or without consulting the agency's or school system's attorney. Professional counselors should take the following steps when receiving a subpoena:

1. Contact the client or the client's attorney and ask for guidance. If you work for a school system, contact the school system's attorney to seek guidance.
2. If the aforementioned parties advise you to comply with the subpoena, discuss the implications of releasing the requested information.

3. Obtain a signed informed consent form to release the records. That form should specify all conditions of release: what, to whom, and so forth.
4. If the decision is made not to release the records, the attorney should file a motion to quash (or, in some areas, ask for a protective order). This will allow the counselor to not comply with the subpoena.
5. Maintain a record of everything the counselor and attorneys did; keep notes regarding all conversations and copies of any documents pertaining to the subpoena.

An attorney who wants information may ask a judge to issue a court order. A **court order** permits the release of confidential information but does not mandate its release. If both a subpoena and a court order are received, the counselor must release the information with or without the client's consent. Failure to do so may result in the counselor being held in contempt of court.

The important things to remember about subpoenas are not to panic and to consult an attorney. Subpoenas are legal documents, but the counselor has enough time to consider the implications to the client of releasing the information and to seek legal advice.

Voices From the Field 5.2 Garnering a License: A Cautionary Tale, *by James R. Rough, Executive Director of the Ohio Counselor, Social Worker, and Marriage and Family Therapist Board*

Many licensure applicants struggle to navigate the licensure process because of a lack of understanding or knowledge of a state's laws and rules and regulatory board-related processes. What follows are several examples of licensure-related problems that I commonly see:

1. Graduates with a master's degree in counseling get jobs and hold themselves out as licensed counselors because they passed the NCE exam (even though they are not yet licensed in the state).
2. Students attend CACREP-accredited programs and assume this accreditation will automatically provide them licensure, when in fact many states have additional coursework or training requirements.
3. Students complete their internship in settings that are not acceptable to the regulatory board (e.g., a school setting) or they do mostly case management and little clinical work.
4. Licensure applicants with felony convictions want to get licensed and/or counsel with a license but cannot get a license or find a job.

With regard to the first point, what is the difference between a licensed professional counselor and a graduate of an approved master's counseling program? A licensed professional counselor can legally call himself or herself a counselor and perform services for fees, whereas an unlicensed graduate with a master's degree cannot. To practice without an actual license is a violation of the law in most states and can result in disciplinary action being taken.

With regard to the second point, if you want to be a licensed counselor after you graduate, then you need to know the laws in the state in which you want to practice. Each state has its own law, rules regarding which degrees lead to counselor licensure and scope of practice for services counselors can perform. The best way to find the answers to these questions is to use the NBCC website under the "For Counselors"—"prepare for your state licensure exam"—"State Board Directory," or this link: www.nbcc.org/directory. There is a link to each state website, which will have the application form and other information you will need.

For example, in Ohio the most common problem for out-of-state graduates is that they need additional clinical course work for Ohio licensure due to a 20-semester-hour clinical course work requirement. In addition, Ohio requires an advanced assessment course focused on the use of assessment instruments in diagnosis and treatment planning. Proper research of the licensure requirements in the state in which you wish to seek licensure will invite an easier licensure process. Do your due diligence to find out the requirements in the state where you want to be licensed, even if it is the state in which your graduate program exists. When it comes to licensure, the five Ps most certainly apply: "Prior Planning Prevents Poor Performance."

Confidentiality

For clients to feel free to share sometimes sensitive and personal information during a counseling session, they must feel that they can trust the professional counselor not to share what is disclosed during sessions with anyone else without their permission. This sense of trust and privacy, called confidentiality, is essential for counseling to be successful. **Confidentiality** is the cornerstone of counseling and is what separates the counseling relationship from other relationships in which information is shared. Confidentiality belongs to the client, not to the counselor. The client always has the right to waive confidentiality or to allow information to be shared with a third party.

Counseling minors presents particular challenges to the issue of confidentiality. Every state sets the age of majority; for most states, it is 18 years of age. Most students are minors younger than age 18 years, who are not legally able to make their own decisions. Students have an ethical right to confidentiality, but the legal rights belong to their parents or guardians (Remley & Herlihy, 2020). Most states protect counselor–client confidentiality. Approximately 20 states protect professional school counselor–student confidentiality through statutes (Cottone & Tarvydas, 2021), but many include significant restrictions.

Counselors-in-training often ask what to do if parents want to know what is discussed during counseling sessions with their minor children. Legally, parents have the right to know what is being discussed. However, the child might not want the information shared with the parent. Section B.5.b, Responsibility to Parents and Legal Guardians, of the ACA *Code of Ethics* states that:

> Counselors inform parents and legal guardians about the role of counselors and the confidential nature of the counseling relationship. Counselors are sensitive to the cultural diversity of families and respect the inherent rights and responsibilities of parents/guardians over the welfare of the children/charges according to law. Counselors work to establish, as appropriate, collaborative relationships with parents/guardians to best serve clients.
>
> (ACA, 2014, p. 8)

This statement leaves professional counselors with a dilemma. To resolve this dilemma, Remley and Herlihy (2020) suggested that the counselor first discuss the issue with the child to determine if the child is willing to disclose the information to the parent. If the child does not want to disclose, the counselor should try to help the parent understand that the best interests of the child are not served by disclosure. If this does not work, the counselor should schedule a joint meeting with the parent and child to discuss the issue. If the parent is still not satisfied, the counselor may have to disclose the information without the child's consent.

Some professional counselors would suggest that this type of situation may reflect some deeper family issue. Although the parent or guardian has a legal right to the information, there may be an underlying "family secret" that the parent does not want known, and the counselor should be sensitive to any difficulties the child may be exhibiting. Or, this situation may be the result of cultural differences, and the counselor needs to be sensitive to the family's traditions and beliefs.

A related dilemma concerns who has the rights to make decisions for the child and therefore has access to information about the counseling process. In this document, the term *parent* is used to mean the person legally recognized as having responsibility for the child. In many cases this person is the biological parent or parents of the child but may also be a guardian or someone else designated by the courts. The situation may become more complex when the parents are divorced, separated, or never married. In school settings, under federal law, both parents have the same rights to information about the child unless the courts have limited or terminated the rights of either or both parents. It is not required that the school request a copy of the document from the courts; usually the parent who has the decision-making rights will provide a copy for the school. In clinical settings the counselor would be wise to determine the legal status of custody for the child and to involve all parties having custody in a discussion of confidentiality prior to beginning the counseling relationship (Remley & Herlihy, 2020).

Many professional counselors suggest that at the beginning of the first session of each new counseling relationship, the professional school counselor should discuss confidentiality with the client, explain what it means, and point out the limits of confidentiality. Some counselors choose to hang a sign on the wall of their office that outlines this information as a reinforcement to what is discussed in the first session. Although this issue seems simple on the surface, in reality it is a very complex issue that has generated a significant amount of research and professional discourse. As the use of technology increases in counseling settings, the discussions will continue and expand. There are significant challenges to keeping electronic information confidential.

Limits to Confidentiality

According to section B.1.a of the ACA *Code of Ethics* (2014, p. 2), "Counselors respect client rights to privacy . . ." Section B.1.c states, "Counselors do not share confidential information without client consent or without sound legal or ethical justification." Section B.1.d states, "At initiation and throughout the counseling process, counselors inform clients of the limitations of confidentiality and seek to identify foreseeable situations in which confidentiality must be breached." There are several instances, however, in which counselors must break confidentiality. These are delineated in Section B.2.a. The most important of these is the **duty to warn**. When a professional counselor becomes aware that a client is in danger of being harmed, such as in instances of abuse or suicide, or when the client is likely to harm someone else, the counselor may break confidentiality and tell an appropriate person.

The basis for the duty-to-warn standard began with the 1974 *Tarasoff* case in California. In this case, the client, a graduate student told his psychologist about his intent to kill a girl (named Tarasoff) who had rejected his advances. The psychologist told the campus police and his supervisor but did not warn the intended victim or her family. The majority of the California Supreme Court ruled that the psychologist had a duty to warn a known, intended victim. This case established the legal duty to warn and protect an identifiable victim from a client's potential or intended violence and has formed the basis of many other court decisions across the United States. The ACA *Code of Ethics*, Section B.2.a, now reads, "The general requirement that counselors keep information confidential does not apply when disclosure is required to protect clients or identified others from serious and foreseeable harm" (p. 2).

In the ensuing decades, some cases have extended the duty-to-warn standard to include types of harm other than violence and foreseeable victims in addition to identifiable victims. Several other situations constrain the limits of confidentiality, as *delineated* in the *ACA Code of Ethics* (2014):

- **Subordinates:** Confidentiality is not absolute when subordinates, including employees, supervisees, students, clerical assistants, and volunteers, handle records or confidential information. Every effort should be made to limit access to this information, and the assistants should be reminded of the confidential nature of the information they are handling.
- **Treatment teams:** The client should be informed of the treatment team and the information being shared.
- **Consultation:** The professional counselor always has the right to consult with a colleague or supervisor on any case. In such instances, the counselor should provide enough information to obtain the needed assistance, but should limit any information that might identify the client.
- **Groups and families:** In group or family counseling settings, confidentiality is not guaranteed. The counselor may state that what goes on in the sessions is confidential, and the members may agree. However, because there is more than one client in the group, it is impossible to guarantee confidentiality.
- **Third-party payers:** Information will sometimes have to be sent to a mental health provider, insurance company, or other agency that has some legitimate need for the information. The counselor must disclose this information only with the client's permission.
- **Minors:** There are special considerations regarding confidentiality and minors; these are discussed in detail in the next section.
- **Contagious, life-threatening diseases:** In contrast to the duty-to-warn standard, the ACA *Code of Ethics* states that the counselor is justified in disclosing information about a client to an identifiable third party if that party's relationship with the client is such that there is a possibility of contracting the disease and the client does not plan on telling the third party. The word used is *justified*, not *should* or *must*. This wording leaves it up to the counselor to decide if the third party is at risk and must be warned.
- **Court-ordered disclosure:** Subpoenas were previously discussed. Even if ordered to reveal confidential information by a judge, counselors should limit what they reveal to only what is absolutely necessary.

In summary, confidentiality is a very complex issue, but it is essential to the effectiveness of counseling. Clients have an ethical right to confidentiality, and counselors must make every effort to ensure this right. There are specific cases, however, in which it is not only permissible, but also essential to break confidentiality to protect the client, or others from the client.

Confidentiality and Privileged Communication

The term confidentiality is used in discussions about counseling, whereas the term **privileged communication** is the legal term used to describe the privacy of the counselor–client communication. Privileged communication exists by statute and applies only to testifying in a court of law. The privilege belongs to the client, who always has the right to waive the privilege and allow the counselor to testify.

Clients have an ethical right to confidentiality, and the ethical standards for the mental health professions detail the boundaries of confidentiality. Privileged communication is more limited; federal, state, and local mandates determine its parameters. Whether a counselor–client relationship is covered by privileged communication varies widely across jurisdictions. Even within a jurisdiction, a counselor in private practice may be covered by privileged communication, but the school counselors who work in that same jurisdiction may not be. It is essential that counselors become familiar with their local mandates and policies to determine the extent to which privileged communication applies to their situation. Self-Assessment Activity 5.3 provides an opportunity to think ahead and consider how you might handle circumstances when confidentiality may need to be compromised.

Self-Assessment Activity 5.3 Limits to Confidentiality

What precautions will you take as a professional counselor to forewarn your clients about the possible limits to confidentiality? Consider how you will approach your client if a breach of confidentiality is necessary, and then practice this approach with a peer.

Minor Consent Laws

All states have a **minor consent law** that allows certain minors to seek treatment for certain conditions, usually involving substance abuse, mental health, and some reproductive health areas. These laws are based on the federal regulation 42 U.S.C. §§290dd-3; 42 C.F.R. Part 2, which references the confidentiality of patient records for drug and alcohol abuse assessment, referral, diagnosis, and treatment. The law further prohibits the release of these records to anyone without the client's informed consent and includes clients younger than age 18 years, even if they are in school and living with parents or guardians.

Over the past decade, there has been a movement to increase the number of student assistance teams and programs in schools. These teams usually consist of an administrator, one or more student services professionals (e.g., professional school counselor, school social worker, pupil personnel worker, school psychologist, school nurse), and teachers and may include a substance abuse assessor from a local agency or similar professional. School staff members refer students who are suspected to have a substance abuse problem to this team. The team is trained to deal with substance abuse issues and, if they believe the student has a substance abuse problem, have the student assessed and referred for appropriate assistance.

The controversy surrounding this program concerns the role of the parents or guardians in this process. Under the federal law, the student may go from referral through completion of treatment without the parents' or guardians' knowledge. Substance abuse professionals are divided regarding whether it is possible to successfully treat teens who abuse substances without the family's involvement. Other professionals have concerns about the ability of young adolescents to seek treatment without any family knowledge or involvement.

As this federal law has been incorporated into state statute, states have taken different approaches to deciding to whom this law applies and for what. Generally, the patient must be old enough to understand the problem, the treatment options available, and the possible consequences of the problem and the treatment options. Some states may have no age limits and maintain that a minor has the same capacity as an adult to consent to certain services. Some states have decided on a specific age at which the minor may consent to mental health treatment, reproductive or substance abuse services, and treatment for sexually transmitted diseases and AIDS/HIV. According to the Guttmacher Institute's *State Policies in Brief* reports (see www.guttmacher.org/statecenter/spibs/spib_OMCL.pdf), various states handle minor consent issues differently.

There is tremendous variation across the 50 states in what is permissible under the law. There is also some question about the applicability of this law to school settings. The laws clearly cover medical personnel and certain conditions. A school nurse is covered, but a professional school counselor or school psychologist may not be covered. It is critical that professional counselors become familiar with the minor consent law in the state in which they work to ensure compliance. A state law may allow a professional counselor to address reproductive issues and substance abuse without parental consent or notification, but a local policy may prohibit such counseling. The laws cover minors seeking advice or treatment or both. If a minor is not seeking help, the law may not apply, and the counselor would follow other policies or procedures in dealing with these issues.

The legal issues aside, this is the law that raises a tremendous number of ethical issues for professional counselors. Numerous professionals have difficulty with the ability of young adolescents, in particular, to access these services without the family's involvement. Should a professional counselor help a 13-year-old with a substance abuse problem seek treatment without the family's knowledge? How successful will the adolescent's recovery be? What about a 15-year-old who is abusing drugs and engaging in risky sexual behaviors? What is the counselor's ethical responsibility in such cases?

The problem this law presents for many professional counselors is that it allows them to assist adolescent clients legally but may conflict with their personal beliefs. Some professionals believe that behaviors such as these can cause harm to oneself, and they have a duty to warn, which supersedes all other responsibilities. Some professional counselors work with the adolescent to help the adolescent involve the family, whereas others believe that telling the family will work against the adolescent's ability to obtain help.

Another issue is that many parents do not understand that their children can seek treatment in these areas without parental consent. Parents will be understandably angry and distrustful when they discover their child has a sexually transmitted disease or is abusing substances, and that the professional counselor knew but did not tell them about it. Professional counselors need to be prepared to deal with the aftermath of such discoveries. They need to think through their positions on these issues carefully and be honest with clients about their beliefs. Professional counselors should not wait until they are faced with a situation to figure out where they stand on an issue.

Records and Personal Notes

Educational Records

Educational records include all records of a student's achievement, attendance, behavior, testing and assessment, school activities, and other information that the school collects and maintains. Schools frequently divide student records into cumulative records, health records, special education records, and confidential records, including psychological evaluations. This division of records is done for the convenience of the school; all these records are considered to be a part of the educational record. The only exceptions are personal notes, reports to Child Protective Services for abuse or neglect, and, in some states, reports from law enforcement agencies regarding students' arrests for reportable offenses.

The inspection, dissemination, and access to student educational records must be in accordance with the **Family Educational Rights and Privacy Act (FERPA)** of 1974 (20 U.S.C. 1232g). This law, which is often referred to as the Buckley Amendment, applies to all school districts, preK–12 schools, and postsecondary institutions (colleges) that receive federal funding through the U.S. Department of Education. Nonpublic schools that do not accept federal funding are exempt from this law.

The FERPA has several provisions. The first provision requires that schools or systems annually send a notice to parents or guardians regarding their right to review their children's records and to file a complaint if they disagree with anything in the record. The system has 45 days in which to comply with the parents' request to review the records. There are penalties, including loss of federal funding, for any school or system that fails to comply.

Second, the law limits who may access the records and specifies what personally identifiable information can be disclosed without informed consent—that is, what constitutes directory information or public information. Under FERPA, only individuals "with a legitimate educational interest" can access a student's record. This includes the new school when a student transfers. The sending school may send the records without the parents' consent, but should make every attempt to inform the parent that it has done so. The major exception relates to law enforcement; the school must comply with a judicial order or lawfully executed subpoena. The school must also make whatever information is needed available to the school's law enforcement unit. In emergencies, information relevant to the emergency can be shared (see www.ed.gov/print/policy/gen/guid/fpco/ferpa/index.html). All states and jurisdictions have incorporated FERPA into state statutes and local policies, with some variance among aspects such as what constitutes directory information.

The rights of consent transfer to the student at age 18 years, or when the student attends a postsecondary institution. The law does not specifically limit the rights of parents of students older than 18 years of age who are still in secondary school. For students in higher education, if the child is considered a dependent on the parent's tax returns, the parent may access information about the child. Noncustodial parents have the same rights as custodial parents, unless their rights have been terminated or limited by the courts. Stepparents and other family members who do not have custody of the child have no rights under FERPA, unless the court has granted authority.

The **Protection of Pupil Rights Amendment (PPRA)** of 1978, often called the Hatch Amendment, gives parents additional rights. It establishes certain requirements when surveys are given to students in preK–12 schools; it does not apply to postsecondary schools because students can consent on their own. If the survey is funded with federal money, informed consent must be obtained for all participating students if students in elementary or secondary schools are required to take the survey, and questions about certain personal areas are included. It also requires informed parental consent before the student undergoes any psychological, psychiatric, or medical examination, testing, or treatment or any school program designed to affect the personal values or behavior of the student. The Hatch Amendment also gives parents the right to review instructional materials in experimental programs.

The **No Child Left Behind (NCLB) Act** of 2001 included several changes to FERPA and PPRA and continued to increase parents' rights. The changes apply to surveys funded either in part or entirely by any program administered by the U.S. Department of Education. NCLB made minor changes to the seven existing categories concerning surveys and added an additional category. PPRA now requires that:

- Schools and contractors make instructional materials available for review by the parents of participating students if those materials will be used in any Department of Education–funded survey, analysis, or evaluation.
- Schools and contractors obtain written, informed parental consent before students' participation in any Department of Education–funded survey, analysis, or evaluation if information in any of the following areas would be revealed:
- Political affiliations or beliefs of the parent or student.
- Mental and psychological problems of the family or student.
- Sex behavior or attitudes.
- Illegal, antisocial, self-incriminating, or demeaning behavior.
- Critical appraisals of other individuals with whom the student has close family relationships.
- Legally recognized privileged or analogous relationships such as those of lawyers, ministers, and physicians.
- Religious practices, affiliations, or beliefs of the student or parent/guardian (newly added).
- Income other than such information as required to determine eligibility or participation in a program (20 U.S.C. 1232h).

The new provisions of PPRA also apply to surveys not funded through the U.S. Department of Education programs. These provisions give parents the right to inspect, on request, any survey or instructional materials used as part of the curriculum if created by a third party and involving one or more of the eight aforementioned areas. Parents also have the right to inspect any instrument used to collect personal information that will be used in selling or marketing. Parents always have the right to not grant permission or to opt their child out of participating in any activity involving the eight previously delineated areas. PPRA does not apply to any survey that is administered as part of the **Individuals with Disabilities Education Improvement Act** (IDEA).

As can be seen from the previous discussion, there are many constraints in schools to assessment, testing, and surveying students. Because individual school systems, districts, or colleges may have defined this legislation further, it is essential that professional counselors become familiar with the requirements of the policies and procedures for their specific school system.

The word *parents* has been used in the preceding discussion about student records. The law does recognize the right of students older than age 18 years to access their own records and accords them the same rights as parents of students younger than age 18 years. However, the law does not specifically limit the right of parents whose children are 18 years of age or older to access their child's records, particularly in cases where the child is still living at home and is financially dependent on the parents. The law also gives noncustodial parents the same rights as custodial parents. Unless there is a court order in the child's file that limits or terminates the rights of one or both parents, both parents have the same access to the child's records. School personnel also must provide copies of records such as report cards to both parents if requested.

The word *parent* is used to reference the legal guardian of the child, who may not be the biological or adoptive parent of the child but rather some other legally recognized caregiver. Stepparents and other family members have no legal right to the student's records without court-appointed authority, such as adoption or guardianship. This is particularly problematic in situations where a relative provides kinship care—that is, the relative has physical custody 24 hours a day, 7 days a week, but no legal custody of the child. Legally, this person has no educational decision-making rights for the child and cannot access the child's record or give consent. The crack epidemic, incarcerations, and AIDS/HIV have created a situation in which millions of children younger than 18 years of age are involved in informal kinship care situations. Kinship care may be the best situation for these children, but these situations present significant legal implications for schools.

Outside agencies may not access the records of any student without the signed consent of the parent or legal guardian. Some states have worked out interagency agreements wherein a parent signs one form that designates what records may be shared with which agencies, making individual forms unnecessary. Local policies dictate whether signed informed consent is needed to share information at school team meetings, such as student assistance programs, IEPs, or student services meetings, when the agency personnel are regular members of the team.

Voices From the Field 5.3 Client Records: A Common Ethics Problem, *by William L. Hegarty, JD*

For 15 years, I have been the chief investigator for the Ohio Counselor, Social Worker, and Marriage and Family Therapist Board. During my time with the board, I have seen every issue imaginable (e.g., counselors having sex with clients, counselors having sex with clients' family members, counselors borrowing money from clients, insurance fraud, counselors acting outside scope of their practice). One issue that has been a constant yet steadily growing problem over the years is the issue of proper record keeping. More recently, we have seen a sharp rise in counselors backdating case files. This backdating is usually an effort to correct a mistake when the record was originally created. Sometimes the record is backdated to make it appear that services were offered on a date when in fact they were not. The backdating of records is not permissible, and in some states this is considered falsifying records and possibly even insurance fraud. Depending on the type of record falsified, this practice may also invite federal prosecution. A licensee can go back into a file and add or amend a note but the date then has to reflect the date the note was amended in addition to the original date the document was created.

Another problem we are seeing with records is the outright creation of false case notes. These cases almost universally involve licensees who provide home-based counseling services as an employee of an agency. We are increasingly seeing counselors who do not go to a scheduled home-based session yet create a case note as if they had. These faux sessions are then submitted for billing purposes. Of course, this action is illegal and harms the clients because the clients are not receiving the necessary services. But these instances also reduce the number of services the client can obtain because they have reduced the client's entitlement. I have seen agencies have to repay tens of thousands of dollars due to the falsification of notes. The rise in occurrence of this type of situation may be related to the increased agency productivity pressures being placed on counselors; that is, agencies are asking counselors to provide an increasing number of billable hours.

Another issue related to record keeping is their legibility. When records are illegible, client care is compromised. In some client files the treatment plan, client goals, and client statements are totally illegible. When I inquire about the utility of an illegible file, I tend to get blank stares before the realization settles in that the file is of no functional use.

Although record-keeping case violations are not as sensational as, say, sexual violations, they are extremely common. Most of these issues can be avoided by proper supervision and peer review within an agency setting. All counselors must police themselves to ensure that they are devoting the appropriate amount of time to ensuring that their records are accurate, timely, and able to be comprehended by those who may need to review them.

Personal Notes

Personal notes are notes written by professional counselors to serve as an extension of their memories; they are an impression of the client or session. These notes must remain "in the sole possession of the maker" and cannot be shared with anyone except "a substitute maker." A substitute maker is someone who takes over for the counselor in the counselor's position, in the same way a substitute teacher takes over for the regular teacher. In the case of school counselors, a substitute maker is not the counselor who becomes responsible for the child the next year or in the next school.

Personal notes must remain separate from the educational record. When any information in the personal notes is shared, it is no longer confidential. If professional counselors keep their personal notes in their offices, they should keep them separate from all other records and secure, such as in a locked file cabinet. Some counselors keep them in their car or house, but this is unnecessary, unless there are problems with security in the counselor's office.

As technology becomes more common in counseling offices, professionals may prefer to keep their personal notes on the computer. This is not a good idea, unless the counselor can absolutely guarantee that no one can access the program or break through network firewalls. Even keeping the notes on disk is questionable. Stories of computer hackers breaking codes and paralyzing websites for hours are frequently reported in the news. It is preferable to keep notes separate and not tell anyone they exist, even if there is nothing of particular interest in them. The information is confidential, and the professional counselor needs to ensure its security. Information from the notes would be shared only in cases in which there is a clear duty to warn, or when a judge requires that confidentiality be broken and the information shared.

The Health Insurance Portability and Accountability Act (HIPAA) of 1996

The **Health Insurance Portability and Accountability Act** (**HIPAA**) of 1996 required that the U.S. Department of Health and Human Services adopt national standards for the privacy of individually identifiable health information, outlined patients' rights, and established criteria for access to health records. The requirement that the U.S. Department of Health and Human Services also adopt national standards for electronic health care transactions was included in this law. The Privacy Rule was adopted in 2000 and became effective in 2001. The Privacy Rule set national standards for the privacy and security of protected health information. The rule specifically excludes any individually identifiable health information that is covered by FERPA. Health records in schools that are under FERPA are specifically excluded from HIPAA.

However, the situation is not that simple, particularly in the area of special education. Many schools receive mental, physical, and emotional health assessments of students that have been conducted by outside providers whose practices are covered by HIPAA regulations. In previous years, such assessments and reports automatically became part of the educational record. This may no longer be the case, particularly if the provider requests that the report not be redisclosed. As HIPAA continues to impact health information, agencies and school systems must develop policies and procedures to address any potential conflicts between FERPA and HIPAA. Professional counselors must be aware of these issues and any school policies.

Child Abuse and Neglect

Another issue professional counselors must deal with that has clear legal mandates is child abuse and neglect. Efforts to recognize and intervene in child abuse cases began in the late 1800s and were modeled on the prevention of cruelty to animals laws. In 1961, the "battered child syndrome" was legally recognized, and by 1968, all 50 states had laws requiring the reporting of child maltreatment. In 1974, the **National Child Abuse Prevention and Treatment Act** (P.L. 93–247) became a federal law. The act was later reauthorized with changes and renamed the **Keeping Children and Families Safe Act** of 2003. The law defined **child abuse** as physical or mental injury, sexual abuse or exploitation, negligent treatment, or maltreatment of a child younger than age 18 years or the age specified by the child protection law of the state in question, by a person who is responsible for the child's welfare, under circumstances that indicate that the child's health or welfare is harmed or threatened (42 U.S.C.S. §5101).

The law is clear regarding who must report cases of child abuse and neglect. Every health practitioner, educator, human services worker, and law enforcement officer must report suspected abuse or neglect, generally within 24 to 72 hours of first "having reason to suspect." It is incumbent on the individual who first suspects the abuse or neglect to call Child Protective Services to report. The oral report must be followed up by a written report in most cases. Each state may have slightly different procedures for reporting; some states allow as many as seven days for submission of the written report and identify different agencies to which the report must be made. What does not change is the legal mandate to report.

There is no liability for reporting child abuse, even if a subsequent investigation determines no evidence that abuse or neglect occurred, unless the report is made with malice. Most states do have serious penalties for failure to report, however. These penalties may include loss of certification or license, disciplinary action, or termination of employment.

Parents or guardians have no rights to information during this process. The agency, school, or other entity making the report should not inform the parents that a report is being made. It is the responsibility of the department of social services and the law enforcement agency to contact the parent and conduct the investigation. It is critical that professional counselors understand the laws regarding cases of child abuse and neglect and follow the procedures exactly. The individual submitting the report does not have to prove that abuse has occurred; it is enough to have reason to suspect.

Professional counselors are sometimes put in an awkward position when they are not the first person to suspect abuse, but the staff member who does is not willing to make the report and asks the counselor to do it. In such cases, if the staff member will not make the report, professional counselors should do it, but should apprise the administrator of the circumstances surrounding the report. Regardless of who submits the report, the client will need support and assistance throughout the process.

Custody Issues*

One of the most common complaints filed against licensed counselors are inappropriate practices in the context of child custody cases. For parents involved in custody disputes, the stakes are high, and the counselor's actions are being scrutinized and well documented through the court system. Most counselors who are sanctioned for custody-related issues unknowingly engage in unethical practices simply because they are unaware of their state laws that relate to counselors' role in custody cases. It is important that counselors know and abide by their state laws related to custody cases.

Many states have language in their counselor practice law that indicates they should not conduct a court evaluation or make a custody recommendation in a case in which he or she served in a therapeutic role for the client or his or her immediate family or has had other involvement that may compromise counselor objectivity. The reason counselors cannot make these recommendations when in this role is because they are unable to be impartial or objective. Any recommendation would be based on limited facts and not within their role as the client's counselor.

With appropriate releases, counselors can testify in custody cases as fact witnesses concerning treatment. In other words, they can report the facts of clients' treatment and their progress in treatment (e.g., how many sessions they have attended, the details of the client's progress, compliance with treatment goals). On the witness stand, counselors are often asked by attorneys, and even judges, to make custody recommendations. In these cases, counselors should clarify to the parties involved their role in the case and the state laws that dictate counselor practice. More specifically, licensed counselors who have a client involved in a custody, visitation, and/or guardianship case, if asked by a client or their lawyer or the guardian ad litem to make a recommendation about custody, visitation, and/or guardianship, should cite their role as the primary counselor for their client. Licensees should inform the requestor that they have not performed a custody, visitation, and/or guardianship evaluation, and it would be unethical for them to make any recommendation outside their role as a treating counselor.

Some counselors may serve in the role of custody evaluator. In these situations, it is appropriate for counselors to make recommendations to the court. In addition, during the course of a court evaluation, a counselor should not accept any of the involved participants involved in the evaluation as a therapy client.

Harm to Self and Others

For many years, the standard that was used in the counseling profession for dealing with potential suicide cases was based on the *Tarasoff* case, which was previously discussed. As a result of the *Tarasoff* case ruling, professional counselors had a duty to warn if there was a foreseeable victim. According to Remley and Herlihy (2020), subsequent court decisions interpreted the case differently; some judges ruled that the duty exists even when there is no foreseeable victim, if individuals are unintentionally injured by the client, such as classes of persons of which the victim is a member, bystanders, and other individuals. Generally, when dealing with a potentially suicidal client, the professional counselor conducts a lethality assessment, determines the seriousness of the threat, and based on the seriousness of the threat, decides whether the duty to warn applies.

The *Eisel* case in Maryland changed the standard for many professional school counselors. In that case, two middle school students became involved in Satanism and obsessed with death and self-destruction. Friends of Nicole Eisel went to their school counselor and told her that Nicole was thinking about killing herself. That counselor consulted with Nicole's school counselor. Both professional school counselors spoke with Nicole, who denied thinking about killing herself. Shortly thereafter, on a school holiday, Nicole's friend, who attended another school, shot Nicole and killed herself in the park behind the school. Mr. Eisel sued the school, the

* Author Note: We are grateful to Dr. Victoria E. Kress for contributing this section.

school system, and the professional school counselors. The circuit court dismissed the case. Mr. Eisel appealed to the court of appeals. Its decision of October 29, 1991, stated,

> Considering the growth of this tragic social problem in the light of the factors discussed above, we hold that school counselors have a duty to use reasonable means to attempt to prevent a suicide when they are on notice of a child or adolescent student's suicidal intent.
>
> (*Eisel v. Board of Education*, 1991)

Based on the facts of this case as developed to date, a trier of fact could conclude that the duty included warning Mr. Eisel of the danger. The case was remanded back to the circuit court to decide the issue of liability for the school system and the professional school counselors. The case finally concluded eight years after it began and found the school and professional school counselors had acted appropriately given the circumstances, their training, and the policies in place at the time.

The court's decision had a major impact on professional school counselors in the state of Maryland. This decision removed the counselor's ability to determine whether duty to warn is applicable. As a consequence, professional school counselors in Maryland must always tell the parent whenever there is any indication from a child or someone else that the child is thinking about suicide, regardless of the seriousness of the threat. They must also inform the principal or the principal's designee. Many of Maryland's school systems now apply this procedure to all student services personnel employed by the school system, and other states have implemented similar provisions and policies.

Although this case is legally binding only on professional school counselors in Maryland, it has become the standard by which subsequent cases have been decided. For example, a Florida court subsequently made a similar ruling in a similar case, and several other courts are following suit. Professional school counselors must be aware of the policies within their system. The courts clearly are ruling in favor of duty to warn, as opposed to counselor discretion. Professional counselors practicing outside schools should abide by state statute and policy, but deciding to warn when there is any reason to suspect the client is in danger to self or others is probably a good practice in almost all circumstances, particularly when the client is a minor child.

As this chapter comes to a close, Self-Assessment Activities 5.4 and 5.5 will help you integrate the information on ethical and legal issues in counseling and apply ethical decision-making principles to numerous scenarios.

Self-Assessment Activity 5.4 Applying the ACA *Code of Ethics*

For each numbered situation, indicate whether the behavior is ethical (E) or unethical (U), and cite the ACA *Code of Ethics* Standard or Standards that apply. The person in question in each scenario is *underlined* .

Situation #1: Judy, a counselor educator at a university, has a colleague named *John*, who is opening a private practice in addition to his teaching job. John is building his client caseload by offering special rates to recent graduates of the university counseling program in exchange for providing supervision, which is required for licensing.

E U Standard(s) ______________________________

Situation #2: A *rehabilitation counselor* is conducting a research study. Because raw data includes confidential information about individual participants, the counselor deletes all identifying data before giving the material to the secretary for computer entry.

E U Standard(s) ______________________________

Situation #3: *Larry* Adams has a PhD in history and is a university professor. He also has a master's degree in counseling and is an LPC. He wants to open a part-time private practice and has business cards printed that say, "Dr. Larry Adams, Individual and Group Counseling."

E U Standard(s) ______________________________

Situation #4: A woman enters into a counseling relationship with a male *counselor* at a mental health center after finishing a treatment program for alcohol addiction. The woman has a history of violent behavior when intoxicated. Although she has maintained her sobriety for several months, one evening, obviously intoxicated, she calls the counselor and threatens to kill her mother. Despite the client's incoherence, the counselor discerns that she has a gun. The counselor calls the client's mother, but is unable to reach her, and then calls the police.

E U Standard(s) ________________________________

Situation #5: A *residence hall director* who is responsible for hall discipline at a university has a master's degree in counseling. He is approached by students living in his hall who say they would like to address some personal concerns and want him to be their counselor. The residence hall director arranges weekly sessions for counseling with the students.

E U Standard(s) ________________________________

Situation #6: A male professional *counselor* in a mental health center works daily with clients who are taking medications. One of the clients, who is taking Prozac, tells the counselor that she continues to be quite depressed. The counselor says, "No problem, you may need your medication changed. I'll arrange that," and refers the woman to the staff psychiatrist.

E U Standard(s) ________________________________

Situation #7: A professional *counselor* has been encouraging a client to get involved in more social activities to get her out of the house more often. One day, the client unexpectedly shows up at an art class that the counselor is enrolled in, saying that she signed up for the same class. The counselor decides to stay enrolled.

E U Standard(s) ________________________________

Situation #8: A professional *counselor* has been seeing a married couple who have decided to divorce. During the week between sessions, the couple has an argument, and the husband moves out of the house. The wife obtains a restraining order because she fears her husband will harm her or the children as he has in the past. The husband calls the counselor and threatens to bomb the house if his wife does not allow him to see the children. The husband sounds rational, but definitely wants to get even with his wife. The counselor believes the husband is just spouting off.

E U Standard(s) ________________________________

Situation #9: *Sharon*, a counselor in private practice, receives a phone call from a former male friend with whom she has had a sexual relationship. He tells her that he is grieving the death of his father and requests counseling from her. Because Sharon specializes in grief counseling and has not dated him in more than a year, she agrees to counsel him.

E U Standard(s) ________________________________

Situation #10: A female *graduate student* in counseling is doing her internship in a community agency. The administrators tell her that they do not want her to inform clients that she is a student intern. They explain that the clients might think they are getting second-class service if they knew their counselor was in training. The administrators contend that clients are paying (on a sliding scale) for services they receive, and that it would not be psychologically good to give them any information that might cause them to believe they were not getting the best help available. The student did as she was told.

E U Standard(s) ________________________________

Situation #11: Robert requests counseling from a counselor in private practice. He indicates that he and his wife are involved in marriage counseling as a couple through an agency in town. Robert says he is undecided about continuing the marriage and would like to sort out his feelings and reach a decision. He intends to continue couples counseling in the meantime. The professional *counselor* agrees to provide counseling for Robert without requesting permission to contact the other marriage counselor.

E U Standard(s) ________________________________

Situation #12: A professional *counselor* has administered a personality inventory for a Mexican-American client. The counselor is aware that this inventory contains several race-sensitive items, but has decided to use it anyway because this particular client seems so well acculturated.

E U Standard(s) ________________________________

Situation #13: A *family counselor* in a mental health clinic has been having weekly sessions with two parents and their adolescent child, a juvenile offender who is about to be released from a detention center. In the past, the juvenile was known to be extremely dangerous and violent and had made generalized statements of hostility, but with no intended or identifiable victim. The counselor took no action to block his release.

E U Standard(s) ________________________________

Situation #14: A professional *school counselor* is working with a student who is distressed about her family situation, which involves the use of crack cocaine. The counselor has little training in drug counseling, but continues working with the student even though a local family service center has an excellent program for teenagers with parents who abuse substances, and this service is available at no charge.

E U Standard(s) ________________________________

Situation #15: As a private practitioner, a professional *counselor* decides not to purchase malpractice insurance and proceeds to practice without it.

E U Standard(s) ________________________________

Situation #16: A high school *counselor* is contacted by a teacher who reports that Diane, a student in her English class, has written a poem about death. When the teacher talked with Diane, she threatened to kill herself. The counselor calls Diane into her office, and Diane admits to being deeply despondent and wanting to end her life. Diane begs the counselor not to tell her parents or anyone else. The counselor is concerned for Diane's safety, so she calls her parents to tell them of Diane's suicidal ideation.

E U Standard(s) ________________________________

Situation #17: A professional *counselor* is seeing a client who had been sexually abused as a child. The client expresses frustration that she cannot remember the earliest incidents of abuse and insists that hypnosis would help her break through this barrier. Although the counselor has no specific training in hypnosis, she agrees to purchase a hypnosis audiotape and attempt the procedure with the client.

E U Standard(s) ________________________________

Situation #18: Steve, an HIV-infected man, reveals to his professional *counselor* that he is infected. After the counselor probes the situation a bit, Steve admits to his counselor that he is embarrassed, is confused, and finds it difficult to talk about his condition. Steve admits that he has unprotected sexual relations and does not disclose his condition to his partners. The counselor agrees to continue providing counseling services only if Steve gives a verbal agreement that he will not have sexual relations with others until he is less confused.

E U Standard(s) ________________________________

Situation #19: Joe, a 23-year-old college student, was convicted of illegal possession of controlled substances and is now serving a two-year probation sentence. He is seeing the *college counselor*. Joe's probation officer contacts the counselor and requests a report. Although Joe has not signed a release of information, the counselor complies, fearing that not to do so might cause the probation officer to file a negative report on Joe to the court.

E U Standard(s) ____

Situation #20: Before seeing a family for counseling, a *professional counselor* gives a written document explaining the process of counseling to the parents. After reading the informed consent document, the parents sign it and bring the family to counseling. The informed consent document is not given or described to the children.

E U Standard(s) ____

Self-Assessment Activity 5.5 Reflection on Ethics

As a future professional counselor, write a reflection on: (a) your ethical decision-making process (with emphasis on self-awareness and analysis of the various codes of ethics), and (b) the implications of your values for counseling practice, including the role of your cultural values in counseling.

Summary

If one were to survey practicing counselors regarding the "hot issues" in counseling, the list would likely include eating disorders, HIV/AIDS, self-mutilation, autism and Asperger's syndrome, bullying, harassment, changing family structures, mobility, cultural diversity, sexual orientation, depression, loss and grief, students with special needs, emotional disturbance, gangs, and a host of other topics. So how does a counselor help a 21-year-old who believes he is gay? Or a 16-year-old who is starving herself to death? Or an incarcerated parent who wants the professional counselor to read his letters to his children because the mother will not let him have any contact with his children?

Here are some final words of wisdom to help guide you as a professional counselor.

- Always document in writing what you did and why you did it.
- If you did not follow a policy, document why you did not (e.g., not calling the parent in a suicide case because it was handled as an abuse case).
- Know federal, state, and local laws, regulations, policies, and guidelines.
- Consult with a colleague or supervisor when you have questions or doubts.
- Read and use resources.
- Consult with a lawyer when appropriate.

Professional counselors must be prepared to deal with these issues and more every day of their professional lives. Many of these areas do not have clear laws, regulations, court cases, or policies to guide counselors toward legal and ethical behavior. Professional counselors need to try to do what is in the best interests of their clients and to help the clients see what that is. They must advocate for their clients because frequently the professional counselor is the only support that the client has. Professional counselors must never stop believing that what they do makes a difference in the lives of clients.

6

Special Populations and Issues

Victoria E. Kress, Matthew J. Paylo, Nicole A. Stargell, and Christine A. McAllister

Preview

Counselors regularly face complex client or student presenting issues that require the synthesis of information spanning multiple areas. The topics presented in this chapter cover a variety of issues and populations that counselors will confront in clinical practice but are likely not addressed in detail in other areas of the counseling curriculum. In approaching these topics, an emphasis was placed upon presenting basic, practical information to serve as a starting point to help counselors navigate their work with the indicated populations.

Special Populations and Issues

Counseling issues important in working with a number of special populations will be reviewed in this chapter, including: child maltreatment, academic problems, substance use, issues with older adults and the terminally ill, self-injury, intimate partner violence, and issues specific to working with clients with military service. First, child maltreatment, which includes child abuse and neglect, is addressed. Most counselors regularly encounter children being maltreated. Consideration is given to counselors' role as mandated reporters and assessors of child maltreatment. Information related to the short and long-term effects of maltreatment, and the related counseling needs of maltreated children, are also discussed.

Issues that counselors should consider when working with children who are gifted, have learning disabilities, or are otherwise differently abled are also addressed. An emphasis is placed upon how counselors can best support this population in the context of their unique learning and cognitive needs. Psychosocial and developmental counseling issues, such as the importance of addressing self-esteem and identity, are presented in the context of counseling this population.

Substance abuse counseling will be addressed next, along with a discussion of how co-occurring mental disorders (dual diagnosis) relate to substance abuse and its treatment. The importance of enhancing clients' motivation to change is highlighted.

Counseling considerations related to working with clients who are in relationships involving intimate partner violence (IPV) are also discussed. Safety considerations and safety planning are discussed, as are various counseling considerations that are important to address when working with this at-risk population. Counseling and intervention considerations are presented with a special focus on the value of using evidence-based treatment approaches.

Issues associated with counseling adults who are older or terminally ill are also addressed. The stages of death and dying and their application to counseling terminally ill clients are detailed. Various issues associated with counseling older adults and the terminally ill are also described.

People who self-injure present counselors with a number of unique challenges. In this chapter, safety and risk management issues that are important to consider when counseling people who self-injure are addressed. Ethical issues (e.g., attempts to force clients to stop self-injuring) and suggestions for ethical practice are also addressed in this chapter. Additionally, treatment methods and practical suggestions for counseling those who self-injure are provided.

Military veterans carry with them the lasting effects of war-related experiences. Whether dealing with future deployment, PTSD, or anxiety and depression, counselors can benefit from understanding the specific aspects of this population and the common issues they present in counseling. Additionally, counselors-in-training need

DOI: 10.4324/9781003305521-6

to be knowledgeable about the specific treatment considerations of this population as well as evidence-based treatment approaches that are beneficial in helping to treat common issues with which they present.

We enter new relationships with a plethora of past relationship experiences that color our contexts. Counselors and clients are no exception, and it is inevitable that they will, at times, bring these past experiences and reactions into the counseling relationship. Counselors need to be aware of their own internal reactions to clients, as well as clients' reactions to them. These personal reactions are commonly described as transference (i.e., clients' reactions to counselors) and countertransference (i.e., counselors' reactions to clients). Recommendations are made for how counselors can assess and manage transference and countertransference issues in real-world practice.

Clients with little motivation to change are typically resistant to the counseling process. Legal offenders and court-ordered clients are populations who often lack a motivation to make behavioral changes. This chapter will highlight the nuances associated with counseling these populations and will provide practical applications to aid counselors in their work.

Child Maltreatment

Counselors frequently find themselves working with children who have, or are experiencing, some type of child abuse or neglect. **Child abuse** includes physical, emotional, or sexual abuse (Centers for Disease Control and Prevention [CDC], 2022). **Neglect** involves the failure of caretakers to provide adequate emotional and physical care for a child. Child abuse typically receives more attention than neglect, which is unfortunate due to well-documented high rates of neglect. For example, the U.S. Department of Health and Human Services (USDHHS, 2021) reported that of the 3.6 million cases of reported and alleged child abuse and neglect, 78% of the reports involved allegations of neglect. Since mental health professionals often make these reports, it is imperative that counselors are aware of the signs and symptoms of maltreatment and neglect.

The effects of child maltreatment are exceptionally diverse and dependent upon several factors, including the resources available to the child, the duration and frequency of the abuse, the nature of the child's relationship with the perpetrator, use of force or the severity of assault, and the number of perpetrators (Briere & Lanktree, 2012). Possible reactions to child maltreatment may include disruptions to the child's emotional well-being (e.g., lowered self-esteem), difficulty with making and sustaining attachments, anger that can be manifested in behavioral problems, depression and anxiety, and academic struggles (Gardner et al., 2019; Lo et al., 2019; Villalba et al., 2018). Posttraumatic stress disorder (PTSD) was recognized as a common effect of child abuse, and these symptoms might include avoidance symptoms (e.g., avoiding situations or places that remind them of the abuse, dissociation, or emotional numbing to deaden or block the pain); re-experiencing the abuse (e.g., flashbacks or recurrent nightmares), and a general sense of increased anxiety and emotional arousal. More specifically, children with PTSD may experience worries about dying at an early age, a loss of interest in activities, somatic symptoms such as headaches and stomachaches, moodiness or showing sudden and extreme emotional reactions, sleep problems, irritability or angry outbursts, difficulties concentrating, regression or acting younger than their age (e.g., being clingy or whiny, thumb sucking), increased alertness (arousal) to the environment, and repeating behaviors that remind them of the trauma (e.g., through play or in art).

Children who have experienced chronic maltreatment are especially vulnerable and may have additional developmental disruptions due to repeated or long-term maltreatment (Herman, 2015). In addition to the PTSD symptoms previously described, these developmental or complex trauma reactions might include difficulties regulating emotions, alterations in self-perception (e.g., a sense of chronic guilt, shame, helplessness), alterations in relationships with others (e.g., being distrustful, isolating), and alterations in their sense of meaning (e.g., a sense of hopelessness and despair). These developmental reactions can have significant, long-term effects on one's functioning, and it is important that these developmental reactions be addressed in counseling in addition to the traditional PTSD symptoms more typically targeted in treatment.

Certain characteristics appear to insulate children from the long-term potentially deleterious effects of maltreatment, and these factors should be considered when counseling this population. These factors include: internal factors such as ability to make meaning; being optimistic about the future; and agency and mastery; and contextual factors such as having a supportive family and supportive environment (Haffejee & Theron, 2017). When possible, the aforementioned factors should be identified, developed, and amplified in clients via counseling.

Despite the negative effects that child maltreatment can invite, it is also important for counselors to understand that most children do not develop ongoing trauma reactions secondary to maltreatment; they can and do move forward, adapt, and live productive lives (Ewert & Tessneer, 2019). Secondary to their maltreatment experiences, children can even experience posttraumatic growth and develop resources such as additional survival skills, a greater self-knowledge and self-appreciation, increased empathy for others, and a broader and more complex view of the world. It is important that counselors believe that all maltreated children with whom they work can heal and thrive.

Adult victims of childhood abuse seek therapy for a number of reasons, but rarely just because of a history of maltreatment. Many adults fail to recognize the effects past abuse and neglect may have had on their development. Similarly, the caregivers of children who are being maltreated sometimes seek counseling for their children, but they often fail to identify current or past abuse or neglect as related to the child's struggles. Many caregivers who act with abuse or neglect do not have a lot of insight into their behaviors (Cohen et al., 2017). They often do not know exactly what constitutes abuse or neglect, especially if they were raised under similar circumstances. They might not understand how their own childhood maltreatment might affect their parenting (e.g., difficulty with emotional regulation, ineffective coping skills, unhealthy attachment styles). Additionally, some caregivers might not understand the ways in which maltreatment affects their children's development, creating a cycle of undesirable feelings, behaviors, and reactions. Counselors working with youth must also work with their families, and these factors can further complicate efforts to support maltreated children.

When counseling children, safety should always be a counselor's first priority (Kress et al., 2012). Counselors should be vigilant about reporting child maltreatment and monitor for any new instances of abuse or neglect that may need to be reported. Counselors should consider consulting with other qualified professionals before reporting child maltreatment and should err on the side of caution if unsure whether reporting is necessary. Reporting child abuse or neglect can be stressful. Counselors should ensure informed consent throughout the therapeutic process (not just at session one), and counselors should openly speak about the limits to confidentiality (one of which is the knowledge of child abuse or neglect). Counselors should tell caregivers if they are required to make a report, and clients might even be given the opportunity to participate in the report themselves if that is a viable option. It is helpful for parents to express their commitment to change. Attempts to enhance and promote a child's safety should be a part of the ongoing counseling process.

A client in the child welfare system (i.e., a client who has been identified as a victim of maltreatment) will have the support of many professionals. It is important that counselors work with the child's support team to ensure optimal treatment. Team members might include: a child welfare system worker, medical personnel who follow the child's growth and development, and if removed from the home, the team may include foster parents. Oftentimes, an hour a week of counseling is not enough to help a child, and a team approach can serve to further enhance and supplement the work done in individual counseling.

When working with maltreated children, it is important that counselors provide a consistent, safe space and a nurturing relationship to help the child experiment and adapt to a safer world. This safety can be created in a literal sense by verbally expressing a client's rights and value. Safety is created in the therapeutic setting with items that youth might find enticing or comforting. Examples include fun pictures, activities, games, and toys. Professional counselors might create a toolbox that includes go-to materials for working with youth (e.g., paper, crayons, toys, games). If meeting youth in their homes, counselors should intentionally seek a space that is private for individual work, and counselors should take care to verbalize ground rules when working with family members.

Children who have been abused or neglected also often do well when counselors work with them in group settings (Kress & Hoffman, 2008). Group counseling can be especially empowering with children who have been sexually abused as it reduces their feelings of shame and differentness, and depending on the tone of the group, it can help them co-create a strength-based identity.

Counseling services should be provided to maltreated children and their families using **evidence-based practices (EBP)** that have research to support the effectiveness of the approach. Numerous studies have pointed to the value of using EBPs, which include structured, manualized, and empirically supported models over other methods of treatment (Reinbergs & Fefer, 2018). There are a variety EBPs that can be used by counselors in school settings (e.g., cognitive-behavioral intervention for trauma in schools, bounce back, support for students exposed to trauma, DBT skills groups, social emotional learning curricula, school-wide positive behavior interventions & supports (PBIS), *Helping traumatized children learn*, psychological first aid in schools). Counselors will need to research and choose EBPs based upon the client's unique needs and circumstances.

An example of an EBP that can be used with abused children receiving clinical services is trauma-focused cognitive-behavioral therapy (TF-CBT; Cohen et al., 2017). TF-CBT is a conjoint child and caregiver psychotherapy approach used with children and adolescents who are experiencing significant emotional and behavioral difficulties secondary to traumatic life events. It is a model that integrates trauma-sensitive interventions with cognitive-behavioral techniques, humanistic principles, and family involvement. Through TF-CBT, children and caregivers learn new skills to help them process thoughts and feelings related to traumatic life events; manage and resolve distressing feelings, thoughts, and behaviors that are related to the traumatic life event(s); and develop an enhanced sense of safety, personal growth, parenting skills, and improved family communication. Resources and a certificate training program on TF-CBT can be completed through the Medical University of South Carolina (see https://tfcbt2.musc.edu/). This training program is an excellent means of deepening one's understanding of CBT treatment principles in general and trauma treatment in particular.

Counseling maltreated children may arouse complex feelings within the counselor. Counselors may feel anger toward the child's caregivers and/or the perpetrators of the maltreatment. Counselors may feel sadness and a sense of protectiveness over the child. Counselors may feel a sense of anxiety around protecting the child from further maltreatment; they may become overly involved with the child and feel a need to rescue them. It is important that counselors working with children who are maltreated seek regular supervision, peer consultation, and, if necessary, personal counseling. Counselors who work with maltreated children should also regularly self-monitor for vicarious trauma, burnout, and compassion fatigue. Any professional counselor who feels exhausted or begins having trouble accessing empathy for clients should take actions (e.g., seek additional supervision; increase self-care initiatives; engage in personal counseling) to rebuild their health and competency.

Voices From the Field 6.1 The Birth of a Superhero, *by Bethany Garr*

I remember the first time Cody walked into my office. He bounded in, nearly knocking me over, and proceeded to pick up and examine everything on my desk, the bookshelves, and the table. When he finally sat next to his mother, this little ball of excited energy continued to move frenetically, unable to sit still. But despite the way his excitement and energy seemed to fill the room, as I heard his story, he seemed almost to shrivel and shrink.

Cody was adopted as a toddler; his birth parents had significant mental health and substance abuse issues, and he had experienced a great deal of neglect as a result. When the police came to remove Cody and his brother from his birth parents, he was found in a boarded-up house, wearing a soiled diaper, with no food in the home except for a few bags of chips.

Cody had been drug-exposed in-utero, which had resulted in a cleft palate. Cody had been diagnosed with AD/HD, which the doctors also theorized was due to this drug exposure. To compound matters, he had also been diagnosed with autism spectrum disorder; while he was quite intelligent and creative, he also had very poor social skills. He had few friends and frequently argued with his peers.

Cody's adoptive mother was frustrated; it seemed that no amount of therapy or medication could alleviate the laundry-list of symptoms with which he presented. He had recently been hospitalized for the first time, which greatly upset both Cody and his mother. He had been on multiple combinations of medications, all of which seemed to help for a bit, before the effectiveness would taper off. His adoptive mother stated that she believed Cody was worsening; he rarely slept, seemed depressed, and was extremely defiant.

Initially, Cody was resistant to exploring the abuse and neglect he had endured when he lived with his birth parents. Although he had been quite young when he was removed from his birth parents' custody, he still had strong memories about them. Despite his claims to the contrary, it was evident that these thoughts still haunted him. He frequently had nightmares about people chasing and trying to kill him, which caused him to wake up screaming almost nightly. He often obsessed about stories of child abductions on the news. Although he trusted his adoptive mother, he questioned her ability to protect him.

I attempted to use trauma-focused cognitive-behavioral therapy with Cody. Although he responded well to the skills-based portions, he did not want to write a trauma narrative. Because of his resistance and fear, I knew I had to find an alternative way to approach Cody. He had always been interested in video games and cartoons, especially those involving superheroes. He also loved writing and drawing. So, one day, I asked if he would like to write a comic book, one in which he could be the superhero. He eagerly agreed.

We started by developing a Super-Cody character, one that was equipped to handle the stress of his past. Super-Cody had a strong, protective suit that was able to repel any weapons used against him. He had several superpowers, including super-speed, invisibility, and the ability to throw fireballs.

We began writing stories about Super-Cody's exploits as he faced all sorts of villains and bad guys, most of whom were trying to steal him away. Even when a villain had trapped Super-Cody, he was always able to summon the strength to save the day. As Super-Cody became stronger and more self-reliant, so did Cody.

One day, I suggested that we write a story about a pair of villains who were trying to abduct Super-Cody. I wondered if we could incorporate the names Tim and Sandy—his birth parents' names—into the villains' names. Cody looked at me with uncertainty but agreed—while the traditional trauma narrative seemed too daunting for him, it seemed that a comic book version was something he felt capable of doing. It took several weeks for Cody to write the story about his battle against Terrifying Tim and Scary Sandy; at first, he seemed reluctant to write each word and draw each picture, but over time, Cody's fear and hesitation seemed to transform into confidence and excitement. As he finally drew the panel in which he threw the villains into jail, he smiled widely to himself. He shared his comic book with his mother, whose face reflected the pride she felt for a son who had accomplished so much.

I continued to work with Cody on other concerns after we had finished writing about and reflecting on Super-Cody. His alter ego seemed to provide him with a sense of strength and resilience that continued to follow him as he struggled with shaky peer relations and difficult family problems. By the time we terminated, he seemed to be a different child. He had good grades and had even made a few new friends. He no longer argued with his parents or the other children at school. He had a healthy sense of self-esteem and seemed to really believe that he deserved to experience good things in his life. Super-Cody and Cody were no longer two separate people, but one strong, secure being.

Children With Learning Disabilities or Giftedness

Counselors must use a unique set of skills and tools when working with children who are gifted or have learning differences or disabilities. For a counselor to effectively work with any child, it is important to understand the child's cognitive ability and method of processing the information received from the world. An understanding of young clients' cognitive abilities can help counselors address any associated mental health consequences in developmentally appropriate ways (Sigelman & Rider, 2022; Stephens et al., 2010).

Generally, children's cognitive abilities are assessed in relation to their intelligence quotient (IQ), academic performance, and social skill abilities (Rix et al., 2009; Sigelman & Rider, 2022). Although there are many different opinions and types of intelligence tests, it is commonly accepted that an IQ of 85–115 indicates average intelligence. Intelligence quotients of 70 to 84 and 116–130 lie outside of the average range, but do not indicate considerable intellectual disability or giftedness. However, an IQ from 52–70 indicates mild intellectual disability, 35–51 indicates moderate, and 20–34 indicates severe intellectual disability. On the opposite end of the spectrum, an IQ of 130 or above indicates intellectual giftedness (Sigelman & Rider, 2022).

When considering how cognitive abilities affect or relate to children's mental health, it is important to have knowledge of their overall sense of well-being. Although a child's sense of belonging, achievement, and personal identity can be heavily influenced by academic achievement, it is also developed through relationships with family, friends, and school personnel (Stephens et al., 2010). By assessing all facets of the client's life, it is possible to determine the area in which counseling can be most beneficial. Counselors work with children, their families, and their teachers in order to help children learn optimally, develop a strong sense of personal identity, and thrive academically and personally.

Intellectual Disability

Academic difficulty (i.e., an IQ of 70 or below and difficulty with developmentally appropriate behaviors and social cues) can create disruptions in children's sense of self: self-esteem, self-concept, and self-efficacy (Sigelman & Rider, 2022; Stephens et al., 2010). Children's responses to these difficulties may include feelings of sadness and depression, withdrawal, avoidance, or anger. Although these feelings often develop as a reaction to academic struggles, they also further inhibit healthy learning. It is important to help children learn how to address these feelings so that they can develop adaptive behavior patterns both in and out of the classroom (Stephens et al., 2010). Individual mental health counseling can be helpful in allowing some of these feelings to be constructively expressed and validated and to help teach children coping and social skills.

When counseling children, it is important to maintain an active counseling style, avoid prolonged use of silence, and appropriately use self-disclosure (Stephens et al., 2010). These techniques can help children feel more at ease and allows for a more interactive mental health process. Children with intellectual disabilities often experience inattention or difficulty concentrating. It is helpful to reduce distracting stimuli and to be appropriately directive when communicating with these children. Counselors can guide a child with attentional difficulties through any simple, enjoyable task and then process the steps as they apply to other activities that are more difficult for the child.

Some counselor-generated techniques suggested by Stephens et al. (2010) include using group counseling interventions as an effective way to address mental health needs of children with intellectual disability. Stephens et al. reported that it can be helpful to include socially accepted children in these groups to reduce social stigma and to have peers who can model socially appropriate behaviors. Issues of impulsivity can be addressed through games that require physical restraint or activities that clearly explain and rehearse appropriate responses to common situations. This can effectively address behaviors that are further contributing to academic difficulties and can even reduce the use of aggressive coping strategies commonly used by children with intellectual difficulty (Rix et al., 2009; Stephens et al., 2010). Over time, group process can effectively help children learn to recognize others' emotional and social cues, which can work to reduce anxiety and emotional lability in children with intellectual difficulties. Children's self-esteem is likely to improve from increased social acceptance, which will further promote children's sense of self-efficacy and academic success (Stephens et al., 2010).

School counselors might consider using both individual and group counseling in collaboration with students' teachers (Rix et al., 2009; Stephens et al., 2010). Individual counseling can address clients' overall well-being, group counseling can be used to address specific aspects of difficulty, and collaboration with teachers can be used to identify helpful teaching and behavioral management techniques. Clinical mental health counselors can also be a valuable resource for these students and may find it helpful to work in collaboration with the school counselor and the parents. It might even be possible for some counselors to work with children in their school setting and in their home, as opposed to providing outpatient counseling.

It is also important to consider the social consequences experienced by many who have an intellectual disability. Group counseling can be especially helpful for teaching social skills and normalizing complex feelings that can result from having an intellectual disability (Rix et al., 2009; Stephens et al., 2010). Children with an intellectual disability can address negative feelings in a safe environment that normalizes and validates their feelings, while increasing social interaction.

An additional consideration for children with intellectual disabilities is the child's family and home life. Often, intellectual disability is genetic, which means that one or both parents may experience similar struggles (Sigelman & Rider, 2022). Some parents might have their own mental health challenges that inhibit them from providing fully attentive and responsive parenting. Additionally, parents with intellectual difficulties may not have the skills or abilities to help their children with schoolwork, healthy coping skills, or social interactions.

Giftedness

The mental health needs of children who are intellectually gifted (i.e., IQ above 130) are similar to those experienced by children with intellectual disability. These children may struggle with issues of self-identity as they notice that their cognitive ability is different from the majority of their peers (Wood, 2010). Additionally, their increased moral awareness may make it difficult for gifted children to relate to their less introspective peers. Although it seems counterintuitive, children with high intellectual ability might experience struggles surrounding academic difficulties. Gifted individuals have a high need for achievement and stimulation. If gifted children are not adequately challenged, they might actually disengage from school activities. Additionally, many gifted children are used to easily understanding academic material; if not challenged appropriately, they may begin to doubt their academic abilities and lose some of their identity related to ease of academic success.

When addressing the mental health needs of gifted children, counselors should remember that intellectual giftedness is an asset, but also can be a burden (Peterson, 2015). Boredom and disengagement from schoolwork can lead to negative self-esteem, social isolation, and depression. Although intelligence is typically viewed as a protective factor, intelligence can lead to existential thoughts that children are not able to understand or accurately interpret. Consequently, children who are gifted may feel overwhelmed, depressed, and isolated.

When working with gifted children, the primary goal of the counselor is to form a safe, therapeutic alliance with the child through acknowledgment of the child's difficulties, while also facilitating the child's self-awareness (Wood, 2010). Some may ignore that these children progress through the same developmental stages as other children (Sigelman & Rider, 2022). Also, many intellectually gifted children are not used to feeling challenged in an academic setting. When they do encounter demanding academic circumstances, it will be important for counselors to help children develop appropriate organizational and time-management skills (Wood, 2010). Counselors should also help children understand that when they struggle or feel frustrated, this is normal and serves to help their character develop, and it is not a sign of weakness (Peterson, 2006). Additionally, adopting a psychoeducational approach to help gifted children make sense of themselves, others, and challenges in life is pertinent (Peterson, 2015).

It is also important to understand the social difficulties some gifted children experience. Parents who do not understand the needs of their gifted children may pathologize behaviors such as underachievement or behavioral expressions of frustration or boredom (Peterson, 2015). In addressing the needs of a gifted child, it is important to help parents gain an understanding of their children's needs and desires. Gifted children also often feel isolated and different from their peers; working with children to develop appropriate social skills and self-esteem will also be important (Wood, 2010).

Although there are many aspects of mental health that are affected by a child's cognitive abilities, it is important to address each one in a systematic way that addresses the child's most serious needs first. It is important to remember that all children are unique individuals who will express their mental health needs in a variety of ways. Ultimately, when working with any child, especially those with academic disability or giftedness, it is important to be compassionate, open-minded, and holistic.

Voices From the Field 6.2 Rose-Colored Glasses, *by Emily C. Campbell*

We are all human, we are all different, and we all experience struggles. Our differences aren't always negative and struggles do not necessarily equate to failure. In fact, our challenges can often become our successes.

As a counselor-in-training, I interned in a child and adolescent hospital unit providing mental health and family counseling services to patients and their families. Many struggles brought my 16-year-old client, Beth, to our unit. She had been actively involved in the mental health system, but because of her behavioral issues, many people had struggled to connect with her strengths and frame her situation in context.

Upon completion of an educational evaluation, it became evident that Beth had a preexisting learning disorder that had not previously been identified secondary to the dominance of her behavioral issues. Her learning disability was compounded too by a history of sexual abuse and trauma, and subsequent rotations through the foster care system. Due to her lack of social skills, traumatic childhood experiences, and inability to regulate her emotions appropriately, Beth found great difficulty in accepting support from the staff and other patients on the unit, and her learning disability had been overlooked.

My work with Beth was brief, but memorable. Others found her to be negative and disruptive, but I was able to see her untapped skills and talents. Although she was challenging to work with, I provided her with kindness, structure, and patience. She was able to significantly improve socially and scholastically, which was visible even to the hospital staff.

Unfortunately, Beth had not been socialized appropriately or received services such as counseling to help her process through her trauma issues. In counseling, Beth and I worked on processing her traumatic past. We also worked on developing her social and coping skills, especially those that related to interacting with others (e.g., tone and pitch of her voice, eye contact, and other nonverbals). It became a topic of discussion with the clinical staff that it was possible that her learning "disability" was not one that was a product of genetics, but possibly evolved secondary to the circumstances she had endured. If nothing else, it appeared the unresolved trauma symptoms were agitating her learning disability. In fact, as she worked through her trauma issues, the symptoms of her learning disability appeared to diminish.

I have found that when I view clients through a humanistic and strength-based lens, this enables our relationship to flourish and to move toward positive growth. Every person has knowledge and experience to share, and my training and experience as a counselor provided me with the tools deemed necessary to focus on Beth's strengths, rather than her weaknesses. Just like anyone else, clients with learning disabilities have a need to feel heard, accepted, and valued.

Self-Assessment 6.1 Assessing Your Biases About Working With Differently Abled Populations

1. Gifted children sometimes have mental health difficulties. T F
2. Children with intellectual disabilities are not able to benefit from counseling as much as others. T F
3. How would you establish therapeutic rapport with a differently abled child?

Answers: 1. T, 2. F.

Nonsuicidal Self-Injury

Nonsuicidal self-injury (hereafter referred to as self-injury) is the direct and deliberate destruction of body tissue in the absence of suicidal intent (Washburn et al., 2012). While people self-injure in a variety of ways, the most common forms include self-cutting, self-burning, and self-scratching (Nock & Favazza, 2009). It is estimated that 21%–80% of clinical samples (Nock & Prinstein, 2004), 21.5% of high school students (Mohl & Skandsen, 2012), 8% of 6th–8th grade students (Hilt et al., 2008), and 15% of college students (Whitlock et al., 2011) have engaged in some form of self-injury, thus making it probable that all counselors will encounter clients or students who self-injure.

There are a variety of reasons people self-injure, and the behavior generally serves various evolving functions that are dependent upon time and experiences. There are multiple reasons why people self-injure, but all explanations are founded on the idea that self-injury is a form of emotion regulation; people self-injure to manage strong, generally painful emotions (Izadi-Mazidi et al., 2019). Self-injury serves various functions at different times, and it may serve as a means of (a) increasing positive emotions and cognitions; (b) decreasing aversive emotions and cognitions; (c) social negative reinforcement (i.e., it reduces aversive social events, or it serves to decrease feelings of isolation and loneliness); and/or (d) social positive reinforcement (i.e., it increases perceived positive social events).

People who self-injure possess a variety of mental health diagnoses, as well as varied developmental and personal contexts that typically contribute to the development and maintenance of the behavior (Washburn et al., 2012). The multifarious nature of self-injury can make it difficult for counselors to conceptualize a client's treatment needs, and they may struggle to know where to begin in helping this population. As such, when working with someone who self-injures, it is important to provide a comprehensive assessment in which the frequency, severity, duration, and onset of the self-injurious behavior is assessed along with the antecedents, consequences, functions, and dynamics of the behavior. More specifically, counselors might inquire about: age of onset, course of the behavior, longest period free of behavior, lifetime and current frequency of self-injury, changes in the behavior over time, emotional states when injuring, triggers leading to the self-injurious behavior, immediate and more long-term aftermath of injuring, medical complications (e.g., infections, stitches, surgeries, corrective surgeries), impulsivity of self-injury, dystonicity (e.g., a wish to stop oneself), resistance (e.g., effort to stop oneself), control (e.g., success in stopping oneself), use of substances before and after the behaviors, and past interventions to stop behavior (Kress, 2003).

The literature offers little guidance on effective treatment of self-injury; empirical research and evidence-supported treatment guidelines are limited (Washburn et al., 2012). In general, therapeutic approaches that emphasize problem solving, emotion regulation, and functional assessment and analysis of the behavior (i.e., developing an understanding of what thoughts, feelings, and behaviors led to the self-injury, and what behaviors could be altered to preclude further self-injury) are cited as important treatment elements. Cognitive restructuring and a strong therapeutic relationship are also suggested as essential when counseling those who self-injure (Flaherty, 2018).

Dialectical behavior therapy (DBT) is one treatment approach that shows promise in supporting those who self-injure (Flaherty, 2018). In an attempt to reduce or eliminate self-injury, a DBT approach focuses on assisting clients in developing alternative coping skills, identifying obstacles to the use of alternative skills, and enhancing skill generalization outside of the therapeutic setting. DBT uses several treatment modalities, including group skills training, individual therapy, phone coaching, and supervision or team consulting for the counselor.

The possible health risks (e.g., cutting too deeply, medical complications such as infections) that can occur secondary to self-injury contribute to some counselors feeling intimidated **at even the prospect of working with this population.** Adding to many counselors' apprehension is that many people who self-injure may not view the behavior as problematic and may not elect to select self-injury cessation as a counseling goal (Kress & Hoffman, 2008). Counselors' challenge when working with clients who do not wish to stop self-injuring is to assess how to best facilitate a client's desire to change while avoiding power struggles and attempts to control the client (e.g., forcing clients to stop injuring, demanding they stop injuring; Nelson & Piccin, 2016). Attempts to control clients often increase their resistance to change and are typically considered unethical. Some counselors may want the cessation of the self-injury to be the primary treatment goal, yet clients may not be ready to change. Motivational interviewing (MI) techniques can be helpful in enhancing clients' motivation to want to change and stop self-injuring (Kress & Hoffman, 2008). Motivational interviewing techniques are discussed in greater detail in the section in this chapter on counseling clients who are mandated and/or have a low motivation for change.

Case Study 6.1 The Case of Sarah

Sarah, a 21-year-old nursing student, presents for counseling at the college counseling center. She would like to receive counseling services to better manage conflicts she is having with her boyfriend. During the interview process, the counselor comes to understand that Sarah is shy and reserved and has difficulty expressing emotions and needs to her boyfriend. When Sarah cannot express herself, or becomes withdrawn, her boyfriend becomes frustrated. In turn, this increases Sarah's inability to express her emotions and thus increases her sense of feeling overwhelmed. Sarah goes on to casually mention that she sometimes uses delicate self-cutting as a method of coping to deal with her unexpressed emotions. Sarah reports that while she feels embarrassed about the self-cutting and self-conscious about her scars, she finds this to be an effective way to manage her frustrations. The counselor is aware of a strong desire to push the client to stop injuring, and to force her to work on behavioral alternatives to self-injury. The counselor considers several options, including having Sarah evaluated for a psychiatric placement at a hospital. The counselor also considers forcing Sarah to sign a contract stating that she will no longer self-injure. Based on this information:

1. What are preliminary safety-related questions that should be considered before continuing to provide counseling services to a client who self-injures, like Sarah?

The counselor might first consider safety-related questions as follows: Has Sarah has ever needed medical attention for her injuries? Does she care for her wounds, or has she experienced wound infections? Does she share cutting implements with others?

2. In this scenario, the counselor appears to be very uncomfortable with Sarah's self-injuring behavior. What might be your initial personal reactions and attitudes toward working with a client who self-injures? What steps might you take to monitor these reactions?

People typically have a variety of reactions toward those who self-injure. It is not uncommon to have negative reactions toward people who self-injure. Consultation with a supervisor, peer supervision, education about self-injury, and increased exposure to those who self-injure are a few of the ways that counselors can manage their personal reactions toward this population.

Intimate Partner Violence

Intimate partner violence (**IPV**), more popularly referred to as domestic violence, is the term used to encompass violence perpetrated by a relationship partner (Campbell et al., 2003). The scope of IPV is far-reaching, with 34% of women spanning varied socioeconomic, age, and racial backgrounds being victims of IPV at some point in their lives (Browne, 1993). Intimate partner violence also affects children, with estimates suggesting that at least that 3.3 million children each year witness IPV, and many of these children experience enduring long-term effects secondary to this exposure (American Psychological Association [APA], 1996).

Intimate partner violence can have serious short and long-term consequences for its victims. Most seriously, 30–55% of female homicides are perpetrated by intimate partners (Campbell et al., 2003), and IPV is the direct cause of 21% of female emergency room visits each year (Browne, 1993). For victims, the psychological consequences of IPV can include depression, anxiety, an increased risk of suicide, PTSD, psychosomatic complaints, substance abuse, and lowered self-esteem (Dokkedahl et al., 2019; Evans & Feder, 2016).

The increased risk of psychological problems associated with IPV increases the likelihood that victims will become consumers of counseling services. Counselors' early and accurate assessment and detection for IPV is important. Clients should be routinely asked about relationship experiences with violent and controlling partners (Evans & Feder, 2016). Many clients do not identify or recognize their experiences as abusive and as such, the first step in completing a thorough assessment of relationship violence is psychoeducation (Murray & Graves, 2012). Clients benefit from having abuse and violence clearly defined and these efforts may help them to recognize that abuse has occurred. Assessment of IPV should include a determination of the duration, nature, extent, and intensity of violent, controlling, and abusive acts. Inquiries into the following areas can help counselors better identify the nature of the abuse: (a) detailed descriptions of a typical abuse experience, (b) the most severe abuse experience, (c) the most recent abuse experience, and (d) the frequency of the abuse.

A first priority when counseling those is abusive relationships is monitoring and enhancing their safety. One of the most important efforts a counselor can take to minimize risk and facilitate client safety is to help the client draft a safety plan (Kress et al., 2008). A safety plan is a detailed plan that highlights the client's role in making the safest decisions possible when managing violent situations. It should be emphasized to clients that although they do not have control over their partner's violent behavior, they do have a choice in how to respond and how to best enhance their safety as well as the safety of their children. Any discussion of safety should be tailored to the unique needs of the individual. For example, a teenager in an abusive dating relationship will require a different safety plan than a woman living with an abusive partner. Safety plans might address the following: (Murray & Graves, 2012): (a) an accessible place to store personal items when a quick exit is necessary, (b) safe places to go when the client decides to leave the abuser, (c) telling friends or neighbors about the violence and requesting that they call the police if they hear suspicious noises or witness suspicious events, (d) identifying safe rooms in the house, school, etc., (e) developing emergency escape routes, (f) where they can go if they fear an argument will develop storing an escape kit, and (g) processing the safety plan with children (when age appropriate).

In addition to the safety plan, areas of discussion might be exploration of issues related to police protection, legal action, domestic violence shelters, community resources, and social supports (Browne, 1993). Counselors should become familiar with both the state laws that relate to IPV and local resources that may be useful in supporting clients seeking safety. It is also important to discuss with clients the importance of trusting their intuition and judgment related to the violence. Many victims who are experiencing IPV have an excellent understanding of their partner's abuse patterns and sense when more serious harm is a possibility. Encouraging clients to trust their instincts and to do what they can to de-escalate the situation may be helpful in promoting client safety, and should be discussed in relation to the safety plan.

Many clients who are or have been in an abusive relationship sustain trauma reactions. Golding's (1999) meta-analysis of 11 studies indicated that PTSD is one of the most prevalent mental disorders in women in abusive relationships. The presence of PTSD symptoms can be potentially devastating for victims. Since when unaddressed, PTSD is related to a risk of future revictimization (Herman, 2015), the resolution of trauma is an important treatment goal. Generally, exposure-based cognitive-behavioral approaches are recommended as front-line treatments for people in abusive relationships (Johnson & Zlotnick, 2009). Clients not yet living in safe, stable living environments, or clients who are managing a great deal of chaos may need to wait to begin exposure-therapy; the exposure-therapy aspect of treatment may be agitating and thus contraindicated during the early stages of treatment.

Substance Abuse

Because of the complexity of addictions and the high prevalence of co-occurring mental disorders, counseling those who abuse substances is a challenging task. The *Diagnostic and Statistical Manual of Mental Disorders* (DSM-5; APA, 2013) classifies substance use disorders resulting from the use of ten separate classes of drugs: alcohol; caffeine; cannabis; stimulants (including amphetamine-type substances, cocaine, and other stimulants); hallucinogens (phencyclidine or similarly acting arylcyclohexylamines, and other hallucinogens, such as LSD); inhalants; opioids; sedatives, hypnotics, or anxiolytics; tobacco; and other or unknown substances. Substance-use disorders are patterns of symptoms resulting from the use of a substance that people continue to use, despite experiencing problems as a result. Substance use disorders are characterized by clients' use of a substance despite its negative impact on their social, occupational, and financial functioning.

Substance use disorders create a number of consequences and problems, and the symptoms of a substance use disorder include:

1. Taking the substance in larger amounts or for longer than one intended.
2. Attempts to cut down or stop using the substance.
3. Spending a great deal of time getting, using, or recovering from use of the substance.

4. Cravings and urges to use the substance.
5. Not managing to do what one should at work, home, or school because of substance use.
6. Continuing to use, even when it causes problems in relationships.
7. Giving up important social, occupational, or recreational activities because of substance use.
8. Using substances again and again, even when it puts one in danger and creates problems.
9. Continuing to use, even when one knows there is a physical or psychological problem that could have been caused or made worse by the substance.
10. Needing more of the substance to get the effect one wants (tolerance).
11. Development of withdrawal symptoms, which can be relieved by taking more of the substance.

As with any other mental health issue, counselors rely primarily upon their clients for information that can lead to an accurate diagnosis and treatment of substance use disorders. People who abuse substances tend to be poor historians about their use. There are many reasons why people with substance abuse difficulties are not honest with their counselors about their use. Inherent to all addictions is a strong desire to maintain use of the substance at all costs, even by lying. Additionally, the effects of the substances being used may also impair one's ability to connect with their use and its consequences. Perhaps as a psychological defense mechanism which protects them from change, many clients also minimize the extent of their substance use and its consequences, even to themselves. Many clients also receive counseling for substance abuse as the result of a court order. Drug court initiatives operate under the notion that people who are arrested for non-violent, drug-related crimes have underlying mental health concerns that can be addressed more thoroughly through therapeutic interventions, rather than imprisonment (Brown, 2011). Although Brown found these programs to decrease recidivism across diverse groups, including women, people of color, older adults, and people with more serious criminal histories, many people still resent participating in mandated counseling.

In addition to the difficulties associated with mandated substance abuse services, many people who have suffered with substance use issues have suffered significant losses in their lives (APA, 2013). Some clients fear that truthful discussion about their substance use will further contribute to the loss of their family, social supports, or employment opportunities. This fear can be partially alleviated by the privileged communication between a client and counselor, but many still struggle to be candid about their use (Kress et al., 2013).

At least 60% of people who abuse substances also have other comorbid mental health disorders, and the combination of substance abuse and a second mental health disorder is referred to as **dual diagnosis** (U.S. Department of Health and Human Services, National Institutes of Health, National Institute on Drug Abuse, 2018). Although it is impossible to say that one causes the other, additional mental health disorders must be addressed when working with substance abuse and dependence. It is imperative to gain clients' trust to fully understand their mental health in the context of their past experiences, personal struggles, and future goals. It is also important to identify the benefits of drug use, such as escape from painful circumstances and social reinforcement.

Most commonly, depressive/bipolar and anxiety-related disorders accompany substance use (U.S. Department of Health and Human Services, National Institutes of Health, National Institute on Drug Abuse, 2018). For some clients, it may be helpful to address the substance abuse separately from other mental health diagnoses, but it is often more realistic to address the client in a more holistic way. One therapeutic intervention that is especially helpful with clients who experience comorbid disorders is motivational interviewing (MI; Miller & Rollnick, 2013). This clinical interviewing approach supports clients in enhancing their personal motivation to stop using substances. Using collaboration and encouragement, MI techniques help clients to identify their own desire to change and locate resources to help them modify their lifestyles.

Although MI is a helpful resource when working with those who have substance use disorders, there are many other treatment alternatives, such as cognitive-behavioral techniques and 12-step programs (Miller & Rollnick, 2013). Ultimately, counselors must understand the complexity of substance use and how it interacts with clients' other mental health needs, their coping strategies, and their motivation to change.

Self-Assessment 6.2. Substance Abuse Attitudes.

1. Are substance use issues always caused by other mental health disorders?
2. Would you enjoy the challenge and complexity of working with clients who use substances? Explain.

Older Adults and the Terminally Ill

When working with older adults, it is important to consider their cognitive and emotional development as this may help to illuminate their personal struggles and identify appropriate counseling interventions. Adults over the age of 65 years usually have entered Erikson's psychosocial stage of integrity versus despair (Sigelman & Rider, 2022). A key challenge to this final stage of life is identifying ways in which an individual's life was meaningful and positively influenced the world. This struggle can be addressed in counseling through techniques such as reminiscence therapy, which was supported by Erikson as a natural way to cope with circumstances of older age (Lök et al., 2019; Sigelman & Rider, 2022).

Reminiscence therapy techniques invite clients to verbally construct their life stories and identify how they have used the skills and gifts given to them by their ancestors to make an influence in the world (Lök et al., 2019). Furthermore, reminiscence therapy allows older clients to identify how their beliefs and values have been passed on to benefit future generations (Syed Elias et al., 2019). Reminiscence therapy may also effectively alleviate symptoms of depression that are often present in older populations and those with Alzheimer disease (Lök et al., 2019). Although many older adults suffer with feelings of isolation and helplessness, countless older adults successfully overcome the challenges of the integrity versus despair stage and find peace in old age (Sigelman & Rider, 2022). In fact, older adults who perceive that they have good health and low stress feel a certain peace with their situation and may even live more in the moment and appreciate and enjoy life more than they did in their younger years (Fullen et al., 2018).

Many older adults face end-of-life issues, and each person experiences these issues in a unique way. It is important to appreciate and understand peoples' relationship with death and how they approach death and dying. As they have aged and experienced loss, older adults have had the opportunity to contemplate the meaning of death in a developmentally normal way. In contrast, and depending upon a person's developmental stage, some people who experience terminal illness may not progress through natural developmental stages; they may be caught unprepared to cope with the realities of death and dying (Sigelman & Rider, 2022).

People with terminal illness often learn of their diagnosis from a physician, and for many, this moment can prove to be traumatic, even haunting. As a counselor, it is important to process these disclosure events with clients. Some doctors might be very sensitive about the issue of death and dying, but some may avoid discussing death due to their own denial or anxiety or because of limited ability to communicate such information (Kübler-Ross, 2014). Processing the way in which clients learned of their illness might prove to be a helpful step in the therapeutic process. Counselors can learn about the clients' initial reactions to the news, and they can also learn about the client's level of awareness of and relationship with death.

Kübler-Ross (2014) developed five stages of dying which provide a general framework for working with clients who are terminally ill and/or facing death. Not every person will experience these stages; in fact, some might experience only a few, and others might experience them in a different order. The first stage, denial and isolation, is characterized by clients refusing to believe they will die; this can be psychologically adaptive when the initial shock of receiving a terminal diagnosis may feel as though it pulls too heavily on a person's ability to cope and adapt. Next, clients experience anger; this anger could be directed toward loved ones, themselves, the external world, or even a higher power. It is important for counselors to educate clients' loved ones about this stage of dying so that they understand any confusing, or even hurtful, client behaviors. After anger, clients often accept their fate, but attempt to bargain for slightly better circumstances, such as extended time or reduced pain.

After the first three stages, clients often experience depression. The depression stage is multifaceted and is experienced by every person, whether an older adult or the terminally ill, differently. Older adults may experience increased physical limitations, and their depression might lead to consideration of how their lives could have been different or better. Additionally, older adults often experience isolation due to the loss of other close loved ones and physical limitations, and this also contributes to depression in older people. People with terminal illness may feel a sense of hopelessness and regret about things that they will not be able to experience. For any person, the reality of leaving loved ones can also be a source of depression (Sigelman & Rider, 2022). Counselors can work with older clients who are depressed by helping them identify their legacy, or their personal accomplishments and relationships that have given their life meaning (Syed Elias et al., 2019). A review or reminiscence of their life allows clients to identify what they have inherited from the world, and what they will contribute to future generations. In addition to material possessions, clients' legacies include the values and beliefs that they will leave behind, and their relationships and the people they have influenced. Helping clients identify their legacy can allow them to make meaning of their lives, and therefore their deaths.

The final stage in the dying process is acceptance. Regardless of the stage in which a counselor first joins with the client, the goal is to help lead them to a place of acceptance and readiness. Just as with any other mental health issue, it is not always possible to reach maximum gains and some clients may struggle and not have time to reach a place of full acceptance. It is always necessary to have a treatment goal that reflects clients' personal aspirations.

In addition to working with clients who are experiencing death and dying, it is important to work with their loved ones, and when helpful, integrate them into the counseling process. Family members can experience feelings of denial, anger, uselessness, and depression as the result of a loved one's dying (Kübler-Ross, 2014). Family members' reactions can inhibit their ability to support the dying person and could result in mental health difficulties of their own. As a counselor, it is important to promote the mental health of clients' loved ones and to make referrals as necessary.

Death and dying lies at the core of human existence and is an issue that every person will eventually face. Counseling this population can prove to be challenging for some counselors. Counseling terminally ill or older adults can be difficult due to time constraints and a lack of control over clients' life circumstances. Additionally, in order to be present and fully available to their clients, counselors must have a firm understanding of their own beliefs and feelings surrounding death. Overall, counselors who have a healthy understanding of their relationship with death, are open and honest with themselves, and willing to empathize with clients in their greatest time of need will find fulfillment and success in their work with the older adult or terminally ill populations.

Voices from the Field 6.3. Living with Dying by Jamie Crockett

Working with a 43-year-old agnostic White woman with rapidly progressing colon cancer was, for me, especially challenging. The client wished to use her time in counseling to cope with her approaching death and address her fears that her two teenage daughters and husband of 25 years "couldn't handle" her illness and end-of-life related issues. Her belief that she had no one else to talk with about her death lent a sense of urgency to the counseling process. It was important that I stayed connected with my role as her counselor; respecting and trusting in her process and ensuring that I did not impose my personal values were critically important.

In order to meet the client where she was, I had to recognize my own bias that successful end-of-life counseling would include family and legacy work. The client believed that her family did not understand the gravity of her illness, yet she adamantly did not want to work on communicating with them about her dying process. Through self-evaluation and invaluable supervision, I learned to let go of my own hopes for what should be accomplished, and instead honored the client's hopes and needs. I had to trust that the client knew what she needed to prepare for her death.

The client emphasized a desire for increased relaxation amidst the physical, emotional, and relational pain she was experiencing. She spoke about death, processed her life experiences, and wondered about an afterlife. The client vented about insensitive things that friends and family said to her and appreciated that I did not tell her "don't think like that, you have to be positive." As we worked together, she grieved the physical and emotional losses she experienced, including an emerging distance she felt between herself and her loved ones. Yet as her time approached, she also felt increasingly ready to go and her curiosity about afterlife increased. Though she never stopped hoping for a miracle to prolong her life she began saying, "I'd rather stay than go, but when it's my time I'm ready."

Our work together was humbling and difficult; it was not about what I wanted for her, it was about what she wanted for herself. By allowing the client to direct her therapeutic process, she felt more confident and relaxed as she passed. Reflecting on our work together, I still find myself second-guessing: *Could I have done more for her and her family? Was it enough?* While I recognize that this questioning is a good thing and is part of my growing edge as a counselor, I know that the best work happens when I trust and support clients' wishes rather than impose my own beliefs and values.

Case Study 6.2: The Case of John.

John is a 78-year-old man who recently learned that he has stage-IV lung cancer. He remarried after divorce ended his first marriage, which produced one daughter who lives on the opposite side of the United States. He lives with his second wife, Sally, who is considerably younger than he is. John has decided to undergo chemotherapy in hopes of a brief period of "rest" in which he will experience little to no symptoms. Upon his third treatment, his doctor asked if he would still like to continue, and John asked his wife. With a heavy heart, Sally replied that it may be better to stop the painful chemotherapy treatments. John replied that he wished to continue with the therapy and said to his wife, "We're going to beat this." Two weeks later, John became too weak for another treatment and hospice was assigned. He passed shortly after in his bed at home with Sally.

1. In what stage of dying was John when he passed away?
    a. Acceptance
    b. Bargaining
    c. Depression
    d. Denial
2. Is it possible for clients to pass from a later stage of dying back to an earlier stage. Explain.
3. In what stage was John when he decided to undergo chemotherapy?
    a. Acceptance
    b. Bargaining
    c. Depression
    d. Denial
4. How aware are you of your own beliefs surrounding death and dying
5. Could you effectively counsel clients who are older or terminally ill? Explain.

Answers: 1) d; 3) b

Military Populations

Counseling Military Service Members and Veterans

Counselor exposure to service members and veterans who have experienced difficulties stemming from military involvement continues to increase (Hall, 2016). The sustained involvement of the United States in several wars, as well as the evolution of warfare, technology, and modern medicine have all contributed to a growing number of military personnel and veterans seeking counseling. Additionally, Houppert (2006) contended military members have not only experienced a drastic increase in overall deployment in the past decade (i.e., 300%), but have had to navigate the issues associated with cutting the general military force by a third. Counselors must understand counseling issues that relate to this growing population and develop appropriate evidence-based treatment plans in order to be most effective.

As military veterans return to the United States with the lasting emotional and psychological effects of war, there is a significant need for professional counselors' services (Mustillo et al., 2015). The most common mental health issues that veterans experience includes depression, PTSD, and alcohol use disorder. The prevalence rate of veterans with mental health issues is high, with as many as 27% exhibiting mental health symptoms. Combat duty and exposure to combat has been associated with a higher utilization of mental health services and a greater attrition rate in counseling (Crawford et al., 2015). Conversely, it has also been documented that those with mental health conditions often do not seek mental health treatment; it is estimated that only 18 to 42 percent of military service members with mental health issues seek out mental health care (Quartana et al., 2014). However, the utilization of mental health services among this population has been increasing over the years.

Stigma continues to be a prevailing theme among veterans and many hesitate to seek counseling services (Hall, 2016). This stigma may be influenced by service members' internalized paradigm that they would not need assistance to cope with the normal demands and stress of the military if internally strong enough. Some military members believe that the utilization of counseling services and/or human service programs may adversely affect their military careers. Additionally, there is often concern that confidentiality will not be maintained. First and foremost, counselors must acknowledge these threats and make every effort to educate military service members and veteran of the limits to confidentiality.

Treatment Considerations and Issues

Hall (2016) outlined two concepts that need to be fully considered when working with military members. These concepts include: a) the concept of honor, and b) the 'us versus them' mentality. The concept of honor relates to the idea that getting killed is an honorable choice if it is within the framework of carrying out a mission. Counselors must learn how to respect and even use this concept of perseverance (even through difficulties) to help an individual also honor family and career. The 'us verse them' mentality is a sense that civilians cannot possibly understand the military world. Civilian counselors need to assume the 'one down position,' and allow the service member or veteran to explain the situation. This stance provides the military member with the confidence that one is the expert of one's own life and military experience.

Carrola and Corbin-Burdick (2015) outlined eight recommendations for counselors who work with this military population. The recommendations are as follows:

1. Formulate a holistic case conceptualization by considering all possible causes of distress, not just combat exposure and military experience.
2. Encourage family involvement in counseling and addressing family-related concerns with the individual.
3. Become knowledgeable about posttraumatic growth and incorporate growth promoting interventions if trauma is present.
4. Focus heavily on the establishment of the therapeutic alliance and increase your understanding about this population even if you do not have military experience; a safe relationship with someone outside the military could increase clients' ability to establish healthy relationships within their community and increase social support.
5. Advocate, encourage, and challenge clients to see themselves as having an important role as a civilian.
6. Focus on cultural competency and sensitivity and enhance client growth and development through a multicultural framework.
7. Utilize evidence-based practices that have been shown to be effective for military clients, such as motivational interviewing, cognitive-behavioral therapies, and brief exposure therapies.
8. Be familiar with government guidelines such as U.S. Department of Veterans Affairs and Department of Defense while working with this population but do not rely exclusively on these guidelines.

These considerations can significantly assist counselors in creating a safe environment and providing the foundation for further treatment with this population.

The military population experiences the same mental health concerns as the civilian population. Hall (2016) suggested that counselors must be prepared to work with veterans on some (if not all) of the following areas: change, grief, and loss; reunion with family members; PTSD and related combat stress; family violence issues; alcoholism and substance abuse; and stress and anxiety regarding finances. These treatment issues are not always evident during the initial interaction with a counselor; therefore, continued assessment of these issues should occur throughout all phases of treatment.

Counselors should take into account if a client is active duty or retired. Current or future exposure to combat exacerbates the stress and anxiety of service members (Hall, 2016). Deployment and the emotional ramifications of leaving family are also significant stressors for service members. Service members who are deployed and enter combat zones experience an increased risk of PTSD, major depression, substance abuse, functional impairment in social and occupational settings, and increased use of physical health care services (Mustillo et al., 2015). As such, counselors should tailor their approaches and interventions according to a client's current employment status, factoring in when and if a client will need to deploy again in the future.

Evidence-Based Treatments

Much of the evidence-based research on working with military service members and veterans is grounded in cognitive-behavioral therapy (CBT; Foa et al., 2010; Hall, 2016). Cognitive processing therapy is a type of CBT that can help military personnel increase their senses of safety, trust, control and intimacy in the world. Prolonged exposure therapy is another form of CBT that incorporates somatic work (e.g., breathing and grounding techniques). CBT assists service members in forming connections between their thoughts, feelings, and behaviors. It is an evidence-based treatment for addressing the symptoms of PTSD and the associated trauma problems (Foa et al., 2010).

CBT is a model that often addresses cognitions and trauma through the use of psychoeducation, stress management, affective modulation, addressing cognitive distortions, trauma/problem processing, *in vivo* mastery of trauma reminders. In the final stages of treatment, CBT addresses safety and future personal development (Foa et al., 2010). Counselors can work to help veterans shift their thoughts, which should affect their feelings and behaviors in helpful ways. Hall (2016) suggested that when working with military personnel, a family systems approach should also be given consideration, and integrated into CBT. Overall, CBT increases service members' abilities to cope with specific trauma symptoms (Foa et al., 2010).

Case Study 6.3. The Case of Chris.

Chris is a White 23-year-old currently seeking treatment for an inability to sleep at night. During the intake phase, Chris disclosed a past sexual assault. Chris discussed that this incident occurred while being enlisted in the armed services and during deployment in Afghanistan. The incident in question was not discussed with fellow service members and never reported to authorities. After active duty was completed, Chris returned to work in the electronics field and committed to leave that experience in the past. Due to recent issues with sleep, avoidance of areas that may be difficult to escape, and recent nightmares about the incident, Chris has increasingly self-isolated. After the persistence of a close friend, Chris decided to talk with a professional counselor.

Questions:

1. What would you need to know prior to working with this veteran?
2. How would you go about establishing a strong therapeutic alliance?
3. Would it matter if Chris were a man or woman? Would your approach to treatment be different?
4. What specific trainings or experiences would be helpful in working with this veteran with this issue?

Counseling Mandated and Unmotivated Clients

Clients who are mandated to attend counseling often have low motivation for change, and thus treatment, and are frequently non-compliant in attending sessions. Falling into this mandated population are legal offenders and court-ordered clients. However, other initially less obvious populations such as children and adolescents are also frequently forced into counseling by their caregivers and may lack an interest or motivation to make changes. This section will highlight important considerations that may help counselors best approach these challenging populations.

Low Motivation and Non-Compliance

Whether novice or experienced, it is difficult for professional counselors to work with clients who lack motivation to change. To complicate matters, clients who lack motivation are also often non-compliant with treatment (e.g., they may miss sessions, not follow through on between-session work). Thus, these two concepts have become relatively synonymous as a lack of motivation is usually highlighted by a lack of compliance. It is essential when working with low-motivated, non-compliant clients to create a climate of change and actively engage the client (Cohen et al., 2010). Counselors can do so by creating a collaborative working relationship with clients.

Counselors can intentionally use motivational interviewing to support clients with low motivation. First, counselors should consider a client's level of motivation and evaluate whether a client is ready to change, contemplating change, or in a precontemplation stage of change (Miller & Rollnick, 2013). In order to enhance a client's motivation to change, it is important to address the client's ambivalence; counselors should roll with resistance and validate the reasons why a client does not want to change. Miller and Rollnick's approach highlights the importance of *not* attempting to define clients' problems and *not* persuading them that they should change. This approach provides feedback through a nonjudgmental, empathetic stance, and seeks to increase clients' ambivalence concerning whether they should change, or not. Motivational interviewing allows the counselor to address the issues which brought the client into treatment through humanizing, collaborative, respectful, and empowering means. The use of MI restores responsibility to clients, thus theoretically increasing their levels of engagement in the counseling process.

While building the therapeutic relationship and assessing the client's motivation, counselors work to enhance the climate for change (Cohen et al., 2010). This is done through the art of engagement and helping clients increase participation and ownership in the counseling process. The use of motivational interviewing enhances clients' motivational self-statements and deepens their commitment to the change process (Miller & Rollnick, 2013). Counselors should take care to meet clients where they are at in the therapeutic process and work toward change a half-step at a time.

Voices from the Field 6.4. Counseling an Unmotivated Adolescent in a Community Mental Health Agency by Lisa Paylo Meyer

In working with adolescents at a community mental health agency, I frequently counseled clients who were forced by others (e.g., parents, guardians, court system) to seek treatment. Consequently, many of my clients lacked the motivation to genuinely examine their situations and behaviors, let alone consider changing them. They often entered counseling with the belief that it was unnecessary and irrelevant.

In one specific case, upon a mother's urgent request, an adolescent who had engaged in serious self-cutting came in for services. The girl spoke very candidly about the cutting and offered to show me her wounds. She went on to discuss her frequent alcohol use, risky sexual behaviors, truancy from school, and elaborate methods for acting upon her urges to harm self. I assumed that such a forthcoming disposition would translate into therapeutically rich conversations, the discovery of the roots of her struggles, and accompanying behavior change.

Instead, what transpired, were cavalier descriptions of her lifestyle, with minimal insight into her behaviors' function. She expressed that cutting and sex were the best ways she knew to manage her stress. As such, she believed counseling was a futile effort because this was her life and she could choose how to navigate it. Despite such bold statements, her nonverbal behaviors suggested she was angry, lonely, and hurt. Her body often tensed when particular people or events were discussed, as if releasing her grasp would release her floodgates. She tended to share only when the information portrayed her in a tough and invulnerable manner.

It was my hope that after extensively exploring the functions and disadvantages of her behaviors, she would desire to live in a healthier, more satisfying way. After weeks of exploration, no such desire ensued. It became apparent to me that I was inadvertently imposing my own ideas about where and how change needed to occur. The client was resisting change as she perceived no benefit to altering her behaviors.

With this new realization, I spent the next few months helping the client connect with both the benefits and drawbacks of her behaviors. The main goal with this client was now to help her move from the precontemplation stage (i.e., when clients do not consider their behavior to be a problem and they do not want to change) to the contemplation stage (i.e., when clients begin to think about changing, cutting down, moderating, or quitting the addictive behavior by eliciting their own motivators and skills for change). In counseling, I began to focus on my client's autonomy—her ability to make her own decisions about change—which enabled her to take ownership for her actions. As the client settled into the role of being an expert on her situation, she slowly began to see her behavior as problematic. Simultaneously, she began to realize she possessed the strengths to change. I worked with this client for nearly five months before she made movement and terminated therapy.

For me, two lessons emerged from this experience. First, counselors cannot force their plan for change on the client; the client may just naturally push back. Secondly, I learned that if a client continues to be resistant, then perhaps the client has not in fact bought into the idea of counseling. It is then the counselor's responsibility to go back and assess where the client's level of motivation is and aid that client in assuming a greater sense of responsibility for personal actions and for the direction of the counseling process.

Legal Offenders

Legal offenders are frequently forced into counseling and typically have a low motivation to change. The two central aims when counseling legal offenders are to reduce recidivism (i.e., deviant, criminal behaviors) and to help offenders overcome their internal and external conflicts through the development of more accurate cognitions about themselves and their behaviors. Policy makers and the criminal justice system dictate that the counseling services rendered to offenders should increase the public's protection. Ultimately, the success of correctional counseling or treatment revolves around reduction of reoffending behaviors. Failure is measured by recidivism rates as seen through additional legal charges and prosecution (Gendreau & Goggin, 2014).

Regardless of a counselor's theoretical orientation, sound counseling in a correctional setting must aid offenders in the realization of their cognitions and how any distorted thoughts have maintained and perpetuated their crimes or criminal behaviors. This includes confronting the offenders' mechanisms of normalizing and rationalizing their actions and identifying how behavioral consequences build upon one another (Mpofu et al., 2018). A legal offender's rationale for deviant offenses can often be derived from a host of irrational thoughts and beliefs, and counselors work to address these cognitive distortions by challenging attitudes and beliefs that maintain the behaviors. Counselors can use cognitive restructuring as part of a CBT approach to help with: (a) exploring the role of deviant thoughts in the client's offending behaviors; (b) aiding the client with a means to correct deviant or impulsive thoughts; (c) assisting the client in discerning appropriate thoughts from inappropriate ones; and (d) supporting the client in challenging these inappropriate thoughts (Moster et al., 2008).

Court-Ordered Counseling

Court-ordered counseling might be mandated for certain individuals for offenses that might be related to underlying mental health issues (e.g., substance use, interpersonal violence). Court-ordered counseling can involve required inpatient or outpatient treatment and may even go so far as to mandate that offenders use certain medications. Rulings on mandated treatments must come from a judge or magistrate designated for these purposes within a given jurisdiction. Mandated treatments are court-ordered, thus providing offenders with an external motivation to comply with proposed treatments.

One often-forgotten mandated treatment modality is university or college disciplinary sanctions against students. In these situations, counselors are often asked to educate the student on the norms and rules of the campus in addition to offer mental health therapy (Kiracofe & Wells, 2007). The university holds the student's academic future as a means to get the student to increase compliance with the rules and norms of the campus.

Fully using the external demands placed upon the client to receive counseling services may enhance treatment compliance. In other words, while a court-ordered client may be non-compliant and even lack motivation, a counselor should use the external demands of the court to create a sense that a problem may exist and may need to be examined. Often mandated clients are quick to agree that getting out of the arms of the justice system is their personal primary goal of treatment, and this can be leveraged as a common ground between counselor and client.

Counselors should take care to avoid persuading clients or forcing them toward change before they are ready. When working with court-ordered clients, it is important to assess a client's readiness for change and use this information to inform practice. A counselor must select interventions that correspond with the appropriate readiness for change stage. Prochaska and Norcross (2018) constructed a developmental, stage theory based upon a client's readiness for change. These stages are as follows: precontemplation, contemplation, preparation, action, maintenance, and termination:

- In the **precontemplation stage**, a client is not aware that a problem exists and often has little motivation to change any part of the current situation. The client may say things like, "I don't have a problem . . . this person . . . or this system has the problem."
- In the **contemplation stage**, a client is able to acknowledge that a problem exists but is apprehensive about changing anything at this time. Often the client feels as if he or she is at a crossroads because positive and negatives of the behaviors are self-evident. The client may say, "I really must stop going out and partying. I know it is really hurting my marriage and my children, but I can't say no."
- In the **preparation stage**, a client is getting ready to change. More ownership of personal responsibility is evident. A client might say, "I've really got to do something about this . . . this is serious . . . something has to change."

- In the **action stage**, a client begins to change behaviors. The client believes that change is possible and acts on this belief.
- In the **maintenance stage**, a client continues to maintain the behavioral change. During this stage, a client must avoid temptation to slip back into the old habit, old ways of being. A client in this stage needs to continually reflect upon how much change has occurred. This stage requires new skills by the client to deal with and avoid relapsing.
- The **termination (or relapse) stage** is when the client returns to older behaviors and abandons the new changes. It is like "falling off the horse" and the best thing to do is to get right back on it. The ideal is that once relapse hits, then the preparation stage starts again. Ideally, the client will not revert back to the pre-contemplation stage.
- Another term, which is not part of Prochaska's original model, is the ideal of **transcendence** (Prochaska & Norcross, 2018). This concept refers to the idea that after a good amount of time in the maintenance stage, a client not only would not return to old ways, but it would seem abnormal to do so.

These stages of change can be useful in conceptualizing work with any client population where people have low motivation or are non-compliant.

Self-Assessment Activity 6.3.

The following statements are from a potential client. Predict the specific stage the client is in using Prochaska's readiness for change model and prepare a possible response to each statement (Prochaska & Norcross, 2018).

Statement 1: I know I need to stop drinking and partying with my friends. . .. It's really killing my chances at making my marriage work but I don't know if I can.

Your Responses:

Statement 2: I don't have any problem . . . you should be talking to my husband . . . now he is the one with the problem . . . go talk to him.

Your Responses:

Statement 3: I can make this change . . . but it will not be easy and I'll need a lot of support.

Your Responses:

Transference and Countertransference

Counselors must understand and be equipped to deal with transference and countertransference when working with clients. These concepts are often associated with Sigmund Freud and the classic psychoanalysts, even though these terms have recently become common vernacular in clinical supervision relationships and in the field of counseling in general. In this section, these two terms will be explained and presented in the context of real-life situations and scenarios. Self-evaluation is discussed and recommendations made on how to assess and deal with transference and countertransference reactions.

Transference

From a psychoanalytic perspective, **transference**, occurs when a client projects onto the counselor the attributes, characteristics, and motives reminiscent of another individual (Kress et al., 2021). More simply, transference is the transferring of the emotions and feelings of the client onto the counselor. This transferring, or projecting, of the client onto the counselor is often based on a real entity and the client will then respond to the counselor as if is the counselor is really that individual.

From a psychoanalytic perspective, there is benefit in counselors transforming themselves into "blank slates" and being neutral in presentation. This neutrality allows a transference reaction to become probable thus providing rich therapeutic information. As transference reactions develop, counselors who work from a psychoanalytic perspective believe that repressed material and dysfunctional patterns emerge. With this underlying material exposed, insights may develop, with the client eventually relating to others in a healthier way.

Regardless of the counselor's theoretical orientation, transference can be used to increase the client's level of awareness. Once the counselor realizes that transference is occurring, the use of immediacy is an invaluable technique that can be used to address it. Essentially, immediacy is the counselor's intentional directing of the dialogue to focus on the 'here and now' of the session; this moves the conversation to what is currently happening in the counselor–client relationship.

Case Study 6.4. The Case of Karen.

Karen is a 28-year-old Caucasian female currently in treatment for severe depression and relational issues. She is a known entity in the community because she has been in and out of a number of treatment facilities and has been diagnosed with borderline personality disorder (BPD). Additionally, she has a long history of self-injurious behaviors and some violent, threatening behaviors. Karen displays mixed emotions during the counseling sessions. This emotional polarity is conceived by the counselor as appropriate for an individual who has been diagnosed with BPD. She desires the counselor's attention, admiration, and unconditional regard. When she does not get this from the counselor, she has extreme emotional outbursts. On one such occasion she exclaims, "You never cared for me. . . . You never loved me. . . . Why did you even have me?" The counselor was then able to see that the client was transferring her turbulent relationship with her father onto the counselor. Karen eventually shared with the counselor that the counselor's beard was extremely similar to her fathers and often she would see this counselor as a warm father figure that she never had in her real life.

Questions:

1. How might you have dealt with this client, as she was transferring intense emotions onto you?
2. Write out a script for how you may have addressed this with Karen and how you would have utilized this opportunity to increase her awareness and address treatment goals.

Countertransference

Countertransference is the process of a counselor projecting attributes, and motives onto a client based on the client's characteristics or material the client presents within sessions (Reidbord, 2010). This can occur for a host of reasons stemming from the counselor's past experiences and can affect counselors at all stages of their development. Often the counselor's first sign that countertransference is occurring is that the counselor begins to perceive an internal shift in regard for the client. This shift is often incongruent with the presented material.

Since countertransference involves the counselor's own internal process, sufficient awareness is needed for a counselor to detect and address it. Self-assessment and supervision are the most useful means to reveal and deal with countertransference. Reidbord (2010) provided counselors with the following four insight-oriented questions that can aid them in the self-detection of countertransference: (a) Is this reaction or feeling characteristic of the way you normally work with clients?; (b) Is this reaction or feeling triggered by something outside of (e.g., not related) to the client? (c) Is this reaction or feeling related to the client in some obvious way?; and, (d) Is this reaction or feeling uncharacteristic for the counselor and not evident or obvious to you? The fourth question is the one that sheds the greatest light on the subtle yet important dynamics of the client and what that material stirs within the counselor. The counselor or supervisor can use these questions to better understand where these reactions and feelings originate.

Additionally, a counselor should use supervision to explore one's own unresolved difficulties concerning the client and the client's material. Sometimes counselors are unaware of countertransference and the use of supervision can aid in its early detection. Often these reactions and feelings can originate from irrelevant characteristics (e.g., physical resemblance), interactional characteristics (e.g., verbally dominated as in a past relationship), by a prior experience or feeling toward a past client, or by material unrelated to the counselor–client relationship (e.g., a fight with a family member, finances, health issues). Once the counselor becomes aware of where these reactions and feelings originate, the counselor can then identify and address countertransference.

Self-Assessment Activity 6.4.

Is countertransference occurring within the counselor–client relationship in the following scenarios?

Scenario 1: You begin to meet with a client who has had intense trauma experiences involving horrific stories of abuse and neglect. She appears to appreciate your style and the way you create a therapeutic alliance as evidenced by the way she has quickly revealed a great deal of information so early in counseling. You begin to think, "If only this person had a different set of parents, a different upbringing, or maybe if she just knew someone who had shown her love and compassion." You begin to see her as a victim, and even muster the idea that she just needs to find someone in her life who could save her. If she could just find this person, it could help her heal and move on.

Question: Is countertransference occurring in this scenario? What could be done to address this situation?

Scenario 2: You have been meeting with a client who is extremely depressed for the last three months. He has denied suicidal ideation but continues to feel relatively immobilized by his feelings of "worthlessness" and "self-doubt." You have tried ACT (acceptance and commitment therapy) and solution-focused brief therapy as well as CBT. You find that you are starting to dread this appointment each week. You feel frustrated by your client's lack of progress and have found that you are avoiding talking about him during supervision. You always seem to have a more urgent case to discuss. You start to construct statements about the client like: He doesn't want to change. . . . He is just resistant. . . . No one can help this guy. . . . He's hopeless. Then an even quieter voice starts to echo in your mind, "maybe I'm not good enough . . . maybe I'm not experienced enough to help him."

Question: Is countertransference happening in this scenario? What could be done to address this situation?

Summary

In this chapter, issues associated with providing counseling to consumers from a variety of populations were addressed. All of the populations have in common that their counseling needs are complex; all require that counselors are dynamic and thoughtful in considering their counseling approaches. The information presented in this chapter provides a starting place for working with these populations. Counselors will need to conduct additional research and garner information for their unique clients in order to ensure a solid understanding of these populations and their counseling needs.

When counseling maltreated children, many important considerations emerge. Among the most important is having a thorough understanding of counselors' roles as mandated reporters of child maltreatment. Counselors are not charged with investigating maltreatment and making determinations about whether maltreatment occurred, or if it will occur again. Our role is simply to ensure that we report all suspected maltreatment. Counselors must have an understanding of state laws related to counselor reporting of maltreatment. Additionally, counselors must also take care to not overlook or fail to report child neglect, the most common form of child maltreatment. Counselors must vigilantly assess for maltreatment on an ongoing basis and report new incidents as warranted.

With regard to child maltreatment, this chapter also addressed the varied and layered effects of child abuse and neglect. Factors that may insulate some children from the ill effects of maltreatment were also addressed and readers were urged to consider how these protective or resiliency factors could be developed or promoted via counseling. It was highlighted that children who experience repeated, ongoing abuse may demonstrate developmental trauma reactions which include symptoms that are unique from the reactions that typically occur after an isolated trauma incident. Because children who are maltreated often need multiple supports and different levels of intervention, the importance of counselors working as part of a team was also discussed.

When counseling maltreated youth, it was emphasized that counselors' interventions should be grounded in evidence-based practices. These evidence-based practices include the use of structured, manualized, and empirically supported models. All counselors who work with children and adolescents should become familiar with at least one evidence-based treatment approach (e.g., trauma-focused cognitive-behavioral therapy; Cohen et al., 2017).

Counseling issues associated with youth who have unique learning needs were also addressed. Although every child has their own individual learning needs, additional considerations must be taken into account when working with those who have learning disabilities or giftedness. It is important to gain a firm understanding of their cognitive abilities and how these affect their overall sense of well-being. A healthy academic identity must be achieved in context alongside a youth's relationships with family, friends, teachers, and peers. This understanding can be used to inform the counseling interventions that will have the greatest positive impact.

Individual counseling can be an effective way to measure individuals' learning abilities and can help identify the successes and struggles that are specific to them. It is helpful to implement family or group counseling to create change in the context of the clients' real-life situations. Family therapy can be used to educate parents and relatives of the struggles faced by youths and can promote the presence of healthy supports for students. Group counseling is especially helpful in addressing issues related to social skills and healthy development, with academic ability being just one part of students' larger personal identities.

Clients who self-injure can be personally activating to counselors, and as such, efforts must be made to ensure counselor personal reactions do not get in the way of effective clinical decision-making. Counselors' fear of clients' accidental death and health risks associated with SI can lead some counselors to feel anxious about a client's self-injurious behavior and push them to stop self-injuring. Instead of focusing treatment on pushing a client to stop self-injuring, counselors are encouraged to enhance a client's desire to change (Kress et al., 2010) through motivational enhancement techniques. Peer consultation, supervision, and education related to self-injury are helpful ways to ensure that counselors' personal reactions are monitored.

When treating self-injury, therapeutic approaches that emphasize problem solving, emotion regulation, and functional assessment and analysis of the behavior may be helpful (Washburn et al., 2012). A solid therapeutic relationship and cognitive restructuring are also important to the effective treatment of self-injury (Flaherty, 2018). Dialectical behavior therapy (DBT) and its emphasis on developing alternative coping skills, identifying obstacles to the use of alternative skills, and enhancing skill generalization outside of the therapeutic setting (Linehan, 2015) show promise in addressing self-injury.

Clients who are in relationships that involve intimate partner violence (IPV) are at a significant risk of being victims of homicide, and as such, counselors working with this population are challenged with the additional task of considering and supporting their safety. Many people who experience IPV may not recognize their relationship as problematic, and counselors must be vigilant about assessing for IPV. Safety plans are an important tool that counselors can use to promote their clients' physical well-being. A good safety plan highlights the client's role in making the safest decisions possible when managing violent situations (Kress et al., 2008). Important elements of safety planning include information related to police protection, legal action, domestic violence shelters, community resources, and social supports.

Research suggests that PTSD is the most common mental disorder in the IPV population (Golding, 1999). Exposure-based cognitive-behavioral approaches are considered the best treatments for those who have PTSD secondary to being in abusive relationships (Johnson & Zlotnick, 2009). Counselors are cautioned that clients who are not yet living in safe living environments or clients who are managing a great deal of chaos may need to wait to begin exposure-therapy treatment as cognitive exposure to past abusive incidents may be too agitating in addition to current stressors.

Substance abuse is a stigmatized mental health disorder in our society, with many people believing that substance use and abuse are matters of choice and will power. The complexity of this disorder makes it difficult for the general population, and even counselors, to fully understand. Due to the complexity of substance abuse issues, high rates of comorbidity with other mental disorders, and high rates of relapse, counselors should accept that multiple interventions over a long period of time might be necessary to produce positive changes in this client population.

More than half of all people diagnosed with substance use disorder have at least one additional diagnosed mental health difficulty. These findings might suggest that people initially begin to use drugs to alleviate the symptoms of their other mental health difficulties. As clients use substances in order to cope with losses that result from the substance use, a vicious cycle emerges and substance dependence ensues.

Interventions that have been found effective with this population are motivational interviewing techniques, CBT techniques, and 12-step programs (which are not a replacement for counseling, but a helpful supplement). Counselors who work with this population must have patience and perseverance. It will benefit counselors to assume the perspective of the client to understand the motivations for client substance use and their possible recovery options. With the ability to understand the client's private logic, counselors might identify a combination of helpful client-specific interventions.

Death and dying can be an uncomfortable subject. However, death lies at the core of human existence. To better serve clients who are experiencing difficulties surrounding death and dying, counselors should take care to evaluate their own struggles and biases related to this natural part of life. Whether it is the client or a client's loved one who is experiencing death and dying, it is important to identify ways in which the individual's life was meaningful and positively impacted the world. Reminiscence therapy allows clients to identify how they have used the skills and gifts given to them by their ancestors to leave a positive legacy with future generations. This intervention implements verbal storytelling to reduce depression in those who are dying as well as their loved ones.

Some clients encounter the impending reality of dying due to the developmental imperatives of old age. However, issues surrounding death and dying will also accompany the diagnosis of a terminal illness. Although distinct spectrums of issues are present in each situation, the five stages of dying developed by Kübler-Ross (2014) are an especially helpful framework for working with youth, adults, and their loved ones. It should be noted that not all people will experience all stages of the model, and some may experience the stages in different orders.

There is no standard way to identify the needs of those facing issues of death and dying, but it is possible to identify how to best help clients by empathically joining with their feelings and allowing them to direct you to the sources of their struggle. Whether they are dealing with grief, guilt, denial, anger, or frustration, it is important to normalize clients' feelings and help them to understand that there is no correct way to deal with death and dying. Effective grief counselors have a healthy relationship with death and loss and are willing to serve as a nonjudgmental, helpful presence in their clients' journeys.

Because combat duty and exposure to combat have been associated with an elevated risk of mental health issues, there is a significant need for professional counselors trained to work with military populations (Mustillo et al., 2015). As exposure to combat increases, service members display an increased risk of PTSD, major depression, substance abuse, and functional impairment in social and occupational settings. Counselors need to consider that even the potential deployment of a service member can create significant emotional ramifications that should be addressed in counseling (Hall, 2016).

Counselors must be ready to work with veterans in the following areas: grief and loss; reunion with family members; PTSD and related combat stress; family violence issues; alcoholism and substance abuse; and stress and anxiety regarding finances (Hall, 2016). Most of the evidence-based approaches are grounded in CBT (Foa et al., 2010; Hall, 2016), which aids service members in forming connections between their thoughts, feelings, and behaviors. Additionally, CBT assists in the reduction of PTSD symptoms by reframing unhelpful thoughts and shifting feelings and behaviors (Foa et al., 2010).

Clients mandated to receive counseling often have a low motivation for change and are frequently non-compliant with treatment expectations. Mandated clients can include court-ordered clients, legal offenders, students who break school rules, or even children and adolescents brought to treatment by guardians/caregivers. A counselor can consider ways to use these mandates to enhance the client's treatment compliance. At a minimum, the mandate can be highlighted as evidence that a problem exists and needs to be examined. Throughout this process, a counselor must consider the client's readiness for change (i.e., precontemplation, contemplation, preparation, action, maintenance, and termination stages; Prochaska & Norcross, 2018) and select interventions appropriate to that stage. When considering a client's level of motivation, a counselor must evaluate whether a client is ready to change, is contemplating change, or is not even at a stage to contemplate change (Miller & Rollnick, 2013).

Legal offenders are frequently mandated to treatment and typically have a low motivation to change. Regardless of a counselor's theoretical orientation, counseling in a correctional setting must assist offenders in the realization of their cognitions and how those thoughts have maintained and perpetuated their crimes and criminal behaviors. The aim of this type of counseling is to reduce offenders' deviant behaviors through the development of their awareness of the connection between cognitions and behaviors, and to confront distorted thinking.

Whether a novice or seasoned professional, it is difficult for counselors to work with clients who lack motivation to change. It is essential when working with low-motivated, non-compliant clients to create a climate of change and actively engage the client (Cohen et al., 2010). In addition to assessing the client's level of motivation, a counselor must enhance the climate for change by creating a collaborative working relationship with the client through the agreement of shared goals and shared expectations of treatment.

Counselors must understand and be equipped to deal with the concepts of transference and countertransference. Regardless of the counselor's theoretical orientation, transference can be used to increase the client's level of awareness. Once the counselor realizes that transference is occurring, the use of immediacy is an invaluable technique to enhance effectiveness in the counselor–client relationship.

Countertransference is when a counselor projects attributes and motives onto a client based upon the client's characteristics or material the client presents within counseling sessions. Countertransference can occur for a host of reasons stemming from the counselor's past experiences and can affect counselors at all stages of development. Often the counselor's first indication that countertransference is occurring is that counselors notice an internal shift in how they perceive the client. This shift is often incongruent with the client's presenting problems. Often the counselor's reactions and feelings are rooted in irrelevant characteristics (e.g., physical resemblance), interactional characteristics (e.g., feeling verbally dominated as in a past relationship), or material unrelated to the counselor–client relationship (e.g., a fight with a spouse; Reidbord, 2010). Counselors should consider using supervision to explore their own unresolved difficulties concerning the client and the client's material. Once counselors become aware (through self-reflection or supervision) of where these reactions and feelings originate, counselors can then address and overcome countertransference reactions.

Overall, counseling is a complex practice that requires much self-reflection, self-control, insight, research, preparation, and personal care. Professional counselors are urged to maintain a curiosity regarding their clients' unique needs and a humble approach to learning and growing alongside clients. Professional counselors work to support clients toward their unique wellness goals in ways that are intentional, effective, and well informed. Counselors engage in lifelong learning, and the principles associated with special populations are likely to emerge in many diverse counseling relationships.

7

Applying Multicultural Counseling

José Villalba and Bradley T. Erford

Preview

This chapter will enhance the reader's clinical experiences by exploring ethnocentrism, intersectionality, personal values and biases, and strategies for reducing personal biases. The historical and contextual nature of cultural sensitivity are examined using the Multicultural and Social Justice Counseling Competencies (Ratts et al., 2015), delving into your self-awareness and the role self-awareness plays when working with individuals identifying with different societal groups, and finally, emphasizing the benefits of working with clients from a strengths-based approach. To facilitate your heightened multicultural counseling competence while in clinical placements, each of the four sections of this chapter will conclude with a series of self-assessment activities and case scenarios. Furthermore, the case study included at the end of the first section will be carried throughout the chapter, allowing you to explore many facets of a hypothetical "encounter with" and "treatment of" the client.

Developing Cultural Sensitivity: Historical and Current Contexts

In 1991 Paul Pedersen acknowledged that multicultural counseling should be considered part of systems theory as the fourth force of counseling and psychology (after psychoanalysis, behaviorism [cognitive-behavioral], and humanistic-existential), and the fields have not looked back since. Because multicultural counseling is best carried out by competent and skilled individuals, the push for multicultural counseling competence of clinicians-in-training and mental health practitioners was operationalized shortly after Pedersen's proclamation. To this end, the major professional associations in counseling and psychology (e.g., American Counseling Association [ACA], American Psychological Association [APA]), as well as national credentialing organizations (e.g., Council for the Accreditation of Counseling and Related Educational Programs [CACREP], National Board of Certified Counselors [NBCC]) and state-level licensing boards, all include multicultural counseling competence requirements in their bylaws, professional standards of practice, and/or ethical codes. So, with most in the field of mental health services advocating for the training and credentialing of multiculturally competent clinicians, why the need for this chapter and this information? Why not leave it at: "Okay. I got it. It's important. I learned about this in undergrad. I've taken a graduate-level course on this topic. Besides, aren't we all just people, and counseling should focus on the individual?"

As seen in the next few pages, the current "need" for this chapter, in this particular book, is to make sure that clinicians-in-training don't lose sight of the fact that multicultural counseling competence "looks" very different in a clinical placement than it does in books, vignettes, or films. The identity development of all clients is influenced by an intersection of their gender, race, ethnicity, first language, religion, sexual orientation, age, ability level, socioeconomic status, immigration status, and so on, so your experiences in clinical placements are precisely the most opportune time to explore the meaning and manifestation of multicultural counseling competence. The information contained over the next few pages should help readers better understand themselves, their clinical placement clients, and the impact that society has on working effectively with *all* current and future clients.

The process whereby clinicians-in-training grow as multiculturally competent counselors is, quite frankly, different from one trainee to the next. Individuals, in that they are all unique and special in their own ways, will experience multicultural issues from their own worldviews. And though Hays and Erford (2022) talk

DOI: 10.4324/9781003305521-7

about the development of one's worldview as being unique, they also emphasize the importance of the era in which one lives, or the city they grew up in, or their family's background, as all playing a role in an individual's worldview. In other words, though one's multicultural counseling competence develops at a personal level, it does so, not in a vacuum, but in a series of contexts that are, simultaneously, historical, political, economic, and social. It is within these four lenses people must frame their cultural sensitivity. And, because it is quite difficult to separate one's cultural sensitivity outside the clinical placement from what happens inside the clinical placement, it becomes paramount for the reader to think of intersectionality and cultural sensitivity as something to which they must be always attuned. Intersectionality involves the crossing of various cultural identities (e.g., gender and race makes the experiences of Black women different from Black men). The purpose of this chapter is to challenge your personal values and biases and consider strategies for reducing personal biases.

Historical Context

What does the phrase "all counseling is historical" mean to you? It is an important question to ponder, specifically as one struggles to find out about a client's history, whether it be their family of origin, experiences with peers, academic challenges, or work-related successes, to name a few. When it comes to multicultural competence, however, the phrase "all counseling is historical" also takes into account not only the history of the client, but also how the history of a community, society, or country has influenced the societal groups that make up the identity of the client in question. For example, working with a female client who is an Afghani refugee in the United States will require the counselor to consider, at the very least, how the many military conflicts in Afghanistan have affected the client's personal experiences. Furthermore, the counselor will also have to consider how the United States' past history with Afghanistan can influence the perception of the client's neighbors, coworkers, or school peers, and how these perceptions may influence the relationship between the client and these individuals. This is not to say that counseling issues related to the client's country-of-origin's history may come up in counseling, but if they do, a multiculturally competent counselor will have already anticipated this possibility and will not shy away from talking about these issues related to the history of both nations.

Probably the most salient, negative historical context for health care (including counseling services) in the United States is the collection of injustices committed against African Americans, from as far back as the pre–Revolutionary War use of slaves in early colonization of what would become the United States of America, through the Civil War, Reconstruction, *Brown v. Board of Education*, and even the current manifestations of health disparities between African Americans and most other ethnic and racial groups (Asim, 2007; Hays & Erford, 2022). It is America's ugly and historical treatment of African Americans (and members of other ethnic groups) that has further contributed to lower-than-average usage rates of mental health services, due to a mistrust of the medical and mental health systems . The sadder and more troubling contexts of the Black experience also has contributed to a stigma surrounding the use of formal mental health services in the Black community. Counselors and counselors-in-training need not raise their hands and say, defensively, we are not the cause of these issues and we do not represent the roots of this history; no one is blaming us. However, history, particularly with Black Americans, influences mental health and reactions to mental health care, and these issues should not be overlooked for Black Americans or any other societal group that may have been marginalized, oppressed, discriminated against, or persecuted.

Current Social, Political, and Economic Contexts

Though any of these three contexts can "stand on their own," social, political, and economic contexts are grouped in this section to encourage counselors-in-training to examine the intricate contexts of their clinical placement, and all intersectionalities therein. Because each clinical placement and the clientele served by it are affected by the current political climate, social and community-based values, and economic realities, special care should be paid to assessing clients' reactions to these three contexts. These three contexts go so far as to also influence the public policies, budgeting, and provision of mental health services, which are unique to communities and municipalities.

Consider, for example, your current clinical placement setting. What city is it located in? What are some of the local or regional customs? What are the predominant places of worship in this community? What are the racial and ethnic demographics of this community? In other words, how would the "local society and local social norms" influence what is seen as normal and abnormal? The responses to these questions and related questions provide a backdrop of not only the type of counseling issues with which clients might present, but also how a potential client views their current situation.

Similarly, consider the political climate, of not only your local community but also the country at large. For example, what are the hotly debated political issues in your community? Are there controversial public policy debates going on (e.g., immigration reform, availability of financial aid for first-generation college students, construction of a local jail) that clients may feel strongly about on any dimension of the political debate? Is there state-level funding of character education programs? What about the current state of health care and health care reform or funding, particularly as it relates to funding mental health services? And, for that matter, are there local, state, or national elections that are arousing strong feelings for or against political parties and ideologies? Again, the responses to these questions may influence some of the questions you ask of your clients, as well as the type of services you provide.

And, finally, the economic status of your clients, as well as national and international fiscal policies, will have some bearing on your experiences at your clinical placement. As an initial, informal self-assessment, consider the following questions related to the clientele at your current and previous placements, and expected future placements. Consider how your clients' income plays a role in meeting economic and personal–social needs.

- What stressors are associated with unmet needs related to income status?
- How has the local economy helped or hindered your client's ability to remain employed?
- To what extent is your client's (or their parents) level of education, family history, and health status influenced by past and present economic status?
- How does the local and state economy support or hinder the ability for your current clinical placement to remain in business, or the funding of the positions held by current colleagues and supervisor(s)?
- How does the local and state economy affect the number of clients on your caseload, or the school counselor-to-student ratio in your school?

As with political and social contexts of counseling, economic contexts have some bearing on the types of issues clients present with, their ability to follow through on clinical goals, and, in the case of access to health insurance, whether or not potential clients can seek out and pay for the help of a mental health professional.

Application: How Contexts Help and Hinder Development of Cultural Sensitivity

The following experiential activities are designed to facilitate personal exploration of the importance of contexts in current clinical sites. As you read the self-assessment activities and case studies, bear in mind the complexity of each response and challenge yourself to be genuine about your feelings and experiences. It also helps if the reader can envision current or anticipated clients when reading these activities, to make the activities and case studies that much more salient. Finally, you should complete all the activities and case studies in a journal to get in the routine of collecting and revisiting multicultural insights gained from the information provided in this chapter, the content and experiences shared in a graduate-level multicultural counseling course, and the overlap between multicultural awareness and your experiences in a current clinical placement.

Self-awareness, as you'll see in the second section of this chapter, is one of the most important aspects of multicultural counseling. Therefore, throughout this chapter, you will encounter a series of self-awareness questions, scenarios, and activities that will challenge how much you know about yourself in relation to multicultural counseling issues, as well as where and how you have acquired this knowledge. Please complete Self-Self-Assessment Activities 7.1 and 7.2.

Self-Assessment Activity 7.1 Perceptions of Cultural Sensitivity

In the first section of this chapter, you have been provided with historical events that have influenced the need for health and human service providers, such as counselors, to be more culturally sensitive. Some individuals and societal institutions (like the media and the educational system) use the term "woke" to be synonymous with "cultural sensitivity." The term "woke" can have some positive and negative associations. In the space provided, please list at least three ways in which you think being culturally sensitive or "woke" is a *positive* thing in a clinical setting, and three ways in which you think being culturally sensitive or "woke" is a *negative* thing in a clinical setting.

Positive connotations of being culturally sensitive: ______________________________

Negative connotations of being culturally sensitive: ______________________________

And

Two political factors influencing your work with clients: ______________________________

Two economic factors influencing your work with clients: ______________________________

Two societal factors influencing your work with clients: ______________________________

The most difficult factor to address in relation to your work with a particular client and why:

____

____

____

Self-Assessment Activity 7.2 Economic, Political, and Social Issues

In this section, we have explored the current contexts of cultural sensitivity, specifically the reasons why now, just as in critical times of our nation's cultural history (e.g., the women's suffrage movement, the civil rights movement, farm workers' rights), it remains important for counselors and human service providers to stay up to date on current economic, political, and societal issues. To this end, please list two economic, two political, and two societal factors in your local community (either where you are currently attending school, or perhaps your hometown if you are going to school away from home) that would impact your work with clients at your current clinical placement. Then, pick one of the six factors listed and write down your own feelings about why this particular factor is "the most difficult factor for you to deal with in relation to your work with a particular client."

Now let's apply your experiences and knowledge of cultural sensitivity and intersectionality to help identify and reduce personal biases. The following case will be used throughout this chapter. What follows is a description of a client similar to one you may come into contact during your practicum or internship. Immediately following the case study, you will find two case scenarios to consider related to developing cultural sensitivity (Case Scenarios 7.1 and 7.2). Refer to this description as you address the case scenarios, both in this section and throughout the chapter. The case scenarios will provide you with opportunities to process different aspects of the case as you seek to address your own values and biases, and to increase your multicultural counseling competence and sensitivity. To this end, please make sure to write your reactions to each case scenario on a separate sheet of paper, to provide you (and peers) with an account of efforts to become more multiculturally counseling competent.

> Consider the case of Sara, to which we will return to from time to time throughout the rest of this chapter. Sara is a 22-year-old client of African American and Latino descent, who identifies herself as a "recovering Catholic" because she no longer practices the religion in which her parents raised her. She was born in the

United States, as was her mother; however, her father was born in Costa Rica. Her parents divorced when she was 12 years old, during a time that was quite tumultuous for her. She is the oldest of three children in her family, and neither of her parents have children from other relationships. Sara is a first-generation college student, who will be graduating with a Bachelor of Science in Nursing (BSN) degree in the next few months. The university she attends is close to her mother's home, where she has lived since her parents' divorce. Sara has come to talk with you because she feels that the counselors at the university counseling center on campus are only there to "help the rich kids who live on campus" and because she really needs help with talking with someone "impartial" about her fears. Specifically, she reports being "anxious and afraid" of getting a job soon after graduation, as well as worrying that she will "never be happily involved in a relationship." She indicates that she's particularly worried about her potential for a healthy romantic relationship like "most of her other friends," because her parents are not together anymore, and because she is bisexual and unsure how future partners will feel about her affective orientation. She indicates that both her parents are aware and "fine" with her affective orientation, though her father's mother (i.e., paternal grandmother) is not pleased with her affective orientation and has not spoken to her in the three years since she shared her affective orientation with her family, which she did through Facebook. Between her immediate and long-term concerns of getting a job and finding a person with whom to have a "meaningful and long-term relationship," you are asked by her to "please help me get my life in check before it all comes crashing down around me."

Case Scenario 7.1 Affective Orientation

What would you do if Sara were to ask you to help her "rationalize" why her grandmother is so against her affective orientation, particularly because she states that others in her family and support network have made "so many strides in the past few years to recognize different types of couples and partnerships, yet not my grandmother?"

Processing Questions:

1. How capable do you think you would be of providing Sara with a response as free as possible from your opinions or reactions to individuals with similar or different affective orientations than your own?
2. How might you experience countertransference with the client if you and she share any societal group membership(s) (e.g., same gender, similar ethnic background, both are first-generation college students, both are Catholic)?

Case Scenario 7.2 Multiracial Client

Assume this is your first time working with a client with a multiracial heritage, in this case, African American and Latino. Therefore, because it is your first time working with a multiracial client, you seek supervision from a colleague in your practice.

Processing Question:

1. Based on what we have reviewed in this section of the chapter with regard to the historical and current contextual nature of multicultural counseling, how would you respond to your supervising colleague posing the following question: "So, how do you think your client's current goals to find a job right after graduation can be facilitated or complicated by the current economic data?"

The Multicultural and Social Justice Counseling Competencies: Attitudes and Beliefs, Knowledge, and Skills

In the spring of 1992, the *Journal of Counseling & Development* published the seminal article by Sue et al. titled "Multicultural Counseling Competencies and Standards: A Call to the Profession." The article was a direct offshoot of the Association for Multicultural Counseling and Development's (AMCD) production of a set of professional standards of practice for clinicians working in an ever-diverse American society. This article came to be seen as the first comprehensive collection of what multicultural counseling competence entailed and how a counselor and counselor-in-training may practice from a position that demonstrates cultural sensitivity. In addition, as the title of the article suggests, the article served as a "grounding point" for the counseling profession to focus on as it strived to become a profession that would serve individuals from all backgrounds. As a "grounding point," the authors wished to not merely outline what multiculturally competent clinicians should do, but also what professional counseling organizations, credentialing bodies, and training programs and institutions should do to ensure the training and professional development of multiculturally competent students and learners.

Ratts et al. (2015) published the Multicultural and Social Justice Counseling Competencies to reflect changes in the profession and society since the original Sue et al. (1992) set of standards. At the core of the revised competencies is that counselors must develop competence related to: (a) counselor self-awareness, (b) client worldview, (c) counseling relationship, and (d) counseling and advocacy interventions. And embedded within each of these domains are additional competencies related to (a) cultural attitudes and beliefs, (b) cultural knowledge, (c) a willingness to learn and apply culturally relevant skills and techniques for clients from various backgrounds, and (d) a willingness to take action as appropriate. Whereas Sue et al. proposed 31 competencies, Ratts et al. (2015) reported 116 competencies organized under these four domains across these four general areas. The competencies are designed so that clinicians can demonstrate an ability to learn about their attitude and beliefs and those of their clients, to gain empirical and anecdotal knowledge of themselves and clients, and to acquire skills and convey those skills in a manner that is culturally sensitive. This tripartite model of multicultural self-awareness, knowledge, and skills has served as the foundation of many of multicultural counseling courses, as well as an effective method for organizing the types of activities in which counselors need to engage to continue their growth as ethical and effective practitioners.

Counselors-in-training can increase their understanding of multicultural competence by reviewing the Ratts et al. (2015) document. Considering that the Multicultural and Social Justice Counseling Competencies (MSJCCs) stress the importance of self-awareness, knowledge, culturally relevant skills, and actions, it is imperative that counselors and those training to enter the field explore these concepts in relation to the MSJCCs themselves. By doing so, the clinician and preservice student demonstrate an ability to intentionally and deliberately view their present and future clinical placements through the lens of the MSJCCs. More specifically, attention should be paid to which of the competencies and exploratory statements are most in line and least in line with the reader's feelings toward the MSJCCs.

Applying the Multicultural and Social Justice Counseling Competencies

The following experiential activities are designed to facilitate your personal exploration of the essential aspects of the MSJCCs. Specifically, the self-assessment activities encourage the reader to place themselves in situations in which they may not be too knowledgeable. The case scenarios further expand on this line of question by considering the many "layers" to the case of Sara, and how working with a client like Sara can push you to consider the four domains of the MSJCCs and perhaps even the dimensions of a personal identity model.

Before beginning the exercises in this section, consider a more general idea of exploring the MSJCCs. Specifically, read the Ratts et al. (2015) document and identify two or three competencies in which you already feel proficient, and two or three that you see as areas of growth. After you have produced this list, take into account how the competencies in which you are proficient might facilitate the current clinical experience, and identify how the competencies listed as needing to be developed might serve as a limitation in the current clinical experience. This activity is a good precursor for embarking on the more detailed questions and topics presented in the next few pages. Now that you have read about the impetus for infusing self-awareness into multicultural counseling competency presented by Ratts et al., let's explore a series of questions for enhancing your self-awareness by completing completing Self-Assessment Activities 7.3 and 7.4.

Self-Assessment Activity 7.3 Experiential Activities for Self-Awareness

List five experiential activities you could engage in that would help you learn about yourself and preconceived notions *while* you learn about members of other societal groups. For example, suppose you are a Methodist Christian and you want to learn more about Judaism. You want to learn more about Judaism because you recently learned that the Old Testament is, essentially, the Jewish Torah. You decide to stop by a local synagogue, speak to the rabbi, and ask if it would be okay for you to come to one of their services. The rabbi emphatically extends an invitation to the Friday night Shabbat service, and you decide to attend. At the end of the service, which you are surprised to find out is not on Sunday morning, you take the time to write down some things that you learned from your first experience with a Shabbat service and how these similarities and differences with your own faith have helped you learn more about yourself and explore your preconceived notions about Jews and Judaism. With this type of activity in mind, use the following five lines to list the type of experiential activities like this one that you would complete. You do not need to elaborate on how they would affect you, just the type of experience that you might have.

Experiential Activity 1:

____

Experiential Activity 2:

____

Experiential Activity 3:

____

Experiential Activity 4:

____

Experiential Activity 5:

____

Self-Assessment Activity 7.4 Learning From Being Wrong

For this activity, reflect on a time when you were proven wrong about someone because of a preconceived notion you had about their gender, ethnic group, second-language ability, sexual orientation, and so on, and how being proven wrong propelled you into learning more about the individual and the societal group(s) of which they were a part. And, if applicable, share how this experience of personal growth and learning more about others may have affected a particular skill set needed to work with members of this group (e.g., if you were a summer camp counselor and your newfound knowledge about members of a particular group helped you better empathize with or provide services to children who were members of this particular group).

In the following pair of scenarios, you will explore how self-awareness, knowledge of other societal groups, and the establishment of culturally relevant interventions all contribute to the multicultural counseling competence of the counselor. Use Case Scenarios 7.3 and 7.4 to practice what you would say and do when similar opportunities and challenges present themselves in your current clinical experiences.

Case Scenario 7.3 Dissatisfaction

Sara presents a particular "challenge" for you as a client because her direct goals of finding a job after graduation and a fulfilling relationship are affected by several factors outside your control or hers. During your fourth session with Sara, you decide to share these feelings of being challenged with her immediately after she tells you that she's "unhappy with the progress in counseling up to this point" because she's no less "scared or anxious" than she was before the first session. Although there is nothing "wrong" with your response to Sara's opinion of the counseling process to date, she seems put off by your response.

Processing Question:

1. Based on what you know about her history and societal groups membership, how might you improve your initial response to her concerns about being unhappy with counseling?

Case Scenario 7.4 Sexuality and Religion

Suppose that Sara told you in your fifth session that she has decided to confront her father and her paternal grandmother about her relationship with her paternal grandmother. However, she would like your suggestions for best talking with them both about how hard the last three years have been on her to be so "distant" from her paternal grandmother. She specifically asks you to provide her with tips for convincing her paternal grandmother that "there's nothing wrong with being bisexual." She also mentions that her paternal grandmother also is upset that Sara has "left the teachings of the Church," and that there's no way she's ever "stepping foot in another church as long as she lives."

Processing Questions:

1. What are your specific reactions to Sara's request that you help "convince" her paternal grandmother on both points?
2. What are your feelings about people "being bisexual" and "never stepping foot in another church," particularly if your views differ from Sara's?
3. How would you reconcile differences in opinion if they do exist or how would you maintain objectivity if there is "100% overlap" between your opinion and Sara's?

Confronting Oneself: Self-Awareness, Overcoming Bias, and Working With Differences

Although Ratts et al. (2015) do not indicate which of the domains are "most important," it is clear that clinicians and those in training who fail to acknowledge their cultural identity development, examine their biases, and challenge their notions of comfort will struggle to become multiculturally competent service providers. Hodges (2015) further expanded on this point by indicating that self-awareness is the first step in developing multicultural competence. From this notion it is quite logical to extrapolate that people must first explore their own experiences, thoughts, beliefs, values, assumptions, stereotypes, prejudices, and behaviors *before* starting to learn more about members from different societal groups or applying clinical skills to diverse populations. As a result, exercises wherein you push your understanding of what it means to be a member of particular ethnic, racial, gender, economic, religious, and sexual/affectional orientation groups (to name a few) is paramount to providing culturally appropriate and ethical mental health care.

Expanding Our Notion of Self-Awareness

Where do your ancestors come from? How many generations of your family have lived in your country, or your particular community? What are the facets of your religious or spiritual beliefs that are most important to you? What privilege do you think your affective orientation affords you, if any? How have you been discriminated against, and how did you know? When have you discriminated against others, to whom, and what was the context for your behaviors and thoughts? Your responses to questions like these go a long, long way toward increasing how much you know about yourself, particularly as a cultural being. This notion of viewing yourself as a cultural being is one that needs to be considered before moving on to personal biases, concepts of privilege, and working with individuals who are different than you or the members of your family.

For years now, researchers and writers in the counseling and psychology fields have argued that we are all cultural beings (e.g., Helms, 1995; Moore-Thomas, 2018; Phinney, 1996). Another way to phrase this is that we all have a culture that influences the way we see the world and our place in that world, specifically in the communities in which we reside, the places in which we work, and the schools we attend. Holding this statement to be true, however, depends on a couple of factors. First, the individual must be willing to see "culture" (e.g., customs, routines, patterns of behavior, ideas handed down from generation to generation, mental schemas, traditions) in many aspects of one's identity. Second, the individual must also acknowledge that culture and how each aspect of culture is affected by messages received from a variety of individuals, including family members, peers, colleagues, and acquaintances, as well as social systems and institutions, such as the media, the judicial system, and the educational system. Combined, these two factors allude to one's ability to self-reflect, which is the cornerstone of self-awareness (Jun, 2018). Once one's ability to self-reflect is considered, it becomes much more likely that individuals will become more self-aware, not merely about their own thoughts, beliefs, values, ideas, interests, and skills, but also about the rationale and history behind their thoughts, beliefs, values, ideas, interests, and skills. For counselors, in particular, being self-aware of the cultural lens with which we develop our worldviews is an integral part of being an effective counselor and a more compassionate person (Sue et al., 2019).

The one thing to keep in mind when expanding one's view of self as a cultural being is that this realization oftentimes comes with both pleasant and unpleasant consequences (Jun, 2018). Specifically, as a mental health practitioner begins to more intentionally and deeply examine all aspects of cultural identity through increases in self-awareness, it becomes more likely to find some deep-seated notions of prejudicial thoughts, or discriminatory behaviors in their past, or the notion that cherished loved ones or pivotal moments in their upbringing were actually manifestations of racism, or homophobia, or socioeconomic privilege. These unpleasant realizations not only clash with the mental health practitioner's notion of what it means to be a helping professional; one also may react to these unpleasant emotions by negating or minimizing the more pleasant realizations, such as a lifelong devotion to altruistic endeavors, or a genuine desire to be an advocate for social justice, or the not-so-common ability to listen to others with dignity and respect.

Overcoming Biases

Once a counselor-in-training or clinician begins to assess and learn from exercises in self-reflection and self-assessment, there exists the possibility that the individual will become so debilitated by unpleasant realizations that the person could be rendered incapacitated to work with future clients. Of course, this should not be the goal of increasing self-awareness as a cultural being. So, to put it in more simplistic terms, how do providers move on without forgetting what they have learned about themselves?

One of the main ways of not stalling the cultural competence developmental process is to not react defensively to the realization that most, if not all, of us have room for growth as culturally sensitive individuals. Exploring our defense mechanisms and realizing our biases and privilege increase our abilities to empathize with others, while minimizing the likelihood of intellectualizing reasons behind the biases (Jun, 2018). Examples of intellectualization of the "why" behind our biases include dwelling too much on the historical nature of racism, or the notion that one has not been the oppressor, or that society is to "blame" for a family member's racist remarks, keeps the practitioner mired in trying to "explain away" the biases, rather than owning up to them and moving on. Anderson and Middleton (2011) elaborated on the importance of "acknowledging and moving on" by encouraging mental health practitioners and those in training to focus more on how to minimize the influence of their biases on their work with clients or potential clients.

An equally effective method to "move on" from acknowledging one's biases is to further immerse oneself in situations that challenge or negate the biases (Hodges, 2015; Hogan-Garcia, 2012). Also known as cultural immersion activities, an individual can make a concerted effort to immerse oneself in knowledge, locations, rituals, experiences, literature, cultural festivals, and even foods; the level of how "deep" one is willing to go is truly up to the individual. Some of the activities in this chapter are aimed particularly at increasing the reader's opportunities in this realm, such as visiting places of worship or interacting with members of different societal groups. But the onus truly is on individuals to seek safe experiences outside of their comfort zone to increase the opportunities for growth and learning. Counselors may then use this growth toward enhancing work with diverse clients in clinical placements.

Working With Differences

If increased self-awareness and self-reflection are the first steps in multicultural counseling competence, then the obvious next set of steps is to learn more about the individuals with whom one will work, as well as the development of culturally relevant counseling skills. It is in these steps that counselors begin to seek more information, more professional development, and more informal and formal meetings with individuals from different societal groups, all done to provide the clinician with a foundation for the implementation of clinical skills that will be effective with a wide range of clients and potential clients.

Many writers in the area of multicultural counseling have produced textbooks, articles, and webinars (e.g., Hays & Erford, 2022; Robinson-Wood, 2016; Sue et al., 2019) with specific information about a variety of societal groups, including, but not limited to, Black Americans, Native Americans, individuals with disabilities, women, older adults, and Muslims. This literature is a great starting place to learn about the types of obstacles and strengths that potential clients representing these societal groups can bring into the counseling relationship. Summative literature of this type also typically provides a synopsis of research studies that indicate which counseling theories and techniques are better suited for members of certain societal groups. Furthermore, information on identity development and the role that culture plays in the identity development of individuals often is included in this line of literature. Therefore, one can see how consuming this type of information can be very helpful, particularly to novice mental health professionals, as they strive to provide ethical services to clients. However, both the novice and the seasoned counselor should always look at this type of information as a "starting point" for working with diverse clients, lest one runs the risk of acting on or providing services that adhere to or come off as stereotypical.

The well-intentioned and multiculturally competent counselor and counselor-in-training is one that takes an open mind to the clinical site, rather than a mind-set that assumes all they need to know about counseling diverse others was learned in a book chapter or from attending a three-hour professional development workshop. Having an open-minded attitude will go a long way toward establishing effective clinical rapport, as well as getting "buy in" from potential clients to the benefits of engaging in a therapeutic relationship with the mental health worker.

Application: Self-Awareness, Overcoming Bias, and Working With Differences

The following experiential activities are designed to facilitate the reader's personal reactions to confronting self-awareness and moving beyond the pleasant and unpleasant "aha moments." The activities are designed to elicit self-reflection, which means the reader must be ready for a bit of "honest soul searching." Because "soul searching" can happen in a variety of places and spaces, notice the wide range of possibilities presented in the self-study activities. Building on self-assessment results, the case scenario encourages the reader to move to the next step of overcoming biases and working with differences by asking the reader to reconsider the case of Sara, the many layers, facets, and intersections of Sara's identity and presenting counseling concerns, and where the reader might find some challenges as Sara's counselor. As has become the underlying pattern to this chapter and these experiential activities, think of these activities and scenarios within the context of your current clinical setting to increase the usefulness and applicability of your responses.

Up to this point, you have explored your self-awareness and preconceived notions about members of different societal groups. But where do these preconceived notions come from, and what influences the development of your self-concept and self-awareness? Self-Assessment Activities 7.5 through 7.7 are designed to further expand your self-awareness in an effort to better facilitate your abilities to connect with others and improve your current clinical experiences.

Self-Assessment Activity 7.5 Social Influences

Think of all the people in your family and group of friends who have contributed to your preconceived notions, both positive and negative, regarding members of different societal groups. Chances are that the number of people in your family and friend circles, coupled with the many different societal groupings, would make for quite the exhaustive list. So, in the name of efficiency, it would probably be helpful to pick one societal group of which you are not a member (e.g., Muslim women, undocumented immigrants, poor families, students from wealthy families, Asian American college students, older adults in the workforce). Now, once you have identified the societal group on which you want to focus, use a separate sheet of paper to list at least five individuals who are close to you who have influenced how you view members of this group. Next, answer the following questions:

- What was it about these individuals close to you that contributed to the level of influence they had on your opinion of this particular societal group?
- Where do you think they received their ideas about members of this societal group?
- How "right" and "wrong" were they about their opinions of these individuals?
- How did you establish they were "right" and "wrong," and how did your feelings about members of this societal group change once you had time to question certain information for yourself?
- Have there been opportunities in your current clinical experience to work with individuals of this societal group?
- How do you think the influence of those close to you has affected your work with members of this societal group in your clinical placement?

Self-Assessment Activity 7.6 Media Influences

Apart from members close to you, messages we see and hear from the media can have great bearing on our opinions and preconceived notions. For this activity, pick one media source (e.g., television, radio, social networking, Web-based content) that you depend on for information on a regular basis. Now, over a weeklong period, "log" on a separate sheet of paper how many times you notice receiving a "stereotypical" message about members from different societal groups. The group or groups you select, how you choose to "code" messages, their frequency, their duration, and so on is up to you; however, the focus should be on heightening your awareness of the effect of these messages on how you come to construct, "validate," and "negate" your preconceived notions of members of different societal groups. Finally, similar toSelf-Assessment Activity 7.5, conclude this activity by reflecting on your work with societal groups at your site and how the media influences your perceptions of members from particular societal group(s) at your site.

Self-Assessment Activity 7.7 Challenging Yourself

The final activity in this section is designed more like a "call to action" in that it challenges you to engage in your future self-awareness as it relates to multicultural experiences. In the space provided, list five ways you plan to challenge yourself to become more self-aware, specifically about your preconceived notions of members of societal groups, even groups of which you are a member. Think of these self-awareness (SA) exercises as both things you can do in the present **and** in the future, with the end goal of maintaining a high level of multicultural counseling competence (MCC).

Current/future SA-MCC exercise 1:

____

Current/future SA-MCC exercise 2:

____

Current/future SA-MCC exercise 3:

____

Current/future SA-MCC exercise 4:

____

Current/future SA-MCC exercise 5:

____

With the emphasis of this section of the chapter on self-awareness and confronting one's biases, Case Scenarios 7.5 and 7.6 challenge the reader to explore the types of "cultural buttons" that potential clients may "push." The contents in Case Scenario 7.5 are particularly controversial in the United States and tend to energize individuals on both sides of the argument. Clinicians who fall on either side of the argument have the potential to have their effectiveness stunted. As a result, now is the time for you to explore your reactions to "hot-button issues," particularly because the availability of supervision in the university and clinical placement setting provides ample chances to seek out feedback from peers and experienced supervisors.

Case Scenario 7.5 Immigration Status

After meeting for seven sessions, Sara mentions to you that she would like to share something she's "never told anyone before." She shares with you that one of the reasons she decided to move in with her mom after her parents got divorced was because her dad was in the country as an undocumented worker, and she was scared that if she "picked her dad over her mom," she could "get in trouble" if immigration officials ever found out that her dad was in the United States without proper documentation. She also confides in you that, in retrospect, what scared her more than anything else was that her mother was the one who "planted this seed" about her dad possibly being "deported" and that, in hindsight, this initial information from her mother has driven a long-term wedge between Sara and her father.

Processing Questions:

1. Knowing what you know now about her dad's undocumented status and her mother's decision to share this type of information with a 12-year-old, how does this information coincide with your own feelings about individuals in the United States without proper documentation, in addition to individuals who would make parental decisions that you may be in agreement or disagreement with?
2. How might your reactions to Sara's new information impact your future work with Sara, if at all?

Case Scenario 7.6 Countertransference

As with Case Scenario 7.2, you have decided to seek supervision with a colleague after your seventh session with Sara. Specifically, you want to share some countertransference issues that you are having with Sara, and you want to be able to explore ways to mitigate the impact of this countertransference.

Processing Questions:

1. Considering that Sara is a member of several societal groups (e.g., woman, mixed heritage, first-generation college student), what might be some countertransference issues you would discuss with your supervisor?
2. What recommendations do you envision your supervisor might give you to limit the effects of your countertransference on your clinical work with Sara?

Keep in mind that countertransference can have effects where you either overidentify with the client (which limits your ability to be as objective as possible) or negatively judge the actions of your client or their loved ones.

Counseling Diverse Clients From a Strengths-Based Perspective

One of the reasons multicultural counseling competence is so important is because traditional psychology was built on the medical model, which assumes that individuals are "sick" and therefore need to be "cured" (Hays & Erford, 2022). As one reviews the earliest psychology theories, such as psychoanalysis or behaviorism, it is easy to see how many theorists viewed individuals as "unwhole," "neurotic," or "programmable," which tends to imply that if clients were to follow a certain set of suggestions, or make certain behavioral changes, then these "deficits" could be more easily resolved and/or minimized (Arredondo et al., 1996). Even the less deficit-based theories, such as humanism and existentialism, have a certain set of assumptions, such as the need to find meaning for oneself or the need to be autonomous, which may run contrary to notions of collectivism that readers may have learned about in their multicultural counseling courses (Kress et al., 2021). So, to work with individuals from a strengths-based approach essentially entails that counselors acknowledge that all individuals have the strengths or abilities to solve their own problems and to persevere.

Social Capital as a Framework for Strengths-Based Perspectives

Adding the notion of cultural sensitivity to this framework means that an individual's race, gender, ethnicity, first language, socioeconomic status, age, ability level and challenges, affective orientation, religion, and so on all contribute to an individual's strength, and that membership and awareness of these societal groupings may provide the client with access to unique skills, perceptions, experiences, and traditions that can facilitate their own mental health and holistic well-being. One way of acknowledging the strengths and benefits of societal group membership is to consider the notion of social capital. Though the origins of social capital as it is used in the literature can be traced to Hanifan (1916), contemporary references to the term typically are credited to Bourdieu (1977). According to Bourdieu, every individual is engaged in a set of relationships, or social networks, that provides them with social capital. This social capital is somewhat synonymous with economic capital, so that the social capital generated by group memberships affords each of us with "currency" that helps us solve problems, provides us with a system of support, helps us learn new information, and so on. However, just like some "capital" is valued more than other "capital" in certain situations (e.g., think about the fact that you cannot use the euro to purchase goods in the United States, rather that currency must be exchanged and the rate of exchange varies along several economic variables), the social capital provided to individuals by their religion or gender or ethnicity may be of "more value" in, for example, the home or local community, than they are in a school or work setting. Clients from all walks of life and who value their societal group membership(s) have experienced the valuation and devaluation of their social capital in various settings and may even share some of their unpleasant reactions and experiences to social capital devaluation in a counseling setting. One example of this devaluation may be a Spanish-speaking client who is learning English as a second language and tells of a time when they were ridiculed at school for speaking in their native language, but who also tells of the time they were offered a receptionist job at a doctor's office solely because of being bilingual and can therefore speak with both English- and Spanish-speaking patients.

With this notion of social capital in mind, the challenge for counselors and counselors-in-training becomes twofold. First, the clinician must be attentive to times when a client's social capital has been minimized, ignored, or worse, viewed by others as a deficit (particularly those in "power," such as a boss, teacher, professor, administrator, politician, or family member). Second, and more salient to the notion of counseling from a strengths-based approach, the clinician must find opportunities in the clinical relationship and discourse to value the social capital that the client possesses. This does not mean the counselor begins to "romanticize" the client's social capital (e.g., "How great is it that you are bilingual!" or "It must be wonderful to have a Jewish mother and a Catholic father because you celebrate both Passover and Easter, right?"); but, rather, that they make aware to the client the potential for social capital in their societal group memberships and to challenge clients to see if they, too, are aware of their social capital's potential for addressing mental health concerns.

Eliciting Client Strengths Through Strengths-Based Counseling

One of the hallmarks of person-centered counseling is the notion that all clients are experts on their own experiences, which provides perspective and insight to address the issues that bring them to counseling (Kress et al., 2021). With this philosophy as a core belief of most counselors and counseling training programs, believing in the client's personal potential to solve some of their counseling issues can oftentimes be rooted in some cultural, gender, ethnic, or language proficiency lens through which the client views the world and community. The challenge for counselors is how to elicit the client's ability to share and acknowledge strength they can draw from societal group membership, without: (a) negating the client's presenting problems, or (b) discrediting the reality that, for most members of different societal groups, group membership oftentimes is at the root of several stressors, negative experiences, or systemic oppression. For example, Black clients and students have experienced oppression because of their race; some Latinas/os are assumed to be in the country as undocumented residents, even though they were born here; Asian Americans are assumed to be intellectually more capable and, therefore, steered more toward careers in science, technology, and math, even though individuals may want to pursue careers in the arts or humanities.

Saleeby (2012) provided a framework for strengths-based services that helps the counselor avoid the two aforementioned concerns. According to Saleeby, strengths-based approaches require the clinician to: (a) believe that every individual, group, family, and community has the internal strengths needed to solve their problems; (b) believe that the most hurtful and difficult experience can at least present individuals, groups, families, and communities with chances for growth and for problem-solving initiatives to evolve; (c) believe that all individuals are in a process of perpetual growth and development, which points to a limitless potential for growth; (d) believe that clients are best served when counselors collaborate instead of directing clients about what to do and not to do at all times; I believe that individual, family, and group environments and surroundings can provide resources to assist them in problem solving; and (f) believe that individuals, families, groups, and communities are more likely to see the strength in the counselor and the clinical experience if they trust in the genuineness of the counselor. Rothman (2008) expanded on Saleeby's suggestions by stressing the importance of viewing a client, group, or family's strengths from a cultural context, acknowledging that cultures help give meaning to certain events.

For example, if working with a Black client, a counselor can listen to the individual's concerns while being attentive to the cause of their problems. If the client fails to indicate that the client's family is at the root of the problems, but rather indicates feeling lost or isolated in the current environment, the counselor may elect to ask the client about the importance being placed on the family unit, collectivism, and support from one's extended network. Because research and the literature on counseling Black clients points to the power of extended family support for addressing counseling concerns, the counselor is facilitating the client's ability to drawn on the social support system through the lens that African Americans, in general, place great importance on the support of nuclear and extended family members (Robinson-Wood, 2016; Rothman, 2008). Inherent in this example is the notion that the counselor must have a working knowledge of the literature as it pertains to counseling Black clients, as well as a level of self-awareness that helps the clinician not "assume" that all Black clients are going to focus on their family as a source of support. Similar examples of strengths from a cultural perspective also include the bilingual abilities of immigrant clients, the resiliency of many individuals with disabilities to navigate physical and/or systemic obstacles, and the ability for those with economic limitations to find the strength and perseverance to work one or more jobs to provide for their families, particularly during challenging economic times. Again, the emphasis is not for the counselor to ignore the counseling concerns of the client, but rather to understand the successes and resiliency of the client.

Application: Counseling From a Strengths-Based Perspective

The following experiential activities are designed to facilitate the reader's ability to "see" strengths in present and future clients, where clients may have only "seen" deficits or, at the very least, obstacles. Though the activity and scenarios are designed as "culminating" experiences to this chapter, the challenge for the reader is to use these exercises as templates for experiencing current and future clinical settings, settings that continue to become more and more diverse as our society continues to become more and more culturally rich with diversity. The final self-assessment (Self-Assessment Activity 7.8) is the wrap-up experience to help solidify how much you have learned about yourself in this process and how to continue to push yourself to learn even more through a commitment to a lifelong pursuit of self-awareness activities and the ability to process these experiences.

Self-Assessment Activity 7.8 Representative Client

Write down the "name" (for confidentiality reasons, use a pseudonym) of the student or client at your current clinical site who you think represents the type of clients you would like to work with the most once you secure postgraduation employment. Next, write down all the different societal groups of which this individual is a member, starting with the group that you think is the most "dominant" factor of the individual's identity. Third, for each societal group, jot down two preconceived notions you had about the group, whether these notions are positive or negative. Fourth, write down how your preconceived notions of these societal groups positively and negatively influenced your work with the client in question, paying particular attention to the rapport you developed with the individual, the clinical goals you established with the individual, and the type of theoretical orientation you decided to use with this individual. Fifth, share at least three strengths that you now "see" in your client that you may not have "seen" prior to your self-reflection. Sixth, in what ways have you "grown" as a counselor-in-training from your experience with this client, particularly as you've focused on your level of self-awareness in relation to becoming a more multiculturally competent professional counselor? And, finally, how do you plan to "not forget or take for granted" what you've learned from this clinical relationship so that it continues to inform your professional progress and growth after completion of your training program?

A strengths-based approach to multicultural counseling competence calls on the clinician to help the client realize personal strengths and attributes. This is not done in a naive, myopic manner that circumvents the client's need to talk about their fears, inabilities, or concerns, but, rather, to balance the client's opportunities for growth, success, and accomplishment. Therefore, these last two scenarios (Case Scenarios 7.7 and 7.8) provide you the opportunity to replace possible "deficit-based thinking" with "strengths-based approaches" for working with Sara, as well as present and future clients.

Case Scenario 7.7 Termination

After nine sessions with Sara, you both realize that the clinical goals have been met and that the time to terminate is upon you both. You decide at the end of this 9th session that the 11th session will be the last one. Even though Sara agrees that the time to terminate the counseling relationship is at hand (in fact, she initiated this line of talk at the beginning of session nine), she still feels a bit anxious about not coming to see you on a regular basis. She no longer feels worried about getting a job after graduation because she has accepted a job offer to work as a nurse for a hospital about 40 miles from home. However, she still feels that her grandmother is no closer to reconciling with her, and she continues to worry about never finding a fulfilling relationship.

Processing Questions:

1. What might you say to reframe her current worries, based on what you have discussed with her over the past eight sessions?
2. What are your reasons for pinpointing specific examples of her "strengths," particularly as it relates to your own growth as a multiculturally competent counselor over the past few weeks?

Case Scenario 7.8 New Perspective

At the conclusion of the 11th session, Sara thanks you "for everything you've done." You, in turn, say you're welcome and you proceed that thank **her** for all that she's taught you. She appreciates your comment; however, she is intrigued by what exactly it is that you've learned from Sara.

Processing Question:

1. How would you respond to Sara's following, and final, question: "If you don't mind me asking, and I know we are about to part ways, what exactly have I taught you over the past few months that you didn't already know? And thanks for answering my question; it means a lot to me."

Summary

The contents of this chapter, as well as the recommended activities and scenarios, are intended to help you get the most out of the clinical placement. Because social, cultural, economic, political, and historical factors all influence the counseling relationship, getting the most out of the clinical placement runs parallel to striving for multicultural competence. To miss opportunities to grow as a multiculturally aware clinician is a disservice to not only the student but also clients and colleagues.

Developing cultural sensitivity from historical and current contexts helps the clinician demonstrate honor and respect for experiences of members from different societal groups, as well as the events shared by clients' families and ancestors. Acknowledging and seeking the influence of these contexts on the lives and mental health of clients also positions the culturally competent counselor as a model to other colleagues and mental health practitioners of how to provide culturally respectful service. Part of serving as a model for other mental health practitioners is a commitment to exploring one's own preconceived notions of certain societal groups different from those with which one is a member. As a result, developing treatment plans and establishing treatment goals with clients within the historical, political, economic, and social contexts of a client's reality is one way to demonstrate an intentional development of multicultural counseling competence in a clinical internship setting.

The Multicultural and Social Justice Counseling Competencies (Ratts et al., 2015) provides counselors with clear ideas and standards for providing culturally relevant services in practicum and internship settings. These competencies are organized around clinicians being aware of their own attitudes and beliefs (and their origins), knowledge of members of various societal groups, and developing skills and actions that manifest as culturally appropriate interventions. This model of multicultural competence serves as the mental health clinician's springboard for a commitment to multicultural counseling competence.

If there is a first step to this springboard, it would be the need to engage in exercises that stimulate self-awareness. Before a counselor gets too involved or even bogged down in overintellectualizing why members of certain societal groups act in certain ways or choose certain options, the practitioner must pursue activities that increase personal insight. Framing this insight in a genuine manner while confronting potentially unpleasant realities related to stereotypes held of members of other societal groups and related to one's family of origin is critical to conveying to clients the genuine empathy and willingness to be with the client. Additional work on the part of the clinician to explore the meaning of privilege, times when they have been discriminated against unfairly (or even gained an unfair advantage), and their own ethnic, racial, and gender identity development (to name but a few societal groups) should serve to enhance the client–clinician relationship, while further cementing the clinician's role within the internship setting as a multiculturally competent counselor.

Although overcoming one's biases is neither a "final step" toward multicultural counseling competence, nor some sort of singular cathartic event, it is nevertheless an important component of providing culturally appropriate services in practicum and internship settings and beyond. Although this chapter includes many different components of biases and methods for overcoming them, it is important to remember that mental health practitioners who react defensively to accusations of behaving in, for example, a racist or sexist manner by clients or colleagues hinder their ability to work effectively with clients and colleagues. Furthermore, practicum students and interns can work to overcome their biases by working with those different from themselves, as they increase their exposure to the experiences, history, customs, and lessons of others. As a result, cultural immersion activities—from those that place the practitioner in an "observer" role to those that provide an opportunity to have a participatory role—are pivotal ways that practitioners can demonstrate their desire to make connections with clients from all backgrounds.

Working with clients from all backgrounds from a strengths-based approach, whether in practicum and internship settings or after graduation, is one of many ways to provide culturally appropriate counseling services. Considering the social capital that all clients and coworkers bring to clinical and professional relationships is an effective way to frame strengths-based counseling approaches. However, all clinicians should remember the importance of balancing the concepts of social capital and providing services from a strengths-based approach with validating the obstacles and negative experiences of clients, for which Saleeby (2012) provided a useful framework. Therefore, clinicians-in-training are encouraged to see all clinical opportunities as openings to practice a strengths-based approach to counseling services.

The content provided in this chapter is but a supplement to the reader's lifelong commitment to the counseling field and the many, many individuals and families who will assist in the professional journey. And, as an added "bonus," the information can help the reader make more meaningful connections in one's personal life as well, a life that is no doubt enriched by the cultural fabric that continues to cover the schools, campus, and communities in which we all work and live.

8

Assessing and Intervening With Clients in Danger and Crisis

Linda Foster, Paul Hard, and Eric Darch

Preview

The focus of this chapter is assessment and intervention with clients in crisis. Counselors must be prepared to assess and intervene with clients who may be a danger to themselves (i.e., suicidal) or others (i.e., homicidal) or who have experienced traumatic events due to either natural disasters or man-made events. Topics of suicide, homicide, and large-scale shock can be uncomfortable for field experience students, so we have included self-assessment examples and activities to help you gain insight and create a personal philosophy for working with these issues. Also included are voices from the field from seasoned professionals to help you learn firsthand from practicing counselors who have vast experience in these areas.

The Importance of Training in Risk Assessment and Suicide and Crisis Prevention

One of the most traumatic and stressful events that can occur during the counseling relationship is the loss of a client to suicide (Baird & Mollen, 2019). Research indicates that as many as 71% of counselors will encounter a suicidal client during their career and that nearly one-fourth of professional counselors have worked with at least one client who died by suicide (Granello, 2010). For field experience students, it is vital that training in the assessment of suicide risk is included in preparation programs. For counselor education programs, accreditation standards guide the curriculum and provide rigor and uniformity in training future counselors. The importance of suicide risk assessment and crisis intervention is supported by the Council for Accreditation of Counseling and Related Educational Programs (CACREP, 2016). Suicide prevention and crisis intervention are mentioned in the 2016 CACREP Standards in key areas, including (a) Counseling and Helping Relationships and (b) Assessment and Testing, and this includes in both knowledge and skills and practice areas. As a result, this chapter will cover how to assess both suicidal and homicidal clients, identify best practice crisis intervention strategies with clients, and provide activities to help you assess your views of suicide and your ability to work with suicidal or homicidal clients.

Suicide is the 10th-leading cause of death in the United States (Whiston, 2016). Professional counselors must have the ability to accurately assess a client's risk of suicide because it is an essential component of prevention. Given the staggering statistics around death by suicide, including suicide attempts, field experience students can and should be prepared to thoroughly assess and intervene with clients who present with suicidal ideation. Before you read the next section, use Self-Assessment Activity 8.1 to assess your knowledge and perceptions of suicide prevalence.

Self-Assessment Activity 8.1 Suicide Prevalence

Before reading the next section, answer the following questions according to your current knowledge and perceptions of suicide prevalence in the United States.

1. How many suicide attempts are made each year?
2. How many suicide attempts occur every minute in the United States?
3. How many attempts are made each year for every person who dies by suicide?
4. Do females or males attempt suicide more often?
5. Of the group that attempts suicide the most, at what frequency does this behavior occur?
6. Which age group attempts suicide most frequently: children, youth, or adults?

DOI: 10.4324/9781003305521-8

7. Among college students, what is the most common means used to attempt suicide?
8. Among all suicide attempts, what method is most common?
9. Are underrepresented sexual/affectional people (e.g., gay, lesbian, bisexual, or transgender) more likely to attempt suicide than their heterosexual counterparts?

Facts About Suicide Attempts:
And the answers are . . .

1. It is estimated that approximately 500,000 suicide attempts occur each year.
2. It is estimated that one attempt occurs each minute.
3. It is estimated that for each death by suicide in the United States there are 25 attempts.
4. Males die by suicide at a rate of 3.5 times more than females.
5. It is estimated that females attempt suicide three times more frequently than men.
6. Youth attempt suicide more frequently than children or adults.
7. The most common form of suicide attempts among college students involves either jumping from a structure or hanging.
8. Firearms are the most common means of suicide across the United States.
9. LGBTQ persons are not more likely to attempt suicide than their heterosexual counterparts. Although some studies suggest there are higher numbers of suicides among LGBTQ youth, there are no studies that suggest an increased likelihood due to sexual orientation.

Granello and Granello (2007) estimated the incidence of encountering a client with suicidal ideations is as high as 71%, suggesting that most practicing counselors will experience clients with suicidal ideation. Statistics today reflect that suicide is now ranked 10th as a leading cause of death and is the second-leading cause of death in the United States for those ages 15 to 34 years (American Foundation for Suicide Prevention [AFSP], 2020). Although the statistics reflect an increase in the number of suicides in the United States, the statistics do not reflect the impact that suicide has on survivors—those left behind after losing a loved one to suicide. Peripheral damage to families and friends is estimated to be almost 1 in 60 Americans and rising due to the increasing number of persons dying by suicide (Laux, 2002).

Effective assessment of suicide risk is essential knowledge. Despite best efforts to adequately assess clients for suicide risk, one is never completely certain that a client will not attempt or complete suicide. Still, suicide risk assessment is the first step in understanding clients' difficulties, coping skills, and social support systems (Juhnke & Granello, 2005) Suicide risk assessment is essential to identify treatable risk factors, protective factors, and warning signs that guide counselors in selecting and using interventions.

The assessment process for suicide risk relies on your understanding of the mind-set of clients with suicidal ideation. Suicidal behavior is very difficult to study, for various reasons; sadly, chief among these reasons is the fact that those who complete suicide are obviously not available for any type of assessment or research. Reasons that lead a person to consider suicide generally involve hopelessness and helplessness, a sense of not belonging, and a perception of oneself as a burden (Van Orden et al., 2010).

Historically, Shneidman (1993), founder of the American Association of Suicidology (AAS), coined the term *psychache*, which refers to a state in which a person experiences extreme and excruciating psychological pain that intensifies the perceived need to take one's own life. The mind aggregates a wide array of negative emotions that perhaps trigger pain, including shame, anxiety, rejection, guilt, threat, unhappiness, and fear-based pressure. The pain experienced by an individual in psychache makes consideration of death by suicide a viable option, and although not all suicidal individuals experience psychache, this notion explains the rationale for ending one's life (Shneidman, 1995). Suicidologists agree there are a series of factors that converge, including biological, social, and environmental. Along with those factors, often there is an interpersonal storm that occurs in an individual who becomes suicidal, and the element of psychological chaos and culmination of events leading to death by suicide is difficult to comprehend (Joiner et al., 2009).

The interpersonal theory of suicide further expounds on psychache and describes that the pain resulting from one's own death is perhaps worth more than life. Causal factors associated with an individual's desire to die by suicide may result from self-perceptions of being a burden to others or feelings of disconnection or non-belongingness (Joiner et al., 2009). Further, acquisition of fearlessness toward death and tolerance of self-inflicted pain may contribute to one's growing capacity of suicide completion. There is an intersection between the factors of burdensomeness, belongingness, and acquired capacity that may overwhelm the psychache, thus resulting in a fatal outcome (Bartlett et al., 2012).

Cook et al. (2006) stated that understanding what drives people to suicide is the first step in the counselor's ability to intervene and gain respect and empathy for clients with suicidal thoughts. Field experience students oftentimes have extreme difficulty putting themselves in the place of a suicidal client. Examination of how one might plan and complete a suicide can afford practicum students and interns with a unique chance to understand the emotional and spiritual turmoil involved in suicidal thinking. Understanding the mind-set of a suicidal client will assist in selecting interventions and enhance counselor empathy for clients with suicidal ideation. In addition, self-awareness of the client's experience will assist field experience students in creating interventions and enhance counselor empathy for clients with suicidal ideation.

Part of what complicates the understanding of the suicidal mind is the many misconceptions that permeate society and even the counseling profession. Some commonly identified myths about suicide that have been debunked include (Granello & Granello, 2007; Joiner, 2007):

- Discussing suicide will lead a client to go forward with a plan to die.
- Only severely mentally ill people die by suicide.
- Suicide is a hereditary trait.
- Those who threaten suicide are just seeking attention.
- Suicide is an impulsive act and occurs without warning.
- Suicide is an act of cowardice.
- Suicide is selfish.
- People who die by suicide do not make future plans.
- There is nothing that can stop people if they really want to die.
- Most suicides occur around the holidays.
- Once a person gets through a suicide crisis (or attempt) there is no more danger.

It is important for you to evaluate the degree to which myths have impacted your understanding of the suicidal mind. The practicum and internship experiences are a unique educational component allowing you to explore the facets of working with suicidal clients. Practicum promotes an understanding of self, biases, and one's impact on clients (Scott et al., 2014). During the practicum and internship training, students are challenged to view their own patterns of thinking and their own characteristics that may impede the counseling relationship. Further, when counseling students examine their feelings, values, background, and perceptions, practicum and internship can provide enhanced self-awareness. As a result, insights gained contribute to professional growth and development of knowledge.

As mentioned earlier, most counselors will eventually be faced with the care of a suicidal client, a family member struggling with supporting a loved one who has suicidal thinking, or survivors of attempted suicide. One way to be prepared for client suicide is to be trained early in one's counseling career. Counselor educators debate how to best provide this training, and various methods have been proposed to enhance student awareness and knowledge about suicide (Juhnke & Granello, 2005; Laux, 2002). You can enhance your awareness and knowledge about suicide through researching and reading professional literature, and by examining your values, thoughts, and feelings. Use Self-Assessment Activity 8.2 to begin thinking about your beliefs about suicide.

Self-Assessment Activity 8.2 Beliefs About Suicide

1. Why do you think people die by suicide?
2. What are your beliefs about suicide?
3. What have you learned about suicide in your life?
4. What type of person kills oneself?
5. Who do you know that has died by suicide?
6. What is your emotional reaction to suicide?

Self-awareness of your attitudes, feelings, thoughts, and values about suicide must be addressed not just in the training experience, but throughout your professional counseling career. Practicum students and interns may not expect, and therefore may not be prepared for, problems such as suicide or sexual and physical abuse. Initially field experience students may experience extreme distress when such problems are presented. Practicum and internship can provide the opportunity for students to recognize their own reactions and, through supervision, move through their distress.

Assessing Client Suicide Risk

Although addressing psychache is fundamental to the treatment of suicidal persons, a practicum student or intern may consider that the presentation of symptoms is complex and may include identification, understanding, and mitigation. The use of a multi-symptom approach is at the core of effective work with suicidal clients and begins with the assessment process (Granello & Granello, 2007; Shneidman, 2005). Although counselors are not able to predict which client will attempt or die by suicide with complete accuracy, if the situation were to arise, field experience students must take the necessary steps to meet the standard of care in the profession, which includes performing risk assessments and implementing an appropriate treatment plan (Simon, 2002). To provide comprehensive care, counselors should assemble a complete client profile by infusing a risk assessment early on, and throughout the case work to identify warning signs; elicit risk and protective factors to make intervention decisions; elicit information about imminent risk, ideation, and behavior to identify lethality; obtain records to complete the client profile; and consult with experienced practitioners so treatment decisions are not made in isolation (Shea, 2011; Suicide Prevention Resource Center and American Association of Suicidology [SPRC/AAS], 2019).

Risk Factors, Warning Signs, and Protective Factors

As mentioned previously, part of the client profile involves gathering information about risk factors, which are those aspects of a client's life that may place the client in a higher risk category but not necessarily presuppose suicide. Therefore, field experience students must be aware of potential risk factors for suicide and engage a client in conversation to elicit risk factors. Counselors can find additional information about risk factors, warning signs, and protective factors on the website of the American Association of Suicidology at www.suicidology.org (Alonso & Gearing, 2017; SPRC/AAS, 2019). Warning signs are different from risk factors. When warning signs are noted, imminent danger is likely indicated (SPRC/AAS, 2019). It is also important to evaluate protective factors that exist in the client's life. Protective factors strengthen and shield a client from increased suicide risk. Exploring protective factors can yield valuable information for a rich discussion regarding matters that impact the client's risk. The more protective factors a client can identify, the more fortified a person is against the risk for suicide. Protective factors include, but are not limited to, family and support systems, spirituality, community connections, children, dependents, or a significant other (Granello & Granello, 2007; SPRC/AAS, 2019).

Indicators that suicide is being contemplated may range from overt statements to more veiled remarks. The practicum student or intern should bear in mind that assessment should be based on a holistic examination, including the content of client remarks, affect, and other aspects of process. It is not uncommon for clients to make statements that seem passive, but such statements may actually indicate suicidal ideation. Being alert and tuned into such statements is a way for practicum students and interns to pursue a discussion about suicidality so that an evaluation can be accomplished. A few examples of veiled comments include: "It's all going to be better soon." "It's not worth it." "It doesn't matter." "This is too hard." "I can't do this anymore."

Comments that are more direct may include: "I don't want to live." "I want to die." "I can't live this way." "I (or my family) would be better off if I were dead." "I want to end it all myself." According to the SPRC/AAS (2019), a counselor can begin inquiring about suicide with the following questions: "Have you ever felt that life was not worth living?" and "Did you ever wish you could just go to sleep and not wake up?" Then follow up with specific questions that inquire about thoughts of death, self-harm, or suicide, including: "Is death something you've thought about recently?" and "Have things ever reached the point that you've thought of harming or killing yourself?" and "Do you want to kill yourself?" Whether the client makes a veiled threat or a direct comment, practicum students and interns should not presume to understand what the client means. Asking the client for clarification and detail is critical. Following the protocol of the counseling site is also essential to the safety and care of the client, as is consulting with a supervisor to determine the next step in providing quality care.

Evidence-Based Suicide Risk Assessment

Suicide assessment should be clear, unambiguous, direct, and nonjudgmental. It is critical to ask the direct question, "Are you suicidal?" or "Are you thinking of death by suicide as an option?" If asked in a genuine, neutral, open manner, the client will most likely respond honestly. This core question begins a conversation required for an effective clinical suicidal assessment. It should be understood that even a clear denial to the question requires follow-up. It is a clinical error not to ask direct questions (Alonso & Gearing, 2017).

In assessing a client for suicidal ideation, examine these seven areas: (a) demographic data, (b) identified problem and symptom history, (c) current suicidality, (d) suicide history, I family and peer suicide history, (f) risk factors, and (g) protective factors. The more detailed the assessment of these areas, the greater the likelihood that an effective plan and subsequent interventions can be implemented. However, it is recognized that it is not always possible to obtain information in all these areas, which makes the assessment process a necessary ongoing event (Rudd et al., 2008).

When examining the seven primary areas, practicum students and interns should be aware that evidence-based assessments exist and should be used with all clients, rather than relying on best clinical impressions. There are 12 underlying principles of suicide risk assessment proposed by Granello (2010). The principles are not hierarchal (i.e., following a first to last order), and practitioners will develop their own process of implementation. Suicide risk assessment (a) is unique to each person; (b) is complex and challenging; (c) is an ongoing process; (d) errs on the side of cautiol(e) is collaborative; (f) relies on clinical judgment; (g) takes all threats, warning signs, and risk factors seriously; (h) requires asking tough questions; (i) acknowledges that assessment is treatment; (j) tries to uncover the underlying message and pain; (k) is done in a cultural context; and (l) is documented.

The application of risk assessment frameworks begins with assessing for past suicidal behavior, which is often the most potent predictor of subsequent suicidal ideation, suicide attempts, and death by suicide (Bartlett et al., 2012). The Suicide Risk Assessment Decision Tree Interview developed by Joiner et al. (2009) is widely endorsed because it is empirically supported. The decision tree involves assessing three "core" indicators of suicide risk: past suicidal behavior, current suicidal desire and ideation, and current resolved plans and preparations. These core indicators guide the practicum student or intern in determining a plan of action based on evaluated risk. It should be noted that with all other risk factors being equal, having resolved plans and preparations for suicide is more concerning than a client expressing only suicidal desire and ideation. A typical interview would include the following questions, moving through the aforementioned interview steps:

1. **Assessing history of suicidal behavior:** Have you attempted suicide in the past? How many times? Methods used? What happened? Do you have a history of self-injury?
2. **Assessing suicidal desire and ideation:** Have you been having thoughts or images of suicide? Wanting to be dead? How often do you think about suicide? What reasons do you have for dying? For continuing to live?
3. **Assessing resolved plans and preparations:** When you have these thoughts, how long do they last [look for preoccupation]? How strong is your intent to kill yourself on a scale of 1 to 10, with 1 meaning not at all and 10 meaning definitely? Do you have a plan for how you would kill yourself? Do you possess the means? Do you think you will have an opportunity? Have you prepared for an attempt? When do you expect to do it? How scared/how courageous/how able do you feel about trying?
4. **Assessing other significant findings:** Has anything especially stressful happened to you recently? Do you feel hopeless? How do you cope when you are feeling badly? Has anyone in your family made a suicide attempt or died by suicide? What are your thoughts and feelings about that attempt/suicide event? Do you feel connected to other people? Live alone? Who do you call when you are feeling badly? Do you believe you are a burden to those significant in your life? In what ways do you believe you contribute meaningfully to those around you?

In addition, the interviewer determines if the client has adequate social support, if there is a presence of any psychopathology, if the person has responsibility to or for others, if the client has cultural and religious beliefs against suicide, and if the client has good problem-solving abilities (Joiner et al., 2009).

Assessment Instruments

A specific assessment instrument is one part of the overall assessment process. A multitude of instruments can be used to assess suicidality. Both the number and complexity may make selection difficult for a practicum student or intern. It is recommended that practicum students and interns have a discussion early into their field placement with their site supervisors regarding preferred suicide risk assessment inventories. In the event the site does not have a preferred instrument, the practicum student or intern should consult a course instructor for recommended evidence-based tools. Factors to consider in selecting an assessment instrument include availability, cost, ease of use, ease of interpretation, and empirical validation. Instruments for use with children, teens/adolescents, adults, and the elderly can be located and evaluated at:

- Buros Center for Testing: Mental Measurements Yearbooks at www.unl.edu/buros/
- Neurotransmitter.net: Psychiatric Rating Scales for Suicide Ideation at www.neurotransmitter.net/suicidescales.html
- The American Association of Suicidology: Translating Suicide Research into Practice at www.suicidology.org/web/guest/current-research

Determining Risk Level

Often, difficulty assessing clients with suicidal thinking involves determining perceived risk level. In part this is because there are no absolute, scientific categories of suicide risk; rather, suicide risk can exist along a continuum (Alonso & Gearing, 2017). Field experience students are encouraged to glean information from the Suicide Risk Assessment Decision Tree Interview to categorize the suicide risk as *low*, *moderate*, or *high*. Ordinarily, multiple suicide attempts would be assigned to a higher risk category than a non-attempter or single-attempter. The counselor should assess for significant findings (e.g., precipitant stressors, such as a recent divorce) and protective factors (e.g., strong social support). Positive endorsement of additional findings should result in possibly increasing the risk designation of the client (e.g., from low to moderate). In contrast, clients who endorse many important protective factors might be placed in a lower risk category, although it is prudent to err on the side of caution when making the decision to adjust a risk category downward based on protective factors (Bartlett et al., 2012).

Once collateral information and evidence is obtained and considered, it must be prioritized. For example, if collateral information indicates a client has attempted suicide multiple times, this client would be considered high risk. The client's current suicide intent and lethality significantly determine the counselor's perception of risk and action steps (Jobes, 2016). The decision tree compares risk factors that are more pernicious than others (e.g., a history of multiple suicide attempts is weighted more heavily than a family history of suicide). These risk categories help the clinician identify the most appropriate actions for interventions.

Having a chart or graph that categorizes risk factors and compartmentalizes them into specific levels is nearly impossible and can be misleading. Each factor has to be evaluated individually as well as in the overall context of the evaluative process. One of the most important things to bear in mind when determining risk level is that although you may use all the information elicited throughout the assessment to make the decision, ultimately, the final determination is subjective. Therefore, a counselor must be able to explain how they concluded a client was rated at the identified risk level and how the determination drove the interventions selected from it. This can be very challenging and is why practicum students and interns are advised not to complete an assessment of suicide (i.e., determining risk level and appropriate interventions) without assistance from a field supervisor. The same is true even for experienced counselors. Given that collaborating with other professionals is part of the overall process, no one should work in isolation. This practice helps to best protect the client from suicide and the counselor from liability should the client die (Lee & Bartlett, 2005; Reid, 2010; Simon, 2004).

Risk level determines counselor actions. Counselor actions are informed by the risk assessment. Once completed and consensus with your field placement supervisor is reached, it would be appropriate to keep clients who have been assessed with a low suicide risk in counseling on an outpatient basis. Should a moderate risk assignment be determined, an outpatient referral and a medication regimen may be considered. In a developing situation, those presenting with high suicide risk should be referred for medical observation and medication reevaluation (Alonso & Gearing, 2017). In circumstances where a pen-and-pencil assessment instrument is not available or timely, a mnemonic (e.g., acronym) can be used. There are various mnemonics, such as SLAP—gathering *specific* details about suicidal thoughts, gauging *lethality* level of plan, determining *availability* of the method, and inquiring about *proximity* of the client to the method. The SPRC/AAS (2019) suggests using the "IS PATH WARM" mnemonic device to guide questions in the assessment process:

I—Ideation

S—Substance Abuse

P—Purposelessness

A—Anxiety

T—Trapped

H—Hopelessness

W—Withdrawal

A—Anger

R—Recklessness

M—Mood Change

A mnemonic can help a counselor remember major areas that need to be covered in an assessment when suicidal thinking is introduced. Counselors are advised to identify a mnemonic that comes most naturally for them, whether it is SLAP, IS PATH WARM, or another assessment (Granello & Granello, 2007). See Case Study 8.1 for practice in identifying aspects of suicide risk.

Case Study 8.1 Alex

Alex is a 67-year-old, widowed, Caucasian, male, who retired recently. He is coming to counseling on referral from his primary care physician, who reported that Alex "presented with depressive symptoms." Alex was prescribed an antidepressant by his primary care physician, which Alex says he only takes on "bad days." The client explained that when he participates in church activities he feels good; however, lately he hasn't been attending church. A change in appetite and sleep is noted, as well as Alex's increasing dependence on taking a sleeping aid for his reported recent sleep disturbance. Alex described having a conflicted relationship with his son, who lives nearby, and a close relationship with his two daughters, who live outside his state of residence. Alex also noted that he had been close to his brother, who Alex described as mentally ill and who had died some years ago as the result of a suicide. Alex reports concern about his finances and becoming a burden to his children, particularly as his arthritis and chronic pain increasingly prevent him from walking his dog (which he loves to do) and from participating in activities at the senior center (which he recently joined at his daughters' encouragement). Alex stated that he would return for another visit but didn't see it as necessary.

- Identify risk factors, warning signs, and protective factors.

What level of risk would you assign to Alex?

Some Best and Not So Best Practices

Let's start with some practices to use with caution. Self-report suicide risk assessment checklists may be used in clinical settings but have not been subjected to rigorous psychometric validation. Checklists may have a place in the counseling setting and may be used for other topics; however, they are not recommended for assessing suicide.

Next, no-suicide contracts (NSCs) continue to be used in clinical practice, despite no clear evidence of efficacy with suicidal clients. An NSC is an agreement in which the client commits not to die by suicide. Literature has suggested the following as potential benefits of including an NSC in a suicide assessment: (a) acknowledges the severity of the situation, (b) reinforces that suicide is a poor choice, (c) affirms a decision not to suicide, (d) enhances the working alliance, and (e) provides diagnostic information (Bartlett, 2008; Jobes, 2016). However, NSCs have little empirical support in the actual prevention of suicide among clients (Bartlett, 2008; Bartlett et al., 2009; Rudd et al., 2006). In fact, potential disadvantages include (a) creates an illusion of safety for the counselor and client, (b) may be overvalued as a risk-management tool, (c) is often instigated by the emotional reactions of the counselor, (d) entrusts a disturbed client to adhere to an agreement, (e) has limited effectiveness due to unpredictability, (f) is invalid as a legal contract, (g) a client may sign only to appease the counselor, and (h) it short-circuits a more comprehensive suicide assessment (Bartlett, 2008; Jobes, 2016, Simon, 2004).

Now for a best practice to do. It is recommended that practicum students and interns collaborate with clients to create a crisis response plan, which is an empirically driven intervention used in place of a no-suicide contract (Jobes, 2016). A crisis response plan: (a) focuses on what the client will do rather than not do; (b) provides direction for collaboration negotiation of stability and client safety; (c) emphasizes mutual give and take; (d) encourages a good faith, time-specific willingness to give treatment a chle; and (e) moves the focus of treatment on increasing pain tolerance, alternative coping skills, and making life worth living.

Interventions With Suicide

Once it is determined that a client is having suicidal thoughts, interventions must be considered. The signs of an effective treatment strategy include (a) a clearly articulated model in which suicidality is the focus; (b) targeting skills deficiencies, self-reliance, self-awareness, and internalized locus of control; (c) ensuring that clients have access to emergency services; and (d) restriction or elimination of lethal means (Bartlett et al., 2012). The most effective intervention in terms of preventing death by suicide appears to be a restriction in access to lethal means. Ironically, many counselors are reluctant to ask clients about available means, in particular firearms, for fear of being too invasive. Just as you are encouraged to ask the core question, "Do you want to kill yourself?" you also are responsible to ask, "Do you own or have any access to firearms?" (Bryan et al., 2011; Coombs et al., 2010).

It is noted that limited empirically validated treatments exist to prevent suicide. However, the strongest clinical interventions and techniques with demonstrated effectiveness with clients with suicidal ideation include dialectical behavior therapy (DBT; Linehan et al., 2006), problem-solving therapy (PST; Rudd et al., 1996), and cognitive therapy (CT; Brown et al., 2005).

Dialectical Behavior Therapy (DBT)

DBT is a type of cognitive behavior therapy that, even in the face of intense emotions, facilitates change by assisting the client in achieving a life worth living (Linehan et al., 2006). The four components of DBT are mindfulness, distress tolerance, interpersonal effectiveness, and emotional regulation. DBT is effective in reducing suicide attempts among clients with recent suicide attempts, self-harm behaviors, and borderline personality disorder. In DBT, clients are taught to: (a) use a behavior chain analysis in which clients dissect their behaviors, identifying urges, thoughts, and situations that contribute to their behavior; (b) engage in live coaching through between-session phone calls, which reduces suicidality by strengthening the client–therapist relationship; (c) use mindfulness to approach situations with perspective rather than emotionality, and with a stance of acceptance rather than judgment; and (d) increase distress tolerance to experience and accept intense emotions rather than acting on them in self-destructive ways. The dual focus of DBT on acceptance and change addresses the ambivalence in clients with suicidality. Further, counselor authenticity builds interpersonal connection that may reduce suicidality (Alonso & Gearing, 2017; Bartlett et al., 2012; Joiner et al., 2009).

Problem-solving Therapy (PST)

Although some research has shown that PST is no more effective than other research indicates that it decreases suicide attempts and suicidal ideation (Donaldson et al., 2005). PST centers on the notion that persons who are suicidal have faulty, poor interpersonal problem-solving skills (Sourander et al., 2001; Wingate et al., 2005). The seven steps (i.e., define the problem, identify the goal, generate alternatives, evaluate alternatives, implement an alternative, evaluate efforts, and modify the approach as needed) center on problem-solving skills as alternatives to suicide and may be written on a portable note card (e.g., Crisis Coping Card) for easy accessibility to reduce impulsive coping (Berk et al., 2004). These cards can be used as part of the client's crisis response plan of what to do when feeling overwhelmed, providing a simple plan of action when the client is overwhelmed or distressed, such as calling a friend, focusing on positive statements, or listening to music (Berk et al., 2004; Wenzel et al., 2009).

Cognitive Therapy (CT)

Central to cognitive therapy is the concept that behaviors and emotions are a result of meanings a person assigned to events (Wenzel et al., 2009). Cognitive therapy has its impact by addressing depression and hopelessness, rather than focusing on suicide itself (Brown et al., 2005). This approach involves three stages: (a) building a framework for treatment, (b) a focus on behavior that uses cognitive restructuring and behavioral interventions to reduce suicidality, and (c) relapse prevention (Berk et al., 2004; Henriques et al., 2003). Two specific cognitive therapy techniques are the hope kit and guided imagery. In the hope kit, clients compile mementos, pictures, souvenirs, and reminders of their reasons for living (Henriques et al., 2003). Building the kit may strengthen hope by correcting cognitive errors regarding reasons to die as opposed to reasons for living. The completed kit serves as a reminder of reasons for living. Guided imagery is a relapse-prevention intervention in which the client is instructed to envision a future suicidal episode and is led through cognitive restructuring, problem solving, and coping skills. This method acts as a rehearsal for future stresses and creates a vision of self-mastery, which strengthens resilience in preparation for actual events (Alonso & Gearing, 2017; Wenzel et al., 2009).

Documentation of Assessment and Intervention Efforts

Clinical documentation demonstrates the actual work of the practicum student or intern. If a suicide assessment and formulation of risk process is not comprehensively documented, courts may suggest that preventative actions were not established (Granello & Granello, 2007; Remley & Herlihy, 2020). "In malpractice litigation, or administrative, or ethics proceedings, an adequately documented, legible patient record is the clinician's 'best friend'" (Simon, 2004, p. 212). Some counselors believe less documentation when treating suicidal clients is more protective when in fact the exact opposite is true. Common risk management intervention errors include not completing an adequate assessment, poor treatment planning, inappropriate management of care, and failure to document (Simon, 2004; SPRC/AAS, 2019). There may be multiple documentation styles used to evidence that an appropriate standard of care was demonstrated. Counselors are responsible to select a documentation format that is setting appropriate. The style of documentation incorporated is often different among agencies and dependent on licensing requirements, mental health governing bodies, and professional organizations.

A widely used and historically established risk–benefit model is that of VandeCreek et al. (1987), who suggested documenting: (a) a description of a comprehensive assessment of risk, (b) information obtained alerting the counselor to the risk, (c) indication of which high and low risk factors are present, (d) what questions were asked of the client and resples given, (e) how the clinical information directed the actions of the counselor, and (f) why other actions were rejected. A counselor needs to justify and articulate decisions via detailed client notations (Jobes, 2016) in a timely manner. Assessment and treatment methods are extremely important should a lawsuit arise. Counselors unable to demonstrate how and when assessment information was obtained and used may invite a charge of negligence. The formulation of risk is not possible to prove in court if the appropriate level of documentation does not exist; the request for documentation in court is to be expected, and inadequate documentation of clinical procedures utilized and actions taken leaves the practitioner susceptible to adverse litigation.

The importance of documenting your work with suicidal or homicidal clients, as noted earlier, can become a legal issue in which you must demonstrate the standard of care provided to your clients. This should not lead you to *fear* working with suicidal clients but to adopt a preventive protocol for documenting your work that fits with your counseling style, your practice setting, and state and local laws.

The process for working with a client who may be suicidal would be easier if there was a standard risk management chart or checklist that could be used to assess and treat suicide. Unfortunately, there is not one list because assessing for suicide is complex and multifaceted. Documentation of the standard of care provided by the counselor is vital. One helpful tool for practicum and internship students to learn is the SCATTT mnemonic (Balkin & Juhnke, 2014). By following SCATTT, counselors can have a step-by-step process to follow utilizing a specific intervention (i.e., Stay, Consult, Apprise, Terminate, Truncate, and Transport):

The SCATTT Mnemonic

- Stay with the client.
- Consult with supervisors and professional peers.
- Apprise the client of assessment findings and your professional judgment.
- Terminate the threat (e.g., remove any identified suicide instruments [e.g., guns, weapons, knives]).
- Truncate threats that cannot be terminated (e.g., remove easy access to medications; ensure only supervised access to cars).
- Transport to the psychiatric hospital or least-restrictive environment deemed best by you and your supervisors (e.g., partial hospitalization, monitored foster care).

SCATTT should be explored in depth by practicum and internship students and is provided here as an overview in recognizing the importance of acting and documenting that action as part of the suicide intervention plan. SCATTT is only one helpful tool; there are other approaches as well to minimize counselors' liability. Recommendations from several leading suicidologists include an overall risk management approach (Joiner et al., 2009; Rudd et al., 2008; SPRC/AAS, 2019). A suicide risk management checklist includes the following:

- Assess for and rule out emergency risk.
- Assess history of suicidal behavior.
- Assess suicidal desire and ideation.
- Assess resolved plans and preparations.
- Elicit warning signs of imminent risk.
- Elicit risk and protective factors.
- Plan to conduct multiple assessments.
- Integrate assessment early and routinely.
- Obtain records from collateral sources.
- Consult with other professionals.
- Formulate risk level.
- Execute treatment and continue assessing.
- Manage treatment and continue assessing.
- Document all work.

Postvention

Postvention, another term first coined by Shneidman (2004), is used to describe helpful acts initiated after a crisis event. Suicide postvention is a concept related to the prevention of subsequent suicides, provision of mental health services, and the community response following a completed suicide. People are affected in different ways by the loss of a family member or person of close connection to suicide. Field experience students should recognize that death by suicide is final for the decedent; however, prevention risk is just beginning for the survivors.

The survivor, or a person who has lost a loved one to death by suicide, should not be confused with an individual who has survived a suicide attempt. Counselors should be aware that active postvention should take place immediately by providing a list of survivor support groups. Survivors can plan to attend bereavement groups and make connections to others who have experienced suicide loss immediately. Suicide survivors often need more care, comfort, and compassion than people who anticipated the death of a loved one, but the needs of survivors are often left unmet (Bartlett et al., 2015; Jordan & McIntosh, 2011; Talbott & Bartlett, 2012).

Treating Survivors

The responses of parents, spouses, and siblings may vary, with parents often experiencing guilt, spouses suffering the accusation of others, and siblings not receiving adequate support. Familiarize yourself with how suicide affects clients at different ages and stages of life. When providing initial assistance to survivors of suicide, all counselors should be aware of their own reactions to suicide, be familiar with community and national survivor support resources, let the survivors talk at their own pace, and refer to the decedent by name rather than saying "your son" or "your husband." Losing someone to suicide is highly personal, and survivors indicate finding comfort when another person refers to their loved one lost to suicide by name. Long-term goals include helping survivors reconcile feelings of anger, to forgive the decedent and others they may perceive were involved in the suicide death, reducing isolation and increasing engagements in social networks, accepting the mysteries of the unknown factors surrounding the suicide loss, and increasing survivors' sharing of the grieving process with others (American Foundation for Suicide Prevention [AFSP], 2021; Jordan & Harpel, 2007).

Treating Returning Clients Who Attempt Suicide

You may face working with a client who returns to counseling following a suicide attempt. For a person who attempted suicide, their risk to attempt again remains relatively high even after discharge from a hospital. Further, the stigma associated with the experience; the reactions of family, friends, and peers; and the degree to which the attempt affects the client should be monitored and addressed by the counselor. Follow-up questions and statements for use when a client returns after an attempt may include the following: "Have your thoughts about suicide increased, decreased, or remained the same since we last met?" "Since I last saw you, give me an update on your suicide thoughts." "Tell me what you have done this week to deal with your suicidal thoughts more effectively." "How successful were you in modifying your thoughts regarding suicide?" "Describe how effective your thought modification has been." "Do you feel more in control of your thoughts?" Using these questions and statements may help to promote smooth reintegration back into home, work, and social communities and can be an opportunity to rebuild resilience for the returning attempter, affected peers, and family members (SPRC/AAS, 2019). Thus, prevention and intervention without postvention supports fails to complete the cycle of full prevention and potentially undermines the work of the former two efforts (Granello & Granello, 2007; SPRC/AAS, 2019).

Losing a Client to Suicide

The loss of a client to suicide will affect you on both personal and professional levels. Should client death occur during the field placement, a practicum student or intern may question their own competence and self-esteem and may even consider another profession. These feelings are normal and should be discussed with supervisors. Aside from feelings of guilt, field experience students and practicing counselors may realistically wonder about the potential for litigation (Farberow, 2005).

Complicating your own recovery from a client suicide is the fact that you may experience discomfort and isolation from other counseling colleagues, staff, and supervisors. Secondary trauma can have a remarkably strong influence on counselors who have experienced suicide of a client (Baird & Mollen, 2019). This vicarious traumatization can result in counselors being ambivalent about disclosing their own feelings and reactions to the loss of a client to suicide. This kind of loss will impact the continued clinical work of a practicum student or intern. It is important to seek close supervision, individual counseling, and the support of peers who have also experienced a similar loss. Many counselors report increased compassion and understanding about the suicidal crisis and report becoming better educated about suicide following their loss of a client to suicide. The AAS now has a clinician survivor task force that provides consultation, support, and education to assist in understanding and responding to loss resulting from the suicide death of a client or family member, and it is highly advised that, in addition to the aforementioned recovery suggestions, counselors access support through the AAS clinical survivor group (AAS, 2012; Bartlett et al., 2015). In addition to the risk of having a client die, you may also have other concerns about working with suicidal clients; use Self-Assessment Activity 8.3 to reflect on these concerns.

Self-Assessment Activity 8.3 Concerns as a Counselor

Take a few moments and journal about your concerns with assessing and working with suicidal clients. Consider the following as you reflect:

1. What is your greatest anxiety about this work?
2. What do you believe to be your current knowledge level on working with suicidal clients?
3. What concerns do you have about assessing for suicide in children and teens?
4. What concerns do you have about assessing for suicide in various adult populations?
5. What concerns do you have about assessing for suicide in diverse populations?
6. What do you consider to be your strengths and weaknesses as a counselor in general?
7. How will those strengths and weaknesses affect your capacity to assess and work with clients who may be suicidal?

Legal and Ethical Issues

Legal standards in treating suicidal clients vary among states, so counselors must exercise additional consideration when treating these vulnerable clients. Comprehensive assessments, risk formulation, and documentation contribute to effective case management. Attention to these details may reduce litigation related to negligence and malpractice should a client die by suicide, which in turn may help to reduce the fear counselors may experience. Field experience students often lack sufficient education on legal aspects of the assessment, management, and malpractice associated with patient suicides. As a result of changing trends and standards, periodic reevaluation of clinical methods is essential, especially given the litigious nature of U.S. society. The best defense against liability tort should a client die by suicide is for the counselor to have followed acceptable standards of care to guide interventions and carefully documented all clinical actions. Through familiarity with evidence-based assessment protocols, professional consultation, and training, field experience students improve their understanding of suicidal clients and legal complications .

Cultural Considerations

Many populations warrant special attention and require specific training to respond appropriately to a suicidal crisis (e.g., children, young adults, persons with physical illnesses, LGBTQ). Cultural, racial, and ethnic differences exist among clients who present with suicidal ideation. Successful intervention is accomplished when the differences are considered and treatment adapted. Prevention efforts should be guided by culturally relevant risk and protective factors for suicide and attitudes toward suicide (Alonso & Gearing, 2017). Recommendations for field experience students to achieve cultural competence working with diverse clients who have suicidal ideation include (a) developing an awareness of personal assumptions, biases, and value; (b) understanding that cultural views differ from clients; (c) developing culturally sensitive and relevant strategies when assisting diverse clients (Sue et al., 2019); and (d) adapting assessment protocols based on language and cultural customs. Field experience students should be aware that the assessment, intervention, and postvention processes with these and other populations are different, and a review of specific assessment and intervention protocols is essential. Field experience students should seek additional training to ensure they are adequately prepared to meet the special needs of various populations (Bartlett et al., 2015).

Duty to Warn

The sentinel case related to a provider's duty to warn that has resounded throughout the helping professions is the 1976 decision in *Tarasoff v. Regents of the University of California*. In this significant case, Prosenjit Poddar was seeing a psychologist at the university counseling center. Poddar threatened to kill a female acquaintance, Tatiana Tarasoff, when she returned from a trip. Tarasoff was not warned of the threat to her life, and shortly after her return, Poddar followed through with his threat by stabbing her to death (Corey et al., 2019; Remley & Herlihy, 2020). In the ensuing lawsuit, the California Supreme Court ruled that there are circumstances in which a therapist should break confidentiality, particularly when it is necessary to prevent harm to others. The act of breaking confidentiality in such circumstances is labeled as the duty to warn.

The effects of *Tarasoff* continue to impact the counseling profession both ethically and legally. This impact is particularly felt in the wake of widely publicized acts of violence by persons who are or have been in counseling. The American Counseling Association (ACA) *Code of Ethics* (2014) indicates that disclosure of client information is required "to protect clients or identified others from serious and foreseeable harm or when legal requirements demand confidential information must be revealed" (Standard B.2.a, p. 7). This standard was adopted as a direct result of the *Tarasoff* ruling. Following the landmark *Tarasoff* ruling, many state legislatures enacted laws reflecting the concerns of the case. According to Herbert and Young (2002) these states fall into four categories, those with: (a) a mandatory duty to warn; (b) a permission to warn; (c) a rejection of a duty or permission to warn (e.g., so-called anti-Tarasoff laws; and (d) those states with no such law. Edwards (2013) noted that the majority of states (33) impose a mandatory duty to warn, whereas 11 jurisdictions give permission to warn at the therapist's discretion. In either case, the counselor has some level of legal protection from prosecution arising from the consequences of such a warning. Six states currently have no law regarding a duty or permission to warn, and the Supreme Court of Virginia rejected Tarasoff-type laws (Edwards, 2018). States with duty or permission to warn laws vary widely on who may be identified as a victim, what constitutes a viable threat, and how the counselor should proceed to issue a warning. In addition, the application of state laws varies with regard to the responsibilities of the practitioner depending on their professional identity (e.g., counselor, psychologist, social worker). Herbert and Young pointed out the absence of any federal law regarding duty to warn; therefore, counselors should be aware of the laws of their own state and the wide differences between state laws as well as the rapidly changing nature of legislation.

Homicidal Clients

Voices From the Field 8.1 Understanding the Homicidal Mind, *by Nancy Slicner, Lt Col (ret.) Air Force, Forensic Psychologist and Independent Consultant*

People who kill others may look and act completely normal. A counselor has to have an ear tuned into what is making another person concerned about the behavior. Counselors aren't always prepared to ask questions to explore the possibility of homicide. They need to ask, "Are you afraid that your spouse may kill you?' and take a step beyond what is comfortable in the assessment experience.

At some point in your professional career, you will likely encounter a homicidal client (Walfish et al., 2010). Similar to the fear and stigmatization associated with the suicidal clients, field experience students often feel anxious and uncomfortable working with homicidal clients and the risks they pose. But the duty to warn and duty to protect also apply to the homicidal client. Protection of public safety is always the primary clinical consideration and preventing harm to others is imperative. Anticipation of interactions with a homicidal client is not enough. The practicum student or intern must prepare to assess, intervene, and treat this client type. Counselors should individualize their intervention styles and participate in continuing education to ensure a proper response.

Homicide is an act of murder and nonnegligent manslaughter that involves the willful killing of one human being by another (U.S. Department of Justice, Office of Justice Programs, Bureau of Justice Statistics, 2020). Over the past decade, a significant decline in homicide rates has been observed in the United States, and consistencies continue to imply that males are most commonly both the victim and perpetrator of these violent acts (U.S. Department of Justice, Office of Justice Programs, Bureau of Justice Statistics, 2019). To further illustrate the decline, general homicide rates were 9.1/100,000 (in 1991) in contrast to that of 4.8/100,000 (in 2010). Of note, homicide rates among young adults aged 18 to 24 years were the highest of any age group reported in 2008 (13.4 homicides/100,000 persons); thus, the need for increased prevention and intervention efforts is warranted. Field experience students must take appropriate steps when a client presents with homicidal thoughts or behaviors (Schwartz, 2008). From time to time, counselors may serve persons with a history of mental disorders and violent offenses who pose an elevated risk to the public—and the counselor. The challenge is to balance personal, professional, and public risk while ensuring the client's rights are not violated (Anderson & West, 2011). Field experience students must provide the appropriate level of documentation related to both inpatient and outpatient care provided and the escalation of risk (Rossi et al., 2010).

Assessment of Homicide Risk

The risk of homicide and factors associated with interpersonal violence should be interpreted with caution during the assessment process. A practicum student or intern may encounter a client that exhibits risk factors, but this does not necessarily mean that the individual will become violent. HowevIt would be naive to think that a client devoid of risk factors could not develop homicidal intentions. The lack of familiarity with violence-based risk assessments should lead the counselor to err on the side of caution and evaluate each case independently (McNiel et al., 2008).

The prevalence of homicide is in some way associated with problem-laden interpersonal relationships, and the majority of victims are killed by someone known to them. The majority of homicide perpetrators are male, and the most common lethal means is the use of a firearm (Papadopoulosa et al., 2009). Research supports that males exhibiting a family history of mental illness, family violence, job instability, and impulsivity are more likely to express homicidal tendencies (Swinson et al., 2011).

Violent outbreaks may also be attributed to substance abuse or changes in psychotropic medication but simply cannot be dismissed as acceptable behavior. One may suspect the homicide rate among those with mental illness to be dramatically higher than the general population; however, this is not particularly true (Kleespies & Richmond, 2009). Further, acts of violence such as homicide and war may require deeper explanation and clinical interventions (Liddle et al., 2012), and client history of military service may be a viable discussion to hold. The increase in homicides by those with schizophrenia and by those with psychotic symptoms at the time may likely be related to drug misuse. The intern and practicum student should be prepared to ask questions of potentially homicidal clients that pertain to the sudden onset of drug use or changes in drug-use patterns (Swinson et al., 2011).

In addition, offenders of homicide may have previously assaulted someone, but that incident may not be on record and documented by the police, community services, shelters, or physicians previously in contact with the client. However, the occurrence of domestic incidents should be assessed and an intimate partner homicide (IPH) risk assessment completed to determine particular risk, as it is unlikely that the initial offense would have raised attention of the police, social services, or mental health systems beforehand (Eke et al., 2011).

Comparable to suicide, counselors must be aware of the potential for litigation regarding harm to others caused by a homicidal client. Assessment of the potential threat for homicidal actions among clients requires counselors to stay up to date on professional literature and advances in the assessment process. In doing so, the client, those the client may potentially hurt, and the counselor are better protected. To better assist practicum and internship students, an overall risk management checklist for assessing homicide may include the following items (Collins & Collins, 2006; Foster et al., 2012; Klott & Jongsma, 2004):

- Assess for and rule out emergency risk.
- Assess for interpersonal discord.
- Assess for substance use.
- Determine history of mental illness.
- Gauge access to firearms.
- Monitor impulsivity.
- Explore job instability and termination.
- Obtain details on experiences with justice system.
- Integrate assessment early.
- Refer for evaluation by forensic specialist.
- Obtain records from collateral sources.
- Formulate risk level.
- Execute and manage treatment.
- Document all work.

This checklist is provided to practicum and internship students as an overview of basic steps in the assessment of homicide and risk management. This checklist is not exhaustive, and counselors are urged to be informed and up to date on state laws, professional guidelines, and best practices to ensure a quality standard of care for all clients, especially when assessing for homicide risk.

Media Influence

Depictions of violent acts and terrorism are readily available and sensationalized by traditional media outlets (e.g., television, newspaper) and reinforced by access to violent video games and Internet content (Savage, 2008; Ybarra et al., 2008). The uncontrolled access to violence presented in different forms of media exposes segments of the population to this type of behavior and can have a profound impact on the actions of youth (Ferguson & Kilburn, 2009). Media outlets leave lasting impressions on vulnerable populations. When violent content is not regulated, it normalizes these behaviors and is one reason that acts of violence are underreported (Herrenkohl et al., 2008; Wolitzky-Taylor et al., 2011). Although seemingly senseless, these acts occur in social networks, families, schools, colleges, the workplace, and all across the country (Smith, 2009).

School Violence

Schools pose a natural gathering place for children, adolescents, and young adults for the purposes of cultural and educational enrichment. Once thought to be a community safe haven, schools have become the focus of violent acts and homicide in recent decades in both the United States and internationally. In particular, events surrounding the Columbine High School, Virginia Tech University, and Northern Illinois University tragedies come to mind as heinous acts resulting in the loss of lives at the hands of young homicidal persons in possession of firearms (Borum et al., 2010). It is important that field experience students not discount the lethality or intent to harm a student or faculty member. Interns selecting employment in the school setting should be particularly in tune with risk factors for homicide. It is difficult to predict when acts such as these may occur; however, learning from historical responses to school crises can be helpful. Each school and geographic region has differing beliefs about the value of education, and cultural issues around respect for others vary widely (Brown et al., 2009). Administrators, counselors, and concerned others have taken steps to create school threat assessment or crisis plans that perhaps did not exist prior to aforementioned incidents (Allen et al., 2008).

Workplace Violence

Ordinarily, a work setting is a public place where individuals can freely enter a facility without restriction. The free range of motion poses a direct opportunity for violent acts should a homicidal individual stalk a victim or carry out homicidal intentions in a particular location. The perpetrator may represent an outside entity, be linked to an external or personal relationship, or be a member of the workplace staff themselves. Increased job stress, uncertain conditions of employment, and disputes with superiors can be factors leading to escalation and homicidal intent (Barling et al., 2009). If a client is referred by an employee assistance program (EAP) for exhibiting outward signs of frustration, counselors should determine if there is the potential for threat escalation and ask direct questions.

Intimate Partner Violence

Intimate partner violence (IPV) is the most common form of violence linked to homicide and is defined as "physical, sexual, or psychological harm by a current or former partner or spouse that may occur among heterosexual or same-sex couples and does not require sexual intimacy" (Centers for Disease Control [CDC], 2010). IPV may involve just one hit, but also can escalate on a continuum to chronic violent beatings. Saltzman et al. (2015), described several types of IPV: (a) physical violence, (b) sexual violence, (c) threats of physical or sexual violence, and (d) psychological/emotional violence. According to the National Intimate Partner and Sexual Violence Survey, one in three women and one in four men in the United States will experience rape, physical violence, and/or stalking by an intimate partner in their lifetime (Black et al., 2011). The most documented rationale for IPV as well as homicide is male sexual jealousy (Goetz et al., 2008) and men's partner-directed violence linked to perceived infidelity (Kaighobadi & Shackelford, 2009). Field experience students should be aware that males are most likely to be the victims of homicide and also the offenders (Farington & Lober, 2011). IPV is more likely to occur when couples are cohabitating, and often homicide is a result of more violent beatings (Mize et al., 2009). Further, the risk of IPV and homicide increases when a prominent age difference between partners exists, the victim has a child from a previous relationship, and the offender has unregulated access to a weapon (Campbell, 2007; Eke et al., 2011).

Assessing Your Views

Field experience students must be prepared to handle cases involving violence despite varying degrees of training in assessment, intervention, and treatment. Prior to working with violent clients, all counselors must take inventory of their personal and family history, which may also include violence attributed to a friend or family member. In fact, you may have witnessed a particular event or be the survivor–victim of a homicide attempt and could subsequently impede the client–counselor relationship. You must explore personal biases, have an action plan, and be able to show openness and clear judgment because each case is deserving of individual attention and assessment without bias. Although this chapter discusses violence and homicide with an emphasis on interpersonal violence, it is noted that field experience students may also shy away from working with clients who are victims of other personally injurious acts, such as stalking or rape. Use Self-Assessment Activity 8.4 to begin to reflect on how your personal experience with violence may influence your work as a counselor.

Self-Assessment Activity 8.4 Your Experience With Violence

1. If you have a family history that includes interpersonal acts of violence, how will this affect your willingness to work with clients presenting with homicidal ideation?
2. Would you be suited to seek employment in the criminal court that required clinical evaluation of persons who have completed a homicide attempt?
3. What level of comfort do you have when working with clients presenting with homicidal ideation? Has your curriculum prepared you to handle these situations?
4. What level of trust or mistrust do you have in the legal system and its ability to prevent homicidal acts if you report concerns about a client?

5. What level of continuing education will you seek should you decide to work in the criminal court system as a clinician?
6. What dialogue have you initiated with your course instructor about your desire to work or refrain from working with violent clients?

Counselor Safety Plan

Counselors must exhibit a level of restraint when interacting with potentially violent clients, including projecting a calm, controlled demeanor. A client who senses fear may choose to act on the counselor's vulnerability and become violent. Field experience students may experience anxiety in this situation that is difficult to control; however, careful evaluation of the situation, despite fear, can help elicit a personal safety plan. If you are new to a clinical setting, complete an assessment of your surroundings that would best protect you from a now-anticipated attack (e.g., sit closest to the door, remove unnecessary objects from the environment that may provide access to means of harm; Stinchfield et al., 2010). Although some statements regarding potential harm to others such as "I could just kill someone" are not uncommon and often dismissed, you are responsible for assessing lethality or level of threat associated with these statements by a homicidal client, whether stated or implied.

Threat Level Assessment

Conducting a homicide assessment is paramount in determining the homicidal threat level and intent. The assessment may provide field experience students with valuable information, such as the names and locations of the people being threatened or targeted. As previously discussed, counselors are required to keep client records confidential under federal laws; however, the duties to warn and protect are altered when a client intends to impose harm on others. Based on the level of threat and violent nature of the information disclosed, counselors are required to notify law enforcement and persons who are the direct target of the proposed violence.

The clinical skill of active listening is important when working with homicidal clients and occurs when a counselor says little to the client but shows a high level of interest in the information disclosed. Active listening clarifies a homicidal client's feelings and attitudes and may help determine if cognitive distortions are present. Further, open-ended questions allow the homicidal client to provide detailed responses and deeper information (Gekoski et al., 2012). Many situational factors contribute to violent acts, and the response of the client is in part dependent on their stage of developmental cognition, motivation, and environmental cues. Research suggests that counselors should employ violence prevention and reduction tactics rather than violence prediction (Douglas & Skeem, 2005), as there is generally not a single cause of malicious acts. Field experience students must consider a client's family history of violence, stress connected to a particular violent event, use of substances that increased violent responses, client ability to reason in a particular circumstance where an intimate partner is involved, and their immediate access to a weapon or other means of force to carry out the harmful behaviors disclosed.

A variety of risk factors are associated with acts of homicide and violence, and the level of risk should be assessed with caution. You should note that each client exhibiting risk factors may not become violent; however, without a working knowledge of risk factors, you may overlook a potentially dangerous situation if the client assessment is not evaluated on an individual basis. A combination of interpersonal, intrapersonal, community, and societal factors contribute to the risk of becoming a victim or perpetrator (Stith et al., 2004).

Threat assessment has two parts: (a) an evaluation of the threat itself, and (b) the expression of intent to do harm. Together, these evaluations can help lead to an informed judgment on whether someone who has made a threat is likely to carry it out, causing you to differentiate when someone is making a threat versus posing a threat. The Federal Bureau of Investigation's National Center for the Analysis of Violent Crimes (O'Toole, 2000) states that threat assessment should evaluate the: (a) details of the threat, (b) identification of victims, (c) means to carry out a threat, (d) emotional Ite of the client, (e) affect presented by the client, (f) level of exposure to stressors, and (g) predisposition to violent behaviors. In doing so, the level of homicidal threat can be assessed and the course of action for treatment determined.

A **low level of threat** poses a minimal risk to the victim and public safety. A low-level threat:

- Is vague and indirect.
- Contains inconsistent information that is implausible or lacks detail.
- Lacks realism.
- Content suggests the person is unlikely to carry out violent acts.

A **medium level of threat** could be carried out but may not appear entirely realistic. A medium level threat:

- Is direct and more concrete than a low-level threat.
- Suggests that the offender has given thought to how the act will be carried out.
- Indicates a possible place and time, though the signs still fall well short of a detailed plan.
- Gives no strong indication that the offender has taken preparatory steps (e.g., an allusion to a book or movie that shows the planning of a violent act or vague, general statement about the availability of weapons).
- May involve a specific statement seeking to convey that the threat is not empty: "I'm serious!" or "I really mean this!"

A **high level of threat** is defined as an occurrence that appears to pose an imminent and serious danger to the safety of others. A high level of threat occurs when the threat:

- Is direct, specific, and plausible.
- Suggests concrete steps have been taken toward carrying it out (e.g., statements indicating that the client has acquired or practiced with a weapon or has had the victim under surveillance).
- Involves the use of warning behaviors offering an escalating perspective in threat assessment.

Warning behaviors are acts that constitute evidence of increased risk. The counselor should document acute, dynamic, and particularly erratic changes in patterns of behavior, which may aid in structuring a professional decision that an individual of concern now poses a threat (Meloy et al., 2011).

Homicide Survivors

A homicidal crisis may leave long-lasting impressions on the community and those involved who are left to figure out how to move forward with life following the tragic event. Counselors should be a referral source for individuals surviving a homicide loss and also involved in community support efforts. Cofacilitation of groups with other mental health professionals can assist field experience students to practice and improve discussion skills with bereaved family and close others. Counselors should be prepared to offer services to the bereaved family of the victim when experiencing grief and also offer resources to the family of the homicidal offender who are also grieving the loss of a family member or are faced with the loss of vitality due to imprisonment.

Counselors should note that African Americans are more likely to become the victims and offenders of homicidal events (Currier et al., 2008). Loss of a loved one through homicide is very difficult to accept, and it is common that one's faith is used as a primary coping resource (Neimeyer & Burke, 2011). Field experience students must understand that clients grieving the loss of a loved one due to homicide and employing religiosity or spirituality may also experience complicated grief.

Regarding health concerns, men and women who have experienced rape or stalking by any perpetrator or physical violence by an intimate partner are more likely to report frequent headaches, chronic pain, difficulty with sleeping, activity limitations, poor physical health, and poor mental health than men and women who did not experience these forms of violence. Women who have experienced sexual assault, stalking, or IPV are also more likely to report having asthma, irritable bowel syndrome, and diabetes than women who have not experienced these forms of violence.

Homicide survivors may contend with economic stressors, stigmatization, fear of recurrence, anxiety when encountering reminders of the event, negative beliefs about themselves and the world, and feelings of guilt and responsibility. Homicide survivors often face greater intrusion from the media and the criminal justice system, strained relationships, and a preoccupation with revenge (Zinzow et al., 2009). These stressors may contribute to the risk for mental health problems among homicide survivors.

Little research has examined the prevalence of homicide survivorship or its relationship to psychiatric disorders. However, research has demonstrated that horror, disbelief, and shock give way to devastating grief and is further complicated by the incomprehensible manner in which a friend or close other died. Murder is an irreplaceable loss without the permission or any appeals process on the behalf of the decedent, so the feelings of outrage, offense, and helplessness leave a survivor feeling physically violated over a relationship now forever terminated without warning (Blakely & Mehr, 2008).

Legal and Ethical Concerns

Limitations about duty to warn vary according to each state's statutes, and field experience students are well advised to learn applicable state laws, regulations, and agency or school procedures (Ivers & Perry, 2014). When the risk level is determined and the decision to break confidentiality is made, the obvious question becomes what legal ramifications exist regarding duty to warn. It is generally not advisable for a counselor to be alone in a room with a client who has a history or perceived risk of violence. Transporting a client at risk for violent acts also poses concerns for counselor safety and the ability to prevent unwanted assaults while retaining control of the vehicle. Counselors are advised to decline such requests providing a rationale that fear for personal safety is of concern. When assessing homicidal clients, it is important to know that forms of documentation may be different than in standard client care, as such notes may need to be immediately shared with law enforcement or the court system.

Field experience students should be equipped with resource information that would facilitate referral of a homicidal client or those experiencing a loss due to homicide. Losses that take place in rural communities are a special challenge because it is sometimes difficult for survivors to locate services that will assist in the recovery and healing processes.

Disaster: Large-Scale Shock

Prior to the terrorist attacks of September 11, 2001, crisis counseling tended to be conceptually limited to individual client needs. Since that devastating large-scale attack, our understanding of disasters and crisis intervention has expanded considerably. Field experience students need exposure to crisis counseling skills so they can quickly respond to the extreme needs of clients when disaster strikes.

A **disaster** is a situation in which both the individual and larger community are faced with circumstances in which normal coping skills and resources are overwhelmed. The forms disaster may take ordinarily are described as natural or man-made. Man-made disasters may be intentional, such as with acts of terrorism, school shootings, or workplace violence. Man-made disasters may also be unintended, as in the case of an industrial accident accident (Hard et al., 2018). Large-scale shock is the reaction of the wider community to catastrophic loss experienced through some form of disaster, whether man-made or natural. McGlothlin (2018) described this circumstance as trauma occurring on a communitywide level. For the purposes of this chapter, the terms *disaster* and *crisis* may be used interchangeably and will refer to broader circumstances affecting the wider community, rather than a normal developmental crisis. This section will examine disaster response, reactions, safety issues, interventions, and available trainings, as well as ethical, legal, and cultural aspects of disaster intervention.

Disaster Response Phases

Disaster recovery is developmental in nature. Survivors will experience or process their circumstances based on the phase of the crisis in which they find themselves. It is, therefore, important that practicum students and interns be aware of the client's adjustment through the phases of disaster response. The Substance Abuse and Mental Health Administration's (2018) adaption of various models for envisioning adjustment to disaster are as follows:

1. **Phase 1, the pre-disaster (warning or threat) phase:** Generally characterized by fear and uncertainty, when there is advanced notice of a disaster, people may also experience feelings of guilt or self-blame for failure to heed the warnings. When there is no warning, people may express feelings of being unsafe, vulnerable, or lacking control. Defense mechanisms vary from attitudes of invincibility to despair. This phase may last as little as minutes or even months in the case of hurricane season.
2. **Phase 2, the impact phase:** Marked by intense emotional reactions ranging from shock to overt panic depending upon the type of disaster, this phase resolves to a focus on self and family preservation. This is normally the shortest of the six phases.
3. **Phase 3, the heroic (or rescue) phase:** This phase is characterized by high levels of activity, low actual productivity with a sense of altruism, and often adrenaline-fueled rescues. Citizens may engage in community activities directed at rescue, such as rushing in to save others, self, or possessions. Risk assessment may be impaired in this phase, which often passes swiftly into Phase 4.
4. **Phase 4, the honeymoon phase:** Survivors express gratitude at having made it through the crisis, as well as both personal and community pride at how they have handled it. There is a sense of community bonding, and many will be engaged in cleaning, salvaging, and working on their plan of recovery. During this phase,

optimism is high and many may be heard to say, "We're going to build it back better than it was before!" This phase normally lasts only a few weeks.

5. **Phase 5, the disillusionment phase:** The true impact of the disaster on people's lives is realized as well as how far they must go to recover. The limits of helping agencies become apparent. Media moves on to other matters as the disaster becomes "old news." Survivors may feel abandoned, angry, or depressed. As a result, other negative responses such as substance abuse and physical exhaustion become evident. Extended by trigger events or anniversaries, this phase can last months or years.
6. **Phase 6, the reconstruction or recovery phase:** This phase is marked by a general sense of recovery. Survivors come to terms with their changed circumstances, the tasks before them, and assume greater responsibility for rebuilding their lives. Grief, emotional recovery, and the rebuilding of lives and homes may continue for years as people adjust to the new normal. Anniversary reactions are also common in this phase, which may last for years.

Survivor Responses

Field experience students must be aware that survivors may be in a heightened state of physical arousal, emotional arousal, or exhaustion, depending on both the phase of recovery and their respective individual condition. Routine survivor responses to disaster have been described as normal reactions to abnormal circumstances, and indeed, most survivors do not suffer from mental illness.

Typical responses have been categorized as cognitive, physical, emotional, and behavioral. Common cognitive responses include confusion; poor concentration, memory, or problem solving; reduced self-esteem; blaming; or nightmares. Physical responses are consistent with fight-or-flight arousal and include fatigue, headache, rapid respiration, sweats, reduced libido, fainting, tremors, or weakness. Emotional reactions may run the continuum of human loss and experience, including denial, loss of control, fear, guilt, anger, despair, helplessness, irritation, apathy, sadness, or being overwhelmed. Behavioral responses may include increased drug or alcohol use, isolation, interpersonal conflicts, loss of interest in social activities, poor sleep or appetite, or restlessness (McGlothlin, 2018).

Demographically, researchers (Carlson et al., 2018) have found that female survivors have more adverse reactions to disaster, perhaps due to traditional caregiving roles. This reaction appears to be more severe in more traditional cultures. Children's reactions to loss from disaster range across the developmental spectrum. According to Hamblin and Barnett (2019), children are more profoundly affected by disaster when: (a) they are exposed to higher levels of life threat, witnessing death, injury, or calls for help; (b) they are located closer to the actual disaster; (c) they have experienced prior trauma; and (d) their parents have a poor response or are mentally ill. Younger children tend to express their distress in terms of somatic symptoms, acting out, or regressive behaviors. Older children may evidence some of the same symptoms, but their responses may also include cognitive confusion, self-attribution, and high attunement to parental response.

Adolescents will have many of the same symptoms already described but will show more advanced emotional responses, anxiety, and even self-injurious behaviors. Field experience students should be aware that for older clients the disaster-related losses may be compounded due to other age-related losses (e.g., limited resources, unplanned or inadequate disaster response, health and roles changes, loss of friends and spouse), potential health concerns, and a higher likelihood of being victimized by criminal elements. For example, news sources at the time noted that over 70% of deaths related to Hurricane Katrina were among adults 60 years and older (Simerman et al., 2005).

Safety Issues

Disaster circumstances produce a variety of safety and security concerns. When working in a disaster location, the counselor must be aware of their own health and safety needs as well as those of the client. These needs include basic safety and nutrition, as well as addressing both environmental dangers and dangers from clients or others. Because of the nature of disasters, counselors need to be aware of their environment and possible threats to their personal safety. Harrington and Daughhetee (2018) recommended being prepared for disaster through establishing a crisis plan for the agency or school. Individual practitioners are encouraged to pursue preparedness through some form of standardized training and coordination with crisis teams through a community agency such as the American Red Cross (ARC) or their local Emergency Management Association (EMA). Counselors working in disaster circumstances must coordinate with local authorities to assist survivors in securing access to the basic needs of medical care, safety, shelter, food, and water, as well as mental health care. Counselors are used in these circumstances to provide support and to prevent normal emotional distress due to the disaster from escalating further. Most survivors of a disaster are not mentally ill and do not require more than supportive care. However, disaster mental health workers are vital in identifying those who may need to be directed to more intensive levels of care.

Voices From the Field 8.2 Words of Wisdom From a Red Cross Volunteer, *by Caroline M. Brackette, PhD, LPC, Disaster Mental Health Volunteer, American Red Cross*

As a disaster mental health (DMH) relief volunteer with the American Red Cross, it is important to understand your role in working with survivors of a disaster. DMH counselors are trained to assist survivors in coping with the emotional and personal impact of a disaster through performing mental health screenings and triage, making referrals to community resources, providing emotional support, providing education about common reactions and recovery, and listening. Crisis intervention may be necessary to address negative thinking patterns and introduce effective coping strategies.

It has been my experience that it is most important to allow survivors the opportunity to tell their story. Listening and using basic counseling helping skills is critical. I have received many gracious "thank yous" after just being available to listen to individuals express how they were feeling and share their experiences during the disaster. This is the time not to trade "war" stories, but to focus on the client's feelings, experiences, and resiliency. It is also important to be mindful of compassion fatigue and its possible effect on you, your volunteer colleagues, and community workers and members assisting with relief efforts. It may be necessary for you to intervene and advocate for the self-care and well-being of those assisting in relief operations.

Intervention Approaches

It is vital for field experience students to understand that the effectiveness of any disaster or crisis intervention approach is dependent on and unique to the type of disaster, the extent of the disaster response, and the phase of disaster response at which the counselor engages the client. In choosing the best approach to address client needs related to disaster, examine multiple models of intervention. Sample models include (a) crisis in context theory (CCT; Myer & Moore, 2006), (b) preparation, action, recovery framework (PARF; McAdams & Keener, 2008), (c) resistance, resilience, and recovery model (RRR; Kaminsky et al., 2006), and (d) Roberts' 7-stage crisis intervention model (Roberts & Ottens, 2005). Such models share similar concepts, including stabilization, assessment, and exploration of feelings and identification of effective coping strategies, as well as referral or follow-up. You can use one of these models as a framework for developing a larger understanding of disaster to effectively train in and use intervention techniques. Once you have a conceptual framework for crisis work, being trained in specific disaster approaches will seem more logical. Although a variety of crisis trainings exist, the following are widely accepted and considered best practice.

Psychological First Aid (PFA)

The PFA approach is a preferred model of disaster intervention (Everly et al., 2006). PFA is based around eight core actions: (a) contact/engagement, (b) safety/comfort, (c) stabilization, (d) information gathering, (e) practical assistance, (r) connection with social supports, (g) information on coping support, and (h) linkage to collaborative services. This approach is based on the philosophy that when these core actions are provided, clients will be able to return to their normal functioning unless there are other mental health issues that complicate the process (Ruzek et al., 2007). Although this intervention approach is typically designed for individual care, it has been found effective in group settings as well. PFA is designed to be applicable to a variety of critical events, including traumatic crises, existential crises, and psychiatric crises. This application is soundly based on a hierarchy of needs in which the counselor first addresses the basic physical needs (e.g., food, shelter, safety) and then moves on to psychological needs (e.g., emotional support, empathy, consolation).

Crisis Counseling Program (CCP)

The crisis counseling program (CCP) program is noteworthy for its strength or wellness perspective as a treatment modality (McIntyre, 2010). Often used for responses to disasters, the CCP model consists of the following five components:

1. **Assess strengths:** Identify the human and material resources available to the client in addition to what problems they face.

2. **Restore pre-disaster functioning:** Reduce the chaos of the disaster by restoring life to what it was before the disaster.
3. **Accept the face value:** Help clients reorganize their lives by accepting the impact of the disaster.
4. **Provide validation:** Demonstrate unconditional positive regard, validation, and acceptance.
5. **Provide a psychoeducational focus:** Provide group and individual psychoeducation on the normal and abnormal reactions to disaster, thereby enabling survivors to monitor their own recovery.

Critical Incident Stress Management (CISM)

The critical incident stress management (CISM) intervention approach originated in the early 1980s for the use of emergency medical services personnel in the United States. Critical incident stress debriefing (CISD), also known as psychological debriefing (PD), is a component of the overall CISM and represents a structured group crisis intervention with discussion and review of the traumatic event. Since its inception, many major international humanitarian aid agencies, such as the International Federation of Red Cross and Red Crescent Societies, as well as the United Nations High Commissioner for Refugees, have come to use PD as part of their CISM programs, along with many other law enforcement agencies and emergency service providers across Europe, the United States, and Australia (Regel, 2007). Although as a practicum student or intern you may be encouraged to engage in only the psychological debriefing element, when properly used, CISM actually consists of six components: (a) acute crisis counseling provided by peer counselors, (b) executive leadership program, (c) the multidisciplinary team, (d) acute traumatic stress group training sessions, (e) hotline, and (f) reentry program (McGlothlin, 2018; McIntyre, 2010).

Controversy has developed around this approach because attention has focused on one component of CISM, which is debriefing. This one aspect of the CISM process became the focus of attention for both intervention and research because it was erroneously perceived that this feature of the approach would prevent the development of posttraumatic stress disorder (PTSD) as a stand-alone process. Research does not support a one-time recital of the emotional and factual events of a traumatic situation as effective in reducing the development of trauma-related disorders. Critical incident stress debriefing that is not a part of an overall CISM intervention process may actually be harmful (McIntyre, 2010). The research does not suggest abandoning debriefing because that intervention has a vital psychoeducational role and is useful in identifying survivors experiencing acute stress reactions that could develop into long-term disorders. However, CISD should be used only as a part of an overall intervention.

Training Programs

As a future professional counselor, you are encouraged to obtain recognized training that is empirically based and provides linkage to national and internationally recognized disaster intervention programs. By obtaining training from such programs, you not only receive valuable skills but are also provided linkage to an organization that can facilitate their service placement and support in the event of a large-scale disaster. Two such programs are disaster mental health (DMH) training, which is provided by the American Red Cross, and community emergency response team (CERT) training, provided by state and local emergency management agencies (EMA).

Disaster Mental Health (DMH) Training

Disaster mental health (DMH) training is based on the PFA model that is implemented within the overall ARC intervention strategy. Once you are trained in PFA, you will be eligible to assist in both local and international recovery efforts. Field experience students should contact their local Red Cross chapter for more information.

Community Emergency Response Team (CERT) Training

Community emergency response team (CERT) training involves a full community-based approach, of which PFA is only one part. Based on the concept that community members may be temporarily cut off from assistance and must be self-reliant until help arrives, certified CERT members are taught a wide range of rescue, triage, and assistance skills in addition to PFA. Field experience students should contact their local office of the EMA for more information (U.S. Department of Homeland Security, 2019).

Disaster Legal and Ethical Issues

Ethics and the laws governing client care are more fully explained in Chapter 6 are complex topics that we will not cover in this chapter. This section is intended to act as a quick guide to just those ethical and legal matters most closely associated with proper practice in crisis and disaster circumstances.

HIPAA and FERPA

The Health Insurance Portability and Accountability Act (HIPAA) and Family Educational Rights and Privacy Act (FERPA) guard the privacy of client and educational records, respectively. Crisis situations typically occur quickly and often in unanticipated ways, so counselors must respond quickly. Therefore, there may be limited time to obtain HIPAA-required releases when critical care is needed, or it may be impossible to obtain such releases due to severe injury, unavailability of family members, or other unforeseen consequences of the disaster. According to the U.S. Department of Health and Human Services, Office of Civil Rights (2013), HIPAA is not intended to interfere with the provision on emergency medical care associated with declared emergencies. Covered health care providers may exercise their professional judgment and act so long as such actions are in the best interests of the patient.

In such circumstances, actions permitted by mental health workers may include disclosure of individually identifiable medical information to government officials, police, emergency first responders, public health officials, or anyone whom the provider deems necessary to best serve the patient. Regardless, the U.S. government has the authority to waive sanctions and penalties associated with violations of the Privacy Rule, even in cases where a public health emergency is not declared (U.S. Department of Health and Human Services, Office of Civil Rights, 2013).

Likewise, FERPA is not intended to impede care in a disaster. The U.S. Department of Education (2022) indicates that an emergency situation creates an exception, and schools may release information from records to protect the health and safety of others. However, this exception exists only for the time of the emergency and is not a blanket consent to release student information. The information may be released to appropriate health and safety individuals such as law enforcement, medical personnel, and public officials.

Documentation

Crisis counselors must keep documentation of their interventions with clients. Of course, disaster conditions (e.g., a fire, flooded area) are not always conducive to writing case notes, but counselors need to clearly document exact dates, pertinent details, assessments, and treatment decisions to the best of their ability. This may mean writing basic notes on returning to a more stable location. Case notes must be specific enough to demonstrate that the treatment reflected prevailing standards of care. The documentation must clearly illustrate the session with details that capture the essence of what occurred and validate treatment decisions. The need for client records to be in a locked and secured location applies during crisis events. Providing for locked and secure confidential file storage in crisis situations must be addressed in crisis planning (Hard et al., 2018).

Confidentiality

When a client is a danger to self or others or where the professional counselor is mandated by law to report abuse or is required by a court of law to disclose information, confidentiality can be legally breached. In situations other than these, a client must give consent for the release of information. In crisis and disaster circumstances, provisions for confidentiality are certainly more challenging; however, the ethical standards and requirements of the profession still apply. Counselors should be aware of the latitude that may be allowed for confidentiality in difficult circumstances, yet strive to ensure the protection of client information. Obtaining a written consent in disaster circumstances may be difficult or impossible. In such circumstances, oral consent to release information may be accepted (see the preceding discussion of HIPAA), but the counselor should obtain clear communication from the client on what they wish to have disclosed, and to whom, and then only the minimum necessary information should be shared (Hard et al., 2018).

Informed Consent

In situations of crisis or large-scale disaster, obtaining informed consent will rarely involve a clipboard and paper. Written consent in such circumstances may be impossible, impractical, or, at least, delayed. For example, a counselor may be called on to provide support to a survivor wrapped in a blanket at the scene of a fire. Crisis counselors should introduce themselves, describe their role, explain the basic limitations of confidentiality, and ask permission to speak with them. It is possible that the survivor may refuse assistance, and in such cases the counselor should withdraw, while offering to be of future service if requested. If the client agrees to work with the counselor, the verbal consent needs to be reevaluated throughout the discussion and may be retracted at any point the survivor desires (Hard et al., 2018). The client's privacy should be protected as much as the circumstances of the disaster allow. Protecting confidentiality may simply involve moving the survivor from more public or trafficked areas or lowering one's voice to limit the possibility of being overheard. Often the counselor may be asked to contact others on the survivor's behalf, such as community resources or loved ones. In disaster circumstances, it may not be possible to obtain a written release of information. The counselor should clarify with the survivor that they give consent for the contact, who they wish to have contacted, and what specific information to share, being mindful to share only the minimal amount necessary. A few suggested questions the counselor may ask are, "What would you not want me to disclose when I contact those you have asked me to?" "How would you like me to identify myself and my connection with you when I call?" "If I call someone, and he or she is not there, may I leave a recording and identify myself?" Linkage such as this may often be deferred to disaster case managers if necessary (Hard et al., 2018).

Death Notification

There may be circumstances under which you may be asked to provide a death notification to a family member or loved one. Although not a comprehensive treatment of the circumstance, the following are best practice suggestions suggestions (Jackson-Cherry & Erford, 2018) for this sad but necessary duty.

- *Get permission.* Never give notice of a death unless you are given permission by a supervisor, team leader, or disaster coordinator.
- *Go in person and in pairs.* Give the notification in person and as a team (e.g., with another counselor, clergy, family member, or loved one of the deceased).
- *Use plain language.* Example, "I have bad news. James was in a wreck and was killed." Avoid euphemisms like he was lost, passed away, and so on.
- *Use compassion.* Offer support and caring; avoid imposing beliefs or other gestures that suggest the death was "for the best."
- *Follow up.* Leave a business card or other contact information and make a follow-up contact to check on the bereaved. They may need other help or direction with the funeral or other arrangements, and this may also facilitate access to mental health care if needed.
- *Debrief.* Take time to process the notification with the other team members as soon as possible to evaluate how it went, if other help is needed, and to process any triggers that may have been activated in the team.

Termination

As mentioned previously, termination in a mass crisis or disaster situation should be understood from a special perspective. Formal admission, assessment, and ongoing counseling are normally not possible under disaster circumstances. Victims in need of ongoing care and provision of counseling services should be referred to local counseling services, case managers, and area providers to avoid therapeutic abandonment.

Wellness

Lambert and Lawson (2013) observed that counselors working in disaster or crisis circumstances are particularly vulnerable to secondary trauma or compassion fatigue. Such a compromised condition may leave the counselor vulnerable to ethical or legal issues. Therefore, a focus on the well-being of the counselor is essential prevention. Erford (2023) noted a variety of strategies for crisis counselors to use to promote and maintain wellness, including (a) leisure activities, (b) social support via friends and family, (c) spirituality, (d) time spent in nature, and (e) receiving supervision, Not only are these important to maintain ethical practice, but Lambert and Lawson (2013) noted that wellness and self-care are vital to counselors because the care that they provide to others is only as effective as that they give themselves. It is for this reason that many disaster response organizations not only recommend but also require some form of psychological debriefing on leaving the disaster site. This is done to identify any stress reactions that the counselor may be developing and refer them to assistance, if necessary.

Large-Scale Shock, Disasters, and Cultural Considerations

There may be a need for interns or practicum students to advocate for cultural minorities in post-disaster circumstances. Researchers have found that disaster is not a social leveler, and marginalized populations will often find their post-disaster reality is worse than before (Enarson et al., 2018). Following Hurricane Katrina, for example, LGBTQ persons reported difficulty locating loved ones or accessing services because relief organizations' policies or volunteers did not recognize their relationships (Hard et al., 2018). Counselors may also discover spiritual or religious distress among survivors as they attempt to fit the disaster into their worldview (Zalaquett et al., 2009).

The crisis response team should be as culturally diverse as possible. When persons from different cultural groups observe cultural diversity and representation on the crisis team, it enables them to feel connected to mental health professionals. When diverse representation is not possible, the team should adopt an open, accepting approach to limit barriers. For counselors to be effective in crisis intervention with culturally different clients, they must be sensitive to differences in the client's worldview, self-aware, and able to provide interventions that are culturally and contextually responsive. These culturally sensitive components must be applied to the counselor's crisis intervention approach (Bartlett et al., 2015).

Summary

The focus of this chapter was to give field experience students insight into the assessment process for clients in danger. Clients may be in danger from self-harm or may be in crisis resulting from homicidal behavior. Clients may also be in crisis and experience shock on a large scale resulting from a natural or man-made disaster. Because of the high likelihood that all counselors will experience a suicidal client (or family member), assessment of clients who are at risk of suicide is important in your training as a counselor. In addition, because of increased awareness of the impact of disasters, assessment and intervention for clients experiencing large-scale shock is also vital to counselor education.

Assessment of client suicide risk begins with an assessment of the counselor's values and attitudes toward suicide. Topics such as suicide and homicide can often evoke feelings of inadequacy for practicum students and interns, but this can be alleviated somewhat through education and training. Awareness of risk factors, warning signs, and protective factors helps the counselor to recognize the danger for clients and intervene in meaningful ways. Field experience students, as well as seasoned counseling professionals, can benefit from learning as much as possible about evidence-based suicide risk assessment as well as other available assessment tools.

Once suicidal risk has been assessed, interventions should begin quickly, but the novice counselor (and sometimes seasoned professionals as well) may be unsure of which interventions to use. This chapter specifically outlined several approaches shown to be effective with suicidal clients, including DBT, PST, and CT. Finally, documentation of intervention efforts was also addressed because of the legal and ethical issues involving suicidal clients.

Homicidal clients may also be encountered by you as a professional counselor. It goes without saying that the legal parameters and ethical guidelines of our profession dictate our actions with homicidal clients. This chapter highlighted some of the staggering statistics surrounding homicide and some of the influences in our environment that may contribute to homicide. These influences include the impact of the media, which can range from television to movies to newspapers and, increasingly, social networking. You have no doubt witnessed the evidence of school violence or workplace violence and the impact on communities. A likely impetus for potential homicidal clients coming to counseling might stem from intimate partner violence. These incidences of violence also are a reason for you as a future counselor to assess your viewpoint and ideas about working with violent clients. This chapter provided information on how to assess threat levels, and hopefully by understanding the levels of threat you will be able to assess the danger. We hope that this chapter has provided information to help you consider your counseling role with homicidal clients.

Finally, professional counselors need to be prepared to work with clients who have experienced large-scale shock from disasters, either man-made or natural. Information about response phases of disaster recovery, information about survivor responses, and safety issues were provided. Intervention approaches used with disaster response are included, and these intervention approaches include an initial assessment phase to determine the best possible interventions for survivors of disasters. Even disaster response includes adherence to ethical and legal guidelines, and this chapter outlined aspects to consider. We would be remiss if we did not mention the cultural aspects to be considered throughout the assessment and intervention of clients in danger, whether it is suicide or homicide or those suffering from large-scale shock. Culturally competent professional counselors have a duty to recognize the importance of respecting diversity in our clients. We must be social justice advocates in our assessment and interventions with our clients in crisis. We must recognize the impact and intersection of age, gender, ability, race, ethnic group, national origin, religion, sexual orientation, linguistic background, or other personal characteristics as we assess and intervene with our clients to provide effective treatment. Other aspects to be considered as part of our clients' diversity might also be involvement with the military, their legal status, geographic location, previous trauma, communication styles, and cultural differences that may be invisible. Working with diverse populations can run the gamut in terms of differences, but focusing on client well-being and helping our clients move out of crisis is the ultimate goal.

We began this chapter with staggering statistics about suicide, about the prevalence of encountering suicidal clients, and the importance of counselors' ability to assess suicide risk and completion. Our goals for this chapter include helping you as a student and future professional counselor become aware of the potential risk of losing a client to suicide, providing some basic assessment tools, and providing some basic suicide prevention and intervention strategies. Another chapter objective included introducing you to the importance of assessing for homicidal risk and the potential effect. Finally, we introduced the notion of large-scale shock as it impacts our clients from disasters, either man-made or natural. Presented here is a simple list of *rules* designed to help you create a plan for working with clients in danger:

1. **Ask questions:** Do not assume you understand what a client means by phrases such as "I'm at the end of my rope." Ask the client to describe in detail what phrases (such as this one) mean specifically to the client. Encourage the client to be open and honest with their answers.
2. **Do not ignore your "gut feeling":** If you have an inner voice or an uncomfortable feeling in your gut, follow it. It is critical to follow your intuitive concern about your client. Go *out on a limb* and stretch your comfort zone by checking it out with your client. Refer to #1 above . . . ask questions!
3. **Go there:** Approach the topic of suicide or homicide with your client in a nonjudgmental and genuine and caring manner. Let your clients know that you are willing to "go there" with them. Although you may be reluctant to have the conversation, it is your responsibility. Show the client you are willing to talk about the tough stuff.
4. **Better safe than sorry:** Always err on the side of caution, and with the client's permission, involve family members or a support network as an intervention. If suicide or homicide is an imminent threat, involving family members (or other supportive people identified by the client) becomes your ethical responsibility.
5. **Be smart:** Learn as much as you can about all aspects of clients in danger and particularly how to assess the risk in your clients. Continuing education throughout your career about the risk factors and treatment of suicide and homicide is essential. Being prepared to assist in crisis situations becomes increasingly important for our changing society.

We do not believe that this list is exhaustive when working with clients in danger. We do stress the importance of having a personal plan that works effectively for you and your clients. Creating your own personal protocol for working with clients in danger should happen early in your career and be reviewed often and updated regularly throughout your career. Eagerly anticipate your future as a professional counselor and continue to gather helpful information, continually adding to your toolbox to provide the best possible counseling outcome for all your clients!

9

Practicing Professional Responsibility

Stephanie G. Puleo, Charlotte Daughhetee, and Jason M. Newell

Preview

This chapter explores the theoretical foundations of ethical, proficient counseling practice and the developmental process of ongoing advancement of therapeutic expertise. In particular, the chapter discusses the sacred nature of the counseling relationship and the professional behaviors that are expected of the counselor in service of that relationship. Clients entrust aspects of their lives to counselors, placing a daunting amount of responsibility on counselors. The counseling relationship and the welfare of the client are contingent on professional, responsible practice by the counselor; therefore, the continuing improvement of one's counseling practice is fundamental to best practice. A major key to proficient counseling practice is the self-awareness of the counselor and the counselor's ability to assess areas of personal and professional growth. It is suggested that counselors seek opportunities for mentoring, consultation, supervision, and professional activity in organizations such as the American Counseling Association (ACA) to enhance therapeutic proficiency. Commitment to continuing competency as a lifelong professional value is stressed, and the importance of advocacy for the profession and for clients is posited as essential to responsible professional practice. The development of the Puleo-Daughhetee Longitudinal Evaluation Objectives (PD-LEO) is discussed, and a description of the 16 resultant professional dispositions is provided. The dispositions are grouped into five categories: microskills, themes and theories, facilitating change, world of work and managing, and caring for the counselor. A thorough description of these dispositions and how the PD-LEO can be used for competency evaluation is offered. Counselors are encouraged to integrate ongoing self-assessment and improvement into their core professional identities.

What Does It Mean to Practice Responsibly?

What does it mean to be a responsible professional? Throughout the pages of this text have been discussions of the counselor's role in the counseling relationship, putting theory into practice, attending to the needs of diverse client populations, and adhering to the values, ethical guidelines, and laws that pertain to the counseling profession. Each of these discussions is integral to the concept of professional responsibility. In a section specific to professional responsibility, the American Counseling Association (ACA) *Code of Ethics* (2014) provides guidelines addressing counselor competency, qualifications, and evidence-based practice, as well as the counselor's role in advocacy and interacting with the public and other professionals. The topics presented in this chapter are intended to help counselors think about the foundations necessary for practicing responsibly and within these ethical guidelines.

Many discussions of professional responsibility begin with an examination of professional behaviors, practices, and conduct that are spelled out in codes of ethics and guidelines for practice. **Codes of ethics** reflect the values of a profession and serve to facilitate professional decision making. In general, they are guidelines that members of the profession agree represent good or acceptable practice and serve as standards against which the behaviors of professionals may be judged (Cottone & Tarvydas, 2021; Mazzula & LiVecchi, 2018; Remley & Herlihy, 2020). The standards are enforceable and may be used to hold members of the profession accountable. Additional discussions of professionalism and professional behavior highlight professional **dispositions**, which are the values, attitudes, and commitments that influence behavior toward those served by the professional.

DOI: 10.4324/9781003305521-9

The *Code of Ethics* of the American Counseling Association (2014) is based on six critical principles: autonomy, nonmaleficence, beneficence, justice, fidelity, and veracity. These general principles are discussed comprehensively elsewhere in this book. Also included in the ACA *Code of Ethics* is an entire section (Section C) outlining professional responsibility. Section C delineates aspirations and expectations regarding competence, credentials, and training, nondiscriminatory and non-harassing attitudes toward others, as well as the way counselors represent themselves and communicate with the public and other professionals. These important principles of ethics, standards of practice, and professional dispositions will be woven throughout the discussion of professional responsibility during the remainder of this chapter.

Counseling has been defined as "a professional relationship that empowers diverse individuals, families, and groups to accomplish mental health, wellness, education, and career goals" (Kaplan & Gladding, 2011). Professional counselors are responsible for the relationship to the clients served. In addition, counselors are responsible for what they bring to the relationship and for how they represent and carry out the intent of the relationship. Key elements revolve around three questions: (a) To whom is the counselor responsible? (b) How should a responsible counselor be? and (c) How do counselors know if they are practicing responsibly?

The Counselor Is Responsible To . . .

The Client

"The primary responsibility of counselors is to respect the dignity and to promote the welfare of clients" (ACA, 2014, p. 4). This ethical guideline reflects a central value of the counseling profession and provides the basis for ethical decision making. To safeguard client welfare, counselors are responsible for honoring their clients' diversity and autonomy.

A central responsibility of counselors is accountability (Erford, 2015, 2023). Counselors are accountable to their clients. Responsible counselors demonstrate their accountability to clients by maintaining their focus on the clients. They establish goals and objectives specific to client needs, implement interventions directed toward those goals and objectives, and measure the results of those efforts. It is imperative that counselors keep their clients' needs, concerns, and goals in focus, while also being cognizant of the contexts of clients' lives.

Many times, clients come to counseling at the request of someone else, perhaps a relative, a teacher, or an employer. Often the request is in the form of an order, and the client faces the choice of being in counseling or suffering negative consequences such as incarceration. In these times, developing counselors sometimes struggle in their roles, aware of participating in a triangle but unsure of their allegiance or position in the triangle. Very often, consciously or unconsciously, counselors see themselves being more accountable to the referral source than the client. From this stance, however, the client becomes secondary rather than primary, and the counseling relationship will be less than optimal. It is important to consider that although some clients have been "mandated" to participate in counseling, they have, in fact, been given a choice. It also is important to remember that regardless of how the client got to counseling, it is the counselor's duty to do no harm, work toward promoting the best interests of the client, and treat the client with the same level of dignity and respect as any other client.

The Counseling Relationship

The therapeutic relationship is of prime importance to the counseling process. Numerous studies have examined the therapeutic relationship from every angle imaginable. The one consistent theme that has emerged from the research is that, regardless the treatment modality, applied theory, or other variables, the outcome of counseling is strongly related to the quality of the therapeutic alliance (Jennings & Skovholt, 2017; Norcross & Lambert, 2018; Sullivan et al., 2017). Thus, counselors are encouraged to make the creation and cultivation of the therapy relationship a primary aim (Norcross & Lambert, 2018, p. 309). Furthermore, they have a responsibility "to create a therapy relationship environment that is flexible and sensitive to client differences" (Sullivan et al., 2017, p. 55).

The counseling relationship is special and different from every other relationship in the client's life. The relationship is intimate, often intense, and, unlike other relationships, intended to end. In addition, the counseling relationship is characterized by a power differential. In contrast to other relationships, the manner of sharing in a counseling relationship is predominantly unidirectional; clients disclose intimate details of their lives and have their needs addressed, but counselors do not (Corey, 2016; Welfel, 2015). Because of the intimate nature of the counseling relationship, the client is vulnerable, and it is the counselor's responsibility to create and maintain a relationship structure that is safe and supportive.

Several interpersonal characteristics and behaviors have been identified in counselors who are considered experts or "master counselors." These counselors are responsive to their clients and seek strong, deep, collaborative relationships. They engage their clients throughout the therapeutic process and, while remaining objective, become agents of change in the relationship (Sullivan et al., 2017).

In using the "self" as an agent of change in the counseling relationship, counselors have a responsibility to make sure that the instrument is in good working order. Counselors have a responsibility to be aware of their own biases, values, and needs. Counselors must be culturally sensitive and must take steps to ensure that their values and needs do not impede the counseling process. Responsible counselors take care of their own needs and participate in the counseling relationship with objectivity (Puleo, 2004). In addition, responsible counselors make efforts to avoid burnout and compassion fatigue by engaging in self-care, issues that are discussed more thoroughly in Chapter 12. The therapeutic relationship will be enhanced if the counselor not only is well, but also is trustworthy, objective, and culturally sensitive.

COUNSELING RELATIONSHIPS AND STRUCTURE

In addition to being aware of what the counselor brings to counseling, it is important for the counselor to accept responsibility for the boundaries of the therapeutic relationship. A **boundary** may be thought of as a structure around a relationship. The structure defines the parameters of the relationship, including its limits and the roles of the individuals in it (Remley & Herlihy, 2020). As noted, counseling relationships are intimate, however, and their structure includes a power differential. Self-disclosure is, for the most part, unidirectional, often leading clients to feel exposed and vulnerable. Boundaries serve the purpose of preserving the integrity of the counseling relationship and safeguarding the welfare of clients. Most responsible counselors are cognizant of potential ways that they might compromise therapeutic boundaries. Confidentiality must be protected, and beneficial multiple relationships are established with caution, consideration, and consent.

In describing their approach to family therapy, Napier and Whitaker (1978) discussed the importance of winning the "battle for structure." They argued that the potential benefit of counseling is greatest when both clients and counselors adhere to clearly delineated terms. The conditions and expectations that must be disclosed and managed include administrative issues as well as boundaries and limitations. Many of these issues can be spelled out in disclosure statements, informed consent documents, or service contracts. See Think About It 9.1.

Think About It 9.1

As you develop as a counselor, what challenges have you had to struggle with to win the "battle for structure?"

COUNSELING RELATIONSHIPS AND INITIATIVE

Issues related to structure sometimes become challenges, as reluctant clients attempt to distract themselves from doing the work of counseling. Napier and Whitaker (1978) also described a "battle for initiative." It was their view that clients must win this battle. It is the responsibility of clients to expend the energy necessary for change. Initiative is seen in clients' motivation, attitude, and movement toward goals. By insisting that clients win the battle for initiative, counselors provide opportunities for clients to make decisions, gain competence, and feel empowered.

Erik Erikson (1963) discussed the concept of initiative as a developmental task to be mastered. Having learned to trust others and construct a sense of autonomy in early childhood, children learn that they can make things happen. If the environment is structured in the right way, and parents and other adults offer appropriate encouragement and support, children develop a sense of initiative. With initiative comes self-efficacy and confidence. In many ways, the concept of initiative that Napier and Whitaker (1978) described parallels this stage of development. Clients need to be supported, but also challenged and encouraged to make things happen for themselves. In this way, autonomy is fostered, and clients are empowered to develop self-efficacy and confidence.

Counselors Are Responsible for Being . . .

Competent

Professional counseling involves the integration of theoretical knowledge, analytical and critical thinking skills, practice experience, and ongoing professional development to maintain the highest level of competency and integrity with clients. According to the ACA *Code of Ethics* (2014), responsible counselors practice within the boundaries of their competence. Determining the boundaries of one's competence might be a difficult task, but suffice it to say that practicing outside those boundaries increases the potential to harm clients and decreases the potential benefit of counseling.

Competence may be thought of as an integration of three components: **knowledge**, **skill**, and **diligence** (Welfel, 2015). To be competent, counselors must have a specific knowledge base and must be able to apply that knowledge base in practice. The development and integration of the components of competency occur through education, training, and experience.

Knowledgeable

COMPETENCE AND KNOWLEDGE

The knowledge base of responsible counselors is rich with information about the history and philosophy of the profession as well as the theories and current research that guide practice. Professional counselors employ a holistic approach when interacting with clients, which often requires working knowledge in multiple content areas such as medicine, pharmacology, social work, and education. Further, many counselors work from an integrative approach, which requires grounding in a number of theories (Corey, 2016). Knowledge of the efficacy of various evidence-based treatment approaches ensures that clients are treated with the most appropriate methods given their individual needs and the uniqueness of their situations.

The Council for Accreditation of Counseling and Related Educational Programs (CACREP, 2016) has delineated eight core areas that comprise the knowledge foundation of professional counselors. These areas include professional orientation and ethical practice, social and cultural diversity, human growth and development, career development, helping relationships, group work, assessment, and research and program evaluation. Knowledge in these areas is acquired through graduate degree programs in counseling and validated by examinations such as the Counseling Preparation Comprehensive Examination (CPCE) or the National Counselor Examination (NCE).

Counseling theory permeates core knowledge for counselors and provides the foundation for intentional counseling (Erford, 2023; Halbur & Halbur, 2018). Theory functions as a roadmap that directs the counseling process (Corey et al., 2019; Hackney & Bernard, 2017; Halbur & Halbur, 2018), and a basis from which counselors may explain how humans develop, learn, and change. Over 400 theoretical approaches to counseling have been identified in the professional literature (Hackney & Bernard, 2017), most of which were derived from four or five major schools of thought.

No one theory stands out in the literature as being better than the others; in fact, studies comparing theories have demonstrated that variation in outcome has little to do with the approach taken. If theory doesn't matter so much, then some developing counselors might question why theory is necessary. Although studies have demonstrated that there is little difference in outcome between theoretical approaches, there *is* importance in having some theoretical framework to provide structure for the therapeutic process.

Theory is based on a set of beliefs about human nature and the change process. For the most part, the theoretical framework from which a counselor works is a reflection of that counselor's values and personality (Corey et al., 2019; Halbur & Halbur, 2018). Just as a spiritual belief system provides guidance for everyday life, a theoretical belief system related to counseling provides guidance for practice. When working with clients, theory helps counselors organize information they have learned about their clients and generate hypotheses about client behavior and experiences. Further, theory serves as a tool for making predictions that can be applied to choosing appropriate intervention strategies, anticipating client outcomes, and evaluating success. It would not be possible to be intentional without theory.

In part because there seems to be little difference in outcome attributed to theory and in part because there are so many new perspectives and interventions proposed in the literature, many counselors consider themselves to function from an "eclectic" orientation. But to be truly **eclectic** would be to suggest that counselors change their fundamental beliefs from situation to situation and client to client (Corey, 2016; Halbur & Halbur, 2018). It is important to distinguish an eclectic approach from one that employs a variety of techniques and intervention strategies in an integrated manner. Theory and technique are related but distinct. It is most likely that counselors who refer to themselves as eclectic actually work from an **integrated theoretical approach**, one that is woven together from strands of several theories fitting the counselor's values, beliefs, and personality. Responsible counselors, therefore, would maintain strong personal systems of beliefs (theory), but might employ an assortment of techniques in the service of those beliefs. As an example, see Think About It 9.2.

Think About It 9.2

What techniques do you frequently employ in your counseling practice? What is the result you anticipate from these techniques? Explain how the techniques should produce the results you anticipate. Is there a common theme or theory?

In addition to being guided by theory, responsible counselors are guided by their knowledge of research and evidence for best practices. It is important for counselors to participate in the research process—if not as producers, then as consumers. Technology allows counselors to connect and communicate. The launching of new ideas, completion of research, and dissemination of results are facilitated through technology and communication. As the world becomes more connected and populations served by counselors become more diverse, the responsibility of counselors becomes to know, understand, and apply approaches appropriate for a diverse clientele (Erford, 2023).

Counseling involves bringing balance to very difficult and often complex problems of life; given the significance of this charge to the profession, there is an ethical imperative for counselors to treat their clients with validated therapeutic techniques and methodologies. Evidence-based practice (EBP) is the professional skill of actively evaluating and using evidence from the research literature to support the practice methods and techniques employed in the treatment of clinical issues. The philosophy of evidence-based practice originated in the field of medicine under the premise that health care and medicine are ever-changing and evolving. Therefore, physicians have an ethical responsibility to be knowledgeable of research and development that could influence the care and well-being of their patients (Adams et al., 2009; Hodge, 2011). This is also true of counseling and other helping professions, as new information and knowledge is continuously developing and circulating into the professional literature.

Think About It 9.3

Is there a technique or practice that you have incorporated as a counselor that you have learned from reading an article in a professional counseling journal? Share the technique and the journal reference with others.

An important principle of responsible practice is that professional counselors consider their knowledge in research methodology as an essential part of clinical practice. Counseling students in professional training programs often question why an entire course (or multiple courses) in the curriculum is dedicated to learning and understanding research methodology. Students may question, "Do I need to be skilled in conducting research if my goal is to counsel people in a practice?" The answer to this simple question is "yes." Although it may not be necessary for professional counselors to conduct clinical research studies, it is important to be able to apply empirical knowledge in a pragmatic way. To achieve this practice goal, professional counselors should have a basic understanding of both qualitative and quantitative research paradigms. These concepts easily can be infused into traditional counseling environments. For example, qualitative methodologies can be useful to assist in learning and documenting client stories as lived experiences. Thematic data on clients and their collective life experiences can be useful tools in understanding individual client or group behavior patterns. Qualitative research methods also can be used in structured interviewing and in interpreting client narratives. Quantitative skills such as use of diagnostic or self-report scales to measure client behaviors add scientific validation to diagnostic and psychosocial assessment work. Also, basic knowledge of data entry and analysis is helpful in analyzing behavioral patterns over time or with large groups of clients and can be done in a time-efficient manner in comparison to most qualitative approaches to client data collection.

Although many professional counselors, particularly at the master's level, do not actively pursue careers in the field of clinical research, counselors in practice have a responsibility to the vulnerable clients they serve to be mindful of the current state of science in the profession. This is particularly important for professional counselors working within specialty care settings (e.g., grief and loss; marital, couples, and family counseling;

trauma; children's mental health). From a consumer's perspective, when seeking services from a professional counselor, there is an understood level of trust between the client and the counselor that the counselor has both intellectual and pragmatic knowledge in a stated area of expertise. It serves to weaken the therapeutic relationship if the consumer is not sure that the interventions used in practice can be validated. Clients have the right to ask the very reasonable question, "How do you know if this is actually going to work? Has it been tried before with other people who have this problem?" The way to answer this question and to feel competent when recommending and using therapeutic techniques in practice is to have the professional skills not only to be a good consumer of the research literature, but also to synthesize information from the literature in a concise and meaningful way and to use this knowledge in practice efficaciously. The responsibility for being consciously and deliberately aware of information in the research literature and applying that information in practice is a key feature of ongoing professional development and lifelong learning. Now complete Think About It 9.4.

Think About It 9.4

In what ways do you use the skills you learned in your research class in your everyday practice as a counselor?

Basic knowledge of assessment, research, and program evaluation allows counselors to assess their own work as well as the work of others. Counselors should have knowledge of evaluative research practices. Basic evaluative research skills help counselors assess individual practice, program effectiveness, agency or school policies, and overall service delivery. Knowledge of evidence-based practices and ethical standards in scientific research also are an invaluable practice skill for counselors involved with grant writing for agency or program funding and development. Finally, as a profession, embracing the ethical obligation to use evidence-based practices ensures that counseling stays on the "cutting edge" as a leader among the helping professions.

COMPETENCE AND SKILLS

Competency means that the counselor not only has a knowledge base but also is able to apply that knowledge in practice. A second aspect of competency identified by Welfel (2015) is the responsibility to be skilled. It is important for responsible professional counselors to possess strong relationship skills (Jennings & Skovholt, 2017). Many individuals enter the profession of counseling because they believe, and perhaps have demonstrated, that they have good relationship skills. They have the ability to listen, observe, and care for the welfare of others (Jennings & Skovholt, 2017) while being sensitive and responsive (Sullivan et al., 2017). Through professional training programs, these fundamental skills are shaped and honed until practicum students and interns can successfully facilitate change in clients.

The types of counseling skills necessary to be considered competent include clinical skills, judgment, technical skills, and cultural competence (Hackney & Bernard, 2017; Welfel, 2015). Central to a wide range of clinical skills, responsible counselors are adept at engaging clients in the counseling relationship, facilitating client expression, conceptualizing client needs, and implementing intervention strategies. As these skills are acquired, responsible counselors learn to trust their clinical judgment; they learn to shift their attention to what they are doing and thinking as they work with clients and to use their own knowledge and critical thinking to inform professional decisions. Part of this shift for beginning counselors involves letting go of their self-consciousness and preoccupation with saying the right thing. As developing counselors learn to relax and turn down the volume of their inner critics, they become more present and better able to hear and attend to clients.

Technical skill refers to the ability to choose and implement specific intervention strategies in specific situations. Often this skill is predicated on knowledge of evidence-based practice and research. Cultural competence also calls on counselors to be responsive to the uniqueness of their clients and to choose interventions that are contextually appropriate. Often this means that counselors must recognize if client concerns originate in societal oppression, marginalization, or discrimination, necessitating that they perform alternate, socially responsible roles such as advocates, consultants, liaisons with community support (Remley & Herlihy, 2020), and agents of social justice.

COMPETENCE AND DILIGENCE

A third component of competence is diligence, the notion that counselors prioritize and are consistently attentive to client needs (Welfel, 2015). This concept ties the ethical principle of competence to the ethical principle of respecting the dignity and welfare of clients, the primary responsibility of counselors. To be diligent, counselors are deliberate in the care they apply to clients. They appropriately conduct assessments and employ interventions fittingly selected for specific clients and client concerns. Diligent counselors are thorough and maintain an appropriate level of care for the duration of the counseling relationship. Being diligent further requires responsible counselors to be self-aware enough to know how their strengths and limitations fit their clients' needs. While maintaining professional boundaries, diligent counselors advocate, consult, and seek further knowledge and training on behalf of their clients. These efforts ensure that individual clients are served effectively while enhancing the counselor's professional growth and ability to serve future clients.

Lifelong Learners

In addition to thinking about diligence as the way counselors maintain focus and attention on their clients, diligence also may be thought of as the way counselors maintain focus and attention on their own competency. Competence crystallizes as developing counselors move through stages from novice to expert. Knowledge attained through graduate study is only a starting point in the development of competence. Research in counseling continues to evolve, rendering a great deal of information obtained while in graduate school obsolete within a short period of time (Welfel, 2015). Thus, it is the professional counselor's responsibility to be a lifelong learner.

It is sometimes the case that counselors-in-training are hesitant to work with new populations or new client concerns. As a rationale for not entering into counseling relationships in these new situations, they cite the ethical standards and maintain that they are being called on to practice beyond the boundaries of their competence. The spirit of these standards is not intended to be exclusionary, however. The standards allow for the development of new skills so long as there is adequate education, training, and supervision, and clients are protected from harm. It would be irresponsible and perhaps unethical for counselors not to continue to acquire competencies.

Whereas validating initial or minimal competencies is accomplished through examinations and the awarding of credentials, validation of continued competency is not so easy. No substantial requirements for post-entry level assessment of competence appear to exist (Daughhetee et al., 2010). To ensure that counselors keep their practices and knowledge base current, thereby assuring protection for the public, most state licensure laws and NBCC require that counselors participate in continuing education activities. Although the intent of these mandates is admirable, the actual requirements often are too minimal to warrant the desired outcome. Many counselors register for seats in continuing education programs, collect their documentation, and renew their credentials, without being renewed themselves. As their skills and competencies erode, and their lack of awareness of new practices continues, these "stagnant" counselors may present risks to their clients.

Clients will be best served by individuals who are intrinsically motivated to seek out lifelong learning and professional development, regardless of the existence of external regulatory requirements. Daughhetee et al. (2010) have suggested several avenues through which professional growth and further competency may be pursued, including mentoring, supervision, consultation, and professional involvement.

LIFELONG LEARNING THROUGH MENTORING, PEER SUPERVISION, AND CONSULTATION

Through mentoring, counselors have the opportunity to crystallize competencies. The mentoring relationship is an enriching association for both experienced and less experienced counselors as opportunities for discovery learning are available for both participants (Daughhetee et al., 2010). By providing mentoring, more experienced counselors continue to explore the same issues that perplex beginners and are exposed to different perspectives as they examine the meaning of their own vantage points (Puleo, 2004).

A threshold of competency has been crossed when developing counselors no longer consider participation in supervision an academic class exercise and begin to see it as an opportunity for growth and professional development. Peer supervision and consultation are effective vehicles for counselors to acquire specific knowledge, develop skills, and obtain help with difficult cases after they have met the criteria for initial competencies and credentials. These activities are particularly important for counselors who work in isolation and may have limited opportunities to debrief or process with colleagues.

LIFELONG LEARNING AND MEMBERSHIP IN PROFESSIONAL ORGANIZATIONS

One of the advantages of membership in ACA, state branches of ACA, Chi Sigma Iota, and other professional organizations is that counselors receive newsletters, journals, and a plethora of digital information and electronic correspondence. Opportunities to expand, enrich, or refresh competencies are ample and include the annual ACA convention, ACA division conferences, annual state conferences, chapter meetings, workshops, seminars, and online courses. Reading and active participation in continuing education expose counselors to new ideas and perspectives and facilitate professional growth (Puleo, 2004). Explore this issue further in Think About It 9.5.

Think About It 9.5

To what professional organizations do you currently belong? What benefits do you enjoy by being a member? If money were no object, what other organizations, divisions, chapters, or groups you would join? Why?

CHALLENGES TO CONTINUING COMPETENCY

There is a wealth of knowledge and practice wisdom to be offered in the professional counseling literature, knowledge that is far too often used only by counselor educators and their students for class projects. After graduating from professional counseling programs, many new counselors inadvertently abandon the valuable skills learned in accessing and synthesizing data from the research literature as an ongoing practice behavior. It can be speculated that this phenomenon in practice occurs for several reasons. First, new counselors may quickly become engaged in daily clinical practice with clients and allow service delivery and client appointments to dominate their daily schedules. New counselors also may find that simply practicing counseling is both liberating and empowering after years of graduate professional training and may see the ongoing practice of research, reading, and learning as more reflective of academic activity. Another challenge to continuing competency is that when professional counselors enter the workforce, whether in schools, agencies, or hospital settings, they often lose access to valuable resources readily available in university settings. Access to comprehensive library systems and online academic databases can be quite costly to maintain independently after graduation. In addition, the developing counselor must take the initiative to actively seek new material as part of lifelong learning, whereas in a classroom setting this information is provided within the context of the curriculum and teaching environment. Therefore, maintaining this important practice behavior after graduation actually becomes more difficult for many professional counselors (see Think About It 9.6). On the other hand, with ongoing advancements in public Internet resources and databases, information on most any clinical issue and treatment methodology is readily available and easily accessible for professional counselors. However, counselors should be mindful that not all online information is scientifically valid; indeed, only a small minority is. Therefore, counselors should be well trained in their professional programs to be "good consumers" of the research literature, especially online information, which tends to be the first, and sometimes primary, source of knowledge for answering practice questions.

Think About It 9.6

How might you recognize a counselor who has not engaged in continuing competency?

Good Citizens of the Professional Community

To be a good citizen of the professional community, counselors must be responsible to not only clients but also the profession. Counselors who are good citizens of the professional community know who they are, advocate for the profession as well as their clients, and communicate with and represent themselves to others appropriately. In addition, responsible counselors maintain membership in the American Counseling Association along with its divisions and branches and abide by the values and ethical guidelines of the association.

PROFESSIONAL IDENTITY

Being a good citizen of the professional community begins with a clear sense of professional identity. Although there is a great deal of overlap in the work performed by counselors and other mental health professional groups (e.g., psychologists, social workers), counselors with a strong professional identity are able to explain the differences between themselves and these other professionals. Responsible counselors can describe the services they offer, the philosophy that informs their activities, the training that prepared them for practice, and the credentials that validate their training and competency. From a clear sense of professional identity emerges a sense of pride in being a member of the profession (Remley & Herlihy, 2020).

ADVOCACY AND SOCIAL ACTION

Compared to other helping disciplines, counseling is a relatively young profession, continuing to strive for recognition and respect from the public, legislators, and other mental health professions (Erford, 2023). The maturation of counseling as a profession would not be possible without the advocacy efforts of members of this community. Advocacy involves activities and attitudes that support, justify, and promote meaningful change. When counselors advocate for the profession, they indirectly advocate for their clients as well. Advocacy efforts may involve simple acts performed by individual counselors or organized group efforts undertaken to influence public policy. Many times, efforts to practice professional advocacy are subtle, as when a counselor encourages someone to seek the services of professional counselors. Other advocacy efforts might be directed at employers who might not otherwise know how professional counselors might contribute to their businesses or organizations. More public advocacy efforts might involve pressing for legislation or public funding that would increase accessibility to qualified professional counselors by expanding opportunities for training, employment, and compensation. All these advocacy activities involve providing information and increasing awareness about the counseling profession. See Think About It 9.7.

Think About It 9.7

How have you engaged in professional advocacy? What are some specific activities that you might initiate during the remaining days of this academic term? In what advocacy activities might you become involved in the future?

REPRESENTATION

Advocating for the profession requires counselors not only to have strong professional identity, but also to communicate and represent their identity properly (see Think About It 9.8). Within the professional responsibility section of the ACA *Code of Ethics* (Section C; 2014), several standards address how professional counselors should interact with others as well as how counselors should represent themselves to the public and to other professionals. When representing themselves, counselors are responsible for being accurate in disclosing the degrees they have earned, whether the degrees were earned through programs that were accredited at the time (e.g., accredited by the CACREP), the credentials they hold, and the professional organizations to which they currently belong. Although the CACREP standards are widely accepted in the counseling profession as the model for counselor training and preparation, the majority of counseling programs in the United States are not accredited by this body (Remley & Herlihy, 2020). Furthermore, degrees awarded for completion of counselor preparation programs vary by institution (e.g., Master of Arts, Master of Science, Master of Education). Credentials also vary. The national certified counselor (NCC) credential, awarded by the National Board for Certified Counselors, is recognized across the United States; however, the licenses to practice that are awarded by state governments vary in name and in requirements. Counselors have a responsibility to clarify all this confusion when they introduce themselves to members of the community. Accuracy also is imperative for information disseminated through advertising, media presentations, and reports to third parties. Finally, professional counselors have a responsibility to be socially sensitive and culturally competent. Counselors who are good citizens of the community do not discriminate against or sexually harass others, nor do they condone these behaviors by other counselors.

Think About It 9.8

Suppose you are traveling on a commercial airliner, and the passenger sitting in the seat next to you asks what you do. You tell that person that you are a professional counselor, and the person asks you to explain what you mean. How would you respond?

NETWORKING

Being part of a community involves being connected to others. Advances in technology augment connections and provide avenues through which information may be shared. Counselors use technology to stay abreast of the latest research and trends in the profession. Mentoring relationships, supervision, and consultation all may be enhanced through communication technology. Communication technologies and social media also provide vehicles through which counselors may reach out to the community. As these advances become more complex and far-reaching, their benefits increase, but opportunities for harm do as well. Counselors who are good citizens of the professional community are connected; however, they must be vigilant about their boundaries.

Given the intimate nature of counseling relationships, along with the power differential and vulnerability of clients, most counselors know that they have a responsibility to protect the structure and boundaries of the relationship. The intimacy and vulnerability aspects of counseling sometimes are confusing for clients, however, and they are uncertain about the limits and boundaries of the relationship. In years past, a clear message about the relationship boundary might have been communicated simply by protecting the counselor's home telephone number. In a digital, wireless, networked society, however, boundaries are much less distinct, and counselors have a responsibility to be aware of the ways in which social media and other technologies may affect the nature and structure of counseling relationships.

The use of digital and social media to interface with clients inevitably presents professional counselors with challenges to maintaining professional boundaries. Difficulty maintaining ethical boundaries and avoiding multiple relationships with clients is a common challenge for professional counselors, one that has become even more difficult in recent history as counselors engage social media platforms within the context of clinical practice. Multiple relationships occur when personal and professional statuses conflict with one another, leading to role conflicts for both the counselor and the consumer of counseling services. The ambiguity of online identities is further complicated by the use of terms by social networking sites such as "friend request," which suggests multiple relationships ("online friend" versus client) by the label itself (Bryant & Marmo, 2012). Professional boundary issues occur if counselors choose to grant clients access to information made available through social networking sites that might not otherwise be available through traditional methods of self-disclosure to clients (Daly & Mansfield, 2014). Minimally, counselors who choose to disclose their profession and agency affiliation on social networking sites are responsible for upholding the mission and values of the profession and their employing agency online in the same manner they would in real time. Now complete Think About It 9.9.

Think About It 9.9

Suppose a client asks to "friend" you on Facebook. How will you respond?

How Do Counselors Know If They Are Practicing Responsibly?

Responsibility Is Revealed in Professional Dispositions

Perhaps informed by the ACA *Code of Ethics*, many counselors describe their expectations for professional behavior in terms of professional "dispositions." **Dispositions** are behaviors that reflect the values, attitudes, beliefs, and commitment of individuals in the profession. These professional behaviors support growth, empowerment, and change. By having and displaying these positive dispositions, counselors are demonstrating professionalism. The evolution of counseling professionalism is a developmental process that initiates during the counselor education program as trainees, under supervision, acquire basic skills and knowledge about professional practice (Storlie et al., 2017).

With the attainment of enhanced professional dispositions, counselors' expertise can continue to be enriched across their careers as they assume responsibility for their ongoing growth and development. Puleo and Daughhetee (2000, 2004) asked counselor supervisors and employers to describe the dispositions they looked for in developing professional counselors. Professional counselors serving in positions as employers and clinical supervisors of developing counselors were invited to participate in focus groups in which they were asked to identify characteristics, attitudes, behaviors, and competencies that represent professionalism. The supervisors and employers described 16 types of behaviors that they thought represented professionalism in counseling. From these 16 identified dispositions, the 16-item Puleo-Daughhetee Longitudinal Evaluation Objectives (PD-LEO) instrument was developed. The dispositions identified ranged from relationship building and microskills (similar to the concepts discussed in Chapter 5 of this text) to self-care (discussed comprehensively in Chapter 12) and being proactive in pursuing professional development.

Table 9.1 contains a list of the dispositions along with individual objectives that illustrate each. To facilitate discussion, the dispositions are grouped into five categories: microskills, themes and theories, facilitating change, connecting to the world of work, and managing and caring for the counselor. The PD-LEO can be used as an evaluation instrument in training programs, as well as an assessment tool for postgraduate disposition review.

Table 9.1 Puleo-Daughhetee Longitudinal Evaluation Objectives (PD—LEO)

1. Demonstrates appropriate respectful, genuine, empathic, multiculturally competent attitude toward clients.
    - Verbally and nonverbally communicates genuine interest and concern for client(s).
    - Demonstrates genuineness and congruence.
    - Uses humor and self-disclosure appropriately.
    - Maintains focus on client(s).
2. Demonstrates ability to engage clients.
    - Communicates to client the nature of the counseling relationship.
    - Identifies expectations of client.
    - Establishes rapport.
    - Facilitates client expression and self-exploration.
3. Demonstrates facilitative communication skills.
    - Uses specific, concrete language.
    - Appropriately uses probes/questions.
    - Uses clarifying statements appropriately.
    - Summarizes appropriately.
4. Demonstrates understanding of clients' nonverbal as well as verbal communication.
    - Attends to clients' nonverbal behavior.
    - Distinguishes feelings from content.
    - Accurately identifies feelings of client(s).
    - Accurately reflects feelings of client(s).
5. Demonstrates an understanding of clients' presenting problems/concerns.
    - Formulates verbal responses that accurately and concisely reflect the content and feeling of client messages.
    - Communicates understanding of client's perception.
    - Articulates client concerns/problems during supervision.
    - Appropriately applies current record keeping standards.
6. Demonstrates an understanding of themes presented by clients as they relate to the presenting concerns.
    - Challenges client appropriately.
    - Demonstrates advanced accurate empathy.
    - Uses comprehensive responses rather than responding only to the client's last response.
    - Articulates client themes during supervision.
7. Demonstrates the ability to conceptualize client themes/problems within a theoretical framework, exhibiting multicultural competency.
    - During supervision, articulates client themes/problems within a theoretical framework.
    - Within a theoretical framework, articulates relationship between client behavior and themes using principles and practices of diagnosis (current edition of the DSM).
    - Using theoretical language, links intervention strategies to themes/problems.
    - Applies theory consistently while working with client(s).
8. Demonstrates ability to develop and implement treatment/program goals.
    - Objectively states treatment/program goals and relates them to presenting concerns/issues including addiction and co-occurring disorders.
    - Communicates treatment/program goals to client(s).
    - Articulates strategies for pursuing treatment/program goals.
    - Demonstrates implementation of strategies for pursuing goals.

Table 9.1 (Continued)

9. Articulates a personal theoretical approach for working with clients grounded in relevant research and best practice.
    - Articulates a personal view of human nature and development.
    - Articulates a personal view of the change process.
    - Links intervention and change strategies to theory.
    - Evaluates change process and counselor effectiveness from theoretical perspective.
10. Assesses the counseling process/relationship (with appropriate assessment techniques and instruments), assesses for suicide, addiction, harm to others, and making appropriate modifications to benefit client progress, exhibiting multicultural competency.
    - Verbally identifies small increments of change.
    - Responds appropriately and with immediacy to important material as it arises in counseling sessions.
    - Responds appropriately regarding assessment and counseling in crisis situations.
    - Terminates counseling sessions and relationship appropriately.
11. Demonstrates knowledge of organizational structure of site.
    - Articulates program administration issues related to clients (i.e., referral sources, admission criteria, assessment process, policies and procedures).
    - Articulates role of counselor relative to the site.
    - Demonstrates knowledge of site's relationship to families, schools, agencies, or organizations in the community and maintains a resource list for referrals.
    - Recognizes and articulates strengths and challenges of site.
12. Engages in program development.
    - Recognizes and assesses needs of client population.
    - Proposes appropriate prevention/intervention and consultation strategies to meet needs of client population, including referral.
    - Implements program strategies to meet needs of client population with awareness of public or school policy, financing, and regulatory processes.
    - Evaluates effectiveness of program strategies with regard to client population needs.
13. Demonstrates appropriate professional behavior.
    - Honors commitments to clients, site, and supervisors.
    - Presents self in a "professional" manner (including appropriate dress for work setting, identifying self as professional counselor-in-training, etc.).
    - Manages time appropriately regarding professional responsibilities.
    - Engages in advocacy for the profession and clients.
14. Examines issues of self (values, beliefs, strengths, challenges) in the counselor–client relationship, and in the counselor–supervisor relationship, including ability to recognize limitations.
    - Accepts feedback, constructive criticism, suggestions.
    - Expresses clear understanding of personal needs, values, strengths, challenges, feelings, and motivations that may influence effectiveness.
    - Demonstrates ability to put aside personal concerns to focus on client/program.
    - Appropriately accepts responsibility in counselor–client relationship and in counselor–supervisor relationship, including referral of clients when necessary.
15. Demonstrates an understanding of and adherence to the ethical and legal responsibilities of the counselor.
    - Upholds legal standards of professional conduct.
    - Upholds standards of ethical conduct.
    - Applies ethical principles to practical situations in counseling (e.g., informed consent).
    - Demonstrates ability to recognize and articulate ethical dilemmas.
16. Takes responsibility for professional growth and development through identification of specific experiences and opportunities.
    - Meets with supervisor(s) regularly.
    - Demonstrates initiative in selecting professional development opportunities.
    - Identifies learning relative to specific experiences.
    - Demonstrates ability to outline plan of supervision.

Microskills

The term **microskills** refers to the basic skills of counseling. These skills are used to enter into and establish relationships with clients and include behaviors such as attending, active listening, and participating in the therapeutic dialogue. Possessing microskill competency is a central responsibility and disposition of counselors.

DEMONSTRATING AN APPROPRIATE PROFESSIONAL ATTITUDE TOWARD CLIENTS

At the core of professional practice is the counseling relationship. Numerous books written about models of helping and the acquisition of helping skills begin with a discourse on the counseling relationship and what the counselor must bring to it. In his seminal work published in 1957, Carl Rogers identified six conditions that are necessary for the therapeutic relationship to affect change. According to Rogers, the counselor must be "congruent" or genuine and must communicate unconditional regard and empathy to the client. Decades later, these conditions continue to be identified by professional counselors as core dispositions. Participants in focus groups conducted by Puleo and Daughhetee (2000, 2004) considered a professional attitude toward clients as one that is respectful, genuine, empathic, and multiculturally competent. Counselors entering relationships with clients should be genuine and congruent themselves and should demonstrate focused attention and genuine caring for their clients.

ENGAGING CLIENTS

Once the counseling relationship has been initiated, it is important for counselors to establish rapport with clients. Clients must feel invited into the counseling relationship. Although legal and ethical standards stipulate that clients must be informed about the nature of the counseling relationship, responsible counselors place value on being certain that the nature of the counseling relationship is communicated in a way that clients understand. It is equally important that counselors understand the perspective and expectations of clients who enter the relationship. Key to engaging clients is facilitating expression and self-exploration.

FACILITATING COMMUNICATION

Professional counselors value effective communication skills. To facilitate client expression and self-exploration, counselors must employ very specific communication skills. By using concrete language, counselors provide clarity and focus and grant permission to discuss sensitive content (Egan & Reese, 2018). Summarizing statements focus further and communicate to the client that the counselor is listening and engaged.

UNDERSTANDING COMMUNICATION

Communication is not just talk. Responsible counselors ask questions and formulate responses that facilitate client expression. Perhaps more importantly, they hear and understand the answers they receive. Active listening, an important responsibility of counselors, involves being able to discern what clients are communicating without words. Responsible counselors sense what clients are feeling and are able to convey to clients that they understand their feelings.

Themes and Theories

Counseling requires more than having a conversation with another person. During the course of therapeutic dialogue, responsible counselors attempt to understand the client from a holistic point of view. They listen for themes, patterns, and relationships among the ideas, content, and feelings that clients express. In essence, responsible counselors look for the "bigger picture." Attending to the bigger picture means developing a comprehensive understanding of clients and their needs in the contexts of their lives. Operating from a theoretical foundation facilitates the conceptualization of client concerns and therapeutic needs.

UNDERSTANDING CLIENTS' PRESENTING CONCERNS

Counselors must be able not only to hear and understand what clients are communicating but also to put that understanding into context. Clients tell their stories in many ways. Some present themselves as "victims," some as complainers, and others as people who do not require help. It is the counselor's responsibility to ascertain what clients are saying about themselves, regardless of the ways in which their stories are told. They must then be able to communicate that they understand the client's perspective. Having a theoretical framework helps counselors explain the relationship between clients' experiences, thoughts, feelings, and behavior. To get at the heart of the matter, responsible counselors must listen with intent and focus their conversation through challenging and empathic responses.

CONCEPTUALIZING

Case conceptualization requires counselors to be able to see relationships between the client's feelings, behaviors, and thoughts against the backdrop of contextual factors such as culture. Using theory helps counselors understand how clients have arrived at their points of view and how their presenting concerns fit into a diagnostic picture. By using theory as a guide, counselors can anticipate client actions and reactions and can select appropriate intervention strategies to promote change.

HAVING A PERSONAL THEORY

It is important for counselors to be intentional in their work, and in being intentional, they must be able to articulate the direction they are going. Theory serves as a road map for counseling, and evidence-based practices serve as vehicles. Responsible counselors articulate their ideas about human nature and the change process. Theoretical framework allows responsible counselors to explain how the practices they intend to employ should work and how subsequent client changes might be identified.

Facilitating Change

Case conceptualization is the first step in treatment planning. For change to occur, counselors and clients need to work together in pursuit of goals. Responsible counselors help clients articulate goals for themselves that will be realistic, substantive, and challenging. These goals may be conceptualized as the client's desired outcomes of counseling. At the same time, counselors work toward therapeutic goals that are suggested by their theoretical orientation. Client goals and therapeutic goals, although stated differently, support one another. For example, a client goal representing "anger management" might be a reduction in fight frequency, whereas the therapeutic goal of a counselor working from cognitive theory might be a change in thought patterns that trigger fighting.

TREATMENT AND PROGRAM PLANNING

Planning for change involves being able to articulate desired outcomes and to select specific strategies for intervention that would facilitate the desired change. Numerous techniques, methods, and tools are available to counselors, and choosing from this vast array must be done with intention. The choices made by responsible counselors are informed by knowledge of evidence-based practices as well as theory.

ASSESSING

Responsible counselors assess throughout the entire counseling relationship. Assessment early in the relationship provides information important for conceptualization and diagnosis as well as information about the counselor's and client's suitability for working together. Once engaged, counselors are responsible for assessing whether progress is being made toward goals. Counselors identify small increments of change in their clients and are willing to examine their own choices and effectiveness if no change is noted. Assessment is an ongoing process, and responsible counselors are diligent in their efforts to assess. Small changes as well as critical changes in clients are noted, and the actions of responsible counselors are adjusted accordingly. In addition, to be able to engage in assessment as an informal, ongoing procedure, responsible counselors are familiar with and able to use formal and standardized assessment practices. The results of assessment guide the course of counseling; intervention strategies are adjusted, referrals are made, or counseling is terminated successfully.

ENGAGING IN PROGRAM DEVELOPMENT

It is important for counselors to have knowledge of the client populations they serve. Responsible counselors apply assessment skills to not only individual clients, but also communities. Communities are served when counselors recognize needs of client populations and develop strategies for addressing those needs. Programs should be developed that are culturally sensitive, take into consideration the needs of underrepresented populations, and apply practices that are supported by research.

Connecting to the World of Work

Counselors work in contexts. Some work in school settings; some work in offices and outpatient settings; some work in hospital or inpatient settings. In addition to working in a variety of settings, counselor interests, emphases, and scopes of practice vary. Responsible counselors are aware of their roles within the contexts of their work environments. They understand their own relationships to their work settings and the relationship of their work settings to other systems in the community. By being connected to other professionals in the world of work, counselors are able to consult with others on behalf of clients and make appropriate referrals when necessary.

SOCIALLY INFLUENCING OTHERS

Counselors are responsible for the way they represent themselves and for being aware of how others perceive them. Interpersonal attractiveness is an important source of influence in counseling relationships (Cormier, 2016). Factors such as demeanor, attitude, and appearance contribute to assessments of attractiveness. Other professional behaviors that make a difference in the way counselors are perceived include honoring commitments made to others. It is important to keep appointments, be punctual, and be prepared, with not only clients but also supervisors, colleagues, and other professionals.

ADVOCATING FOR THE PROFESSION

Responsible counselors recognize that they represent not only themselves, but also the counseling profession. Counselors with strong, clear professional identities can represent the value of counseling to others. They can describe the services that counselors offer and explain the unique qualities of those services. According to the *Code of Ethics* of the American Counseling Association, "Counselors actively participate in local, state, and national associations that foster the development and improvement of counseling" (2014, p. 9). By being members of the American Counseling Association, counselors have a role in advocating for the values of the profession and for the individual and societal changes that may be brought about by implementing those values.

Managing and Caring for the Counselor

To be effective with clients, communities, and the profession, counselors are responsible for themselves, both professionally and personally. Counselors have a personal responsibility to be well (Puleo, 2004). Counselors are responsible for monitoring and maintaining their own physical, mental, and emotional health, and those who do not pose a risk to clients.

Counselors also pose a risk of harm to clients if they do not attend to their own professional growth. Counselors have a responsibility to be lifelong learners (Daughhetee et al., 2010). Professional growth is maximized when counselors assume responsibility for continuing the development of their competencies. Numerous avenues for learning and growth are available, including supervision, consultation, mentoring, participating in continuing education activities, and staying abreast of the professional literature, and responsible counselors take advantage of all these opportunities.

Assessment of Professional Dispositions

The PD-LEO

Puleo and Daughhetee (Attaway et al., 2002; Puleo & Daughhetee, 2000, 2004) developed the Puleo-Daughhetee Longitudinal Evaluation Objectives (PD-LEO) as a tool for assessing professional development (see Table 9.1). The PD-LEO is a representation of the 16 dispositions identified by supervisors and employers of developing professional counselors. Four behavioral objectives are associated with each area. To assess a

Table 9.2 Rating scale for use with the PD-LEO

- **Level 1**—Does not appear to be familiar with this concept, skill, or practice. Requires didactic instruction or formal coursework to gain knowledge in this area.
- **Level 2**—Has some familiarity with this concept, but has not demonstrated knowledge, skill, or practice.
- **Level 3**—Has attempted to demonstrate knowledge, skill, or practice, but with specific direction and close monitoring and supervision.
- **Level 4**—Has demonstrated this knowledge, skill, or practice with some initiative. Requires close monitoring, training, and supervision to further develop this competency.
- **Level 5**—Demonstrates this knowledge, skill, or practice independently, but at a rudimentary level. Requires monitoring, training, and supervision to further develop this competency.
- **Level 6**—Demonstrates this knowledge, skill, or practice adequately. Requires ongoing training and supervision to further refine this competency.
- **Level 7**—Consistently demonstrates this knowledge, skill, or practice adequately, independently, and with minimal prompting. Requires ongoing supervision to continue to advance this competency.
- **Level 8**—Routinely demonstrates this knowledge, skill, or practice independently and with proficiency. Requires ongoing supervision to continue to advance this competency.
- **Level 9**—Demonstrates expertise in this knowledge, skill, or practice. Could benefit from supervision or consultation to apply this competency in nonroutine circumstances.
- **Level 10**—Consistently demonstrates expertise in this knowledge, skill, or practice. May benefit from consultation. Is capable of teaching others this competency.

counselor's level of professional growth, it is recommended that a 10-point developmental scale (see Table 9.2) be applied to each objective on the checklist. A score at the lowest level of the scale would represent no exposure or growth in each area. A score of 10 would reflect maximum growth and would be an indication of readiness to teach, mentor, or supervise someone else. By scoring each item individually, a profile emerges that suggests emerging strengths as well as areas of challenge in need of further growth. See Think About It 9.10 to begin considering your own dispositions and use the PD-LEO to assess the professional development of the early career counselors in Case Studies 9.1 through 9.3.

Think About It 9.10

Find excerpts from your own counseling activities that reveal each of the dispositions listed in the PD-LEO. Use the rating scale in Table 9.2 to indicate your level of development of each.

Case Study 9.1 Gaining Experience in a College Counseling Center

Anni is a 25-year-old counseling practicum student placed in a counseling center at a large public university. She is very excited about this placement. At the beginning of the semester she helped with various freshmen orientation programs and will begin seeing individual clients after orientation week. Some of the freshmen orientation programs provided information about counseling, career development services, and tutoring, and some of the programs were fun social events sponsored by the university's Division of Student Affairs. Anni loved the social events; it brought back memories of her fun days in college a few years ago. Anni believes that college is the best time in life, and she wants to help students adapt to their new environment so they can enjoy these precious years.

After orientation, Anni was assigned an 18-year-old freshman client named Graziella. Graziella came to the counseling center of her own volition during the second week of classes. She is having a tough time and was reminded of the counseling center by her resident advisor (RA). Graziella's home is about 20 miles from the university. She has an older brother who is a junior at another university about 90 minutes away. Graziella's mother was diagnosed with cancer about ten months ago. After multiple surgeries and chemotherapy, she seems to be doing well, but Graziella still worries. Graziella is a quiet, introverted person who enjoys writing poetry. She plans to get her BA degree in English and go on to graduate school for an MFA in creative writing. She is very talented and has had a few of her poems published. Graziella's boyfriend broke up with her over the summer, and she is still having a hard time getting over him. She believes she has nothing in common with the other girls in her residence hall and feels very isolated. A part of her just wants to leave and go home, but she doesn't want to be a burden to her parents, whom she believes are struggling with more dire problems. She needs to figure out a way to survive here and is hoping that a counselor can help her.

Anni: So, Graziella, what brings you to counseling?

Graziella: I don't know, I'm not feeling so great about being here, but I also don't want to go back home. I need help in making this college thing work.

Anni: Well, homesickness is very common and lots of other people feel the same way. Usually by the third week people have made friends and are involved in activities, and they don't give home a second thought. Maybe you haven't given this enough time?

Graziella just looks at Anni blankly, so Anni continues

Anni: Were you at the orientation events?

Graziella: Yes.

Anni: Good, so you know about all the clubs and activities you can join. Once you join some groups, you'll make friends, and this will feel like home. Have you been meeting people, going to games and events?

Graziella: Well, I'm not much into that sort of thing.

Anni: What have you been doing?

Graziella: Well, I've been reading ahead in some of the novels for my World Lit class, and I've been working on some poems.

Anni: Yes, I saw you are an English major. What type of job do you hope to get after graduation?

Graziella: I don't know yet. Maybe grad school.

Anni: OK . . . what about friends? Have you met any new friends or any boys you might be interested in?

Graziella: There is one girl in one of my classes that seems kind of nice. My boyfriend broke up with me before school started, and I'm still not ready for another relationship.

Anni: Well, when you are ready, there are plenty of fish in the sea, you know. Are you going to Rush?

Graziella: No, I'm not into that.

Anni: Well, even if you don't join a sorority, Rush is a great way to meet people, and you might be surprised.

The session wraps up with Anni giving Graziella a homework assignment to go to two campus events before the next session and to look into sorority Rush. Anni also sets up an appointment for Graziella in the Career Center. Graziella cancels both the counseling and the career center appointments the next day. Anni is surprised and disappointed.

What do you think of Anni's session with Graziella? Using the PD-LEO, analyze this session segment. What could Anni have done differently? How might Anni's own experiences be getting in the way of her counseling in this setting?

Case Study 9.2 "I'm There to Be a Counselor"

Tori had a positive experience during practicum at a well-regarded non-profit agency that serves a diverse clientele in a small city. She saw individual clients and co-facilitated a grief group with her site supervisor. At the beginning of the next semester, her first semester of internship, her site supervisor indicated that, as an intern, she would have additional responsibilities and duties. For the first month of internship, Tori takes on more clients and assumes sole responsibility for the grief group. She is very pleased with her site and feels that she is gaining valuable experience. Then, at a staff meeting, the site supervisor states that she wants Tori to come up with ideas for additional groups the agency can offer. Tori makes a note to ask her university supervisor what types of groups she should suggest. The site supervisor then asks

Tori to work with another counselor to come up with ideas for outreach to the surrounding community and ways the agency can serve the community better. Additionally, there is a fundraiser coming up in a few months and the site supervisor adds Tori to the fundraising planning committee. Tori is furious. When she meets with her university supervision group she states, "I'm there to be a counselor, not an event planner." She also says that she suspects the site supervisor is using her as cheap labor for these frivolous activities and events. Tori worries that she will not get enough experience working with clients if she is pulled away for fundraising planning and community outreach. Which PD-LEO items would apply to this situation? How would you evaluate Tori on those items?

Case Study 9.3 Little League Dilemma

Jordan and Kamari are a married couple with a 5-year-old child. Jordan is a counselor intern about to complete requirements for a master's degree in counseling. The couple is watching their child's Little League baseball game when another parent, Terry, approaches them expressing concerns about a child on the team who may be neglected and physically abused at home. Aware that Jordan is a counseling intern, Terry proceeds to show Jordan and Kamari inappropriate comments made by the child's parents on a social networking site (Facebook) and asks them to review some posted photos of the child and the child's parents. One of the photos is a "selfie" of the parents driving with the child while using alcohol. The photo reveals an alcohol container visible in the cup holder adjacent to the parent operating the vehicle while holding the child in her lap.

What is Jordan's professional responsibility in this situation? What potential boundary or role conflicts exist between Jordan, Kamari, and Terry? What competencies and skills should Jordan be using?

Summary

In essence, this entire text is a discussion of professional responsibility. Professional responsibility involves being accountable, being competent, and working well with others. Professional responsibility goes beyond adhering to the ACA *Code of Ethics*; responsible counselors possess dispositions through which they express their professional attitudes, values, beliefs, and commitments.

The questions raised in this chapter were intended to help developing counselors reflect on their own growth and the degree to which they are accepting and practicing professional responsibility. Developing counselors enrolled in practicum and internship are guided toward assuming greater responsibility but are afforded a level of safety that is provided by their supervisors' responsibility for them and their work. Within this safety net, developing counselors may gain experience, competence, and confidence as professionals.

Counselors are responsible to their clients and to the counseling relationship. To practice responsibly, counselors should be cognizant of the power differential that exists in counseling relationships as well as the vulnerability of clients. Counselors should take caution not to abuse their power and to safeguard the welfare and dignity of all clients. Counselors are responsible for relationships that empower others in the pursuit of their goals. To promote successful outcomes, counselors need to take responsibility for the structure and parameters of those relationships while guiding clients toward taking the initiative to change.

Counselors have a responsibility for being competent. Initial competencies are acquired during graduate training programs, but to practice responsibly once a degree and credentials have been awarded, counselors must continue to gain competency as they mature. Competency includes knowledge, skill, and diligence (Welfel, 2015). Knowledge competencies should include core areas such as those proscribed by CACREP and NBCC, as well as knowledge of research and professional trends communicated through the professional media. As counselors mature, they are responsible for incorporating current, evidence-based practices into their repertoires of skill competencies. To function optimally, counselors are responsible for being lifelong learners and for maintaining their own wellness.

Counselors are responsible for being counselors; that is, counselors must know what sets this profession apart from other professions. Counselors are responsible to the American Counseling Association as they adhere to the ACA *Code of Ethics*, espouse the values of the profession, and advocate for the profession and the communities they serve. Being clearly identified as a professional counselor is requisite for responsible communication with others.

Professional dispositions are necessary for practicing responsibly. In this chapter, knowledge, skills, and practices that exemplify dispositions were presented as longitudinal objectives for developing counselors. Counselors who practice responsibly will monitor their growth, development, and continuing competencies in a variety of areas to be optimal agents of change.

10

Wrapping It Up

Nicole A. Stargell and Bradley T. Erford

Preview

Throughout this text, we have provided practical knowledge and skills that will support successful practicum and internship experiences. We have discussed how to merge expectations with reality, how to get the most out of supervision, ways to promote effective practice, the importance of counselor wellness, and ongoing legal and ethical considerations. This chapter offers opportunities to reflect on what has been learned and provides information about termination. We also explore the idea of meta-learning and explain how this can be used to support lifelong learning in the counseling profession.

Termination

Termination is the act of wrapping up a process and bringing it to a close. There are many relational processes in the counseling profession that can be terminated, and professional counselors should have an eye toward termination when working toward measurable goals and objectives with clients and colleagues. We will discuss the termination of the supervisory relationship, which has its own unique dynamics associated with the evaluative nature of the process. We will also discuss termination of professional relationships with clients and the special considerations that must be made in this fundamental counseling process. We will first explore the familiar terminations all counselors-in-training have experienced in the academic setting as semesters close and commencement eventually arrives.

Counselors-in-training experience a form of termination each term when their courses end. On the first day of class, the professor provides a syllabus that includes course objectives, concrete ways to measure if these objectives have been met, and a timeline of the work students will complete. When courses finish, the relationship between professor and student concludes. Reflect upon how it feels to terminate this type of professional relationship.

It can be nice to feel a sense of accomplishment after successfully concluding a semester, but students and professors might feel a sense of loss in some ways. Although school is often associated with stress and hard work, it can also be quite exciting, predictable, and supportive. Students often meet likeminded individuals at school, and students often turn to their professors for consultation and encouragement. After their training programs, graduate students leave a somewhat comfortable environment and enter the workforce, which can be competitive and somewhat scary (Tod et al., 2011). Recent graduates might struggle to develop a routine that helps them maintain productive and healthy lifestyles.

Students who complete a master's program in counseling have become familiar with the ebbs and flows of the university calendars. However, when students have completed all coursework and program requirements, they graduate, and termination from school can be harder than students sometimes anticipate. How do you think the termination of counseling relationships with clients might compare to terminating the classroom relationship? How might terminating a relationship with your supervisor be similar or different?

It can be helpful for students to prepare for the time when the constant demands of graduate school are suddenly lifted. Intentional preparation can help to foster an effective and healthy termination of the student role. New graduates can be encouraged to notice and reflect upon the times they would normally be in class

DOI: 10.4324/9781003305521-10

or working on assignments and intentionally form new habits that promote personal and professional growth. Self-care would be a great consideration to integrate into this plan (Myers & Sweeney, 2008)! It may be helpful to keep a journal that can be used to express the feelings and worries associated with closing one chapter and opening a new one.

An important consideration regarding termination is sustainability. We strive to only terminate relationships with clients when they have ample resources to thrive without counseling. It is likewise important to plan for the loss of resources that students might experience upon graduation. When enrolled in school, students have access to resources such as university events, the career center, counseling services on campus, student organizations, the library, fitness centers, and social relationships that naturally evolve in vibrant campus settings. Although alumni associations serve to connect graduated students with campus resources, this can be limited by school policy or geographic location of alumni. It can be helpful to intentionally consider the resources you find particularly useful while in graduate school and start thinking about ways to maintain access after graduation.

Enrollment in classes brings a sense of community with other students who are learning the same material and completing the same assignments. Students join with one another in the classroom and engage in dynamic learning processes. Students can get peer supervision from their classmates, and they are able to validate each other in unique ways. It might be smart for students to exchange contact information with one another before graduation; consider using personal email addresses in case school accounts are ended. Professional counselors are also encouraged to join professional associations to maintain a connection to regular continuing education opportunities and a sense of professional community. Reflect upon the ways in which staying in touch with other professionals differs from keeping in touch with former clients. What are the reasons that our ethical codes (American Counseling Association, 2014) encourage counselors to maintain firm boundaries with former clients after termination?

Professional relationships with supervisors and clients might follow a similar pattern to school-based terminations in which individuals come together to pursue a common goal, and termination occurs when the work has been completed. However, there are unique and important ethical and practical considerations when terminating both these types of relationships. Let's review some important facets to consider when terminating relationships with supervisors and clients.

Termination of Supervisory Relationships

The relationships between practicum students or interns and their supervisors are special in that supervisors can assume many roles throughout the supervision process. A supervisor may act as a mentor, counselor, and teacher over the span of the supervision relationship or even within a single supervision session (Bernard & Goodyear, 2019). In addition, supervisors are responsible for gatekeeping activities and are often required to evaluate the student's performance. This creates a need for the supervisor to assume a careful balance between encouraging interns and realistically evaluating their abilities.

Training programs will likely have their own forms for use in student evaluation. Sample evaluation forms that you might encounter as an intern in a school or clinical mental health counseling program are provided in Tables 10.1 through 10.4. It is important to provide evaluation forms to supervisors well in advance so that they have ample time to review the evaluation criteria and complete the evaluation thoughtfully and accurately. Some practicum students and interns might find this process awkward, but it is important to view the evaluation process as an opportunity to improve counseling skills, rather than an obstacle to overcome (Hodges, 2015). Invite critical feedback from your supervisor; spend time reviewing areas in which you have excelled and areas for further improvement. It will also be helpful to discuss concrete ways in which you can develop your competency. Your supervisor is a valuable resource; no matter a counselor's age or level of experience, there is still room for growth and improvement.

Table 10.1 An example criterion-referenced counseling practicum performance evaluation to be completed by a supervisor

The following counseling experiences must be successfully completed by the end of practicum. Place an (x) beside each outcome achieved and a (—) beside each outcome not fully achieved. Please return this form to the university supervisor.

The practicum student must be able to:

___Demonstrate high-quality personal and professional traits.

___Describe through observation the role of the counselor as a community liaison and counseling advocate.

___Demonstrate competence in individual counseling through a rotating caseload of at least two individuals.

___Demonstrate competence in group counseling: at least one group consisting of at least eight sessions.

___Use counseling literature to address issues of importance to counseling practice.

___Use a variety of counseling tools, resources, and strategies to facilitate client growth.

___Observe and participate in consultation and collaboration with colleagues and parents.

___Discuss and network with the interdisciplinary treatment team.

___Demonstrate knowledge of and ability to use a variety of counseling assessment tools.

___Apply referral procedures for clients in need of specific help.

___Demonstrate adherence to ethical and professional standards.

___Facilitate appreciation for cultural, lifestyle, and gender diversity.

Table 10.2 An example criterion-referenced counseling internship performance evaluation to be completed by a supervisor

The following counseling experiences must be successfully completed by the end of the internship experience. Please place an (x) beside each outcome achieved and a (—) beside each outcome not fully achieved.

On the completion of the internship, the intern is able to:

___Demonstrate multicultural competencies in relation to diversity, equity, and opportunity in client learning and development.

___Provide small-group counseling.

___Engage in consultation with stakeholders and colleagues.

___Use current methods of data to inform decision making and evaluation.

___Use appropriate referral procedures.

___Use a variety of career development tools and strategies to foster career planning

___Use procedures for assessing and managing suicide risk as well as other crisis plans or procedures.

___Demonstrate knowledge of and participate on various interdisciplinary teams.

___Understand societal problems facing clients.

___Develop measurable outcomes for counseling services and interventions.

___Demonstrate skills in advocacy.

___Communicate evaluation results of counseling services to stakeholder groups.

Table 10.3 An example school counseling disposition, competencies, and skills rating scale

Personal Dispositions and Traits	*Needs Improvement*	*Meets Expectations*	*Above Average*	*Exceptional*
1. Voice quality				
2. Professional appearance				
3. Energy/initiative				
4. Punctuality				
5. Self-confidence/perseverance				
6. Humility/willingness to seek help				
7. Trustworthiness				
8. Sense of humor				
9. Flexibility				
10. Emotional maturity				
Guidance and Counseling Knowledge and Skills				
1. General knowledge of school counseling program				
2. Ability to apply individual counseling skills				
3. Ability to apply group counseling skills				
4. Ability to plan/conduct developmental guidance lessons				
5. Ability to consult and collaborate with colleagues and parents				
6. Ability to use original and imaginative ideas				
7. Ability to follow up on cases				
8. Ability to work independently				
9. Ability to manage unexpected situations				
10. Ability to work with others				
11. Ability to plan and coordinate				
12. Ability to respect and appreciate the diversity of the student population				
13. Ability to plan and implement a developmental comprehensive school counseling program				
Professional Dispositions and Traits				
1. Rapport with students				
2. Relationships with colleagues				
3. Interest in the total school program				
4. Attitude toward counseling and assigned duties				
5. Response to suggestions				
6. Oral communication				
7. Written communication				
8. Respect for confidentiality				
9. Attitude toward, and respect for, diverse populations				
10. Adherence to ethical standards				

Table 10.4 An example clinical mental health counseling disposition, competencies, and skills rating scale

Professional and Personal Traits	*Needs Improvement*	*Meets Expectations*	*Above Average*	*Exceptional*
1. Openness to present one's work for critique				
2. Hears and incorporates feedback				
3. Initiates pertinent discussion in supervision				
4. Demonstrates ability to elicit and understand essential data				
5. Formulates and modifies a working diagnosis				
6. Distinguishes between the presenting problem and underlying issues				
7. Attends/responds empathically, initiates, and accepts clients nonjudgmentally				
8. Formulates short- and long-term counseling goals				
9. Intervenes in a manner consistent with stated theoretical orientation				
10. Recognizes personal limitations				
11. Shows successful use of therapy to further one's personal and professional growth				
12. Uses countertransference issues in a promotive manner				
13. Reacts in an emotionally appropriate manner in difficult situations				
14. Communicates clearly, routinely and effectively engages clients, peers, faculty, supervisors, and support staff				
15. Displays sensitivity to multicultural issues				
16. Demonstrates an awareness of the multiple levels inherent in each interaction				
17. Functions skillfully as a counselor				
18. Willingness to learn through active participation in individual, small-group, and other supervisory situations				
19. Effectively performs roles in clinical setting				
20. Sensitive to ethical issues as they emerge in the counseling relationship				
21. Respects the confidential nature of the counseling relationship				
22. Establishes, maintains, and respects boundaries				
23. Grasps one's role as a professional counselor				
24. Demonstrates knowledge and use of at least one of the four theoretical approaches (psychodynamic, humanistic, cognitive/behavioral, family)				
25. Demonstrates knowledge of the field of counseling according to student's level of training				
26. Communicates ideas well in reports, summaries, and case studies				
27. Speaks and writes clearly, articulately, and in grammatically correct English				
28. Is prompt, thorough, and conscientious with assignments				

Supervisors are often asked to evaluate university programs as well (see Table 10.5). This evaluation allows training programs to ensure that their students are receiving satisfactory internship learning experiences (Baird & Mollen, 2019; Hodges, 2015).When completing these evaluations, supervisors should be careful to identify areas in which the program did well and areas in which the program could improve. Likewise, students are often asked to evaluate their site supervisor. It is often difficult to separate any personal biases from the professional relationship, but this practice will prove helpful as a new professional. For example, it is possible that a supervisor and supervisee do not have much in common; perhaps they enjoy different things and have different communication styles. Keep this in mind when objectively identifying overall strengths and weaknesses of the supervisor. This is good professional practice and displays your ability to be objective and work with a variety of people.

Table 10.5 School-based supervisor evaluation of a university counseling education program

Area	*Poor*	*Fair*	*Adequate*	*Good*	*Exceptional*
On the basis of your experience with this university's school counseling intern, please check one response for each area presented below to indicate the level of intern preparedness. This evaluation is not meant to assess any single intern but rather is meant to help program faculty more effectively evaluate the effects of the training program. To that end, please feel free to comment on particular strengths noticed in the intern as well as any suggestions the program could use for improvement.					
1. Managing a comprehensive program. Apply the knowledge base of counseling to develop, implement, and evaluate data-driven, comprehensive developmental school counseling programs. Strengths: Improvements:					
2. Professional roles. Assume professional roles and functions of the professional school counselor as described by CACREP, ASCA *National Model*, and MSDE Pupil Services Regulation. Strengths: Improvements:					
3. Effective interventions. Translate personality theory, learning theory, and normal and abnormal behavior theory into effective research-based interventions for individuals, groups, and families. Strengths: Improvements:					
4. Multicultural society. Describe and adjust to societal changes and trends in a multicultural society. Strengths: Improvements:					
5. Individual counseling skills. Demonstrate the ability to form effective helping relationships with diverse individuals and groups. Strengths: Improvements:					
6. Understanding the helping process. Understand the facilitative factors that influence the helping process, including counselor and client characteristics; racial, ethnic, and gender factors that might bear on the success of the helping process; collaboration/consultation skills; and philosophical and theoretical frameworks that undergird the process. Strengths: Improvements:					
7. Group counseling skills. Translate group development, dynamics, leadership styles, and counseling methods and skills into effective interventions with students, parents, faculty, staff, and community initiatives. Strengths: Improvements:					

Table 10.5 (Continued)

Area	*Poor*	*Fair*	*Adequate*	*Good*	*Exceptional*
8. Classroom guidance skills. Integrate an understanding of instruction and classroom management into effective classroom guidance interventions. Strengths: Improvements:					
9. Career counseling and educational planning. Demonstrate the capability to apply educational planning, career development and decision theory, and knowledge of sources of career information to student development and aspirations. Strengths: Improvements:					
10. Using assessments. Use formal and informal assessment procedures to identify needs, focus interventions, and assess counseling interventions and programmatic outcomes and effectiveness. Strengths: Improvements:					
11. Using counseling research. Understand and use counseling research and evaluation results to guide counseling practice. Strengths: Improvements:					
12. Professional and personal behaviors. Exhibit professional and personal behaviors, skills, and attitudes associated with competence in the core areas specified by CACREP Standards. Strengths: Improvements:					
13. Ethical and legal behavior. Demonstrate ethical behavior based on the ethical standards for ACA and ASCA and understand the legal issues relevant to school counseling. Strengths: Improvements:					
14. Leadership and advocacy. Exhibit the professional leadership and social advocacy skills necessary to serve as an effective change agent and advance the cause of oppressed or underrepresented groups, parents, and students. Strengths: Improvements:					

Evaluations are only one step in the process of terminating supervisory relationships. Be sure to review all necessary termination paperwork that must be completed for the school, agency, or practice in which you are interning. This paperwork might be related to payroll or other agency record-keeping methods. It will also be necessary to identify termination paperwork that needs to be completed for each client on your caseload (Baird & Mollen, 2019). Termination with clients is a process discussed in further detail in the next section.

The final step in terminating the practicum or internship supervisory experience is reflecting with your supervisor about your experience to become emotionally ready for your next journey. This is a time in which any past difficulties can be resolved, and the supervisor and supervisee can celebrate the successful completion of a practicum or internship. It may be helpful to process the emotions that you are feeling about graduation in general, termination of the internship, hopes and fears for the future, and the accomplishments of which you are most proud caseload (Baird & Mollen, 2019). Self-Assessment Activity 10.1 contains some important internship termination questions to reflect on.

Self-Assessment Activity 10.1 Internship Termination

As you reach the end of your internship, reflect on and answer the following questions:

- What have I learned as a result of this internship?
- What are my strengths as a counselor?
- What areas of counseling should be the focus of further growth?
- What qualities of my supervisor do I hope to remember and emulate in the future?
- What would I have done differently as a supervisor?
- Is there any professional relationship that needs to be mended before internship termination?
- Will I have any opportunity to maintain communication with individuals from this internship site after termination?
- Have I completed all necessary paperwork before my last day?
- Who should I say good-bye to in person and who should I send a quick electronic good-bye note?
- What is the next step in my plan toward graduation and employment?

Termination of Counseling Relationships

It is essential for practicum students and interns to focus on how best to terminate therapeutic relationships or transition clients from their care to the care of another mental health professional. A wise supervisor suggests that counselors should be thinking about termination during their first meeting with a client and in every session thereafter. Although it is important to be present in the moment with clients and to allow the counseling process to unfold at its own pace, the ultimate goal of counseling is to create client change. Once the client's desired changes have come to fruition, termination is a natural and desirable part of the counseling process. Realistically, not all terminations occur in a planned manner as the result of goal attainment, and every practicing professional will experience client termination for a variety of other circumstances. Open and honest discussion about eventual termination allows clients to process this occurrence at their own pace (Baird & Mollen, 2019; Hodges, 2015). Questions that may be helpful to ask clients in a first session include the following:

- When our work together is done and you have made the changes you desire to make, how will you know?
- What will look different?
- How will you feel different?
- How will you behave differently?
- How will you think differently?"

If clients struggle to develop responses to these questions, you might also ask them: If I were a fly on the wall watching you once you reached your counseling goals, what would I see and observe?

Although it is possible for clients to realize their desired changes and then continue therapy to gain increased wellness or as a maintenance tool, it should not be assumed every client has this luxury. With the implementation of managed care and insurance companies' reluctance to reimburse for "nonessential mental health services," many clients are not able to receive counseling once their diagnosable mental health difficulties have been resolved (Kress & Paylo, 2019). In addition, life circumstances often prevent clients from maintaining long-term counseling relationships. Many clients experience housing challenges, have transportation difficulties, or have jobs and other obligations to which they must attend first. Therefore, it is smart for counselors to realize that any session with a client could potentially be the last time the client will receive mental health services.

The counseling process takes time and cannot be rushed; it could take weeks or years to help clients overcome mental health-related difficulties. However, counselors can end each session in a manner that prepares clients to continue their growth between sessions or on their own, if necessary. Counselors might ask clients to articulate one thing they learned from the session, or to specify one small change they feel comfortable making over the next week. This is a helpful practice because it promotes autonomy and places responsibility on the client. In addition, it allows each client to identify personal progress and a plan to lead to the achievement of actual goals. Additional end-of-session termination strategies may include use of scaling (e.g., On a scale of 1–10 how close are you to achieving [goal]?), sentence completion, process questions, or an assigned journaling activity. Mindful remembrance of the termination goal facilitates the change process and places focus on achieving maximum gains in a relaxed, engaging manner (Kress & Paylo, 2019).

At the end of each session, counselors might also inquire how clients feel they are moving toward their counseling goals. They might ask questions such as: "How do you feel you are doing in moving toward your counseling goals? How far do you believe you are away from reaching your counseling goals? What can I be doing to better help support you in moving toward your counseling goals?" Counselors can also ask the client to provide a summary of what occurred in that session. The counselor can add any necessary information, but this helpful tool allows counselors to learn what clients are getting from the sessions, and future meetings can be tailored accordingly. For example, a counselor and client may have spent 20 minutes discussing a relationship, and the counselor might believe that the client resolved to speak with the partner about their difficulty. However, the counselor might learn through the client's summary that the client plans to wait one more week before speaking with the partner. This is valuable information, as it provides clues to the client's internal processes and areas for continued improvement during the next session.

After the client provides a summary of the current session, the counselor could ask the client to describe how things have, or have not, changed since the very first meeting. This allows clients to identify areas in which they have succeeded and provides a sense of hope and control. It also allows clients to verbalize what desires they still have for themselves and how they might achieve their goals. This future-oriented thinking allows the counselor to understand what the client wishes to achieve on completion of the counseling relationship. The counselor can also contemplate termination and visualize a plan for the remainder of the counseling process. Of course, the actual process might look very different from what the counselor visualizes, but it is helpful to operate from a goal-oriented perspective.

Now that the client and counselor have taken five or ten minutes to discuss the client's progress and future goals, the counselor can invite the client to identify one way to work for change in the time between the next session. This increases clients' self-efficacy, whereas reviewing the client's progress at the beginning of the next session places responsibility on the client to facilitate forward progress. This process for terminating an individual session can also be applied to termination of a counseling relationship (Baird & Mollen, 2019; Hodges, 2015).

Counseling relationships can be terminated for a variety of reasons. Ideally, the client has reached maximum gains in counseling and feels as though more sessions are not needed. It is also possible that extenuating circumstances, such as a counselor or client move or other client obligations, will prevent the counseling relationship from continuing. Another possible reason for termination is that the counselor determines that the counselor–client match is not a good fit, which could occur if the client presented issues outside the counselor's area of expertise or would benefit from a different counseling approach or style. Finally, clients may decide not to return for counseling because they do not feel as though it is helpful, do not feel as though the counselor is a good fit, or are not ready to address their mental health issues at the time. For each of these circumstances (whether planned or unplanned), counselors must take necessary steps to ensure they accomplish a satisfactory termination.

In terms of termination paperwork, each agency and private practice will have different procedures and policies in accordance with state laws and rules of affiliated mental health boards or other funding sources. In general, it is important to document the reason for termination and that appropriate referrals have been made, if necessary (Hodges, 2015). In addition, it is important to formally close any terminated case either by having the client sign a termination agreement or by documenting that sufficient attempts have been made to reach the client to have the agreement completed. This protects the counselor or agency; if a case is left open, but inactive, and the client engages in self-harm or harms others, the mental health provider could potentially be held liable for this unfortunate occurrence (Remley & Herlihy, 2020).

In addition to necessary termination paperwork, the counselor has the responsibilities of beneficence and autonomy (Remley & Herlihy, 2020). Throughout the entire counseling process, as mentioned before, the counselor should be working to provide the clients with necessary self-help skills. Upon a planned termination session, counselors can take similar steps to identify the client's current progress, future goals, and how the client will facilitate these goals. Therefore, even the termination session is helpful for the client and promotes their own sense of self-efficacy. In the case of an unplanned termination (e.g., the client does not return and cannot be contacted), it is good practice to provide a small-scale termination review at the end of each session, as previously mentioned.

Termination is a natural part of the counseling process; it can be a celebration of the client achieving maximum gains. However, it can also be a difficult process, such as when a counselor's internship is ending, or the client wishes to cease counseling despite an obvious need for continuing it. Regardless, it is a necessary part of counseling and can be beneficial for the client and counselor. Counselors should take time to reflect on any termination to identify areas in which they could improve and ways in which they were successful helpers. This information could even be processed with colleagues or a supervisor supervisor (Bernard & Goodyear, 2019).

To help clients through the termination process, termination should be discussed regularly. For some counselors, discussing termination during the initial intake might feel premature, and counselors might feel concerned they are pushing clients away before they begin their work. However, creating a treatment plan implies that the counselor and client are working toward a goal that will hopefully be achieved. Also, research suggests that most clients want to attend counseling sessions only until their presenting problems have been resolved; most clients are not seeking lengthy counseling experiences (Hays & Chang, 2019) The counselor could spend time during the treatment planning session to discuss what will happen on achievement of goals; the client could decide to create new, more challenging goals or the counseling relationship can be terminated. This is a natural way to assist the client in thinking about termination without feeling rushed. In addition, some clients might like to know that there will be an end to the process and that they can hope to achieve their desired goals.

As a planned termination approaches, the counselor should discuss with the client any final needs. The counselor might also consider a creative way to bring closure to the relationship. The use of symbolic objects or tangible reminders provides clients with an item to take away and use to reconnect with the concepts learned in counseling (Hays & Chang, 2019). For example, if clients responded well to any metaphors used in counseling, a symbolic object such as a picture or a small item representative of the metaphor might be given to the client to help them reconnect with the metaphor once they have moved on from counseling. The client and counselor might also create a book or a picture (using collage, drawings, words, or symbols) that illustrates the change that occurred through the counseling process. Clients might be asked to complete one picture of where they were during their first session and a second picture that highlights where they are at present. A third picture might depict where the client will be in the future, as the client continues to move forward. Regardless of how the counselor and client choose to spend their last session, a summary of the client's progress and a goal-oriented, hopeful future plan should be created.

Counselors are also expected to have thoughts and feelings about termination procedures. As previously suggested, it can be helpful to process these emotions with a supervisor. It is also helpful to use some self-assessment strategies to feel confident in termination procedures. For example, answering the following queries may yield helpful insights about the client's progress:

- What are the client's goals?
- Have these goals been met?
- Do I feel uneasy about terminating this relationship?
- What is different about this client that might be contributing to these feelings?
- Is the client resistant to termination?
- What needs or past experiences might the client have that may be contributing to this resistance?
- What referrals, if any, should be made?

Voices From the Field 10.1 Holding Onto Hope, *by Jessica A. Headley*

For over six months, a yellow Post-It with the word *hope* written on it rested in my top drawer. Each week, it made its way into the light, as a reminder to my client that I was holding onto her hope. "Are you ready to take your hope back?" I regularly asked her. And in every instance, I received similar responses: "Things are never going to get better," "There's no point for hope," and "I wish I didn't exist."

As a beginning counselor, such responses were difficult to hear—especially because our time together was dwindling. I truly believed she was making progress. She had obtained a new job that gave her a sense of purpose, improved her relationships with family members and friends, and had begun to engage in self-care activities. She was even contemplating moving into a new apartment to reclaim her independence. Why wasn't she ready to relieve me of my caretaking responsibility? What was she holding onto?

With a few remaining weeks together, I made sure to give her gentle reminders of when our last day would be. I explained that termination is a process, and together we decided how we wanted to spend our remaining time. The Post-It still sat out as a reminder, but I had stopped asking about it. I had assumed that work still needed to be done, and so together the client and I made arrangements for her to continue counseling with a new counselor.

The week before our final session, she began to cry and I thought, "Oh no, this can't be good." But to my surprise, she told me that she was ready to say good-bye *and* that she was ready to take back her hope. She told me that she was getting ready to pick up the keys to her new apartment. "Why hadn't she told me about this?" I thought. I was hurt. But before the situation became about me, she explained that taking back her hope meant that she had accomplished all her counseling goals and that it was time to say good-bye. *She* decided it was time for her to make a new beginning—a beginning that did not include me.

This experience taught me that a client must say good-bye on their own terms and in their own special way. Picking up her hope, and then her keys, signified a new journey for my client. Handing over her hope reminded me of two important things: change doesn't happen on a timeline, and in counseling, change occurs on the client's terms.

Meta-Learning: Learning From What You've Learned

Counseling training programs are compact and intense. The Council for Accreditation of Counseling and Related Educational Programs (CACREP) requires training programs to provide 60 semester credit hours of coursework, including within the eight core areas of counseling: human growth and development, social/cultural foundations, the helping relationship, group dynamics/counseling, career development, appraisal, research, and professional orientation/ethics (CACREP, 2016). After taking a number of courses that are reading intensive and require an extensive amount of time and energy, it is difficult to step back and truly grasp what was learned throughout the training process.

Meta-learning is a concept that encourages people to take control of and integrate their learning. Meta-learning encourages learners to understand the ways in which they learn and retain information and methods that allow learners to be aware of their cognitive processes (Colthorpe et al., 2018). Meta-learning goes beyond metacognition (thinking about the way you think) to encourage learners to think about the ways in which they are learning (Jackson, 2004). Meta-learning creates new ways of thinking; as learners begin to ponder the process of learning, their understanding of the learning process is altered, and their attitudes about learning change. As a result of altered thoughts and attitudes, behaviors related to learning, such as study and organizational methods, change in accordance. Finally, knowledge is acquired as the result of thinking about meta-learning.

Counselors should use meta-learning at all stages of their development. To reach graduate school, students must have identified a basic set of learning techniques that are effective. These techniques were probably further refined throughout their master's education and to accommodate the complex and critical thinking required at this level of study. However, it is possible that students had never thought of the complexity of their learning as is required through meta-learning. The process of meta-learning requires scholars to actively and mindfully evaluate and alter their learning strategies to maximize their abilities (Colthorpe et al., 2018; Jackson, 2004). The earlier this complex thought is integrated in your training program, the better. Use Self-Assessment Activity 10.2 to begin working with meta-learning.

Self-Assessment Activity 10.2 Meta-learning

- What is my motivation for learning?
- What emotions do I feel when learning something new?
- In what setting is it easiest for me to learn (e.g., in a classroom, at a work site, online)?
- What behaviors do I alter to increase my learning ability?

Meta-learning can be actively applied throughout the internship process. In understanding your organizational preferences, it is possible to acquire the materials needed to best learn in a class. Some people prefer binders, others prefer folders, and some use notebooks. However, it should not be taken for granted that the tools you are currently using are actually maximizing your learning capacity. Analyze your motivation for procuring the supplies (e.g., money, habit, convenience), and identify any other more optimal solutions.

Before entering the classroom or an internship site, analyze the behaviors that allow you to be most present and absorb information the best. For example, some people enjoy exercising before going to class to achieve an attentive sense of calm. Others prefer to read a book or take a car ride to settle their minds into their tasks. In forming an understanding of the behaviors that best help you learn, it is possible to maximize retention of information (Colthorpe et al., 2018). In addition, it is more likely that you will be able to identify alternative behaviors to increase learning if the preferred methods are not accessible.

Meta-learning is unique to everyone, just as each individual's learning style is unique (Jackson, 2004). Learners who are aware of their own personal experiences can better identify the ways in which they make sense of new knowledge. Subjective awareness of these learning biases can allow learners to process new knowledge in alternative ways to gain a different set of knowledge or skills. In addition, understanding the value learners place on a certain type of information and how they will use this knowledge in the future will allow scholars to intentionally retain information that they might otherwise disregard.

The Reflections on Learning Inventory was developed to help students identify their specific meta-learning needs (MeyerMeyer, 2004). Although this instrument is not free, other instruments are available on the Web to help students identify similar constructs, such as preferred study methods (e.g., rereading the text, memorizing, or using repetition). It can also be helpful to reflect upon students' motivations for learning and ways in which learners are best able to remember material. Because the counseling field is constantly expanding, every counselor (regardless of age or educational level) is a perpetual learner; it is never too late to begin exploring meta-learning techniques.

When entering an internship, meta-learning techniques can allow students to process their surrounding environment in dynamic and informative ways. An awareness of one's biases toward information collection could allow someone to focus on more relevant information throughout the internship process. For instance, an intern could focus on remembering new colleagues' faces and job titles, rather than pairing faces with names. Interns might also focus on retaining clients' treatment goal rather than their home address or mother's name. In understanding our learning biases, we can retrain our brains to retain more helpful information.

As graduating students reflect on their classroom and field experiences, it will be helpful to identify the optimal ways that information can be processed. If students prefer linear processing, it might be helpful to create binders of course information beginning with the first semester's courses and working through the last semester. However, a categorical learner may prefer to file their educational materials in a binder according to the eight core areas as defined by CACREP (2016). This will allow students to easily access the palpable information they gained in their program. This level of thoughtful organization might also help students retain the information they have stored in their cognitions, as they will better know how they processed and stored the data (Colthorpe et al., 2018; Jackson, 2004; Meyer, 2004).

Often, counselors find their first employment opportunity at an establishment other than their internship site. It will be important for these new counselors to be able to apply the information they learned at their internship site to their new place of employment. Students who have explored their meta-learning are better able to carefully retain information from their internship and generalize that learning to their next job. For example, instead of memorizing the wording of each question on a case note, the learner would internalize the basic categories of data that will need to be explained on any case note in their state (e.g., treatment goal, interventions, client response, and future plans). Learning to retain general data can be much more helpful for interns than focusing on site-specific information.

Meta-learning is a helpful concept for counselors at any stage of their career; although it requires a great deal of introspection and self-discipline, the benefits of learning from what you've already learned are endless. Counselors who can understand why they retained the information they chose to retain are able to understand areas in which they need further education and specific aspects of counseling that are most important to them. Counselors who can learn through an objective lens can incorporate new information into their existing cognitions and retain information in a way that is most beneficial to themselves and their clients. The ability to reflect on past learning to optimize future success will prove to be a valuable skill in a variety of settings. Consider the importance of meta-learning for the counselor described in Case Study 10.1, and look back at your own experience using Self-Assessment Activity 10.3

Case Study 10.1 Julie

Julie is a clinical mental health counseling student who is preparing for graduation in two months. She is preparing to take the National Counselor Examination (NCE) to become a licensed counselor and feeling a great deal of anxiety. Julie feels as though the past two years have been a blur for her; she was working full time and taking classes at night, then she quit work to begin internship and increased her coursework. She has been financially strained and often found herself thinking about expenses and bills during class. She is typically an organized person but feels disheveled and very stressed about the condition of her course materials. At the end of each semester, she placed the folders for each of her classes on her bookshelf and has not touched them since. Her bookshelf used to be filled with movies that were carefully organized by genre; now, she couldn't find her favorite romantic comedy if you paid her!

Julie used to work in logistics before her company announced financial difficulties. She didn't love her job, but she was good at it. In fact, she could remember 13-digit tracking numbers as soon as the trucking companies shouted them out! Julie is especially stressed about the NCE because she has had some trouble in her classes; no matter how many times she copies her notes or reads the texts, she just doesn't seem to retain the information. Do you think there is anything else Julie can do to pass this test? She really wants to help clients, but she is struggling to help herself!

Discussion: Julie is having difficulty concentrating in class, and she is thinking about life stressors instead of her learning. It would be helpful for Julie to identify her motivation for going back to school. If Julie is able to clearly identify why the class is important, she might find it easier to pay attention. She should also clearly identify what she wants to learn from the class. If she is able to identify aspects of the class that are truly important to her, she can mindfully focus her attention to acquiring those bits of knowledge.

Julie liked to organize her movies in genres, but she is organizing her class material chronologically. It may be helpful for Julie to create a filing system that separates her course material by genre, which would be the eight CACREP core areas. She might purchase eight large three-ring binders and insert the appropriate class material into each one. This would allow Julie to review the information as she organized her binders and would allow her to more easily access the data when studying for her exam.

It sounds like Julie can remember things very well when they are said aloud. However, she must be unaware of her preference for verbal processing due to her use of written study techniques. Julie probably should study for the NCE through verbal methods such as repetition of key points out loud and listening to audio study guides for the NCE. She might even consider having a fellow student or loved one read information to her and verbally quiz her.

Finally, Julie should work to understand the types of information she finds important. She might like to memorize specific numbers, such as dates (as evidenced by her recollection of tracking numbers). However, it may be more helpful for Julie to remember more general information for the NCE. With mindful awareness of her own personal biases, Julie should have success with the NCE exam!

Self-Assessment Activity 10.3 Progress During Clinical Experience

1. I feel comfortable confiding in my supervisor about my own thoughts and feelings. True or false? Explain.
2. When would you feel comfortable discussing long-term termination with a client?
3. Termination can be a positive experience for counselors. True or false? Explain.
4. Termination can be a positive experience for clients. True or false? Explain.
5. If clients terminate before reaching maximum gains, they made no progress in counseling. True or false? Explain.
6. I know how I best retain information I learn in the classroom. True or false? Explain.
7. I know how to best retain information I learn at my internship site. True or false? Explain.

Summary

Termination is a sensitive subject and can bring mixed emotions for counselors, supervisors, and clients. It is important to be mindful and deliberate when addressing termination to avoid regret, confusion, or unresolved feelings. Confide in your supervisors and other mentors for guidance in this process.

It may be helpful to view all relationships with clients as temporary. The ultimate goal of counseling is to create change, so planned termination is the sign of success. Take care, however, to carefully prepare clients for this transition and be sensitive to and aware of their feelings surrounding termination discussions and actions. It is especially helpful to end each counseling session with a hopeful look to the future and a discussion about the ultimate goal of the counseling process. This helps clients to understand that they are in control of their progress and gives them autonomy and responsibility in the relationship. This practice also makes it clear that termination is a desirable and realistic part of the counseling relationship.

Meta-learning is a helpful practice to adopt as a counselor and a lifelong learner. In addition to simply thinking about your thoughts, meta-learning is the practice of examining your learning processes. In gaining an in-depth understanding of your learning and retention, your attitudes and practices can be altered to create more meaningful and productive patterns of learning and memory. This technique can be helpful when working through difficult situations, such as terminations, in that students and counselors can be more confident that their practices were helpful and that all necessary tasks have been completed. Meta-learning can be helpful for new counselors so they can generalize their skills to new environments, and it is a helpful practice for counselors at any stage of their career. Mindful incorporation of the most salient learning practices will prove to be beneficial for supervisors, counselors, and their clients.

Although there is a great deal of information to learn and process as a counselor-in-training, it is important to work at a pace that is comfortable for you. Most important, incorporate the concepts discussed in this chapter into your daily routine so that it becomes habit, rather than extra stress. In the end, these tips and tricks should help you work more reflectively and intelligently!

11

Other Pertinent Issues in Counseling Practice

Elisabeth Bennett and Mark A. Young

Preview

Previous chapters have addressed many of the activities, issues, and responsibilities of the professional counselor. This chapter provides an overview of other such pertinent issues/roles in counseling practice, including as consultation, academic advising and career guidance, and advocacy. Supportive and collaborative services such as psychological, educational, and vocational assessment; compliance support for the psychopharmacological regimen set by the medical professional; and practice consistent with the requirements of third-party payers or managed care companies are also discussed. Understanding the role and function of the counselor is imperative in maintaining an ethical position and providing best practice throughout one's counseling career. An examination of each counseling role performed by a counselor, Meghan, in her typical day is provided. A self-assessment at the end of each section assists the reader in the application of knowledge in each area to the practice of counseling.

A Day in the Life of a Counselor

In considering the role of the professional counselor, many students beginning a graduate degree envision days spent in one-on-one sessions with clients who are extremely motivated and ready to change and grow to alleviate their own and others' suffering. This is a marvelous dream. And some of it is accurate. Most professional counselors, though, do much more than orchestrate the process of growth for individuals, groups, couples, or families. Most play a host of other roles throughout the day. Consider the following typical day of Meghan, a professional counselor at the mental health center in a midsized city where she is employed full time. Throughout Meghan's day, she addresses a variety of issues and offers services and resources aimed at increasing the potential for many people to have a more fulfilling life (see Case Study 11.1).

Case Study 11.1 A Day in the Counseling Life of Meghan, Licensed Professional Counselor

8:00 a.m.	Arrive at the office. Respond to business email and phone messages and finish preparations for meeting with Mr. Henderson, bachelor degree-level supervisor of the mental health center's crisis line volunteers in the Urgent Care Department.
8:45 a.m.	Meet with Urgent Care Team manager, Mr. Henderson. Bring materials for consultation regarding Mr. Henderson's agenda: training of volunteers for suicide hot line and restructuring of volunteer duties.
10:30 a.m.	Work on notes and treatment plans from prior day.
11:00 a.m.	Meet with client, Kevin. Explore results of Myers-Briggs Type Indicator (MBTI) and Strong Interest Inventory (SII) in light of interests and interview. Discuss further assessment as well as potential visit with college counselor.

DOI: 10.4324/9781003305521-11

12:00 noon	Lunch at desk. Catch up on paperwork.
12:30 p.m.	Meet with clients, Raul and Salina, who are raising their grandchildren. They are making progress with grandparenting plans but continue to feel isolated as well as concerned about their abilities to have energy and material resources to meet the needs of their grandchildren. Both want to make connections with other grandparents in this position and not feel alone as grandparents raising their grandchildren. A support group may be very useful, but none presently exist locally. (Fourth set of grandparents parenting grandchildren currently on my caseload.) Make appointment with program manager to discuss beginning a support group for grandparents raising their grandchildren. Schedule meeting with Aging Services Program coordinator to advocate for services in the community for grandparents raising grandchildren.
1:30 p.m.	Meet with client, Kathleen. Celebrate goal attainment (assertive with boyfriend about not smoking in the house). Review symptom reduction since prescription changes. Send note to/call Dr. Brown (MD) with concerns about facial tic and other symptoms since beginning new medications two weeks ago.
2:30 p.m.	Supervise interns (Kellie, Jackson, and Maria). Review center protocol for suicide assessment and prevention. Provide contact information for shift supervisors for consultation in case of client crisis. Prepare suicide assessment packages for interns and others at site.
4:00 p.m.	Review student case notes. Complete case notes. Write summary for court case. Prepare treatment plans. Sign documentation for billing department.
5:00 p.m.	End of business day.

The Role of the Counselor

The role of a professional is defined by the profession's governing entities, which most often are professional associations and/or accrediting organizations. Such bodies generally prescribe the educational program standards and clinical experiences required of the institution preparing future counselors. The profession's defined practices are aligned with the resulting knowledge and skills (Staton et al., 2018). For the counseling profession, these organizations include the American Counseling Association (ACA) and the Council for Accreditation of Counseling and Related Educational Programs (CACREP). State by state, counseling laws and regulations mandate the requirements for licensure and certification for professional counselors. Professional counselors provide assistance to individuals, groups, couples, families, organizations, and communities across a number of specialties, all with the goal of increasing the insights and abilities of the counselee to assist in the resolution of developmental conflicts or to help with challenging day-to-day struggles and decisions.

Nearly 25 years ago, Nugent and Jones (2008) defined the role of the counselor as a professional relationship through which the healthy growth and development of a client occurs by way of an increase in the client's self-understanding, as well as the client's understanding of relationships with others. Healthy and accurate understanding would result in the resolution of normal developmental conflicts. Almost a decade later, Altekruse et al. (2001) proposed that the role of the counselor needed a clearer and more inclusive definition representative of the activities of the counselor, including diagnosis and treatment for disorders that move beyond normal development into the abnormal arena. Another decade of marked efforts toward counseling identity definition clarified that the activities of the professional counselor are evolving, varied, and critical to the mental health profession. The ACA defines counseling as "a professional relationship that empowers diverse individuals, families, and groups to accomplish mental health wellness, education, and career goals" (Kaplan et al., 2014). Given the sum of the roles and activities of the counselor, it is prudent that counseling students understand the counselor's role in consultation, academic advising/career guidance, advocacy, supporting compliance to medically prescribed psychopharmacology, assessment, and ethical involvement with both public and private insurance providers.

Consultation

In the example of a day in the life of the professional counselor provided in Case Study 11.1, Meghan began her day in the role of consultant. She had been approached by Mr. Henderson to gain her expertise regarding the training of volunteer crisis line workers. Meghan's role was not to provide the training; rather, she was to assist Mr. Henderson in determining *his* actions. This is consultation. Later in the day, Meghan provides instruction and training to interns who must act as directed. This is supervision.

Consultation was defined as early as 1963 by Caplan as a process whereby the assistance of an expert is sought with the goal of increasing the seeker's capacity for addressing a particular issue involving a third party (i.e., target of the consultation). The role of the counselor as a consultant varies in that consultation may be sought by a broad variety of professionals, including but not limited to teachers, doctors, attorneys, clergy, business leaders, and fellow counselors who are working with students, patients, clients, parishioners, and employees. Anyone who seeks the input of another qualified individual to better address a situation for yet another person or group of persons is a potential consultee (see Figure 11.1).

The counselor-as-consultant's role is not limited to any particular counseling specialty. School counselors are asked by administration, staff, and faculty to provide consultation regarding students, parents, other

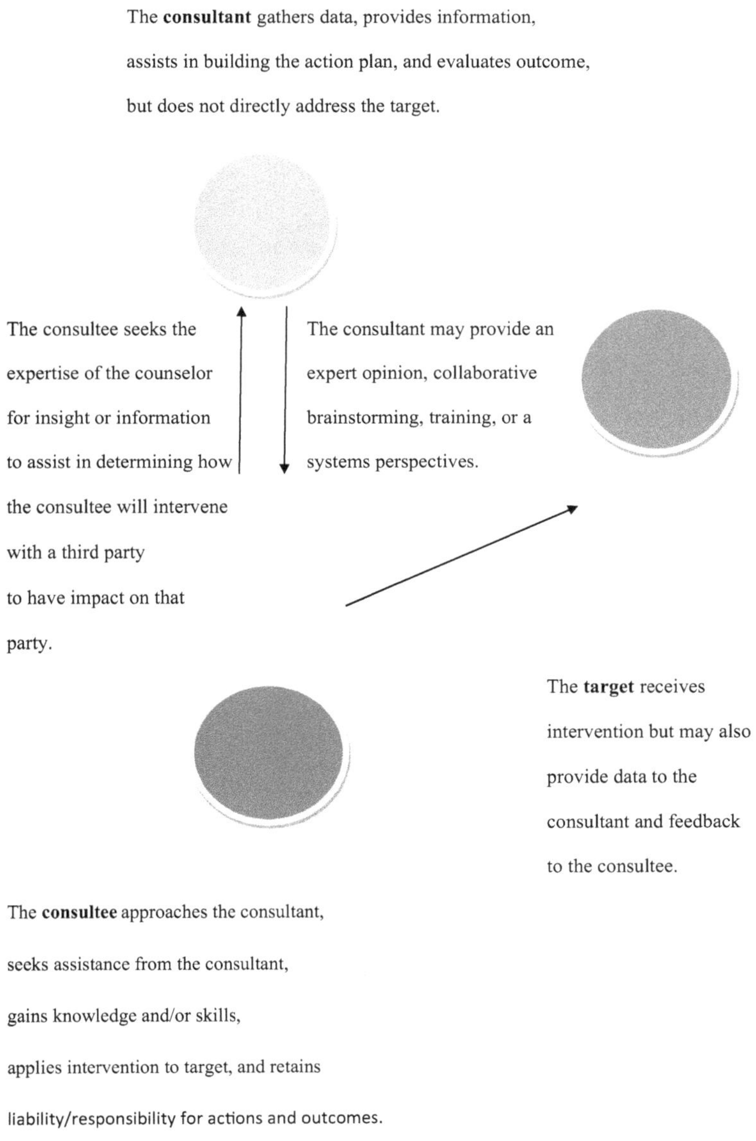

Figure 11.1 Consultation roles and process

school personnel, and community members across a wide range of issues. College counselors provide advice and assistance to various consultees, such as faculty, residence life personnel, administration, academic advisors, and student groups. Mental health counselors might provide consultation for parents, schools, businesses, social service agencies, attorneys, doctors, and hospitals as well as for other counselors or mental health personnel in need of the counselor's particular expertise. In any case, the ethical obligations of a counselor to be beneficent and nonmaleficent remain consistent when consulting. Different from supervision, there is no power to enforce that a consultee behaves as the consultant suggests, and the consultee remains fully liable for actions implemented. The consultant is liable to provide best practice within the scope of their expertise.

Various models of consultation have been developed and employed, placing emphasis on content versus process, expert versus collaborative versus system centeredness, various theoretical foundations, and inward versus outward focus (Keys et al., 1998). There have been several models of the process of consultation proposed, all of which delineate stages covering entry to exit. Whether the counselor is the expert, a collaborator, or facilitator of a systems-based approach, consultation activities can be categorized into five stages: (a) orientation, (b) design, (c) implementation, (d) review/revision, and (e) follow-up/termination. These stages are noted and applied to associated activities and samples in Table 11.1.

Table 11.1 The consultation process

Stage	*Brief Explanation*	*Activities*	*Example*
Orientation	Consultee contacts consultant and proposes the issue. Consultant works to build relationship, to understand the issue, and to clarify the conditions of the consultation.	Meet, greet, define issue, set contract defining the roles and responsibilities of each party involved, limitations of expertise with referral where appropriate.	The Dean of Student Life at the university contacts the counseling center regarding the increase in reports from resident directors involving violation of the "no alcohol in the dorms" policy. Opal, a professional counselor, is assigned to consult. Opal has both education and training in chemical dependency and has worked in student life at another university. Opal meets with the dean to gather a clear picture of the issue and assess her expertise to provide consultation. Roles and responsibilities are identified.
Design	Consultant works collaboratively with consultee to gather information, further define the issue, set goals, and determine potential solutions for goal attainment. An action plan is developed as is a means of data collection to measure outcomes.	Information gathering regarding all parties involved, which may mean interviewing individuals or groups, or obtaining quantitative data, to clarify and confirm the issue. Both parties work to discover probable outcomes, including the potential impact each option could have on the target and system(s) involved.	Opal meets with a group of resident directors to gather information to assess the details of the issue. Opal also meets with a focus group of residents to discuss their perspectives of the rise in violations of the alcohol policy. After determining a clearer picture of the issue, Opal reviews the most current literature regarding college life and alcohol use with recommended interventions and preventative actions. She meets with the dean to discuss the potential steps the dean could take to assist residents in adhering to the alcohol policy.
Implementation	Consultee implements the action plan with the target (e.g., individual, group, organization) and connects with the consultant to support/problem solve any issues that may arise throughout implementation.	Consultee implements the action plan and is ultimately responsible for the outcome, whereas the consultant remains responsible for providing best practice strategies concerning the issue within the consultant's expertise.	The dean implements one of the prevention programs recommended by Opal in addition to weekend late-night campus activities that do not involve alcohol and that are hosted by resident directors. The dean meets with Opal twice to gain her expertise in determining who should be required to complete the prevention program and who may not need the education.

Table 11.1 (Continued)

Stage	*Brief Explanation*	*Activities*	*Example*
Review/Revision	Consultant and consultee meet to review and revise the goals and action plan throughout the process (formative review) to ensure ongoing success of consultee's implementation; review is also conducted after the action plan is concluded to evaluate and determine what worked and what did not (summative evaluation) and what could have been done differently to best ensure success.	Consultee provides information regarding the impact of the implementation of the action plan, which may include numerical or anecdotal data. The consultant integrates the data and determines what to retain and what to revise for the next consultation. The consultant furthers assesses the process and outcome to determine where further education and/or training may be beneficial to maintain expertise in best practice regarding the issue.	The dean meets with Opal and reviews monthly reports of issues related to alcohol use by residents. They brainstorm additional actions the dean could take to assist in reduced alcohol-related issues. They determine that there is a reduction in issues each month and that there appears to be less of an issue when there are more supports available such as the late-night activities and the greater contact with the resident directors. Revisions to increase the number of hosted activities are made within the dean's budget.
Follow-up/ Termination	The consultant lays out a plan with the consultee to follow up after the action plan has been completed to fortify changes that were made during implementation and to provide any further advice or information to secure that the goals that were met are sustained. The consultant concludes the consultation.	The follow-up period is designed to meet the needs of the particular consultation and therefore varies in length and activity. In any case, follow-up includes an analysis of the data, a review of the success or lack thereof with all involved parties, the collaboration between consultant and consultee regarding any unfinished issues, and a formal ending of the relationship once all contracted work is completed.	The dean and Opal meet six months later at the end of the academic year and agree that the objectives were met. The consultation is then formally concluded.

The counselor-as-consultant holds an expertise that is sought by a consultee for the consultee to facilitate a change that benefits an individual, group, or community. The consultant and consultee work together to create an action plan that is fulfilled by the consultee, evaluated and revised as needed again in collaboration, and assessed for outcome and process to improve the next consultation (Staton et al., 2018). The most common form of consultation in the counseling profession occurs between helping professionals where one counselor seeks the expertise of another counselor for the first to provide best practice designed for a particular client or type of client. This kind of consultation is a mainstay of the profession, and every counselor must both seek consultation when it best serves the client and be prepared to provide it within one's expertise. Regardless of the type of consultation, the counselor-as-consultant consistently demonstrates altruistic behavior and clear concern for increase in consultee capacity and target well-being (Legowo et al., 2017). As you think about consultation, consider the questions in Self-Assessment Activity 11.1.

Self-Assessment Activity 11.1 Consultation

1. An area of expertise for which I could currently be an effective consultant is ________.
2. Limitations that would lead me to refer a potential consultee to another expert are ________.
3. To develop and/or maintain an expertise necessary for consultation, I would ________.

4. As a graduate student, you are becoming an expert in attentive listening. Assume the local high school has begun a program aimed at student leadership development. They have contacted you for assistance in creating a set of experiences for their students that would increase the students' capacities to be good listeners and effective communicators. Complete the following chart according to your role as consultant.

Stage	*Consultation Regarding Graduate School Application*
1. Orientation	
2. Design	
3. Implementation	
4. Review/Revision	
5. Follow-up/Termination	

Career Guidance

Meghan's day (see Case Study 11.1) included a meeting with Kevin, a college sophomore, to discuss his Myers-Briggs Type Indicator results as well as an upcoming meeting with his college counselor. Kevin came to see Meghan initially because of his increasing uncertainty about his future and the resulting anxiety. In their first meeting, Meghan learned that Kevin had earned a C– in Biology and D+ in Organic Chemistry the prior semester and was in jeopardy of losing his scholarships. Kevin's anxiety occurred as he realized he did not have the requisite skills and motivation to be a medical doctor as he had planned. Meghan helped Kevin realize that he needed to identify a major and develop a career plan that fit his interests, values, and abilities. She helped him understand that his motivation would increase as his academic work and career aspirations aligned. Meghan assisted Kevin in gathering information about his lifetime of career development, and they began formulating a plan for his career in relationship to other life roles.

Counselors across specialties must be prepared to integrate career guidance where needed throughout their counseling practices. As a lifelong critical aspect of human development, career guidance has its place in nearly every aspect of counseling. Career counseling is a required component of the CACREP (2016) standards across all counseling preservice programs. Career counseling also comprises a major section of the National Counselor Examination (NCE; National Board for Certified Counselors & Affiliates, Inc. [NBCC], 2012). The American School Counselor Association's (ASCA, 2019) *National Model* focuses on career development as one of three domains of comprehensive program delivery. This keeps career guidance at the forefront of the school counseling profession. Still, many other specialties spend little if any time in direct focus on career guidance or academic advising, a career counseling component.

Historically, theorists have postulated various approaches to career development. Case Study 11.2 and Table 11.2 illustrate how a range of theoretical approaches might be used to interpret and respond to the situation of the client in the case study. These theories are outlined in the remainder of this section.

Case Study 11.2 Rob

Rob Rutherford is a 57-year-old married male who has been referred for counseling services after his job as associate vice president of a small power company was eliminated as the company downsized. He worked for the last 24 years at the same company beginning just after his graduation with a master's degree in business administration. Although Mr. Rutherford has no debt with his mortgage paid and his children completely independent, he states that he must have employment soon or he will not be "the man" of the house—especially given that his wife's income has been the only real source of financial support for the last few months. He states he has scoured the job market for the last six months and has found nothing similar to the job he held at the power company. He is not averse to a new type of employment, but he states he has no idea in what direction he would want to look. Consequently, he feels depressed and has never considered his life less valuable than he does presently. Table 11.2 depicts each theory, the basic premise for each theory, and an application of each theory to Case Study 11.2.

Table 11.2 Career theory application

Theory (Theorist)	Premise/Foundation	Sample
Trait and Factor Theory (Parsons)	Assesses the client's strengths and interests and considers the job market to assist the client in career decision making.	Counselor assists Mr. Rutherford by assessing his strengths and interests. It is discovered that Mr. Rutherford has exceptional logical and mathematical abilities coincident to his bachelor's degree in mathematics. He enjoys working with numbers and enjoyed the component of budget and projections most in his last job. The counselor assists Mr. Rutherford in finding different access points to the current job market in addition to the local paper and word of mouth. Mr. Rutherford now approaches the possibilities with ideas about other employment related to these interests that go beyond his past career that will fit him. As a result, he has new places to begin to look.
Psychodynamic (Roe)	Parenting styles and emotional climate ultimately result in one of eight orientations to the world of work that combine with gender, physical appearance, temperament and personality, genetics, family background, and economic circumstance to lead to occupational choice.	Counselor engages Mr. Rutherford in talking about his early life experiences and the shaping of his career decisions. Mr. Rutherford shares that his parents were warm, accepting, and loving and that he had enjoyed learning to keep his father's books in their hardware store business during summers while in college. Mr. Rutherford confirms that he is geared toward business and finance in particular and is rejuvenated to continue looking with a scope toward another business/finance venture.
Life-Span Development (Super)	Five predictable and orderly stages of career development across the life span during which humans learn about interests and abilities, developing self-concept, and awareness of the world of work; test their occupational fantasies in leisure, school, and early work; and solidify their preferences in occupational decision making. In later life, humans disengage from work and invest in retirement and leisure/avocation activities.	Counselor determines that Mr. Rutherford has experienced a disruption in his self-concept and developmental progression that has him unsure of his capacities and interests, keeping him from moving forward into a new job. The counselor works to assist Mr. Rutherford in rediscovering his interests and helping him to define more fully these interests and his abilities to make an effective match to the job opportunities that do exist for Mr. Rutherford.

(Continued)

Table 11.2 (Continued)

Personality (Holland)	Humans play out personalities by career decisions and are content if occupations match personalities (six types including realistic, investigative, artistic, social, enterprising, and conventional). Counselors assess occupational codes comprised of a predominant type and secondary types. Careers are also coded in *The Dictionary of Holland Occupational Codes*. Matching individual code to occupational code leads to satisfaction.	Counselor assesses Mr. Rutherford using the Self-Directed Search and determines his Holland code with Enterprising as his primary and Conventional and Social as his secondary types (ESC). Together they perused *The Dictionary of Holland Occupational Codes* to determine a list of potential jobs that would likely be most satisfying to Mr. Rutherford. This rejuvenated Mr. Rutherford and provided direction to him for expanding his job search in a direction fitting him.
Social Learning Theory of Career Decision Making/Learning Theory of Career Counseling (Krumboltz)	Environmental factors, learning, and task approach skills interact, producing self-observation generalizations, an emphasis on task approach, and action outcomes. Positive and negative influences shape career decisions. Interventions include defining/gathering information about problems and goals, identifying solutions/ outcomes, and generalizing to new situations. Techniques include modeling, improving and influencing learning experiences, increasing self-observation, task approach, cognitive, and performance skills to enhance self-efficacy. Seven stages: DECIDES. LTCC added emphasis to counselor intervention in shaping decision making. Happenstance added to account for chance, creativity, and exploration.	Counselor works with Mr. Rutherford through the DECIDES model by which they define the issue of his current career decision point, establish a plan to clarify his interests and reestablish his direction concerning his career world, clarify his values by examining his observations of self and the world, identify alternatives to the career path he was just derailed from, discover probable outcomes of the options before him, eliminate alternatives that are not a fit to his desired outcome, and start action aimed toward a resolution of the defined problem. The counselor encourages Mr. Rutherford to see the happenstance of his employment loss as an opportunity for creative exploration of a new direction that might prove to have a silver lining.
Constructive Development (McAuliffe)	One's career challenge adaptability is informed by the meaning one construes throughout one's life span. Each person creates one's own reality via an organized self-created story across the life span dependent on stages of development with more advanced stages allowing for more multifaceted and complex solutions to career problems. Counselors accept clients' stories and gently push for increased development using receptive inquiry, pattern recognition, primacy of life experience, mindfulness, writing, metaphor, and creating meaning through activity.	Counselor encourages Mr. Rutherford to share his life's stories, especially with regard to the formation of his career decisions to date. He listens carefully and affirms Mr. Rutherford's perspectives as they are yet encourages him to consider stretching outside his current patterns via writing what life would be like with some small changes to his daily interactions with himself, others, and his environment. Mr. Rutherford begins to see himself more fully in relation to his world and begins to think of alternative patterns he could develop that would allow him to maintain his lifestyle as he desires yet to move beyond his job loss. He begins to consider the options that are definitely outside the box he had believed was his work world and has become enthusiastic about the new career adventure that has come via his job shift.

Table 11.2 (Continued)

Systems Theory Framework (McMahon & Patton)	Considers career issues within the comprehensive context of one's life reflecting content (intrapersonal and context variables) and process (recursiveness, change over time, and chance). Consider the dynamic reciprocal relationship between and with the individual (gender, ability, interests, age, etc.) and social and environmental/societal systems (socioeconomics, political, religious, etc.). Counselors assist clients in examining parts of self in concert with systems and the whole via the individual's sharing of and reconfiguring of story within the counselor-assisted accepting environment.	Counselor builds a relationship with Mr. Rutherford in which they explore Mr. Rutherford's patterns of connection within himself, with others, and with the world in which he lives. Mr. Rutherford exposes his unfounded perspectives that his world rests solely on his earning capacity and begins to see the reciprocal relationships with his children and spouse that he has heretofore not noted. He begins to define himself not only as valuable for his income, but also as a companion, friend, advisor, and supporter in nonmonetary ways. He begins to consider new career options in addition to the career he has forged within his old employment. He begins talking with his wife and adult children about how they might alter their current environment to better meet what is most valued by each of them and by the family as a family. His job hunt is thereby altered as his desires for potential employment expand to fit his newfound sense of self in his world.

Theories of career development reach at least as far back as Frank Parsons in the early 1900s. He developed the trait and factor approach, which involved the rational process of assessing strengths and interests and considering the job market to assist the client in career decision making (Zunker, 2015).

Ann Roe (1956) developed a psychodynamic career theory in the mid-1950s. She postulated that parenting styles (warm/cold) and emotional climate (emotional concentration toward the child, acceptance of the child, or avoidance of the child) ultimately resulted in one of eight orientations to the world of work, including service, business, organization, technology, outdoor, science, general culture, and arts/entertainment. Roe added that additional influences such as gender, physical appearance, temperament and personality, genetics, family background, and economic circumstances contributed to occupational choice.

Donald Super's theory of predictable and orderly stages of career development across the life span has been a marked force in the career counseling world. He proposed that career development occurred across a five-stage (multiple substages) process during which people learn about their interests and abilities while developing self-concept, gaining an awareness of the world of work; testing their occupational fantasies in leisure, school, and early work; and solidifying their preferences in occupational decision making, including specialized education and training. In later life, people disengage from work and invest their interests progressively more into retirement and leisure/avocation activities.

John Holland's proposed personality theory of occupational choice also helped to frame early career counseling practice by suggesting that humans play out their personalities (preferred ways of social and environmental situations) through their career decisions (Zunker, 2015). He posited that humans would be most fulfilled or content if their occupations were chosen to fit their unique personalities. He conceptualized personality into six types, including realistic, investigative, artistic, social, enterprising, and conventional (RIASEC Model), that are represented along points of a hexagon. By Holland's theory, humans are not bound to personalities of a single type or hexagon point but have occupational codes comprised of a predominant type (strongest point) and secondary types (adjacent two points). Holland proposed that careers could also be typed along the hexagon, and some 12,860 plus jobs have been coded and published in The Dictionary of Holland Occupational Codes (Gottfredson & Holland, 1996). Assessing the individual for code and matching codes to occupations of similar code give direction to the options that would lead to the greatest job satisfaction.

Recently, theories have emerged that move beyond traits, temperaments, personality, and interests and into *the process* of development of career decision making. Most prominent of the developmental theories are the evolving theories of Krumboltz, constructive development career counseling, and most recently the systems approach. In the 1970s, Krumboltz proposed the social learning theory of career decision making (SLTCDM). In addition to one's genetic endowment or personality/trait factors offered in earlier theories, Krumboltz included environmental factors (events and settings) as well as learning histories (associative and instrumental learning experiences) and task approach skills (personal standards, work ethics, emotional responses). Outcomes of the interaction of these factors are self-observation generalizations (one's own evaluation and assessment of performance, values, and interests), an emphasis on task approach, and action outcomes. Krumboltz noted positive (reinforcements, observations of a valued model, access to people and resources) and negative (punishments of self or valued model) influences on career decision-making skills. Social learning theory counseling interventions included defining and gathering information about problems and goals, identifying a host of solutions and potential outcomes, and generalizing the process to new situations. Techniques such as modeling, improving and influencing learning experiences, and increasing self-observation, as well as task approach, cognitive, and performance skills to enhance self-efficacy, were applied. Krumboltz's theory hosted a seven-stage model with the acronym DECIDES as follows: (a) define the problem, (b) establish the action plan, (c) clarify the values, (d) identify alternatives, (e) discover probable outcomes, (f) eliminate alternatives, and (g) start action action (Krumboltz et al., 1986).

Some 20 years later, the learning theory of career counseling (LTCC) was added to the SLTCDM (Mitchell & Krumboltz, 1996). This addition moved from explanation of the whys of career decision making to what counselors can do to assist in helping clients resolve career-related issues. Since then, Krumboltz has demonstrated his belief that theories are strongest when they hold the potential to change on the discovery of new ideas. In line with this notion, his efforts have shifted to the inclusion of "happenstance" or "chance" in the role of career decision making. This addition brings the notion that there are benefits found in unplanned events and that exploration, open-mindedness, creativity, and lifelong learning are essential components to healthy career development and decision making (Krumboltz & Levin, 2010). Krumboltz's theory integrates career counseling and personal counseling, making clear the lifelong process of one's career development. This further validates the importance of all counselors being well educated and trained in the application of career counseling theories.

Constructive developmental career counseling was introduced in the early 1990s by McAuliffe (1993) and Peavy (1992), who incorporated Kegan's theory of constructive development into career practice. The premise was that the meaning one construes throughout the life span shapes one's career challenge adaptability. Constructivist concepts assert that each person creates a personal reality with subjective meaning constructed in organized ways into stories that they continually revise over the course of the life span. This formation of meaning is dependent in part on the individual's developmental stage, with later stages allowing greater understanding in more multifaceted and advanced ways. The counselor's role becomes one of acceptance of the client's current developmental stage and cumulative story to lay the groundwork for gently pushing the client's development. As the client develops the capacity to think differently about self in relation to the world (self, work, relationships, career), the client is able to problem solve career issues differently. Counseling activities based in constructive developmental thought might include receptive inquiry, pattern recognition, primacy of life experience, mindfulness, writing, and creating meaning through activity (Peavy, 1994; Stebleton, 2010), all of which aim at supporting development of an altered self-authored story. Similar theory development and application occurs with narrative career counseling with a focus on how the client's story provides personal meaning in career choice and career development. The counselor assists the client in becoming an active agent in identifying the career narrative as it is then outlining the most helpful narrative for the client to live most meaningfully, productively, and fulfilled (Maree, 2011; McAuliffe & Emmett, 2017).

Further focus on client empowerment is espoused in the application of motivational interviewing (MI) in career counseling. MI occurs within an empathetic relationship in which the counselor assists the client in focusing on particular career goals, the client's reason for wanting these goals, and planning of steps the individual is ready to take in moving toward the career goals. This approach is client-centered and aimed toward exploring client motivation in order to increase the client's motivation and commitment actions that promote particular career goals (Rochat & Rossier, 2016).

The systems approach has been considered fundamental to other career counseling modalities in that this approach considers career issues within the comprehensive context of one's life. Systems theory reflects both content (intrapersonal and context variables) and process (recursiveness, change over time, and chance). The core of systems theory is the individual system consisting of intrapersonal influences such as age, gender, interests, and abilities. Systems theory considers this core within the grander contextual social system and environmental/societal subsystems. The social system consists of those with whom the individual interacts, such as family, peers, classmates, and even media. The environmental/societal subsystem includes the whole of the environmental factors within which the individual lives, including location, socioeconomics, politics, and so forth. Interacting systems are not static; rather, they are dynamic, having reciprocal influence on one another. A change in one system or part of a system will create change in others (McMahon, 2005).

Foundational tenants of systems theory include the following conceptual understandings. Just as with constructive developmental theory, systems theory notes that individuals are the experts of their own content. People use language to write multiple stories of their own lives, which produces meaning, which leads to a preferred career. Counselors assist clients in examining all parts possible as they interact within systems, with parts of the system, and with the whole system to understand repeating patterns (recursiveness), change as it occurs over time, and chance. With new information, the client can write different stories leading to new patterns of career decision making. Tools of the system-focused career counselor include the building of connectedness, use of story, and the counseling relationship itself and in relationship to other parts and whole of the system(s), along with genuineness, unconditional positive regard, empathic understanding, and flexibility (McMahon, 2005).

Many tools are available to assess personality traits, interests, values, and abilities in relationship to career decision making. These tools are grounded in theory, have sound score reliability and validity, and should be familiar to the counselor. Table 11.3 depicts some of the most widely used career assessment tools, the theory base of the tool, the publisher, and a brief description.

With the all the ideas of this section in mind, use Self-Assessment Activity 11.2 to explore your thoughts about career guidance.

Self-Assessment Activity 11.2 Career Guidance

1. Of the seven theories discussed earlier, which do you find is aligned with your own thought processes about career development and guidance, and why?
2. How might you synthesize/integrate the components from each theory that align with your perspectives to provide the foundation for your career guidance counseling work?

Table 11.3 Career assessment tools and broad descriptions

Kuder Career Search with Person Match—Identifies interests and aligns interests with most fitting career cluster.
Kuder Skills Assessment—Identifies skills and aligns to the most fitting career cluster.
Super's Work Values Inventory—Identifies values most important to chosen career.
Self-Directed Search (SDS)—Uses test takers' information about interests to determine personality type presented in three-letter Holland code.
Strong Interest Inventory—Measures users' interests based on Holland's six types.
O*Net interest profiler—Educates about occupations based on their code.
O*Net ability profiler—Measures users' skills in nine areas important to many occupations.
O*Net Work Importance Profiler—Measures users' work values in six different categories.
California Occupational Interest Survey (COPS)—168 items, provides activity interests scores to 14 different career clusters. Each cluster corresponds to high school and college curriculum, as well as current sources of occupational information.
Career Beliefs Inventory—Looks at clients' assumptions, generalizations, and beliefs about self related to the world of work.
Jackson's Vocational Interest Inventory—Career assessment and career planning tool that matches interests to careers, job groups, and college majors.
Armed Services Vocational Aptitude Battery (ASVAB)—Originally designed to predict future academic and occupational success in military occupations. Test areas include General Science, Academic Reasoning, Word Knowledge, Paragraph Comprehension, Mathematics Knowledge, Electronics Information, Auto and Shop Information, and Mechanical Comprehension.
Myers-Briggs Type Indicator—Allows clients to see how they prefer to behave as opposed to how they actually behave. Preference drives direction of job search.

3. Belinda is a 15-year-old high school freshman who is considering which courses to take as she contemplates her life beyond high school. Her father and mother are both high school graduates, and she is certain she will graduate from high school. She has always been a good student, and her teachers have been encouraging her to go on to college. She is frightened and intrigued by the prospect, but she feels fairly sure that she doesn't have the capacity to complete college given that no one from her family has ever even applied to college, let alone graduated. She has come to meet with you to get some direction about the decisions she feels she needs to make as she registers for classes. The only thing she has ever considered as a job was a grocery checker because both of her parents work at the local grocery store—her father as a butcher and her mother as a checker. She says she doesn't want to work hard in high school if it isn't going to get her anywhere. What kinds of questions or thoughts come to mind when considering counseling with the following presenting issue?
4. Consider the case of Belinda. Using Table 11.4, complete the sample column with actions the counselor might take if working with Belinda from the theory as noted.

Academic Advising

Your work with Belinda is an example of academic advising in the career guidance process. To effectively advise Belinda, the counselor needs to understand the framework for career development offered at the high school. This includes the courses of study available and the high school's protocols for assisting in college searches and applications as well as applications for scholarships and other financial assistance. An effective tool that may be foundational to the high school's protocol is the ASCA (2019) *National Model*, which contains the key element of individual planning based on assessment and a decision-making process. With this framework in mind, the counselor can assist Belinda in exploring the possibilities in the world of work, in understanding the skills and personal qualities employers want for particular jobs, and in examining Belinda's interests and abilities. The counselor can help Belinda to develop a good decision-making process based on an understanding of the preceding qualities in relationship to the available opportunities. Belinda can then choose from course offerings, experiences within the community such as volunteering or job shadowing in a similar career field to her interests, and other activities such as leadership opportunities that would prepare her for entry into a career or further education or skills training. Once such decisions are made, the counselor and Belinda produce an individualized written career plan that aligns with her high school course of study and career goals beyond high school.

It is clear from this example that **academic advising** involves preparation and planning for the student to select an appropriate direction, a course of study to meet that direction, and a selection of courses to best ensure student success. Academic advising may also include psychoeducation and skill building such as time management, communication skills, test-taking strategies, and effective study habits and skills. Other related counseling activities might include stress reduction/management, test anxiety reduction, communication and social skill building, work readiness skill development, job shadowing, volunteer experiences, service opportunities, and other activities that enhance career maturity.

Table 11.4 Sample actions for the case of Belinda

Theory (Theorist)	*Sample*
Trait and Factor Theory (Parsons)	
Psychodynamic (Roe)	
Life-Span Life-Space Development (Super)	
Personality (Holland)	
SLTCDM/LTCC (Krumboltz)	
Motivational Interviewing (Miller & Rollnick)	
Constructive Development/Narrative (McAuliffe)	
Systems Theory Framework (McMahon & Patton)	

Academic advising does not begin and end with high school. Academic advising occurs throughout one's education. The National Academic Advising Association (NACADA) states in its guiding principles that academic advising is integral to fulfilling the teaching and learning mission of higher education (National Academic Advising Association, 2014) In the samples of the methods used in academic advising to assess student learning outcomes activities, several are familiar to counselors, including to assist students to

> craft a coherent educational plan based on assessment of abilities, aspirations, interests, and values; use complex information from various sources to set goals, reach decisions, and achieve those goals; . . . cultivate the intellectual habits that lead to a lifetime of learning; [and] behave as citizens who engage in the wider world around them.

The counselor's role over the life span includes assistance in attaining accurate knowledge regarding the client's educational world. This requires using appropriate assessment tools (whether the client is a student in elementary school or retraining in later adulthood). It requires assisting the client in gaining the skills and insight that lead to career choice, including decisions within the academic plan. It includes the skill building and coping strategies listed previously as well as guidance and support in gaining employment such as writing skills and confidence building for interviewing. The counselor who is most effective collaborates with other professionals and uses available career resources and support systems to ensure accurate and efficient guidance throughout the process of career guidance and academic advising.

Advocacy in Counseling

Meghan's early afternoon appointment was spent with Raul and Salina, who are grandparents raising their grandchildren (see Case Study 11.1). Meghan recognized a growing need in her community for services related to this population and the lack of resources currently available. She will prepare a rationale for services to present to both her employer and the local Aging Services Program to advocate for resources that would meet the needs of this population. Advocacy work of this kind is a common counseling activity.

The counseling profession was borne out of concern for human beings who were suffering, many of whom were disenfranchised because of little to no access to the kind of assistance that would alleviate such suffering. The meaning of the root word of advocacy, voc, is "voice." The counseling profession has been one of "voice" for clients and assisting the client in becoming empowered or finding "voice" for self since its inception (Smith & Weikel, 2011). The late 1990s gave rise to a renewed call to counselors for social activism regarding a diverse set of client-related issues ranging from anti-drugs in schools campaigns to services for the disabled to issues related to sexual orientation to other cultural injustices (Smaby & Daugherty, 1995; Smith & Chen-Hayes, 2003; Torkelson-Lynch & Gussel, 1996). The renewed call was not only extended to social justice concerns, but counselors were also urged to invest in efforts to promote the counseling profession itself (Eriksen, 1997; Myers et al., 2002).

The response to the call for both social justice and professional advocacy has included advocacy training in counselor education programs. CACREP has required advocacy training in its standards, and counselor educators have developed methodology for the training of effective counselor advocates (Collison et al., 1998; Eriksen, 1997; House & Sears, 2002; Lewis & Bradley, 2000; Steele, 2008). With effective training, education, and dispositions geared to both social justice and the promotion of the profession, the counselor's role can and must include advocacy for both client and profession. A definition of counselor advocacy, an overview of the scope of advocacy with samples of advocacy action and outcomes, and a set of advocacy strategies for counselors follow.

In 2003, the ACA Governing Council officially adopted advocacy competencies that described necessary counselor skills, knowledge, and behavior that address systemic barriers and issues facing students, clients, client groups, or whole populations. The advocacy competencies are organized around two dimensions: Extent of Client Involvement in Advocacy and Level of Advocacy Intervention. These dimensions help counselors examine who is involved in the advocacy intervention and what level may be most effective. The intersection of the two dimensions works across six domains of advocacy: empowerment, client advocacy, community collaboration, systems advocacy, collective action, and social/political advocacy. Counselors acting as an advocate examine multicultural and ethical considerations relevant for the client, group, issue, and approach (Toporek & Daniels, 2018).

Combining the accepted views of **advocacy** in the counseling profession results in the following definition provided by CACREP (2016):

> action taken on behalf of clients or the counseling profession to support appropriate policies and standards for the profession; promote individual human worth, dignity, and potential; and oppose or work to change policies and procedures, systemic barriers, long-standing traditions, and preconceived notions that stifle human development.
>
> (p. 59)

Such a definition provides the foundation for both client- and profession-focused advocacy.

Client-focused advocacy may include outreach to deliver helpful services to those who are in need of but not receiving such services otherwise. Outreach promotes and is promoted by the ideal of social justice when the effort is extended to groups of people rather than individual clients, particularly when applied to those who have diminished influence and power. Another client-focused advocacy counselor focus is the empowerment of clients to help clients develop the necessary skills, abilities, and confidence to have more control over their own lives and advocacy within, or influence over, the environment in which they live. Empowerment may include more than community or client changes; in addition, counselors may work toward creating legislative changes such as reworking of regulations developed within the law or in changes to the law at the most basic levels to secure better opportunities and services for clients.

Counselors also advocate for the counseling profession itself. As noted earlier, promotion of the profession generally allows counselors greater potential for successful social change and client advocacy. **Professional advocacy** includes lobbying for extending counseling services to all populations, such as the recent addition of counselors serving veterans through the Veterans Administration. Gaining state counseling certification and/or licensure has been a focus of professional advocacy, with California becoming the last of the 50 states to achieve that goal (California Association for Licensed Professional Clinical Counselors, 2020). Each of these changes followed countless hours of devoted efforts of counselors across the nation advocating by establishing a sense of urgency via media communication, supporting existing alliances and creating new ones aimed at collaborative efforts, lobbying legislators and policy makers, and persisting until the vision is realized (Lee & Rodgers, 2009).

Outreach, empowerment, social change, and professional advocacy involve particular counseling dispositions, skills, and activities. Resourcefulness, flexibility, and integrity top the list of counselor-as-advocate characteristics (Kurpius & Rozecki, 1992). Kiselica and Robinson (2001) noted that counselors must have compassionate spirits and a deep sensitivity to, and commitment to alleviation of, human suffering. Lee and Rodgers (2009) added to compassion, sensitivity, and commitment the characteristics of leadership, a strategic vision, courage, and skills in data collection and use of data to promote needed change.

Specific steps or strategies assist in securing successful advocacy efforts. Stewart et al. (2009) provided such strategies beginning with the identification of the target, including identity, location, and the nature and extent of the issue or injustice. Next, the counselor-as-advocate hones a rationale for choosing the issue including the potential impact on the client or target population. Next, a clear and concise specific identification of the problem and how it fits the role of the counselor is described. Thorough research, both in the literature and from practical experience of individuals and counselors and other professionals who have been involved in the issue, the details and past efforts at resolution of the issue can be gathered. This leads to better determination of resources needed for change. Turning the outcome of the last step into a reference and resource list can assist in educating others who might assist in making changes happen. Goals are then formulated ranging from the global outcome goal to smaller contributory goals that may be refined and readjusted as needed. Finally, steps are delineated in action format so that the counselor-as-advocate can intervene driven by the information and resources noted earlier.

The counselor is not always involved in every step of an advocacy strategy. It is often the case that counselors are asked to join efforts for advocacy that are well underway. The advocacy steps as applied to licensure and Veterans Administration roles for counselors are two such actions. Counselors from across the country joined in the efforts to secure these outcomes in the form of letters to senators and representatives of Congress, visits to Capitol Hill, educating key community figures, and rallying other professionals at conferences or via other state and regional organization events. Use Self-Assessment Activity 11.3 to reflect on your ideas about advocacy.

Self-Assessment Activity 11.3 Advocacy

1. What is at least one local advocacy opportunity addressing an issue of social justice in which you could participate that would have potential impact on a client population in your area?
2. What is at least one regional or national advocacy opportunity in which you could participate that could impact the profession of counseling?

3. Who are the legislators who represent you at the state and national levels? What stance is each taking regarding the advocacy issues you listed in questions 1 and 2 above?
4. On a scale of 1 to 10, how would you rate yourself on each of the dispositions of a counselor foundational to advocacy (e.g., compassionate spirit, resourcefulness, flexibility, integrity, deep sensitivity to human suffering, leadership, a strategic vision, courage, and skills)?
5. How can you get involved now, as a graduate student, in advocacy efforts aimed at improving situations for clients or promoting the counseling profession?

Psychopharmacology

Meghan advocated for her client, Kathleen, who struggles with schizophrenia, disorganized type. Meghan encouraged Kathleen's empowerment by assisting her to "find her voice" with her boyfriend regarding his not smoking in their apartment. Meghan also used her own power with Kathleen's medical professional by giving voice to Kathleen's struggles with compliance due to the difficult side effects of her new medication. To do the latter and to collaborate well with the medical professional, Meghan must have an understanding of her role as a counselor in collaboration with medical professionals as well as knowledge of the basics of psychopharmacology.

The counselor-as-advocate or collaborator does not necessitate major social reform. Most of the advocacy by professional counselors occurs on a much smaller scale such as the preceding efforts made to assist the client in attaining or maintaining consistent and effective psychiatric services from a medical professional. One might argue that psychopharmacology has no place in the day of a counselor given that the counseling degree is not medically based. Counseling is largely based in the social sciences. Still, the reality under managed care is that the medical provider is most apt to see a client only once every three to four months on average, whereas the counselor often sees the client weekly (Gabbard & Kay, 2001). This gives the counselor much more time to note issues related to medication compliance and impact; hence, the counselor can greatly assist the client by advocating and collaborating with the medical professional.

As noted almost four decades ago, to be an effective advocate and collaborator with medical professionals, counselors need to be prepared with knowledge and the capacity to collaborate with medical professionals (Ponterotto, 1985). This includes understanding basic neuroanatomy, the action of neurotransmitters, the general categories of psychopharmaceuticals, including generic and trade names, the side effects of said medications, and presentation of side effects notable in the counseling office. Counselors must understand their roles, boundaries, and limitations when collaborating and be able to avoid issues of liability and other pitfalls when providing assistance to the medicated client (King & Anderson, 2004). The following will provide an overview of these essentials of psychopharmacology for the counselor.

The basics of psychopharmacology begin with the lobes and structures of the brain to provide a foundation for understanding the impact of psychotropic medications on the brain and subsequently on behavior, thought, and emotion. Figure 11.2 depicts the lobes of the brain.

Frontal Lobe

Toward the back of the frontal lobe is the motor strip, which is responsible for planning and initiating motor movement as well as controlling complex tasks. The rest of the frontal lobe is responsible for higher-order functions. These include metacognition, cause-and-effect or futuristic thinking/planning, reasoning, judgment, impulse control, and memory. Broca's area is found toward the back lower part of the frontal lobe and accounts for speech production. The frontal lobe is the last of the lobes to mature, which occurs for women in their early twenties and men in their mid to late twenties. Due to location and size (behind the forehead), the frontal lobe is more susceptible to damage than other lobes (Giedd, 2002).

Parietal Lobe

Just behind the motor strip begins the parietal lobe containing the sensory strip. Sensory nerves send messages to the sensory strip, where the messages are processed and sent to specialty areas of the brain for coding and responding. The parietal lobe is responsible for integration of sensory information such as pain, touch, and visual perception as well as for spatial orientation, knowledge of numbers and their relations, and the manipulation of objects (Preston et al., 2017).

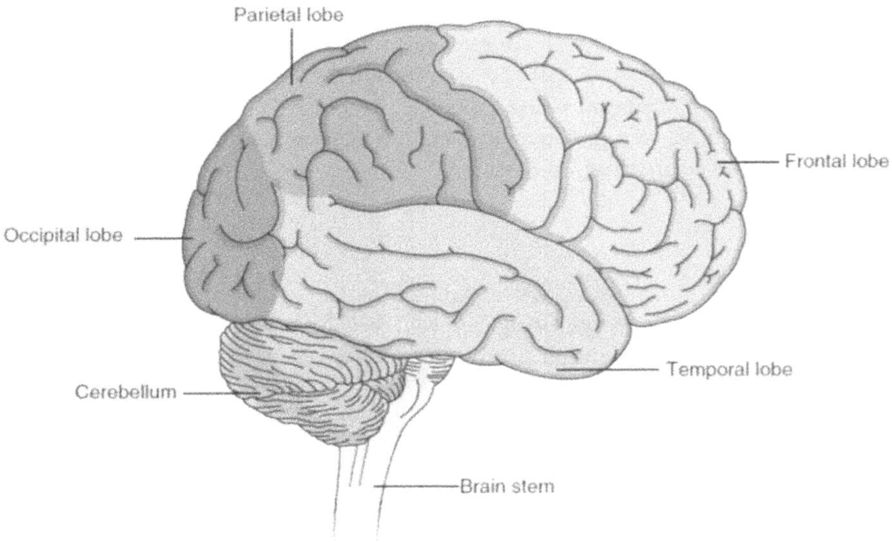

Figure 11.2 Right side view of the lobes of the brain

Occipital Lobe

The occipital lobe controls vision and color recognition. Trauma to this lobe may cause visual defects such as distorted or limited perception fields or misinterpretation of incoming data; however, trauma to this area is less likely due to its location.

Temporal Lobe

The temporal lobe is responsible for hearing, memory, and language comprehension, recognition, interpretation, and semantic processing. These language capacities are housed in Wernicke's area, found at the top and center of this lobe. There are eight major signs of damage to the temporal lobe, including changes in auditory sensation, perception, and attention to input as well as visual perception issues, impaired verbal organization, decline in language comprehension, long-term memory impairment, and altered personality and sexual behavior (Preston et al., 2017).

Limbic System

There are a few deep brain structures that appear to work in conjunction with one another to influence behavior and functions such as olfaction, emotion, motivation, motor coordination and behavior, and the autonomic nervous system. The structures include the hippocampus, amygdala, thalamus, cingulated gyrus, fornix, parahippocampus gyrus, and basal ganglia (which include the striatum, pallidum, substantia nigra, and subthalamic nucleus Preston et al., 2017), some of which are noted in Figure 11.3. Exactly how these structures interact is unclear, making it difficult to isolate the process let alone the struggles that result when damage has occurred.

Endocrine System

The endocrine system involves brain structures including the thalamus, hypothalamus, and pituitary and pineal glands. Glands producing hormones distributed throughout the body include the thyroid and parathyroid, adrenal, pancreas, and reproductive glands (ovaries and testes). The glands of the endocrine system influence almost every cell, organ, and function of the human body, including overall growth and development, mood regulation, tissue function, metabolism, and sexual and reproductive processes (Preston et al., 2017). Likewise, hormone levels are influenced by many factors, including infection, changes in fluid and mineral levels in the

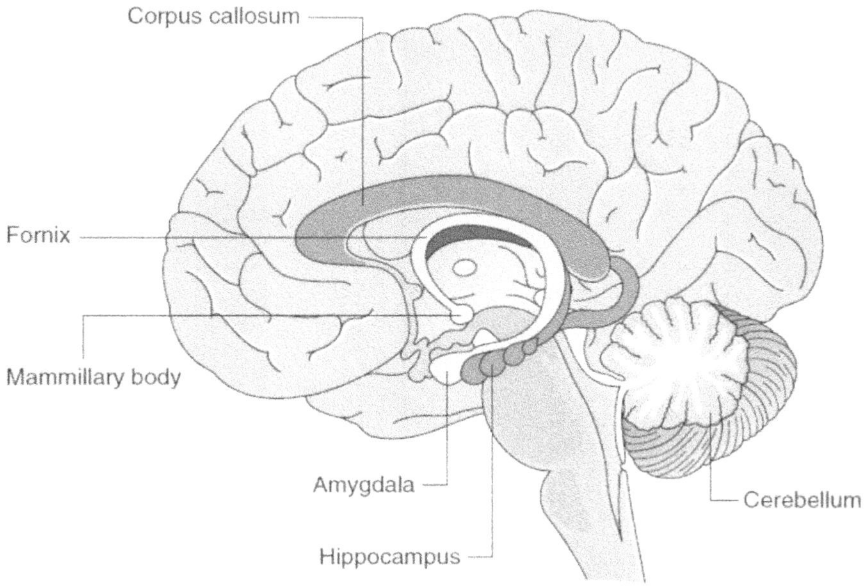

Figure 11.3 Limbic system basic structures

blood, and stress. These factors make it difficult to determine which emotions are due to neurological issues or to other elements of the environment.

Neurons and Synapses

Neurons are the basic cells that comprise each structure of the brain. Figure 11.4 illustrates the critical components of the neuron. The cell body houses the nucleus, which functions like the motherboard of the neuron in determining what the cell is and does. This includes the gathering of ingredients for the specific neurotransmitter made in the cell. There are many primary neurotransmitters and modulators that play a role. Of the ten primary neurotransmitters, acetylcholine, dopamine, epinephrine, norepinephrine, serotonin, GABA, and histamine are most commonly targeted by psychotropic medications.

The axon of the neuron (the shaft extending from the cell body to the terminal button) serves as the corridor for message transmission, which occurs at the terminal button at the axon's end. The axon is covered with rings of insulation called myelin sheath, which is produced by nearby glial cells. Myelin assists in making the transmission effective by insulating all but the nodes of Ranvier (the periodic fraction of the axon that is not insulated by myelin rings) so that the transmission only need occur in those brief spots. The terminal button, or bouton (foot), holds the neurotransmitter in sacs fused to the button until released into the synaptic cleft.

Once released into the synaptic cleft, the neurotransmitter fills in the receptor sites of the neighboring neuron's dendrites (tree branch-like projections coming from the cell body very near the terminal button). When enough dendrite receptors sites are filled, that neuron activates. This begins that neuron's process of transmitting its neurotransmitter into the next synaptic cleft, which continues the process to the next neuron and so on. Neurons are "green" in that they recycle used neurotransmitter, which is broken down into ingredient parts and retaken up into the cell to make the neurotransmitter all over again.

The basic structures of the brain and neuron are important for the counselor to understand to make sense of expected and unexpected drug action and side effects. Each of the psychotropic medications acts on at least one of the neurotransmitters by providing an abundance of necessary ingredients; by mimicking the action the specific neurotransmitter creates at the specific receptor sites; by blocking receptor sites, which limits cell activation; by blocking the reuptake process, which makes the neurotransmitter remain in the synaptic cleft longer; and/or by breaking apart the sac holding the neurotransmitter so that it cannot be dumped as prolifically into the cleft (Preston et al., 2017).

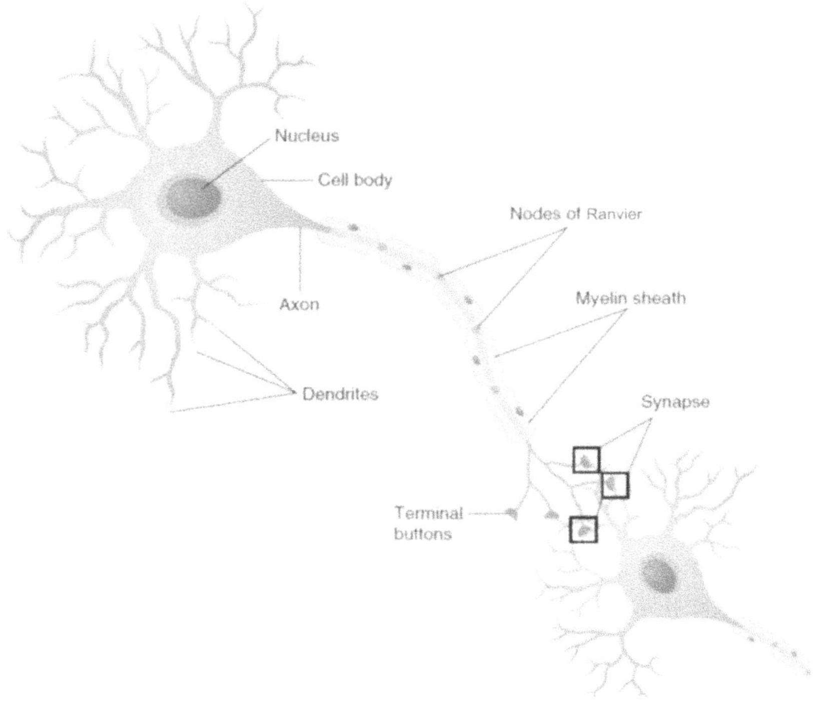

Figure 11.4 The neuron and synapse

Table 11.5 denotes types of drugs and their targeted benefits. Generic name (representative of the active ingredient), the trade name (representing the name applied by manufacturing company), and common side effects are provided for each type of drug. This table is designed to be helpful, but it is neither conclusive nor exhaustive and should not be assumed to suffice for medical advice. Counselors should consult with medical professionals such as physicians, physician's assistants, nurse practitioners, and pharmacists for complete, up-to-date, and thorough advice regarding these and all medications. Of further note is the reality that prescribers vary in their tendencies to prescribe or not prescribe particular classes of medications and types within classes. Additionally, there are shifts within the various prescribing professions that may markedly influence the use of particular classes or types of medications within a class. For example, a beginning trend in psychiatry is a movement away from benzodiazepines and other medications thought to be addictive and potentially deadly. This decline follows what had been a doubling of the number of prescriptions of benzodiazepines over the prior 15 years with a rise in related deaths (Agarwal & Landon, 2019). The counselor can be more helpful and supportive of client compliance if the counselor is aware of current trends and rationales for such trends in addition to knowing each class and type of medication and related signs and symptoms of effectiveness and side effects.

Given that the counselor generally spends a great deal more time both in a single session and over time with the client on medication than does the medical professional, the counselor who can denote side effects, monitor symptoms, and collaborate and advocate with the medical professional can be critical to client medical compliance and ultimate therapeutic success. Suggested strategies for working collaboratively with medical professionals include five guidelines. First is to make certain both the counselor and the medical professional have a signed release from the patient consenting to the collaboration. This step is necessary for all conversations divulging any data about the client to medical professions except for those involving the client as a danger to self or others that warrant duty to warn or duty to protect. The next is to be ready with a written list of the issues to address to be respectful of the medical professional's time. Third is to be clear about your role regarding the collaborative effort and to not overstep your professional role (e.g., you are not a medical professional, so do not offer medical advice to anyone—especially not the medical professional). Be prepared to offer your opinion when asked, but also make clear what you are not prepared to address. Finally, ask questions that might help you assist the medical professional such as, "What would you like me to watch for?" or "When

Table 11.5 Psychotropic medications by class with side effects

Group by Use/Indication	*Common US Agents* *Generic Name (Trade Name)*
Anxiolytic Medications/ Antianxiety Medications	**Antihistamines**
	Diphenhydramine (Benadryl)
	Hydroxyzine HCl (Atarax)
	Hydroxyzine Pamoate (Vistaril)
	Benzodiazepines
	Alprazolam (Xanax)
	Chlordiazepoxide (Libritabs, Librium)
	Chlordiazepoxide/amitriptyline (Limbitrol)
	Clonazepam (Klonopin, Ceberclon)
	Clorazepate (Tranxene)
	Diazepam (Valium, Dizac)
	Lorazepam (Ativan, Loreev XR)
	Oxazepam (Serax)
	Herbal products
	Ashwagandha Root
	Cannabinoid
	Passion Flower
	St. John's Wort
	Miscellaneous
	Buspirone (BuSpar)
	Propranolol (Inderal)
Antidepressant Medications	**Monoamine Oxidase Inhibitors (MAOIs)**
	Isocarboxazid (Marplan)
	Phenelzine (Nardil)
	Selegiline (Eldepryl, EMSAM)
	Tranylcypromine (Parnate)
	Selective Serotonin Reuptake Inhibitors (SSRIs)
	Citalopram (Celexa)
	Escitalopram (Lexapro)
	Fluoxetine (Prozac, Sarafem)
	Fluvoxamine (Luvox)
	Paroxetine (Paxil, Brisdelle, Pexeva)
	Sertraline (Zoloft)
	Serotonin Norepinephrine Reuptake Inhibitor (SNRIs)
	Desvenlafaxine (Prestiq, Khedezla)
	Duloxetine (Cymbalta, Drizalma)
	Venlafaxine (Effexor)
	Tetracyclic Antidepressants
	Maprotiline (Ludiomil)
	Mirtazapine (Remeron)
	Tricyclic Antidepressants
	Amitriptyline (Elavil)
	Clomipramine (Anafranil)
	Desipramine (Norpramin)
	Doxepin (Adapin, Sinequan)
	Imipramine (Tofranil)
	Nortriptyline (Aventyl, Pamelor)
	Protriptyline (Vivactil)
	Trimipramine (Surmontil)
	Miscellaneous
	Bupropion (Wellbutrin, Zyban)
	Ketamine (Ketalar)
	Nefazodone HCL (Serzone)
	Trazodone (Desyrel)

(Continued)

Table 11.5 (Continued)

Group by Use/Indication	*Common US Agents* *Generic Name (Trade Name)*
Antipsychotic Medications/ Neuroleptics Medications	**Atypical Antipsychotics**
	Aripiprazole (Abilify, Aristada)
	Asenapine (Saphris, PERSERIS, SECUADO)
	Clozapine (Clozaril, Fazaclo, Versacloz)
	Ilopoeridone (Fanapt)
	Lurasidone (Latuda)
	Olanzapine (Zyprexa)
	Paliperidone (Invega)
	Quetiapine (Seroquel)
	Risperidone (Risperdal)
	Ziprasidone (Geodon)
	Conventional Antipsychotics
	Chlorpromazine (Thorazine)
	Fluphenazine (Prolixin)
	Haloperidol (Haldol)
	Loxapine (Loxitane, ADASUVE)
	Perphenazine (Trilafon)
	Pimozide (Orap)
	Thioridazine (Mellaril)
	Thiothixene (Navane)
	Trifluoperazine (Stelazine)
Attention Deficit/CNS Stimulant Medications	**CNS Stimulants**
	Amphetamine/Dextroamphetamine (Adderall, Mydayis)
	Dexmethylphenidate (Focalin)
	Dextroamphetamine (Dexedrine, Detrostat, Liquadd, ProCentra)
	Lisdexamfetamine Dimesylate (Vyvanse)
	Methamphetamine (Desoxyn)
	Methylphenidate (Daytrana, Methylin, Metadate, Ritalin, Cotempla, QuilliChew, Quillivant, Jornay, Adhansia, Aptensio, RELEXXII, Concerta)
	Selective Alpha2-Adrenergic Adjunctive Therapy
	Clonidine (Catapres, Kapvay)
	Guanfacine (Tenex, Intuniv)
	Miscellaneous
	Atomoxetine (Strattera)
Antimanic Medications Mood stabilizers	**Anticonvulsant Medications**
	Carbamazepine (Tegretol, Carbatrol, Epitol, Equetro)
	Divalproex sodium (Depakote, Stavzor)
	Gabapentin (Neurontin, Horizant, Gabarone, Gralise)
	Lamotrigine (Lamictal, Subvenite)
	Topiramate (Topamax, Quedexy XR, Topiragen, Trokendi XR)
	Valproic Acid (Depakene)
	Miscellaneous
	Lithium Carbonate (Eskalith, Lithobid)

Table 11.5 (Continued)

Group by Use/Indication	*Common US Agents* *Generic Name (Trade Name)*
Sleep Aids/Hypnotic agents	**Benzodiazepine medications** Estazolam (ProSom) Flurazepam (Dalmane) Quazepam (Doral) Tasimelteon (Hetlioz) Temazepam (Restoril) Triazolam (Halcion) **Herbal products** Cannabinoid/CBD Catnip/Nepeta cataria Chamomile Hops/Humulus lupulus Lavender/Lavandula Melatonin Passionflower/Passiflora incarnata Tryptophan Valerian root **Over-the-Counter Medications** Dimenhydrinate (Dramamine, Driminate) Diphenhydramine (Benadryl, Nytol, Sleepinal, Sominex, Banophen) Doxylamine (Unisom) **Miscellaneous** Butabarbital (Butisol) Doxepin (Silenor) Eszopiclone (Lunesta) Ramelteon (Rozerem) Secobarbital (Seconal) Suvorexant (Belsomra) Zaleplon (Sonata) Zolpidem (Ambien, Zolpimist, Edluar, Intermezzo)

Disclaimer: This chart does not represent all currently available medications and supplements. The counselor should consult with the prescriber for any issues related to the client's medication or suspected/potential adverse events. The information in this table was compiled from a variety of sources, including Physicians' Digital Reference (PDR; www.pdr.net/drug-summary;), the Food and Drug Administration (www.fda.gov/media/77381/download; www.fda.gov/media/76700/download; www.dbsalliance.org/pdfs/medication_charts/BPmedication_chart.pdf), Brunton et al. (2011), Foster (2007), and Awang (2009).

would you like me to provide a verbal report to you regarding any effect I may notice?" or "Are there any compliance issues you would like me to be aware of or assist with regarding our shared client?"

Occasionally, medical professionals will ask mental health professionals for input regarding medications they have seen to be effective with clients with similar issues to the one under consultation. Counselors may offer an opinion when asked but must steer clear of assuming any roles belonging to the medical professional and not to the counselor (e.g., counselors do not instruct medical professionals regarding what or how they should or should not prescribe medication or conduct other actions belonging to the medical profession). Furthermore, occasionally the counselor may be aware of prescriptions, over-the-counter medications, or other altering substances (illicit or otherwise, such as alcohol, drug, or herbal remedy) that the client is consuming. A report of such behavior can be critical and should be made to the medical professional when known (King & Anderson, 2004).

Counselors can be critical components of effective medical treatment when working in collaboration and consultation with medical professionals. That said, there are clear limitations to the counselor's role. Most important, counselors must never assume the roles or responsibilities of the medical profession. Counselors do not alter, in any manner, the regimen outlined for the client (King & Anderson, 2004). Counselors do not prescribe any substance (medical, herbal, or otherwise). Counselors do not instruct clients to begin or end medical treatments or to adjust dosages or timing of medical practices. Rather, counselors support the medical regimen as outlined by the medical professional. Should the counselor note a need for medical intervention (side effects, negative drug interactions, or any other medically managed issue), the counselor makes an immediate referral to the medical professional, sends the client to the emergency room, or calls emergency services as the situation warrants. The counselor never acts in the role of the medical professional. Use Self-Assessment Activity 11.4 to begin thinking about psychopharmacology as it relates to counseling.

Self-Assessment Activity 11.4 Psychopharmacology

1. Think about the kinds of symptoms and side effects you might notice a client exhibiting. How do you determine when to contact the medical professional for collaboration? How do you determine when to act more urgently, such as sending the client to the medical professional's office, the emergency room, or even more emergent services such as calling for an ambulance?
2. Practice with a fellow student counselor role-playing a conversation you might have with a medical professional regarding a client who is exhibiting excessive and uncomfortable side effects. How can you make your conversation conducive to collaboration? How can you demonstrate your respect for the medical professional's expertise and role while being helpful and advocating for your client?
3. Suppose a medical professional has just prescribed medication (Alprazolam) for your client presenting with anxiety. Your client explains to you that she is bothered by excessive tiredness and periods where she doesn't feel as "sharp" as she typically does. What might your role as her counselor be in supporting the medical regimen prescribed as well as supporting and assisting your client?
4. Suppose your client has talked to her medical doctor, who has suggested she begin a course of Duloxetine (Cymbalta). Your client is apprehensive because she worries about side effects of the medication. How can you educate her about the potential side effects she might experience? How can you assist her in making a decision regarding compliance with the medical doctor's regimen? What must you avoid doing to act ethically?
5. Your client who is diagnosed with bipolar disorder has been taking Gabapentin (Neurontin) for three weeks. He is threatening to stop taking it entirely and informs you he has missed today's dose. He is doing this because he has experienced diarrhea since beginning it. What would you do to assist your client in being compliant with the medical regimen as outlined by the prescribing professional?

Psychological, Educational, and Vocation Assessment

Meghan spent her 11:00 hour with her client, Kevin, reviewing the results of the life planning assessment and information for Kevin. The assessment included a structured interview, observations, client report, review of Kevin's academic record including current transcripts, Myers-Briggs Type Indicator results, Strong Interest Inventory results, and World of Work review in medically related areas. Meghan has conducted this assessment because Kevin has indicated that the greatest source of his current near-debilitating anxiety is his uncertainty about his academic and career future. They determined together that it would be helpful to assess his interests and personality to determine potential occupational goals to give direction to, and motivation toward, his educational pursuits. Assessment is an ongoing role of the counselor.

Humans spend much of their lives assessing. No matter what the situation may be, humans gather data, consider it, organize it, and construct meaning from the data, which is then used to determine the course of action to be taken. Counseling practice requires an organized means of assessment that involves defining the question, gathering data related to the question from as many sources as reasonably possible, organizing the data and looking for consistent patterns, determining meaning of the patterns, and making recommendations regarding courses of action given the conclusions drawn from the assessment process. Three areas of assessment in which counselors are often involved (conduct or refer for formal assessment) are psychological, educational, and vocational. An overview of the assessment process and a brief examination of each area comprise this section.

The counselor begins the process of assessing the client from the first moment of contact. The astute counselor gathers observations, client report, histories (e.g., social, emotional, medical, educational), reports of others (concerned teachers, spouses, parents, children, coworkers), records (scholastic, medical, past counseling), and many other sources of assessment data to both formulate an assessment question and respond to the question with as much accuracy and helpfulness as possible Erford, 2021). Most assessment questions center around one or more of three main areas, including the client's psychological functioning, intellectual and educational capacities and achievements, and vocational interests and capacities.

Psychological assessment involves gathering data and developing summaries of the client's mental well-being, including personality, cognitive, behavioral, and emotional states (current functioning) and traits (general long-term functioning). In addition to the data sources listed earlier, the counselor may formally assess the client using interviews (structured and unstructured) and psychological tests.

The interview can vary from little structure with more open-ended guidance to a detailed set of questions intentionally chosen by the counselor to assess a particular area of functioning or specific history. A common interview used for over half a century is the mental status examination (MSE), which is often conducted during the first interview. The MSE assesses general appearance, attitude, activity level and quality, mood and affect, speech and language, thought process/content and perception, cognition, insight, and judgment. It provides structure that can lead to the diagnosis in addition to a general understanding of the client's level and style of ffunctioning (Erford, 2021). A very brief and structured mental status examination is the mini-mental state examination (Folstein et al., 1975), which assesses for basic memory, cognitive process, and content issues.

Most psychological tests are standardized; they have structure that details the way in which the test is administered, scored, interpreted, and otherwise used. Most have norms for defined populations that assist the assessor in accurately determining what tests are appropriate to employ given the client's demographics, the question being addressed, and the outcome desired. Most psychological tests require particular education and supervised training of the assessor. Psychological testing can be categorized as projective or nonprojective. Projective tests have little directive stimuli to elicit the client's unconscious thoughts, feelings, or actions. Examples include the Rorschach, the House-Tree-Person, or Sentence Completion tests. Nonprojective tests have more obvious structure that directs the client toward the desired area to be assessed. Examples include the Minnesota Multiphasic Personality Inventory-2, the Beck Depression Inventory, and the Myers-Briggs Type Indicator (Erford, 2021; Gladding & Newsome, 2018).

Educational assessment refers to data gathering and summation regarding the individual's levels of knowledge, aptitude, capacities/limitations, interests, and beliefs. School counselors spend a significant portion of their time participating in the process of educational assessment. Educational assessment involves achievement and ability tests such as the American College Testing Program Assessment (ACT), Scholastic Aptitude Test (SAT), Graduate Record Examination (GRE), or Miller Analogy Test (MAT) for entrance to various levels of educational programs. Education assessment can be specific to educational issues such as the improvement of instruction, which is the goal of the Iowa Tests of Basic Skills (ITBS). Another common form of educational assessment is various states' high stakes testing to determine if students meet levels of knowledge and application required for graduation. The counselor's role in educational assessment can vary greatly from simply proctoring tests, to conducting in-depth observations and testing, to assisting in assessing students' learning disabilities. Time is spent on interpretation and application with students to set goals, plan, motivate, promote the development of self-knowledge, and increase confidence in students as learners. In addition to aptitude and achievement, school assessments include interest, career maturity, and personality inventories.

Vocational assessment is the category containing the example of Meghan and Kevin noted earlier. Clients bring to counseling various issues relating to vocational struggles ranging from unemployment due to downsizing at midlife, to confusion regarding good fit of career choices at high school graduation, to difficulties in retirement planning and adjustment. Literally hundreds of assessment tools are available related to vocational guidance. Those that are most common are listed in Table 11.3 (Career Assessment Tools). General categories of vocational assessment include academic skill, aptitude, interest, intelligence, learning style, occupational skill, personality, transferable skills, and values.

For each type of assessment, the process is consistent. The client and counselor work together to determine the type of assessment needed via a clear statement of the issue at hand. The counselor works with the client to determine the appropriate assessment strategies to employ including both tests and non-test means of data collection. The counselor uses those strategies that the counselor is competent to administer and interpret and seeks assistance from, or refers to, qualified professionals where the counselor is not educated and/or trained to act. The counselor diligently works to gather a well-rounded and complete set of data related to the defined issue. Data is synthesized so that potential answers can be formulated to address the defined issue. The counselor incorporates client feedback and input to ensure that the synthesis has produced accurate results fitting to the client, whether it be a DSM diagnosis, clarity regarding educational preparation, or a list of occupational choices that might fit the client. The counselor and client work together whenever possible to determine the action to be taken related to the assessment results, and the counselor assists the client in taking those action steps toward a successful outcome regarding the issue.

All along the assessment path, the counselor remains adherent to professional ethical standards and uses a healthy decision-making model consistent with beneficence and nonmaleficence. The counselor never provides any service beyond the scope of the counselor's education and training without supervision fitting to the level of ethical practice. Critically important to ethical practice is the adherence to the practice of informed consent for assessment; appropriate distribution and retention of results with written release of information when any information is disseminated beyond the client or immediate treatment team within the assessing agency; careful and fitting selection of assessment tools; conditions of assessment administration in accordance with both ethical practice and standardization of specific testing tools; and finally assessment security, keeping assessment tools protected from all inappropriate use or availability (ACA, 2014).

Furthermore, the counselor-as-assessor must be mindful of diversity issues. The counselor must select assessment tools particularly fitting to the purpose of the assessment, ensuring availability of appropriate norm groups for comparison, maintaining awareness of cultural limitations or insensitivity of tools that may impact the client or the accuracy of the summations from the data gathered, and being ever mindful of the impact of assessment on the relationship between the counselor and client (ACA, 2014). Table 11.6 presents the process of assessment with a sample application. See Self-Assessment Activity 11.5 to reflect on your assessment skills and use Case Study 11.3 to practice them.

Self-Assessment Activity 11.5 Counselor-as-Assessor

1. What assessment tools are you aware of that are available for your use as a counselor?
2. What are your current skills in using each of these assessments?
3. How might you go about securing increased skills/abilities in using these tools?
4. What are your ethical responsibilities as a counselor conducting assessments?

Table 11.6 Assessment process with sample application

Stage of Assessment	Activities	Sample
1. Orientation	Meet the client, discuss rights of the client and limitations of service as well as fee structure and other policies, build rapport, discuss issue, background, and client's focus.	Sue meets with Jim, a client who, at the recommendation of his boss, is seeking assessment of his depression symptoms that have persisted since his wife passed away following breast cancer approximately two years ago. She reviews her disclosure statement and explains the process of assessment to Jim, who understands and agrees to work with Sue and complete a formal assessment. Jim shares his marital history, the period of his wife's illness, and her subsequent death. He states that he has never been an outgoing person and thinks he is probably okay—just not as extroverted as his wife was making him seem. He does divulge his decline following her death and is concerned that he may be clinically depressed, even though he is functioning well at work and with his grown children.
2. Construct the question(s)	Formulate the questions to be answered by the assessment. Get specific and concrete. Ensure accuracy with client to ensure buy in and client rights.	Sue and Jim discuss Jim's and the boss's concerns and determine that Jim could be assessed to determine if his withdrawal from activities is due to a treatable depression or due to his introverted personality that is more prominent now that his extroverted wife is not there to drag him out of his shell.

Table 11.6 (Continued)

Stage of Assessment	Activities	Sample
3. Select the assessment tools	Review appropriate available tools for assessment and select those most fitting to the client's demographics, issue, and assessment question(s).	Sue determines that the Beck Depression Inventory (BDI-II) and the Myers-Briggs Type Indicator (MBTI) are useful tests to employ in addition to a detailed structured interview with an embedded mental status examination. She and Jim agree that an interview with his two grown children who live locally might also prove helpful.
4. Administer the assessment tools	Administer chosen assessment tools to client, ensuring appropriate testing conditions and following the protocols and procedures of the standardized instructions of each tool.	Jim attends two appointments for his assessment. The first appointment involves an interview with mental status examination for the first 45 minutes and 30 minutes shared with his two adult children. The second session includes both the MBTI and BDI-II.
5. Score, interpret	Follow all protocols and procedures for scoring and interpreting test results as provided using appropriate norm groups for comparisons. Organize results to discover themes and important outcomes.	Sue scores the MBTI and the BDI-II and interprets them according to the manuals. She summarized the interview results from both Jim and his adult children and finds themes in each.
6. Write report	Organize themes and outcomes in structured report concisely and clearly while avoiding professional jargon and unnecessary redundancy.	Sue organizes the results of the testing and the interviews as well as her own observations and writes a detailed, organized report concluding that Jim's testing results do indicate introversion as well as a low level of depression symptoms. She further supports these findings with reports of both Jim and his children that he is functioning well at work and in family gatherings, is keeping his home in good repair and cleanliness, and appears to be enjoying his solitary activities when not with family or at work.
7. Share report with client	Summarize report and highlight important outcomes with the client, avoiding jargon or complicated language to ensure client understands what you have concluded. Seek input from client regarding conclusions and integrate feedback the client provides in disagreement. Adjust as appropriate.	Sue shares the results with Jim, who states his agreement with the findings. He expresses a desire to branch out a little more in his activities than he has been over the past two years and discusses with Sue the option of seeking a few sessions of counseling to work on increasing his activities and contacts with others in a social setting to make his world a bit more fun. Sue includes in her report the recommendation that he may find benefit in counseling to that end.

Case Study 11.3 Casey

Casey is a 16-year-old 10th grader at the local high school. He is an excellent student, a better than average athlete, and vice president of the sophomore class. His mother has insisted that he come to see you after noticing that Casey has become somewhat irritable and withdrawn the last couple of months. Casey has refused to talk with his mother about his struggles, but he has consented to meet with a counselor. He tells you at your first meeting that he thinks he is going crazy because he feels like he is pressured all the time to do things perfectly. He says he feels anxious all the time and cannot sleep at night. He reports being distracted in class and at basketball practice. His symptoms began after a basketball trip with the juniors and seniors (he is on the varsity team) during which time several of them complained about their workloads, college applications, and their pressures to go to college and/or get jobs. Casey came home upset stating he had no idea what he could possibly study in college or what he wanted to do career wise. Both Casey and his mother want an assessment to see if his anxiety and sleeplessness are as severe as his mother perceives and to assess what he might focus his activities and studies on to prepare for college and his future.

Write up an assessment, following the "Sample" section of Table 11.6, based on your capacities and understanding of the process of assessment. What are the areas for which you are not yet educated and trained, considering this case? What can you do to become prepared?

The "Business" of Counseling: Third-Party Payers

The last hour of Meghan's day is spent ensuring all paperwork regarding her workday has been completed. Some of the paperwork completed by counselors promotes quality care, some paperwork documents ethical treatment, and some satisfies the requirements of organizations that pay for the services provided to the client. These organizations (e.g., private insurance companies, government programs, managed care agents, employee assistance programs) are known as **third-party payers**. Third-party payers tend to be diligent guardians of their funds and insist on particular protocols to ensure their clients are receiving necessary care aimed at resolving the issues that led to the need for care or for adequate services that make for the least expensive maintenance for long-term issues.

Private insurance companies make up a large number of third-party payments. From individuals to large corporations, private insurance companies contract to collect premiums from their patrons in return for a guarantee that certain types of health services will be paid for by the insurance company up to a designated amount. Although mental health services have not always topped the list of those services generally covered, most insurance companies now do provide mental health benefits. Recent laws have required that insurance plans serving more than 50 employees provide coverage for mental health services in accordance with the rates of physical health coverage. The federal law providing for this action, the Wellstone-Domenici Mental Health Parity and Addiction Equity Act (MHPAEA), was passed by Congress in 2008 and was enacted initially in January of 2010 and fully in January of 2011. State laws vary, but many require the same parity of plans serving fewer than 50 employees (American Psychological Association, 2010).

Private insurance companies often utilize structures such as PPOs (Preferred Provider Organizations), which require services be provided by panel members or "preferred providers." To become a preferred provider, counselors must complete an application; provide documentation of their education, training, and capacities; and sometimes serve a particular niche the insurance company believes necessary in the counselor's geographic region. Counselors not on provider panels may be allowed to provide services at a lesser reimbursement rate. The rate of payment and number of sessions allotted are generally defined by the policy or plan, and insurance companies keep careful track of "going rates" (average amount charged in an area for counseling services) as well as number of billed sessions. Some insurance companies will consider extending the number of sessions allowed via an appeals process—especially when the appeal documents a savings of funds in the long run. Finally, some insurance companies require preauthorization of services and will not pay for services rendered outside said contract.

Several legal changes have been enacted to extend health insurance coverage to people unable to garner insurance through employment and to include mental health and substance abuse treatment as part of the health care benefit. The 2008 Mental Health Parity and Addiction Equity Act (MHPAEA) incorporated coverage for addiction treatment as well as general mental health care, and the Affordable Care Act (ACA) aimed to extend benefits to more people and included ten categories of services within health insurance. Mental health services were one of the ten categories covered under ACA. It is estimated that a total of 62 million people will see a gain in coverage for mental health and substance abuse care as a result of the interaction of MHPAEA and the ACA (Frank et al., 2014).

With the electronic age, billing services have shifted from handwritten bills sent directly to the client, who might then submit the tab to the insurance company for re-imbursement, to hand-completed forms the counselor submitted to the insurance company for payment, and often now to electronic payments submitted online with payment systems, including automatic deposits, and emailed explanations of benefit (EOBs). Many services are now available for counselors in private or group practices or agencies that wish to have another party complete their billing to both clients and third-party providers.

Several government-run and funded programs function much like private insurance, including Medicare, Medicaid, Labor and Industry Benefits (L&I), and Victims' Compensation. Medicare is a federally funded program that began in the 1960s providing insurance for the aged, blind, and disabled. Medicaid is a similar program with joint federal/state funding extending services to those with financial need regardless of age. Presently, publicly funded insurance programs (Medicare) only reimburse master's-level counselors for mental health services under particular circumstances and not under others for which other mental health professionals (e.g., psychologists, psychiatrists, social workers) are reimbursed (Medicaid, 2011). Thanks to the efforts of the American Counseling Association, active house and senate bills are under consideration to extend said reimbursement to services by counselors. The inclusion of mental health counselors for Medicaid programs varies by services and differs from state to state. The future inclusion of counselors at both state and federal levels provides professional advocacy opportunities. In any case, both federal and state programs provide detailed parameters for the practice and billing of mental health providers as well as a process by which said professionals become Medicare certified. Medicare- and Medicaid-approved fee schedules are markedly lower than most insurance companies and lower still than most private practitioner fees. Certified providers agree to take these fees as full payment (they "take assignment"; Terry-McElrath et al., 2011).

The institutions of Medicare and Medicaid and the growing number of insurance programs offering mental health coverage increased the global costs of mental health services. In response to these escalating costs and resulting concerns, the Health Maintenance Organization Act (HMOA) of 1973 was passed to assist in cost containment while ensuring quality of care. The act required that employers offer managed care alternatives to employees and made available federal money for the development of managed care programs. The impact of the HMOA has progressively grown, and a boom of managed care companies arose in the 1990s and remain a primary factor influencing mental health care today (Gottlieb & Cooper, 2000).

Labor and Industry (L&I) and Crime Victims (CV) are two other government-sponsored third-party payers. L&I provide payment for counseling services to those who have been injured on the job when those services are warranted in relationship to the injury or when those services are deemed necessary for reentry into the workforce. CV is a program intended to assist in amending the psychological harm created via crime on its victims. In many cases, the perpetrator of the crime is required to pay into the system, and CV pays for services to the victim to assist in recovering mental health to precrime levels. Counselors with expertise in each area may contract with L&I and/or CV to become providers of mental health services to these populations.

Employee assistance programs (EAPs) are another method by which organizations are attempting to keep costs contained and mental health services available. Some organizations create their own in-house EAP programs, whereas others contract with independent counselors for services through which employees can seek limited assistance with issues ranging from stress to marital issues—each of which may have an impact on the employee's productivity. These services are typically included in employee benefits or offered at very low rates. Most EAPs provide referrals to outside providers for concerns that extend beyond the limited number of sessions allowed or the scope of practice defined for services within the EAP (Gladding & Newsome, 2018). Use Self-Assessment Activity 11.6 to reflect on issues surrounding third-party payers

Self-Assessment Activity 11.6 Third-Party Payers

1. What ethical dilemmas can you foresee facing as a counselor working within the policies and procedures of third-party payers?
2. How will you ensure quality of care when a client's insurer limits care to a number of sessions you believe are too few, given the client's presenting issue?
3. What are at least five third-party payers you could consider if you were involved in assisting someone with very limited resources in securing mental health services? List the specific resources particular to your area.
4. What challenges might you face in making the business end of a counseling practice work efficiently?

Summary

The activities comprising the role of the counselor have grown tremendously over time. Most counselors now have complex duties, including providing consultation, career guidance, academic advising, advocacy, medical or psychopharmaceutical compliance support, and assessment, as well as business practices with third-party payers. It is critical that counselor preparation include a basic understanding of these activities as well as a foundation for practical application. To review, each role is briefly summarized.

The **counselor-as-consultant** provides service to a broad range of consultees who seek expert advice, opinions, or information. The counselor-as-consultant gathers data to ensure that the consultation provides accuracy and current best practices for the consultee to consider. The consultee then determines what services will be provided to yet a third party, or target. The consultant may provide assistance to the consultee in creating an action plan for implementing the decision. Finally, the consultant evaluates the effects of the consultee's actions.

The counselor provides **career guidance** as needed throughout clinical practice, given that career development is a lifelong process. Seminal works in career guidance provide the foundation for assisting clients through the process of career development. These works include the early trait and factor work of Frank Parsons, Ann Roe's psychodynamic career theory, Donald Super's five-stage theory, and John Holland's personality theory of occupational choice, as well as the more recent work of Krumboltz's Social Learning Theory, McAuliffe's and Peavy's constructive development theory, and the systems approach of Patton and McMahon. Many tools have been developed based on these theories to assess clients' needs from, preferences for, and matches to various potential careers.

A facet of career counseling includes **academic advising**. In this role, the counselor assists the student is ensuring success through planning and preparations in selecting a direction and the course of study to meet that direction. Additional academic advising activities include psychoeducation and skill building such as time management and communication skills as well as testing strategies and study habits. Counselors may also assist students in creating job shadowing, volunteer, and service opportunities that enhance career maturity.

Counselors have acted as **advocates** for the disenfranchised and suffering since the beginning of the counseling profession, with a particular emphasis in assisting others in finding their voice. Over the decades, counseling advocacy has grown to include not only social justice issues, but also advocating for the counseling profession itself. Indeed, the standards set for professional education and training make clear that counselors must act on behalf of both clients and the profession to promote human development. Such advocacy has resulted in major changes, including actions to allow counselors positions within Veterans Administration facilities, recent enactment of parity laws, and laws for counseling licensure in all 50 states.

Counseling advocacy has also grown to include having a voice for clients undergoing **psychopharmacotherapy** to ensure effective compliance with the medical professional's regimen and to keep the medical professional apprised of the client's condition. The counselor must understand the basic structures and functions of the brain, its neurotransmitters, and intertwined endocrine and peripheral nervous systems. The counselor must also know the desired and potentially harmful effects of medications prescribed to treat the various symptoms experienced by the client. To be effective in this supporting role, the counselor must build respectful relationships with medical professionals and exercise effective communication with clients, significant others, and the medical professional.

Counselors continually engage in informal **assessment** as they consider the client's symptoms, issues, and desired outcomes of counseling. Formal assessment tends to center around three main areas, including the client's psychological functioning, intellectual and educational capacities and achievements, and vocational interests and capacities. When conducting formal assessment, the counselor is clear regarding the question at hand, the process of gathering data related to that question from as many sources as reasonably possible, the organization of the resulting data into patterns, the determination of meaning or themes of those patterns, and the making of recommendations for a course of action. When psychological tests are employed as part of the assessment process, counselors carefully adhere to the standardization procedures required of each tool. Counselors use the least invasive protocols and sensitivity to the needs of the client and tend to issues of confidentiality, client rights, and the fit of testing procedures given issues of diversity.

Finally, the role of the counselor involves the **activities of business**—particularly those involving third-party payers. Third-party payers are those organizations, such as insurance companies, government programs, managed care agents, and employee assistance programs, that pay for the services provided to the client. Counselors need to understand the structure and function of third-party payer organizations to become allowable and payable providers and to meet the requirements of each organization, including payment systems, record keeping, types of services covered, preauthorization for services, and limitations of coverage.

The counselor's role is varied and complex. Understanding each facet of the counselor's workday requires a solid foundation of knowledge and skill as well as dispositions conducive to the successful practice of counseling. The counselor who stays abreast of the current professional literature will likely find the role of counselor expanding as the profession continues to address the needs of our diverse and changing society.

12

Counselor Self-Care

Kerry Thon

Preview

Up until this chapter, the focus has been on your relationship and interactions with clients, how to provide outstanding services, and how to get the most out of your practicum and internship. In these final two chapters, the focus shifts and is now squarely on you as the counselor-in-training, with needs and goals. This chapter reviews the importance for all counselors to have an effective self-care plan to help prevent burnout and to deal with the stressors inherent in the counseling field. Clinical supervision allows you to seek advice and consultation from experienced counselors, just as you might seek knowledge from others in your life who have gone before you. This can assist you in sidestepping common pitfalls and mistakes made by beginning counselors and provide much-needed support as you come to the limits of your competence. Your self-care plan is much like your protective gear, which can help you weather the storms as you navigate through your first counseling experiences. Many professionals have tools of their trade that they need to keep in tip-top shape. As counselors, we are our own best therapeutic tool, so we have an obligation to keep ourselves in shape mentally, physically, and spiritually. Be mindful of the parallel process that happens with stress and wellness. What you learn about stress and wellness applies to not only your clients but also yourself. This chapter will highlight areas to focus on as you create your own self-care plan, but let's first explore stress and its effects.

Stress and the Helping Professions

As I was writing this chapter, I was reminded yet again of the importance of taking care of oneself. This reminder came late one night after I had been writing for several hours in a café. Toward the end of the night the server came by and suggested that I take a break to stretch. Here I was writing about self-care and at the same time ignoring my body signs that I needed a break. The irony of the situation was not lost on me. I decided to heed his advice and felt much better for taking the time to engage in a few self-care practices. Reminders to take a break for our own self-care are all around us. A self-care plan is not just for counseling students; rather, it is a critical tool for all counselors that needs to be reviewed and revised on a consistent basis.

Becoming a counselor is an exciting and rewarding adventure. And, just like other journeys and adventures, you must prepare yourself to get the most out of your experience. When traveling I try to anticipate what I may need on my journey, so I read up on the locale, gain insights from others who may have traveled there, and pack appropriately for the climate. This is similar to your clinical training in that your classroom knowledge has prepared you with basic clinical tools and skills that you will hone on this journey, but it is always important to keep learning about the population you are serving.

The helping profession is filled with, well, helpers. Some of the personal characteristics of those interested in helping others make them excellent candidates to become counselors. Interestingly, these same characteristics also put those helpers at risk for burnout, secondary trauma, and compassion fatigue.

It is critical for counselors, and counseling interns, to understand themselves as a person if they are to grow into competent counselors. Understanding your strengths, areas for improvement, and triggers allows you to know what you are bringing to the counseling session and to better assess your own level of functioning. Counselors are certainly not immune to bad days, relationship troubles, or difficult life situations. It is almost always easier to work on someone else's life, but we also need to apply what we teach to ourselves. There have been many times where I have been working with a client, and the ideas being discussed could easily be applied to my own life. Coming up with a self-care plan is not just for those in counseling; it is a necessity for everyone.

DOI: 10.4324/9781003305521-12

We should not be asking our clients to do anything that we ourselves are not willing to do. Take some time to explore your relationship with stress by completing Self-Assessment Activity 12.1.

Self-Assessment Activity 12.1 Stress

- Rate yourself from 1 to 10 (10 being the highest level of stress and 1 being the lowest) regarding how stressed you are feeling in your current life situation. Take the time to jot down what factors you took into consideration when identifying this number.
- Gain an understanding of what triggers stress for you: What life circumstances tend to create the most stress for you (e.g., financial stress, frequent life hassles versus major life stressors, interpersonal conflict)?
- Explore how stress affects your mind, body, and spirit. When you are stressed:

  - What thoughts tend to pop up?
  - What body reactions do you notice (e.g., tight shoulders, headaches, getting run down and sick)?
  - What influence does this have on your mood (e.g., increased irritability, depression, anxiety), and how you express your emotions (e.g., emotionally shutting down, unable to contain emotion)?
  - Which areas of your life do you focus on the most? The least? Does this help you or just lead to avoidance?
  - Do you tend to neglect your own well-being to ensure other aspects of your life are taken care of? How does this help you? How does this hurt you?

Our Obligation to Help Ourselves

All counselors have an obligation to take care of themselves. If you are not at your best, then you will be less likely to be present and focused for your clients. By taking care of yourself, you are taking care of your best therapeutic tool. As a graduate student, you are often pulled in many directions and play a multitude of roles. Your student role may be taking up a significant amount of time, and along with other possible roles of employee, partner, parent, friend, and so on, you may find that you have a limited amount of time to focus on yourself. It is often tempting to put off your own self-care so that you can meet all the other needs around you. As difficult as it may be to take time for oneself, it is a wise investment. You can only put off your own self-care for so long before you feel the effects physically, emotionally, and spiritually.

When talking about stress management to counseling students, their reaction sometimes is, "Yeah, right, like I have time for exercise or meditation when I'm working, going to school, and taking care of a family." This reaction implies that self-care is a luxury, not a basic need. Finding balance among our life roles is quite difficult, and we all struggle at times to maintain it. There are periods of time when I am successful at setting limits with work and making sure to balance other aspects of my life, and then there are other times when I am putting in many hours of overtime and neglect my personal time. The key is knowing when one area of your life is taking over and you are starting to lose balance.

I see similarities between my need for self-care and when my cell phone battery starts to die. The battery icon on my phone will change colors as it loses power; and when it reaches a certain color, I know I had better plug it in or I will lose use of the phone altogether. This is much like what happens with my body when I am feeling stress, although it is unfortunate our bodies don't come with battery icons. I guess in many ways our bodies do give us warning signs that we are out of balance, such as when we feel the aches and pains, or when we succumb to a virus due to a compromised immune system. Your body can handle only so much, and if you don't recognize the signs, you will lose energy and functioning, much like your cell phone when it has not been properly charged.

In counseling, we may educate our clients about how their seemingly unimportant decisions and the "slippery slope" can contribute to them going down an unhealthy path. It is important to remember this when it comes to our own self-care. Oftentimes we make unhealthy choices, smaller choices that we don't think will have a significant impact on us. Making one decision to stay up later results in less sleep, which then affects the way you feel the next day, further affecting your decision to work out that next morning. The cycle of poor choices may then contribute to other poor choices throughout the day, eventually resulting in unhealthy habits and patterns in the long run.

As helpers, we may put others' needs before our own, but to assist others we need to have something to give them. It is also important to practice what you preach. If you don't have an active self-care practice, then you won't be able to use it when you really need it. One day while working in a high-end residential treatment facility, I was heading back to my office after an especially difficult meeting about budget cuts and billing quotas when I unexpectedly ran into a client. She stated that she needed to see me right away, which was typical for this client. I explained that I really needed a few minutes to myself and that I would check on her after that. I went into my office and started to use my coping skill of deep breathing. After about three deep breaths I heard a voice coming from the other side of the door saying, "You're doing a great job with your breathing!" My client had followed me to my office and had been listening to me engage in this self-soothing technique. My well-engrained coping skill not only helped decrease the amount of stress I was feeling, but it also provided an impromptu role-modeling opportunity.

Helpful Models for Understanding Stress

Stress is a natural part of life but left unmanaged it can become quite destructive. Hans Seyle (1974) defined "stress," a term that is now widely accepted, as "the nonspecific response of the body to any demand upon it" (p. 6). In other words, regardless of cause, the body will respond and attempt to cope with the demands placed on it to restabilize. Cannon (1929) coined the term homeostasis, which refers to the body's drive to return to a previous level of usual functioning after changes are detected. We are constantly making adjustments physiologically and emotionally to deal with outside forces, which highlights our keen adaptive and regulatory abilities; however, when we respond to a perceived threat for a prolonged period of time, we can experience mental and physical illness (Goldstein & Kopin, 2007).

Although stress can have deleterious effects on our mental and physical health, not all stress is unhealthy and leads to distress. Seyle's (1974) term, eustress, describes a more positive psychological response to a stressor, which is often associated with higher levels of hope, energy, and a sense of meaningfulness when coping with that stressor (McGowan et al., 2007; Nelson & Cooper, 2005). All change to an organism or system involves some level of discomfort or stress, even when the changes are positive or could lead to growth. It requires an evaluation of the stressor, as well as our ability to manage it effectively. Lazarus's (2006) cognitive-transactional model referred to this phenomenon as the appraisal of demands, in which we assess whether or not the demand is threatening to our well-being. If it is deemed threatening, then we conduct an assessment of the resources we possess to meet this demand. Distress results when we have determined the demands to be greater than our resources. Our interpretation of both the demands and our resources plays a significant role in whether or not we experience the negative psychological response of distress

As you begin your clinical experiences, you may be faced with significant demands that have the potential to lead to distress or to significant personal and professional growth. Lazarus and Folkman (1984) posited that when one assesses that they have adequate resources to manage the given demand, one will appraise the demand as a challenge and not as a threat. Whereas appraising a demand as threatening can lead to a high arousal state, appraising a demand as a challenge allows you the opportunity to grow from the experience and leads to a more positive emotional response.

Identifying Personal Stressors

In counseling programs, we stress the importance of viewing the counselor as not only a professional, but also a person who inherently brings with them to the counseling session all their own unique characteristics and experiences. As competent counselors and counselors-in-training, it is essential that we understand and recognize our personal stressors and the effects they are having on us in the moment. Counselors are certainly not immune to the same types of personal stressors with which we are often assisting our clients. We too may be dealing with our own interpersonal stressors with family, friends, and significant others. We are also subject to life events that are beyond our control, as well as daily hassles such as getting stuck in traffic, losing items, and technology problems.

Just as you would assess a client at the onset of counseling, so should you assess yourself on the current personal stressors you are dealing with and how they may be affecting your overall functioning. Being able to honestly evaluate your level of functioning in all areas of your life is a skill that needs to be practiced at length. Venart et al. (2007) identified several important areas for counselor self-care, including physical, cognitive, emotional, social, and spiritual domains. In the next section we will explore each of these dimensions. As you explore each dimension of health, identify any stressors that you have in this area and think about the influence this has on your overall functioning, as both a person and a professional counselor. Identifying possible strengths and resources you have that can assist you in dealing with stressors in this area is also important. As previously mentioned, it is not necessarily the demands that are placed upon us, but rather our interpretation of whether we have the resources to manage those demands, that determines our level of functioning.

Coping With Personal Stressors—Dimensions of Health and Intervention

Once you have assessed your personal stressors and resources, then you need to put your coping skills into action. While in fourth grade, I was in a play called *The GIGO Effect.* GIGO stood for "garbage in, garbage out." Although my only detailed memory of the play is one of an embarrassing dance number, the underlying principle has always stuck with me. This simple concept of what we put into something is directly proportional to what we get out has been invaluable to me both personally and professionally. I have used this concept with numerous clients to illustrate their progress, or lack thereof, in counseling. We often want significant change in our lives without making much personal effort. Just as it is improbable that our clients will make change without effort, we as professional counselors cannot expect to be fully functioning without putting effort into our own self-care. If you find you are lacking in resources in one area or are not using the resources you already have, then you may want to explore the effect this has on your well-being in this particular area, as well as your overall functioning. Use Self-Assessment Activity 12.2 to begin this exploration.

Self-Assessment Activity 12.2 Personal Stressors

- Think about what you have been "putting" into yourself, as both a person and a professional. Where have you been spending your time and energy? How might this affect you in your role as a counselor?
- Next, create a list of your personal stressors and resources. Based on your assessment of the stressors and your personal resources, do you find the stressors to be threatening or challenging?

For any personal stressor you find threatening, determine what resources may need to be gained to turn this threatening demand into an opportunity for growth and learning.

Counselor Self-Care

Many students take on clinical experiences like they would any other class, but there are specific demands related to clinical experiences that make it especially difficult. Up until now you have only read about or practiced your counseling skills with fellow students or volunteers. The pressures of working with real clients, as well as the additional hours in your schedule, can take its toll on your overall health if you are without an adequate self-care plan. As you review the following areas of self-care, think about how you might apply the GIGO effect to each area. As you take on additional responsibilities within your clinical experiences, think about what you are putting into each of these areas.

Physical Self-Care

Taking care of your body is essential in managing stress and maintaining adequate self-care. Schafer (2000) highlighted daily exercise, healthy eating habits, and adequate sleep as necessary tools to help your body ward off both physical and emotional stress and illness. Although this probably does not come as much of a surprise to you, it is interesting how these aspects of self-care are often neglected. Although simple to understand, it is often difficult to implement, and these basic tools for physical self-care are the first to go when other demands are competing for your time and energy. When you have school, work, and family obligations, it is tempting to stay up late to finish projects, grab fast food on your way to your internship, and skip your physical exercise routine because there just aren't enough hours in the day. Unfortunately, the first areas to be sacrificed when we are overworked and overscheduled are the areas that are most crucial to our own mental and physical well-being. In the long run these healthy activities make us more productive, less fatigued, and less susceptible to burnout. It would be wise to invest time in creating a realistic plan for how you are going to meet your basic physical needs. Try creating a schedule where you first input these key basics into a self-care plan, and then work in your other obligations. Making them a priority can be a difficult transition from your current schedule, but it may be the only way for you to ensure that they are met. Self-Assessment Activity 12.3 to take a close look at how you are handling your physical self-care.

Self-Assessment Activity 12.3 Physical Self-Care

- On a scale of 1 to 10 (10 being the best), how would you rate your overall physical self-care?
- What efforts have you been putting into regular physical exercise?
- What efforts have you been putting into getting adequate sleep?
- What efforts have you been putting into maintaining a healthy diet?
- As you evaluate each area of physical self-care, identify one small action you would be willing to commit to that would make an improvement in that area. These are some examples:

    - *Physical exercise routine*: Take a midday walk break a couple of times a week, take the stairs at work, during commercials do squats/sit-ups/jumping jacks, or other exercises. Although it would be beneficial to have a consistent exercise routine, you can still make progress one step at a time. It is not necessary for you to go immediately from leading a sedentary life to working out five days a week. Any activities you add to your routine is progress.
    - *Adequate sleep*: Again, you don't have to go to extreme measures if you are a late-night person. Just try going to bed ten minutes earlier than you normally would and keep moving that up until you reach your target bedtime. Being a late-night person, I could come up with a million excuses why it is difficult to get to bed earlier, but in the end if it is negatively affecting me, then I have to make the choice to change or to deal with the effects of maintaining the same unhealthy behaviors.
    - *Healthy diet:* This could include drinking more water, eating a healthy breakfast, cutting down on fast food, swapping out one junk food option for nuts, berries, or a healthier snack, skipping dessert 1–2 x/week, and so on. Again, think about small steps that you can build on. It is unrealistic to think you could go from eating fast food frequently throughout the week to cooking all your own meals with organically grown foods every day. If it were that easy, you would already be doing it.

Voices From the Field 12.1 Lack of Self-Care and Lorna Doones, *by Nicole Bradley*

After completing my master's degree in community counseling, I began working full time with children and adolescents at a community mental health agency. I was ecstatic to have found a job close to home and to begin working only weeks after graduation. Previously, I had spent years working with children in multiple non-counseling capacity, including day cares, direct care in a residential treatment facility, a center for autism, and school settings. As I tried on the role of professional counselor, I was excited and eager to continue my work with children and use the skills I had worked hard to cultivate over the past two years.

In addition to working with children, self-care had also always been a priority for me; I had been a runner since the age of 11 years, maintained supportive friendships, and was always conscious about eating healthy. Despite my attempts to take care of myself, I was not prepared for how emotionally draining counseling could be.

A year and a half into my first counseling position, I was beginning to feel burned out. I was not running as much as I typically had, I was working through lunch, regularly eating the Lorna Doone cookies that I kept in my office, and experiencing guilt about going home to a safe home, where I had food, heat, and clean clothes and knew that no one would hurt me. Thankfully, I recognized that I wasn't pulling on my healthy coping skills and began to make changes in my life. I look back now and reflect on what a valuable learning experience this was for me.

To overcome the stresses of my counseling job, I created rituals. I committed myself to running with my friends a few days a week—as I had previously done—and asked them to help me be accountable to this commitment. To facilitate focus at work, I began taking my lunch breaks that I had gotten into the habit of skipping. In addition, not only did I take my lunch break, but I would also call a friend or leave the office area to help take my mind off work and my clients. Finally, probably one of the most important changes that I made was the creation of a daily routine to leave my work at work and not bring it into my personal life. Each day before I left the office, I would stand in front of my door after locking it and say to myself out loud,

"I am leaving it here until tomorrow." I found that having that concrete behavior at the end of my day really helped me transition into my personal life in a healthier way. Now did it *always* work? No! But it significantly decreased my emotional stress, and it helped me to set a work–home boundary. At present, I work clinically and teach master's-level counseling courses. I make sure to continue to engage in these self-care strategies as well as others, and I actively promote the importance of self-care to my students.

Cognitive Self-Care

The area of cognitive self-care relates to our ability to identify and manage our own self-talk, as well as our ability to organize our thoughts and make decisions. As counselors, often we are aware of the importance our cognitions have on our emotional and behavioral reactions. This is the basic tenet of cognitive-behavioral therapy: Our interpretations of events, not the events themselves, influence the way we feel and then react. Accurately assessing situations and our abilities to manage them is part of our cognitive self-care. Take a moment to complete Self-Assessment Activity 12.4 and reflect on the points in Think About It 12.1 and 12.2. Throughout your career, you will be faced with ethical dilemmas, but during your clinical experiences you may be faced with them for the first time. You also will begin to recognize the expansive gray area of ethics.

Self-Assessment Activity 12.4 Cognitive Self-Care

- Identify distorted cognitions or negative self-talk that limits your daily functioning. What influences do these distorted cognitions or negative self-talk have on you? Becoming aware of these distortions is a key step to stopping them.
- Identify healthy and realistic cognitions and self-messages that you can use to replace the more negative self-messages. How can healthy and realistic cognitions help you deal with stressors related to practicum and internship?

Think About It 12.1

While in graduate school, I wrote myself a support letter in anticipation of difficult times. This letter identified my strengths, empathized with potential issues my future self might face, and encouraged me to keep going even when things got difficult. You may find it useful to write a supportive letter to yourself that can help ease distress you may feel throughout your clinical experience.

Think About It 12.2

Check out www.counseling.org/docs/default-source/ethics/practioner-39-s-guide-to-ethical-decision-making.pdf and review the *Practitioner's Guide to Making Ethical Decisions*. Having a clear understanding of how to make difficult decisions can help ease the pressure when you find yourself in an ethical dilemma. It is critical for all student counselors to be able to identify at least one ethical decision-making model that they are comfortable using before they graduate. This will be your go-to model when faced with an ethical dilemma. As with theoretical orientations, it may be your beginning practice model that may change as you put it to the test with real-life clinical situations. The key is to have at one model that fits with you already in place before ethical dilemmas arise.

Emotional Self-Care

Managing emotions, those of your clients as well as your own, is crucial for all counselors. Oftentimes beginning counselors are not prepared when they are triggered by their client's emotional responses. Working with adolescents with emotional and behavioral issues has taught me a significant amount about managing intense emotions. It is a matter of when, not if, you will be triggered. The ability to manage your own feelings of anxiety, anger, fear, frustration, helplessness, and shame is essential in the counseling relationship. We are less capable of sitting with our clients' emotions if we are already overwhelmed by our own. Later we will review the idea of personal counseling for the counselor, which may be especially helpful for counselors who have a history of depression, anxiety, or personal trauma, but all counselors need an outlet to maintain their emotional self-care. Just as we would promote healthy emotional expression with our clients, we too need to find a healthy balance between shutting down emotionally and becoming emotionally saturated. Use Self-Assessment Activity 12.5 to reflect on the state of your emotional self-care practices.

Self-Assessment Activity 12.5 Emotional Self-Care

- How do you typically manage intense emotions you may be experiencing? Do you shut down or feel it so intensely that you become immobilized by the emotion?
- Which emotions tend to be most difficult for you to manage?
- How might you manage intense emotions (your own and others') within a counseling session?
- Although it is important to have a certain amount of comfort being in the presence of emotion, how might you assist a client to manage the intensity of their own emotions?

Social Self-Care

Interpersonal connections are crucial in managing stress. Assessing your own social roles and expectations will be beneficial during your practicum and internship. If you can gain an accurate assessment of all your personal and professional roles and obligations, you will be better prepared to balance all these roles. Maintaining healthy and supportive social connections will be key throughout your journey as a counselor. Just as we would encourage our clients to seek positive social connections to serve as a buffer to life stressors, counselors too can benefit from strong interpersonal relationships to help them deal with stress and prevent burnout.

Gaining and maintaining social connections are a priority. So are skills related to boundaries such as setting limits and learning when to say "no." This can be especially difficult as we wear many personal and professional hats. As your role of student and beginning practitioner intensifies, you may feel the demands of your professional connections, as well as feel strain on your personal connections. Use Self-Assessment Activity 12.6 to examine your resources for social self-care.

Self-Assessment Activity 12.6 Social Self-Care

See Figure 12.1, the social connections wheel, and respond to these questions regarding social self-care.

- Identify the roles and obligations you have in each area. Feel free to add additional social connections.
- Rate each area: 1 = few or no demands, 10 = intense level of demands.

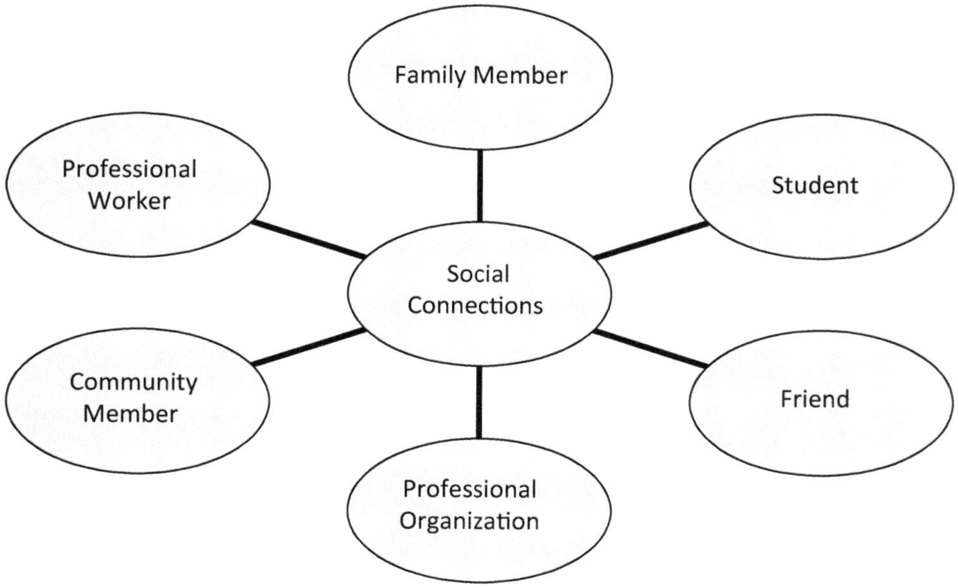

Figure 12.1 The social connections wheel

- After reviewing this wheel, which area is most demanding of your resources (e.g., time, energy, money) at this time?
- If there is a need to balance these areas, what is one small step you can take to make that happen?

Spiritual Self-Care

Myers and Sweeney (2008) originally placed spirituality at the center of their Wheel of Wellness as the most important contributor to well-being. Although not supported empirically to be the epicenter of well-being, it remains a critical aspect of wellness. Exploring and connecting with our spiritual self is one way to be present and mindful in our everyday lives. Maintaining a mindfulness practice enhances our spiritual and emotional self-care practices. Greason and Cashwell (2009) found connections between mindfulness and counseling students' ability to fully engage and be present in the counseling session. In this study, students were less focused on doing counseling than they were on just being present with their client. This also allowed them to be more tolerant of intense emotions within the session. Attuning to our spiritual center can assist in being genuine and nonjudgmental in a session, as we are less likely to be overly attached to the thoughts and emotions that are evoked throughout the session. Many counseling theory books do not cover issues of spirituality in depth, but Jones-Smith (2014) included an entire chapter in her text on counseling theories due to the increased focus on the significance of this life domain.

Jones-Smith (2014) holds the view that "spirituality influences the way that people interpret their experiences and make meaning out of life" (pp. 451–452). Exploring the influence that spirituality may have had on one's purpose and meaning in life, as well as how one perceives the world and themselves in it, would be a valuable exercise for all counselors. Robertson (2010) makes a clear link between spiritual and religious beliefs and one's overall mental and physical well-being, which is helpful as we discuss tools to enhance counselor wellness, but this also has important implications for how we counsel clients. Having cultural competence in the spiritual and religious realms will become ever more present in counselor education and training, and the counseling field. If this is an area of wellness that you have never nurtured or have recently neglected, here are some ideas on how to connect to your spiritual self:

- Start a meditation practice.
- Practice being mindful in everyday activities (i.e., cooking, eating, cleaning, walking a pet).
- Take up yoga or tai chi.
- Connect to a spiritual or religious community.
- Spend more time in nature.
- Use prayer or mantras.
- Take time to explore your spiritual journey and purpose in life.
- Attend a kirtan or chanting group.
- Read poetry, books, or articles or watch movies that stimulate your curiosity of spiritual matters.

You cannot make excuses and progress at the same time, so now is the time to get started on your self-care plan. Now see Figure 12.2, where you will find a form to assist as you begin creating your own self-care plan.

I. Demands and Resources: Identify all the stressors or demands you are experiencing in each domain. Then identify all resources and strengths you have that will assist you in meeting the demands. Based on your assessment of the demands/resources ratio, check the box of whether you view the demands on this domain as a threat or a challenge.

Domain of Self-Care	Demands	Resources/Strengths
Physical		
Threat		
Challenge		
Emotional		
Threat		
Challenge		
Social		
Threat		
Challenge		
Spiritual		
Threat		
Challenge		
Cognitive		
Threat		
Challenge		

Figure 12.2 Your own personal self-care plan!

II. Choose one domain that you would like to focus on first. Please complete the next chart based on this domain. Which domain did you choose? ______________________

III. Identify a large, overarching goal that describes which domain you have chosen to work on. Then create two to three more specific objectives that will result in you making progress in your overall goal. Finally, identify specific and measurable interventions that will lead to achieving your objectives. See the example here for a model. Remember—think small steps!

The plan in the example states that by increasing the amount of exercise and eating a healthy diet, the person will achieve the goal of improving one's overall level of physical health. If your objectives don't meet the overall goal, then they should be changed. Once you are sure your objectives will meet your goal, then make sure your interventions have a reasonable chance of meeting your objectives. This is the checks and balances of treatment plans. What you are doing here is creating a treatment plan for yourself, but this format can also be used with clients. Now, it's your turn . . . choose a domain and get started preparing your wellness plan!

Self-Care Plan Example

Large Goal #1: *To improve the overall level of physical health.*

Objective 1: *To increase the amount of physical exercise.*
Intervention 1: *Will take the stairs at work at least 3 out of 5 workdays.*
Intervention 2: *Will go for a walk during lunch at least 2 out of 5 workdays.*

Objective 2: *To maintain a healthy diet.*
Intervention 1: *Will plan out weekly meals every Sunday for the following week.*
Intervention 2: *Will have a nutritious breakfast 5 out of 7 days.*

My Self-Care Plan

Large Goal #1:

Objective 1:
Intervention 1:
Intervention 2:
Intervention 3:

Objective 2:
Intervention 1:
Intervention 2:
Intervention 3:

Objective 3:
Intervention 1:
Intervention 2:
Intervention 3:

Recognizing and Avoiding Burnout

Burnout has become a hot topic in recent years, and you can find many workshops on combating the symptoms and signs of burnout and compassion fatigue. When it comes to burnout, prevention should be the goal, not treatment. We often wait until there are already signs of a problem and then react with a treatment response. Instead of actively working to avoid burnout, we spend time trying to counteract the negative physical and emotional effects it has already had on the individual, as well as the surrounding systems. Primary prevention is a central concept in community psychology, and this approach argues the benefits of taking a more proactive stance, rather than treating emerging or already existing problematic symptoms (Moritsugu et al., 2019).

The human services field in general is conducive for stress and burnout reactions. Counselors may face intense billing and budget pressures, long hours, high caseloads, ineffective policies and procedures, and lack of appreciation. Obviously, there are many reasons why counselors join and remain in the field, but it is important to recognize the most typical stressors that plague the counseling and human services field. Recognizing and targeting organizational factors is one way to intervene before burnout sets in, but it may also be necessary to address individual factors such as your own personal characteristics and motivations for joining the field. Just as knowing how your work culture plays a role in burnout and then taking action to prevent it can be beneficial, so too can assessing ways to intervene on a personal level.

Taking the potential stressor of "counseling being a thankless job," let's address this on a personal level. It is important to know that you will not always receive confirmation that you are doing a good job or see the progress you were expecting with clients; therefore, it can be helpful for you to prepare for those rough patches when you are questioning your effectiveness. Many beginning counselors equate clients doing well with their counseling skills. They often fail to realize that treatment ebbs and flows, and clients often take one step forward and two steps back. If you solely rely on your clients' progress as an indicator of your skill as a counselor, you will be quickly disappointed and discouraged. Further, it can be highly detrimental when we are overly invested in our client's progress as a way to validate ourselves as a counselor, rather than for the sake of our client. Some counselors may overidentify with being a helper and may risk having their clients become dependent on them to serve out their role. The American Counseling Association [ACA] (2014) is clear in its ethical guidelines that counselors should safeguard their clients' ability to be autonomous. One question I consistently ask myself as a counselor, as well as a question I ask supervisees, is whose needs are being met? If the answer is not your client's needs, then you will need to reassess what is happening in the counseling session. Self-Assessment Activity 12.7 will help you identify whether you are facing burnout and alert you to some of the related issues.

Ways to manage our personal reactions to clients and our own issues with competence, fear of failing, and desire to help are all worthy topics to explore in supervision. Even if we are aware that our impatience with lack of client progress is our own personal issue, we still need to learn how to manage it. I often tell supervisees that they are planting the seeds for growth in their clients even if they aren't there to witness the end result. Although this can be frustrating, I find it comforting to know that at some time in the future my work with the client will grow into something beneficial and positive for them. I know there have been times when a client quickly progresses, and in part this may be due to the hard work of another clinician, and I just happened to be there when the client finally reached the goal. Savoring the small moments can lift you up and keep you going during times of discouragement. I always found it ironic that during really difficult days when I was contemplating whether or not I was really having an influence on the system, I would receive a call from a previous client who wanted to share with me their progress or to tell me about the impact I had on them. Those moments remind me why I continue to do this work and how special it truly is when others allow you to take part in their personal journeys.

Self-Assessment Activity 12.7 Recognizing Burnout

- Go to www.proqol.org and take the ProQOL (Professional Quality of Life Questionnaire).
- Take a burnout quiz: You can find a free burnout quiz at www.mindtools.com/stress/Brn/BurnoutSelfTest.htm . Christina Maslach's burnout assessment is available for purchase at www.mindgarden.com/products/mbi.htm.
- Assess and improve your time management skills. Lack of effective time management skills can lead to increased stress and burnout. The Mayo Clinic provides numerous suggestions on how to improve your ability to manage your time at the following website: www.mayoclinic.com/health/time-management/WL00048. Instead of trying to make too many changes at one time, they suggest you choose one technique and practice it for a couple of weeks. You should determine whether or not this technique has been effective and should be continued. Once you have embraced the technique, then you can start adding additional techniques.

Vicarious Trauma, Compassion Fatigue, and Secondary Trauma

The term *burnout* is often interchangeably used with secondary trauma, vicarious trauma, and compassion fatigue, leading to confusion for counselors on what they are experiencing. There are several key differences among these terms, which are important to note so you can gain an accurate understanding of what you are experiencing. These differences relate to type of onset, the cause of the condition, and the effects on the counselor. Whereas burnout and compassion fatigue come about more progressively, the onset of vicarious and secondary trauma tends to be more immediate (Newell & MacNeil, 2010). Let's review the similarities and differences between vicarious trauma, compassion fatigue, and secondary trauma.

Vicarious traumatization, a term credited to McCann and Pearlman (1990), relates to one's exposure to trauma and disrupts one's frame of reference in one of five core areas: safety, trust, esteem, control, and intimacy. Vicarious traumatization targets the counselor's belief systems and self-concept and focuses on the cognitive changes that occur within the counselor as a result of empathic interactions with traumatized individuals. We develop our self-concept over time as we make assessments about the world and our place in it. When a counselor experiences vicarious traumatization, self-concept and overall belief systems change, greatly affecting a counselor personally and professionally. We open ourselves up when empathically engaging with our clients and let the trauma in as a way to assist our clients. When this negatively impacts the way we view the world, then we are experiencing signs of vicarious trauma. Some examples of cognitive shifts that can occur include viewing the world as basically unpredictable and unsafe, others as untrustworthy, and yourself as incompetent.

As a case example, Ann is a 28-year-old, single counselor who is working with Jane in an outpatient clinic. Jane has been diagnosed with PTSD after being sexually assaulted. Both Ann and Jane are similar in age, race, SES, and even live in nearby neighborhoods. As Ann works with Jane on her trauma, Ann notices some differences in the way Ann has been thinking. Perhaps due to their similarities, Ann started to think that everything Jane was talking about could also happen to her. As Ann leaves work, she is suspicious of males around the facility and in her neighborhood. She starts to view the world as more dangerous and less predictable, which alters the way she reacts to her environment. It did not take prolonged exposure to the trauma for Ann to experience these symptoms. She is not feeling burned out or exhausted, nor is she experiencing actual symptoms of PTSD like her client, but her worldviews have been significantly altered. If you were Ann, what do you think you should do as you noticed the cognitive changes?

Vicarious traumatization and secondary traumatic stress have similarities but have distinct manifestations. Vicarious traumatization focuses on the cognitive changes that occur after direct work with those who have been traumatized, whereas secondary trauma manifests itself in the behaviors, in particular symptoms of PTSD. Vicarious traumatization and secondary traumatic stress may occur independent of one another, or a counselor may both experience a shift in their cognitive process and exhibit behavioral symptoms of PTSD (Newell & MacNeil, 2010).

Early in my career I worked with a therapist who was struggling in her work with traumatized individuals. She began experiencing symptoms of both vicarious and secondary trauma, although I did not have a full understanding of these concepts at the time. She began to struggle with her own intimacy with her partner, became hypervigilant, and began to view the world as being unsafe and full of potentially threatening situations. The work she was doing had changed her cognitive schemas, and she also began to report symptoms of PTSD such as hypervigilance, nightmares, a disconnection from others, and avoidance of trauma stimuli. This last symptom greatly impacted her ability to counsel her clients, as she was more avoidant of trauma-related material in sessions, and she more readily allowed her clients to avoid this issue due to her own discomfort. She ended up leaving her position at the facility because of the effects that trauma work had on her.

Now, not all counselors experience vicarious trauma or secondary trauma even though they may do intense trauma work, but it is imperative that if signs are noted that they be addressed early. I do wonder whether or not there would have been a different outcome with my colleague if she received the support and supervision she desperately needed at that time, instead of people perhaps thinking that trauma work was just not for her. There is risk in counselors just assuming something is wrong with them if they notice these changes, so talking openly in supervision about changes in cognitive schemas or experiencing PTSD symptoms is imperative. Many times, both new and experienced clinicians suffer in silence, as there is shame associated with these experiences and fear that others will view them as incapable.

Another related term is *compassion fatigue*, which is like burnout in that it develops over time. As counselors we are not just exposed to our clients' suffering, we become a container for it. Working with trauma day in and day out takes great amounts of empathy, and this can take its toll on the counselor's well-being and lead to fatigue. Figley (2002) identified cognitive, emotional, and behavioral effects of the chronic use of empathy and being overexposed to the suffering of one's clients. Cognitively, counselors may have trouble concentrating, apathy, increased negativity, and decreased self-esteem. Counselors may begin to feel helplessness and powerlessness, guilt, depression, and emotionally drained. These cognitive and emotional effects may lead to sleep disturbances, impatience and irritability, and somatic complaints (Berzoff & Kita, 2010).

Being cognizant of factors that put one at risk for compassion fatigue is critical to prevention. Craig and Sprang (2010) found that having a high percentage of one's caseload dedicated to clients with PTSD and not using evidence-based practices as significant indicators for compassion fatigue, whereas significant indicators for burnout were "younger age, having no special trauma training, having an increased percentage of individuals on the caseload with PTSD, being an inpatient practitioner, and not using evidence-based practices" (p. 334). Talking from my own experience as a counselor working with trauma, I would agree that these indicators can lead to negative effects on counselors. We don't always have control over our caseloads when we work in agencies, but it would be wise to make sure your supervisors are aware of the concepts described if you are frequently dealing with traumatized clients. Making supervisors aware of the potential effects may result in redistribution of caseloads, or at the very least will ensure that everyone is aware of the possible cognitive, emotional, and behavioral outcomes of this type of work.

Make sure to seek supervision, as well as consultation with other colleagues, if you notice any cognitive, emotional, or behavioral changes in yourself. As you begin your practicum or even when you start out as a new professional, you may not have all the tools you need to treat your clients, which may lead to the symptoms of compassion fatigue, vicarious trauma, or secondary trauma. If you will be working with traumatized individuals, then seek specific trauma trainings, learn about evidence-based practices, and attend related professional development opportunities. The more you know about trauma and how to treat it, the more prepared and less overwhelmed you will be when working with your clients. It is also helpful to seek consultation on the therapy process. Many new professionals start to question their professional abilities if clients are not making progress.

By talking to other professionals about the therapy process, you may be able to combat unrealistic expectations of the therapy process, which could have damaging effects on your sense of professional competence. If you are noticing symptoms of PTSD as a result of the work you are doing, then you should consider seeking professional counseling, as well as talking to your supervisor to find ways to assist you in the workplace.

So why in the world would any counselors want to do trauma work if they have all these potential problems to look forward to? Well, first, not all counselors experience these negative effects, so make sure to invest in your prevention efforts so that you limit your risk. Compassion satisfaction might also be a reason for doing this work for many counselors. This refers to the satisfaction one gets from helping others (Bride et al., 2007). Personally, I have found trauma work to be intrinsically very rewarding. You are assisting clients as they work through intense suffering. They are allowing you to come along on this incredible journey of healing. The intensity of the work can be overwhelming, draining, and yet so very rewarding for both you and your client. It is the intense satisfaction that you get from doing meaningful work that has a direct positive impact on another's life.

Common Sources of Stress for the Beginning Counselor

Lack of Delegating

Learning what to delegate to others when you are first beginning your internship can be difficult. You are often the one to whom others delegate and not the other way around. Having an accurate understanding of your skills in time management and problem solving will help you delegate. Knowing how long it takes you to accomplish tasks is vital when planning projects, as is effectively communicating to your team the resources you will need to complete your tasks and projects. There may be times when it is not feasible to complete all your assigned tasks, so taking initiative to find alternative solutions such as delegating will be much appreciated by your supervisors. Taking on whatever tasks are given to you may seem like a great way to be a team player, but this only works if you can realistically accomplish all the tasks.

Difficulty With Boundaries

Many counselors underestimate how difficult it will be to maintain healthy boundaries. Going into graduate school, I held a pretty dichotomous view of ethics where situations were either black or white, right or wrong. Do not have sex with clients . . . check. Don't break confidentiality . . . got it. Although there are obviously clear-cut examples of ACA *Code of Ethics* violations, most situations will be varying shades of gray that are not always so simple to decipher. Even with the example earlier with not having intimate relationships with clients, the ACA *Code of Ethics* (2014) has guidelines for this behavior, and it is not an all or nothing as many would assume. Hopefully your legal and ethical issues graduate course will shed light on the legal, ethical, and moral complexities of the counseling profession.

Sometimes, unsuspecting interns go down the slippery slope, eventually finding themselves smack dab in the middle of a boundary violation and not knowing exactly how they got there. Terms such as *SUDs* (seemingly unimportant decisions) are used when working with clients with sexually problematic behaviors or those in recovery from substance abuse. This concept can also be applied to the boundary violations of counselors. The small, seemingly unimportant decisions that we make can lead us down a path that is fraught with ethical dilemmas and boundary violations. Each small decision leads us either closer to or further away from high-risk situations and therefore is quite important in the long run. It is equally important to remind counselors-in-training that some boundary violations result from an immediate lapse in clinical judgment and don't require a slippery slope.

When I work with clients with significant trauma histories, I often explore the three Ts: how they *talk*, *trust*, and *touch* others. This can help me assess issues with boundaries as they may talk, trust, and touch others indiscriminately due to poor, diffuse boundaries, or they may have become so rigid in their boundaries that they have difficulty trusting or connecting to anyone. Exploring the three Ts can also be helpful for counseling interns in assessing their own boundaries as they begin to practice. Think about the differences in how you talk, trust, and touch a romantic partner, a friend, a client, and a stranger on the street. You would treat them all differently. These areas reflect boundaries, physical and emotional, both in and out of the counseling session. When we start to treat our clients like we would a friend, family member, or significant other, we may be violating boundaries.

Supervision is a great time to explore small decisions you are questioning that may lead to larger ethical issues if left unchecked. This is also a time when you and your supervisor can explore any countertransference reactions you may be having related to these decisions. It is important to note that not all boundary violations are related to countertransference, and not all countertransference leads to boundary violations. Being open in supervision about the reactions you are having toward clients can be uncomfortable, as you want your supervisor to see you as competent, but countertransference reactions that are not openly explored about are more likely to be acted on.

Several types of boundaries need to be addressed in a counseling setting, such as physical boundaries, which tend to be easier to assess in terms of appropriate versus inappropriate, as well as emotional, generational, and time boundaries. Physical boundaries relate to how physically close we get to our clients and how close we allow them to get to us. It is important for counseling interns to understand cultural difference that may affect comfort levels related to physical proximity. I have had clients who wanted to give me a hug upon meeting me for the first time and others who sit many arm-lengths away. Negotiating physical boundaries can be uncomfortable, as you do not want to offend your clients if you prefer more distance, but you should trust your instinct and respect not just your client's comfort zone of physical closeness, but your own as well.

Some populations of clients struggle more with healthy, appropriate boundaries. You should know the population with which you are working and ask your supervisor to help you to anticipate possible situations that may come up at your internship site. A client's request for a hug may have an underlying meaning of which you are not aware. When looking at physical contact, I tend to assess my clients in the following areas: gender, age, length of treatment, the context of the situation, treatment issues, and treatment setting. I would assess the request for a hug differently from an 8-year-old client I'd been seeing for six months who just found out about a death in the family differently than with the 17-year-old male client with a history of sexually problematic behaviors with whom I have just started working. Every clinical setting will also have expectations related to physical contact with clients. Working in settings such as residential treatment facilities can make maintaining boundaries (physical and emotional) more challenging. You may see your clients frequently outside their therapy sessions as they wake up, go to school, in the hallway, in groups, and even as they get ready for bed. This obviously differs significantly from an outpatient setting where you only see your clients at their weekly therapy appointment.

Looking at countertransference reactions can be helpful when assessing for generational and emotional boundaries. Do you spend more time with a particular client? Do you share more personal information, or specific personal information, with a particular client that you wouldn't typically share with other clients? There may be times when you feel more protective of a particular client or have clients with which building a connection is more of a struggle. Acknowledging and exploring these reactions in supervision is beneficial to learn not only about your triggers, but also how to manage these reactions so that you are effective in therapy. Included in this area are time boundaries, which I've personally found to be the most difficult to manage and the most damaging to one's own self-care. Not being protective of your time and having an unhealthy work–life balance can contribute not only to the decline in self-care, but also potentially to further boundary violations. Robinson (2000) found that those categorized as workaholics were more likely to overcommit to the point of fatigue, resulting in being less productive than what he called *optimal performers*. Although those categorized as workaholics spent more time at work, they were less focused and capable of completing projects. This sounds like a similar result for workers who are experiencing burnout. I was told by a supervisor that human services would "suck you dry" if you let it. In a field where the demands significantly outweigh the resources, you will be called on to do more with less. As an intern you may be asked to take on additional tasks or to stay later than required to help an overly stressed system. This is the beginning of being "sucked dry," as you are asked to put in more and more until you have nothing left to give. It is our responsibility as counselors to learn what we can give and set healthy boundaries with not only our clients, but our employers as well.

This is another area where it is essential to evaluate yourself as a person and a worker. What role does work have in your life? What motivates you in your work role? Robinson (2000) defined typologies of workaholics and the implications for counselors, but what about when the counselor is the workaholic? His recommendations to moderate workloads, explore underlying work motivations, and incorporate time for social, leisure, and family activities into one's self-care plan seem fitting for all workers, including counselors. Use Self-Assessment Activity 12.8 to identify your own perceptions and strategies regarding boundaries.

Self-Assessment Activity 12.8 Boundary Issues

- Write out the three Ts (talk, trust, touch), and compare the ways you would treat clients, family members, romantic partners, friends, and acquaintances differently. Explore with your site any expectations they have regarding boundaries. Always bring up concerns with boundaries with your supervisor.

- Think about how you will handle a client trying to break generational boundaries. How might you answer if your clients ask you about whether or not you are married, have a significant other, or about other personal aspects of your life? We do not want to hide behind a professional façade and avoid being genuine with clients, but we do want to maintain healthy boundaries. How might you find a balance between these two when being asked personal questions?
- How can you use your self-care plan to manage time boundaries with your clinical experience and/or work setting?

Inability to Compartmentalize

The inability to compartmentalize our roles as a professional and person often come out in boundary issues as we allow one area of our life to influence the other. At times this may mean that our role as a professional impedes our personal roles. Often clinical supervision addresses issues of allowing your personal role to impinge on your professional role. At my previous place of employment, the term *detached concern* was used to communicate a need to maintain balance and boundaries. This term implied that as counselors we need to have genuine care and concern for our clients and their success in treatment, but there must be a certain amount of detachment so that we do not lose objectivity and perspective. If our personal needs play a significant role in our clinical decisions, then we risk losing objectivity. It can be difficult to enter fully into the world of another and then be able to pull back out without becoming overly attached. It takes practice and supervision, as I found out when I first started counseling and was drawn to a particular client who needed intense services. I found myself engaging in small boundary violations such as giving her more counseling time than other clients. Although treatment should be individualized based on the needs of the client, I was providing extended sessions more out of my enjoyment of spending time with this client and feeling personally rewarded by these sessions than by her need for additional services. I felt she was making progress, which made me feel good as a counselor.

In supervision I explored how I could manage my feelings of caring and concern for her well-being, address my need to feel competent in my role as counselor, and yet still maintain healthy boundaries. In the end, this experience was invaluable for me as a counselor, and I learned how to recognize when I was acting more out of getting my needs met than meeting the needs of my client. Reinforcing healthy boundaries also allowed me to show genuine concern for my client without connecting my worth as a counselor to her success in treatment. This is not a lesson that one learns once, never to be repeated. It involves a constant practice of self-examination.

Two additional areas of compartmentalization are (a) leaving work at work and (b) the inability to compartmentalize different aspects of living. Beginning counselors may frequently think about clients after they get home or have difficulty transitioning to other life roles. It can be helpful to find a transition ritual to signal a switch from a work to personal mode. Some ideas for a transition ritual include the following:

- Change out of your work clothes once you get home.
- Have a period of time to share about your day when you first get home. Once that time period is up, then it is time to move on to other roles.
- Engage in self-care activities on returning home (e.g., journal about your day, listen to soothing music, take a bath, engage in a preferred hobby) to de-stress.

Some counselors may not get the opportunity to engage in self-care activities when they return home because they are immediately thrust into their other role as parent or partner. If this is the case, then use your ride home to ease the transition. When I was living in Chicago, I had multiple routes I could take to get back home from work, but when I was a bit stressed, I always took Lake Shore Drive. This way my view included Lake Michigan, which I found to be very relaxing. Other times I would listen to specific music or a great audiobook so that I could immerse myself in another world. By the time I was home, I was ready to transition from my counselor mode into my personal mode.

Role Confusion

It is imperative that you know what will be expected of you at your practicum or internship site. Many sites will have orientation activities where you learn about your clinical site, but you can alleviate problems down the road by sitting down with your supervisor to ensure that you both have the same view of your role. Even with clear role expectations, you may be called on to complete tasks not in your job description throughout your clinical experience, which can result in role confusion and blurred boundaries. Some helpful areas to clarify before or as you begin your clinical experience include the following:

- Knowing the days and hours you will be expected to work, whether you will be on call, and the extent of internship hour requirements.
- A review of your primary job duties. Ask about whether you will be shadowing other counselors before taking on clients, whether your supervisor will be observing you in individual/group sessions, and your role when co-leading groups with other counselors.
- Identifying who will be your primary supervisor and other evaluators of your performance. Also, it can be helpful to identify anyone else on site who will be giving you tasks to complete or to whom you will be reporting. It can become confusing when you are asked to complete tasks for others who are not your supervisor, so clarify how they want you to handle this. At some sites, if other professionals would like your assistance, they must first go through your primary supervisor so that your supervisor is aware of all additional tasks that you may be working on.
- What if you should find yourself without enough work to do? I had one practicum student report that she was frequently asked to do non-work-related tasks such as cleaning out closets when she was done with other counseling duties. Although organizing therapeutic materials can be a job responsibility, this was not what she was being asked to do. Your primary role is as a student and assigned tasks should assist you in further learning about the field. Obviously, there may be times when you are asked to pitch in to assist with tasks that are less counseling-based, but this should not become a pattern. As you get settled into your internship, you may have your own ideas on projects you would like to work on. Being proactive and taking initiative is often appreciated by site supervisors, and this can also help avoid situations where you are assigned busywork to keep occupied.

Being All Things to All People

Ah, the superhero syndrome. For interns, this can be a challenging time as you put into practice all you have learned up until this point. Obviously, we all want to do well when our skills are being evaluated, so we may be tempted to take on additional tasks to demonstrate our competence or show vigor for the field. Knowing your skills, abilities, motivations, and limitations will be key in recognizing and managing any vulnerabilities to being all things to all people. What are the roles and commitments you have already taken on? What motivates you to take on tasks? How strong is your desire to please?

Feelings of Incompetence

When I was first starting out, I wanted there to be a structured manual on *How to be a Great Counselor*. I wanted to read the manual, put it into practice, and, voilà, be a great counselor. Unfortunately, becoming a competent counselor takes time and practice, and although there are helpful resources out there, you must work at it. All experienced counselors have struggled with feeling unsure of themselves at one point or another. In the beginning, I had several moments where I thought to myself, "Graduate school did not prepare me for this!" No amount of classroom experience can fully prepare you for the professional journey you are about to embark on, and many beginning counselors feel woefully underprepared as they begin to see clients. It can be helpful to take a few deep breaths and realize that your classroom experience was not a waste of time; it prepared you to critically think about your cases, and during your clinical experiences you will put that knowledge into action. It can be exciting when the interventions you have read about actually work with a real client. But even if they don't, you get the experience of having to adjust your methods or approach. This is why good supervision is such an essential part of your counseling education.

Nothing can bring out feelings of incompetence like an ethical dilemma. Beginning counselors tend to overestimate how much others know and underestimate their own abilities, which leads to beginning counselors doubting themselves. In their attempts to avoid appearing incompetent, some beginning counselors try to handle the ethical dilemma on their own. Seeking consultation and having a firm grasp on how to make ethical decisions can decrease the amount of distress you feel as you begin your work as a counselor. Knowing the steps to ethical decision making and who to turn to for support can prepare you for the inevitable situations that will come up in your internship and throughout your career. Counselors who are uncertain how to proceed when faced with an ethical dilemma and who feel unsupported can quickly become overwhelmed by the situation. Use Self-Assessment Activity 12.9 to begin to identify your own professional support system.

Self-Assessment Activities 12.9 Professional Support Systems

Identify your professional support system, making sure to identify the following types of support people:

- A peer who is at a similar stage of practice as you. This person may be best able to identify with the stressors associated with this stage of practice.
- An experienced, fully licensed counselor working with a similar population.
- An experienced, fully licensed counselor or legal advocate who can assist you in legal and ethical matters.
- A professional who is connected to a professional counseling association or other related professional organization. This person may be able to mentor you and get you connected and involved in professional opportunities within the field. This can lead to writing, teaching, and practicing opportunities in the future.

Personal Counseling

I am often asked my opinion by internship students about personal counseling. There is considerable debate in the field about mandating counseling students to undergo personal counseling as part of their core requirements, although there is consensus on the benefits of personal counseling for counselors. Here are a few assumptions that I have about those entering the counseling field:

- You think that counseling is beneficial and helps people overcome life struggles.
- You understand that going to counseling does not make you "crazy."
- You think those who seek help in dealing with their life struggles, or wanting to explore interpersonal and intrapersonal processes, are showing courage by reaching out for help.

Given these assumptions, it seems natural that counselors would be open to their own individual counseling. Engaging in your own treatment gives perspective as a client and provides an opportunity for personal growth and a pathway to work on personal issues that may affect your ability to be a competent counselor. A common question is, "Can you ask others to do what you have not done yourself, or are too afraid to do?" What are your reactions to this question?

Feelings of fear are common when deciding to enter into counseling, as it takes a considerable amount of courage to truly explore your inner world. I have heard from both counselors and clients alike that they fear they will fall apart if they engage in the counseling process. This is a legitimate concern, as most people do not feel like they have the time or ability to lose any amount of functioning, although, ironically, this can lead to avoiding significant issues resulting in a loss of functioning. For some, dealing with the surface symptoms without delving deeper is like the old adage "Ignorance is bliss." To be a competent counselor, it is important to know yourself as a person. Without this knowledge, you lack insight into your cognitive processes, emotional responses, and significant relationship patterns, which may make you less likely to recognize when you are being triggered in a session.

Whether or not you engage in your own counseling, it is your responsibility to explore how your life experiences affect the way you think and respond to the world. The ACA (2014) *Code of Ethics* clearly identifies practicing counseling while impaired as an ethical breach in conduct. The question is, how impaired do you need to be before you are no longer meeting ethical standards? As a counselor, how do you know when you have crossed the line? Although supervision can assist the counselor in determining when the line has been crossed, personal counseling allows the counselor an opportunity to explore the impairment or issues that may lead to impairment. Use Self-Assessment Activity 12.10 to explore your views about personal counseling.

Self-Assessment Activity 12.10 Personal Counseling

- What are your thoughts about requiring counseling for counseling students?
- If you were to go into counseling, what would your therapeutic work focus on?
- What issues or types of clients are most likely to trigger a countertransference reaction in you? How might you recognize and subsequently manage these reactions when they come up?
- How might counseling help you to become a better counselor?

Summary

By exploring your personal stressors, as well as strengths and resources in each of the wellness domains, you are well on your way to creating your self-care plan. Oftentimes we already know what needs to be done, yet we fail to make the desired changes or are unable to sustain the improvements we've made. People are often eager to make changes and may become overzealous in their goal setting without a realistic plan on how to maintain their progress. Other times they set lofty goals that are ideal, but difficult to achieve. Corey (2016) reviewed many theoretical approaches to goal setting, but one that I've found to be particularly useful is the solution-focused brief therapy's focus on "small, realistic, achievable changes that can lead to additional positive outcomes" (p. 381). By starting out with small goals, we are setting the foundation for future progress. These small incremental changes that eventually lead to larger goal attainments further support a successful outcome. Once we get a taste of success, we become more confident in our abilities, increasing our level of motivation. Feelings of empowerment can also result as we feel we have the resources needed to make healthy changes. The goal is to have a long, healthy career in the human services field and to avoid burnout, but first we must invest in our ability to take care of ourselves physically, emotionally, cognitively, socially, and spiritually.

13

From Envisioning to Actualization

Marketing Yourself in the 21st Century

Nicole A. Stargell and Jessica A. Headley

Preview

This final chapter addresses the importance of finding your place in the counseling market as a 21st-century counselor. The first part ("*Temet Nosce*") will address the significance of self-evaluation and reflection, utilizing the SELF acronym. The second part ("Understanding the Field Around You") will highlight current trends and opportunities in the field. The third part ("Securing a Job the Old-Fashioned Way") will cover the logistics of the job search and traditional self-promotion strategies. The fourth part ("Carving Out Your New-Age Niche") will outline how social media can be used to establish counselor identity and credibility. Finally, part five ("The Advantages of Continued Learning") will discuss how advanced training and postgraduate education can increase your marketing opportunities. Ultimately, the integration of information from all these sections will enhance your ability to promote yourself to potential employers and clients, giving you the edge you need to compete in the current professional market.

From Envisioning to Actualization: Marketing Yourself in the 21st Century

For mental health practitioners, the U.S. Bureau of Labor Statistics (2020, 2021) projects a relatively optimistic employment outlook, calling for favorable job opportunities in years to come. Although counseling services will be needed and valued in future job markets, Savickas (2012) asserted that "the new job market . . . calls for viewing career not as a lifetime commitment to one employer but as a recurrent selling of services and skills to a series of employers who need projects completed" (p. 13). In the postindustrial technology boom, the selling of services is now dependent on our knowledge of technology-based delivery methods and the use of the Internet as a marketing tool (Anthony et al., 2010), in addition to more conventional self-marketing strategies (e.g., print advertisements, face-to-face networking).

Temet Nosce

As the Latin phrase *temet nosce* goes, "know thyself." As counselors, if we are to market ourselves in a competitive economic and social climate, it is imperative that we understand who we are as helping professionals and the main strengths and skills that we can provide diverse employers and consumers. A developed understanding of your professional identity will enable you to select an environment that is personally and professionally stimulating and will be helpful to the individuals you will serve. This initial section will provide a simple way to examine the characteristics that define you as a counselor. We have devised the "SELF" acronym to guide you in this evaluation. The SELF acronym is composed of the following action areas: select your strengths; examine your values, biases, and beliefs; live with limitations; and formulate your counseling approach.

Select Strengths

Part of developing your professional network as a counselor involves identifying and being recognized for your professional strengths. If you can clearly communicate your strengths and interests to other professionals, you will be sought after for opportunities that allow you to use and promote your skills and talents. By *selecting*

DOI: 10.4324/9781003305521-13

and *developing* your strengths, you are then able to *sell* your strengths. Use Self-Assessment Activity 13.1 to begin assessing your strengths.

Self-Assessment Activity 13.1 Personal Strengths

Take a moment to reflect on your personal strengths and how they fit into the following framework. First, reflect on your basic strengths (e.g., rapport building, punctuality, thorough documentation). Next, reflect on the strengths that make you special or even unique. For example, do you have specialized training or certifications? Do you have extensive field experience? Third, reflect on the strengths you would like to further develop. You may ask yourself: Do I want to seek additional education? Do I want research experience? Last, devise some development strategies that you can employ to achieve these desired strengths. If you want to seek additional education by pursuing a doctoral degree, you may consider reviewing accredited programs and talking with current doctoral students. Or if you want to gain research experience, you may want to consider reaching out to faculty or professionals who share similar interests.

Basic Strengths	Special Strengths	Desired Strengths	Development Strategies

The ability to reflect on and acknowledge your strengths will enable you to envision the environment in which you will thrive. For instance, if you find that one of your strengths involves working with children in crisis, you should consider focusing your attention on gaining employment that serves this population. Some of the questions you may ask yourself might be: What age group best suits my comfort level or abilities? What environment will allow me to practice effectively? Am I part of a supportive team? Overall, working in an atmosphere that best suits your strengths will allow you to further develop and enhance your skills and talents as a clinician, leading toward a more fulfilling career in the counseling profession.

Last, the ability to verbalize and demonstrate your strengths will allow you to sell yourself with ease and confidence in the interview process. Employers are looking for self-assured and enthusiastic practitioners. Remember, it is not always about the quantity of your strengths or abilities, but rather the quality and how you express them. Imagine for a moment that you are in an interview and asked the following question: "So, what would you say are your clinical strengths?" *What* examples would you provide in response, and more importantly, *how* confidently would you respond? Whether you are interviewing for a position or building an online image, as we will discuss later in the chapter, keep in mind how important it is to deliver a convincing and positive first impression.

Examine Values, Biases, and Beliefs

Along with evaluating your strengths, it is essential to examine your own values, biases, and beliefs and how those may influence your work with clients. Your values, biases, and beliefs are influenced by the sociopolitical and cultural environment in which you live and are shaped by your intersecting identities (e.g., age, gender, ethnicity, religion; Kress et al., 2019). The context of your life experiences allows for differing degrees of power and privilege in our society, determining your worldview, and ultimately influencing your professional impact on micro-, meso-, and macro-levels.

When thinking about these levels, you should take an integrated approach. Consider how making a difference on the micro-level (e.g., empowering a client in session) will inevitably influence the meso-level (e.g., the client's interaction with community) and macro-level (e.g., the broader social structure). Broad questions that you should consider may include: "Do my values, biases, and beliefs align with the vision of counseling and the standards of practice that guide the profession?"; "Do they mirror the mission of the agency or organization that I see myself a part of?"; and "Do they interfere with my client's growth and development?" Knowing these aspects of your identity will allow you to search for corresponding opportunities in the professional counseling market.

Once you have identified your values, biases, and beliefs—as well as corresponding opportunities—it is time to incorporate them into your self-marketing image. Prospective employers and clients want and need to know where you stand (Corey et al., 2019). Discussing these issues is a collaborative effort of both parties to ensure that you are a good fit for either a therapeutic relationship or employment position. Appearing to waver on your values, biases, and beliefs; seeming unsure or undecided of them; or having a complete lack of insight into them can all have a negative effect on your marketing image. Therefore, it is important that you take the time to explore your worldview so that you can market yourself with confidence and competence in hand.

Live With Limitations

Reflecting on all that you learned at your field placement, you may feel pressured by high expectations and standards. This pressure may in turn contribute to perfectionism, which is increasingly common in graduate students (Cowie et al., 2018). When perfectionism takes a maladaptive form, you may create self-standards and goals that are unrealistic at the moment given your lack of experience. You may find yourself engaging in negative self-talk, telling yourself that you *should* work harder, have *everything* under control, and know *exactly* what to do. These messages will likely lead to self-doubt and criticism, adversely affecting your growth and development.

Instead of focusing on what *should be*, try focusing on *what is* and *what can be*. By doing so, you engage in adaptive perfectionism in which you continue to challenge yourself in the same way, but instead of complying with negative self-talk, you view your experiences as opportunities for self-growth and development without excessive self-doubt and criticism.

In an ever-changing environment, we strive to be the best counselors we can be. Yet, we must accept the same message we impart to our clients: We are human, and each of us has limitations. As you progress through your training, it is crucial to be honest with yourself and admit these limitations. If not, then you risk putting yourself in a position where, despite your best intentions, you may do more harm than good to your clients and self. Remember that recognizing your limitations does not mean you are an ineffective counselor; rather, you become a model for your clients in that you are seeking self-understanding and using your strengths most effectively.

In the professional marketing context, acknowledging your limitations is just as important as promoting your strengths. By acknowledging your limitations, you send a clear message to employers and clients that you are aware of your ethical responsibilities and will not risk putting them in harm's way. Neither your employer nor client want to hear excuses if you make a mistake. Therefore, by taking ownership of your limitations, you convey to them that you are not only aware of your shortcomings but, more important, are willing to address them. From a self-marketing standpoint, acknowledging your limitations within reason can increase the positive image you send out to the public.

Formulate Your Counseling Approach

How many times have you been asked about your counseling approach? Chances are that you have had to answer this question often. However, just as with evaluating your values, biases, and beliefs while acknowledging your strengths and limitations, understanding your counseling approach will enable you to market yourself toward organizations that value and respect the ways in which you practice. When formulating your counseling approach, you will want to consider the following questions: "How do I promote trust in the therapeutic relationship??"; "How do I create an affirmative space for growth?"; and "What is the role of social justice in my work?" All these are valid questions to consider and will ultimately influence how you view your clients and how you will work with them throughout the counseling process.

Having a solid theoretical orientation, as part of your overall counseling approach, will help you attract agencies, organizations, and clientele who share your beliefs. Remember, an interview is a two-way process: employers are not only interviewing you, but you are evaluating your fit with them as well. Take a moment to imagine yourself as a potential employer or client. How important would your applicant's or counselor's theoretical orientation be to you? Chances are that the explicit or implicit response to this question would be an important determinant of how well the applicant would fit into the organization and the likelihood of establishing rapport throughout sessions. Thus, like the SELF acronym, be clear about your theoretical orientation, as this will enhance your image when networking, interviewing for a job, or building your clientele. Use Self-Assessment Activity 13.2 to strengthen your understanding of your own counseling orientation.

Self-Assessment Activity 13.2 Your Inner Counselor

1. I am comfortable with self-promotion. True or False? Explain.
2. What are my strengths, values, biases, and beliefs; limitations; and theoretical orientation?
3. How can I become aware of agencies or organizations that share my counseling approach?

Understanding the Field Around You

Professional counselors have the opportunity to work in many different capacities and settings while they promote health and wellness among individuals, couples, families, and groups. A counselor may not just be found in a community agency or private practice. You see professional counselors in schools working with our youth and across college campuses, empowering students of all ages to reach their full potential. Professional counselors can be found conducting workshops and groups for both professionals outside the field of counseling and nonprofessionals looking for tools to improve their quality of life. Counselors may be found on the front lines of a natural disaster aiding those in need and connecting them with critical services. If you have a family member who is a veteran of our armed services, a counselor may be working with them on a wide variety of issues from rehabilitation to reducing trauma symptoms. Counselors can also practice in a variety of specialty areas such as marriage and family therapy, art therapy, school counseling, addictions counseling, and career counseling. These are just a few of the many roles that counselors may play. If you are unsure of where you see yourself fitting among this diverse population of professionals, it may be helpful to look at statistics highlighting growing trends in the field of counseling. The remainder of this section will be devoted to providing helpful information on two broad categories of professional counselors: substance abuse, behavioral disorder, and mental health counselors; and school and career counselors.

For clinical mental health counselors, future employment prospects remain positive. In 2018, substance abuse, behavioral disorder, and mental health counselors held about 304,500 jobs with an average salary of \$44,630 (up from \$42,590 in 2010). The Bureau's job outlook for the years spanning from 2018 to 2028 estimates an increase of 22%, which is much faster than average job growth. This results in an increase of around 68,500 new jobs for clinical mental health counselors during the current decade. Table 13.1 presents a breakdown of the industries with the highest percentages of mental health counselors in 2018, whereas Table 13.2 presents estimated projected job growth by industry among mental health counselors.

Table 13.1 Percentage of mental health counselors by industry

Outpatient mental health and substances abuse centers	19%
Individual and family services	16%
Hospitals; state, local, and private	10%
Residential mental health and substance abuse facilities	10%
Government	9%

Source: Adapted from the U.S. Bureau of Labor Statistics (2020).

Table 13.2 Percentage of projected job growth for mental health counselors by industry

Substance abuse, behavioral disorder, and mental health counselors	22%
Counselors, social workers, and other community and social service specialists	12%
All occupations in the U.S. economy	5%

Source: Adapted from the U.S. Bureau of Labor Statistics (2020).

Table 13.3 Projected job growth for school and career counselors by industry

Elementary and secondary schools; state, local, and private	44%
Junior colleges, colleges, universities, and professional schools; state, local, and private	35%
Health care and social assistance	8%
Other educational services; state, local, and private	4%
Self-employed workers	3%

Source: Adapted from the U.S. Bureau of Labor Statistics (2020).

For school and career counselors, future employment prospects remain average despite local and state funding cuts. In 2018, school and career counselors held about 324,500 jobs with an average yearly salary of $56,310 (up from $53,380 in 2010; U.S. Bureau of Labor Statistics, 2020). The Bureau's job outlook for the years spanning from 2018 to 2028 estimates an increase of 8%, which is faster than average job growth. This results in an increase of around 27,200 new jobs during the current decade. Table 13.3 presents estimated projected job growth by industry among school and career counselors.

Based on these projections by the U.S. Bureau of Labor Statistics (2020), counseling positions at both the master's and doctoral levels will be in demand throughout the current decade. Although this remains encouraging, it is important to assess current and future employment trends, as you likely will not remain in the same position throughout your professional career. Having reliable information on employment trends will better enable you to market yourself toward counseling careers that best fit with the current economic climate. Remember to always keep your options open, be willing to adapt to narrow economic conditions, and remain flexible choosing in which industries you see yourself within the counseling profession. These traits will allow you to weather less-positive employment conditions while giving you an increased advantage over individuals who have less information or who attempt to target counseling industries with declining projected growth.

Using Networking Opportunities and Embracing Mentorship

No matter where you are in your counseling career, a helpful mentor can be a catalyst for marketing yourself to other professionals and organizations. Finding the right match, at times, may require considerable time and effort. For some, a mentorship can be initiated with a faculty member in a department, a supervisor from a practicum or internship site, or a professional from the surrounding community. For others, a mentoring relationship can blossom after networking at a conference, through state or national mentoring programs, or by reaching out to respected professionals in the field (e.g., sending an email to a researcher who shares your interests).

Before you consider reaching out to a potential mentor, consider the following questions: "What are my expectations?"; "Are my expectations realistic?"; "How will this professional relationship allow me to market to others?"; "Does my potential mentor have a thorough understanding of the counseling field?"; and "Can my mentor connect me with other individuals and organizations that will help me market my skills and abilities?" Finding and building a mentoring relationship helps foster professional growth and development in the counseling field. Use Self-Assessment Activity 13.3 to begin thinking about mentorship.

Self-Assessment Activity 13.3 Your Knowledge of the Profession

1. What are three current trends in the counseling profession?
2. What are the benefits of counseling to the general public?
3. Who are several professionals in the field I can contact about issues related to my professional growth and development?

Voices From the Field 13.1 Personal and Professional Growth, *by Julie Lenyk*

I have had a unique experience at every conference I attended, and I think it is important to take the time to attend conferences because they can really benefit you personally and professionally. As I look back, I can mark very important points in my career that involved attending conferences both statewide and nationally. They all offered me the opportunity to network with other professionals in this field, enhance my knowledge of the counseling profession, and develop a professional identity.

One memorable experience occurred at a conference by the American Counseling Association. This conference was significant to me for many reasons, but most important, it led me on the path of my professional goals of being a clinical counselor and obtaining my doctorate. Attending the presentations, meetings, and social gatherings gave me the chance to network with many leaders in this field, thus opening the door to many possibilities for my future career. It was these people who really motivated me to pursue my area of clinical work and my doctorate. I established strong relationships with these individuals, and they are people who I continue to connect with both personally and professionally today.

I think that conferences offer a unique environment because it really is the only time that so many students, counselors, and faculty can all gather. Conferences are a great way to meet new people and build relationships with other professionals. They can help you to establish new opportunities that can assist you in further achieving your goals.

As I reflect on the conferences I have attended, I realize that each one was vital for my professional development because of the strong relationships I built through networking. I also think they enhanced my personal development as I built strong relationships that continue to influence my life today. I am confident in saying that I would not be where I am today if I did not use the many opportunities conferences offer to network with others, learn about the counseling profession, and develop a professional identity.

Securing a Job the Old-Fashioned Way

Now that you have explored your identity as a counselor and have a vision of where you want to go, what is the next step? It is likely that the next logical step toward beginning your career as a professional counselor is the job search. Although this may seem simple enough, finding employment that aligns with your needs and goals is a multifaceted process (Hodges & Connelly, 2010). After identifying your personal and professional identity as a counselor and exploring the many employment options that are available for counselors, it is important to approach the job market with knowledge and confidence. In this section, we will present the materials you will need to gain entry into the workforce and the knowledge you will need to successfully navigate within it.

Preparing a Curriculum Vita or Resume

In the counseling profession, most counselors-to-be and licensed professionals focus on developing a curriculum vitae (CV) or a resume (depending on the employment position). A resume is typically a one- to two-page document highlighting the most relevant professional information, whereas a CV is multiple pages (translated from Latin, CV means "course of life"). You would use a CV to outline all your academic accomplishments, achievements, and experiences as they relate to your career in counseling. On the other hand, a resume may be more appropriate for employers who desire a more succinct description of your skills and abilities based on your previous work history. This chapter will use the term CV for consistency, but these guidelines can be applied to the creation of either a resume or CV.

The CV should be easy to read, and the major points should be easily found. The language on your CV should be succinct and professional. Given the importance of this document, it is important that you (a) evaluate whether the information that you choose to include is relevant, (b) ensure that the document is error free, and (c) organize the flow of information using appropriate headings and formatting. A polished CV will set you apart from other candidates and often serves as the first impression that potential employers (or doctoral programs) have of you. It is important to have a wide variety of skills and activities on your CV to display your full range of talents and abilities.

To organize these attributes, it is important to start with a foundation. All CVs are organized with the use of headings. Although there is variation, common headings (and corresponding information) include the following: *personal information* (name, address, phone number, email, Web page address if applicable); *education* (degree, major, minor, institution, graduation dates, program accreditation); *work or related experience* (job title, name of organization and location; dates of employment; responsibilities, achievements); *leadership experience* (leadership roles, organizational membership, community involvement); *honors or awards* (academic or nonacademic awards, scholarships, fellowships, special recognitions, and year received); *professional affiliations* (on the local, state, national, and international levels); *technical competencies* (computer programs); *licenses or certifications*; *languages* (fluent, conversational, novice); *service* (community involvement, campus involvement, volunteerism); and *research* (grants, publications, presentations). Take care to make sure all information of equal importance is displayed with the same level of headings and maintain the same font and spacing throughout the document.

Begin your CV with your contact information, including your phone number and an appropriate email address. After graduation, it is likely that your university email will no longer be accessible. If you do not have a professional alternative email address, create one for free through Google or whichever service you prefer. Email addresses using your name or initials make it easy to contact you; avoid any slang or unprofessional terms in the address (e.g., flirtyflower@mail.com is not professional).

After your contact information, you may wish to list some of your most relevant qualifications and an objective statement (Hodges, 2015). The objective statement, if included, should be one sentence that states exactly what you are seeking and why you are qualified for that position. However, you could choose to list your education next; take care to indicate if your master's program was CACREP-accredited, as this indicates the focus of your education. Be sure to list any internship positions or other jobs in the helping profession, and make sure your publications and presentations are formatted using the most recent edition of the APA (American Psychological Association, 2019) *Publication Manual*. It is also important to organize your CV so that your most important information is first, which may differ depending to whom you are sending your CV.

The next step, after filling in your headings, is to evaluate the message you are sending to the reader. You may ask yourself: Did I overlook anything? Are all of my special strengths highlighted? Is my passion represented? Are there areas for improvement? Some areas that may be particularly important to look at beyond the basic information (contact information, education) are the sections that address your volunteer or professional service. Both emphasize that you are invested in the counseling profession for more than just money, and they emphasize your dedication to the mission of counseling, which is helping others. Another area that you may want to turn your attention toward is your involvement in professional organizations, as they are excellent sources of volunteer and professional service opportunities. Your school's chapter of Chi Sigma Iota is a valuable resource; consider running for an officer position and take advantage of volunteer activities your chapter organizes.

Another great way to build your CV is to join the American Counseling Association (ACA), ACA divisions, or your state ACA branch. You can list your membership on your CV, any conferences that you have attended, and any activities that you have participated in on behalf of your local chapter. Not only is this excellent information for your CV, but also every professional meeting and event is a rich networking experience.

In addition to carefully planning your CV, it is important to include anything that could help explain who you are as a person, counselor, and employee. Although it would be unethical to embellish your accomplishments or activities, it is desirable to present yourself in the most positive light (Hodges, 2015). Do not forget to list the hour you spend every Sunday at the nursing home, the informal mentoring you have provided to first-year counseling students, or the training that you attended to work toward a counseling specialty area. These things may seem inconsequential, but they help your reader gain an accurate picture of you.

Ultimately, the goal of a CV is to help position yourself in the professional marketplace. As you can imagine, many CVs will tend to look similar due to similar coursework, trainings, and internship experiences. It is the extra lines on your CV that will help you stand out from the crowd. So, make sure to include extracurricular activities and leadership positions that highlight who you are as a counselor, employee, and coworker. Take time to complete Self-Assessment 13.4 and review Figures 13.1 and 13.2, which include a sample resume and CV, respectively.

Self-Assessment 13.4 CVs and Resumes

1. How does my resume or CV accurately reflect my personal and professional qualities?
2. Have I participated in professional activities that reflect my passions? Explain.

3. What aspects of my resume or CV promote high-quality achievements?
4. What additional experiences should I seek out to enhance my resume or CV quality?

Brandy V. Ackers

1645 Bowling Court 336-275-9290

Greensboro, NC 27455

bvackers@gmail.com

EDUCATION

MS Ed. December 2019	**Clinical Mental Health Counseling** (CACREP-Accredited)	State University City, State
BA with Honors May 2016	**Psychology**	State University City, State

CREDENTIALS

- Licensed Professional Counselor Associate, C000098 (January 2020)
- National Certified Counselor (NCC), 980098 (January 2020)

RELEVANT EXPERIENCE

Graduate/Research Assistant August 2017–December 2019

State University—City, State

Dr. Olivia Don, Supervisor

- Developed and edited manuscripts for publication
- Collected and analyzed research data
- Presented at state and national conferences with supervisor
- Created documents; updated master's-level syllabi

Clinical Counseling Intern January 2019–December 2019

Agency—City, State

Mr. Quinn Pierce, Supervisor

- Diagnosed and treated mental and emotional disorders
- Utilized cognitive-behavioral, trauma-focused, and creative interventions
- Served as a behavioral consultant for four Multidisciplinary Student Achievement Teams

Direct Care Staff June 2017–June 2018

Agency—City, State

Mr. Ronald Brick, Supervisor

- Supervised female adolescents
- Promoted use of positive coping skills
- Implemented concrete, behavioral aspects of therapeutic treatment plans

SELECTED PUBLICATIONS AND PRESENTATIONS

Ackers, B. V. (2018). Title of article. *Newsletter Title*, *25*(3), 11–12.
Peters, R., & **Ackers, B. V.** (2018, November). *Title of presentation*. Poster session presented at the State Conference, City, State.

PROFESSIONAL AND HONORS MEMBERSHIPS

- American Counseling Association
- Chi Sigma Iota (Counseling Academic and Professional Honor Society International)

Figure 13.1 Sample resume

Brandy V. Ackers

1645 Bowling Court 336-275-9290

Greensboro, NC 27455

bvackers@gmail.com

EDUCATION

MS Ed. December 2010	**Clinical Mental Health Counseling** (CACREP-Accredited)	State University City, State
BA with Honors May 2008	**Psychology**	State University City, State

CREDENTIALS

- Licensed Professional Counselor Associate, C000098 (January 2020)
- National Certified Counselor (NCC), 980098 (January 2020)

RESEARCH AND SCHOLARSHIP

Graduate/Research Assistant August 2017–December 2019

State University—City, State

Dr. Olivia Don, Supervisor

Developed and edited qualitative and theoretical manuscripts for publication; collected and analyzed research data. Presented at state and national conferences with supervisor and independently. Created documents for the department's counselor training clinic and updated master's-level syllabi according to 2016 CACREP standards.

CLINICAL COUNSELING EXPERIENCE

Clinical Counseling Intern January 2019–December 2019

Agency—City, State

Mr. Quinn Pierce, Supervisor

Diagnosed and treated mental and emotional disorders in children, adolescents, and families; utilized cognitive-behavioral, trauma-focused, and creative interventions in outpatient and in-home settings. Served as a behavioral consultant for Multidisciplinary Student Achievement Teams at four urban schools.

Direct Care Staff June 2019–June 2019

Agency—City, State

Mr. Ronald Brick, Supervisor

Supervised female adolescents in a residential treatment facility; served meals, created and enforced chore schedule, assisted with online school assignments, developed and implemented leisure activities, promoted use of positive coping skills, and otherwise implemented concrete behavioral aspects of therapeutic treatment plans.

AWARDS

- NBCC Foundation Rural Scholarship Semifinalist 2018

GRANT FUNDING

- 2018—State University—Graduate Studies Internal Grant, Undergraduate Student Research Grant. *Title of Grant*. $500

PUBLICATIONS

Ackers, B. V. (2018). Title of article. *Newsletter Title*, *25*(3), 11–12.
Ackers, B. V., & Lindley, J. L., (2017). Title of article. *Newsletter Title*, *2*, 5–7.

PRESENTATIONS

Peters, R., & **Ackers, B. V.** (2018, November). *Title of presentation*. Poster session presented at the State Conference, City, State.

PROFESSIONAL SERVICE AND LEADERSHIP

Secretary

Chi Sigma Iota, Our Chapter

State University

April 2018 to April 2019

- Organized workshops for professional continuing education
- Advocated for the counseling profession
- Sponsored social events
- Organized philanthropic endeavors
- Increased chapter participation

PROFESSIONAL MEMBERSHIPS

- American Counseling Association

HONOR SOCIETY MEMBERSHIPS

- Chi Sigma Iota (Counseling Academic and Professional Honor Society International)

Figure 13.2 Sample CV

Using Your Resume or CV

Your resume or CV will be invaluable when searching for an internship or your first counseling job. It is helpful to email potential interviewers your resume or CV before a face-to-face meeting so that they can learn more about your accomplishments. Also, bring a paper copy to your meeting or interview. It is sometimes nice to use resume paper, rather than regular printing paper, for the first page of your resume or CV. Subsequent pages should be standard printing paper. Resume paper can be found at any office supply store in a variety of professional colors, but white is always appropriate.

Your resume or CV will also be useful to anyone who is writing a letter of recommendation for you. Although this person should know you very well, you cannot expect them to know all your accomplishments. Send your resume or CV to those who you trust to write a supportive letter of reference several weeks before the letter is needed (Hodges, 2015). This allows the writer ample time to create a thoughtful and persuading letter. There are often many applicants interested in internship, job, or doctoral positions; your resume or CV and letters of reference can set you apart from other candidates.

As a graduate student and new professional, you are doing things every day that deserve to be on your resume or CV. It is helpful to update your resume or CV at least once per month so that nothing is forgotten. This practice also prevents you from being caught with an outdated resume or CV when opportunity knocks. As a professional in the job market, it is important to be prepared at all times to secure a job that is right for you. Although there are many job opportunities for counselors, your resume or CV can be used as a reflective tool to help you and an employer gain an understanding of a career choice that would be best for you.

Voices From the Field 13.2 The Course of Life: My Curriculum Vitae, *by Ron Del Moro*

I never knew the difference between a resume and its fancier cousin, the curriculum vitae (more commonly referred to as a CV). I figured if I mumbled both words interchangeably I could not go wrong. As time marched on, though, it became necessary to learn about these documents and how to provide an overview of my life in a few pages or less.

CV is a Latin expression that can be translated to "the course of life." Some say CVs are exclusive to academia, and others will contend they are becoming more popular outside the walls of education. The main difference between a resume and CV is length; resumes typically run one or two pages at most, whereas CVs can go on, and on and on. (Consult one of your successful professors' CVs for an example.)

Resumes and CVs are "living" documents that must constantly be updated as your professional identity grows. I find it easiest to update regularly, rather than waiting until I need my CV and then trying to remember what I have done since the last update. It is also helpful to have someone else check it out before sending it.

Resumes and CVs are representations of ourselves; they are often the first impression we leave with others. Countless formats, designs, and styles can be chosen, and there does not seem to be one universally agreed upon "right" design, as long as there are no smiley faces or butterflies! I have learned that this "summation of life experiences" cannot be prepared at the last minute. Do it right the first time, update it regularly, and life will be a lot easier down the road.

Cover Letters

Cover letters are an integral part of your job search. These brief letters act in conjunction with your resume or CV to provide a first impression, clearly explain why you are a viable job candidate, and invite employers to contact you for follow-up (Hodges & Connelly, 2010). Cover letters should be addressed specifically to the person (or group) who will be overseeing the hiring process and should not exceed one page. Ultimately, the cover letter allows you to add personality to your CV but should also be concise and meaningful. Use specific examples to illustrate your points. For example, instead of stating "I was a helpful addition to the team" provide a more detailed explanation such as "I covered more than ten shifts for coworkers and reorganized the filing system." The cover letter provided in Figure 13.3 can serve as a template for your personalized cover letter, which should be written intentionally and specifically for each opportunity to which you apply.

Tiffany A. Herring
204 Country Rd.
Winston, Ohio 54321

April 2, 2019

Brett Logan, Supervisor of Guidance

Winston City Schools

20 Levitt Street

Winston, Ohio 54321

Dear Mr. Logan:
I am aware of an available school counseling position within Winston City School District, and I would like to convey my interest in this opportunity. Unlike many other candidates, I am a Licensed School Counselor as well as a Licensed Clinical Counselor. My passion for working with inner-city youth combined with my strong academic and leadership background make me an especially valuable school counseling candidate.

As an employee in a residential treatment facility and an intern at Winston Early College, Kale Elementary School, and Sage Counseling Center, I served diverse student populations whose learning and social functioning levels covered a wide spectrum. I particularly enjoyed working with at-risk students to help resolve interpersonal conflicts. One of my greatest strengths is my ability to increase students' academic self-efficacy through individual and group counseling and by paying close attention to the quality of the school environment. I also enjoy professional development endeavors and have made scholarly presentations on school counseling topics at the state and national conferences.

My experience in the nationally accredited Daley University Counseling Program and my passion for helping students has allowed me to serve as a successful school counseling intern. I have excellent initiative and organizational skills, and I am excited about the opportunity to find employment within your school district. I believe you will discover that my warm personality, strong communication skills, maturity, and honesty are characteristics that make me an outstanding choice for this position. I thank you for your time and consideration and look forward to speaking with you through email or over the phone.

Sincerely,

(Signature)

Tiffany Herring

Figure 13.3 Sample cover letter

The Job Search

The job search is a process that intersects your personal desires, practical needs, realistic skill set, and job market availability. Although complicated, this process can be navigated by a prepared counselor. However, luck and chance also play a role in this process, so try not to become discouraged if things do not go exactly as planned—your hard work will pay off soon. If possible, choose an internship in a setting that you would like to work. Many sites that accept interns also hire their interns, so take your internship seriously. Practica and internships help you gain experience and fulfill graduation requirements but can also serve as a year-long interview with a future employer. It might be beneficial to have conversations with your on-site supervisor or administrator about your graduation date and any possible employment opportunities.

If you find that you do not wish to work at your internship site, or there are no available positions, plan backward from your graduation date. Often, before you can be hired as a professional, you must attain the necessary licensure. Although you may not be able to formally apply until you have graduated, you can take any necessary licensure exams ahead of time. You should begin registering for such exams as you enter the last semester of your program. However, you can definitely start sooner if you feel comfortable doing so.

Each counseling license is associated with different examinations depending on the state in which you plan to be licensed. Currently, there is not a unified licensure process in the United States for all 50 states, but there is a way to show potential employers that you have nationally recognized qualifications. The National Board for Certified Counselors (NBCC) has developed the National Counselor Examination for licensure and certification (see www.nbcc.org). This exam serves two functions in the counseling profession. First, many state boards recognize successful completion of this exam as an indicator that a candidate should receive a counseling license. In addition, this exam indicates that the counselor is eligible to become nationally certified. National certification is not the same as licensure; it does not allow someone to practice as a counselor. However, it does indicate the candidate has met national standards and is endorsed by NBCC. If this credential can be listed on your CV, it shows employers that you meet national counseling standards.

The credentials that you have chosen to earn are an indicator of the job positions that would be best for you. Once you have created a CV that accurately represents you and displays credentials that indicate your high achievements, it is important to stay abreast of employment opportunities. Opportunities may be sent through listservs (e.g., mass emails sent through your state branch of the ACA or from your university or school system), and it is important to take note of these helpful opportunities. Make sure to follow the directions specified in the message and to accompany your CV with a formal cover letter.

Word of mouth is an excellent way to learn of new job opportunities. It is estimated that almost two-thirds of all jobs are not formally advertised (Hodges & Connelly, 2010). If you are looking for a job, communicate with other students in your program; ask them if their internship sites are hiring. This is also helpful because you can find out about the culture of the organization. When attending conferences, make sure to network with your peers, speakers, and other professionals in attendance; mention that you are looking for a counseling position. It might even be worthwhile to send a CV and cover letter to an agency that is not currently advertising any employment positions but matches your personal and professional career needs.

When interacting with colleagues in person, business cards are an important networking tool (Hodges & Connelly, 2010). Take care to ensure that your business cards have updated contact information and accurately convey your qualifications. Also, choose a business card format that is simple, professional, and easy to read. It is helpful to exchange business cards when at any networking function. Someone may learn of a job opening after meeting you (although they did not know about it when you initially met) and contact you in the future. In addition, if you happen to get an interview at a place with which you are unfamiliar, you might be able to search through your collection of business cards to find a personal contact in the area.

When networking in person, it is especially important to be cognizant of your professional appearance. Remember that you are a counselor at all times of the day; whether you are at a party on the weekend or eating a meal during the week at a local restaurant, your community now views you as a professional, and it is important not to prove them wrong. Especially when job hunting, but from here on out, think before you act. This applies to activities you do in public and at home, such as Facebook or Twitter. Think about how the things you say or do reflect on you and the counseling profession; you never know who is watching. As a new professional marketing yourself for the best possible employment position, it will be important not to lose any opportunities over events that occur in your personal life.

Voices From the Field 13.3 The Importance of Comfort and Support During the Job Search, *by Emily Herman*

My job as a graduate student was clear: attend classes, work in groups, write papers, and complete internship. However, as graduation approached, the daunting task of the job search loomed ahead. I felt uncertain about finding not only a job, but also a career in counseling. My goal was to work with children and adolescents, but I soon found that there are a limited number of agencies that work with that population. This realization led me to ask myself, "What would I say to a client who was in a similar position?"

It became apparent that my next step was to identify other options and avenues that could serve as a stepping-stone. After searching local newspapers, online postings, and listservs, I realized that the most useful tool I had was the network of peers, professors, and adjunct instructors that I had worked with and admired for the past two years. It was also beneficial that they knew me and my training; this trust led to more personal interactions with people who could help me begin my professional life. I had finally found the comfort and support that I was looking for in the job search.

For me, the most overwhelming part of the job search was questioning if I was making the best decision and feeling isolated in the process. In graduate school and during internship, there was a safety net of advisors, university mentors, and site supervisors to help me with scheduling and internship placement. Although the job search is an individual decision, I used these same resources to search for a job in which I could begin my career. Ultimately, I had to make the final decision, but I found the path clearer when I had support from people I had grown to trust throughout my graduate studies.

Landing the Interview and Following Up

After submitting a carefully constructed cover letter and professional CV, it is important to follow up with the organization. If possible, it is helpful to go to the agency in person to ensure that your information was received. This also serves as an initial meeting during which your personality can be associated with your qualifications. Bring a hard copy of your resume and be respectful if the person you are wishing to see is busy; you can leave your resume and follow up via phone or email later. Also, if you are able to meet with the person, only stay 10 or 15 minutes to be respectful of their time (this only applies if you did not make an appointment). If it is not possible to physically go to the organization, call three to five days after your resume and cover letter should have been received. Ask to speak with the person in charge of the job search (call them by name if possible), or graciously leave a message or speak with someone else in the organization if that person is unavailable. Your efforts to be professional will be noticed and connected to your stellar CV or resume.

Sometimes the job search process takes months, and you might plant a seed that doesn't blossom for quite some time. Work through discouragement and disappointment in healthy ways; keep working on the process. If you receive a call for an interview, be polite, calm, and appreciative. Make sure to write down the date and time of your interview, the name of the interviewers, and confirm the address of the location. Arrive to your interview at least 15 minutes early. If you are unfamiliar with the area to which you are going, take a practice drive a day or two before. Arrive at your interview with proper business attire, minimal jewelry, and no perfume or cologne; it is not worth risking the chance that your scent could offend one of the interviewers. In a dark blue or black folder, carry one or two hard copies of your CV (you may wish to print the first page on resume paper) and your business cards. It is also helpful to bring a portfolio of accomplishments you achieved while working in a related position or internship.

Take care to speak and act professionally in your interview; try to avoid slang terms and sit still if possible (Hodge, 2011). However, it is important to be yourself. It would not be beneficial to falsely represent yourself in the interview, as the employers are sure to learn your true personality if you are offered the job.

In many instances, several rounds of candidates are interviewed for one job opening, so practice patience. After the interview (no more than a day or two after), send a handwritten thank-you note or email to your interviewers. In your message refer the interviewers by name, reiterate your qualifications and passion for the position, and refer to specific conversations during the interview that demonstrate a good fit between you and the organization. These details show that you are personable, invested, and professional. Generally, it would be acceptable to make a follow-up call if you have not heard anything for about two weeks. If you are informed that you did not get the position, gracefully thank them for the opportunity and request that they keep your information on file. However, if you are informed that you were selected to fill the position, congratulations!

Carving Out Your New-Age Niche

Counseling students and licensed professional counselors who use social networking tools have a unique ability to reach out to thousands and even millions of individuals, groups, and organizations across the globe. Whether promoting the profession, a cause, or oneself, those seeking to self-market can gain from the benefits of social networking tools, as they provide a direct and accessible medium to achieve these aims. However, with increased connectivity comes increased risk and liability. In the sections that follow, we will discuss the most up-to-date and popular social networking tools that you can use to build your professional network and market yourself to potential clients and employers. We will also discuss some of the potential pitfalls of relying too heavily on social media and how it can potentially damage your image and practice.

Reaching Out with Social Networking

As technology expands, more and more social networking tools will become available to the public. Many of these are user friendly and free of charge. However, perhaps the most enticing incentive to use social networking tools is the ability to connect with, and distribute information to, a larger audience while sitting at your home or office computer. Take, for example, YouTube, one of the most accessed websites across the world. Many people visit this site to listen to and watch videos ranging from personal biographies to contemporary and historical media events to professional lectures from esteemed experts. If you were to type the word "counseling" into the search box, there are countless unique videos related to this topic, each with the potential to be watched by millions of viewers who have access to this website. Recognizing the advantages of this tool, you as a counselor have endless opportunities to market yourself. Possibilities may include presenting informed consent videos to potential clients, performing a presentation or lecture on a given research topic, promoting a social justice initiative, or uploading a video diary of your own experience as you work through your master's program and beyond. This is a great way to make a strong first impression and to promote the profession as a whole.

Another social networking medium is Facebook. Originally created as a networking site for U.S. college students, Facebook has gone global. This audience includes everyone from young adults to nationally known organizations. Your Facebook page can allow you to connect with family and friends, but in the context of marketing, it can also serve as an outlet to connect with other counseling professionals, reach out to other mental health organizations, or promote the latest research, depending on your interests. Think of Facebook as a way for your clients, colleagues, or potential employers to perform their own background check on you. You may wish to keep two separate profiles: one personal (for family, friends, and loved ones), and one professional (for the broader community). Information that you choose to include on your professional profile can be your education, current employment, trainings and certifications, professional interests, relevant professional experiences, and other organizations that you belong to. Facebook also allows you to post status updates and messages to those who are linked, or "friended," in your profile. It is important to note that you should not "friend" clients or potential clients on personal or professional Facebook sites. Friendships with clients are unethical (ACA, 2014) and it can break confidentiality for clients to be associated with your professional site. It might be helpful to note a social media policy in your professional disclosure statement.

Along with YouTube and Facebook, another website and application called Twitter can allow instantaneous access to spreading information to millions of individuals. This social networking tool can allow you to post immediate updates to those who "follow" you and share your own interests. If you find yourself traveling and giving lectures or presenting at conferences, you can use Twitter to promote these events. You can also follow the leading experts in the field who have a Twitter account, receiving immediate notifications about the who, what, where, and when of their professional endeavors.

Selling Yourself on the Virtual Job Market

Numerous websites will allow you to search for employment as well as promote your practice and skills. For example, LinkedIn has quickly become the world's largest professional network with more than 600 million users, allowing you to post your professional profile to potential organizations and employers. If individuals type your name into a search engine (for example, Google, Bing, or Yahoo!), your LinkedIn profile is usually among the first five links that show up on the results page. If they choose to review your profile, you are just one click away from connecting, conversing, and collaborating. To help your LinkedIn profile stand out, a few recommendations include: use a professional (rather than casual) headshot, include the same information that is on your resume or CV, list your skills, create a profile summary, and include an email address that you check often. Similar to your resume or CV, it is important that you update your profile regularly.

Other websites afford you the opportunity to post your resume and search for jobs specifically tailored to your counseling interests. These sites include, but are not limited to: Monster.com, Careerbuilder.com, and

Indeed.com. One option when using these sites is uploading a resume or CV in your account for potential employers to review. If interested, the employers initiate contact. For some, this laid-back approach is ideal; however, for those who are on an aggressive job hunt, this approach may not be beneficial. Thus, the latter group may lean toward option two: searching for positions of interest and sending/uploading their resume or CV to the prospective employer. This is a more direct approach that not only gives the applicant more control but also shows the employer that the applicant views the position as a professional investment in career development. Using a combination of these options and sites can further enhance your ability to self-market.

A consideration to keep in mind when building your professional profiles on these websites is maintenance. Specifically, you will want to ask yourself: "Is my profile up to date?"; "Is it accurate?"; and, "Does it reflect my skills, abilities, and passions in the field of counseling or related fields?" Taking an objective stance will allow you to critically evaluate your online profile and make adjustments based on current trends and the needs of employing agencies or organizations.

Building a Professional Website

So far, we have discussed using other websites as a means to market your practice and professional identity. Now we will discuss using your own website to build on and enhance your professional career in counseling. You may be asking yourself, what are my options if I decide to start my own website? The answer to this question lies heavily on the intent of your website. For instance, if the overall intent of your website is to educate individuals about your professional career and services, you will more likely have a website with fewer features. If, however, the goal of your site is to market your independent practice, then you may have more enhanced features embedded in your website that enable clients to schedule appointments, make and collect payments, or even post comments on a dedicated forum included on your site. Neither example presented should have more appeal than the other. Rather, the success of your website to attract and keep viewers will rely heavily on how well the site functions to achieve its goals.

Beginning a website can be an overwhelming task. Thus, it might be wise to start off slowly by developing your own professional blog. According to Todd (2009), blogs serve two purposes. First, they provide a sense of community to those individuals and organizations that you serve or are trying to attract. Second, blogging allows you to connect with them directly so that you may better understand the services they need and what is most important to them. When developing your blog, you will have the opportunity to incorporate graphics, visuals, and other functions that will not only help stimulate the content of your blog but also serve as a foundation for creating tools to enhance the goals of your future website. The experience of maintaining a blog will give you a solid foundation of working within a website and connecting with viewers while preparing you to build your own site.

When you have had some practice in the blogging world and are ready to develop your own website, what are some goals to keep in mind? Todd (2009) stated that your website should accomplish three goals, including making a great first impression to the viewer about who you are and your practice, building satisfaction and loyalty, and reducing labor and costs of conducting business. Making a great first impression will help draw the viewer in and keep them interested in the information you are presenting. Building satisfaction and loyalty will not only keep them coming back to your site but also help spread positive word of mouth, thus increasing the traffic on your site. Reducing labor and costs only makes sound financial sense if the intent of your website is to sustain a counseling business or practice, allowing you to allocate financial resources to other appropriate business needs. For example, clients may fill out and submit forms via your website instead of you having to pay hundreds of dollars yearly in printing fees.

Although it may be tempting to assume that looks are everything about a website, this could not be further from the truth in the counseling profession. Potential clients are not interested in fancy graphics or animations. They are looking for direct and clear information, so keep your main page organized to reduce confusion. This may be the case if a potential client is in distress and trying to access information quickly about your services to determine appropriateness of fit within your practice. However, it is still important to allow your personality to be reflected through your website.

If you happen to visit counseling professionals with their own website, you may notice common headings on the main page of the site. Here is a list of important headings to consider on your home page, and you may also incorporate others: counselor biography, business information, scheduling, client resources, treatment populations served, and how you approach counseling Todd (2009). As we discussed in managing profiles on other social networking sites, it is crucial to keep the information within these headings updated continuously.

If viewers visit your website and are met with outdated information, they may develop the impression that you have less interest in and commitment to your site and, by extension, to them.

When building your website, remember to have the following criteria in mind to provide a better experience for your viewers and to reduce your own frustration when managing your site: Keep your site user friendly to allow clients to access and download information with as few clicks as possible. A client or colleague should not have to spend ten minutes or more searching for your contact information. As you become familiar with your website, you may consider adding videos, links to other social media accounts, documents, and podcasts. Depending on the nature of your counseling website, you may consider adding forums or discussion boards so clients or professionals can comment on their experiences or connect with others in a positive and meaningful way.

Ensure that you are always looking ahead when designing your website so you can modify it to your public's liking. Few things can be more frustrating than trying to build in a feature that viewers are requesting only to find out that it is not functioning properly. For instance, if you decide to incorporate the ability for individuals to view or download documents, make sure they can be converted to a PDF (portable document format); that way the file cannot be manipulated and is easily accessible Todd (2009). Making the website interactive will keep clients and professionals interested and on your site for longer periods of time. However, if viewers are met with confusing information, broken links, or dysfunctional features, they will become frustrated and leave the site, never to return.

Virtual Liabilities

Nowadays, all these tools can be accessed using a variety of modes—a personal or public computer, your cell phone, and tablet computers. All these tools allow for quick and easy access, along with a cost-effective way to promote yourself to a large-scale audience. However, it is important to note that although self-promotion is just a click away, so is self-destruction. It is essential that you consider the short-term and long-term consequences of what you post on these sites.

Although interacting with clients via personal websites may be beneficial for building trust and self-esteem, there are drawbacks worth considering. For example, personally disclosing information (such as posting your views on a particular subject) may potentially harm the therapeutic relationship, blur boundaries, and put counselors in a position where they may cross or violate boundaries. Consider the following questions when evaluating your own presence in the online world: How many online sites do I belong to? How easy would it be for a client to find me on these sites? How will I balance my personal and professional online identity? If my clients reviewed my online profiles, how would that affect our therapeutic relationship?

With the rise of online security breaches and personal data being compromised, it is recommended to always act with caution and safety when presenting personal details to the online world. With the right information, computer hackers may access personal and private information about you and your family. Not only may they access this information, but they may also sell it on a black market for their own profit. Therefore, it is prudent to refrain from posting any information about yourself on a website should you feel uncomfortable or unsure.

Overall, there are a variety of positive ways in which your professional identity may grow using social media and websites. However, there are numerous possibilities and events that may occur that can harm the process of building your online image. No matter how well your online image is built, keep in mind the impact of word of mouth. Word of mouth can just as easily ruin your reputation and professional identity as it can launch your career. In the digital age, word of mouth may spread not just from person to person but from blog to blog, online article to online article, chatroom to chatroom, and message board to message board. In the past, news took days and weeks to circle the globe, whereas in the 21st century, information is posted, available, and accessed in seconds.

The Advantages of Continued Learning

Part of marketing yourself as a mental health professional includes not only the delivery of content but also the quality of your content. A mistake new counselors may make is feeling like they have to know everything or be all things to all people. According to Diana (2010), counselors become generalists, creating a sense of mediocrity and placing them in the middle of the professional marketplace. The following section will help guide you in developing your professional skills so the quality of your words and presentations demonstrates expertise, thus positioning you at the front line for career opportunities.

Keep Up to Date

If you are attempting to market yourself in the counseling profession, it is imperative that you keep up to date with the latest information. Otherwise, you risk tarnishing your reputation by appearing uninterested in the profession or incompetent by having the wrong information at hand. There are many ways to keep up to date within the counseling profession. Academic journals and professional magazines are a great way to stay involved with the latest research and trends. You should visit your state board's website on a regular basis to keep abreast of any changes in laws or regulations, and always keep the most recent and relevant ethical codes handy for consultation. Remember, you are ultimately responsible for seeking this information. Having a thorough knowledge of the latest trends, laws, and regulations will say to others that you take the profession seriously and will help build your marketing image.

Become an Expert

In the field of counseling, there are numerous avenues to explore when obtaining advanced training to become an expert. Training institutions and certifications allow individuals to seek additional experience in a variety of formats. For example, institutions and certifications can be tailored to working with specific populations, theoretical approaches, treatment modalities, and in particular settings such as disaster relief training. When seeking these opportunities, it is important to consider the level of commitment required at the time of training and whether there are additional requirements following the initial training, the location of the training, and the financial costs. Some training may only take one day, whereas becoming an expert requires a lifetime commitment.

In their journey to become experts, some individuals seek advanced education at the postgraduate level. Pursuing a doctoral degree can seem like an impossible task, especially when you have just finished your master's degree. Whether you choose to pursue the degree immediately after your master's or decades later, a doctoral degree can provide countless opportunities for personal and professional growth. Opportunities include conducting research with faculty in a particular subject, presenting at conferences, teaching counseling-related coursework, and obtaining additional experience and hours toward your counseling and supervision licensure.

Although rigorous and demanding, obtaining a doctoral degree in counselor education and supervision will communicate to others that you have gone through advanced training and education in your field. You will have opportunities at the doctoral level that may have never been available to you while in your master's program. Depending on your professional interests, you can enhance your knowledge by conducting research, writing essays, publishing articles, writing books or book chapters, and even developing your own courses. These are just some of the numerous ways in which a doctoral program can allow you to become an expert in the counseling profession and in a particular specialty area.

Becoming an expert through advanced training will open many networking opportunities. Traveling to conferences, workshops, and meetings will afford you the advantage of networking with other professionals and build stronger relationships with your colleagues, all of which allows you to promote your expertise. Through active promotion, "you will be able to use your expanding knowledge base to build systems and service offerings that will earn you increased credibility, authority, and recognition in the field" (Diana, 2010, p. 76). As a result of successful self-promotion opportunities will arise; as opportunities arise, you will be afforded new ways to market yourself to others!

Voices From the Field 13.4 Mindfulness: The Personal Becomes Professional, *by Andy Davis*

I can remember starting my master's program and realizing quickly that I had to face many uncertainties and fears: Am I making the right choice? What does it mean to be a counselor? How do I see myself fitting into that mold? What if this does not work out? These were just some of the many questions that plagued my mind. My undergraduate degree was in engineering, and to change careers to counseling felt quite different. I was also faced with confronting my conservative Christian background, which had taught me to be suspicious of psychology and its attacks on religious values. Friends were verbally supportive of my decision to change careers, yet I could see from their facial expressions that they too were just as confused as I was. As a source of strength, I could hear my mother, who had passed away one year earlier, saying to me, "Andy, you can be whatever you want to be!"

Up until I began my master's program, I had been living up to expectations from others and was now faced with developing my own self-expectations and defining who I was going to be as a counselor. To add to the uncertainty and role confusion, I was getting married and trying to be a father to five children. My life seemed to be moving quickly, and I was trying to catch up with it. While working at a mental health practice, I came into contact with clients who were attending a dialectical behavior therapy (DBT) class, where mindfulness is one of the core skills taught. This immediately caught my undivided attention, and I set out to learn more about this clinical approach by attending several workshops and retreats.

One day, while attending a mindfulness workshop, I had a profound and life-changing experience that allowed me to develop an identity as a counselor and approach to my practice with clients. That morning, I was intentionally and slowly eating a bowl of oatmeal. While mindfully consuming the oatmeal, I began to see the beauty in this intricate process of eating that contrasted with my stressful and fast-paced lifestyle. I was overwhelmed with emotion, tears began to flow, and it was at this moment that I experienced mindfulness.

From that moment, I began incorporating mindfulness-based interventions into my own practice and witnessed clients experiencing positive results. Since then, I have had opportunities to run classes for cancer patients, persons suffering from depression, and nonclinical college students. Invitations have been offered to do public workshops and teach a graduate-level course in mindfulness in counseling. In my doctoral program, I have also had the pleasure of connecting with other practitioners interested in research and clinical practice of mindfulness-based interventions. From my own experience, opportunities have seemed to come together based on my own passion for mindfulness and incorporating it into my clinical work. I have allowed my personal experience with mindfulness to transform my professional identity, reaching out to clients and professionals in ways I had not thought were possible.

Summary

The SELF acronym is a useful tool to navigate the job search process and promote your career advancement. As an ever-changing and growing counseling professional, your personal and professional needs and aspirations will certainly continue to evolve. By maintaining a clear idea of your strengths and acknowledging your limitations, it is likely that you will enjoy your work as a counselor and prove to be an asset to your clients and employers. It is important to maintain an understanding of your values as they relate to your personal and professional needs and aspirations, and to maintain employment that aligns with your beliefs and passions.

Traditional methods of networking, such as personal conversation, word of mouth, attending conferences, and sharing business cards, are commonly used and effective self-marketing strategies. Similarly, the use of technology to self-market is now commonplace because it allows professional counselors fast and easy access to employment opportunities and numerous ways to digitally connect with opportunities. Therefore, it is important to remain informed of the latest technological advances. This includes the importance of staying updated with social networking tools that can be utilized to launch your career into the 21st century.

It is important to create a CV that conveys your interests and understanding of counseling skills. Your CV should be organized and succinct to catch readers' attention in a way that showcases a broad range of skills and talents. Take care to list continued education that aligns with your professional interests and the trends in the counseling profession. Consistent revision of your CV allows you to take advantage of job opportunities quickly, which could make quite a difference in your job search. In addition, cover letters should accompany every CV that is sent to a potential employer.

The job search is multifaceted and requires quite a bit of time and energy. If applicants take time during the application process to identify the assets they offer as a professional, as well as the accommodations and opportunities they need from a potential employment opportunity, it will be worthwhile in the end. Careful use of your CV and interviewing skills, in combination with face-to-face interaction and social networking, will result in a fulfilling career and an opportunity to help others in meaningful ways.

References

Adams, K. B., Matto, H. C., & LeCroy, C. (2009). Limitations of evidence-based practice for social work education: Unpacking the complexity. *Journal of Social Work Education*, *45*(2), 165–186. https://doi.org/10.5175/JSWE.2009.200700105

Agarwal, S. D., & Landon, B. E. (2019). Patterns in outpatient benzodiazepine prescribing in the United States. *JAMA Network Open*, *2*(1), e187399. https://doi.org/10.1001/jamanetworkopen.2018.7399

Allen, K., Cornell, D., Lorek, E., & Sheras, P. (2008). Response of school personnel to student threat assessment training. *School Effectiveness and School Improvement: An International Journal of Research, Policy and Practice*, *19*(3), 319–322. https://doi.org/10.1080/09243450802332184

Alonso, D., & Gearing, R. E. (2017). *Suicide assessment and treatment* (2nd ed.). Springer.

Altekruse, M. K., Harris, H. L., & Brandt, M. A. (2001). *The role of the professional counselor in the 21st century*. Love Publishing.

American Association of Marriage and Family Therapists (AAMFT). (2022). *AAMFT code of ethics*. www.aamft.org/Legal_Ethics/Code_of_Ethics.aspx

American Association of Suicidology (AAS). (2012). *Clinicians as survivors: After a suicide loss*. www.sprc.org/resources-programs/clinicians-survivors-after-suicide-loss

American Counseling Association (ACA). (2014). *American Counseling Association code of ethics*. www.counseling.org/docs/default-source/default-document-library/2014-code-of-ethics-finaladdress.pdf?sfvrsn=96b532c_2

American Foundation for Suicide Prevention (AFSP). (2020). *Suicide statistics*. https://afsp.org/about-suicide/suicide-statistics/

American Foundation for Suicide Prevention (AFSP). (2021). *Surviving a suicide loss: A resource and healing guide*. www.pfw.edu/departments/cepp/depts/hs/centers/bhi/documents/AFSP%20resource%20healing%20guide.pdf

American Mental Health Counselors Association (AMHCA). (2020). *Principles for AMHCA's code of ethics*. www.amhca.org/publications/ethics

American Psychiatric Association. (2013). *Diagnostic and statistical manual of mental disorders* (5th ed.). American Psychiatric Press.

American Psychological Association (APA). (1996). *Violence and the family: Report of the APA presidential task force on violence and the family*. www.nnflp.org/apa/APA_task_force.htm

American Psychological Association (APA). (2010). *Mental health insurance under the federal parity law*. www.apaservices.org/practice/good-practice/winter11-mhpaea.pdf

American Psychological Association (APA). (2019). *Publication manual of the American Psychological Association* (7th ed.). Author.

American School Counselor Association (ASCA). (2016). *ASCA ethical standards for school counselors*. www.schoolcounselor.org/getmedia/f041cbd0-7004-47a5-ba01-3a5d657c6743/Ethical-Standards.pdf

American School Counselor Association (ASCA). (2019). *ASCA national model: A framework for school counseling programs* (4th ed.). Author.

Ancis, J. R., & Ladany, N. (2010). A multicultural framework for counselor supervision. In L. J. Bradley & N. Ladany (Eds.), *Counselor supervision* (4th ed., pp. 53–95). Routledge.

Anderson, A., & West, S. G. (2011). Violence against mental health professionals: When the treater becomes the victim. *Innovations in Clinical Neuroscience*, *8*(3), 34–39.

Anderson, S. K., & Middleton, V. A. (2011). *Explorations in privilege, oppression, and diversity* (2nd ed.). Brooks/Cole.

Anthony, K., Nagel, D., & Goss, S. (2010). *The use of technology in mental health*. Charles C Thomas.

Arredondo, P., Toporek, R., Brown, S. P., Jones, J., Locke, D., Sanchez, J., & Stadler, H. (1996). Operationalization of the multicultural counseling competencies. *Journal of Multicultural Counseling and Development*, *24*, 42–78. https://doi.org/10.1002/j.2161-1912.1996.tb00288.x

Asim, J. (2007). *The n word: Who can say it, who shouldn't, and why*. Houghton Mifflin Company.

Association for Counselor Education and Supervision (ACES). (2011). *Best practices in clinical supervision*. https://acesonline.net/wp-content/uploads/2018/11/ACES-Best-Practices-in-Clinical-Supervision-2011.pdf

Attaway, T., Barnes, L., Daughhetee, C., & Puleo, S. (2002, November). *Cutting the muster: Evaluating our future peers.* Paper presented at the Alabama Counseling Association, Mobile, AL.

Awang, D. V. C. (2009). *Herbs of choice: The therapeutic use of phytochemicals* (3rd ed.). CRC Press, Taylor and Francis Group.

Baird, B. N., & Mollen, D. (2019). *The internship, practicum, and field placement handbook: A guide for the helping profession* (8th ed.). Pearson.

Balkin, R. S., & Juhnke, G. A. (2014). *The theory and practice of assessment in counseling.* Pearson.

Barling, J., Dupré, K., & Kelloway, E. (2009). Predicting workplace aggression and violence. *Annual Review of Psychology, 60*(1), 671–692. https://doi.org/10.1146/annurev.psych.60.110707.163629

Bartholomew, C. (2003). *Gender-sensitive therapy: Principles and practices.* Waveland Press.

Bartlett, M. L. (2008). The efficacy of no-suicide contracts with clients in counseling on an outpatient basis. *Dissertation Abstracts International, 67*, 3438, 06B. (ProQuest [formerly UMI] No. 3225247).

Bartlett, M. L., Carney, J., & Talbott-Forbes, L. (2009). Clients' perceptions of no-suicide contracts. *Journal of Counseling, Research, and Practice, 1*(1), 23–31.

Bartlett, M. L., Siegfried, N. J., & Witte, T. K. (2012). Best practice clinical interventions for working with suicidal adults. *Alabama Counseling Association Journal, 38*(2), 65–79.

Bartlett, M. L., Trippany, R., & Reicherzer, S. (2015). Prevention and crisis intervention services. In D. Sheperis & C. Sheperis (Eds.), *Clinical mental health counseling: Fundamentals of applied practice* (pp. 225–250). Pearson.

Bem, S. L. (1981). *Bem Sex-Role Inventory: Professional Manual.* Consulting Psychologists Press.

Berg, I. K., & Miller, S. (1992). *Working with the problem drinker.* W. W. Norton.

Berghuis, D. J., Peterson, L. M., & Bruce, T. J. (2014). *The complete adult psychotherapy treatment planner* (5th ed.). Wiley.

Berk, M., Henriques, G., Warman, D., Brown, G., & Beck, A. (2004). A cognitive therapy intervention for suicide attempters: An overview of the treatment and case examples. *Cognitive and Behavioral Practice, 11*, 265–277. https://doi.org/10.1016/S1077-7229(04)80041-5

Berman, P. (2018). *Case conceptualization and treatment planning: Integrating theory with clinical practice* (4th ed.). SAGE.

Bernard, J. M., & Goodyear, R. K. (2019). *Fundamentals of clinical supervision* (6th ed.). Pearson.

Berzoff, J., & Kita, E. (2010). Compassion fatigue and countertransference: Two different concepts. *Clinical Social Work Journal, 38*, 341–349. http://doi.org/10.1007/s10615-010-0271-8

Betan, E. J., & Binder, J. L. (2010). Clinical expertise in psychotherapy: How expert therapists use theory in generating case conceptualizations and interventions. *Springer Science and Business Media, 40*, 141–152. https://doi.org/10.1007/s10879-010-9138-0

Black, M. C., Basile, K. C., Breiding, M. J., Smith, S. G., Walters, M. L., Merrick, M. T., Chen, J., & Stevens, M. R. (2011). *The National Intimate Partner and Sexual Violence Survey (NISVS): 2010 summary report.* www.cdc.gov/violenceprevention/pdf/nisvs_report2010-a.pdf

Blakely, T. L., & Mehr, N. (2008). Common ground: The development of a support group for survivors of homicide loss in a rural community. *Social Work with Groups, 31*(3–4), 239–254. https://doi.org/10.1080/01609510801980971

Borders, L. D. (1991). A systemic approach to peer group supervision. *Journal of Counseling & Development, 69*(3), 248–252. https://doi.org/10.1002/j.1556-6676.1991.tb01497.x

Borders, L. D., & Brown, L. L. (2005). *The new handbook of counseling supervision* (2nd ed.). Routledge.

Borum, R., Cornell, D. G., Modzeleski, W., & Jimerson, S. R. (2010). What can be done about school shootings? A review of the evidence. *Educational Researcher, 39*(1), 27–37. https://doi.org/10.3102/0013189X09357620

Bourdieu, P. (1977). *Outline of a theory of practice.* Cambridge University Press.

Bowen, M. (1966). The use of family theory in clinical practice. *Comprehensive Psychiatry, 7*(5), 345–374. https://doi.org/10.1016/S0010-440X(66)80065-2

Bowen, M. (1976). Theory in the practice of psychotherapy. In P. J. Guerin (Ed.), *Family therapy: Theory and practice* (pp. 42–90). Gardner Press.

Bradley, L. J., Hendricks, B., Lock, R., Whiting, P. P., & Parr, G. (2011). E-mail communication: Issues for mental health counselors. *Journal of Mental Health Counseling, 33*(1), 67–79. https://doi.org/10.17744/mehc.33.1.05208025375v03r7

Bride, B., Radey, M., & Figley, C. (2007). Measuring compassion fatigue. *Clinical Social Work Journal, 35*, 155–163. https://doi.org/10.1007/s10615-007-0091-7

Briere, J. N., & Lanktree, C. B. (2012). *Treating complex trauma in adolescents and young adults.* SAGE.

Brown, G. K., Ten Harve, T., Henriques, G. R., Xie, S. R., Hollander, J. E., & Beck, A. T. (2005). Cognitive therapy for the prevention of suicide attempts: A randomized control trial. *Journal of the American Medical Association, 294*(5), 563–570. https://doi.org/10.1001/jama.294.5.563

Brown, R. (2011). Drug court effectiveness: A matched cohort study in the Dane County drug treatment court. *Journal of Offender Rehabilitation, 50*, 191–201. https://doi.org/10.1080/10509674.2011.571347

Brown, R. P., Osterman, L. L., & Barnes, C. D. (2009). School violence and the culture of honor. *Psychological Science, 20*(11), 1400–1405. https://doi.org/10.1111/j.1467-9280.2009.02456.x

Browne, A. (1993). Violence against women by male partners: Prevalence, outcomes, and policy implications. *American Psychologist*, *48*(10), 1077–1087. https://doi.org/10.1037/0003-066X.48.10.1077

Brunton, L., Chabner, B., & Knollman, B. (2011). *Goodman and Gilman's: The pharmacological basis of therapeutics* (12th ed.). McGraw-Hill.

Bryan, C. J., Stone, S. L., & Rudd, M. D. (2011). A practical, evidence-based approach for means-restriction: Counseling with suicidal patients. *Professional Psychology: Research and Practice*, *42*(5), 339–346. http://doi.org/10.1037/a0025051

Bryant, E. M., & Marmo, J. (2012). The rules of Facebook friendship: A two-stage examination of interaction rules in close, casual, and acquaintance friendships. *Journal of Social and Personal Relationships*, *29*(8), 1013–1035. https://doi.org/10.1177/0265407512443616

California Association for Licensed Professional Clinical Counselors. (2020). *About CACREP*. www.cacrep.org/about-cacrep/

Cameron, S., & Imani Turtle-Song. (2002). Learning to write case notes using the SOAP format. *Journal of Counseling & Development*, *80*(3), 286–292. https://doi.org/10.1002/j.1556-6678.2002.tb00193.x

Campbell, J. C. (2007). Prediction of homicide of and by battered women. In J. C. Campbell (Ed.), *Assessing dangerous: Violence by batterers and child abusers* (2nd ed., pp. 85–104). Springer.

Campbell, J. C., Webster, D., Koziol-McLain, J., Block, C., Campbell, D., Curry, M. A., Gary, F., Glass, N., McFarlane, J., Sachs, C., Sharps, P., Ulrich, Y., Wilt, S. A., Manganello, J., Xu, X., Schollenberger, J., Frye, V., & Laughon, K. (2003). Risk factors for femicide in abusive relationships: Results from a multisite case control study. *American Journal of Public Health*, *93*(7), 1089–1097. https://doi.org/10.2105/ajph.93.7.1089

Campbell, J. M. (2006). *Essentials of clinical supervision*. Wiley.

Cannon, W. B. (1929). Organization for physiological homeostasis. *Physiological Review*, *9*(3), 399–431. https://doi.org/10.1152/physrev.1929.9.3.399

Caplan, G. (1963). Types of mental health consultation. *American Journal of Orthopsychiatry*, *33*, 470–481.

Carlson, S. M. S., Plum, K. C., & Meeker, E. C. (2018). Understanding the psychosocial impact of disasters. In T. G. Veenema (Ed.), *Disaster nursing and emergency preparedness: For chemical, biological, and radiological terrorism and other hazards* (4th ed., pp. 151–166). Springer.

Carrola, P., & Corbin-Burdick, M. F. (2015). Counseling military veterans: Advocating for culturally competent and holistic interventions. *Journal of Mental Health Counseling*, *37*(1), 1–14. https://doi.org/10.17744/mehc.37.1.v74514163rv73274

Centers for Disease Control and Prevention (CDC). (2010). *Intimate partner violence: Definitions*. www.cdc.gov/violenceprevention/intimatepartnerviolence/definitions.html

Centers for Disease Control and Prevention (CDC). (2022). *Child maltreatment prevention*. www.cdc.gov/ViolencePrevention/childmaltreatment/index.html

Chang, C. Y., Hays, D. G., & Shoffner, M. (2004). Cross-racial supervision: A developmental approach. *The Clinical Supervisor*, *22*(2), 121–138. https://doi.org/10.1300/J001v22n02_08

Chester, A., & Bretherton, D. (2001). What makes feminist counseling feminist? *Feminism & Psychology*, *11*(4), 527–545. https://doi.org/10.1177/0959353501011004006

Cohen, J. A., Berliner, L., & Mannarino, A. (2010). Trauma focused CBT for children with co-occurring trauma and behaviors problems. *Child Abuse & Neglect*, *34*(4), 215–225. https://doi.org/10.1016/j.chiabu.2009.12.003

Cohen, J. A., Mannarino, A. P., & Deblinger, E. (2017). *Treating trauma and traumatic grief in children and adolescents* (2nd ed.). Guilford Press.

Collins, B. G., & Collins, T. M. (2006). *Crisis and trauma*. Lahaska.

Collison, B. B., Osborne, J. L., Gray, L. A., House, R. M., Firth, J., & Lou, M. (1998). Preparing counselors for social action. In C. C. Lee & G. Walz (Eds.), *Social action: A mandate for counselors* (pp. 263–277). American Counseling Association.

Colthorpe, K., Sharifirad, T., Ainscough, L., Anderson, S., & Zimbardi, K. (2018). Prompting undergraduate students' metacognition of learning: Implementing 'meta-learning' assessment tasks in the biomedical sciences. *Assessment & Evaluation in Higher Education*, *43*(2), 272–285. https://doi.org/10.1080/02602938.2017.1334872

Cook, K., Juhnke, G. A., Peters, S. W., Marbach, C. R., Day, S., Choucroun, P., & Baker, R. E. (2006). Promoting clinical knowledge, skills, and empathy via a creative self-suicide assignment: Rationale, purpose, and student responses. *Journal of Creativity in Mental Health*, 2(2), 39–46. https://doi.org/10.1300/J456v02_05

Coombs, D., Talbott, L. L., & Harrington, J. (2010). Youth suicides in Alabama: A focus on gun safety. *Alabama State Association for Health, Physical Education, Recreation, and Dance Journal*, *31*(1), 31–35.

Corey, G. (2016). *Theory and practice of counseling and psychotherapy* (10th ed.). Cengage.

Corey, G., Corey, M., & Corey, C. (2019). *Issues and ethics in the helping profession* (10th ed.). Cengage.

Cormier, S. (2016). *Counseling strategies and interventions* (9th ed.). Pearson.

Cottone, R. R., & Tarvydas, V. M. (2021). *Ethics and decision-making in counseling and psychotherapy* (5th ed.). Springer.

Council for Accreditation of Counseling and Related Educational Programs (CACREP). (2016). *2016 CACREP standards*. www.cacrep.org/wp-content/uploads/2018/05/2016-Standards-with-Glossary-5.3.2018.pdf

Cowie, M. E., Nealis, L. J., Sherry, S. B., Hewitt, P. L., & Flett, G. L. (2018). Perfectionism and academic difficulties in graduate students: Testing incremental prediction and gender moderation. *Personality & Individual Differences*, *123*, 223–228. https://doi.org/10.1016/j.paid.2017.11.027

Craig, C. D., & Sprang, G. (2010). Compassion satisfaction, compassion fatigue, and burnout in a national sample of trauma treatment therapists. *Anxiety, Stress, & Coping*, *23*, 319–339. https://doi.org/10.1080/10615800903085818

Crawford, E. F., Elbogen, E. B., Wagner, H. R., Kudler, H., Calhoun, P. S., Brancu, M., Straits, T. K. A. (2015). Surveying treatment preferences in U.S. Iraq-Afghanistan veterans with PTSD symptoms: A step toward veteran-centered care. *Journal of Traumatic Stress*, *28*(2), 118–126. https://doi.org/10.1002/jts.21993

Currier, J. M., Holland, J., Coleman, R., & Neimeyer, R. A. (2008). Bereavement following violent death: An assault of life and meaning. In R. Stephenson & G. Cox (Eds.), *Perspectives on violence and violent death*. Routledge.

Cutts, L. (2011). Integration in counselling psychology: To what purpose? *Counselling Psychology Review*, *26*(2), 38–48.

Daly, M. E., & Mansfield, J. K. (2014). A study of relevance of social network sites and ethics involving undergraduate students. *Journal of Baccalaureate Social Work*, *19*, 83–96.

Daughhetee, C., Puleo, S., & Thrower, E. (2010). Scaffolding of continuing competency as an essential element of professionalism. *Alabama Counseling Association Journal*, *36*(1), 15–22.

DeLettre, J. L., & Sobell, L. C. (2010). Keeping psychotherapy notes separate from the patient record. *Clinical Psychology and Psychotherapy*, *17*(2), 160–163. https://doi.org/10.1002/cpp.654

de Shazer, S. (1988). *Clues: Investigating solutions in brief therapy*. W. W. Norton.

de Shazer, S. (1991). *Putting difference to work*. W. W. Norton.

Diana, D. (2010). *Marketing for the mental health professional: An innovative guide for practitioners*. Wiley.

Dokkedahl, S., Kok, R. N., Murphy, S., Kristensen, T. R., Bech-Hansen, D., & Elklit, A. (2019). The psychological subtype of intimate partner violence and its effect on mental health: Protocol for a systematic review and meta-analysis. *Systematic Reviews*, *8*(1), 1–10. https://doi.org/10.1186/S13643-019-1118-1

Donaldson, D., Spirito, A., & Esposito-Smythers, C. (2005). Treatment for adolescents following a suicide attempt: Results of a pilot trial. *Journal of the American Academy of Child Adolescent Psychiatry*, *44*(2), 113–120. https://doi.org/10.1097/00004583-200502000-00003

Dougherty, J. L. (2005). Ethics in case conceptualization and diagnosis: Incorporating a medical model into the developmental counseling tradition. *Counseling and Values*, *49*, 132–140. https://doi.org/10.1002/j.2161-007X.2005.tb00259.x

Douglas, K. S., & Skeem, J. L. (2005). Violence risk assessment: Getting specific about being dynamic. *Psychology, Public Policy, and Law*, *11*(3), 347–383. https://doi.org/10.1037/1076-8971.11.3.347

Edwards, G. S. (2013). Tarasoff, duty to warn laws, and suicide. *International Journal of Law and Economics*, *34*, 1–8. https://doi.org/10.1016/j.irle.2012.10.004

Edwards, G. S. (2018). *Database of state Tarasoff laws*. https://papers.ssrn.com/sol3/papers.cfm?abstract_id=1551505

Egan, G., & Reese, R. J. (2018). *The skilled helper: A problem-management and opportunity-development approach to helping* (11th ed.). Cengage.

Eisel v. Board of Education, 597 A.2d 447 (Md. Ct. App. 1991).

Eke, A. W., Hilton, N. Z., Harris, G. T., Rice, M. E., & Houghton, R. E. (2011). Intimate partner homicide: Risk assessment and prospectus for prediction. *Journal of Family Violence*, *26*(3), 211–216. https://doi.org/10.1007/s10896-010-9356-y

Enarson, E., Fothergill, A., & Peek, L. (2018). Gender and disaster: Foundations and possibilities. In H. Rodriguez, W. Donner, & J. E. Trainor (Eds.), *Handbook of disaster research* (pp. 205–224). Springer.

Erford, B. T. (2015). *Research and evaluation in counseling* (2nd ed.). Cengage.

Erford, B. T. (2020). *45 techniques every counselor should know*. Pearson.

Erford, B. T. (2021). *Assessment for counselors*. Pearson.

Erford, B. T. (Ed.). (2023). *Orientation to the counseling profession* (4th ed.). Pearson.

Eriksen, K. (1997). *Making an impact: A handbook on counselor advocacy*. Accelerated Development.

Erikson, E. H. (1963). *Childhood and society* (2nd ed.). W. W. Norton.

Evans, M. A., & Feder, G. S. (2016). Help-seeking amongst women survivors of domestic violence: A qualitative study of pathways towards formal and informal support. *Healthy Expectations*, *19*(1), 62–73. https://doi.org/10.1111/hex.12330

Everly, G. S., Phillips, S. B., Kane, D., & Feldman, D. (2006). Introduction to and overview of group psychological first aid. *Brief Treatment & Crisis Intervention*, *6*, 130–136. https://doi.org/10.1093/brief-treatment/mhj009

Ewert, A., & Tessneer, S. (2019). Psychological resilience and posttraumatic growth: An exploratory analysis. *Journal of Experiential Education*, *42*(3), 280–296. https://doi.org/10.1177/1053825919859027

Farberow, N. L. (2005). The mental health professional as suicide survivor. *Clinical Neuropsychiatry*, *2*(1), 13–20.

Farington, D. P., & Lober, R. (2011). *Young homicide offenders and victims: Risk factors, prediction, and prevention from childhood*. Springer.

Ferguson, C. J., & Kilburn, J. (2009). The public health risks of media violence: A meta-analytic review. *Journal of Pediatrics*, *154*, 759–763. https://doi.org/10.1016/j.jpeds.2008.11.033

Figley, C. R. (2002). Compassion fatigue: Psychotherapists' chronic lack of self-care. *Journal of Clinical Psychology*, *58*(11), 1433–1441. https://doi.org/10.1002/jclp.10090

Flaherty, H. B. (2018). Treating adolescent nonsuicidal self-injury: A review of psychosocial interventions to guide clinical practice. *Child & Adolescent Social Work Journal*, *35*(1), 85–95. https://doi.org/10.1007/s10560-017-0505-5

Flynn, S., Abel, K., While, D., Mehta, H., & Shaw, J. (2011). Mental illness, gender and homicide: A population-based descriptive study. *Psychiatry Research*, *185*(3), 368–375. https://doi.org/10.1016/j.psychres.2010.07.040

Foa, E. B., Keane, T. M., Friedman, M. J., & Cohen, J. A. (Eds.). (2010). *Effective treatments for PTSD: Practice guidelines from the International Society for Traumatic Stress Studies* (2nd ed.). Guilford.

Folstein, M. F., Folstein, S. E., & McHugh, P. R. (1975). "Mini-mental state": A practical method for grading the cognitive state of patients for the clinician. *Journal of Psychiatric Research*, *12*(3), 189–198. https://doi.org/10.1016/0022-3956(75)90026-6

Forester-Miller, H., & Davis, T. E. (2016). *Practitioner's guide to ethical decision making* (rev. ed.). www.counseling.org/docs/default-source/ethics/practioner-39-s-guide-to-ethical-decision-making.pdf

Foster, K., O'Brien, L., & Korhonen, T. (2012). Developing resilient children and families when parents have mental illness: A family-focused approach. *International Journal of Mental Health Nursing*, *21*(1), 3–11. https://doi.org/10.1111/j.1447-0349.2011.00754.x

Foster, S. (2007). *Tyler's honest herbal: A sensible guide to the use of herbs and related remedies* (4th ed.). Routledge.

Frank, R. G., Beronio, K., & Glied, S. A. (2014). Behavioral health parity and the Affordable Care Act. *Journal of Social Work in Disability & Rehabilitation*, *13*(1–2), 31–43. https://doi.org/10.1080/1536710X.2013.870512

Frankl, V. (1963). *Man's search for meaning*. Beacon.

Fullen, M. C., Granello, D. H., Richardson, V. E., & Granello, P. F. (2018). Using wellness and resilience to predict age perception in older adulthood. *Journal of Counseling & Development*, *96*(4), 424–435. https://doi.org/10.1002/jcad.12224

Gabbard, G., & Kay, J. (2001). The fate of integrated treatment: Whatever happened to the biopsychosocial psychiatrist? *The American Journal of Psychiatry*, *158*(12), 1956–1963. https://doi.org/10.1176/appi.ajp.158.12.1956

Gardner, M. J., Thomas, H. J., & Erskine, H. E. (2019). The association between five forms of child maltreatment and depressive and anxiety disorders: A systematic review and meta-analysis. *Child Abuse & Neglect*, *96*, 104082. https://doi.org/10.1016/j.chiabu.2019.104082

Gekoski, A., Gray, J. M., & Adler, J. A. (2012). Interviewing women bereaved by homicide: Assessing the impact of trauma-focused research. *Psychology, Crime, & Law*, *18*(2), 177–189. https://doi.org/10.1080/10683161003718692

Gendreau, P., & Goggin, C. (2014). Practicing psychology in correctional settings. In I. B. Weiner & A. K. Hess (Eds.), *The handbook of forensic psychology* (4th ed., pp. 759–794). Wiley.

Giedd, J. (2002). *The adolescent brain—why teenagers think and act differently*. www.edinformatics.com/news/teenage_brains.htm

Gilbert, L. A., & Scher, M. (2009). *Gender and sex in counseling and psychotherapy*. Wipf & Stock Pub.

Gladding, S. T. (2017). *The counseling dictionary: Concise definitions of frequently used terms* (4th ed.). Pearson.

Gladding, S. T. (2018). *Counseling: A comprehensive profession* (8th ed.). Pearson.

Gladding, S. T. (2019). *Family therapy history theory and practice* (7th ed.). Pearson.

Gladding, S. T., & Newsome, D. W. (2018). *Clinical mental health counseling in community and agency settings* (5th ed.). Pearson.

Glasser, W. (2001). *Counseling with choice theory*. Harper Perennial.

Goetz, A. T., Shackelford, T. K., Romero, G. A., Kaighobadi, F., & Miner, E. J. (2008). Punishment, proprietariness and paternity: Men's violence against women from an evolutionary perspective. *Aggression and Violent Behavior*, *13*(6), 481–489. https://doi.org/10.1016/j.avb.2008.07.004

Golding, J. (1999). Intimate partner violence as a risk factor for mental disorders: A meta-analysis. *Journal of Family Violence*, *14*(2), 99–132. https://doi.org/10.1023/A:1022079418229

Goldstein, D. S., & Kopin, I. J. (2007). Evolution of concepts of stress. *Stress*, *10*(2), 109–120. https://doi.org/10.1080/10253890701288935

Goodyear, R. K., Borders, L. D., Chang, C. Y., Guiffrida, D. A., Hutman, H., Kemer, G., Watkins, Jr. C. E., & White, E. (2016). Prioritizing questions and methods for an international and interdisciplinary supervision research agenda: Suggestions by eight scholars. *The Clinical Supervisor*, *35*(1), 117–154. https://doi.org/10.1080/07325223.2016.1153991

Gottfredson, G. D., & Holland, J. L. (1996). *Dictionary of Holland occupational codes* (3rd ed.). Psychological Assessment Resources.

Gottlieb, M. C., & Cooper, C. C. (2000). The future of mental health care delivery: Ideals and realities. *The Counseling Psychologist*, *28*(2), 263–266. https://doi.org/10.1177/0011000000282005

Granello, D. H. (2010). The process of suicide risk assessment: Twelve core principles. *Journal of Counseling & Development*, *88*, 363–370. https://doi.org/10.1002/j.1556-6678.2010.tb00034.x

Granello, D. H., & Granello, P. F. (2007). *Suicide: An essential guide for helping professionals and educators*. Pearson.

Greason, P. B., & Cashwell, C. S. (2009). Mindfulness and counseling self-efficacy: The mediating role of attention and empathy. *Counselor Education & Supervision*, *49*(1), 2–19. https://doi.org/10.1002/j.1556-6978.2009.tb00083.x

Grossman, L. R., & Koocher, G. P. (2012). Privacy, confidentiality and privilege of health records and psychotherapy notes in custody cases. *American Journal of Family Law*, *24*(1), 41–50.

Guillot-Miller, L., & Partin, P. W. (2003). Web-based resources for legal and ethical issues in school counseling. *Professional School Counseling*, *7*(1), 52–60. www.jstor.org/stable/42732535

Gutheil, T., & Hilliard, J. (2001). Don't write me down: Legal, clinical, and risk-management aspects of patients' requests that therapists not keep notes or records. *American Journal of Psychotherapy*, *55*(2), 157–165. https://doi.org/10.1176/appi.psychotherapy.2001.55.2.157

Hackney, H. L., & Bernard, J. M. (2017). *Professional counseling: A process guide to helping* (8th ed.). Pearson.

Haffejee, S., & Theron, L. (2017). Resilience processes in sexually abused adolescent girls: A scoping review of the literature. *South African Journal of Science*, *113*(9/10), 31–39. https://doi.org/10.17159/sajs.2017/20160318
Halbur, D. A., & Halbur, K. V. (2018). *Developing your theoretical orientation in counseling and psychotherapy* (4th ed.). Pearson.
Hall, L. K. (2016). *Counseling military families: What mental health professionals need to know*. Routledge.
Hamblin, J., & Barnett, E. (2019). *PTSD in children and adolescents*. www.ptsd.va.gov/professional/treat/specific/ptsd_child_teens.asp
Hanifan, L. J. (1916). The rural school community center. *Annals of the American Academy of Political and Social Science*, *67*(1), 130–138. https://doi.org/10.1177/000271621606700118
Hansen, J. C., Stevic, R. R., & Warner, R. W. (1993). *Counseling: Theory and process* (4th ed.). Allyn & Bacon.
Hansen, J. T. (2006a). Counseling theories within a postmodern epistemology: New roles for theories in counseling practice. *Journal of Counseling & Development*, *84*(3), 291–297. https://doi.org/10.1002/j.1556-6678.2006.tb00408.x
Hansen, J. T. (2006b). Humanism as moral imperative: Comments on the role of knowing in the helping encounter. *Journal of Humanistic Counseling, Education, and Development*, *45*(2), 115–125. https://doi.org/10.1002/j.2161-1939.2006.tb00011.x
Hard, P. F., Talbott-Forbes, L. L., & Bartlett, M. L. (2018). Ethical and legal considerations in crisis counseling. In L. R. Jackson-Cherry & B. T. Erford (Eds.), *Crisis prevention, assessment, and intervention* (3rd ed., pp. 45–62). Pearson.
Harrington, J. A., & Daughhetee, C. (2018). Risk assessment and intervention: Suicide and homicide. In L. R. Jackson-Cherry & B. T. Erford (Eds.), *Crisis prevention, assessment, and intervention* (3rd ed., pp. 103–132). Pearson.
Harris, E. A. (1995). The importance of risk management in a managed care environment. In M. B. Sussman (Ed.), *A perilous calling: The hazards of psychotherapy practice* (pp. 247–258). Wiley.
Harris, S. M., Brown, A., Dakin, J. B., Lucas, B., Riley, L., & Bulham, R. (2009). Are clinical records really that important? The dearth of research and practice guidelines in MFT literature. *The American Journal of Family Therapy*, *37*(5), 373–387. https://doi.org/10.1080/01926180902754729
Haynes, R., Corey, G., & Moulton, P. (2003). *Clinical supervision in the helping professions: A practical guide*. Brooks/Cole—Thomson Learning.
Hays, D. G., & Chang, C. Y. (2019). Termination. In B. T. Erford (Ed.), *Group work: Processes and applications* (pp. 146–170). Pearson.
Hays, D. G., & Erford, B. T. (Eds.). (2022). *Developing multicultural counseling competence: A systems approach* (4th ed.). Pearson.
Heller, R. J., Gilliam, L. S., Chenail, R. J., & Hall, T. L. (2010). Three authors, one client: A qualitative description of marriage and family therapy initial case documentation. *Contemporary Family Therapy*, *32*(4), 363–375. https://doi.org/10.1007/s10591-1-010-9130-6
Helms, J. E. (1995). An update of white and people of color racial identity model. In J. G. Ponterotto, J. M. Casa, L. A. Suzuki, & C. M. Alexander (Eds.), *Handbook of multicultural counseling* (pp. 191–198). SAGE.
Hendricks, B., Bradley, L. J., Southern, S., Oliver, M., & Birdsall, B. (2011). Ethical code for the International Association of Marriage and Family Counselors. *The Family Journal*, *19*(2), 217–224. https://doi.org/10.1177/1066480711400814
Henriques, G. R., Beck, A. T., & Brown, G. K. (2003). Cognitive therapy for adolescent and young adult suicide attempters. *American Behavioral Scientist*, *46*(9), 1258–1268. https://doi.org/10.1177/0002764202250668
Herbert, P. B., & Young, K. A. (2002). Tarasoff at twenty-five. *Journal of the American Academy of Psychiatry and the Law*, *30*, 275–281.
Herlihy, B., & Corey, G. (2014). *ACA ethical standards casebook* (7th ed.). American Counseling Association.
Herman, J. (2015). *Trauma and recovery: The aftermath of violence—from domestic abuse to political terror*. Basic Books.
Herrenkohl, T. I., Sousa, C., Tajima, E. A., Herrenkohl, R. C., & Moylan, C. A. (2008). Intersection of child abuse and children's exposure to domestic violence. *Trauma, Violence, & Abuse*, *9*(2), 84–99. https://doi.org/10.1177/1524838008314797
Hilt, L. M., Nock, M. K., Lloyd-Richardson, E. E., & Prinstein, M. J. (2008). Longitudinal study of nonsuicidal self-injury among young adolescents. *The Journal of Early Adolescence*, *28*, 455–469. https://doi.org/10.1177/0272431608316604
Hodge, D. R. (2011). Using spiritual interventions in practice: Developing some guidelines from evidence-based practice. *Social Work*, *56*(2), 149–158. https://doi.org/10.1093/sw/56.2.149
Hodges, S. (2015). *The counseling practicum and internship manual: A resource for graduate counseling students* (2nd ed.). Springer.
Hodges, S., & Connelly, A. R. (2010). *A job search manual for counselors and counselor educators: How to navigate and promote your counseling career*. American Counseling Association.
Hoffman, R. M. (2001). The measurement of masculinity and femininity: Historical perspectives and implications for counseling. *Journal of Counseling & Development*, *79*(4), 472–485. https://doi.org/10.1002/j.1556-6676.2001.tb01995.x
Hogan-Garcia, M. (2012). *The four skills of cultural diversity competence* (4th ed.). Cengage.
Holloway, E. L. (1995). *Clinical supervision: A systems approach*. SAGE.
Houppert, K. (2006). *Homes fires burning: Married to the military—for better or worse*. Ballantine.
House, R. M., & Sears, S. J. (2002). Preparing school counselors as leaders and advocates: A critical need in the new millennium. *Theory into Practice*, *41*(3), 154–162. https://doi.org/10.1207/s15430421tip4103_3
Ingram, B. L. (2012). *Clinical case formulations: Matching the integrative treatment plan to the client* (2nd ed.). Wiley.

International Association of Marriage and Family Counselors (IAMFC). (2017). *IAMFC code of ethics*. www.iamfconline.org/ethics

Ivers, N. N., & Perry, R. L. (2014). A time to tell? Legal issues regarding the duty to warn and protect. *Journal of Human Services*, *34*(1), 70–81.

Ivey, A. E., Ivey, M. B., & Zalaquett, C. P. (2017). *Intentional interviewing and counseling: Facilitating client development in a multicultural society* (9th ed.). Cengage.

Izadi-Mazidi, M., Yaghubi, H., Mohammadkhani, P., & Hassanabadi, H. (2019). Assessing the functions of non-suicidal self-injury: Factor analysis of functional assessment of self-mutilation among adolescents. *Iranian Journal of Psychiatry*, *14*(3), 184–191.

Jackson, N. (2004). Developing the concept of metalearning. *Innovations in Education and Teaching International*, *41*(4), 391–403. https://doi.org/10.1080/147032904200027699510.1080/1470329042000276995

Jackson-Cherry, L. R., & Erford, B. T. (Eds.). (2018). *Crisis prevention, assessment, and intervention* (3rd ed.). Pearson.

Jennings, L., & Skovholt, T. M. (2017). The cognitive emotional and relational characteristics of master therapists. In T. M. Skovholt & L. Jennings (Eds.), *Master therapists exploring expertise in therapy and counseling* (10th ed., pp. 31–52). Oxford University Press.

Jobes, D. A. (2016). *Managing suicidal risk: A collaborative approach* (2nd ed.). Guilford Press.

Johnson, D., & Zlotnick, C. (2009). Hope for battered women with PTSD in domestic violence shelters. *Professional Psychology: Research and Practice*, *40*(3), 234–241. http://doi.org/10.1037/a0012519

Joiner, T. E. (2007). *Why people die by suicide*. Harvard University Press.

Joiner, T. E., Van Orden, K. A., Witte, T. K., & Rudd, M. D. (2009). *The interpersonal theory of suicide: Guidance for working with suicidal clients*. American Psychological Association.

Jones-Smith, E. (2014). *Theories of counseling and psychotherapy: An integrative approach* (2nd ed.). SAGE.

Jordan, J. R., & Harpel, J. L. (2007). *Facilitating suicide bereavement support groups: A self-study manual*. American Foundation for Suicide Prevention.

Jordan, J. R., & McIntosh, J. L. (2011). *Grief after suicide: Understanding the consequences and caring for the survivors*. Routledge.

Juhnke, G. A., & Granello, P. F. (2005). Shattered dreams of professional competence: The impact of client suicides on mental health practitioners and how to prepare for it. *Journal of Creativity in Mental Health*, *2*(3–4), 205–223. https://doi.org/10.1300/J456v01n03_12

Jun, H. (2018). *Social justice, multicultural counseling, and practice: Beyond a conventional approach* (2nd ed.). SAGE.

Kaighobadi, F., & Shackelford, T. K. (2009). Suspicions of female infidelity predict men's partner-directed violence. *Behavioral and Brain Sciences*, *32*(3–4), 281–282. https://doi.org/10.1017/S0140525X09990392

Kaminsky, M., McCabe, O. L., Langlieb, A. M., & Everly, G. S. (2006). An evidence-informed model of human resistance, resilience, and recovery. The Johns Hopkins' outcome-driven paradigm for disaster mental health services. *Brief Treatment and Crisis Intervention*, *7*(1), 1–11. https://doi.org/10.1093/brief-treatment/mhl015

Kaplan, D. M., & Gladding, S. T. (2011). A vision for the future of counseling: The 20/20 principles for unifying and strengthening the profession. *Journal of Counseling & Development*, *89*(4), 367–372. https://doi.org/10.1002/j.1556-6678.2011.tb00101.x

Kaplan, D. M., Tarvydas, V. M., & Gladding, S. T. (2014). 20/20: A vision for the future of counseling: The new consensus definition of counseling. *Journal of Counseling & Development*, *92*(3), 366–372. https://doi.org/10.1002/j.1556-6676.2014.00164.x

Kelly, G. A. (1963). *A theory of personality*. W. W. Norton.

Kerr, M., & Bowen, M. (2009). *Family evaluation* (2nd ed.). W. W. Norton.

Kettenbach, G. (1995). *Writing S.O.A.P. notes* (2nd ed.). F. A. Davis.

Keys, S. G., Bemak, F., Carpenter, S. L., & King-Sears, M. E. (1998). Collaborative consultant: A new role for counselors serving at-risk youth. *Journal of Counseling & Development*, *76*(2), 123–133. https://doi.org/10.1002/j.1556-6676.1998.tb02385.x

King, J. H., & Anderson, S. M. (2004). Therapeutic implications of pharmacotherapy: Current trends and ethical issues. *Journal of Counseling & Development*, *82*(3), 329–336. https://doi.org/10.1002/j.1556-6678.2004.tb00318.x

Kiracofe, N. M., & Wells, L. (2007). Mandated disciplinary counseling on campus: Problems and possibilities. *Journal of Counseling & Development*, *85*(3), 259–268. https://doi.org/10.1002/j.1556-6678.2007.tb00473.x

Kiselica, M. S., & Robinson, M. (2001). Bringing advocacy counseling to life: The history, issues, and human dramas of social justice work in counseling. *Journal of Counseling & Development*, *79*(4), 387–397. https://doi.org/10.1002/j.1556-6676.2001.tb01985.x

Kleespies, P. M., & Richmond, J. S. (2009). Evaluating behavioral emergencies: The clinical interview. In P. M. Kleespies (Ed.), *Behavioral emergencies: An evidence-based resource for evaluating and managing risk of suicide, violence, and victimization* (pp. 33–55). American Psychological Association.

Klott, J., & Jongsma, A. E., Jr. (2004). *The suicide and homicide risk assessment & treatment planner*. Wiley.

Koocher, G. P., & Keith-Spiegel, P. (2016). *Ethics in psychology and the mental health professions: Standards and cases* (4th ed.). Oxford University Press.

Koocher, G. P., Norcross, J. C., & Greene, B. A. (2013). *Psychologists' desk reference* (3rd ed.). Oxford University Press.

Kress, V. E. (2003). Self-injurious behaviors: Assessment and diagnosis. *Journal of Counseling & Development*, *81*(4), 490–496. https://doi.org/10.1002/j.1556-6678.2003.tb00276.x

Kress, V. E., Adamson, N. A., Paylo, M., DeMarco, C., & Bradley, N. (2012). The use of safety plans with children and adolescents living in violent families. *The Family Journal*, *20*(3), 249–255. https://doi.org/10.1177/1066480712448833

Kress, V. E., & Hoffman, R. (2008). Empowering adolescent sexual abuse survivors: Application of a solution-focused, Ericksonian counseling group. *Journal of Humanistic Counseling, Education, and Development*, *47*(2), 172–186. https://doi.org/10.1002/j.2161-1939.2008.tb00056.x

Kress, V. E., Hoffman, R. M., & Eriksen, K. (2010). Ethical dimensions of diagnosing: Considerations for clinical mental health counselors. *Counseling & Values*, *55*(1), 101–112. https://doi.org/10.1002/j.2161-007X.2010.tb00024.x

Kress, V. E., Hoffman, R. M., Adamson, N., & Eriksen, K. (2013). Informed consent, confidentiality, and diagnosing: Ethical guidelines for counselor practice. *Journal of Mental Health Counseling*, *35*(1), 15–28. https://doi.org/10.17744/mehc.35.1.5q82020u18r46007

Kress, V. E., & Paylo, M. J. (2019). *Treating those with mental disorders: A comprehensive approach to case conceptualization and treatment* (2nd ed.). Pearson.

Kress, V. E., Paylo, M. J., & Stargell, N. A. (2019). *Counseling children and adolescents*. Pearson.

Kress, V. E., Protivnak, J. J., & Sadlak, L. (2008). Counseling clients involved with violent intimate partners: Mental health counselors' role in promoting client safety. *Journal of Mental Health Counseling*, *30*(3), 200–210. https://doi.org/10.17744/mehc.30.3.e0r87734721l6016

Kress, V. E., Seligman, L., & Reichenberg, L. W. (2021). *Theories of counseling and psychotherapy: Systems, strategies and skills* (5th ed.). Pearson.

Krumboltz, J. D., Kinnier, R. T., Rude, S. S., Scherba, D. S., & Hamel, D. A. (1986). Teaching a rational approach to career decision making: Who benefits most? *Journal of Vocational Behaviour*, *29*(1), 1–6. https://doi.org/10.1016/0001-8791(86)90024-2

Krumboltz, J. D., & Levin, A. S. (2010). *Luck is no accident: Making the most of happenstance in your life and career* (2nd ed.). Impact Publishers.

Kübler-Ross, E. (2014). *On death and dying* (reissue). Scribner.

Kurpius, D. J., & Rozecki, T. (1992). Outreach, advocacy, and consultation: A framework for prevention and intervention. *Elementary School Guidance & Counseling*, *26*(3), 176–189. www.jstor.org/stable/42869014

Lambert, S. F., & Lawson, G. (2013). Resilience of professional counselors following Hurricanes Katrina and Rita. *Journal of Counseling & Development*, *91*(3), 261–268. https://doi.org/10.1002/j.1556-6676.2013.00094.x

Lassiter, P. S., Napolitano, L., Culbreth, J. R., & Ng, K. (2008). Developing multicultural competence using the structured peer group supervision model. *Counselor Education and Supervision*, *47*(3), 164–178. https://doi.org/10.1002/j.1556-6978.2008.tb00047.x

Laux, J. M. (2002). A primer on suicidology: Implications for counselors. *Journal of Counseling & Development*, *80*(3), 380–384. https://doi.org/10.1002/j.1556-6678.2002.tb00203.x

Lazarus, A. A., & Beutler, L. E. (1993). On technical eclecticism. *Journal of Counseling & Development*, *71*(4), 381–385. https://doi.org/10.1002/j.1556-6676.1993.tb02652.x

Lazarus, R. S. (2006). *Stress and emotion: A new synthesis*. Springer.

Lazarus, R. S., & Folkman, S. (1984). *Stress, appraisal and coping*. Springer.

Lee, C. C., & Rodgers, R. A. (2009). Counselor advocacy: Affecting systemic change in the public arena. *Journal of Counseling & Development*, *87*(3), 284–287. https://doi.org/10.1002/j.1556-6678.2009.tb00108.x

Lee, J. B., & Bartlett, M. L. (2005). Suicide prevention: Critical elements for managing suicidal clients and counselor liability without the use of a no-suicide contract. *Death Studies*, *29*(9), 1–19. https://doi.org/10.1080/07481180500236776

Legowo, E., Rachmawati, I., & Hariko, R. (2017). The philosophy of helping (consultation model and altruistic behavior as an important part of the counselor for early childhood). *Advances in Social Science, Education and Humanistic Research*, *169*, 240–245. https://doi.org/10.2991/icece-17.2018.62

Lewis, J., & Bradley, L. (Eds.). (2000). *Advocacy in counseling: Counselors, clients, & community*. ERIC Counseling and Student Services Clearinghouse.

Liddle, J. R., Shackelford, T. K., & Weekes-Shackelford, V. A. (2012). Why can't we all just get along? Evolutionary perspectives on violence, homicide, and war. *Review of General Psychology*, *16*(1), 24–36. https://doi.org/10.1037/a0026610

Linehan, M. M. (2015). *DBT skills training manual*. Guilford.

Linehan, M. M., Comtois, K. A., Murray, A. M., Brown, M. Z., Gallop, R. J., Heard, H. L., Korslund, K. E., Tutek, D. A., Reynolds, S. K., & Lindenboim, N. (2006). Two year randomized controlled trial and follow-up of dialectical behavior therapy vs. therapy by experts for suicidal behaviors and borderline personality disorder. *Archives of General Psychiatry*, *63*(7), 757–766. https://doi.org/10.1001/archpsyc.63.7.757

Lo, C. K. M., Chan, K. L., & Ip, P. (2019). Insecure adult attachment and child maltreatment: A meta-analysis. *Trauma, Violence & Abuse*, *20*(5), 706–719. https://doi.org/10.1177/1524838017730579

Loganbill, C., Hardy, E., & Delworth, W. (1982). Supervision: A conceptual model. *The Counseling Psychologist*, *10*(1), 3–42. https://doi.org/10.1177/0011000082101002

Lök, N., Bademli, K., & Selçuk-Tosun, A. (2019). The effect of reminiscence therapy on cognitive functions, depression, and quality of life in Alzheimer patients: Randomized controlled trial. *International Journal of Geriatric Psychiatry*, *34*(1), 47–53. https://doi.org/10.1002/gps.4980

Magen, R. H., & Magen, J. G. (2010). Revisiting Aunt Fanny: Evaluating professional writing. *Social Work Education*, *29*(7), 792–809. https://doi.org/10.1080/02621547100359327

Magruder, J. A., Adams, B. S., Photo, P., & Smith, T. L. (2018). Clinicians' experiences of transition to electronic health records. *Journal of College Counseling*, *21*(3), 210–223. https://doi.org/10.1002/jocc.12104

Maree, K. (Ed.). (2011). *Shaping the story: A guide to facilitating narrative career counselling*. Sense Publishers.

Maruish, M. E. (2019). *Essentials of treatment planning*. Wiley.

May, R. (1977). *The meaning of anxiety* (rev. ed.). W. W. Norton.

Mazzula, S. L., & LiVecchi, P. (2018). *Ethics for professional counselors: Integrating counseling and psychotherapy standards*. Springer.

McAdams, C. R., & Keener, H. J. (2008). Preparation, action, recovery: A conceptual framework for counselor preparation and response in client crises. *Journal of Counseling & Development*, *86*(4), 388–398. https://doi.org/10.1002/j.1556-6678.2008.tb00526.x

McAuliffe, G. J. (1993). Constructive development and career transition: Implications for counseling. *Journal of Counseling & Development*, *72*(1), 23–28. https://doi.org/10.1002/j.1556-6676.1993.tb02271.x

McAuliffe, G. J., & Emmett, J. (2017). The postmodern impulse and career counselor preparation. In L. A. Busacca & M. C. Rehfuss (Eds.), *Postmodern career counseling: A handbook of culture, context, and cases*. American Counseling Association.

McCann, L., & Pearlman, L. A. (1990). Vicarious traumatization: A framework for understanding the psychological effects of working with victims. *Journal of Traumatic Stress*, *3*(1), 131–149. https://doi.org/10.1007/BF00975140

McGlothlin, J. (2018). Emergency preparedness and response. In L. R. Jackson-Cherry & B. T. Erford (Eds.), *Crisis intervention and prevention* (3rd ed., pp. 379–404). Pearson.

McGowan, J., Gardner, D., & Fletcher, R. (2007). Positive and negative affective outcomes of occupational stress. *New Zealand Journal of Psychology*, *35*(2), 92–98.

McIntyre, J. M. (2010). Federal disaster mental health response and compliance with best practices (Doctoral dissertation). *Dissertation Abstracts International: Section B: The Sciences and Engineering*, *71*(1–B), 218.

McLeod, A. L. (2008). *A phenomenological investigation of supervisors' and supervisees' experiences with attention to cultural issues in multicultural supervision*. Unpublished doctoral dissertation. Georgia State University.

McMahon, M. (2005). Career counseling: Applying the system theory framework of career development. *Journal of Employment Counseling*, *42*(1), 29–38. https://doi.org/10.1002/j.2161-1920.2005.tb00896.x

McNiel, D. E., Chamberlain, J. R., Weaver, C. M., Hall, S. E., Fordwood, S. R., & Binder, R. L. (2008). Impact of clinical training on violence risk assessment. *American Journal of Psychiatry*, *165*(2), 195–200. https://doi.org/10.1176/appi.ajp.2007.06081396

McWhirter, B. T., & Miesch, J. J. (2009). Individual counseling: Traditional approaches. In D. Capuzzi & D. R. Gross (Eds.), *Introduction to the counseling profession* (5th ed.). Pearson.

Medicaid. (2011). *Behavioral health services*. www.medicaid.gov/medicaid/benefits/bhs/index.html

Meichenbaum, D. (1995). Cognitive-behavioral therapy in historical perspective. In B. M. Bongar & L. E. Beutler (Eds.), *Comprehensive textbook of psychotherapy: Theory and practice* (pp. 140–158). Oxford University Press.

Meloy, J. R., Hoffmann, J., Guldimann, A., & James, D. (2011). The role of warning behaviors in threat assessment: An exploration and suggested typology. *Behavioral Sciences and the Law*, *30*, 256–279. https://doi.org/10.1002/bsl.999

Meyer, J. H. F. (2004). An introduction to the RoLI™. *Innovations in Education & Teaching International*, *41*(4), 491–497. https://doi.org/10.1080/1470329042000277057

Miller, W. R., & Rollnick, S. (2013). *Motivational interviewing: Helping people change* (3rd ed.). Guilford.

Mills, G. (2012). Destroying client records. *Therapy Today*, *21*(6), 30–32.

Mitchell, L. K., & Krumboltz, J. D. (1996). Krumboltz's learning theory of career choice and counseling. In D. Brown, L. Brooks, & Associates (Eds.), *Career choice and development* (3rd ed.). Jossey-Bass.

Mize, K. D., Shackelford, T. K., & Shackelford, V. A. (2009). Hands-on killing of intimate partners as a function of sex and relationship status/state. *Journal of Family Violence*, *24*, 463–470. https://doi.org/10.1007/s10896-009-9244-5

Mohl, B., & Skandsen, A. (2012). The prevalence and distribution of self-harm among Danish high school students. *Personality & Mental Health*, *6*(2), 147–155. https://doi.org/10.1002/pmh.191

Moore-Thomas, C. (2018). Cultural identity development. In D. G. Hays & B. T. Erford (Eds.), *Developing multicultural counseling competence: A systems approach* (3rd ed., pp. 32–54). Pearson.

Monk, G., Winslade, J., Crocket, K., & Epston, D. (1997). *Narrative therapy in practice*. Jossey-Bass.

Morgan, M. M., & Sprenkle, D. H. (2007). Toward a common factors approach to supervision. *Journal of Marital and Family Therapy*, *33*(1), 1–17. https://doi.org/10.1111/j.1752-0606.2007.00001.x

Moritsugu, J., Vera, E., Wong, F. Y., & Duffy, K. G. (2019). *Community psychology* (6th ed.). Psychology Press.

Moster, A., Wnuk, D. W., & Jeglic, E. L. (2008). Cognitive behavioral therapy interventions with sex offenders. *Journal of Correctional Health Care*, *14*(2), 109–121. https://doi.org/10.1177/1078345807313874

Mpofu, E., Athanasou, J. A., Rafe, C., & Belshaw, S. H. (2018). Cognitive-behavioral therapy efficacy for reducing recidivism rates of moderate- and high-risk sexual offenders: A scoping systematic literature review. *International Journal of Offender Therapy and Comparative Criminology*, *62*(1), 170–186. https://doi.org/10.1177/0306624X16644501

Murray, C. E., & Graves, K. N. (2012). *Responding to family violence: A comprehensive, research-based guide for therapists*. Routledge.

Mustillo, S. A., Kysar-Moon, A., Douglas, S. R., Hargraves, R., MacDermid Wadsworth, S., Fraine, M., & Frazer, N. L. (2015). Overview of depression, post-traumatic stress disorder, and alcohol misuse among active duty service members returning from Iraq and Afghanistan, self-report and diagnosis. *Military Medicine*, *180*(4), 419–427. https://doi.org/10.7205/MILMED-D-14-00335

Myer, R. A., & Moore, H. B. (2006). Crisis in context theory: An ecological model. *Journal of Counseling & Development*, *84*(2), 139–147. https://doi.org/10.1002/j.1556-6678.2006.tb00389.x

Myers, J. E., & Sweeney, T. J. (2008). Wellness counseling: The evidence base for practice. *Journal of Counseling & Development*, *86*(4), 482–493. https://doi.org/10.1002/j.1556-6678.2008.tb00536.x

Myers, J. E., Sweeney, T. J., & White, V. E. (2002). Advocacy for counselors: A professional imperative. *Journal of Counseling & Development*, *80*(4), 394–402. https://doi.org/10.1002/j.1556-6678.2002.tb00205.x

Napier, A. Y., & Whitaker, C. (1978). *The family crucible*. Harper & Row.

National Academic Advising Association. (2014). *NACADA concept of academic advising*. https://nacada.ksu.edu/Resources/Clearinghouse/View-Articles/Definitions-of-academic-advising.aspx

National Board for Certified Counselors & Affiliates, Inc. (2012). *NBCC code of ethics*. www.nbcc.org/Assets/Ethics/NBCCCodeofEthics.pdf

Neimeyer, R. A., & Burke, L. A. (2011). Complicated grief in the aftermath of homicide: Spiritual crisis and distress in an African American sample. *Religions*, *2*(2), 145–164. https://doi.org/10.3390/rel2020145

Nelson, D., & Cooper, C. (2005). Guest editorial: Stress and health: A positive direction. *Stress and Health*, *21*(2), 73–75. https://doi.org/10.1002/smi.1053

Nelson, M. D., & Piccin, R. (2016). Working with nonsuicidal self-injurious adolescents. In T. P. Remley, Jr., W. D. Rock, & R. M. Reed (Eds.), *Ethical and legal issues in school counseling* (4th ed.). American School Counselor Association. (Reprinted article from *Journal of School Counseling*, *14*. www.jsc.montana.edu/articles/v14n14.pdf).

Newell, J. M., & MacNeil, G. A. (2010). Professional burnout, vicarious trauma, secondary traumatic stress, and compassion fatigue: A review of theoretical terms, risk factors, and preventative methods for clinicians and researcher. *Best Practices in Mental Health*, *6*(2), 57–68.

Nichols, M. P., & Davis, S. D. (2020). *The essentials of family therapy* (7th ed.). Pearson.

Nock, M. K., & Favazza, A. R. (2009). Nonsuicidal self-injury: Definition and classification. In M. K. Nock (Ed.), *Understanding nonsuicidal self-injury: Origins, assessment, and treatment* (pp. 9–18). American Psychological Association.

Nock, M. K., & Prinstein, M. J. (2004). A functional approach to the assessment of self-mutilative behavior. *Journal of Consulting and Clinical Psychology*, *72*(5), 885–890. http://doi.org/10.1037/0022-006X.72.5.885

Norcross, J. C., & Goldfried, M. R. (2005). The future of psychotherapy integration: A roundtable. *Journal of Psychotherapy Integration*, *15*(4), 392–471. http://doi.org/10.1037/1053-0479.15.4.392

Norcross, J. C., & Lambert, M. J. (2018). Psychotherapy relationships that work III. *Psychotherapy*, *55*(4), 303–315. https://doi.org/10.1037/pst0000193

Nugent, F. A., & Jones, K. D. (2008). *An introduction to the profession of counseling* (5th ed.). Pearson.

O'Hanlon, W. H., & Weiner-Davis, M. (1989). *In search of solutions: A new direction in psychotherapy*. W. W. Norton.

O'Toole, M. E. (2000). *The school shooter: A threat assessment perspective*. www.fbi.gov/file-repository/stats-services-publications-school-shooter-school-shooter/view

Papadopoulosa, F. C., Skalkidoub, A., Sergentanisc, A. N., Kyllekidisc, S., Ekseliusa, S., & Petridouc, E. (2009). Preventing suicide and homicide in the United States: The potential benefit in human lives. *Psychiatry Research*, *169*(2), 154–158. https://doi.org/10.1016/j.psychres.2008.06.038

Park, E. H., Ha, G., Lee, S., Lee, Y. Y., & Lee, S. M. (2019). Relationship between working alliance and outcomes: A meta-analysis. *Journal of Counseling & Development*, *97*(4), 437–446. https://doi.org/10.1002/jcad.12292

Peavy, R. V. (1992). A constructivist model of training for career counselors. *Journal of Career Development*, *18*(3), 215–228. https://doi.org/10.1007/BF01321713

Peavy, R. V. (1994). Constructivist career counselling: A prospectus. *Guidance and Counselling*, *9*(2), 3–12.

Pedersen, P. B. (1991). Multiculturalism as a generic approach to counseling. *Journal of Counseling & Development*, *70*(1), 6–12. https://doi.org/10.1002/j.1556-6676.1991.tb01555.x

Perls, L. (1970). One Gestalt therapist's approach. In J. Fagan & I. Shepherd (Eds.), *Gestalt therapy now* (pp. 125–129). Harper & Row.

Peterson, J. (2006). Addressing counseling of gifted students. *Professional School Counseling*, *10*(1), 43–51. https://doi.org/10.1177/2156759X0601001S06

Peterson, J. S. (2015). School counselors and gifted kids: Respecting both cognitive and affective. *Journal of Counseling & Development*, *93*(2), 153–162. https://doi.org/10.1002/j.1556-6676.2015.00191.x

Phinney, J. S. (1996). When we talk about American ethnic groups, what do we mean? *American Psychologist*, *51*, 918–927. https://doi.org/10.1037/0003-066X.51.9.918

Piazza, N. J., & Baruth, N. E. (1990). Client record guidelines. *Journal of Counseling & Development*, *68*(3), 313–316. https://doi.org/10.1002/j.1556-6676.1990.tb01380.x

Ponterotto, J. G. (1985). A counselor's guide to psychopharmacology. *Journal of Counseling & Development*, *64*(1), 109–115. https://doi.org/10.1002/j.1556-6676.1985.tb01046.x

Preston, J. D., O'Neal, J. H., & Talaga, M. C. (2017). *Handbook of clinical psychopharmacology for therapists* (8th ed.). New Harbinger Publications.

Prieto, L. R., & Scheel, K. R. (2002). Using case documentation to strengthen counselor trainees' case conceptualization skills. *Journal of Counseling & Development*, *80*(1), 11–21. https://doi.org/10.1002/j.1556-6678.2002.tb00161.x

Prochaska, J. O., & DiClemente, C. C. (1982). Transtheoretical therapy: Toward a more integrative model of change. *Psychotherapy: Theory, Research, and Practice*, *19*(3), 161–173. http://doi.org/10.1037/h0088437

Prochaska, J. O., & Norcross, J. C. (2018). *Systems of psychotherapy: A transtheoretical analysis* (9th ed.). Oxford University Press.

Puleo, S. G. (2004). Lessons I have learned. *Alabama Counseling Association Journal*, *30*, 21–31.

Puleo, S. G., & Daughhetee, C. (2000, October). *Collaborative evaluation of counselor trainees*. Paper presented at the annual convention of the Southern Association for Counselor Education and Supervision, Greensboro, NC.

Puleo, S. G., & Daughhetee, C. (2004, September). *Supervisor empowerment in the evaluation of counselor trainees*. Paper presented at the convention of the Southern Association for Counselor Education and Supervision, Athens, GA.

Quartana, P. J., Wilk, J. E., Thomas, J. L., Bray, R. M., Rae Olmsted, K. L., Brown, J. M., Williams, J., Kim, P. Y., Clarke-Walper K., & Hoge, C. W. (2014). Trends in mental health services utilization and stigma in US soldiers from 2002 to 2011. *American Journal of Public Health*, *104*(9), 1671–1679. https://doi.org/10.2105/AJPH.2014.301971

Ratts, M. J., Singh, A. A., Nassar-McMillan, S., Butler, S. K., & McCullough, J. R. (2015). *Multicultural and social justice competencies*. www.counseling.org/docs/default-source/competencies/multicultural-and-social-justice-counseling-competencies.pdf?sfvrsn=20

Rawson, R. E., Quinlan, K. M., Cooper, B. J., Fewtrell, C., & Matlow, J. R. (2005). Writing skills development in the health professions. *Teaching and Learning in Medicine*, *17*(3), 233–239. https://doi.org/10.1207/s15328015tlm1703_6

Reamer, F. G. (2017). Evolving standards of care in the age of cybertechnology. *Behavioral Science & The Law*, *36*(2), 257–269. https://doi.org/10.1002/bsl.2336

Recupero, P. R., & Rainey, S. E. (2005). Informed consent to e-therapy. *American Journal of Psychotherapy*, *59*(4), 319–331. https://doi.org/10.1176/appi.psychotherapy.2005.59.4.319

Regel, S. (2007). Post-trauma support in the workplace: The current status and practice of critical incident stress management (CISM) and psychological debriefing (PD) within organizations in the UK. *Occupational Medicine*, *57*(6), 411–416. https://doi.org/10.1093/occmed/kqm071

Reid, W. H. (2010). Preventing suicide. *Journal of Psychiatric Practice*, *16*(2), 120–124. https://doi.org/10.1097/01.pra.0000369973.10650.13

Reidbord, S. (2010). *Countertransference: An overview. Sacramento Street Psychiatry*. www.psychologytoday.com/blog/sacramento-street-psychiatry/201003/countertransference-overview

Reinbergs, E. J., & Fefer, S. A. (2018). Addressing trauma in schools: Multitiered service delivery options for practitioners. *Psychology in the Schools*, *55*(3), 250–263. https://doi.org/10.1002/pits.22105

Remley, T. P., & Herlihy, B. (2020). *Ethical, legal, and professional issues in counseling* (6th ed.). Pearson.

Rix, J., Hall, K., Nind, M., Sheehy, K., & Wearmouth, J. (2009). What pedagogical approaches can effectively include children with special educational needs in mainstream classrooms? A systematic literature review. *Support for Learning*, *24*(2), 86–94. https://doi.org/10.1111/j.1467-9604.2009.01404.x

Roberts, A. R., & Ottens, A. J. (2005). The seven-stage crisis intervention model: A road map to goal attainment, problem solving, and crisis resolution. *Brief Treatment and Crisis Intervention*, *5*(4), 329–339. https://doi.org/10.1093/brief-treatment/mhi030

Robertson, L. A. (2010). The Spiritual Competency Scale. *Counseling and Values*, *55*(1), 6–24. https://doi.org/10.1002/j.2161-007X.2010.tb00019.x

Robinson, B. E. (2000). A typology of workaholics with implications for counselors. *Journal of Addictions & Offender Counseling*, *21*(1), 34–49. https://doi.org/10.1002/j.2161-1874.2000.tb00150.x

Robinson-Wood, T. L. (2016). *The convergence of race, ethnicity, and gender: Multiple identities in counseling* (5th ed.). SAGE.

Rochat, S., & Rossier, J. (2016). Integrating motivational interviewing in career counseling: A case study. *Journal of Vocational Behavior*, *93*, 150–162. https://doi.org/10.1016/j.jvb.2016.02.003

Roe, A. (1956). *The psychology of occupations*. Wiley.

Rogers, C. (1951). *Client-centered therapy*. Houghton Mifflin.

Rogers, C. R. (1957). The necessary and sufficient conditions of therapeutic personality change. *Journal of Consulting Psychology*, *21*(2), 95–103. http://doi.org/10.1037/h0045357

Rossi, J., Swan, M. C., & Isaacs, E. D. (2010). The violent or agitated patient. *Emergency Medicine Clinics of North America*, *28*(1), 235–256. https://doi.org/10.1016/j.emc.2009.10.006

Rothman, J. C. (2008). *Cultural competence in process and practice: Building bridges*. Allyn & Bacon.
Rudd, M. D., Berman, A. L., Joiner, T. E., Jr., Nock, M. K., Silverman, M. M., Mandrusiak, M., Van Orden, K., & Witte, T. (2006). Warning signs for suicide. Theory, research, and clinical applications. *Suicide and Life-Threatening Behavior, 36*(3), 255–262. https://doi.org/10.1521/suli.2006.36.3.255
Rudd, M. D., Cukrowicz, K. C., & Bryan, C. J. (2008). Core competencies in suicide risk assessment and management: Implications for supervision. *Training and Education in Professional Psychology*, 2(4), 219–228. http://doi.org/10.1037/1931-3918.2.4.219
Rudd, M. D., Rajab, M. H., Orman, D. T., Stulman, D. A., Joiner, T., & Dixon, W. (1996). Effectiveness of an outpatient intervention targeting suicidal young adults: Preliminary results. *Journal of Consulting and Clinical Psychology, 64*(1), 179–190. http://doi.org/10.1037/0022-006X.64.1.179
Ruzek, J. L., Brymer, M. J., Jacobs, A. K., Layne, C. M., Vernberg, E. M., & Watson, P. J. (2007). Psychological first aid. *Journal of Mental Health Counseling, 29*, 17–27.
Saleeby, D. (2012). *The strengths perspectives in social work practice* (6th ed.). Pearson.
Saltzman L. E., Fanslow, J. L., McMahon, P. M., & Shelley, G. A. (2015). *Intimate partner violence surveillance: Uniform definitions and recommended data elements, version 2.0*. www.cdc.gov/violenceprevention/pdf/ipv/intimatepartnerviolence.pdf
Savage, J. (2008). The effects of media violence exposure on criminal aggression: A meta-analysis. *Criminal Justice and Behavior, 35*(6), 772–791. https://doi.org/10.1177/0093854808316487
Savickas, M. L. (2012). Life design: A paradigm for career intervention in the 21st century. *Journal of Counseling & Development, 90*(1), 13–19. https://doi.org/10.1111/j.1556-6676.2012.00002.x
Schafer, W. (2000). *Stress management for wellness* (4th ed.). Wadsworth Group.
Schermer, M. (2002). Introduction: Colorful pebbles and Darwin's dictum. In M. Schermer (Ed.), *The skeptic encyclopedia of pseudoscience*. ABC-Cilo, Inc.
Schwartz, R. C. (2008). Psychosocial symptoms and poor insight as predictors of homicidality among clients with psychosis: Implications for counseling practice and research. *Journal of Counseling & Development, 86*(4), 471–481. https://doi.org/10.1002/j.1556-6678.2008.tb00535.x
Scott, J., Boylan, J. C., & Jungers, C. M. (2014). *Practicum & internship: Textbook and resource guide for counseling and psychotherapy* (5th ed.). Routledge Taylor & Frances Group.
Selye, H. (1974). *Stress without distress*. New American Library.
Shea, S. (2011). *The practical art of suicidal assessment: A guide for mental health professionals and substance abuse counselor*. Mental Health Presses.
Shneidman, E. (1993). *Suicide as psychache*. Aronson.
Shneidman, E. S. (1995). *Suicide as psychache: A clinical approach to self-destructive behavior*. Aronson.
Shneidman, E. S. (2004). *Autopsy of a suicidal mind*. Oxford University Press.
Shneidman, E. S. (2005). How I read. *Suicide and Life Threatening Behavior, 38*, 375–386.
Sigelman, C. K., & Rider, E. A. (2022). *Life-span human development* (10th ed.). Cengage.
Simerman, J., Ott, D., & Mellnik, T. (2005, December 30). Katrina affected the elderly the most. *The Charlotte Observer*. www.charlotteobserver.com/
Simon, R. I. (2002). Suicide risk assessment: What is the standard of care? *The Journal of the American Academy of Psychiatry and the Law, 30*(3), 340–344.
Simon, R. I. (2004). Assessing and managing *suicide risk: Guidelines for clinically based risk management*. American Psychiatric Press.
Sklare, G. B. (2014). *Brief counseling that works: A solution-focused approach for school counselors and other mental health professionals* (3rd ed.). Corwin Press.
Smaby, M. H., & Daugherty, R. (1995). The school counselor as leader of efforts to have schools free of drugs and violence. *Education, 115*(4), 612–622.
Smith, D. L. (2009). *The most dangerous animal. Human nature and the origins of war*. St. Martin's Press.
Smith, H. B., & Weikel, W. J. (2011). Mental health counseling comes of age: The first 35 years. In W. A. J. Palmo, W. J. Weikel, & D. P. Borsos (Eds.), *Foundations of mental health counseling* (4th ed., pp. 5–28). Charles C. Thomas.
Smith, S. D., & Chen-Hayes, S. F. (2003). Leadership and advocacy for lesbian, bisexual, gay, transgendered, and questioning (LBGTQ) students: Academic, career, and interpersonal success strategies. In R. Perusse & G. E. Goodnough (Eds.), *Leadership, advocacy and direct service strategies for professional school counselors*. Brooks/Cole.
Sourander, A., Helstelä, L., Haavisto, A., & Bergroth, L. (2001). Suicidal thoughts and attempts among adolescents: A longitudinal 8-year follow-up study. *Journal of Affective Disorders, 63*(1–3), 59–66. https://doi.org/10.1016/S0165-0327(00)00158-0
Sperry, L., & Sperry, J. (2012). *Case conceptualization: Mastering this competency with ease and confidence*. Routledge.
Stansbury, C. D. (2010). Accessibility to a parent's psychotherapy records in custody disputes: How can the competing interests be balanced? *Behavioral Sciences & the Law, 28*(4), 522–541. https://doi.org/10.1002/bsl.949
Staton, A. R., Benson, A. J., Briggs, M. K., Cowan, E., Echterling, L. G., Evans, W. F., McKee, J. E., Presbury, J., & Stewart, A. L. (2018). *Becoming a community counselor: Personal and professional explorations*. Cengage.

Stebleton, M. J. (2010). Narrative-based career counseling perspectives in times of change: An analysis of strengths and limitations. *Journal of Employment Counseling, 47*(2), 64–78. https://doi.org/10.1002/j.2161-1920.2010.tb00091.x

Steele, J. M. (2008). Preparing counselors to advocate for social justice: A liberation model. *Counselor Education & Supervision, 48*(1), 74–85. https://doi.org/10.1002/j.1556-6978.2008.tb00064.x

Stephens, D., Jain, S., & Kim, K. (2010). Group counseling: Techniques for teaching social skills to student with special needs. *Education, 130*, 509–512.

Stewart, T. A., Semivan, S., & Schwartz, R. C. (2009). The art of advocacy: Strategies for psychotherapists. *Annals of the American Psychotherapy Association, 12*(2), 54–59.

Stinchfield, T. A., Hill, N. R., & Kleist, D. M. (2010). Counselor trainees' experiences in triadic supervision: A qualitative exploration of transcendent themes. *International Journal for the Advancement of Counseling, 32*(4), 225–239. https://doi.org/10.1007/s10447-010-9099-8

Stith, S. M., Smith, B. D., Penn, C. E., Ward, D. B., & Tritt, D. (2004). Intimate partner physical abuse perpetration and victimization risk factors: A meta-analytic review. *Aggression and Violent Behavior, 10*(1), 65–98. https://doi.org/10.1016/j.avb.2003.09.001

Stoltenberg, C. D., & McNeill, B. W. (2009). *IDM supervision: An integrated developmental model for supervising counselors and therapists*. Routledge.

Stone, C. B. (2017). *School counseling and principles: Ethics and law* (4th ed.). American School Counselor Association.

Storlie, C. A., Baltrinic, E. R., Mostade, S. J., & Darby, T. (2017). Professional functioning: Exploring developmental narratives of counselor trainees. *Counselor Education and Supervision, 56*(3), 225–240. https://doi.org/10.1002/ceas.12074

Stuart, S., & Robertson, M. (2012). *Interpersonal psychotherapy: A clinician's guide* (2nd ed.). CRC Press.

Substance Abuse and Mental Health Services Administration. (2018). *Phases of disaster*. www.samhsa.gov/dtac/recovering-disasters/phases-disaster

Sue, D. W., Arredondo, P., & McDavis, R. J. (1992). Multicultural counseling competencies and standards: A call to the profession. *Journal of Counseling & Development, 70*, 477–486.

Sue, D. W., Sue, D., Nevill, H. A., & Smith, L. (2019). *Counseling the culturally diverse: Theory and practice* (8th ed.). Wiley.

Suicide Prevention Resource Center and American Association of Suicidology (SPRC/AAS). (2019). *Assessing and managing suicide risk: Core competencies for mental health professionals*. https://sprc.org/resources-programs/assessing-and-managing-suicide-risk-core-competencies-mental-health-professionals

Sullivan, M., Skovholt, T. M., & Jennings, L. (2017). Master therapists' construction of the therapy relationship. In T. M. Skovholt & L. Jennings (Eds.), *Master therapists exploring expertise in therapy and counseling* (10th ed., pp. 53–76). Oxford University Press.

Sweeney, T. J. (2009). *Adlerian counseling and psychotherapy: A practitioner's approach* (5th ed.). Routledge.

Swinson, N., Flynn, S. M., While, D., Roscoe, A., Kapur, N., Appleby, L., & Shaw, J. (2011). Trends in rates of mental illness in homicide perpetrators. *The British Journal of Psychiatry, 198*(6), 485–489. https://doi.org/10.1192/bjp.bp.110.085357

Syed Elias, S. M., Petriwskyj, A., Scott, T., & Neville, C. (2019). Spiritual reminiscence therapy for older people with loneliness, anxiety and depression living in a residential aged care facility, Malaysia: A qualitative approach. *Australasian Journal on Ageing, 38*(1), E25–E30. https://doi.org/10.1111/ajag.12598

Talbott, L. L., & Bartlett, M. L. (2012). Youth suicide postvention: Support for survivors and recommendations for school personnel. *Alabama Counseling Association Journal, 38*(2), 104–119.

Terry-McElrath, Y. M., Chriqui, J. F., & McBride, D. C. (2011). Factors related to Medicaid payment acceptance at outpatient substance abuse treatment programs. *Health Services Research, 46*(2), 632–653. https://doi.org/10.1111/j.1475-6773.2010.01206.x

Teyber, E., & Teyber, F. (2017). *Interpersonal process in therapy: An integrative model* (7th ed.). Cengage.

Tod, D., Andersen, M., & Marchant, D. (2011). Six years up: Applied sport psychologists surviving (and thriving) after graduation. *Journal of Applied Sport Psychology, 23*(1), 93–109. https://doi.org/10.1080/10413200.2010.534543

Todd, T. (2009). *Practice-building 2.0 for mental health professionals: Strategies for success in the digital age*. W. W. Norton.

Toporek, R. L., & Daniels, J. (2018). *American Counseling Association advocacy competencies*. www.counseling.org/docs/default-source/competencies/aca-2018-advocacy-competencies.pdf?sfvrsn=1dca552c_6

Torkelson-Lynch, R., & Gussel, R. (1996). Disclosure and self-advocacy regarding disability-related needs: Strategies to maximize integration in postsecondary education. *Journal of Counseling & Development, 74*(4), 352–356. https://doi.org/10.1002/j.1556-6676.1996.tb01879.x

U.S. Bureau of Labor Statistics. (2020). *Occupational outlook handbook, 2020–21 edition. Substance abuse, behavioral disorder, and mental health counselors*. www.bls.gov/ooh/community-and-social-service/substance-abuse-behavioral-disorder-and-mental-health-counselors.htm

U.S. Bureau of Labor Statistics. (2021). *Occupational outlook handbook, 2020–21 edition*. www.bls.gov/ooh

U.S. Department of Education. (2022). *When is it permissible to utilize FERPA's health or safety emergency exception for disclosures?* https://studentprivacy.ed.gov/faq/when-it-permissible-utilize-ferpa%E2%80%99s-health-or-safety-emergency-exception-disclosures

U.S. Department of Health and Human Services. (2021). *Child maltreatment*. www.acf.hhs.gov/cb/data-research/child-maltreatment

U.S. Department of Health and Human Services, National Institutes of Health, National Institute on Drug Abuse. (2018). *Comorbidity: Substance use disorders and other mental illness drugfacts*. www.drugabuse.gov/publications/drugfacts/comorbidity-substance-use-disorders-other-mental-illnesses

U.S. Department of Health and Human Services, Office of Civil Rights. (2013). *Health information privacy: Is the HIPAA Privacy Rule suspended during a national or public emergency?* www.hhs.gov/hipaa/for-professionals/faq/1068/is-hipaa-suspended-during-a-national-or-public-health-emergency/index.html

U.S. Department of Homeland Security. (2019). *Community emergency response team: Basic training participant manual*. www.ready.gov/sites/default/files/2019.CERT_.Basic_.PM_FINAL_508c.pdf

U.S. Department of Justice, Office of Justice Programs, Bureau of Justice Statistics. (2019). *Homicide*. www.bjs.gov/index.cfm?ty=tp&tid=311

U.S. Department of Justice, Office of Justice Programs, Bureau of Justice Statistics. (2020). *Homicide trends in the United States 1980–2008: Annual rates for 2009 and 2010*. http://bjs.ojp.usdoj.gov/content/pub/pdf/htus8008.pdf

VandeCreek, L., Knapp, S., & Herzog, C. (1987). Malpractice risks in the treatment of dangerous patients. *Psychotherapy: Theory, Research, and Practice*, *24*(2), 145–153. http://doi.org/10.1037/h0085698

Van Orden, K. A., Witte, T. K., Cukrowicz, K. C., Braithwaite, S. R., Selby, E. A., & Joiner, T. E. (2010). The interpersonal theory of suicide. *Psychological Review*, *117*(2), 575–600. https://doi.org/10.1037/a0018697

Venart, E., Vassos, S., & Pitcher-Heft, H. (2007). What individual counselors can do to sustain wellness. *Journal of Humanistic Counseling, Education and Development*, *46*(1), 50–65. https://doi.org/10.1002/j.2161-1939.2007.tb00025.x

Vernon, A. (2004). Counseling children and adolescents: Developmental considerations. In A. Vernon (Ed.), *Counseling children and adolescents* (3rd ed., pp. 1–34). Love Publishing.

Villalba, L., Smith, P., Hickin, N., & Stringaris, A. (2018). Emotion regulation difficulties in traumatized youth: A meta-analysis and conceptual review. *European Child & Adolescent Psychiatry*, *27*(4), 527–544. https://doi.org/10.1007/s00787-018-1105-4

Walfish, S., Barnett, J. E., Zielke, M., & Zielke, R. (2010). "Doc, there's something I have to tell you": Patient disclosure to their psychotherapist of unprosecuted murder and other violence. *Ethics & Behavior*, *20*(5), 311–323. https://doi.org/10.1080/10508422.2010.491743

Walter, J. L., & Peller, J. E. (1992). *Becoming solution-focused in brief therapy*. Brunner/Mazel.

Washburn, J. J., Richardt, S. L., Styer, D. M., Gebhardt, M., Juzwin, K. R., Yourek, A., & Aldridge, D. (2012). Psychotherapeutic approaches to non-suicidal self-injury in adolescents. *Child & Adolescent Psychiatry & Mental Health*, *6*(1), 14–21. https://doi.org/10.1186/1753-2000-6-14

Watts, R. E. (2017). Adlerian and constructivist therapies: A neo-Adlerian perspective. *Journal of Individual Psychology*, *73*(2), 139–155. https://doi.org/10.1353/jip.2017.0012

Welfel, E. R. (2015). *Ethics in counseling and psychotherapy* (6th ed.). Cengage.

Wenzel, A., Brown, G. K., & Beck, A. (2009). *Cognitive therapy for suicidal patients: Scientific and clinical applications*. American Psychological Association.

Wheeler, A. M., & Bertram, B. (2019). *The counselor and the law: A guide to legal and ethical practice* (8th ed.). American Counseling Association

Whiston, S. C. (2016). *Principles and application of assessment in counseling* (5th ed.). Cengage.

White, M., & Epston, D. (1990). *Narrative means to therapeutic ends*. W. W. Norton.

Whitlock, J., Muehlenkamp, J., Purington, A., Eckenrode, J., Barreira, P., Baral Abrams, G., Marchell, T., Kress, V., Girard, K., Chin, C., & Knox, K. (2011). Nonsuicidal self-injury in a college population: General trends and sex differences. *Journal of American College Health*, *59*(8), 691–698. https://doi.org/10.1080/07448481.2010.529626

Wingate, L. R., Van Orden, K. A., Joiner, T. E., Williams, F. M., & Rudd, M. D. (2005). Comparison of compensation and capitalization models when treating suicidality in young adults. *Journal of Consulting and Clinical Psychology*, *73*(4), 756–762. http://doi.org/10.1037/0022-006X.73.4.756

Wolitzky-Taylor, K. B., Resnick, H. S., McCauley, J. L., Amstadter, A. B., Kilpatrick, D. G., & Ruggiero, K. J. (2011). Is reporting of rape on the rise? A comparison of women with reported versus unreported rape experiences in the national women's study-replication. *Journal of Interpersonal Violence*, *26*(4), 807–832. https://doi.org/10.1177/0886260510365869

Wood, J. T., & Fixmer-Oraiz, N. (2019). *Gendered lives: Communication, gender, and culture* (13th ed.). Wadsworth/Thomson Learning.

Wood, S. (2010). Best practices in counseling the gifted in schools: What's really happening? *Gifted Child Quarterly*, *54*(1), 42–58. https://doi.org/10.1177/0016986209352681

Wubbolding, R. E. (2016). Professional school counselors and reality therapy. In B. T. Erford (Ed.), *Professional school counseling: A handbook of theories, programs, and practices* (3rd ed., pp. 338–351). PRO-ED.

Yalom, I. D. (2017). *The gift of therapy: An open letter to a new generation of therapists and their patients*. Harper Collins.

Ybarra, M. L., Diener-West, M., Markow, D., Leaf, P. J., Hamburger, M., & Bozer, P. (2008). Linkages between Internet and other media violence with seriously violent behavior by youth. *Pediatrics*, *122*(5), 929–937. https://doi.org/10.1542/peds.2007-3377

Zalaquett, C., Carrión, I., & Exum, H. (2009). Counseling survivors of national disasters: Issues and strategies for a diverse society. In J. Webber (Ed.), *Terrorism, trauma, and tragedies: A counselor's guide to preparing and responding*. American Counseling Association.

Zinzow, H. M., Rheingold, A. A., Hawkins, A. O., Saunders, B. E., & Kilpatrick, D. G. (2009). Losing a loved one to homicide: Prevalence and mental health correlates in a national sample of young adults. *Journal of Traumatic Stress*, *22*(1), 20–27. https://doi.org/10.1002/jts.20377

Zubernis, L., Snyder, M., & Neale-McFall, C. (2017). Case conceptualization: Improving understanding and treatment with the temporal/contextual model. *Journal of Mental Health Counseling*, *39*(3), 181–194. https://doi.org/10.17744/mehc.39.3.01

Zuckerman, E. L., & Kolmes, K. (2008). *The paper office: Forms, guidelines, resources* (5th ed.). Guilford.

Zunker, V. G. (2015). *Career counseling: A holistic approach* (9th ed.). Cengage.

Zur, O. (2010). *Record-keeping of phone messages, email and texts in psychotherapy & counseling*. www.zurinstitute.com/digital_records.html

Index

Note: Numbers in **bold** indicate a table. Numbers in *italics* indicate a figure

AAMFT *see* American Association for Marriage and Family Therapists (AAMFT)
AAS *see* American Association of Suicidology (AAS)
AASCB *see* American Association of State Counseling Boards (AASCB)
academic advising 232–233, 248; *see also* career guidance/counseling/development
academic difficulty *see* intellectual disability
ACES *see* Association for Counselor Education and Supervision (ACES)
acceptance stage of dying 135; John's case 136 (box)
access to records 80, 88; *ACA Code of Ethics* on 87; client records, ethical issues regarding 116; client requests for 91–93; FERPA on 92, 114, 117; HIPAA on 78, 80, 91, 92, 102, 117; student educational records 114–116
accountability 57, 94, 189, 205; *see also* Health Insurance Portability and Accountability; professional responsibility
accountability initiatives 59
accreditation process and programs: ACA 222; CACREP-accreditation, sample CV indicating 274, 275; Council for the Accreditation Counseling and Related Education Program (CACREP) 2, 3, 22, 110, 147, 191, 196, 217, 222, 274; NBCC 28, 95, 110, 147, 194, 205; state certification/credentialing and licensure 28, 95, 107, 117, 222, 234; The Joint Commission (TJC) on 2; requirements 26; standards 163
accreditation programs: reviewing by student of 269
ACT *see* American College Testing Program Assessment (ACT)
active listening 33; as clinical skill, 178, 200; modeling 53; self-assessment regarding, 69; activities of business, 248
Adams, K. 192
Adler, A. **45**, 49
Adlerian counseling **45**, 49; modern adaptations of 49; social interest theory of, 49
administrative supervisor 31; *see also* on-site supervisors
adolescents: counseling forced on 138; counseling of 64; counseling an unmotivated adolescent (case study) 139; evidence-based treatment approach for 143; loss from disaster, reactions to 181, as mandated client 145; schools as gathering places for 176; SFBC successfully applied to 58; suicidal 119; TF-CBT used on 125; treatment sought by 113–114; working with 6, 72, 143, 255, 281
adolescent-to-adulthood transformation 61
advanced empathy *see* empathy
advocacy: client-focused 234; in counseling 233–235; counselor-as-advocate 235, 248; interventions 152; mental health services 147; post-disaster 186; professional 202, 206, 234; representation and 196; school counselors 104; self-assessment exercise 234–235; social action and 196; social-justice 187; Red Cross volunteer (case study) 182
African Americans: health disparities among 148; homicides, as victims and offenders of 179; importance of family support among 160; injustices committed against 148; letter written by sexually-abused girl 64–65; Sara (case study) 151
Agarwal, S. 238
Allen, K. 177
Alonso, D. 166, 167, 168, 170, 171, 174
Altekruse, M. K. 222
American Association for Marriage and Family Therapists (AAMFT) 95, 103
American Association of Suicidology (AAS) 166, 168, 173
American College Testing Program Assessment (ACT) 243
American Counseling Association (ACA) 95; conference of 273; divisions/branches 28; ethical codes of 208; ethical guidelines followed by 259; membership in 195, 202, 222, 274; multicultural competencies in bylaws of 147; political advocacy by 247; therapeutic proficiency and 188; *see also Codes of ethics* (ACA)
American Foundation for Suicide Prevention (AFSP) 164, 173
American Mental Health Counselors Association (AMHCA) code of ethics, 95, 101–102
American Psychological Association (APA) 147, 274
American Red Cross (ARC): disaster relief volunteer (Voices from the Field) 182; International Federation of the Red Cross 183; Red Crescent Society 183
American School Counselor Association (ASCA) 95; ethical standards for school counselors of 103

Anderson, S. K. 155
androgyny **46**, 66; *see also* feminist counseling
Ancis, J. 39
Anderson, A. 175
Anderson, S. K. 155
Anderson, S. M. 235, 241
anger: manifested as behavioral problems 124; as stage in dying process (Kübler-Ross stages of dying) 134, 135, 145
Anthony, K. 268
antianxiety medications **239**
antidepressants 169 (case study box), **239**
anxiolytics 122, **239**
appraisal of demands 252
ARC *see* American Red Cross (ARC)
Armed Services Vocational Aptitude Battery (ASVAB) **231**
Arrendondo, P. 159
Asians or Asian Americans: hypothetical college student 44, 156; stereotypes regarding, 160
Asim, J. 148
assessment: *ACA Code of Ethics*, Section E 100; *AMHCA Code of Ethics* 102; diagnosis and 27; documentation of intervention efforts and 81, 171–174; evaluation, assessment, interpretation 102; example: uncomplicated bereavement 83–84 (box); follow-up 31; of homicide risk 175–176; *IAMFC Code of Ethics* 103; importance of training in risk assessment 163–166; informal 248; IPV 131–132; lethality 118; of professional disposition 202–205; psychological, education, and vocational 242–246; risk 85; scaling technique for 58; school constraints regarding 115, 117; self-assessment, 1, 28, 142, 155–156; SOAP (Subjective, Objective, Assessment, Plan) 80, 93; therapeutic approaches emphasizing 130; threat level 178–179; *see also* suicide risk assessment
assessment guides 22
assessment instruments 17, 167–168; Ohio's required assessment course using, 110
assessment phase 25–26
Association for Counselor Education and Supervision (ACES) 31, 37
Association for Multicultural Counseling and Development (AMCD) 152
ASVAB *see* Armed Services Vocational Aptitude Battery (ASVAB)
attachment style 68
Attachment Theory 67
Attaway, T. 202
attitude(s): advocacy and 196; changes in 7; client 48, 178; clinicians' own 162; cultural 152; defensive mechanisms and 180; multicultural and social justice counseling competencies and 152; open-minded 156; professionalism expressed by/involving, 188, 189 190, 196, 197, 200, 202, 205; self-awareness of 165; towards suicide 174, 186
autonomy: developing 35; client 139, 189, 190, 215; client communication and 88; emotional 61; ethics principle of 91; Kitchener's moral principle of 94, 104

Baird, B. N.: on abused spouse receiving counseling 85; on economy of expression in case notes 84; on loss of client to suicide 163, 173; on supervisees' coping strategies 37; on supervisee's training experiences 211; on termination paperwork 214, 215; on time-sequenced notes 82
Balkin, R. 171
Barling, J. 177
Barnett, E. 181
Bartholomew, C. 66
Bartlett, M. L. 165, 168, 170, 172, 173, 174, 186
Baruth, N. E. 79, 81
Bateson, G. 64
Beck, A. **45**; cognitive therapy of 55
Beck Depression Inventory 243, **245**
behavioral change, maintaining 141
Behavioral/Cognitive-Behavioral Paradigm 47, 54–61
behavioral counseling 55
behavioral management techniques 128
behavioral modification techniques 18, 55
behavioral responses to disaster 181
behaviors: changes in 76; classic conditioning of 55; client 21, 35, 51; cognitive-behavioural therapy (CBT) 55; counterconditioning of 55; of professional counselors 31; Rational Emotive Behavior Therapy (REBT) **46**, 47, 56, 71; response maintenance to 55; systematic desensitization of 55; token economy of 54
beliefs: about counseling (held by practitioner) 43, 70, 71, 73, 77; assessing client's beliefs 8; cultural, 63t, 66, 67; death and dying-related 135; ethical standards as basis of 94; examining 269; exploring **69**; family 111; irrational, disputing **46**, 47, 56, **60**; laws emerging from 95; maladaptive 55; multicultural and social justice competencies and 152; mythical 64; REBT and 56, 57; religious or spiritual 154; reminiscence therapy and 134; SFBC and 59; students and parents 103, 115; of supervisor/supervisee 38
Bem, S. L. 66
benzodiazepine 238, **239**, 241
Berg, I. K. 58
Berghuis, D.J. 18, 26, 27
Berman, P. 18, 21
Bernard, J. M.: on evaluating supervisees 36, 38; on interpersonal conflict 35; supervisees and supervisor relationship 31–33; *supervision* defined by 30–31; supervisory relationship, scope of 208; on termination of counseling relationship 216; three broad categories of supervision models set out by 39
Bertram, B. 86, 87, 88, 92
Berzoff, J. 261
Betan, E. J. 21
biases: avoiding 101; confronting 158; of counselors-in-training 38, 48, 190; against cultural groups 38; evaluating 144; examining 154; learning 218; overcoming 155–156, 162; personal 211; practicum 165; reducing 147, 148, 150; SELF acronym 268; of supervisees 35; *see also* multicultural competencies
Binder, J. L. 21
binders: course information 218; note keeping 34, 106
Binswanger, L. 52
Black Americans 156; anonymous grieving female 83 (box); anonymous married female 84 (box); as clients 159, 160; Ebony, case study 82–83 (box); *see also* African Americans
Black experience 148
Black women and Black men, differing experiences of 148
Blakely, T. 179
blogs and blogging 86, 88, 283, 284; two purposes served by 283
Borders, L. D. 35, 40
Borum, R. 176
boundaries: between supervisors and students 100; client 96; of competence 104, 191; of confidentiality 113;

detached concern related to 264; difficulty with 197, 262–264; professional, maintaining of 101, 197, 208, 235; setting, 35, 99; therapeutic 190; types of 263
Bourdieu, P. 159
Bowen, M. **45**, 61
Brackett, C. M. 182
Bradley, L. J. 89
Bradley, N. 254
brain *236*; basic functions of, importance of counselors' understanding 248; endocrine system 236–237; frontal lobe 235; limbic system, 236, *237*; neurons and synapses 237–242, *238*; occipital lobe 236; parietal lobe 235; retraining 218; temporal lobe 236
brainstorming **225**; collaborative *223*
Bretherton, D. 66
Bride, B. 262
Briere, J. 124
Brown, L. L. 35
Brown, R. 133
Brown v. Board of Education 148
Bryan, C. 170
Bryant, E. 197
bulimia 43
Bureau of Labor Statistics 268, 271, 272
burnout: avoiding 190, 253, 267; preventing 250, 256; recognizing and avoiding 259–260; self-monitoring for 126; workaholics and 263; *see also* compassion fatigue; stress

CACREP *see* Council for the Accreditation Counseling and Related Education Program (CACREP)
California Association for Licensed Professional Clinical Counselors 234
California Supreme Court 112
California Occupational Interest Survey (COPS) **231**
camera review 92
Cameron, S. 81, 84
Campbell, E.C. 129
Campbell, J. C. 131, 177
Campbell, J. M. 38
Cannon, W. B. 252
Caplan, G. 223
card sort **46**, **65**
career assessment tools **231**, 243
career guidance/counseling/development 226–231, 248; career theory application **227–229**; case study (Rob) 226–227; personality theory of occupational choice 229; social learning theory of career decision making (SLTCDM) 229–230
Carlson, S. 181
Carrolla, P. 137
case conceptualization 8; assumption-based 18; brief 18; clarifying 25; client-focused 18, **19–20**; diagnosis informed by 27; full-scale 18; historically based 18; interpersonally based 18; person-centered, **21–22**; provisional 18; as "road map" for working with client 18, 23; symptom-focused 18; thematically based 48; theory-focused 21, **21–22**; wellness/developmental model of 22
caseloads 3, 259, 261; case notes 31, 35, 79–80; best practices 87; clinical 92; detail of 85; disaster-conditions 184; ethical practice of keeping 79; false 116; FERPA and 92; reviewing 84, 86; "think about it" scenario involving 84–85; unredacted 91; *see also* record keeping; records
case presentations 31, 40, 42
case scenarios 150, 156
case study: adolescent anxiety (Casey) 245–246; career development (Rob) 226–227; counselor's security protocols (Keith and Ibrahim) 88; day in life of counselor (Meghan) 221–222, 223, 233; depression with history of sexual assault (Carlos) 5; depression (anonymous) 28; depression and suicide risk (Alex) 169; depression with grief (Ebony) 82; difficulty concentrating (Julie) 219; dying (John) 136; gaining experience in College Counseling Center (Anni) 203–204; homesickness (Graziella) 203–204; male sexual assault victim and military vet (Chris) 138; outreach practicum (Tori) 204–205; resistance to therapy (Shannon) 4–5; romantic life, fears regarding (Sophie) 9; self-harm and depression (Terry) 47; self-harm and potential IPV (Sarah) 131; severe depression and borderline personality disorder (Karen) 142; suspected child abuse (Jordan and Little League Team) 205
Cashwell, C. S. 257
CCP *see* Crisis Counseling Program (CCP)
CDC *see* Centers for Disease Control (CDC)
Centers for Disease Control (CDC) 124, 177
CERT *see* Community emergency response team (CERT)
certification 1, 31, 38, 282; ACA, 222; listing on CV of 274; loss of 117; national 280; NBCC 95; referral to 101; requirements for 222; state 28, 107, 234
certification agencies 32
Chester, A. 66
child abuse and neglect 117–118; adult victims of 125; caregivers for 125; confidentiality laws and 7, 89; definition of 124; educational records and 114; effects of 124; evidence-based practices (EBP) 125–125, 192; laws and legal issues 106, 109, 117–118; legal definition of 117; liability for reporting 117; Keeping Children Safe Act 117; Kress on 64–65; narrative therapy for (Voices from the Field) 64–65; National Child Abuse Prevention and Treatment Act 117; PTSD and 124; situation involving (hypothetical client) 121; TF-CBT and 125–126; *see also* child maltreatment
child custody cases 109, 111, 115, 116, 118
childhood: adult victims of childhood abuse 125; Adler's theories of, 49; Freud's theories of 48, 49; personality constructed during 70; sense of autonomy from 190; traumatic experiences during 129
child maltreatment 123, 124–127; counselor's role regarding 143
Child Protective Services (CPS) 106, 114, 117
children: cognitive abilities of 127; harm to self and others by 118–119; intellectual disability 127–128; with learning disabilities 127–128; treatment centers for 37; reactions to loss from disaster 181; rights of 28; *see also* child abuse; giftedness
child welfare system, 112
Chi Sigma Iota International (CSI) 28, 36, 194, 274
Choice theory, 57–58; *see also* Reality therapy
CISD *see* critical incident stress debriefing (CISD)
CISM *see* critical incident stress management (CISM)
civil liability 108
Civil Rights Movement 150
Civil War, United States 148
Classical conditioning 55
client-focused advocacy 234
client-focused case conceptualization 18; Teyber's model, sample of **19**

client communication *see* communication
clinical supervisor, 32; *see also* university supervisors
codes of ethics: AAMFT 122; AMHCA 95, 101–102; ASCA 95, 103–104; definition of 188; IAMFC 95, 102–103; Kitchener's five moral principles and 94; NBCC 95; *see also Codes of ethics* (ACA)
Codes of ethics (ACA): advocacy 202; client access to own records 91; confidentiality and privacy 98, 112; counseling relationship, 96–97; disclosure of client information 174; distance counseling, technology, social media 101; duty to warn 112; ethical and best practices in documentation 93; ethical guidelines provided by 188; evaluation 100; maintenance of records and case notes 78, 79, 87, 93; minor children, confidentiality issues and 111; on parents as resources for counselors 7; professional competence 107, 191; professional disclosure statement, sample, **96–97**; professional disposition 197; professional responsibility 99, 196, 205–206; research and publications 100–101; relationships with other professionals 99–100; resolving ethical issues 101; revisions of 95–96; seven step model of 106; six critical principles as foundation of 189; supervision 100; transfer of client files 92
cognitive abilities of children *see* children
Cognitive-Behavioral Therapy (CBT) 55, 50, 67, 73; ACT with (scenario) 132; cognitive restructuring as part of 140; military personally treated using 138; substance use disorder treated with 144; TF-CBT 125–126; *see also* behavioral/cognitive-behavioral paradigm
cognitive self-care **258**
cognitive restructuring 140, 144
Cognitive Therapy (CT) 171; *see also* suicide interventions
cognitive-transactional model, 251; *see also* stress
Collins, B. G. 176
Collins, T. M. 176
Collison, B. 233
Colthorpe, K. 217, 218
common factors, in theories 47, 77
communication: confidentiality and 86, 88–89, 98, 112–113; effective writing 85–86; electronic 89; e-therapy 90; privileged 7, 98, 112–113, 133
communication theory 67
Community Emergency Response Team (CERT) training 17
compartmentalize, inability to 264; *see also* stress
compassion fatigue 126, 250, 259, 260
competence, professional 107; *see also* professional responsibility
competencies 219–224; advocacy 233; crystallizing 194; professional growth and development of 202; professionalism and 197; Ratt on 152; school counseling **210**; Sue on 152; validating 194; *see also* multicultural competencies
computer hackers *see* hackers
confidentiality 6, 110–112; *ACA Code of Ethics* 79, 96, 98, 103, 112; AMHCA code 102; breach of 88, 89, 90, 93, 184; breaking 32, 81, 117, 175, 180; children/minors as clients and 7, 28, 111; client rights regarding 102, 113; email and 86; duty to warn 174; HIPAA 80, 91; legal breach of 184; legal notifications 78; limitations of 101, 112, 185; limits of 89, 112; limits to 111–112, 137; privileged communication and 7, 112–113; protecting 185; relinquishing right to 92
confrontation 57
confronting oneself 154–156
Connelly, A. R. 273, 279, 280
constructive developmental career counseling 229, 230
Constructivist counseling 63, 65–66
Constructivist supervision 58
Constructivist theory 65–66
consultation 112, 223–226; Caplan's defining of 223; counselor-as-consultant 225; lifelong learning through 194; models of 224; peer 144; process **224–225**; professional 174; stages of 224–225
contact information: agency 90; client 78, 85; client intake form **9**; in CV 313; professional disclosure statement **98**; students' exchanging of 208
contacting others, on behalf of survivors 185; death notification-related 185
contemplation stage of change, **70**, 140, 145; precontemplation, **70**, 139, 140, 141, 145
continued learning 284–285
Cook, K. 165
cooking (act of) 254, 257
Coombs, D. 170
Corbin-Burdick, M. 137
Corey, G. 94, 174, 190, 191, 192, 267, 270
Cormier, S. 202
Cottone, R. R. 107
Council for Accreditation of Counseling and Related Educational Programs (CACREP) 147, 222; accredited programs/accreditation by 110, 274; advocacy training required by 233; career counseling required by 226; core knowledge areas for professional counselors 191, 205, 218, 219 (case study box); field experiences standards 2–3, 22, 196; on suicide risk and training prevention 163; training and preparation 217
counseling: advocacy in 233–235; business of 246–248; of children 125–126, 127–128; court-ordered 140–141; of gifted children 128–129; goals of 70, 72; group 144; integrative versus eclectic 73; of intellectually disabled children 127–128; of legal offenders 140; multicultural and social justice 147–161; personal 266–267; practice of 86; strengths-based perspective on 158–161; supervision versus 36–37; of unmotivated adolescent 139
counseling approach, formulating 270–271
counseling competencies, multicultural and social justice 152–154
counseling diverse clients 158–161
counseling mandated and unmotivated clients 138
counseling military service members 136–137
counseling practice, pertinent issues in 221–248
counseling practicum student 30–32
counseling relationship: as core of professional practice 200; establishing rapport with clients 200; informed consent and, 96–97; termination of 214–217
counseling skills 28, 30, 33; *see also* skills
counseling theory 39, 40; ethics of applying, 43
counselor: common ethical dilemmas of 107; common sources of stress 262–266; day in the life of 221; marketing of yourself as 268–286; responsibilities of 189–202; role as professional 71, 72; role of 222; roles as supervisee and 30
counselor safety plan 178
counselor self-care 250–267
counseling relationship: AMHCA code on 102; assessment in 25; boundaries of 197; *Codes of ethics* (ACA) on 96; ethical standards in 194, 197; structure of 190–191; termination of 214–217

Counseling Today 106
countertransference 80, 85; addressing and overcoming 146; assessing and managing 124; boundary violations and 263; case scenario 158; definition of 145–146; reactions, exploring 262; supervisor/supervisee 33; transference and 48, 50, 141–142
court order 103, 110, 115
court-ordered counseling 124, 133, 138, 140–141, 145
court-ordered disclosures 6, 112
cover letters 279, 280, 281, 286
Cowie, M. 270
Craig, C. D. 261
Crawford, E. 136
crimes: criminal behavior and 140; drug-related 133; National Center for the Analysis of Violent Crimes (FBI, US) 178; psychological harm caused by 247; *see also* homicide
crime victim (CV) program 247
Crisis Counseling Program (CCP) 182–183
critical incident stress debriefing (CISD) 183
critical incident stress management (CISM) 183
Crockett, J. 135
cross-cultural communication 51
cross-supervision 32
CSI *see* Chi Sigma Iota International (CSI)
cultural beliefs 67
cultural buttons 158
cultural competence 41, 43, 104, 137, 162; developmental process of 155; recommendations for 174
cultural considerations 174; counseling disaster and 213; suicide interventions and 200
cultural identity 48, 154
cultural immersion activities 162; *see also* multicultural competencies
culturally diverse groups *see* multicultural counseling
cultural sensitivity 48; to client 56–57; developing 147–149, 162; Gestalt counseling and 53
cultural values in counseling 122
curriculum vita (CV): academic use of 278; contact information in 274; credentials listed on 280; developing 273; organizing 274; personal information in 273; preparing 273; resume *vs.* 273, 278; sample *275–278*; uploading 283; using 278; Voices from the Field: De Moro 278; *see also* cover letters
Currier, J. M. 179
custodial/noncustodial parents **98**, 103, 111, 114–115, 126
custodian of records 92, 99, 102
custody-related issues 109, 111, 116, 118
Cutts, L. 73
CV *see* Crime Victims program
CV *see* Curriculum Vita

Daly, R. J. 197
Daughhetee, C. 181, 188, 194, 197, 200, 202
Davis, A. 285
Davis, T. 61, 94
DBT *see* Dialectical behavior therapy (DBT)
death notification 185; *see also* dying
defense mechanisms 48, **50**; exploring 155; psychological 133; variation of 180
delegating, lack of 272
DeLettre, J. L. 92
denial and isolation stage, of dying 134
Department of Defense (U.S.) 137
Department of Education (U.S.) 114, 115
Department of Health and Human Services (U.S.) 117, 124, 133, 184
Department of Homeland Security (U.S.) 183
Department of Justice (U.S.) 175
Department of Veterans Affairs (U.S.) 137
depression stage of dying 134–136
De Shazer, S. 58
detached concern 264
diagnosis 22, 27; role in treatment 22–23
diagnosis debate 22
dialectical behavior therapy (DBT) 170: self-injury and 130, 144; mindfulness and 286; skill groups 125; suicidal clients and 186
Diana, D. 284, 285
DiClemente, C. C. 70
differentiation of self **46**, 61
diligence: competence and 191, 193–194, 205; due diligence 110
disaster: cultural considerations and 186; death notification 185; legal and ethical issues 184; man-made 187; response phases 180–182; safety and security concerns 181; survivor responses 181; termination in 213; training programs 183; wellness and 185
disaster mental health (DMH) training 182, 183
disillusionment phase of disaster response 181
dispositions, professional 188, 189, 205; assessment of 202–203; definition of 197; responsibility revealed by 197–198, **198–199**, 206; school counseling ratings scale including, **210**
distress: in clients 181, 283; in counseling students experiencing fieldwork 166; in counselors 252, 255, 265; in disaster survivors 186; emotional 83; family (hypothetical situation) 121; interpersonal 67; religious 186; resolving feelings of 126; theories on 67
distress tolerance 170
DMH *see* disaster mental health (DMH) training
documentation: auditing of 32; best practices 87; clear and inclusive 93; of clients in danger/crisis 171–174; client-related 2, 86–87; destruction or alteration of 91; ethical requirements 93; questions concerning procedures 80; service 79; SOAP 81; by supervisees/counselor trainees 35, 41
Dokkedahl, S. 131
Donaldson, D. 170
Dougherty, J. L. 22
Douglas, K. S. 178
downcoding 79, 108; *see also* upcoding
drop-ins 31
dual diagnosis 133
duty, military: active 137; combat 136, 145
duty to collaborate with clients 18
duty to do no harm 189
duty to protect 175
duty to warn 28; *ACA Code of Ethics* and 174; *Eisel* case and 118–119; legal limitations to 174–175, 180; superseding status of 114, 117; *Tarasoff* decision and 112, 118, 174–175; *see also* confidentiality
dying: case study: John 136 (box); five stages of 134–135, 145; reminiscence therapy for 144; terminal illness and 134–135, 145; suicide 164; worries about 124

EAP *see* Employee Assistance Programs (EAP)
EBP *see* evidence-based practices (EBP)
eclecticism 191–192; *vs.* theoretical integration 73

economic status of clients 149; socioeconomic status (SES) 33, 148
economic stressors 179
educational assessment 242–244; *see also* assessment
educational records 114–116: FERPA and 92; PPRA and 115
Edwards, G. S. 174
Egan, G. 200
ego 48, **50**
ego psychology **45**
Eisel, Nicole 118–119
Eisel case 118–119
Eke, A. W. 176, 177
electronic data 93
electronic health care transactions 117
electronic information, confidentiality of 111
electronic file 34
electronic records 88, 96
EMA *see* Emergency Management Association (EMA)
email 86, 89–90, 98; on CV 273, 274; personal 208
Emergency Management Association (EMA) 181
emotional abuse 124
emotional climate 229
emotional reactions, to disaster 180
emotional regulation, difficulty with 125
emotional self-care 257, **258**
empathy 51; as basic skill of counseling 69; counselors conveying to clients 162; counselors experiencing trouble accessing 126; encouraged in children 125; psychological first aid and 182; SFBC and 58; suicidal ideation in clients and 165; *see also* person-centered therapy
Employee Assistance Programs (EAP) 247
employment trends 372
empowerment **46**, **68**; client 230; client-focused advocacy and 233–234; feelings of 267; feminist counseling to include 66; professional behaviors to support 197; six domains of advocacy, including 233
Enarson, E. 186
environmental dangers 181
environmental factors **60**; case conceptualization **20**; in suicide 164
environmental/societal subsystem **229**; *see also* systems theory
environmental stimuli 54
EOBs *see* explanation of benefits (EOBs)
Epston, D. **45**, 63, 64
Erford, B. T.: *45 Techniques Every Counselor Should Know* 71; on advocacy and respect for profession of counseling 196; on assessing the client 242; on accountability in professional counseling 189; on counseling theory in intentional counseling 191; on creative CBT techniques 55; on death notification, best practices for 185; on five techniques commonly associated with SFBC 58; on intake interviews 8; on medical model in traditional psychology 158; on mental status exam (MSE) for client 243; on multicultural counseling 147, 156, 158, 192; on overcorrection 54; on use of "I" in statements 53; on worldview, development of 147–148
Eriksen, K. 233
Erikson, E. H. 134, 190
ethical concerns with homicidal clients 180
ethical decision making 106
ethical dilemmas 107–110
ethical issues in disasters 184–185
ethical standards and laws 94–95; ASCA 93, 103–105; definition of 94
Ethical Standards for School Counselors (ASCA) 95, 103–105
eustress 252
Evans, M. A. 131
Everly, G. S. 182
evidence-based practices (EBP) 125, 192
existential anxiety 52
existential counseling 52
existentialism 52
existential vacuum 52
expert/expertise 285; client as expert on what works for themselves 59; moral 58; professional counselor as 48; technical 44
explanation of benefits (EOBs) 247

Facebook 151, 197, 205 (case study box), 280, 282; *see also* social networking
Family Educational Rights and Privacy Act (FERPA) 92, 114–115, 117; Buckley Amendment 114; HIPAA and 184; No Child Left Behind and 115
family system approach 138
family system paradigm **45–46**
family system strategies and interventions **62**
Farberow, N. L. 173
Farington, D. P. 177
feedback: accepting **199**; receiving 38; seeking 158; soliciting and providing 36, 86–88; supervisor 31–34
feminist counseling 63, 66–67
feminist paradigm **46**
feminist theory **45**
Ferguson, C. J. 176
FERPA *see* Family Educational Rights and Privacy Act (FERPA)
field experiences 1–3, 28
Figley, C. R. 261
Flaherty, H. 130, 134
Foa, E. B. 138, 145
Folkman, S. 252
Folstein, M. F. 243
Forester-Miller, H. 94, 106
foster care system 129
Foster, L. 176
foster parents 125
Frankl, V. **45**, 52
Freud, S. **45**, 48, 49, 141

Gabbard, G. 235
Gardner, D. 124
Gearing, R. E. 166, 167, 168, 170, 171, 174
gender 35; intersectionality and 147, 148, 187, 269; Roe on 229; social capital and 159; systems theory on 230
gender identity development 162
gender issues 49
gender role analysis **46**, 67; *see also* feminist counseling
gender roles **69**
gender sensitivity in counseling 66
Gendreau, P. 140
genogram **46**, 61, **62**
genuineness 33, **46**, 51, **53**, 86; PD-LEO on **198**; Saleeby on 160; *see also* person-centered therapy
Gestalt theory 73
Gestalt therapy **45**, 47, 52–53
Giedd, J. 235
giftedness 127, 128–129, 143; *see also* children

GIGO Effect, The 253
Gilbert, L. A. 66
Gilligan, C. 66
Gladding, S. T. 43, 51, 55, 61, 92, 189, 243, 247
Glasser, W. 57–58
goals: of counseling 70–71; developing learning goals with supervisors 35; differentiating between practicum and internship 2; in treatment planning 26
Goetz, A. T. 177
Goggin, C. 140
Goldfried, M. R. 73
Golding, J. 132, 144
Goldstein, D. S. 252
Goodyear, R. K.: on evaluating supervisees 36, 38; on interpersonal conflict 35; supervisees and supervisor relationship 31–33; *supervision* defined by 30–31; supervisory relationship scope of 208; on termination of counseling relationship 216; three broad categories of supervision models set out by 39
Gottlieb, M. C. 247
Granello, P.H. 164–167, 169, 171, 173
Granello, D.H. 163–167, 169, 171, 173
Greason, P. B. 257
Grossman, L. R. 91, 92
group counseling 91: child abuse and 125; intellectual disability and 128; student participation in 103; student teachers and 128
Guillot-Miller, L. 106
Gussel, R. 233
Gutheil, T. 78

hackers 90, 117, 284
Hackney, H. L. 191, 193
Halbur, D. A. 43, 44, 191, 192
Halbur, K. V. 43, 44, 191, 192
hallucination 8, 80
hallucinogens 132
Hamblin, J. 181
Hanifan, L. J. 159
Hansen, J. C. 44
Hansen, J. T. 43, 63, 65
Harpel, J. L. 173
Harrington, J. A. 181
Harris, E. A. 85
Harris, S. M. 86
Haynes, R. 33, 34
Hays, D. G. 147, 148, 156, 158, 216
Health Insurance Portability and Accountability Act (HIPAA) 117; AMHCA code and 102; client confidentiality under 92; electronic health records/storage under 91; FERPA and 184; legal notifications required by 78; need to secure prior to treatment 79; note storage time frame recommended by 87; process notes/psychotherapy notes under 80, 92; US Department of Health and Human Services and 117
Health Maintenance Organization Act (HMOA) of 1973 247
Hegarty, W. 116
Heller, R. J. 86
Helms, J. E. 155
Hendricks, B. 95
Henriques, G. R. 171
Herbert, P. B. 174, 175
Herlihy, B.: on accreditation/CACREP 196; on client access to own records 91; on client consent to release records 92; on counselor's liability re: patient self-harm 216; on counseling relationship and structure 190; on counselors' pride in professional identity 195; on counselor's responsibility of beneficence and autonomy 216; on counselors' varied roles 193; on diagnosis debate 22; on documentation of assessment/intervention with suicidal clients 171; on ethical consideration when counseling minors 111; on ethical standards, three purposes of 94; on FERPA and student records 92; four self-tests to consider when decision has been made 106; on informed consent 88; on professional code of ethics 188; on *Tarasoff* and duty to warn 118, 174
Herman, E. 280
Herman, J. 124, 132
heroic phase of disaster response *see* rescue/heroic phase of disaster response
Herrenkohl, T. I. 176
Hilliard, J. 78
Hilt, L. M. 130
HIPAA *see* Health Insurance Portability and Accountability Act (HIPAA)
HMOA *see* Health Maintenance Organization Act (HMOA) of 1973
Hodge, D. R. 192
Hodges, S.: on cover letters 279; on evaluation process as opportunity to improve 208; on evaluation for supervisors 211; on "moving on" from or negating one's own biases 155; on referring clients after termination 215; on securing a job in counseling 273, 274, 278, 279, 280; on self-awareness in counseling 154; on termination of relationship with client 214, 215
Hoffman, R. M. 66, 125, 130
Hogan-Garcia, M. 155
Holland, J. **228**, 229, **231**, **232**, 248
Holloway, E. L. 39
homeostasis 252
homicidal behavior 186
homicidal clients 175–180: homicidal mind, understanding 175; importance of documenting 171; potential for litigation 176; workplace violence and 177
homicidal crisis 179
homicidal ideation 80
homicidal mind (Voices from the Field) 175
homicide: definition of 175; field experience students and 163, 180, 186; IPV and 131, 144, 177; offenders of 176; threat level assessment of 178
homicide risk, assessment of 163, 175–176
homicide survivors 179
honeymoon phase of disaster response 180–181
hooks, b. 66
Houppert, K. 136
House, R. M. 233
House-Tree-Person test 243
human behavior 61
human emotions 54, 55
humanism 159
humanistic-existential approach 70
humanistic-existential paradigm 51–54, 77, 147
humanistic principles 126
humanitarian aid 183
human nature: articulation of 201; IPT view of 67; view of 70
Human Services: field of 259, 263, 267; providers 137, 149, 150
human subjects 100

IAMFC *see* International Association of Marriage and Family Counselors (IAMFC)
Id 455, 48
IDEA *see* Individuals with Disabilities Education Improvement Act (IDEA)
identity *see* professional identity
immediacy **53**, 141, 145, 199
impulsivity 128, 130, 175; *see also* intellectual disability
individualized treatment planning **23–24**
Individuals with Disabilities Education Improvement Act (IDEA) 115
informed consent: confidentiality and 6, 88–89; counseling relationship and 96, 125; disaster-related situations 184; duty to warn and 19; ethical practice and 244; family therapy and 190; forms, example of **97–98**; forms, signed 110; hypothetical situation involving 122; identity and role of custodian outlined in 92; minor (child) consent laws and 113–114; PPRA and 115; principles of 33; protocols for communicating with counselors and 90; reviewing 6; school/student 116
Ingram, B. L. 23
initiative 33; counseling relationships and 190, 195
initiatives: accountability 58; drug court 133; problem-solving 160; self-care 126
initiative to change 205insurance companies 94, 112, 214, 246
insurance fraud 108, 116
insurance policies 22
intake counselor 7
intake forms 28
intake session/interview: conducting **41**; confidentiality 6; diagnosis 22; gathering information and client history 7; imperative of 25; informed consent 6; mental status exam 8; parents and guardians, initial session 7; psychosocial history 8; *see also* case conceptualization
intellectual disability 127, 129; IQ and 127
intellectualization **51**, 155
intellectually gifted 128
intelligence quotients (IQ) 127
intentionality 44, 72
International Association of Marriage and Family Counselors (IAMFC) 95, 102, 103
Internet 106; content-specific risks 90; general security risks 90; as marketing tool 268; violent content and 176; *see also* online promotion; social networking; websites
interns 2; concerns expressed by 26; ethical standards for 94; individual/triadic and group supervision of 31; "learning curve" for 80; outpatient 3; referral of clients by 5
internship 1, 2; hypothetical situation 120; personal reflection 3–4, 6; practicum/internship 30, 32, 33; Voices from the field: Fawcett 3
interpersonal attractiveness 202
interpersonal psychotherapy (IPT) **45**, **46**, 67–68
intervention approaches, disaster-related 182–183
interventions: coping with personal stressors 253; documenting efforts with suicide 171; selecting, in treatment planning 27–28; with suicide 170
interview, job 281; *see also* intake session/interview
intimate partner violence (IPV) 123, 131–132; assessment of 132, 144; health issues tied to 179; homicide and 177
Iowa Tests of Basic Skills (ITBS) 243
IPT *see* interpersonal psychotherapy (IPT)
IPV *see* intimate partner violence (IPV)
"IS PATH WARM" mnemonic device 168–169; *see also* suicide risk assessment
"I" statements **46**, 50, 53, **53**, **62**
ITBS *see* Iowa Tests of Basic Skills (ITBS)
Ivey, A. E. 34, 44, 63

Jackson, N. 217, 218, 222
Jackson-Cherry, L. R. 185
Jackson's Vocational Interest Inventory **231**
Jennings, L. 189, 193, 293
Jobes, D. A. 168, 170, 171
job search 273–281
Johnson, D. 132, 144
Joiner, T. E. 164, 165, 167, 170, 172
Jones, K. D. 222
Jones-Smith, E. 257
Jongsma, A. E. 176
Jordan, J. R. 172, 173
Journal of Counseling & Development 152
journals 106, 194, 285
Juhnke, G. A. 164, 165, 171
Jung, C. **45**, 49–50
Jungian theory 49–50
Jun, H. 155
justice 94, 106

Kaighobadi, F. 177
Kaminsky, M. 182
Kaplan, D. M. 189, 222
Kay, J. 235
Keener, H. J. 182
Keeping Children and Families Safe Act 117
keeping records *see* record keeping
Keith-Spiegel, P. 80
Kelly, G. A. **45**, 65
Kerr, M. 61
Kettenbach, G. 81
Keys, S. G. 224
Kilburn, J. 176
Kiracofe, N. M. 140
Kiselica, M. S. 234
Kita, E. 261
Kleespies, P. M. 175
Klonopin 239
Klott, J. 176
knowledge: competence and 191–192, 205; meta-learning and 217; multicultural and social justice counseling competencies 152
Koocher, G. P.: 15 domains in comprehensive clinical records 78–79; on process notes 80; on releasing unredacted copies of case records 91–92; on special status of psychotherapy notes/HIPAA 80, 92
Kopin, I. J. 252
Kress, V. E.: 12 categories within mental status exam 8; on client safety plan 132, 144; on client substance abuse 133; on counseling children 125; on deficit-based counseling theories 159; on examining own values, biases, beliefs 269; diagnosis and developmental model of counseling 22; managing boundary issues in counseling (VFTF) 99; on mindful remembrance of termination goals 215; narrative therapy with children who have been abused (VFRTF) 64; on nonsuicidal self-injury 130; on transference 141
Krumboltz, J. D. **45**, 54, **228**, 229–230, **232**, 248
Kübler-Ross, E. 134, 135, 145

Kuder Career Search **231**
Kuder Skills Assessment **231**
Kurpius, D. J. 234

Labor and Industry (L & I) 247; *see also* third-party payers
Ladany, N. 39
Lanktree, C. B. 124
large-scale shock *see* disaster
Lassiter, P. 40, 41
Laux, J. M. 164, 165
Lawson, G. 185
Lazarus, A. A. 73
Lazarus, R. S. 252
learning goals 30, 35
Learning Theory of Career Counseling (LTCC) **228**, 230, **232**
Lee, C. C. 234
legal and ethical concerns 180; disaster-related 184
legal offenders 140
Legowo, E. 225
Lenyk, J. 5–6, 272–273
Levin, A. S. 230
Lewis, J. 233
L & I *see* Labor and Industry (L & I)
licensure 110, 194, 222, 234; laws 248; NBCC 280
licensure boards 22, 32; complaints 87, 92
Liddle, J. R. 175
life span/life space development **232**
limitations: acknowledging 270; multicultural 51
Linehan, M. M. 144, 170
LinkedIn 282
listening 48, 182; active 33, 53, 69, 178, 200
Lober, R. 177
lobes of brain *see* brain
Loganbill, C. 39
Loganbill model 39
low motivation: non-compliance and 138
LTCC *see* Learning Theory of Career Counseling (LTCC)

MacNeil, G. A. 260, 261
Magen, J. G. 87
Magen, R. H. 87
maintenance: boundary 100; of client records 78, 88, 103; developmental stage theory, *maintenance* as stage in 140–141, 145; Health Maintenance Organization Act (HMOA) 247; stages of change **70**; of standards (professional) 104
maintenance tool, therapy as 214
malpractice 108–109; case records, role in event of 87, 171; client record release/right to confidentiality 92; patient suicide and 174; unauthorized release of client information 85
malpractice insurance (scenario) 121
maltreatment of children *see* child abuse
Maruish, M. E. 25, 26, 27
Maslach, C. 260
Maslow, A. 52
MAT *see* Miller Analogy Test (MAT)
McAdams, C. R. 182
McAuliffe, G. J. **228**, 230, **232**, 248
McCann, L. 260
McGlothlin, J. 180, 181, 183
McGowan, J. 252
McIntosh, J. L. 172
McIntyre, J. M. 182, 183
McLeod, A. L. 38
McMahon, M. 231
McMahon, P. M. 229, 232, 248
McNeill, B. W. 39
McNiel, D. E. 175
McWhirter, B. T. 51
media influence, and homicide 176
Medicaid 247
Medicare 247
Mehr, N. 179
Meichenbaum, D. **45**, 55
Meloy, J. R. 179
membership: ACA 96, 195; cultural group 38; listing on CV 274, 276 (example); in professional organizations 104, 194–195; societal group 159
Mental Health Parity and Addiction Equity Act (MHPAEA) 246
Mental Status Examination (MSE) 243
mentor 36, **63**, 203, 207, 220, 281
mentoring **53**, **69**, 194, 196
mentorship 272–273
meta-analysis 132
metabolism 236
metabolizing theory 21
metacognition 235; *vs.* metalearning 216
Metadate 240
metalearning 207, 217–220; case study: Julie 220 (box); metacognition *vs.* 216
metaphors 41, 50, 62, 63, 216
MHPAEA *see* Mental Health Parity and Addiction Equity Act (MHPAEA)
microskills 188, 197–198, 200
Middleton, V. A. 155
military veterans *see* veterans, military
Miller Analogy Test (MAT) 243
Miller, S. 68
Miller, W. R. 133, 139, 145, **232**
Mills, G. 88, 92
Mini-Mental State Examination 243
Minnesota Multiphasic Personality Inventory-2 243
minor clients 6, 7; confidentiality with 28, 103, 111, 112; FERPA 92; parents' rights regarding 92, 97, 103; records keeping and storage 87; text-based interactions with 90
minor consent laws 113–114
minority groups 48
misrepresentation 107
Mitchell, L. 230
Mize, K. D. 177
Mohl, B. 130
Mollen, D. *see* Baird B. N.
Monk G. 63, 64
Moore H. B. 182
Moore-Thomas, C. 155
Morgan, M. M. 35
Moritsugu, J. 259
Moster, A. 140
motivation to change 123, 124; low 138–139, 140, 145; stages of change for conceptualizing 141
motivational enhancement techniques 144
motivational interviewing (MI) 63, **68**, 130, 133, 139, **232**; client empowerment and, 230
Mpofu, E. 140
MSE *see* Mental Status Examination (MSE)
multicultural counseling 147–161; Pedersen on, 147
Multicultural and Social Justice Counseling competencies: AMCD Multicultural Counseling Competencies 152, 162; applying 152
multiple credentials 107

Murray, C. E. 132
Myer, R. A. 182
Myers-Briggs Type Indicator (MBTI) 221 (case study box), 226, 242, 243, **245**
Myers, J. E. 233, 257

NACADA *see* National Academic Advising Association (NACADA)
Napier, A. Y. 190
narrative approach to counseling 63, 64
narrative paradigm **46**
narratives: career 230; client 192; trauma 126, 127
narrative theory **45**; constructive development/narrative theory, **232**
narrative therapy 64, 65, 68
National Academic Advising Association (NACADA) 233
National Board for Counselor Certification (NBCC): career counseling 226; code of ethics 95; continuing education requirements of 194; credentialing by 28; knowledge competencies proscribed by 205; multicultural counseling competencies required by 147; National Counselor Exam (NBCC) developed by 280; website 110
National Certified Counselor (NCC) 28, 196
National Counselor Exam 280
National Intimate Partner and Sexual Violence Survey 177
National Model (ASCA) **212**, 226, 232
NBCC *see* National Board of Certified Counselors (NBCC)
NCC *see* National Certified Counselor (NCC)
neglect 97, 106, 117; *see also* child abuse
negligence 198
Neimeyer, R. A. 179
Nelson, D. 251
Nelson, M. D. 130
networking 196–197, 272; business cards 280; in-person 280; opportunities for 285; self-marketing/promotion and 272; social networking 205, 281–283, 286; traditional forms of 286
neuroanatomy 235
neurons and synapses 237–242
neurotransmitters 235, 237, 248
Newell, J. M. 260, 261
Newsome, D. W. 243, 247
Nichols, M. P. 61
Nietzsche, F. 52
No Child Left Behind (NCLB) Act of 2001 115
Nock, M. K. 130
nodes of Ranvier 237
nonmaleficence 94–95, 104, 189, 224, 243
nonprofessional interactions 79, 96
nonprojective tests 243; *see also* psychological assessment
nonsuicidal self-injury 130–131
nonverbals 8, 41, 53, 90, 120, 139, 198
Norcross, J. C. 73, 140, 141, 145, 189
no-suicide contracts (NSC) 169, 170
Notice of Privacy Practice 80
NSC *see* no-suicide contracts (NSC)
Nugent, F. A. 222

objectives: developing 26–27; establishing 189; examples of 33; of internship 2; of practicum 2; required 36; of treatment 18
object-relations theory 49
O'Hanlon, W. H. 58
older adults 123, 134–136
online self-promotion 284
on-site practicum experiences 2
on-site supervision/supervisors 3, 30, 31–33, 35, 41, 280
open-ended guidance 243
open-ended questions 7, 57, 178
open-mindedness 129, 156, 230
optimal performers 362
O'Toole, M. E. 178
Ottens, A. J. 182

Papadopoulosa, F. C. 175
paradigms *see* theoretical paradigms
paraphrasing 69
Parsons, F. **227**, 229, **243**, 248
Partin, P. W. 106
Paylo, M. 215
PD-LEO *see* Puleo-Daughhetee Longitudinal Evaluation Objectives (PD-LEO)
Pearlman, L. A. 260
Peavy, R. V. 230, 248
Pedersen, P. 147
peer consultation 144
peer group supervision 40–42
peer supervision 99, 144
Peller, J. E. 58
Perls, F. **45**, 52, 53
Perls, L. 52
personal constructs 65
personal counseling 266
personality 35, **228**, 232; Adler's theory of 49; altered 236; borderline personality disorder (BPD) 142 (box), 170; clients' 51; of counselor 191; dynamics of 18, **20**; Freud's theory of 48; Gestalt therapy and 52; Minnesota Multiphasic Personality Inventory-2 243; psychodynamic theory and, 70; reconstruction of 48; style of 21; tools to assess 231*; see also* Heller
personality inventory 121
personality theory of occupational choice 229
personal notes 114, 116–117
person-centered counseling/counselors 51–52, 71, 72–73; hallmarks of 159
person-centered supervision 39
person-centered theoretical case conceptualization **21–22**
person-centered therapy **45**, 51
Peterson, J. 128, 129
PFA *see* Psychological First Aid (PFA)
Phinney, J. S. 155
physical self-care 104, 253–254
Piazza, N. J. 79, 81
political contexts, and multicultural counseling 148
Ponterotto, J. G. 235
population: adult smoking 70; client 4, 6, 31, 36; ethnic 64; preferred client 1, 28; special 123–143
portability *see* HIPAA
posttraumatic stress disorder (PTSD) 123; case example 260–261; child abuse and 124; CISM and 183; in counselors 262; EBT and 138; IPV and 131, 132, 144; military veterans and 136, 137, 138, 145; vicarious traumatization and 261
postvention, suicide 172, 173, 174
PPO *see* Preferred Provider Organizations (PPO)
PPRA *see* Protection of Pupil Rights Amendment (PPRA)
precontemplation, as stage of change **70**, 139, 140, 145
Preferred Provider Organizations (PPO) 246
preparation, action, recovery framework (PARF) 182
preparation stage as stage of change **70**, 140, 141, 145
Preston, J. D. 235, 236, 237
Prieto, L. R. 86

Principles for AMHCA's Code of Ethics (AMHCA) 95, 101
Prinstein, M. J. 130
private insurance 22, 246
privileged communication *see* communication; confidentiality
probes 121, **198**
Problem-Solving Therapy (PST) 170, 186; *see also* suicide interventions
process notes *see* psychotherapy notes
Prochaska, J. O. 70, 140, 141, 145
professional advocacy 234
professional disclosure statement **97**
professional disposition *see* disposition, professional
professional growth (Voices from the Field) 272–273
professional identity 33, 174, 196; temet nosce 268
professional responsibility, practicing 188–205
progress notes, and supervision 86–87
projective tests 243; *see also* psychological assessment
Protection of Pupil Rights Amendment (PPRA) 115
PST *see* Problem-Solving Therapy (PST)
psychache 164, 165, 166
psychoanalysis **45**, 48–49, 52, 141, 147, 158
psychodynamic career theory **227**, 229
psychodynamic counseling 43, 73
psychodynamic paradigm **45**, 48–51, 77
psychodynamic theories 49–50, 70
psychological assessment 242–246; *see also* assessment
psychological debriefing (PD) 183, 185; *see also* critical incident stress debriefing (CISD)
Psychological First Aid (PFA) 182, 183
psychopharmacology 235–242
psychotherapy: existential 52; interpersonal **46**, 67–68; TF-CBT 125; theoretical paradigms in 77
psychotherapy notes 80, 92, 93; HIPAA and 80
psychotherapy theory 39
psychotropic medications 175, 235, 237, **239–241**
PTSD *see* posttraumatic stress disorder (PTSD)
Publication Manual (APA) 274
Puleo-Daughhetee Longitudinal Evaluation Objectives (PD-LEO) 197, **198–199**, 202–203
Puleo, S. G. 190, 194, 195, 197, 200, 202

qualitative research paradigm 192
quantitative research paradigm 192

Rainey S. E. 90
rational emotive behavior therapy (REBT) **46**, 47, 56, 71
Rawson, R. E., 85
reality therapy 57–58
REBT *see* rational emotive behavior therapy (REBT)
recidivism 133, 140; *see also* legal offenders
reciprocity 48, 229, 231
reconstruction/recovery phase of disaster response 181
record keeping: avoiding problems of 87–91; details 84, 85; importance of 78; overview 78; process notes 80; progress notes 86–87; SOAP notes 80; time-sequenced notes 82; *see also* case notes
records: *ACA Code of Ethics* on 79, 87, 91, 96; auditing of 32; backdating of 116; client (Voices from the Field) 116; client requests for 91–92; double-lock guideline 88; FERPA and 114; HIPAA laws 92; laws regarding maintenance of 78; personal notes and 114; release of 110; student 103, 114–115; *see also* educational records; electronic communication; informed consent
records custodian 99
recovery phase of disaster response *see* reconstruction/recovery phase of disaster response
Recupero, P. R. 90
referral: best interests of client 5; by designated custodian 92; documenting/record-keeping 79–81, 215; intervention including 182; offering 102; outpatient 168; treatment plans 27–28; underage or child patient 113
referral source: counselors' accountability to 189; counselors as 179; primary care physician as 169
Reflections on Learning Inventory 218
Reidbord, S. 142
reminiscence therapy techniques 134, 144
Remley, T. P. 88, 91, 106, 111, 118
representation 195; *see also* misrepresentation
rescue/heroic phase of disaster response 180
research: qualitative research paradigm 192; quantitative research paradigm 192
response phases of disaster 207–208
responsibilities *see* professional responsibility
responsive parenting 128
resume 273–279; *see also* curriculum vita (CV)
reuptake process 237; SNRIs **239**; SSRIs **239**
Richmond, J. S. 175
Rider, E. A. 127, 128, 134
rights, of client *see* confidentiality; informed consent
risk assessment: importance of training in 163–166; homicide 175–176; *see also* suicide risk assessment
risk factors 166
risk level, determining 168–169
Rix, J. 127, 128
Roberts, A. R. 182
Robertson, L. A. 257
Robinson, B. E. 263
Robinson, M. 234
Robinson-Wood, T. L. 156, 160
Rochat, S. 230
Rodgers, R. A. 234
Roe, A. **227**, 229, **232**, 248
Rogers, C.: four traits of people becoming actualized **22**; person-centered therapy **45**, 51; six conditions necessary for therapeutic relationship to affect change 200
role confusion **50**, 264; *see also* stress
Rollnick, S. 133, 139, 145, **232**
Rossier, J. 230
Rossi, J. 175, 230
Rothman, J. C. 160
Rough, J. 110
Rudd, M. D. 167, 170, 172
Ruzek, J. L. 182

SA *see* self-awareness
safeguarding: of client records 88, 91; of research participants 100
safety issues in disasters 181–182
safety plan: for at-risk clients 123, 132, 144; for counselors 178; for homicide 205
safe space 125, 128
Saleeby, D. 160, 162
Saltzman L. E. 177
Savage, J. 178
Savickas, M. L. 268
SCATTT mnemonic 171, 172
Schafer, W. 253
Scheel, K. R. 86

Scher, M. 66
Schermer, M. 39
school counselors 6, 73, 92; administrators/supervisors 104; *American School Counselor Association (ASCA) Ethical Standards for School Counselors* 103; *Eisel* case, impact on profession of 119–120; ethical considerations 107; expert witnesses 108; individual and group counseling suggested by 128; intern site supervisors 104; minor consent laws and 113; personal notes taken by 116; school counseling ratings scale **210**; sexual misconduct, accusations of 109; situation involving crack cocaine (hypothetical) 121; violating or failing to follow mandates 109
schools 126; ACA model applied to 106; HIPAA and FERPA 117; opt-in model adopted by 107
school shootings 180
school threat assessment 176–177
school violence 176–177, 186
Schwartz, R. C. 175
Scott, J. 165
Sears, S. J. 233
secondary trauma 260
security risks 90
Selective Serotonin Reuptake Inhibitors (SSRIs) **239**
self-awareness (SA) 45; in children 128; competency in 152; as crucial to counselor development 29, 44; developing **54**; encouraging **53**; existentialism and human capacity for 52; expanding understanding of 154; increasing 34, 35; in multicultural counseling 149, 152, 156, 157, 158, 160; person-centered counseling and 71; role of 147; self-reflection and 155, 156; in suicide intervention 170; in supervisee 31; working with difference and 156
self-care 250–267; cognitive 255; burnout, recognizing and avoiding 259–260; domains of *257*; emotional 255–256; envisioning 34–35; importance of 34–35, 185, 190; maintaining balance and (Voices from the Field: Lenyk) 5–6; physical and mental 104; plan, example 258–259; social 256–257; spiritual 257; vicarious trauma and need for 260–262
self-destruction 56, 118, 284; *see also* suicide
self-disclosure 33; boundary issues presented by 197; cautious 52, **54**; counseling children and 127; PD-LEO **198**; traditional methods of 197; unidirectional character of 190
self-injury (SI) *see* nonsuicidal self-injury
self-marketing 268, 270, 286
Serotonin Norepinephrine Reuptake Inhibitor (SNRIs) **239**
Shackelford, T. K. 177
Shea, S. 166
Shneidman, E. S. 164, 166, 172
Sigelman, C. K. 127, 128, 134
Simon, R. I. 166, 168, 170, 171
site protocols 33, 84
Skeem, J. L. 178
skills: case conceptualization 86; clinical 154, 156; cognitive 36; communication **68**; coping 65, 130, 144, 164, 170, 171, 180; crisis counseling 180; critical thinking 191; developing 1–28, 44; documentation 87; interpersonal 33; microskills 188, 197, 198, 200; problem-solving 55; quantitative 192; ratings scale (sample) **210**, **211**; school-based supervisor evaluation of university counseling education program **212–213**; self-help 216; social 129; survival 125
Sklare, G. B. 58
Skovholt, T. M. 189, 193
SLTCDM *see* social learning theory of career decision making (SLTCDM)
Smaby, M. H. 233
Smith, D. L. 176
Smith, H.B. 233
SNRIs *see* Serotonin Norepinephrine Reuptake Inhibitor (SNRIs)
SOAP notes 80–81, 93; case study 82; note format 83
Sobell, L. C. 92
social action 196
social capital 159, 162; *see also* multicultural counseling; strengths-based approach
social connections wheel *256*, 257
social difficulties 129
social emotional learning curricula 125
social influence 52
social interest 49
social isolation 26
social learning theory of career decision making (SLTCDM) 229–230, **232**, 248
social media 96, 101, 197, 268, 282, 284
social negative reinforcement 130
social networking 186, 205, 281–283, 286; Facebook 151, 197, 205 (case study box), 280, 282
liabilities 284; Twitter 280, 282; YouTube 282
social norms, and multicultural counseling 149
social self-care 256
social support 67, 160
social system 230; *see also* systems theory
social theory 67
solution-focused brief counseling (SFBC) 58–59
Sourander, A. 170
sparkling moments **46**, **62**, 64, **68**
special populations 123–143; child maltreatment 124; children with learning disabilities or giftedness 127; court-ordered counseling 140; intimate partner violence (IPV) 131; legal offenders 140; military populations 136; mandated and unmotivated clients 138; nonsuicidal self-injury 130; substance abuse 132; older adults and the terminally ill 134; transference and countertransference 141
specific factors, in theories 47
Sperry, J. 18
Sperry, L. 18
spiritual distress: disasters and 186
spiritual freedom 52
spiritual guidance: case study (anonymous Black female) 84; case study (Ebony) 82, 83
spirituality 166, 179, 185, 191
spiritual turmoil: suicidality and 165
spiritual self-care 252, 257, **258**, 292
Sprang, G. 261
Sprenkle, D. H. 35
SSRIs *see* Selective Serotonin Reuptake Inhibitors (SSRIs)
stages of change 70, **70**, 141
stages of death and dying 123
Stansbury, C. D. 92
Staton, A. R. 222, 225
Stebleton, M. J. 230
Steele, J. M. 233
Stephens, D. 127, 128
Stewart, T. A. 234
Stinchfield, T. A. 178
Stith, S. M. 178
Stoltenberg, C. D. 39
Stone, C. B. 106, 108

Stone Center 66
strengths 268
strengths-based approach 147, 158–161; *see also* multicultural counseling
stress: being all things to all people 265; compassion fatigue 126, 185, 250, 259, 260–261; feelings of incompetence and 265–266; helping professions and 250; inability to compartmentalize and 264; lack of delegation and 262; role confusion and 264; *see also* burnout; self-care
stressors: coping with 253–254; identifying 252–253
Strong Interest Inventory 242
Stuart, S. 67
subpoena 80, 84, 89, 109–110
substance abuse 132–134
Sue, D. 174
suicide/suicide attempts 97, 112, 118, 119; facts about 164; interpersonal theory of 164; loss of a client to 173; myths about 165; prevalence of 164; statistics about 187; treating returning clients after attempt of 173; treating survivors of 172–173; *see also* postvention; psychache
suicide interventions 170; cognitive therapy 170–171; cultural considerations and 174; DBT and 170; duty to warn in cases of 112; ethical standards and 200; legal and ethical behavior 122; PST and 170; by school counselors 119; survivors and 165, 172–173
suicide risk assessment 166–174; assessment of 186; assessment instruments 167; best practices 169–170; determining the risk level 168–169; documentation 171–174; evidence-based 166–167; Granello's 12 principles of 167
Suicide Risk Assessment Decision Tree 167
Sullivan, M. 189, 190, 193
summarizing 32, 200
Super, D. **227**, 229, **232**, 248
superego **45**, 48, **50**
supervisees: definition of 31; case presentations by **40**, 40–41; responsibilities 34, 35; role as 30
supervision: ACA code on 98, 100, 107; AMHCA code on 102; barriers to 37–38; counseling *vs.* 36; formats 31; IAMFC 103; models of 39; peer 99; peer group 40; process 30–41; progress notes and 86–87, 93
supervisors 15; learning goals with 35–36, 41; on-site 31–32; role of 31; supervisory process and 86; theoretical orientation of 42; university 32–33
supervisory alliance 33, 41
supervisory relationship: communicating needs in 35; expressing doubts and vulnerabilities in 37; feedback in 34, 38; responsibilities as supervisee 17–19; termination of 207, 208–214
survivor responses 181
survivors: disaster 182, 186; homicide 179, 180; suicide 165, 172, 173; Voices from the Field: Brackette 182
Sweeney, T. J. 49, 208, 257
Swinson, N. 175
system paradigm **45**, **46**, 61–63
systems theory 147, **229**, 230–231, **232**

Tarasoff v. Regents of the University of California 112, 118, 174
Tarvydas, V. M. 107
task approach 229, 230
task force, clinician survivor (AAS) 173
technology-assisted counseling 102, 103
technology-based counseling modalities 101, 268
technology in counseling 96, 98, 104, 111, 117; community-building using 192, 196–197' self-marketing using 268, 286; social networking 282
temet nosce 368
terminal illness 98, 123, 134–135, 145; *AMHCA Code of Ethics* 102
termination: of counseling relationship 214–217; definition of 207; in disaster 185; of student roles 207–208; of supervisory relationships 208–214; unplanned 216
Terry-McElrath, Y. M. 247
text-based communication 90
Teyber, E. 18, **19**
Teyber, F. 18, **19**
TF-CBT *see* trauma-focused cognitive behavioral therapy (TF-CBT)
theoretical integration 72–77; integrative versus eclectic counseling 73; reasons for 73–77
theoretical orientations in counseling 38–40, 255
theoretical paradigms 45–63; behavioral/cognitive-behavioral 54–59; humanistic-existential 51–54; psychodynamic 48–51; systems 61–63
theories: common factors 47; good 44–45; integrating into practice 70–72; intentionality in 44; postmodern 63–69; specific factors 47; theoretical integration 72–77; *see also* theoretical paradigms
third-party payers 18, 246–248; *ACA Code of Ethics* and 112; "business" of counseling and 246–247, 248; definition of 246; diagnostic categories expected by 27; HIPAA and 80; number of sessions limited by 108; practice consistent with 221; time-sequenced notes and 82; treatment plans and 25–26
third-party reimbursement 22; client's rights 102
threat phase of disaster response *see* warning/threat phase, of disaster response
time-sequenced notes 82–84
Todd, T. 284, 284
token economy **46**, 54, **59**
Toporek, R. 233
Torkelson-Lynch, R. 233
training: advocacy 233; disaster intervention 183; in risk assessment for suicide 163
Trait and Factor Theory **227**, 229, **232**, 248
transcendence 141
transference 33, 124, 141
trauma-focused cognitive behavioral therapy (TF-CBT) 125–126
treatment planning 23–28; assessment and 81; defining problem 26; designing 79; developing 25–26; developing goals for 26; developing objectives for 26–27; diagnosis 27; electronic records and 91; examining notes in supervision 86; example 27–28; identifying problem 26; individualized **23–25**; informed consent and 96; interventions 27; program planning and 201; record keeping in 87
treatment teams 4, 112; *see also* multidisciplinary team
Turtle-Song, I. 81, 84, 85
Twitter 280, 282

unconditional positive regard **21**, **46**, 51, **53**, 183, 200; *see also* person-centered therapy
unfinished business 52
university mentors 281
university supervisors 32–33, 35–36, 41
upcoding 79, 108

values 269
VandeCreek, L. 171
Van Orden, K. A. 164
Venart, B. 252
Vernon, A. **50**
veterans, military 123, 136–137; CBT and 138; counseling area work focused on 145
Veterans Administration (U.S.) 234, 248
vicarious trauma 126, 173, 260–262
view of human nature 70
violence: domestic 93; family 137, 145; interpersonal 175; school 176; underreporting of 176; workplace 177; *see also* intimate partner violence (IPV)
virtual counseling 104
virtual job market 282–284
virtual liabilities 284; *see also* online promotion; social networking
Vocational Aptitude Battery *see* Armed Services Vocational Aptitude Battery (ASVAB)
vocational assessment 221, 243; *see also* assessment
Vocational Interest Inventory **231**
vocational interests 242, 248
voice mail messages 89–90, 98

Walker, A. 66
Walter, J. L. 58
warning behaviors 179
warning signs: for illness or poor health 251; for suicide 164, 166, 167, 169, 186
warning/threat phase of disaster response 180, 186
Watson, J. B. **45**, 54
Watts, R. E. 49
websites: blogging 284 for career enhancement 283–284; hacking of 117
Weikel, W. J. 233
Weiner-Davis, M. 58
Welfel, E. R. 78, 80, 86, 190; on competence/competency 191, 193, 205; on counselor's right to use client records in defense against complaint 92; on obsolescence of knowledge and importance of lifelong learning 194; on providing clients access to records 91
wellness: counselor 205, 207; disaster and 185; mental health 22; promoting 271; Wheel of 257
wellness/developmental model of conceptualization and treatment 22, 34
wellness movement 59
Wells, L. 140
Wellstone-Domenici Mental Health Parity and Addiction Equity Act (MHPAEA) *see* Mental Health Parity and Addiction Equity Act (MHPAEA)
Wenzel, A. 171
West, S. G. 175
Wheeler, A. M. 86, 87, 88, 92
wheel of social connections *256*, 257
Wheel of Wellness 257
Whisenhunt, J. 39
Whiston, S. C. 163
Whitaker, C. 190
White, M. **45**, 63–64
White people: male victim of sexual assault (case study) 138; woman with cancer 135
White feminism 66
Whitlock, J. 130
Wingate, L. R. 170
Wolitzky-Taylor, K. B. 176
Wood, J. T. 66, 83
Wood, S. 128, 129
workplace violence, and homicide 177
worldviews 147, 155, 269; of clients 5, 152, 261; disaster responses and 186
writing: case notes 80, 84, 91, 93; documenting in 122; letter to self 64; Magen and Magen's guidelines for 87; note-writing 78, 82; other professional 86; professional and effective 85, 87; therapy notes for mental health practitioners 81
Wubbolding, R. E. 57

Yalom, I. D. **45**, 52
Ybarra, M. L. 176
Young, K. A. 175
YouTube 282

Zalaquett, C. 186
Zinzow, H. M. 179
Zlotnick, C. 132, 144
Zubernis, L. 21
Zuckerman, E. L. 85
Zunker, V. G. 229
Zur, O. 89
Zyban **239**

For Product Safety Concerns and Information please contact our EU
representative GPSR@taylorandfrancis.com
Taylor & Francis Verlag GmbH, Kaufingerstraße 24, 80331 München, Germany

www.ingramcontent.com/pod-product-compliance
Ingram Content Group UK Ltd.
Pitfield, Milton Keynes, MK11 3LW, UK
UKHW050235200926
475702UK00020B/3045
9781032304861